The Ethics of Citizenship

The Ethics of Citizenship

Liberal Democracy and Religious Convictions

J. Caleb Clanton
editor

BAYLOR UNIVERSITY PRESS

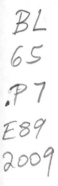

© 2009 by Baylor University Press
Waco, Texas 76798

Cover Design by Jeremy Reiss, J.Reiss Design

Library of Congress Cataloging-in-Publication Data

The ethics of citizenship : liberal democracy and religious convictions / J. Caleb Clanton, editor.
    p. cm.
  Includes index.
  ISBN 978-1-60258-203-3 (pbk. : alk. paper)
  1. Religion and politics. 2. Citizenship--Moral and ethical aspects. I. Clanton, J. Caleb, 1978-
  BL65.P7E89 2009
  201'.72--dc22

                              2009020930

Printed in the United States of America on acid-free paper with a minimum of 30% pcw content.

Contents

Acknowledgments

Several people have been helpful in the completion of this project, and I owe them a debt of gratitude. I would like to thank Adam Coulson and Michelle Perry for their help with formatting texts. I am especially grateful to Jason Eggleston for his technological support, as well as his production and research assistance during the preparation of the manuscript. I would also like to thank Andrew Forcehimes for his help with the index.

For encouraging me to compile this anthology, and for all his advice along the way, I want to recognize my friend and former teacher, Robert Talisse. His mentoring has made an enormous and lasting impact on my life as a philosopher, and I am grateful to him for that.

Lastly, for her patience and gentle love, I am thankful to my beautiful wife, Sophia. Her support and calming presence in my life means the world to me.

Introduction

On the Tension
between Religion and Democracy

J. Caleb Clanton

The issue of whether and to what extent religion should play a role in democratic politics is one of the most salient and hotly debated issues of our day.
How we settle this particular issue informs nearly every aspect of our public
life in America—from the way we deliberate and attempt to justify policy to
the way we run election campaigns to the way we as individual citizens vote.
And how we engage in these activities of the public square either directly or
indirectly impacts our decisions on the most controversial issues our nation
faces—from our decisions about school vouchers, same-sex unions, public
Ten Commandments displays, welfare assistance, and international debt forgiveness to our decisions about abortion, stem-cell research, right-to-die, the
death penalty, the environment, animal rights, and war. Indeed, it is difficult
to locate any substantive issue on the American political landscape that does
not involve at some level the question of whether and how religion should
factor into the public square.

Over the last two decades, there has been a flurry of scholarly debate
concerning whether citizens should allow their religious convictions to
filter into their lives within the political domain. *The Ethics of Citizenship:*

Liberal Democracy and Religious Convictions can be seen as an attempt to compile some of the most significant contributions to that debate from the leading political philosophers, theologians, and legal scholars of our time.

I

Americans are, no doubt, a religious people. Some studies indicate that nearly 95 percent claim belief in God, and approximately 70 percent are members of a church, synagogue, or mosque.[1] Of course, this is not to say that Americans are all religious in the same sense—some are Christian, some Jewish, some Muslim, and so forth.[2] In any case, it remains a sociological fact that most Americans take themselves to be answerable in some sense to a religious source of authority. And it is not uncommon for religiously committed citizens to believe that their moral, social, and political commitments follow either directly or indirectly from these religious sources. According to polls, 48 percent of Americans think of themselves as members of a particular religion when it comes to political matters.[3] Roughly 44 percent admit that their religious beliefs play a role in deciding which candidates to support.[4] Some 49 percent said that their religious beliefs affect how they vote in an election.[5] And over 60 percent of Americans said their religious beliefs and faith would be an important factor when it came to deciding how to vote in the 2004 presidential election.[6]

Clearly, many, if not most, Americans act as though they think religious reasoning has a perfectly legitimate role in the activities of the democratic public square—from public deliberation to political advocacy to voting. But are they misguided? Are citizens stepping out of line when they do things like rally at the Tennessee capitol under religious banners asking "Who Would Jesus Cut?" while protesting decreases in the state's healthcare budget? Are citizens out of order when they cite Jeremiah 1:5 or Psalm 139:13-16 in support of antiabortion policies that aim to govern other citizens who reject the normative authority of Jewish and Christian Scriptures? Are citizens acting improperly when deciding how to vote—or not to vote—on the basis of a candidate's religious affiliation or association with certain religious leaders? The question stated more generally is this: in a religiously and morally pluralistic society such as ours, are citizens wrong to ground their political behavior on sectarian religious reasons?

A March 2005 ruling of the Colorado Supreme Court suggests that they are. In that ruling the court threw out a death penalty in a gruesome rape-and-murder case precisely because several of the jurors had distributed and discussed Bible passages such as "eye for eye, tooth for tooth" while deliberating the sentence.[7] And these judges are hardly alone in thinking that these jurors were acting improperly. Over the last decade or so, one of the prevailing opinions among liberal political theorists has been that citizens ought to bracket their religious convictions when deliberating political matters and deciding how to vote.

But can a compelling case be made that says that nearly half of all Americans are, in fact, *bad* citizens? In many respects, this is the fundamental question animating the essays in this anthology. One should note that the issue at hand is *not* whether these citizens have the legal right to vote as they vote or to participate in public deliberation as they do. Even adamantly anti-religious democratic thinkers avoid making these sorts of arguments against such rights to religious liberty and freedom of expression. And, indeed, it is highly likely in America that religious citizens will continue to exercise their legal rights to be influenced by their respective religions in the course of public deliberation, political advocacy, and voting. The issue, instead, is whether citizens shirk the moral duties of good democratic citizenship when they employ religious reasoning in the public square.

II

Controversy over the issue of religion and democratic citizenship in many respects stems from a tension present in our American public philosophy.[8] As Americans, we conceive ourselves in two different and, at times, conflicting ways: the United States is at once both *liberal* and *democratic*. We see ourselves as liberal in that we maintain that citizens should not be required to submit to any one particular religious, moral, or philosophical authority.[9] This liberal self-conception motivates our public urge to accommodate a wide range of differences, allowing citizens liberty to pursue various goods and ends consistent with individual choice and conscience. Alongside this liberal element stands our democratic self-conception, which (roughly put) motivates our need to seek political legitimacy by means of securing the consent of the governed. Integral to this notion of self-government is the idea that citizens should be free to voice their concerns, beliefs, and preferences *as they understand them* in the political sphere. So, among other things, what falls out of our democratic self-conception is our felt need to pursue common goods and entertain ongoing public dialogue about matters of shared interest, where citizens engage even at fundamental levels.

Traditionally, the liberal self-conception—or more generally, liberal-ism—has been understood by many as being not only consistent with but a necessary supplement to democracy itself. At least since John Stuart Mill, political theorists have argued that democracy should be kept in check by certain institutional limits so as to prevent the tyranny of the democratic majority over individual citizens. Mill famously writes:

> Protection, therefore, against the tyranny of the magistrate is not enough; there needs protection also against the tyranny of the prevailing opinion and feeling, against the tendency of society to impose, by other means than civil penalties, its own ideas and practices as rules of conduct on those who dissent from them; to fetter the development and, if possible, prevent the formation of any individuality not in harmony with its ways, and compel all characters to fashion themselves upon the model of its own. There is a limit to the legitimate interference of collective opin-ion with individual independence; and to find that limit, and maintain it against encroachment, is as indispensable to a good condition of human affairs as protection against despotism.[10]

The concern that Mill aptly expresses here is that, without some con-straints in place, our democratic aims can get out of hand, and democ-racy runs the risk of collapsing into mob rule. Thus, individuals stand in need of a schedule of rights and liberties invulnerable to the changing tides of prevailing majoritarian opinion. Only when our democratic aim is so limited can we expect to protect the value of being free to choose and follow one's own good in one's own way, which, at least according to Mill, is the "only freedom which deserves the name."[11] And it is only when the exercise of this individual freedom brings harm upon others that it can be justifiably encroached by the democratic majority.

Contemporary liberals like John Rawls argue similarly concerning the fit between liberalism and democracy. Accordingly, liberalism is viewed as a type of constraint on democracy that allows it to function properly. For Rawls, this constraint manifests as an idea of political legitimacy according to which "our exercise of political power is proper only when we sincerely believe that the reasons we would offer for our political action . . . are sufficient, and we also reasonably think that other citizens might also reasonably accept those reasons." Imposing this standard of political legitimacy—a standard more stringent than mere majority opinion—effectively guards citizens against oppression. Accordingly, an individual is free to pursue her own conception of the good life unless prohibitions can be justified to her in terms which she can be expected to endorse. That is, only when the use of coercive state power is justified to "every last individual"—even those individuals who differ from the prevailing opinion—is it legitimate.[12] And only when this liberal principle of legitimacy is met, so it is thought, is our democratic ambition properly safeguarded against oppressive mob rule.

But, while these aims—liberal *and* democratic—stand side by side in our public philosophy, they are not always entirely compatible; hence the tension we confront.[13] On the one hand, our liberal aim prompts us to pursue constraints on the kinds of reasons that should be employed in the public square so that the actions of the government can be justified to all individuals despite the diversity of religious, moral, and philosophical convictions among citizens. On this view, political decisions should be made in such a way as to prevent any one particular doctrine from dominating the public sphere and oppressing those who might reasonably reject that doctrine. Thus, only reasoning that remains neutral among conflicting religious, moral, and philosophical doctrines will sufficiently meet our needs to afford individuals enough space to march to the beat of their own drummers and thereby mute any would-be oppressive and homogenizing cadence. Yet, on the other hand, our democratic aim promotes the notion that "we the people" are sovereign. As such, this democratic aim prompts us to think that the commitments, convictions, and voices of the citizens should be taken and heard *as they stand*. Among other things, this means that citizens should not have to bracket their religious, moral, and philosophical doctrines when entering the public square.

It is an uncontroversial sociological fact that citizens disagree about religious, moral, and philosophical authority. This sociological fact of pluralism, when fully acknowledged, pushes to the surface the tension latent in our liberal democratic public philosophy. We want the actions of the state to be justifiable to "every last individual," thereby satisfying the liberal conditions for legitimacy. But these religious, moral, and philosophical doctrines about which citizens disagree are themselves visions of ultimate value—and hence visions of final goods—and so are not easily compromised for the sake of political values. It might seem inevitable, then, that justifications in the public square will need to engage these conflicting comprehensive doctrines. So contemporary political theorists face a difficult question: given the sociological fact of pluralism, how are we to achieve the sort of justification and legitimacy required by our democratic aims? On what grounds can the actions of the state be justified to citizens who are so divided? Restated just a bit, how are citizens to govern themselves when those very citizens do not share fundamental religious, moral, and philosophical commitments? Unchecked majoritarianism threatens to slip into a baser mob rule, as Mill warns, potentially undermining our liberal aims. But it seems that if we impose the sort of neutralist constraints required by our liberal aims when thinking about the public square, we find it increasingly difficult to support our democratic aspiration to allow citizens to come as they are to the public square, complete with their deepest religious, moral, and philosophical views of ultimate value and final good. Consequently, the tension between our *liberal* and *democratic* aims fully emerges, thrusting on us difficult questions that continue to vex our public philosophy in America.

It is unlikely that we will be able to make much progress in answering these deeper theoretical questions unless we pause to figure out exactly what the role of religious, moral, and philosophical doctrines in the public life of citizens should be. Why is this? We are trying to figure out how self-government is possible for a citizenry that is divided on fundamental commitments. Consequently, it makes sense to consider what role those fundamental commitments about which the citizenry is so divided should play in the political arena. And it goes perhaps without saying that those fundamental commitments in question are going to be primarily religious, at least within the American context.

III

There are a variety of responses to the question of whether and to what extent religion should factor into citizenship in the democratic public square. Typically, these views fall into one of two broad categories—what I shall call here *separatism* and *integrationism*. Separatist views seek to keep religion and politics in distinct and separate spheres. Integrationist views argue that the religious convictions of citizens have some legitimate role to play—or are at least permissible under certain circumstances—in democratic politics. Of course, there are variations within each of these categories. And it is worth pointing out that these categories themselves are not hard and fast; some views seem to defy being neatly placed in one or the other category. In any case, I offer these categories simply as a way of (only roughly) organizing the different views in currency. What follows is a brief introduction to each of the essays in this anthology.

Part I: Separatist Views

Liberal political theorists like Thomas Nagel, John Rawls, Robert Audi, Stephen Macedo, Bruce Ackerman, and Richard Rorty tend toward separatism in the sense that they favor keeping religion and politics separate, at least in some important respect. Accordingly, a common theme among their views is that good democratic citizenship requires citizens (in some sense) to bracket their religious views when attempting to justify important public policy matters and deciding how to vote. For instance, in his essay "Moral Conflict and Political Legitimacy" Nagel argues that political justification requires that citizens offer impersonal reasons for their favored positions so that other citizens can "have what you have, and can arrive at a judgment on the same basis." This precludes, on Nagel's view, appeals to one's personal faith or revelation of the truth precisely because such appeals are not something that other citizens in a pluralistic society have access to in the same way. In his seminal essay, "The Idea of Public Reason Revisited," Rawls argues that meeting the demands of his liberal principle of legitimacy (mentioned above) requires citizens to justify their political positions and votes on fundamental matters with *public* reasons, i.e., reasons that are neutral with respect to the diverse assortment of comprehensive moral, religious, and philosophical doctrines at play in a pluralistic society. In this essay, Rawls attempts to widen the view of public reason he previously spelled out in *Political Liberalism* by allowing reasons drawn from a comprehensive doctrine to be expressed in public deliberation, provided that "we give public reasons to support the principles and policies our comprehensive doctrine is said to support." This now famous proviso seems to push Rawls' view closer to the view expressed by Audi in "Religious Convictions and Secular Reasons." There, Audi argues that citizens should abide by a principle of secular rationale that "says that one has a prima facie obligation not to advocate or support any law or public policy that restricts human conduct, unless one has, and is willing to offer, adequate secular reason for this advocacy or support (say for one's vote)." Consequently, while religious reasons are not *per se* impermissible, they can only do the work of overdetermination. Hence, religious reasons by themselves should have no role in the actual justification of political positions. Additionally, on Audi's view, citizens should be careful to make sure they have sufficient secular motivation for their political positions. In his "Liberal Civic Education and Religious Fundamentalism: The Case of God v. John Rawls?" Macedo discusses the

Mozert v. Hawkins case, which prompts a consideration of the claim made
by some fundamentalists that political liberalism is not sufficiently inclusive of their religious views. In defense of political liberalism's aim to seek
justification of public policy on the basis of reasons shared by "reasonable
people whose religious and other ultimate commitments differ," Macedo
argues that liberalism should have "spine" and own up to "the fact that
no version of liberalism can make everyone happy."

Whereas some separatists tend to endorse restrictions (or at least heavy
qualifications) on religious reasoning in the public square by focusing on
the moral duties incumbent on citizens, other separatists like Ackerman
and Rorty advocate the separation of religion from public deliberation on
more practical grounds. For instance, in his "Why Dialogue?" Ackerman
suggests that citizens should employ "conversational restraint" in the face
of certain contentious moral and religious questions about which there
is deep disagreement. Accordingly, "we should simply say *nothing at all*
about this disagreement and put the moral ideal that divides us off the
conversational agenda of the liberal state," says Ackerman. The basic idea
is that, by employing some restraint with respect to the types of reasons
to which we can appeal and the types of issues considered in public
deliberation, there is at least some hope of deliberating other matters with
reasons that remain neutral regarding the moral, religious, and philosophical commitments about which we sharply disagree. The implication
then is that religious reasons are best left out of public deliberation. In
"Religion as Conversation-Stopper," Rorty argues that religion tends to
impede and even kill deliberations in the political arena. For, on Rorty's
view, religious reasons are mostly unconvincing and, as such, just cannot do the sort of work we need our reasons to do in the public square.
Hence, Rorty thinks that religious citizens should strike a Jeffersonian
compromise: employ only useful, secular reasons in the public square
and allow their religious beliefs to remain a private matter.

Part II: Integrationist Views

There are a variety of what I call integrationist views included in the second part of this anthology. A common theme in the integrationist views
of Nicholas Wolterstorff, Christopher J. Eberle, Paul J. Weithman, Jeffrey
Stout, Cornel West, Michael J. Perry, Richard John Neuhaus, Michael J.
Sandel, as well as my own, is that there is no *ex ante* moral restriction on
religious reasoning in the public square. There are, of course, differences
in how these integrationist views are spelled out. For instance, in "The

Role of Religion in Decision and Discussion of Political Issues" Wolter-storff argues that the project of locating an independent source of wholly neutral public reasons (of the sort that Rawls and other liberals advocate) is doomed from the outset. Hence, in spelling out his own consocial position, he argues that citizens should feel free to express whatever reasons they actually hold in the public square. In "What Respect Requires—And What It Does Not," Eberle takes a different approach. While Rawlsian liberals claim that citizens should show respect to their fellow citizens by *successfully* offering public reasons to justify their favored coercive policies, Eberle contends that respect simply requires citizens "sincerely and conscientiously to *pursue* a plausible nonreligious rationale for [their] favored coercive laws" even if they ultimately lack a "plausible nonreligious rationale." The implication is that religious reasoning is perfectly acceptable in the public square, as long as citizens meet this justificatory obligation to *pursue* nonreligious rationales. Weithman argues in "The Principles" that responsible democratic citizenship requires that "citizens advocate and vote only for measures that they sincerely believe would be justified." But, on Weithman's view, this doesn't require that citizens not offer distinctly religious reasons for what they sincerely take to be the justification of their favored views.

In his "Religious Reasons in Political Argument," Stout argues that respect does not require citizens to restrict or privatize their religious views when participating in the activities of the public square. Rather, on Stout's view, a citizen can show respect to his fellow citizens by taking seriously and engaging in immanent criticism "the distinctive point of view *each* other occupies," including an interlocutor's religious point of view. West takes a pragmatic turn in his "The Crisis of Christian Identity in America" and suggests that leftist intellectuals often undermine their own attempts to bring about progressive reform since many of them rely on decidedly antireligious strategies for bringing it about. As such, political theorists should concern themselves less with how to keep religion out of the public square and more with how to forge and support a "new democratic Christian identity in America" that draws upon the "prophetic legacies" of the civil rights movement, while avoiding the "imperial realities" of what he what deems Constantinian Christianity. In "Why Political Reliance on Religiously Grounded Morality Is Not Illegitimate in a Liberal Democracy," Perry argues that reliance on religious reasoning in the public square does not violate the core moral commitments of liberal democracy to the inviolability of persons and the protection of basic

human freedoms. He contends that we should not discourage but rather
"*encourage* the presentation of such [religious] belief in public political
argument—so that we can test it there" and, in turn, be tested by it.

In "The Vulnerability of the Naked Public Square," Neuhaus argues that
neutralist liberals have a dangerously myopic view of our shared political
culture and, as such, construct models of public reasoning that overlook
the sociological reality of the religious element in our society. On his
view, the exclusions of particularist religion in the naked public square
(to use his metaphor) ultimately move us in the direction of embracing
the "state-as-church, toward totalitarianism." In "The Public Philosophy
of Contemporary Liberalism," Sandel offers a civic-republican critique of
liberal conceptions of neutral public reasoning. He contends that requiring religious and moral commitments to be bracketed in the public square
poses problems for maintaining the "moral energies of a vital democratic
life." Moreover, he argues that the neutralist requirements of liberalism
are problematic insofar as they presume a flawed conception of the self as
unencumbered—a conception that "cannot account for certain moral and
political obligations that we commonly recognize." In my own contribution to this anthology, "Democratic Deliberation *after* Religious Gag Rules,"
I propose a roughly Peircean model of the public square that encourages
citizens to express whatever lines of reasoning they may hold, as long as
they do so in a manner that is open to truth-seeking inquiry and, hence,
to the possibility of deliberative defeat. I offer an epistemic justification for
this fallibility requirement, following the work of Cheryl Misak. My aim in
this essay is to provide a strategy for accommodating religious citizens and
their modes of reasoning in the democratic public square in a way that *also*
provides a framework for holding them accountable.

IV

Unfortunately, no single anthology can possibly include *all* of the useful
and significant contributions to the debate concerning the role of religion in the public square and the ethics of citizenship; there is simply
too much literature on this subject to compile in one place. At best, an
anthology of this sort can only hope to provide insight into the some of
the most significant twists and turns of this important dialectic. Moreover, the important issues surrounding this particular debate are numerous. One of the most notable omissions of this anthology is the important
work related directly to church-state issues, though clearly some of the
essays in this volume are relevant to that debate. And this anthology does

not include important discussion related directly to the issues of religion in politics within the global context. But concerning these omissions, one needs to offer no apology. The issues concerning the role of religion in the American public square are important and expansive enough in their own right to warrant serious reflection. The aim of this anthology is to provide readers—students, teachers, and scholars alike—with a helpful resource for understanding the basic contours of a debate that is central to citizenship in American democracy.

Part I

SEPARATIST VIEWS

Chapter 1

Moral Conflict
and Political Legitimacy

Thomas Nagel

I

Robert Frost defined a liberal as someone who can't take his own side in an argument. A bit harsh, but there is something paradoxical about liberalism, at least on the surface, and something obscure about the foundations of the sort of impartiality that liberalism professes. That is what I want to discuss.

Ethics always has to deal with the conflict between the personal standpoint of the individual and some requirement of impartiality. The personal standpoint will bring in motives derived not only from the individual's interests but also from his attachments and commitments to people, projects, and particular things. The requirement of impartiality can take various forms, but it usually involves treating or counting everyone equally in some respect—according them all the same rights, or counting their good or their welfare or some aspect of it the same in determining what would be a desirable result or a permissible course of action. Since personal motives and impartiality can conflict, an ethical theory has to say something about how such conflicts are to be resolved. It may do this by according total victory to the impartial side in case of conflict, but that is only one solution.

The clash between impartiality and the viewpoint of the individual is compounded when we move from personal ethics to political theory. The reason is that in politics, where we are all competing to get the coercive power of the state behind the institutions we favor—institutions under which all of us will have to live—it is not only our personal interests, attachments, and commitments that bring us into conflict, but our different moral conceptions. Political competitors differ as to both the form and the content of the impartial component of morality. They differ over what is good and bad in human life, and what kind of equal respect or consideration we owe each other. Their political disagreements therefore reflect not only conflicts of interest but conflicts over the values that public institutions should serve, impartially, for everyone.

Is there a higher-order impartiality that can permit us to come to some understanding about how such disagreements should be settled? Or have we already gone as far as necessary (and perhaps even as far as possible) in taking up other people's point of view when we have accepted the impartial component of our own moral position? I believe that liberalism depends on the acceptance of a higher-order impartiality, and that this raises serious problems about how the different orders of impartiality are to be integrated. To some extent this parallels the familiar problem in moral theory of integrating impartiality with personal motives; but the problem here is more complicated, and the motive for higher-order impartiality is more obscure.[1]

It is so obscure that critics of liberalism often doubt that its professions of impartiality are made in good faith. Part of the problem is that liberals ask of everyone a certain restraint in calling for the use of state power to further specific, controversial moral or religious conceptions—but the results of that restraint appear with suspicious frequency to favor precisely the controversial moral conceptions that liberals usually hold.

For example, those who argue against the restriction of pornography or homosexuality or contraception on the grounds that the state should not attempt to enforce contested personal standards of morality often don't think there is anything wrong with pornography, homosexuality, or contraception. They would be against such restrictions even if they believed it *was* the state's business to enforce personal morality or if they believed that the state could legitimately be asked to prohibit anything simply on the grounds that it was wrong.

More generally, liberals tend to place a high value on individual freedom, and limitations on state interference based on a higher-order impartiality among values tends to promote the individual freedom to which liberals are partial. This leads to the suspicion that the escalation to a higher level of impartiality is a sham, and that all the pleas for toleration and restraint really disguise a campaign to put the state behind a secular, individualistic, and libertine morality—against religion and in favor of sex, roughly.

Yet liberalism purports to be a view that justifies religious toleration not only to religious skeptics but to the devout, and sexual toleration not only to libertines but to those who believe extramarital sex is sinful. Its good faith is to some degree attested in the somewhat different area of free expression, for there liberals in the United States have long defended the rights of those they detest. The American Civil Liberties Union is usually glad of the chance to defend the Nazis when they want to demonstrate somewhere. It shows that liberals are willing to restrain the state from stopping something that they think is wrong—for we can assume most supporters of the ACLU think both that it is wrong to be a Nazi and that it is wrong for the Nazis to demonstrate in Skokie.

Another current example is that of abortion. At least some who oppose its legal prohibition believe that it is morally wrong but that their reasons for this belief cannot justify the use of state power against those who are convinced otherwise. This is a difficult case, to which I shall refer again.

Of course liberalism is not merely a doctrine of toleration, and liberals all have more specific interests and values, some of which they will seek to support through the agency of the state. But the question of what kind of impartiality is appropriate arises there as well. Both in the prohibition of what is wrong and in the promotion of what is good, the point of view from which state action and its institutional framework are supposed to be justified is complex and in some respects obscure. I shall concentrate on the issue of toleration and shall often use the example of religious toleration. But the problem also arises in the context of distributive justice and promotion of the general welfare—for we have to use some conception of what is good for people in deciding what to distribute and what to promote, and the choice of that conception raises similar questions of impartiality.[2]

II

This question is part of the wider issue of political legitimacy—the history of attempts to discover a way of justifying coercively imposed political and social institutions to the people who have to live under them and at the same time to discover what those institutions must be like if such justification is to be possible. "Justification" here does not mean "persuasion." It is a normative concept: arguments that justify may fail to persuade, if addressed to an unreasonable audience; and arguments that persuade may fail to justify. Nevertheless, justifications hope to persuade the reasonable, so these attempts have a practical point: political stability is helped by wide agreement to the principles underlying a political order. But that is not all: for some, the possibility of justifying the system to as many participants as possible is of independent moral importance. Of course this is an ideal. Given the actual range of values, interests, and motives in a society, and depending on one's standards of justification, there may not be a legitimate solution, and then one will have to choose between illegitimate government and no government.

The practical and the moral issues of political motivation are intertwined. On the one hand, the motivations that are morally required of us must be practically and psychologically possible, otherwise our political theory will be utopian in the bad sense. On the other hand, moral argument and insight can reveal and explain the possibility of political motivations which cannot be assumed in advance of moral discussion. In this way, political theory may have an effect on what motives are practically available to ground legitimacy, and therefore stability.

Defenses of political legitimacy are of two kinds: those which discover a possible *convergence* of rational support for certain institutions from the separate motivational standpoints of distinct individuals; and those which seek a *common standpoint* that everyone can occupy, which guarantees agreement on what is acceptable. There are also political arguments that mix the convergence and common standpoint methods. A convergence theory may begin from motives that differ widely from person to person, or it may begin from a single type of motive, like self-interest, which differs from person to person only because it is self-referential. In either case, the difference of starting points means that the motivational base itself does not guarantee that there is a social result which everyone will find desirable. A common standpoint theory, by contrast, starts from a single desire that is not self-referential, and this guarantees a common social aim, provided people can agree on the facts.

Hobbes, the founder of modern political theory, is a convergence theorist par excellence. Starting from a premoral motive that each individual has, the concern for his own survival and security, Hobbes argues that it is rational for all of us to converge from this self-referential starting point on the desirability of a system in which general obedience to certain rules of conduct is enforced by a sovereign of unlimited power. This is a convergence theory because the motive from which each of us begins refers only to his own survival and security, and it is entirely contingent that there should be any outcome that all of us can accept equally on those grounds: our personal motives could in principle fail to point us toward a common goal. And as is generally true of convergence theories, the political result is thought to be right because it is rationally acceptable to all, rather than being rationally acceptable to all because it is by some independent standard right.

Utilitarianism, on the other hand, is an example of a common stand-point theory. It asks each person to evaluate political institutions on the basis of a common moral motive which makes no reference to himself.[3] If all do take up this point of view of impartial benevolence, it will automat-ically follow that they have reason to accept the same solutions—since they are judging in light of a common desire for everyone's happiness. A political result is then rationally acceptable to everyone because by the utilitarian standard it is right; it is not right because it is universally acceptable. There are other types of convergence theories—notably those which find political legitimacy in a compromise among conflicting eco-nomic, social, and religious interests, acceptable to all as an alternative to social breakdown. And common standpoint theories can be based on motives other than general benevolence—commitment to the protec-tion of certain individual rights, rejection of severe social and economic inequalities, even nationalism or a shared religious commitment. But what I want to concentrate on is a type of mixed theory that is charac-teristic of contemporary liberalism. Recent political philosophy has seen the development of a new type of liberal theory, exemplified by the work of Rawls and others, whose distinctive feature is that it bases the legiti-macy of institutions on their conformity to principles which it would be reasonable for disparate individuals to agree on, where the standard of individual reasonableness is not merely a premoral rationality, but rather a form of reasoning that includes moral motives. In contrast with Hobbesian convergence, reasonable agreement is in these theories sought by each person as an end and not merely as a means necessary for social stability. At the same time, the moral motives which contribute to convergence are not sufficient by themselves to pick out an acceptable result: more individual motives also enter into the process. So the prin-ciples converged on are right because they are acceptable—not generally acceptable because they are by independent standards morally right.

With regard to Rawls, I am referring here not to the reasoning inside the Original Position (from which moral motives are excluded), but to the wider argument within which the Original Position plays a subsidiary role, the argument that we should regulate our claims on our common institutions by the principles that *would* be chosen in the Original Position.

It may seem surprising to characterize Rawls' theory as a mixed theory, for in asking us all to enter the Original Position to choose principles of justice, he seems simply to be proposing a common standpoint of impartiality which guarantees that we will all approve of the same thing. But an important element of Rawls' argument is his reference to the strains of commitment: even in the Original Position, not knowing his own conception of the good, each person can choose only such principles of justice as he believes he will be able to live under and continue to affirm in actual life, when he knows the things about himself and his position in society that are concealed by the Veil of Ignorance.[4] This introduces an element of convergence.[5]

True principles of justice are those which can be affirmed by individuals motivated both by the impartial sense of justice as fairness and by their fundamental personal interests, commitments, and conceptions of the good. As with other convergence theories, it is not logically guaranteed that there are such principles, but if there are, they will be shaped by the requirement of such convergence, and their rightness will not be demonstrable independent of that possibility. That is what Rawls means by describing the theory as a form of constructivism.

The other position I would like to mention is T. M. Scanlon's. The criterion of moral wrongness he proposes in "Contractualism and Utilitarianism" employs the notion of a rule which no one could reasonably reject, provided he had among his motives a desire to live under rules which no one who also had that motive could reasonably reject. This notion can be used to construct a mixed theory of political legitimacy, where the common standpoint is represented by the said harmonious desire and convergence enters because what people can and cannot reasonably reject is determined in part by their other, divergent motives as well.

Note that the standard is not what principles or institutions people will *actually accept*, but what it would be unreasonable for them not to accept, given a certain common moral motivation in addition to their more personal, private, and communal ends. As with Rawls, there would be no standard of political legitimacy or rightness independent of this possibility of convergence.

It is a distinctive feature of both these theories that they set moral limits to the use of political power to further not only familiar social and economic interests, but also moral convictions. They are mixed theories based not just on a mixture of benevolence and self-concern but on limits to the *content* of benevolence. They distinguish between the values a person can appeal to in conducting his own life and those he can appeal to in justifying the exercise of political power.

III

What I want to know is whether a position of this type is coherent and defensible. I am concerned less with the specific views of Rawls or Scanlon than with the fundamental moral idea behind such a position, which is that we should not impose arrangements, institutions, or requirements on other people on grounds that they could reasonably reject (where reasonableness is not simply a function of the independent rightness or wrongness of the arrangements in question but genuinely depends on the point of view of the individual to some extent). The question is whether an interpretation of this condition, or something like it, can be found which makes it plausible, despite an initial appearance of paradox.

It is not clear why the possibility of this kind of convergence should be the standard of political legitimacy at all. Why should I care whether others with whom I disagree can accept or reject the grounds on which state power is exercised? Why shouldn't I discount their rejection if it is based on religious or moral or cultural values that I believe to be mistaken? Why allow my views of the legitimate use of state power to become hostage to what it would be reasonable for *them* to accept or reject? Can't I instead base those views on the values that I believe to be correct?

An antiliberal critic of Rawls could put the point by asking why he should agree to be governed by principles that he would choose if he did not know his own religious beliefs, or his conception of the good. Isn't that being *too* impartial, giving much authority to those whose values conflict with yours—betraying your own values, in fact? If I believe something, I believe it to be *true*, yet here I am asked to refrain from acting on that belief in deference to beliefs I think are false. What possible moral motivation could I have for doing that? Impartiality among persons is one thing, but impartiality among conceptions of the good is quite another. Why isn't true justice giving everyone the best possible chance of salvation, for example, or of a good life? In other words, don't we have to start from the values that we ourselves accept in deciding how state power may legitimately be used?

And it might be added, are we not doing that anyway if we adopt the liberal standard of impartiality? Not everyone believes that political legitimacy depends on this condition, and if we forcibly impose political institutions because they do meet it (and block the imposition of institutions that do not), why are we not being just as partial to our own values as someone who imposes a state religion? It has to be explained why this is a form of impartiality at all. To answer these questions we have to identify the moral conception involved and see whether it has the authority to override those more particular moral conceptions that divide us—and if so, to what extent or in what respects. Rawls has said in a recent article that if liberalism had to depend on a commitment to comprehensive moral ideals of autonomy and individuality, it would become just "another sectarian doctrine."[6] The question is whether its claim to be something else has any foundation.

IV

If liberalism is to be defended as a higher-order theory rather than just another sectarian doctrine, it must be shown to result from an interpretation of impartiality itself rather than from a particular conception of the good that is to be made impartially available. Of course any interpretation of impartiality will be morally controversial—it is not a question of rising to a vantage point above all moral disputes—but the controversy will be at a different level.

In the versions of liberalism formulated by Rawls, Ronald Dworkin, and Bruce Ackerman, exclusion of appeal to particular conceptions of the good at the most basic level of political argument is one of the ways in which it is required that social institutions should treat people equally or impartially. But since this is much less obvious than the requirements of impartiality with respect to race, sex, social class, or even natural endowments, it requires a special explanation by reference to more fundamental moral ideas. The requirement itself may be modified as a result of the explanation: the proposal I end up with does not correspond perfectly to the views from which I begin.[7]

What form should impartiality take, in the special conditions which are the province of political theory? The specialness of the conditions is important. We have to be impartial not just in the conferring of benefits, but in the imposition of burdens, the exercise of coercion to ensure compliance with a uniform set of requirements, and the demand for support of the institutions that impose those requirements and exercise that coercion. (Even if the support is not voluntarily given, it will to some degree be exacted, if only through payment of taxes and passive conformity to certain institutional arrangements.) I suggest that this element of coercion imposes an especially stringent requirement of objectivity in justification.[8] If someone wishes simply to benefit others, there can in my view be no objection if he gives them what is good by his own lights (so long as he does them no harm by theirs). If someone wants to pray for the salvation of my soul, I can't really complain on the grounds that I would rather he gave me a subscription to *Playboy*. The problem arises when he wants to force me to attend church or pay for its upkeep instead of staying home and reading *Playboy*. The real problem is how to justify making people do things against their will.

We can leave aside the familiar and unproblematic Hobbesian basis for coercion: I may want to be forced to do something as part of a practice whereby everyone else is forced to do the same, with results that benefit us all in a way that would not be possible unless we could be assured of widespread compliance. This is not really forcing people to do what they don't want to do, but rather enabling them to do what they want to do by forcing them to do it.

There are two other types of coercion whose justification seems clear: prevention of harm to others and certain very basic forms of paternalism. In both these types of case, we can make an impersonal appeal to values that are generally shared: people don't want to be injured, robbed, or killed, and they don't want to get sick. The nature of those harms and the impersonal value of avoiding them are uncontroversial and can be appealed to to justify forcibly preventing their infliction. From an impersonal standpoint I can agree that anyone, myself included, should be prevented from harming others in those ways.

I can also agree that under some conditions I should be prevented from harming myself in those ways, as should anyone else. The clear conditions include my being crazy or seriously demented or radically misinformed about the likely results of what I am doing. Paternalism is justified in such cases because when we look at them from outside, we find no impersonal value competing with the values of health, life, and safety. If I say I would want to be prevented from drinking lye during a psychotic episode, it is not because the dangers of internal corrosion outweigh the value of self-expression. We are not faced here with a conflict of impartialities.

But in other cases we are. I have gone over these familiar examples for the sake of contrast. There are cases where forcing someone to do what he doesn't want to do is problematic—not just because he doesn't want to do it, but because of his reasons for not wanting to do it. The problematic cases are those in which either the impersonal value to which I appeal to justify coercion would not be acknowledged by the one coerced, or else it conflicts with another impersonal value to which he subscribes but which I do not acknowledge, though I would if I were he. In such a case it seems that I shall have failed in some respect to be impartial whether I coerce him or not.

An example may help. I am not a Christian Scientist. If I ask myself whether, thinking of it from outside, I would want to be forced to undergo medical treatment if I *were* a Christian Scientist and had a treatable illness, it is hard to know what to say. On the one hand, given my beliefs, I am inclined to give no impersonal weight to the reasons I would offer for refusing treatment if I *were* a Christian Scientist, and substantial weight to the medical reasons in favor of treatment. After all, if I believe Christian Science is false, I believe it would be false even if I believed it was true. On the other hand, I am inclined to give considerable impersonal weight to the broader consideration of not wanting others to ride roughshod over my beliefs on the subject of religion, whatever they may be.

Or suppose a Roman Catholic who believes that outside the Church there is no salvation asks himself whether if he were not a Catholic he would want to be given strong incentives to accept the Catholic faith, perhaps by state support of the Church and legal discouragement of other religions.[9] He may be torn between the impartial application of his actual religious values and the impartial application of a more general value that he also holds, of not wanting other people's religious convictions to be imposed on him.

Which of these should dominate? It is really a problem about the interpretation of the familiar role-reversal argument in ethics: "How would you like it if someone did that to you?" The answer that has to be dealt with is "How would I like it if someone did *what* to me?" There is often more than one way of describing a proposed course of action, and much depends on which description is regarded as relevant for the purpose of moral argument.

V

This general problem is familiar in the context of interpreting universalizability conditions in ethics, but I am thinking of a particular version of it. Should a Catholic, considering restriction of freedom of worship and religious education for Protestants from an impersonal standpoint, think of it as

(1) preventing them from putting themselves and others in danger of eternal damnation;

(2) promoting adherence to the true faith;

(3) promoting adherence to the Catholic faith;

(4) preventing them from practicing their religion; or

(5) preventing them from doing something they want to do?

For the purpose of argument, let me suppose that as far as he is concerned, he would be doing all of these things. The question then is, which of them determines how he should judge the proposed restriction from an impersonal standpoint?

The defense of liberalism depends on rejecting (5) as the relevant description, and then stopping with (4) rather than going on to (2) or (1). Roughly, the liberal position avoids two contrary errors. To accept as an authoritative impersonal value everyone's interest in doing what he wants to do, for whatever reason (that is, to rely on description [1]), is to give too much authority to other people's preferences in determining their claims on us. To accord impersonal weight to our own values, whatever they are (that is, to rely on descriptions [1] and [2]), is on the other hand not to give others enough authority over what we may require of them.

The characteristic of description (4) that the others lack is that it has some chance of both (a) being accepted by all parties concerned as a true description of what is going on (something it shares with [3] and [1]), and (b) being accorded the same kind of impersonal value by all parties concerned (something it shares, more or less, with [1] and [2]).

This makes (4) a natural choice for the morally relevant description which provides a basis for impartial assessment. However, several objections have to be dealt with.

First, why isn't (5) at least as impartial as (4)? No one wants to be prevented from doing what he wants to do. Why can't we all agree that impersonal value should be assigned to people's doing or getting what they want, rather than to something more restricted like freedom of worship?

But the fact is that we cannot. To assign impersonal value to the satisfaction of all preferences is to accept a particular view of the good—a component of one form of utilitarianism—which many would find clearly unacceptable and which they would not be unreasonable to reject.[10] The objection to making it the basis of political legitimacy parallels the objection to making any other comprehensive individual conception of the good the basis of political and social institutions. A liberal who is a utilitarian should no more impose his conception of the good on others than should a liberal who is a Roman Catholic or a devotee of aesthetic perfection—that is, he should pursue the good so conceived for himself and others only within the limits imposed by a higher-order impartiality.

This reply, however, leads to another objection: if (5) is ruled out, why shouldn't (4) be ruled out for parallel reasons? The value of liberty seems more neutral than the value of preference-satisfaction, but perhaps it is not. The problem with assigning impersonal value to the satisfaction of preferences per se (description [1]) is that if a nonutilitarian is asked, "How would you like to be prevented from doing something you want to do?" he can reply, "That depends on what it is, and why I want to do it." A similar move might be made against assigning uniform impersonal value to religious toleration (description [4]). If a Catholic is asked, "How would you like to be prevented from practicing your religion?" why can't he reply, "That depends on whether it's the true religion or not"?

But in that case we are left with no version of what is going on that permits a common description resulting in a common impersonal assessment. If the description can be agreed on, the assessment cannot be, and vice versa. Impartiality has been ruled out.

VI

A solution to this impasse requires that we find a way of being impartial not only in the allocation of benefits or harms but in their identification. The defense of liberalism requires that a limit somehow be drawn to appeals to *the truth* in political argument, and that a standpoint be found from which to draw that limit. It may seem paradoxical that a general condition of impartiality should claim greater authority than more special conceptions which one believes to be, simply, true—and that it should lead us to defer to conceptions which we believe to be false—but that is the position.

Gerald Dworkin discusses this issue in an essay called "Non-neutral Principles." He means principles like "The true religion should be taught in the public schools"—whose application to particular cases "is a matter of controversy for the parties whose conduct is supposed to be regulated by the principle in question."[11]

Dworkin argues that the liberal position has to rest on a skeptical epistemological premise—"that one cannot arrive at justified belief in religious matters."[12] That, he claims, is the only possible justification for suppressing knowledge of the parties' religious beliefs in Rawls' Original Position—a condition essential to Rawls' argument for tolerance. "If there were a truth and it could be ascertained," asks Dworkin, "would those in the original position who contemplated the possibility that they would be holders of false views regard their integrity as harmed by choosing that it [sic] should be suppressed?"[13]

Rawls, however, claims that his position depends on no such skepticism.[14] "We may observe," he says, "that men's having an equal liberty of conscience is consistent with the idea that all men ought to obey God and accept the truth. The problem of liberty is that of choosing a principle by which the claims men make on one another in the name of their religion are to be regulated. Granting that God's will should be followed and the truth recognized does not as yet define a principle of adjudication."[15]

He intends to put forward not a skeptical position about religious knowledge but a restriction on the sorts of convictions that can be appealed to in political argument. In his recent discussion he says: "It is important to stress that from other points of view, for example, from the point of view of personal morality, or from the point of view of members of an association, or of one's religious or philosophical doctrine, various aspects of the world and one's relation to it, may be regarded in a different way. But these other points of view are not to be introduced into political discussion."[16]

I believe that true liberalism requires that something like Rawls' view be correct, that is, that exclusion of the appeal to religious convictions not rely on a skeptical premise about individual belief. Rather it must depend on a distinction between what justifies individual belief and what justifies appealing to that belief in support of the exercise of political power. As I have said, liberalism should provide the devout with a reason for tolerance.

But is Rawls right? It is not sufficient to exclude knowledge of one's religious beliefs from the Original Position on the grounds that this is needed to make agreement possible. The question is whether there is a viable form of impartiality that makes it possible to exclude such factors from the basis of one's acceptance of political institutions, or whether, alternatively, we have to give up the hope of liberal legitimacy.

I believe that the demand for agreement, and its priority in these cases over a direct appeal to the truth, must be grounded in something more basic. Though it has to do with epistemology, it is not skepticism but a kind of epistemological restraint: the distinction between what is needed to justify belief and what is needed to justify the employment of political power depends on a higher standard of objectivity, which is ethically based.

The distinction results, I believe, if we apply the general form of moral thought that underlies liberalism to the familiar fact that while I cannot maintain a belief without implying that what I believe is true, I still have to acknowledge that there is a big difference, looking at it from the outside, between my believing something and its being true.

On the view I would defend, there is a highest-order framework of moral reasoning (not the whole of morality) which takes us outside ourselves to a standpoint that is independent of who we are. It cannot derive its basic premises from aspects of our particular and contingent starting points within the world, though it may authorize reliance on such specialized points of view if this is justified from the more universal perspective. Since individuals are very different from one another and must lead complex individual lives, the universal standpoint cannot reasonably withhold this authorization lightly. But it is most likely to be withheld from attempts to claim the authority of the impersonal standpoint for a point of view that is in fact that of a particular individual or party, against that of other individuals or parties who reject that point of view. This happens especially in the political or social imposition of institutions that control our lives, that we cannot escape, and that are maintained by force.

Morality can take us outside ourselves in different ways or to different degrees. The first and most familiar step is to recognize that what we want should not depend only on our own interests and desires—that from outside, other people's interests matter as much as ours do, and we should want to reconcile our interests with theirs as far as possible. But liberal impartiality goes beyond this by trying to make the epistemological standpoint of morality impersonal as well.

The idea is that when we look at certain of our convictions from outside, however justified they may be from within, the appeal to their truth must be seen merely as an appeal to our beliefs and should be treated as such unless those beliefs can be shown to be justifiable from a more impersonal standpoint. If not, they have to remain, for the purpose of a certain kind of moral argument, features of a personal perspective—to be respected as such but no more than that.

This does not mean we have to stop believing them—that is, believing them to be *true*. Considered as individual beliefs, they may be adequately grounded, or at least not unreasonable: the standards of individual rationality are different from the standards of epistemological ethics. It means only that from the perspective of political argument we may have to regard certain of our beliefs, whether moral or religious or even historical or scientific, simply as someone's beliefs rather than as truths—unless they can be given the kind of impersonal justification appropriate to that perspective, in which case they may be appealed to as truths without qualification.

We accept a kind of epistemological division between the private and the public domains: in certain contexts I am constrained to consider my beliefs merely as beliefs rather than as truths, however convinced I may be that they are true, and that I know it. This is not the same thing as skepticism. Of course if I believe something, I believe it to be true. I can recognize the possibility that what I believe may be false, but I cannot with respect to any particular present belief of mine think that possibility is realized. Nevertheless, it is possible to separate my attitude toward my belief from my attitude toward the thing believed and to refer to my belief alone rather than to its truth in certain contexts of justification.

The reason is that unless there is some way of applying from an impersonal standpoint the distinction between my believing something and its being true, an appeal to its truth is equivalent to an appeal to my belief in its truth. To show that the two are not equivalent I would have to show how the distinction could be applied, in political argument, in a way that did not surreptitiously assume my personal starting point—by, for example, defining objective truth in terms of the religion to which I adhere, or the beliefs I now hold. I have to be able to admit that I might turn out to be wrong, by some standards that those who disagree with me but are also committed to the impersonal standpoint can also acknowledge. The appeal to truth as opposed to belief is compatible with disagreement among the parties—but it must imply the possibility of some standard to which an impersonal appeal can be made, even if it cannot settle our disagreement at the moment.

VII

The real difficulty is to make sense of this idea, the idea of something which is neither an appeal to my own beliefs nor an appeal to beliefs that we all share. It cannot be the latter because it is intended precisely to justify the forcible imposition in some cases of measures that are not universally accepted. We need a distinction between two kinds of disagreement—one whose grounds make it all right for the majority to use political power in the service of their opinion, and another whose grounds are such that it would be wrong for the majority to do so.

For this purpose we cannot appeal directly to the distinction between reasonable and unreasonable beliefs. It would be an impossibly restrictive condition on political power to say that its exercise may be justified only by appeal to premises that others could not reasonably reject (though less restrictive than the condition that the premises be *actually* accepted by all). If the impossibility of reasonable rejection comes in at all, it must come in at a higher level, in justifying some less stringent standard for the justification of particular employments of political power.

Reasonable persons can disagree not only over religious doctrines and ultimate conceptions of the good life, but over levels of public provision of education and health care, social security, defense policy, environmental preservation, and a host of other things that liberal societies determine by legislative action. What distinguishes those disagreements from the ones where liberalism rejects majority rule? When can I regard the grounds for a belief as objective in a way that permits me to appeal to it in political argument, and to rely on it even though others do not in fact accept it and even though they may not be unreasonable not to accept it? What kinds of grounds must those be, if I am not to be guilty of appealing simply to my belief, rather than to a common ground of justification?

By a common ground I do not mean submerged agreement on a set of premises by which the claim could in principle be settled in a way that all parties would recognize as correct. Public justification in a context of actual disagreement requires, first, preparedness to submit one's reasons to the criticism of others, and to find that the exercise of a common critical rationality and consideration of evidence that can be shared will reveal that one is mistaken. This means that it must be possible to present to others the basis of your own beliefs, so that once you have done so, *they have what you have,* and can arrive at a judgment on the same basis. That is not possible if part of the source of your conviction is personal faith or revelation—because to report your faith or revelation to someone else is not to give him what you have, as you do when you show him your evidence or give him your arguments.

Public justification requires, second, an expectation that if others who do not share your belief are wrong, there is probably an explanation of their error which is not circular. That is, the explanation should not come down to the mere assertion that they do not believe the truth (what you believe), but should explain their false belief in terms of errors in their evidence, or identifiable errors in drawing conclusions from it, or in argument, judgment, and so forth. One may not always have the information necessary to give such an account, but one must believe there is one, and that the justifiability of one's own belief would survive a full examination of the reasons behind theirs. These two points may be combined in the idea that a disagreement which falls on objective common ground must be open-ended in the possibility of its investigation and pursuit, and not come down finally to a bare confrontation between incompatible personal points of view. I suggest that conflicts of religious faith fail this test, and most empirical and many moral disagreements do not.

The large question I have not addressed is whether there are significant differences of fundamental moral opinion which also fail the test—and if so, how the line is to be drawn between those cases and others which fall into the public domain. My sense is that the sort of liberal restraint I have been describing should apply, in the present state of moral debate, to certain matters besides the enforcement of religious views. I would include abortion, sexual conduct, and the killing of animals for food, for example. Admittedly, if we refrain from enforcing any moral position on these matters, it has the same effect as we would get if the law were based on the positive position that whatever people choose to do in these areas is permissible. But the two justifications for restraint are very different, and if I am right, the first is available to those who may not accept the second.

To defend this claim would require serious analysis of the issues. I would try to argue that such disagreements come down finally to a pure confrontation between personal moral convictions, and that this is perceptibly different from a disagreement in judgment over the preponderant weight of reasons bearing on an issue. Of course there are reasons and arguments on both sides, but they come to an end in a different and more personal way than arguments about welfare payments or affirmative action, for example. This does not mean that such disagreements cannot move into the public category through further development of common grounds of argument. But at any given stage, the justifications on opposite sides of an issue may come to an end with moral instincts which are simply internal to the points of view of the opposed parties—and this makes them more like conflicts of personal religious conviction.

I realize that this is vague. It also raises a further problem: Why can't the same be said of some fundamental issues that clearly fall within the public domain? Aren't people's disagreements about the morality of nuclear deterrence and the death penalty just as ultimate and personal as their disagreements over abortion?

The question requires much more discussion than I can give it here. Briefly, these issues are poor candidates for liberal toleration because they are not matters of individual conduct, which the state may or may not decide to regulate. So no conclusion about what the state should do can be derived from the refusal to justify the use of state power by reference to any particular position on the moral issue. The application of the death penalty or the possession by the military of nuclear weapons cannot be left to the private conscience of each individual citizen: the state *must* decide.[17]

The same question might also be raised about fundamental issues of social justice—the conflicts of economic liberals with radical libertarians, or with radical collectivists who regard individualism as an evil. Here I would give a more complex answer. I do not believe these moral oppositions are as "personal" as the others: even radical disagreements about freedom and distributive justice are usually part of some recognizable public argument. On the other hand, social provision is not so essentially the function of the state as is warfare: voluntary collective action is certainly possible. So to the extent that some of these disagreements are like religious disagreements, there would be a place for liberal toleration in the economic sphere—for example, toleration of private ownership even by those who think it is an evil.

VIII

It is important to stress that the nondogmatic moral disagreements which fall within the public domain may nevertheless be irresolvable in fact. That there is common ground does not mean that people will actually reach agreement, nor does it mean that only one belief is reasonable on the evidence. I may hold a belief on grounds that I am willing to offer in objective justification, suitable for the public domain, while acknowledging that others who consider that justification and yet reject the belief are not being irrational or unreasonable, though I think they are wrong.

The idea is that in such a case there is a common reason in which both parties share, but from which they get different results because they cannot, being limited creatures, be expected to exercise it perfectly.[18] Differences in evidence result from the different experiences people have had and the different testimony and arguments to which they have been exposed. Even more important are differences in assessment of the evidence and the arguments, and these inevitably involve differences of judgment. In most significant cases reasonable belief is not strictly determined by the grounds that can be explicitly offered: that is why there can be reasonable disagreement—disagreement in judgment—even among those who are in general agreement about what kinds of grounds are relevant to the matter at hand, and what the evidence and arguments in the case are. (In some cases they may agree more precisely on what evidence not now available would demonstrate decisively which of them is right; but this need not be so—either in factual matters, if they are sufficiently general, or in questions of value.)

I believe—though I wish I could express it more clearly than this—that the parties to such a disagreement can think of themselves as appealing to a common, objective method of reasoning which each of them interprets and applies imperfectly. They can therefore legitimately claim to be appealing not merely to their personal, subjective beliefs but to a common reason which is available to everyone and which can be invoked on behalf of everyone even though not everyone interprets its results in the same way.

There is something of a paradox here: How can I believe something if I think others presented with the same grounds could reasonably refuse to believe it? Doesn't this mean I believe it but think also that it would be reasonable for *me* not to believe it—and is that possible?

Well, perhaps if I actually think that as things are and as I am, it would be reasonable for me not to believe *p*, I cannot believe it. But I may think it would be reasonable for someone else either to believe or not to believe *p* on the evidence available to me that I can specifically identify, yet find that I do believe it. Perhaps in that case I must also judge that it would not be reasonable for *me*, as I am, not to believe it on that evidence— though I don't know why. This would be true whether my grounds are highly personal, or impersonal and objective. There may be people enough like me in whatever determines judgment so that if I judge that they could reasonably disbelieve *p*, I cannot reasonably believe it. But if there is such a class of persons, it is not coextensive with my political community and cannot determine the standard of public justification.

We therefore have to recognize that there can be enough consider-ations on more than one side of a question in the public domain so that reasonable belief is partly a matter of judgment, and is not uniquely determined by the publicly available arguments. But I do not believe this makes the distinction between a disagreement in the common, public domain and a clash between irreconcilable subjective convictions too rarefied to be of political significance. Judgment is not the same as faith, or pure moral intuition.

Admittedly it will be controversial in many cases whether an appeal to truth collapses into an appeal to belief—some people might try to deny objective, public status to scientific methods that most of us would take as clear cases of impersonal verification, whereas others might claim objective status for certain theological arguments or forms of revelation. Religious believers no doubt vary in this respect: some would deny that belief is a matter of reasonable judgment; but others would presumably claim that the truth of their doctrines is supported by objective reasons and evidence of a kind available to all. These issues have to be argued out one by one; I do not have a general test of public epistemological justi-fication—which is not, I repeat, the same as intersubjective agreement. But I believe that the basic idea remains intelligible even if its application is problematic.[19] The appeal to truth in political argument requires an objective distinction between belief and truth that can be applied or at least understood from the public standpoint appropriate to the argument in question. Disagreements over the truth must be interpreted as result-ing from differences of judgment in the exercise of a common reason.

Otherwise the appeal to truth collapses into an appeal to what I believe, and belief carries a very different kind of weight in political argu-ments. The fact that someone has certain religious or moral convictions has its own considerable importance, from an impersonal standpoint, in determining how he should be treated and what he should do, but it is not the same as the importance that the truth of those convictions would have, if it could be admitted as a premise in political argument. There would be no inclination to accept impersonally a general right to try to use state power to limit the liberty of others in order to force them to live as I *believe* they should live. None of us would be willing to have our liberty limited by others on such grounds. But if I am right, the appeal to the truth of a certain religion to justify enforcement collapses into just such an appeal to belief.

We can now return to the distinction between (4) and (5), which was left hanging at the end of Section V. Why is liberty a more neutral standard of evaluation than preference-satisfaction? I have tried to explain why a believer, if asked, "How would you like to be prevented from practicing your religion?" cannot legitimately reply, "That depends on whether it's the true religion or not." But why doesn't the same argument rule out the corresponding reply to the question "How would you like to be prevented from doing something you want to do?"—namely, the reply "That depends on what it is, and why I want to do it"?

I believe this reply is not in general ruled out, because the judgments appealed to in following it up need not be pure personal beliefs, but may claim the kind of objectivity and admit the kind of public justification which allows them to be used in political argument. Of course sometimes they will turn out to be inadmissibly private or parochial, but they need not be: it can be argued that the satisfaction of some desires is valueless or harmful by public and objective standards. The resistance to preference-satisfaction as a public measure of value can be objective in a way in which the resistance to religious liberty cannot be.

IX

Even if some form of liberal impartiality can be defended in this way, it has to contend with the persistence of those personal convictions which it excludes from political argument, or admits only under strict constraints. This is a general problem in ethics: the impersonal standpoint does not make personal motives go away, and in restricting their operation it may put itself under great strain.

It is difficult to decide how much weight the liberal version of impartiality can bear when it comes into conflict not only with purely personal interests but with the impartial application of more particular values that cannot be generally acknowledged. From an impersonal standpoint, how strongly is my commitment to religious toleration prepared to resist the value of health, when applied to the case of a Christian Scientist? And how strongly can the impersonal value of not being prevented from practicing one's religion resist the less impartial but still impersonal interest of a Catholic in the salvation of souls?

In such cases, the condition of public justification reverses the relative importance possessed by different values in the private domain. To a believer, salvation is more important than liberty, yet in political justification he may not appeal to the importance of salvation to justify the restriction of liberty, because liberty is a publicly admissible value and salvation is not. One might ask whether the standard of liberal impartiality itself meets the condition of impersonal justifiability necessary for admission to the public domain. I believe that it does, because it is defendable, and attackable, by arguments of the right type, some of which I have tried to formulate. And I would add that its claim to objective status is not undermined by the fact that some people may not accept it because they reject the requirement of impersonal justifiability itself. Even those who accept the requirement may disagree about how it is to be applied, but that is another matter.

Liberalism is a demanding doctrine. Still, it is qualified somewhat by a division of the moral territory. Its relatively stringent impartiality applies only to uniform and involuntary social and political institutions. One might ask why. Why doesn't the same standard apply to the justification of all action that has an effect, even indirectly, on the interests of others? Part of the answer, already referred to above, is that when we force people to serve an end that they cannot share, and that we cannot justify to them in objective terms, it is a particularly serious violation of the Kantian requirement that we treat humanity not merely as a means, but also as an end. The justification of coercion must meet especially stringent standards.

The other answer I would give is that we have here an instance of the moral division of labor between society and the individual, corresponding to the division of standpoints in each of us.[20] We literally externalize the demands of the impersonal standpoint by placing in the hands of social and political institutions the task of enforcing the most general claims for assistance and restraint of our fellow human beings. Subject to our contribution to the support of those institutions, this ideally should leave us free to lead our individual lives in obedience to more personal attachments, commitments, and crotchets. It would be for most of us intolerably intrusive to have to live by a morality that required us to justify everything we did, insofar as it affected others, in terms that could be defended from an impersonal standpoint.

The liberal restriction on what kind of thing we may appeal to does not apply to the justification of action generally. It leaves individuals free to regulate their own personal lives (and to a lesser extent, though this is a problematic intermediate case, the lives of their children) according to their full personal conceptions of how life should be lived. And it also, importantly, leaves them free to refer to their own conceptions in determining how they will benefit others or help them avoid harm or misfortune, so far as this goes beyond what is morally or legally obligatory.

Most importantly of all, this extends to the domain of political activity, which in a democracy is left open to the pursuit by individuals of their goals and interests—the large range of legislative and communal issues that are put under the control of the preferences of the majority, or of coalitions among minorities. In these cases it is not that we give the authority of the impersonal standpoint to the point of view of the winning side. Rather, on a certain range of questions, we regard the balancing of all sorts of personal preferences or opinions against one another as impersonally acceptable.

Liberalism certainly does not require us to run our lives, even our lives as political beings, on radically impartial principles. But it does require that the imposed framework within which we pursue our more individual values and subject ourselves to the possibility of control by the values of others be in a strong sense impartially justifiable. That means it must bear up under substantial moral and motivational strain.

The real issue is not just relative strength but relative priority. Liberal impartiality is not in competition with more specific values as one conception of the good among others. If it were, it would be unintelligible, for it would have to advocate impartiality between itself and alternative conceptions, and that would generate a meaningless regress of higher-order standpoints in search of common ground between liberalism and more sectarian views. But liberalism does not require its adherents to step outside liberalism itself to compromise with antiliberal positions. It purports to provide a maximally impartial standard of right which has priority over more specialized conceptions in determining what may be imposed on us by our fellow humans, and vice versa. (This is not just the familiar doctrine of the priority of the right over the good, since some of the specialized views that are subordinated by liberalism may themselves be conceptions of right.)

The real problems with the position arise in its interpretation, not from the fact that it is controversial. It must distinguish two types of grounds for belief, neither of which shows that those who reject the belief are necessarily unreasonable, but one of which justifies the exercise of political power and the other not—and it must explain why the distinction has this consequence, and how it is to be applied. Of course liberal impartiality claims for itself an authority that will not in fact be universally accepted, and therefore the justifications it offers for resisting the imposition of more particular values in certain cases will not secure actual universal agreement. But since it is a substantive moral position, that is not surprising.

Chapter 2

The Idea of Public
Reason Revisited

John Rawls

INTRODUCTION

The idea of public reason, as I understand it,[1] belongs to a conception of
a well-ordered constitutional democratic society. The form and content
of this reason—the way it is understood by citizens and how it interprets their political relationship—is part of the idea of democracy itself.
This is because a basic feature of democracy is the fact of reasonable
pluralism—the fact that a plurality of conflicting reasonable comprehensive doctrines,[2] religious, philosophical, and moral, is the normal result
of its culture of free institutions.[3] Citizens realize that they cannot reach
agreement or even approach mutual understanding on the basis of their
irreconcilable comprehensive doctrines. In view of this, they need to consider what kinds of reasons they may reasonably give one another when
fundamental political questions are at stake. I propose that in public
reason comprehensive doctrines of truth or right be replaced by an idea
of the politically reasonable addressed to citizens as citizens.[4]

Central to the idea of public reason is that it neither criticizes nor attacks any comprehensive doctrine, religious or nonreligious, except insofar as that doctrine is incompatible with the essentials of public reason and a democratic polity. The basic requirement is that a reasonable doctrine accepts a constitutional democratic regime and its companion idea of legitimate law. While democratic societies will differ in the specific doctrines that are influential and active within them—as they differ in the western democracies of Europe and the United States, Israel, and India—finding a suitable idea of public reason is a concern that faces them all.

§ 1: THE IDEA OF PUBLIC REASON

1. The idea of public reason specifies at the deepest level the basic moral and political values that are to determine a constitutional democratic government's relation to its citizens and their relation to one another. In short, it concerns how the political relation is to be understood. Those who reject constitutional democracy with its criterion of reciprocity will of course reject the very idea of public reason.[5] For them the political relation may be that of friend or foe, to those of a particular religious or secular community or those who are not; or it may be a relentless struggle to win the world for the whole truth. Political liberalism does not engage those who think this way. The zeal to embody the whole truth in politics is incompatible with an idea of public reason that belongs with democratic citizenship.

The idea of public reason has a definite structure, and if one or more of its aspects are ignored it can seem implausible, as it does when applied to the background culture.[6] It has five different aspects: (1) the fundamental political questions to which it applies; (2) the persons to whom it applies (government officials and candidates for public office); (3) its content as given by a family of reasonable political conceptions of justice; (4) the application of these conceptions in discussions of coercive norms to be enacted in the form of legitimate law for a democratic people; and (5) citizens' checking that the principles derived from their conceptions of justice satisfy the criterion of reciprocity.

Moreover, such reason is public in three ways: as the reason of free and equal citizens, it is the reason of the public; its subject is the public good concerning questions of fundamental political justice, which questions are of two kinds, constitutional essentials and matters of basic justice;[7] and its nature and content are public, being expressed in public reasoning by a family of reasonable conceptions of political justice reasonably thought to satisfy the criterion of reciprocity. It is imperative to realize that the idea of public reason does not apply to all political discussions of fundamental questions but only to discussions of those questions in what I refer to as the public political forum.[8] This forum may be divided into three parts: the discourse of judges in their decisions, and especially of the judges of a supreme court; the discourse of government officials, especially chief executives and legislators; and finally, the discourse of candidates for public office and their campaign managers, especially in their public oratory, party platforms, and political statements.[9] We need this three-part division because, as I note later, the idea of public reason does not apply in the same way in these three cases and elsewhere.[10] In discussing what I call the wide view of public political culture,[11] we shall see that the idea of public reason applies more strictly to judges than to others, but that the requirements of public justification for that reason are always the same.

Distinct and separate from this three-part public political forum is what I call the background culture.[12] This is the culture of civil society. In a democracy, this culture is not, of course, guided by any one central idea or principle, whether political or religious. Its many and diverse agencies and associations with their internal lives reside within a framework of law that ensures the familiar liberties of thought and speech and the right of free association.[13] The idea of public reason does not apply to the background culture with its many forms of nonpublic reason nor to media of any kind.[14] Sometimes those who appear to reject the idea of public reason actually mean to assert the need for full and open discussion in the background culture.[15] With this political liberalism fully agrees.

Finally, distinct from the idea of public reason, as set out by the five features above, is the *ideal* of public reason. This ideal is realized, or satisfied, whenever judges, legislators, chief executives, and other government officials, as well as candidates for public office, act from and follow the idea of public reason and explain to other citizens their reasons for supporting fundamental political positions in terms of the political conception of justice they regard as the most reasonable. In this way they fulfill what I shall call their duty of civility to one another and to other citizens. Hence, whether judges, legislators, and chief executives act from and follow public reason is continually shown in their speech and conduct on a daily basis.

How though is the ideal of public reason realized by citizens who are not government officials? In a representative government citizens vote for representatives—chief executives, legislators, and the like—and not for particular laws (except at a state or local level when they may vote directly on referenda questions, which are rarely fundamental questions). To answer this question, we say that ideally citizens are to think of themselves *as if* they were legislators and ask themselves what statutes, supported by what reasons satisfying the criterion of reciprocity, they would think it most reasonable to enact.[16] When firm and widespread, the disposition of citizens to view themselves as ideal legislators, and to repudiate government officials and candidates for public office who violate public reason, is one of the political and social roots of democracy and is vital to its enduring strength and vigor.[17] Thus citizens fulfill their duty of civility and support the idea of public reason by doing what they can to hold government officials to it. This duty, like other political rights and duties, is an intrinsically moral duty. I emphasize that it is not a legal duty, for in that case it would be incompatible with freedom of speech.

2. I now turn to a discussion of what I have labeled the third, fourth, and fifth aspects of public reason. The idea of public reason arises from a conception of democratic citizenship in a constitutional democracy. This fundamental political relation of citizenship has two special features: first, it is a relation of citizens within the basic structure of society, a structure we enter only by birth and exit only by death;[18] and second, it is a relation of free and equal citizens who exercise ultimate political power as a collective body. These two features immediately give rise to the question of how, when constitutional essentials and matters of basic justice are at stake, citizens so related can be bound to honor the structure of their constitutional democratic regime and abide by the statutes and laws enacted under it. The fact of reasonable pluralism raises this question all the more sharply, since it means that the differences between citizens arising from their comprehensive doctrines, religious and nonreligious, may be irreconcilable. By what ideals and principles, then, are citizens who share equally in ultimate political power to exercise that power so that each can reasonably justify his or her political decisions to everyone?

To answer this question we say: citizens are reasonable when, viewing one another as free and equal in a system of social cooperation over generations, they are prepared to offer one another fair terms of cooperation according to what they consider the most reasonable conception of political justice; and when they agree to act on those terms, even at the cost of their own interests in particular situations, provided that other citizens also accept those terms. The criterion of reciprocity requires that when those terms are proposed as the most reasonable terms of fair cooperation, those proposing them must also think it at least reasonable for others to accept them, as free and equal citizens, and not as dominated or manipulated, or under the pressure of an inferior political or social position.[19] Citizens will of course differ as to which conceptions of political justice they think the most reasonable, but they will agree that all are reasonable, even if barely so.

Thus when, on a constitutional essential or matter of basic justice, all appropriate government officials act from and follow public reason, and when all reasonable citizens think of themselves ideally as if they were legislators following public reason, the legal enactment expressing the opinion of the majority is legitimate law. It may not be thought the most reasonable or the most appropriate by each, but it is politically (morally) binding on him or her as a citizen and is to be accepted as such. Each thinks that all have spoken and voted at least reasonably, and therefore all have followed public reason and honored their duty of civility.

Hence the idea of political legitimacy based on the criterion of reciprocity says: our exercise of political power is proper only when we sincerely believe that the reasons we would offer for our political actions—were we to state them as government officials—are sufficient, and we also reasonably think that other citizens might also reasonably accept those reasons. This criterion applies on two levels: one is to the constitutional structure itself; the other is to particular statutes and laws enacted in accordance with that structure. To be reasonable, political conceptions must justify only constitutions that satisfy this principle.

To make more explicit the role of the criterion of reciprocity as expressed in public reason, note that its role is to specify the nature of the political relation in a constitutional democratic regime as one of civic friendship. For this criterion, when government officers act from it in their public reasoning and other citizens support it, shapes the form of their fundamental institutions. For example—I cite an easy case—if we argue that the religious liberty of some citizens is to be denied, we must give them reasons they can not only understand—as Servetus could understand why Calvin wanted to burn him at the stake—but reasons we might reasonably expect that they, as free and equal citizens, might reasonably also accept. The criterion of reciprocity is normally violated whenever basic liberties are denied. For what reasons can both satisfy the criterion of reciprocity and justify denying to some persons religious liberty, holding others as slaves, imposing a property qualification on the right to vote, or denying the right of suffrage to women?

Since the idea of public reason specifies at the deepest level the basic political values and specifies how the political relation is to be understood, those who believe that fundamental political questions should be decided by what they regard as the best reasons according to their own idea of the whole truth—including their religious or secular comprehensive doctrine—and not by reasons that might be shared by all citizens as free and equal, will of course reject the idea of public reason. Political liberalism views this insistence on the whole truth in politics as incompatible with democratic citizenship and the idea of legitimate law.

3. Democracy has a long history, from its beginning in classical Greece down to the present day, and there are many different ideas of democracy.[20] Here I am concerned only with a well-ordered constitutional democracy—a term I used at the outset—understood also as a deliberative democracy. The definitive idea for deliberative democracy is the idea of deliberation itself. When citizens deliberate, they exchange views and debate their supporting reasons concerning public political questions. They suppose that their political opinions may be revised by discussion with other citizens; and therefore these opinions are not simply a fixed outcome of their existing private or nonpolitical interests. It is at this point that public reason is crucial, for it characterizes such citizens' reasoning concerning constitutional essentials and matters of basic justice. While I cannot fully discuss the nature of deliberative democracy here, I note a few key points to indicate the wider place and role of public reason.

There are three essential elements of deliberative democracy: one is an idea of public reason,[21] although not all such ideas are the same. A second is a framework of constitutional democratic institutions that specifies the setting for deliberative legislative bodies. The third is the knowledge and desire on the part of citizens generally to follow public reason and to realize its ideal in their political conduct. Immediate implications of these essentials are the public financing of elections and the providing for public occasions of orderly and serious discussion of fundamental questions and issues of public policy. Public deliberation must be made possible, recognized as a basic feature of democracy, and set free from the curse of money.[22] Otherwise politics is dominated by corporate and other organized interests who through large contributions to campaigns distort if not preclude public discussion and deliberation.

Deliberative democracy also recognizes that without widespread education in the basic aspects of constitutional democratic government for all citizens, and without a public informed about pressing problems, crucial political and social decisions simply cannot be made. Even should farsighted political leaders wish to make sound changes and reforms, they cannot convince a misinformed and cynical public to accept and follow them. For example, there are sensible proposals for what should be done regarding the alleged coming crisis in Social Security: slow down the growth of benefits levels, gradually raise the retirement age, impose limits on expensive terminal medical care that prolongs life for only a few weeks or days, and finally, raise taxes now rather than face large increases later.[23] But as things are, those who follow the "great game of politics" know that none of these sensible proposals will be accepted. The same story can be told about the importance of support for international institutions (such as the United Nations), foreign aid properly spent, and concern for human rights at home and abroad. In constant pursuit of money to finance campaigns, the political system is simply unable to function. Its deliberative powers are paralyzed.

§ 2: THE CONTENT OF PUBLIC REASON

1. A citizen engages in public reason, then, when he or she deliberates within a framework of what he or she sincerely regards as the most reasonable political conception of justice, a conception that expresses political values that others, as free and equal citizens, might also reasonably be expected reasonably to endorse. Each of us must have principles and guidelines to which we appeal in such a way that this criterion is satisfied. I have proposed that one way to identify those political principles and guidelines is to show that they would be agreed to in what in *Political Liberalism* is called the original position.[24] Others will think that different ways to identify these principles are more reasonable.

Thus, the content of public reason is given by a family of political conceptions of justice, and not by a single one. There are many liberalisms and related views and therefore many forms of public reason specified by a family of reasonable political conceptions. Of these, justice as fairness, whatever its merits, is but one. The limiting feature of these forms is the criterion of reciprocity, viewed as applied between free and equal citizens, themselves seen as reasonable and rational. Three main features characterize these conceptions:

> First, a list of certain basic rights, liberties, and opportunities (such as those familiar from constitutional regimes);

Second, an assignment of special priority to those rights, liberties, and opportunities, especially with respect to the claims of the general good and perfectionist values; and

Third, measures ensuring for all citizens adequate all-purpose means to make effective use of their freedoms.[25]

Each of these liberalisms endorses the underlying ideas of citizens as free and equal persons and of society as a fair system of cooperation over time. Yet since these ideas can be interpreted in various ways, we get different formulations of the principles of justice and different contents of public reason. Political conceptions differ also in how they order, or balance, political principles and values even when they specify the same ones. I assume also that these liberalisms contain substantive principles of justice and hence cover more than procedural justice. They are required to specify the religious liberties and freedoms of artistic expression of equal citizens, as well as substantive ideas of fairness involving fair opportunity and ensuring adequate all-purpose means, and much else.[26]

Political liberalism, then, does not try to fix public reason once and for all in the form of one favored political conception of justice.[27] That would not be a sensible approach. For instance, political liberalism also admits Habermas' discourse conception of legitimacy (sometimes said to be radically democratic rather than liberal),[28] as well as Catholic views of the common good and solidarity when they are expressed in terms of political values.[29] Even if relatively few conceptions come to dominate over time, and one conception even appears to have a special central place, the forms of permissible public reason are always several. Moreover, new variations may be proposed from time to time and older ones may cease to be represented. It is important that this be so; otherwise the claims of groups or interests arising from social change might be repressed and fail to gain their appropriate political voice.[30]

2. We must distinguish public reason from what is sometimes referred to as secular reason and secular values. These are not the same as public reason. For I define secular reason as reasoning in terms of comprehensive nonreligious doctrines. Such doctrines and values are much too broad to serve the purposes of public reason. Political values are not moral doctrines,[31] however available or accessible these may be to our reason and common-sense reflection. Moral doctrines are on a level with religion and first philosophy. By contrast, liberal political principles and values, although intrinsically moral values, are specified by liberal

political conceptions of justice and fall under the category of the political. These political conceptions have three features:

First, their principles apply to basic political and social institutions (the basic structure of society);

Second, they can be presented independently from comprehensive doctrines of any kind (although they may, of course, be supported by a reasonable overlapping consensus of such doctrines); and

Finally, they can be worked out from fundamental ideas seen as implicit in the public political culture of a constitutional regime, such as the conceptions of citizens as free and equal persons, and of society as a fair system of cooperation.

Thus, the content of public reason is given by the principles and values of the family of liberal political conceptions of justice meeting these conditions. To engage in public reason is to appeal to one of these political conceptions—to their ideals and principles, standards and values—when debating fundamental political questions. This requirement still allows us to introduce into political discussion at any time our comprehensive doctrine, religious or nonreligious, provided that, in due course, we give properly public reasons to support the principles and policies our comprehensive doctrine is said to support. I refer to this requirement as *the proviso*, and consider it in detail below.[32]

A feature of public reasoning, then, is that it proceeds entirely within a political conception of justice. Examples of political values include those mentioned in the preamble to the United States Constitution: a more perfect union, justice, domestic tranquility, the common defense, the general welfare, and the blessings of liberty for ourselves and our posterity. These include under them other values: so, for example, under justice we also have equal basic liberties, equality of opportunity, ideals concerning the distribution of income and taxation, and much else.

The political values of public reason are distinct from other values in that they are realized in and characterize political institutions. This does not mean that analogous values cannot characterize other social forms. The values of effectiveness and efficiency may characterize the social organization of teams and clubs as well as the political institutions of the basic structure of society. But a value is properly political only when the social form is itself political: when it is realized, say, in parts of the basic structure and its political and social institutions. It follows that many political conceptions are nonliberal, including those of aristocracy and corporate oligarchy, and of autocracy and dictatorship. All of these fall within the category of the political.[33] We, however, are concerned only with those political conceptions that are reasonable for a constitutional democratic regime, and as the preceding paragraphs make clear, these are the ideals and principles expressed by reasonable liberal political conceptions.

3. Another essential feature of public reason is that its political conceptions should be complete. This means that each conception should express principles, standards, and ideals, along with guidelines of inquiry, such that the values specified by it can be suitably ordered or otherwise united so that those values alone give a reasonable answer to all, or to nearly all, questions involving constitutional essentials and matters of basic justice. Here the ordering of values is made in the light of their structure and features within the political conception itself, and not primarily from how they occur within citizens' comprehensive doctrines. Political values are not to be ordered by viewing them separately and detached from one another or from any definite context. They are not puppets manipulated from behind the scenes by comprehensive doctrines.[34] The ordering is not distorted by those doctrines provided that public reason sees the ordering as reasonable. And public reason can indeed see an ordering of political values as reasonable (or unreasonable), since institutional structures are open to view, and mistakes and gaps within the political ordering will become exposed. Thus, we may be confident that the ordering of political values is not distorted by particular reasonable comprehensive doctrines. (I emphasize that the only criterion of distortion is that the ordering of political values be itself unreasonable.)

The significance of completeness lies in the fact that unless a political conception is complete, it is not an adequate framework of thought in the light of which the discussion of fundamental political questions can be carried out.[35] What we cannot do in public reason is to proceed directly from our comprehensive doctrine, or a part thereof, to one or several political principles and values and the particular institutions they support. Instead, we are required first to work to the basic ideas of a complete political conception and from there to elaborate its principles and ideals and to use the arguments they provide. Otherwise public reason allows arguments that are too immediate and fragmentary.

4. I now note several examples of political principles and values to illustrate the more specific content of public reason and particularly the various ways in which the criterion of reciprocity is both applicable

and subject to violation. (a) As a first example, consider the value of autonomy. It may take two forms: one is political autonomy, the legal independence and assured integrity of citizens and their sharing equally with others in the exercise of political power; the other is purely moral and characterizes a certain way of life and reflection, critically examining our deepest ends and ideals, as in Mill's ideal of individuality.[36] Whatever we may think of autonomy as a purely moral value, it fails to satisfy, given reasonable pluralism, the constraint of reciprocity, as many citizens, for example, those holding certain religious doctrines, may reject it. Thus moral autonomy is not a political value, whereas political autonomy is. (b) As a second example, consider the familiar story of the Good Samaritan. Are the values appealed to properly political values and not simply religious or philosophical values? While the wide view of public political culture allows us, in making a proposal, to introduce the gospel story, public reason requires us to justify our proposal in terms of proper political values.[37] (c) As a third example, consider appeals to desert in discussing the fair distribution of income: people are wont to say that ideally distribution should be in accordance with desert. What sense of desert do they have in mind? Do they mean that persons in various offices should have the requisite qualifications—judges must be qualified to judge—and all should have a fair opportunity to qualify themselves for favored positions? That is indeed a political value. But distribution in accordance with moral desert, where this means the moral worth of character, all things considered, and including comprehensive doctrines, is not. It is not a feasible political and social aim.

(d) Finally, consider the state's interest in the family and human life. How should the political value invoked be specified correctly? Traditionally it has been specified very broadly. But in a democratic regime the government's legitimate interest is that public law and policy should support and regulate, in an ordered way, the institutions needed to reproduce political society over time. These include the family (in a form that is just), arrangements for rearing and educating children, and institutions of public health generally. This ordered support and regulation rests on political principles and values, since political society is regarded as existing in perpetuity and so as maintaining itself and its institutions and culture over generations. Given this interest, the government would appear to have no interest in the particular form of family life, or of relations among the sexes, except insofar as that form or those relations in some way affect the orderly reproduction of society over time. Thus, appeals to monogamy as such, or against same-sex marriages, as within the government's legitimate interest in the family, would reflect religious or comprehensive moral doctrines. Accordingly, that interest would appear improperly specified. Of course, there may be other political values in the light of which such a specification would pass muster: for example, if monogamy were necessary for the equality of women, or same-sex marriages destructive to the raising and educating of children.[38]

5. The four examples bring out a contrast to what I have above called secular reason.[39] A view often expressed is that while religious reasons and sectarian doctrines should not be invoked to justify legislation in a democratic society, sound secular arguments may be.[40] But what is a secular argument? Some think of any argument that is reflective and critical, publicly intelligible and rational, as a secular argument; and they discuss various such arguments for considering, say, homosexual relations unworthy or degrading.[41] Of course, some of these arguments may be reflective and rational secular ones (as so defined). Nevertheless, a central feature of political liberalism is that it views all such arguments the same way it views religious ones, and therefore these secular philosophical doctrines do not provide public reasons. Secular concepts and reasoning of this kind belong to first philosophy and moral doctrine and fall outside of the domain of the political.

Thus, in considering whether to make homosexual relations between citizens criminal offenses, the question is not whether those relations are precluded by a worthy idea of full human good as characterized by a sound philosophical and nonreligious view, nor whether those of religious faith regard it as sin, but primarily whether legislative statutes forbidding those relations infringe the civil rights of free and equal democratic citizens.[42] This question calls for a reasonable political conception of justice specifying those civil rights, which are always a matter of constitutional essentials.

§ 3: RELIGION AND PUBLIC REASON IN DEMOCRACY

1. Before examining the idea of the wide view of public political culture, we ask: How is it possible for those holding religious doctrines, some based on religious authority, for example, the Church or the Bible, to hold at the same time a reasonable political conception that supports a reasonable constitutional democratic regime? Can these doctrines still be compatible for the right reasons with a liberal political conception? To attain this compatibility, it is not sufficient that these doctrines accept a democratic government merely as a *modus vivendi*. Referring to citizens

holding religious doctrines as citizens of faith, we ask: how is it possible for citizens of faith to be wholehearted members of a democratic society who endorse society's intrinsic political ideals and values and do not simply acquiesce in the balance of political and social forces? Expressed more sharply: how is it possible—or is it—for those of faith, as well as the nonreligious (secular), to endorse a constitutional regime even when their comprehensive doctrines may not prosper under it, and indeed may decline? This last question brings out anew the significance of the idea of legitimacy and public reason's role in determining legitimate law.

To clarify the question, consider two examples. The first is that of Catholics and Protestants in the sixteenth and seventeenth centuries when the principle of toleration was honored only as a *modus vivendi*.[43] This meant that should either party fully gain its way, it would impose its own religious doctrine as the sole admissible faith. A society in which many faiths all share this attitude and assume that for the indefinite future their relative numbers will stay roughly the same might well have a constitution resembling that of the United States, fully protecting the religious liberties of sharply divided religions more or less equal in political power. The constitution is, as it were, honored as a pact to maintain civil peace.[44] In this society political issues might be discussed in terms of political ideas and values so as not to open religious conflict and arouse sectarian hostility. The role of public reason here serves merely to quiet divisiveness and encourage social stability. However, in this case we do not have stability for the right reasons, that is, as secured by a firm allegiance to a democratic society's political (moral) ideals and values.

Nor again do we have stability for the right reasons in the second example—a democratic society where citizens accept as political (moral) principles the substantive constitutional clauses that ensure religious, political, and civil liberties, when their allegiance to these constitutional principles is so limited that none is willing to see his or her religious or nonreligious doctrine losing ground in influence and numbers, and such citizens are prepared to resist or to disobey laws that they think undermine their positions. And they do this even though the full range of religious and other liberties is always maintained and the doctrine in question is completely secure. Here again democracy is accepted conditionally and not for the right reasons.

What these examples have in common is that society is divided into separate groups, each of which has its own fundamental interest distinct from and opposed to the interests of the other groups and for which it is prepared to resist or to violate legitimate democratic law. In the first example, it is the interest of a religion in establishing its hegemony, while in the second, it is the doctrine's fundamental interest in maintaining a certain degree of success and influence for its own view, either religious or nonreligious. While a constitutional regime can fully ensure rights and liberties for all permissible doctrines, and therefore protect our freedom and security, a democracy necessarily requires that, as one equal citizen among others, each of us accepts the obligations of legitimate law.[45] While no one is expected to put his or her religious or nonreligious doctrine in danger, we must each give up forever the hope of changing the constitution so as to establish our religion's hegemony or of qualifying our obligations so as to ensure its influence and success. To retain such hopes and aims would be inconsistent with the idea of equal basic liberties for all free and equal citizens.

2. To expand on what we asked earlier: how is it possible—or is it—for those of faith, as well as the nonreligious (secular), to endorse a constitutional regime even when their comprehensive doctrines may not prosper under it, and indeed may decline? Here the answer lies in the religious or nonreligious doctrine's understanding and accepting that, except by endorsing a reasonable constitutional democracy, there is no other way fairly to ensure the liberty of its adherents consistent with the equal liberties of other reasonable free and equal citizens. In endorsing a constitutional democratic regime, a religious doctrine may say that such are the limits God sets to our liberty; a nonreligious doctrine will express itself otherwise.[46] But in either case, these doctrines formulate in different ways how liberty of conscience and the principle of toleration can cohere with equal justice for all citizens in a reasonable democratic society. Thus, the principles of toleration and liberty of conscience must have an essential place in any constitutional democratic conception. They lay down the fundamental basis to be accepted by all citizens as fair and regulative of the rivalry between doctrines.

Observe here that there are two ideas of toleration. One is purely political, being expressed in terms of the rights and duties protecting religious liberty in accordance with a reasonable political conception of justice. The other is not purely political but expressed from within a religious or a nonreligious doctrine, as when, for example, it was said above that such are the limits God sets on our liberty. Saying this offers an example of what I call reasoning from conjecture.[47] In this case we reason from what we believe, or conjecture, may be other people's basic doctrines, religious or philosophical, and seek to show them that, despite what they might think, they can still endorse a reasonable political conception of justice.

We are not ourselves asserting that ground of toleration but offering it as one they could assert consistent with their comprehensive doctrines.

§ 4: THE WIDE VIEW OF PUBLIC POLITICAL CULTURE

1. Now we consider what I call the wide view of public political culture and discuss two aspects of it. The first is that reasonable comprehensive doctrines, religious or nonreligious, may be introduced in public political discussion at any time, provided that in due course proper political reasons—and not reasons given solely by comprehensive doctrines—are presented that are sufficient to support whatever the comprehensive doctrines introduced are said to support. This injunction to present proper political reasons I refer to as *the proviso*, and it specifies public political culture as distinct from the background culture.[48] The second aspect I consider is that there may be positive reasons for introducing comprehensive doctrines into public political discussion. I take up these two aspects in turn.

Obviously, many questions may be raised about how to satisfy the proviso.[49] One is: when does it need to be satisfied? On the same day or some later day? Also, on whom does the obligation to honor it fall? It is important that it be clear and established that the proviso is to be appropriately satisfied in good faith. Yet the details about how to satisfy this proviso must be worked out in practice and cannot feasibly be governed by a clear family of rules given in advance. How they work out is determined by the nature of the public political culture and calls for good sense and understanding. It is important also to observe that the introduction into public political culture of religious and secular doctrines, provided the proviso is met, does not change the nature and content of justification in public reason itself. This justification is still given in terms of a family of reasonable political conceptions of justice. However, there are no restrictions or requirements on how religious or secular doctrines are themselves to be expressed; these doctrines need not, for example, be by some standards logically correct or open to rational appraisal or evidentially supportable.[50] Whether they are or not is a matter to be decided by those presenting them and how they want what they say to be taken. They will normally have practical reasons for wanting to make their views acceptable to a broader audience.

2. Citizens' mutual knowledge of one another's religious and nonreligious doctrines expressed in the wide view of public political culture[51] recognizes that the roots of democratic citizens' allegiance

to their political conceptions lie in their respective comprehensive doctrines, both religious and nonreligious. In this way citizens' allegiance to the democratic ideal of public reason is strengthened for the right reasons. We may think of the reasonable comprehensive doctrines that support society's reasonable political conceptions as those conceptions' vital social basis, giving them enduring strength and vigor. When these doctrines accept the proviso and only then come into political debate, the commitment to constitutional democracy is publicly manifested.[52] Made aware of this commitment, government officials and citizens are more willing to honor the duty of civility, and their following the ideal of public reason helps foster the kind of society that ideal exemplifies. These benefits of the mutual knowledge of citizens' recognizing one another's reasonable comprehensive doctrines bring out a positive ground for introducing such doctrines, which is not merely a defensive ground, as if their intrusion into public discussion were inevitable in any case.

Consider, for example, a highly contested political issue—the issue of public support for church schools.[53] Those on different sides are likely to come to doubt one another's allegiance to basic constitutional and political values. It is wise, then, for all sides to introduce their comprehensive doctrines, whether religious or secular, so as to open the way for them to explain to one another how their views do indeed support those basic political values. Consider also the abolitionists and those in the civil rights movement.[54] The proviso was fulfilled in their cases, however much they emphasized the religious roots of their doctrines, because these doctrines supported basic constitutional values—as they themselves asserted—and so supported reasonable conceptions of political justice.

3. Public reasoning aims for public justification. We appeal to political conceptions of justice, and to ascertainable evidence and facts open to public view, in order to reach conclusions about what we think are the most reasonable political institutions and policies. Public justification is not simply valid reasoning, but argument addressed to others: it proceeds correctly from premises we accept and think others could reasonably accept to conclusions we think they could also reasonably accept. This meets the duty of civility, since in due course the proviso is satisfied.

There are two other forms of discourse that may also be mentioned, though neither expresses a form of public reasoning. One is declaration: here we each declare our own comprehensive doctrine, religious or nonreligious. This we do not expect others to share. Rather, each of us shows how, from our own doctrines, we can and do endorse a reasonable public political conception of justice with its principles and ideals. The aim of doing this is to declare to others who affirm different comprehensive doctrines that we also each endorse a reasonable political conception belonging to the family of reasonable such conceptions. On the wide view, citizens of faith who cite the gospel parable of the Good Samaritan do not stop there, but go on to give a public justification for this parable's conclusions in terms of political values.[55] In this way citizens who hold different doctrines are reassured, and this strengthens the ties of civic friendship.[56]

The second form is conjecture, defined thus: we argue from what we believe, or conjecture, are other people's basic doctrines, religious or secular, and try to show them that, despite what they might think, they can still endorse a reasonable political conception that can provide a basis for public reasons. The ideal of public reason is thereby strengthened. However, it is important that conjecture be sincere and not manipulative. We must openly explain our intentions and state that we do not assert the premises from which we argue, but that we proceed as we do to clear up what we take to be a misunderstanding on others' part, and perhaps equally on ours.[57]

§ 5: ON THE FAMILY AS PART OF THE BASIC STRUCTURE

1. To illustrate further the use and scope of public reason, I shall now consider a range of questions about a single institution, the family.[58] I do this by using a particular political conception of justice and looking at the role that it assigns to the family in the basic structure of society. Since the content of public reason is determined by all the reasonable political conceptions that satisfy the criterion of reciprocity, the range of questions about the family covered by this political conception will indicate the ample space for debate and argument comprehended by public reason as a whole.

The family is part of the basic structure, since one of its main roles is to be the basis of the orderly production and reproduction of society and its culture from one generation to the next. Political society is always regarded as a scheme of social cooperation over time indefinitely; the idea of a future time when its affairs are to be concluded and society disbanded is foreign to the conception of political society. Thus, reproductive labor is socially necessary labor. Accepting this, a central role of the family is to arrange in a reasonable and effective way the raising of and caring for children, ensuring their moral development and education into the wider culture.[59] Citizens must have a sense of justice and the political virtues that support political and social institutions. The family must ensure the nurturing and development of such citizens in appropriate numbers to maintain an enduring society.[60]

These requirements limit all arrangements of the basic structure, including efforts to achieve equality of opportunity. The family imposes constraints on ways in which this goal can be achieved, and the principles of justice are stated to try to take these constraints into account. I cannot pursue these complexities here, but assume that as children we grow up in a small intimate group in which elders (normally parents) have a certain moral and social authority.

2. In order for public reason to apply to the family, it must be seen, in part at least, as a matter for political justice. It may be thought that this is not so, that the principles of justice do not apply to the family and hence those principles do not secure equal justice for women and their children.[61] This is a misconception. It may arise as follows: the primary subject of political justice is the basic structure of society understood as the arrangement of society's main institutions into a unified system of social cooperation over time. The principles of political justice are to apply directly to this structure but are not to apply directly to the internal life of the many associations within it, the family among them. Thus, some may think that if those principles do not apply directly to the internal life of families, they cannot ensure equal justice for wives along with their husbands.

Much the same question arises in regard to all associations, whether they be churches or universities, professional or scientific associations, business firms or labor unions. The family is not peculiar in this respect. To illustrate: it is clear that liberal principles of political justice do not require ecclesiastical governance to be democratic. Bishops and cardinals need not be elected; nor need the benefits attached to a church's hierarchy of offices satisfy a specified distributive principle, certainly not the difference principle.[62] This shows how the principles of political justice do not apply to the internal life of a church, nor is it desirable, or consistent with liberty of conscience or freedom of association, that they should.

On the other hand, the principles of political justice do impose certain essential constraints that bear on ecclesiastical governance. Churches cannot practice effective intolerance, since, as the principles of justice require, public law does not recognize heresy and apostasy as crimes, and members of churches are always at liberty to leave their faith. Thus, although the principles of justice do not apply directly to the internal life of churches, they do protect the rights and liberties of their members by the constraints to which all churches and associations are subject. This is not to deny that there are appropriate conceptions of justice that do apply directly to most if not all associations and groups as well as to various kinds of relationships among individuals. Yet these conceptions of justice are not political conceptions. In each case, what is the appropriate conception is a separate and additional question, to be considered anew in each particular instance, given the nature and role of the relevant association, group, or relation.

Now consider the family. Here the idea is the same: political principles do not apply directly to its internal life, but they do impose essential constraints on the family as an institution and so guarantee the basic rights and liberties, and the freedom and opportunities, of all its members. This they do, as I have said, by specifying the basic rights of equal citizens who are the members of families. The family as part of the basic structure cannot violate these freedoms. Since wives are equally citizens with their husbands, they have all the same basic rights, liberties, and opportunities as their husbands; and this, together with the correct application of the other principles of justice, suffices to secure their equality and independence.

To put the case another way, we distinguish between the point of view of people as citizens and their point of view as members of families and of other associations.[63] As citizens, we have reasons to impose the constraints specified by the political principles of justice on associations; while as members of associations we have reasons for limiting those constraints so that they leave room for a free and flourishing internal life appropriate to the association in question. Here again we see the need for the division of labor between different kinds of principles. We wouldn't want political principles of justice—including principles of distributive justice—to apply directly to the internal life of the family.

These principles do not inform us how to raise our children, and we are not required to treat our children in accordance with political principles. Here those principles are out of place. Surely parents must follow some conception of justice (or fairness) and due respect with regard to their children, but, within certain limits, this is not for political principles to prescribe. Clearly the prohibition of abuse and neglect of children, and much else, will, as constraints, be a vital part of family law. But at some point society has to rely on the natural affection and goodwill of the mature family members.[64]

Just as the principles of justice require that wives have all the rights of citizens, the principles of justice impose constraints on the family on behalf of children, who as society's future citizens have basic rights as such. A long and historic injustice to women is that they have borne, and continue to bear, an unjust share of the task of raising, nurturing, and caring for their children. When they are even further disadvantaged by the laws regulating divorce, this burden makes them highly vulnerable. These injustices bear harshly not only on women but also on their children; and they tend to undermine children's capacity to acquire the political virtues required of future citizens in a viable democratic society. Mill held that the family in his day was a school for male despotism: it inculcated habits of thought and ways of feeling and conduct incompatible with democracy.[65] If so, the principles of justice enjoining a reasonable constitutional democratic society can plainly be invoked to reform the family.

3. More generally, when political liberalism distinguishes between political justice that applies to the basic structure and other conceptions of justice that apply to the various associations within that structure, it does not regard the political and the nonpolitical domains as two separate, disconnected spaces, each governed solely by its own distinct principles. Even if the basic structure alone is the primary subject of justice, the principles of justice still put essential restrictions on the family and all other associations. The adult members of families and other associations are equal citizens first: that is their basic position. No institution or association in which they are involved can violate their rights as citizens.

A domain so-called, or a sphere of life, is not, then, something already given apart from political conceptions of justice. A domain is not a kind of space, or place, but rather is simply the result, or upshot, of how the principles of political justice are applied, directly to the basic structure and indirectly to the associations within it. The principles defining the equal basic liberties and opportunities of citizens always hold in and through all so-called domains. The equal rights of women and the basic rights of their children as future citizens are inalienable and protect them wherever they are. Gender distinctions limiting those rights and liberties are excluded.[66] So the spheres of the political and the public, of the nonpublic and the private, fall out from the content and application of the conception of justice and its principles. If the so-called private sphere is alleged to be a space exempt from justice, then there is no such thing.

The basic structure is a single social system, each part of which may influence the rest. Its basic principles of political justice specify all its main parts, and its basic rights reach throughout. The family is only one part (though a major part) of the system that produces a social division of labor based on gender over time. Some have argued that discrimination against women in the marketplace is the key to the historical gendered division of labor in the family. The resulting wage differences between the genders make it economically sensible that mothers spend more time with their children than fathers do. On the other hand, some believe that the family itself is the linchpin[67] of gender injustice. However, a liberal conception of justice may have to allow for some traditional gendered division of labor within families—assume, say, that this division is based on religion—provided it is fully voluntary and does not result from or lead to injustice. To say that this division of labor is in this case fully voluntary means that it is adopted by people on the basis of their religion, which from a political point of view is voluntary,[68] and not because various other forms of discrimination elsewhere in the social system make it rational and less costly for husband and wife to follow a gendered division of labor in the family.

Some want a society in which division of labor by gender is reduced to a minimum. But for political liberalism, this cannot mean that such division is forbidden. One cannot propose that equal division of labor in the family be simply mandated, or its absence in some way penalized at law for those who do not adopt it. This is ruled out because the division of labor in question is connected with basic liberties, including the freedom of religion. Thus, to try to minimize gendered division of labor means, in political liberalism, to try to reach a social condition in which the remaining division of labor is voluntary. This allows in principle that considerable gendered division of labor may persist. It is only involuntary division of labor that is to be reduced to zero.

Hence the family is a crucial case for seeing whether the single system—the basic structure—affords equal justice to both men and women. If the gendered division of labor in the family is indeed fully voluntary, then there is reason to think that the single system realizes fair equality of opportunity for both genders.

4. Since a democracy aims for full equality for all its citizens, and so of women, it must include arrangements to achieve it. If a basic, if not the main, cause of women's inequality is their greater share in the bearing, nurturing, and caring for children in the traditional division of labor within the family, steps need to be taken either to equalize their share or to compensate them for it.[69] How best to do this in particular historical conditions is not for political philosophy to decide. But a now common proposal is that as a norm or guideline, the law should count a wife's work in raising

children (when she bears that burden as is still common) as entitling her to an equal share in the income that her husband earns during their marriage. Should there be a divorce, she should have an equal share in the increased value of the family's assets during that time.

Any departure from this norm would require a special and clear justification. It seems intolerably unjust that a husband may depart the family taking his earning power with him and leaving his wife and children far less advantaged than before. Forced to fend for themselves, their economic position is often precarious. A society that permits this does not care about women, much less about their equality, or even about their children, who are its future.

The crucial question may be what precisely is covered by gender-structured institutions. How are their lines drawn? If we say the gender system includes whatever social arrangements adversely affect the equal basic liberties and opportunities of women, as well as those of their children as future citizens, then surely that system is subject to critique by the principles of justice. The question then becomes whether the fulfillment of these principles suffices to remedy the gender system's faults. The remedy depends in part on social theory and human psychology, and much else. It cannot be settled by a conception of justice alone.

In concluding these remarks on the family, I should say that I have not tried to argue fully for particular conclusions. Rather, to repeat, I have simply wanted to illustrate how a political conception of justice and its ordering of political values apply to a single institution of the basic structure and can cover many (if not all) of its various aspects. As I have said, these values are given an order within the particular political conception to which they are attached.[70] Among these values are the freedom and equality of women, the equality of children as future citizens, the freedom of religion, and finally, the value of the family in securing the orderly production and reproduction of society and of its culture from one generation to the next. These values provide public reasons for all citizens. So much is claimed not only for justice as fairness but for any reasonable political conception.

§ 6: QUESTIONS ABOUT PUBLIC REASON

I now turn to various questions and doubts about the idea of public reason and try to allay them.

1. First, it may be objected that the idea of public reason would unreasonably limit the topics and considerations available for political

argument and debate, and that we should adopt instead what we may call the open view with no constraints. I now discuss two examples to rebut this objection.

(a) One reason for thinking public reason is too restrictive is to suppose that it mistakenly tries to settle political questions in advance. To explain this objection, let's consider the question of school prayer. It might be thought that a liberal position on this question would deny its admissibility in public schools. But why so? We have to consider all the political values that can be invoked to settle this question and on which side the decisive reasons fall. The famous debate in 1784–1785 between Patrick Henry and James Madison over the establishment of the Anglican Church in Virginia and involving religion in the schools was argued almost entirely by reference to political values alone. Henry's argument for establishment was based on the view that:

> Christian knowledge hath a natural tendency to correct the morals of men, restrain their vices, and preserve the peace of society, which cannot be effected without a competent provision for learned teachers . . . .[71]

Henry did not seem to argue for Christian knowledge as good in itself but rather as an effective way to achieve basic political values, namely, the good and peaceable conduct of citizens. Thus, I take him to mean by "vices," at least in part, those actions contrary to the political virtues found in political liberalism[72] and expressed by other conceptions of democracy.

Leaving aside the obvious difficulty of whether prayers can be composed that satisfy all the needed restrictions of political justice, Madison's objections to Henry's bill turned largely on whether religious establishment was necessary to support orderly civil society. He concluded it was not. Madison's objections depended also on the historical effects of establishment both on society and on the integrity of religion itself. He was acquainted with the prosperity of colonies that had no establishment, notably Pennsylvania; he cited the strength of early Christianity in opposition to the hostile Roman Empire, and the corruption of past establishments.[73] With some care, many if not all of these arguments can be expressed in terms of the political values of public reason.

Of special interest in the example of school prayer is that it brings out that the idea of public reason is not a view about specific political institutions or policies. Rather, it is a view about the kind of reasons on which citizens are to rest their political cases in making their political justifications to one another when they support laws and policies that invoke the coercive powers of government concerning fundamental political questions. Also of special interest in this example is that it serves to emphasize that the principles that support the separation of church and state should be such that they can be affirmed by all free and equal citizens, given the fact of reasonable pluralism.

The reasons for the separation of church and state are these, among others: it protects religion from the state and the state from religion; it protects citizens from their churches[74] and citizens from one another. It is a mistake to say that political liberalism is an individualist political conception, since its aim is the protection of the various interests in liberty, both associational and individual. And it is also a grave error to think that the separation of church and state is primarily for the protection of secular culture; of course it does protect that culture, but no more so than it protects all religions. The vitality and wide acceptance of religion in America is often commented upon, as if it were a sign of the peculiar virtue of the American people. Perhaps so, but it may also be connected with the fact that in this country the various religions have been protected by the First Amendment from the state, and none has been able to dominate and suppress the other religions by the capture and use of state power.[75] While some have no doubt entertained that aim since the early days of the Republic, it has not been seriously tried. Indeed, Tocqueville thought that among the main causes of the strength of democracy in this country was the separation of church and state.[76] Political liberalism agrees with many other liberal views in accepting this proposition.[77] Some citizens of faith have felt that this separation is hostile to religion and have sought to change it. In doing this, I believe they fail to grasp a main cause of the strength of religion in this country and, as Tocqueville says, seem ready to jeopardize it for temporary gains in political power.

(b) Others may think that public reason is too restrictive because it may lead to a standoff[78] and fail to bring about decisions on disputed issues. A standoff in some sense may indeed happen, not only in moral and political reasoning but in all forms of reasoning, including science and common sense. Nevertheless, this is irrelevant. The relevant comparison is to those situations in which legislators enacting laws and judges deciding cases must make decisions. Here some political rule of action must be laid down and all must be able reasonably to endorse the process by which a decision is reached. Recall that public reason sees the office of citizen with its duty of civility as analogous to that of judge with its duty of deciding cases. Just as judges are to decide cases by legal grounds of precedent, recognized canons of statutory interpretation, and other relevant grounds, so citizens are to reason by public reason and to be guided by the criterion of reciprocity whenever constitutional essentials and matters of basic justice are at stake.

Thus, when there seems to be a standoff, that is, when legal arguments seem evenly balanced on both sides, judges cannot resolve the case simply by appealing to their own political views. To do that is for judges to violate their duty. The same holds with public reason: if, when standoffs occur, citizens simply invoke grounding reasons of their comprehensive views,[79] the principle of reciprocity is violated. From the point of view of public reason, citizens must vote for the ordering of political values they sincerely think the most reasonable. Otherwise they fail to exercise political power in ways that satisfy the criterion of reciprocity.

In particular, when hotly disputed questions, such as that of abortion, arise which may lead to a standoff between different political conceptions, citizens must vote on the question according to their complete ordering of political values.[80] Indeed, this is a normal case: unanimity of views is not to be expected. Reasonable political conceptions of justice do not always lead to the same conclusion;[81] nor do citizens holding the same conception always agree on particular issues. Yet the outcome of the vote, as I said before, is to be seen as legitimate provided all government officials, supported by other reasonable citizens, of a reasonably just constitutional regime sincerely vote in accordance with the idea of public reason. This doesn't mean the outcome is true or correct, but that it is reasonable and legitimate law, binding on citizens by the majority principle.

Some may, of course, reject a legitimate decision, as Roman Catholics may reject a decision to grant a right to abortion. They may present an argument in public reason for denying it and fail to win a majority.[82] But they need not themselves exercise the right to abortion. They can recognize the right as belonging to legitimate law enacted in accordance with legitimate political institutions and public reason and therefore not resist it with force. Forceful resistance is unreasonable: it would mean attempting to impose by force their own comprehensive doctrine that a majority of other citizens who follow public reason, not unreasonably, do not accept. Certainly Catholics may, in line with public reason, continue to argue against the right to abortion. Reasoning is not closed once and for all in public reason any more than it is closed in any form of reasoning. Moreover, that the Catholic Church's nonpublic reason requires its members to follow its doctrine is perfectly consistent with their also honoring public reason.[83]

I do not discuss the question of abortion in itself since my concern is not with that question but rather to stress that political liberalism does not hold that the ideal of public reason should always lead to a general agreement of views, nor is it a fault that it does not. Citizens learn and profit from debate and argument, and when their arguments follow public reason, they instruct society's political culture and deepen their understanding of one another even when agreement cannot be reached.

2. Some of the considerations underlying the standoff objection lead to a more general objection to public reason, namely, that the content of the family of reasonable political conceptions of justice on which it is based is itself much too narrow. This objection insists that we should always present what we think are true or grounding reasons for our views. That is, the objection insists, we are bound to express the true, or the right, as seen from our comprehensive doctrines.

However, as I said in the introduction, in public reason ideas of truth or right based on comprehensive doctrines are replaced by an idea of the politically reasonable addressed to citizens as citizens. This step is necessary to establish a basis of political reasoning that all can share as free and equal citizens. Since we are seeking public justifications for political and social institutions—for the basic structure of a political and social world—we think of persons as citizens. This assigns to each person the same basic political position. In giving reasons to all citizens, we don't view persons as socially situated or otherwise rooted, that is, as being in this or that social class, or in this or that property and income group, or as having this or that comprehensive doctrine. Nor are we appealing to each person's or each group's interests, though at some point we must take these interests into account. Rather, we think of persons as reasonable and rational, as free and equal citizens, with the two moral powers[84] and having, at any given moment, a determinate conception of the good, which may change over time. These features of citizens are implicit in their taking part in a fair system of social cooperation and seeking and presenting public justifications for their judgments on fundamental political questions.

I emphasize that this idea of public reason is fully compatible with the many forms of nonpublic reason.[85] These belong to the internal life of the many associations in civil society, and they are not of course all the same; different nonpublic reasons of different religious associations shared by their members are not those of scientific societies. Since we seek a shareable public basis of justification for all citizens in society, giving justifications to particular persons and groups here and there until all are covered fails to do this. To speak of all persons in society is still too broad, unless we suppose that they are in their nature basically the same. In political philosophy one role of ideas about our nature has been to think of people in a standard, or canonical, fashion so that they might all accept the same kind of reasons.[86] In political liberalism, however, we try to avoid natural or psychological views of this kind, as well as theological or secular doctrines. Accounts of human nature we put aside and rely on a political conception of persons as citizens instead.

3. As I have stressed throughout, it is central to political liberalism that free and equal citizens affirm both a comprehensive doctrine and a political conception. However, the relation between a comprehensive doctrine and its accompanying political conception is easily misunderstood.

When political liberalism speaks of a reasonable overlapping consensus of comprehensive doctrines,[87] it means that all of these doctrines, both religious and nonreligious, support a political conception of justice underwriting a constitutional democratic society whose principles, ideals, and standards satisfy the criterion of reciprocity. Thus, all reasonable doctrines affirm such a society with its corresponding political institutions: equal basic rights and liberties for all citizens, including liberty of conscience and the freedom of religion.[88] On the other hand, comprehensive doctrines that cannot support such a democratic society are not reasonable. Their principles and ideals do not satisfy the criterion of reciprocity, and in various ways they fail to establish the equal basic liberties. As examples, consider the many fundamentalist religious doctrines, the doctrine of the divine right of monarchs and the various forms of aristocracy, and, not to be overlooked, the many instances of autocracy and dictatorship.

Moreover, a true judgment in a reasonable comprehensive doctrine never conflicts with a reasonable judgment in its related political conception. A reasonable judgment of the political conception must still be confirmed as true, or right, by the comprehensive doctrine. It is, of course, up to citizens themselves to affirm, revise, or change their comprehensive doctrines. Their doctrines may override or count for naught the political values of a constitutional democratic society. But then the citizens cannot claim that such doctrines are reasonable. Since the criterion of reciprocity is an essential ingredient specifying public reason and its content, political liberalism rejects as unreasonable all such doctrines.

In a reasonable comprehensive doctrine, in particular a religious one, the ranking of values may not be what we might expect. Thus, suppose we call *transcendent* such values as salvation and eternal life—the *Visio*

Dei. This value, let's say, is higher than, or superior to, the reasonable political values of a constitutional democratic society. These are worldly values and therefore on a different, and as it were lower, plane than those transcendent values. It doesn't follow, however, that these lower yet reasonable values are overridden by the transcendent values of the religious doctrine. In fact, a *reasonable* comprehensive doctrine is one in which they are not overridden; it is the unreasonable doctrines in which reasonable political values are overridden. This is a consequence of the idea of the politically reasonable as set out in political liberalism. Recall that it was said: in endorsing a constitutional democratic regime, a religious doctrine may say that such are the limits God sets to our liberty.[89]

A further misunderstanding alleges that an argument in public reason could not side with Lincoln against Douglas in their debates of 1858.[90] But why not? Certainly they were debating fundamental political principles about the rights and wrongs of slavery. Since the rejection of slavery is a clear case of securing the constitutional essential of the equal basic liberties, surely Lincoln's view was reasonable (even if not the most reasonable), while Douglas' was not. Therefore, Lincoln's view is supported by any reasonable comprehensive doctrine. It is no surprise, then, that his view is in line with the religious doctrines of the abolitionists and the civil rights movement. What could be a better example to illustrate the force of public reason in political life?[91]

4. A third general objection is that the idea of public reason is unnecessary and serves no purpose in a well-established constitutional democracy. Its limits and constraints are useful primarily when a society is sharply divided and contains many hostile religious associations and secular groups, each striving to become the controlling political force. In the political societies of the European democracies and the United States these worries, so the objection goes, are idle.

However, this objection is incorrect and sociologically faulty. For without citizens' allegiance to public reason and their honoring the duty of civility, divisions and hostilities between doctrines are bound in time to assert themselves, should they not already exist. Harmony and concord among doctrines and a people's affirming public reason are unhappily not a permanent condition of social life. Rather, harmony and concord depend on the vitality of the public political culture and on citizens' being devoted to and realizing the ideal of public reason. Citizens could easily fall into bitterness and resentment once they no longer see the point of affirming an ideal of public reason and come to ignore it.

To return to where we began in this section: I do not know how to prove that public reason is not too restrictive or whether its forms are properly described. I suspect it cannot be done. Yet this is not a serious problem if, as I believe, the large majority of cases fit the framework of public reason, and the cases that do not fit all have special features that both enable us to understand why they should cause difficulty and show us how to cope with them as they arise. This prompts the general questions of whether there are examples of important cases of constitutional essentials and basic justice that do not fit the framework of public reason, and if so, why they cause difficulty. In this paper I do not pursue these questions.

§ 7: CONCLUSION

1. Throughout, I have been concerned with a torturing question in the contemporary world, namely: Can democracy and comprehensive doctrines, religious or nonreligious, be compatible? And if so, how? At the moment a number of conflicts between religion and democracy raise this question. To answer it, political liberalism makes the distinction between a self-standing political conception of justice and a comprehensive doctrine. A religious doctrine resting on the authority of the Church or the Bible is not, of course, a liberal comprehensive doctrine: its leading religious and moral values are not those, say, of Kant or Mill. Nevertheless, it may endorse a constitutional democratic society and recognize its public reason. Here it is basic that public reason is a political idea and belongs to the category of the political. Its content is given by the family of (liberal) political conceptions of justice satisfying the criterion of reciprocity. It does not trespass upon religious beliefs and injunctions insofar as these are consistent with the essential constitutional liberties, including the freedom of religion and liberty of conscience. There is, or need be, no war between religion and democracy. In this respect political liberalism is sharply different from and rejects Enlightenment Liberalism, which historically attacked orthodox Christianity.

The conflicts between democracy and reasonable religious doctrines and among reasonable religious doctrines themselves are greatly mitigated and contained within the bounds of reasonable principles of justice in a constitutional democratic society. This mitigation is due to the idea of toleration, and I have distinguished between two such ideas.[92] One is purely political, being expressed in terms of the rights and duties protecting religious liberty in accordance with a reasonable political conception of justice.[93] The other is not purely political but expressed from within a religious or a nonreligious doctrine. However, a reasonable judgment of the political conception must still be confirmed as true, or right, by a reasonable comprehensive doctrine.[94] I assume, then, that a reasonable comprehensive doctrine accepts some form of the political argument for toleration. Of course, citizens may think that the grounding reasons for toleration and for the other elements of a constitutional democratic society are not political but rather are to be found in their religious or nonreligious doctrines. And these reasons, they may well say, are the true or the right reasons; and they may see the political reasons as superficial, the grounding ones as deep. Yet there is no conflict here, but simply concordant judgments made within political conceptions of justice on the one hand, and within comprehensive doctrines on the other.

There are limits, however, to reconciliation by public reason. Three main kinds of conflicts set citizens at odds: those deriving from irreconcilable comprehensive doctrines; those deriving from differences in status, class position, or occupation, or from differences in ethnicity, gender, or race; and finally, those deriving from the burdens of judgment.[95] Political liberalism concerns primarily the first kind of conflict. It holds that even though our comprehensive doctrines are irreconcilable and cannot be compromised, nevertheless citizens who affirm reasonable doctrines may share reasons of another kind, namely, public reasons given in terms of political conceptions of justice. I also believe that such a society can resolve the second kind of conflict, which deals with conflicts between citizens' fundamental interests—political, economic, and social. For once we accept reasonable principles of justice and recognize them to be reasonable (even if not the most reasonable), and know, or reasonably believe, that our political and social institutions satisfy them, the second kind of conflict need not arise, or arise so forcefully. Political liberalism does not explicitly consider these conflicts but leaves them to be considered by justice as fairness, or by some other reasonable conception of political justice. Finally, conflicts arising from the burdens of judgment always exist and limit the extent of possible agreement.

2. Reasonable comprehensive doctrines do not reject the essentials of a constitutional democratic polity.[96] Moreover, reasonable persons are characterized in two ways: first, they stand ready to offer fair terms of social cooperation between equals, and they abide by these terms if others do also, even should it be to their advantage not to;[97] second, reasonable persons recognize and accept the consequences of the burdens of judg-

ment, which leads to the idea of reasonable toleration in a democratic society.[98] Finally we come to the idea of legitimate law, which reasonable citizens understand to apply to the general structure of political authority.[99] They know that in political life unanimity can rarely if ever be expected, so a reasonable democratic constitution must include majority or other plurality voting procedures in order to reach decisions.[100]

The idea of the politically reasonable is sufficient unto itself for the purposes of public reason when basic political questions are at stake. Of course, fundamentalist religious doctrines and autocratic and dictatorial rulers will reject the ideas of public reason and deliberative democracy. They will say that democracy leads to a culture contrary to their religion or denies the values that only autocratic or dictatorial rule can secure.[101] They assert that the religiously true, or the philosophically true, overrides the politically reasonable. We simply say that such a doctrine is politically unreasonable. Within political liberalism nothing more need be said.

I noted in the beginning[102] the fact that every actual society, however dominant and controlling its reasonable citizens may be, will normally contain numerous unreasonable doctrines that are not compatible with a democratic society—either certain religious doctrines, such as those of fundamentalist religions, or certain nonreligious (secular) doctrines, such as those of autocracy and dictatorship, of which our century offers hideous examples. How far unreasonable doctrines may be active and are to be tolerated in a constitutional democratic regime does not present a new and different question, despite the fact that in this account of public reason we have focused on the idea of the reasonable and the role of reasonable citizens. There is not one account of toleration for reasonable doctrines and another for unreasonable ones. Both cases are settled by the appropriate political principles of justice and the conduct those principles permit.[103] Unreasonable doctrines are a threat to democratic institutions, since it is impossible for them to abide by a constitutional regime except as a *modus vivendi*. Their existence sets a limit to the aim of fully realizing a reasonable democratic society with its ideal of public reason and the idea of legitimate law. This fact is not a defect or failure of the idea of public reason, but rather it indicates that there are limits to what public reason can accomplish. It does not diminish the great value and importance of attempting to realize that ideal to the fullest extent possible.

3. I end by pointing out the fundamental difference between *A Theory of Justice* and *Political Liberalism*. The first explicitly attempts to develop from the idea of the social contract, represented by Locke, Rousseau, and Kant, a theory of justice that is no longer open to objections often

thought fatal to it and that proves superior to the long dominant tradition of utilitarianism. *A Theory of Justice* hopes to present the structural features of such a theory so as to make it the best approximation to our considered judgments of justice and hence to give the most appropriate moral basis for a democratic society. Furthermore, justice as fairness is presented there as a comprehensive liberal doctrine (although the term *comprehensive doctrine* is not used in the book) in which all the members of its well-ordered society affirm that same doctrine. This kind of well-ordered society contradicts the fact of reasonable pluralism, and hence *Political Liberalism* regards that society as impossible.

Thus, *Political Liberalism* considers a different question, namely: how is it possible for those affirming a comprehensive doctrine, religious or nonreligious, and in particular doctrines based on religious authority, such as the Church or the Bible, also to hold a reasonable political conception of justice that supports a constitutional democratic society? The political conceptions are seen as both liberal and self-standing and not as comprehensive, whereas the religious doctrines may be comprehensive but not liberal. The two books are asymmetrical, though both have an idea of public reason. In the first, public reason is given by a comprehensive liberal doctrine, while in the second, public reason is a way of reasoning about political values shared by free and equal citizens that does not trespass on citizens' comprehensive doctrines so long as those doctrines are consistent with a democratic polity. Thus, the well-ordered constitutional democratic society of *Political Liberalism* is one in which the dominant and controlling citizens affirm and act from irreconcilable yet reasonable comprehensive doctrines. These doctrines in turn support reasonable political conceptions—although not necessarily the most reasonable—which specify the basic rights, liberties, and opportunities of citizens in society's basic structure.

Chapter 3

Religious Convictions
and Secular Reasons

Robert Audi

The separation of church and state is not the only aspect of the relation between religion and democracy that is a central topic in political philosophy. There is a related battery of issues concerning the role of religious considerations in the conduct of ordinary citizens, people who may be politically active but are not government officials. These issues, almost as much as institutional separation of church and state, have been brought into great prominence by the growth, in recent decades, of religious fundamentalism. It is a powerful force in many parts of the world, and, in some of its forms, it is inimical to democracy.

There is division of judgment regarding the question whether fundamentalism is undermining democracy in the United States, but there is little disagreement on the powerful influence of the "religious right," as it is often called, in American political life. The reference is usually to conservative Christian groups, whether fundamentalist or not, but similar concerns have been expressed about fundamentalist elements in other religions and in other cultures. I propose no assessment of the sociological issue of the actual effects of religious fundamentalism; even the risk of an imbalance between religious and secular considerations in democratic societies is reason enough to indicate a need for principles that help to preserve a good balance between them. Defending such principles is the main concern of this [essay]. If all of the citizens in a democracy adhere to sufficiently good ones, these principles should be able to guide their conduct in a way that can accommodate both a variety of fundamentalist movements and the aggressively secular forces we also find in contemporary Western culture. In Western Europe, Scandinavia, much of Britain, and other countries where there is no "complete" separation of church and state, these principles may seem less important. But they remain important. The recent history of Ireland and Lebanon makes this evident.

It must not be thought that liberal religious groups are not also politically active, nor should it be assumed that religiously conservative people as such are less than strongly committed to preserving democratic government. I shall indeed assume that in the United States, at least, reflective religious people, particularly those in what we might loosely call the Hebraic-Christian tradition, are on the whole committed to preserving not only democratic government but also religious liberty, including the liberty to remain outside any religious tradition.

Both democratic government and religious liberty are values that, from the point of view of any sound political philosophy, are eminently worth preserving. Their joint preservation, however, is far from easy, particularly when politically active religious groups are passionately convinced that certain freedoms are religiously forbidden or are immoral or, as in the cases of abortion and physician-assisted suicide, both. It is in part to achieve that joint preservation that liberal democracies characteristically observe a separation of religious institutions and the state. It is also partly in the interest of this joint preservation that many conscientious citizens seek a related separation between religious and political considerations, for instance between grounds for laws affecting all citizens and standards of purely personal conduct.

The need for this separation brings us to the task of this [essay]. . . . Now suppose that, between religious institutions and the state, there ought to be the kind of separation I have defended, under the libertarian, equalitarian, and neutrality principles at the level of government and the principle of ecclesiastical political neutrality among religious institutions. Should there also be, in our conduct as citizens, a related separation between religious and secular considerations?

RELIGION, POLITICS, AND THE ETHICS OF CITIZENSHIP

By way of background for understanding the rationale for certain principles governing citizens in political matters on which their religion has significant bearing, recall that there are broadly moral arguments supporting liberal democracy as a form of government. If any of these succeeds, then insofar as separation of church and state and, more broadly, of religious and political considerations is crucial for liberal democracy, there is at least indirect support, from broadly moral premises, for preserving that separation both in the design of institutions and in the political conduct of individuals.

* * * *

Moral Grounds for Liberal Democracy

. . . One might mount some version of the following broadly moral arguments, which I state only in outline, that bear on the kinds of principles of sociopolitical conduct one might endorse as part of the ethics of citizenship. A liberal-democratic state might be held to be the only kind that preserves freedom and provides adequate scope for individual autonomy. Second, it may also be thought to be the only kind that can sustain legitimate government, which may be broadly construed as the sort of government that rational citizens are willing to consent to. And third, it may be held to contribute best—or to be essential—to human flourishing.

There are . . . other rationales for preferring liberal democracy over alternative forms of government. Some are moral, appealing for instance to the virtues of statecraft in those who govern and to correlative virtues of citizenship on the part of the governed. Some are economic, for example the case for liberal democracy as the only suitable framework for free-market capitalism. Some are pragmatic, such as the argument that entrenched power corrupts and democratic succession is the only way to minimize its deleterious effects. And there are eclectic approaches combining these and other sorts of considerations. I assume that some broadly moral rationale for liberal democracy will succeed. But it also seems that religious institutions might, for internal reasons, want to subsist in a liberal state. They might, for one thing, religiously endorse a moral case for a liberal state. But they might also see such a state as best for their own flourishing—indeed, even for their own safety—especially in a world of inescapable religious pluralism.

Individual citizens, religious and nonreligious alike, often have a similar considered desire to live in a free and democratic society in which religious liberty is assiduously preserved. I consider this desire to be reasonable, but I will not argue directly for the preferability of liberal democracy over other forms of government. My task here is to explore some appropriate liberal-democratic principles in the conduct of individual citizens.

As individuals living in a liberal democracy, we are less constrained by principles that restrict sociopolitical conduct than are governments and institutions. It is indeed arguable that a citizen in such a society may properly vote or engage in other political conduct on any conscientiously chosen basis.[1] But some of the same grounds—including protection of religious liberty—that underlie separation of church and state at the institutional level may, at the individual level, warrant a measure of separation of religious and secular considerations. I want to explore the extent to which this is so.

Liberal Democracy from a Religious Perspective

Despite the connections between the institutional and individual levels and the bearing of liberal democratic theory on both, I think it is instructive to begin not (as is common) with the implications of some liberal theory of the state for the conduct of citizens or institutions, but instead with the point of view of a morally upright religious citizen who wants to live in a free and democratic society. This strategy will confirm the point . . . that despite appearances, a theological approach to providing a framework of good government might well lead to the choice of liberal democracy.

Let us initially ask, then, whether a version of liberal-democratic theory of a kind favoring a separation of religious and political considerations can be reasonably reached from a certain range of religious perspectives. My main question here is this: what should conscientious and morally upright religious citizens in a pluralistic society want in the way of protection of their own freedom and promotion of standards that express respect for citizens regardless of their religious position?

Suppose that I am devoutly religious and that my faith (a Christian denomination, let us suppose) implies much about how a good life is to be lived. I might subscribe to the Ten Commandments, to the do-unto-others rule, and to Jesus' injunction to love our neighbors as ourselves. I thus have far-reaching, religiously grounded prima facie obligations relevant to my conduct as a citizen, and I might try to lead my daily life with such religious standards in mind.[2] May I, as a conscientious citizen, pursue these obligations as vigorously as possible within the limits of the law? This is a plausible view; but—as is appropriate from a religious point of view—let us go beyond taking legal limits as our baseline for acceptable conduct. The law may be either unjustifiably restrictive or unwarrantedly permissive.

The better question for our purposes is this: may I, as a conscientious citizen, pursue my religious obligations and aspirations so far as possible within the limits of my moral rights? An affirmative answer to the second question also seems plausible, at least if the issue is *moral* propriety; for if I were violating anyone else's moral rights, I would presumably be going beyond mine. If I am not, why should I limit my zeal?

One answer that may occur to me if I am aware of religious diversity in my society is that I should limit my zeal because I would like people in other faiths, with different sociopolitical ideals, to limit theirs. There are surely moral considerations bearing on this issue that go beyond the question of what we have a moral or legal right to do. There are ideals of moral virtue that require of us more than simply acting within our moral rights. In particular, there are, in the sociopolitical domain, *ideals of citizenship* that are supported by the most plausible kinds of groundings of liberal democracy . . . and demand of us more than simply staying within our rights. These ideals can be attractive to religiously committed citizens as well as to those whose standards are determined within a secular perspective. . . .

The standards I have in mind are what might be called *involuntary ideals*; their nonfulfillment (under the conditions to which they are relevant) subjects citizens in a liberal democracy to criticism, even if one may in various cases avoid it because of, say, a stronger conflicting demand. This does not hold of voluntary ideals, such as literary excellence or athletic prowess, which do not obligate us unless we undertake to realize them. There is a sense in which citizens in a liberal democracy *ought* to meet standards of, for instance, mutual concern and mutual respect, even if they have a right not to.[3] Insofar as what we ought to do in this sense is a constitutive element in liberal democracy, a rights-based theory of such democracy is deficient.

Despite appearances, the "ought" in question is not an unusual one; it is commonly recognized that those with enough resources to do more than comfortably sustain themselves ought to make charitable donations, but scarcely anyone thinks they have no right to choose otherwise. As is evident from this example, the kind of ideal in question is not utopian;

it simply represents a high standard. In the main I shall speak here of prima facie obligations; but given that I recognize a moral right to act in ways that fall short of the relevant standards, the terminology of ideals may at times be preferable provided we distinguish between voluntary and involuntary ideals. (We could also speak of standards, but that term seems less apt for the purpose.) Let us consider some of the principles that partially express the ideals of citizenship that concern me.

TWO PRINCIPLES OF DEMOCRATIC CITIZENSHIP

If citizens in a democracy do no more in shaping their society by their political participation and in contributing to public service than they must do by law, their society will at best languish. A liberal state, however, not only protects free expression but also leaves the basis on which one votes—as well as voting itself—up to individual citizens. In this vast area of protected conduct there are high and low standards, and there is virtue and vice. What principles might citizens with high standards—including high standards grounded in their religious commitments—wish to abide by in relation to harmonizing religious and political considerations? I will defend two in particular. In doing this, I will have religious citizens foremost in mind but speak largely in more general terms applicable to citizens irrespective of religious commitments.

Secular Rationale

The first principle I want to discuss—the *principle of secular rationale*— says that one has a prima facie obligation not to advocate or support any law or public policy that restricts human conduct, unless one has, and is willing to offer, adequate secular reason for this advocacy or support (say, for one's vote). Adequate secular reasons may be considerations of, for instance, public health, public safety (as with gun control), educational need, or national defense. It should be stressed immediately that this principle implies no exclusion of the religious, such as that one not also have a religious reason, nor does it imply that no such reason may be offered. It is equally important to see that the adequacy condition by itself is not intrinsically tied to secularity: it may rule out many secular reasons as well as many religious ones but does not automatically rule out any specific kind of reason. There are difficult questions concerning secularity, adequacy, and the appropriateness of offering reasons of various kinds, not just those that are rooted in a particular religion. I address a number of these below. First, it will help to illustrate the principle of secular rationale in a case where religious considerations are central.

Suppose I want to advocate mandatory periods of prayer or meditation in public schools. According to the secular-rationale principle, I should have adequate secular reason for this, such as its being educationally and psychologically essential for the nation's youth.[4] If my only reason is to promote my own or other distinctively religious ideals, then I would not satisfy this principle. Without an adequate rationale independent of my own religious commitments, I would (according to the principle) be moving improperly toward reducing the freedom of students who prefer to avoid such sessions. This might not disturb me insofar as I think of what I am doing as essential for the spiritual well-being of students. But if, for example, I imagine being forced to observe certain dietary laws or to dress in a certain style because another religion gains a majority and makes this legally binding, I may begin to see the advantages of adhering to the principle of secular rationale in matters of coercive law or public policy. I would feel alienated if coerced through the majority vote of another religious group acting as such. My sense of fairness will tend to restrain me from doing likewise.

Advocacy is so common in political action that one may lose sight of the other forms of political support in question. Voting is crucial; so is contributing to political campaigns, encouraging political candidates, preparing letters, pamphlets, and other written material supporting one's view, and attacking a political opponent. The list can be expanded. The principle of secular rationale applies to all of these kinds of conduct, though in different ways and to differing degrees. Nine additional points of clarification are in order immediately.

Two Kinds of Coercion. First, most laws and public policies do restrict human conduct to some extent, and the more restrictive the laws or policies in question, the stronger the relevant obligation. It is useful to distinguish *primary coercion* and *secondary coercion*. The first requires a particular action, such as paying tax at a certain level or submitting to inoculation. The second occurs in at least two ways. It may operate on the basis of the former, as where one's tax payments—already legally required—are spent partly in ways one disapproves of, so one is in a sense funding something against one's will. Secondary coercion may also be only conditional, as where it applies in circumstances that citizens may avoid, say by deciding not to drive and so avoid being forced to go through the process of licensing. Other things equal, primary coercion is more in need of justification than is secondary coercion: showing that a kind of coercive action, such as taxation, is warranted in the first place tends to be more difficult than showing that, *given* a presupposition of its justification, the appropriate authorities may (within limits set by the justifying grounds for the coercion) use the funds in ways that contravene the will of some citizens. One might think that the secondary coercion is permissible wherever the corresponding primary coercion is; but, the other things equal, qualification is crucial. If, for instance, a tax revenue is to be used for a purpose inconsistent with the rationale for imposing the tax, then the secondary coercion in question is (apart from some special excuse) impermissible.

Positive versus Negative Restrictions. Second, my main concern is what I propose to call *positive restrictions*—roughly, coercion or restriction of the conduct of ordinary citizens—as opposed to *negative restrictions*, which are roughly the coercion or restriction of the enforcement of positive restrictions, chiefly by governmental or institutional officials. Negative restrictions are second-order, being restrictions of restrictions, and they amount to *liberalizations*. Restricting the government's power to investigate individuals, for instance, enhances civil liberties. For enhancing liberty, a free and democratic society does not ordinarily require special reasons; nurturing liberty is one of its constitutive purposes. This is why a civil rights movement does not need a special rationale beyond a justified claim of unwarranted restriction of liberty. But consider restricting government from investigating individuals even in legitimate law enforcement; here liberalization might engender exploitation of some individuals by others and thus produce restrictions of freedom that would be justified only if an adequate secular reason can be given for them. Negative and positive restrictions are, then, interconnected, and this must be kept in mind even though the former will not be discussed further here.

Nonrestrictive Laws and Policies. Third, the secular-rationale principle seems to have some force even when widened to apply to nonrestrictive laws and public policies (those that, like laws enabling a certain kind of agreement to be a legal contract, impose no significant positive restrictions); but these less troublesome cases do not concern me here. It would be quite enough to speak adequately to those issues involving religion and politics that raise questions of substantially burdensome coercion, such as the issue of state-sponsored school prayer, as opposed to a city government's decision to give a face-lift to one old building rather than another. Still, a law is a kind of social statement, and a public policy may be that and more, even apart from coercion. It is thus desirable for citizens in a liberal democracy to have adequate secular reason to support such measures, even if it may not be obligatory.

The Notion of a Secular Reason. Fourth, I am taking a secular reason as roughly one whose normative force, that is, its status as a prima facie justificatory element, does not evidentially depend on the existence of God (or on denying it) or on theological considerations, or on the pronouncements of a person or institution *qua* religious authority.[5] Roughly, this is to say that a secular reason is a ground that enables one to know or have some degree of justification (roughly, evidence of some kind) for a proposition, such as a moral principle, independently of having knowledge of, or justification for believing, a religious proposition. Evidential independence of God on the part of reasons does not imply independence of God in general.[6] Nor does it imply that the "faculty" of reason is secular, in the sense that it is not capable of reaching religious knowledge or is not in some way intrinsically religious. My concern here is with *reasons*, not with the faculty of reason overall, except insofar as my points about reasons presuppose certain rational capacities. Moral skeptics may think there *are* no adequate reasons for moral judgments, but I assume that this is not so, that, for instance, an adequate secular reason for making murder and rape punishable is that they violate central moral principles, they constitute serious threats to the security of society, and they require legal punishability at least on grounds of adequate deterrence. Not every category of moral principle is so close to being uncontroversial among civilized people, and there remain disagreements on significant matters of detail, such as the appropriate severity of punishments. But similar moral principles basic to a liberal legal structure can be seen (by nonskeptics) to be adequately justified by secular reasons concerning enslavement, theft, fraud, and many other behaviors that every free and democratic society prohibits by law.[7]

Secularity versus Publicity. My fifth point concerns the contrast between what is appropriately independent of religion and what is simply "public." There may be a use of "public" in which my position implies that public reasons should have the role I attribute to secular ones. But I do not think it wise to substitute "public" for "secular." In addition to the risk this poses of assimilating my position to others (such as Rawls'), the term "public" suggests intelligibility or even likely acceptance on the part of the general public, perhaps even ready intelligibility or even an appropriate familiarity. But a public could be ill-educated or blinded by prejudice. Second, in the work of Rawls and others the term often rules out reliance on "comprehensive views," something that my principles do not do. . . .[8] There is, however, a kind of public accessibility, in the sense in which scientific evidence is supposed to be publicly accessible, that is implicit in the notion of a reason which is *adequate* as well as secular. Let me clarify the notion in question.

Adequacy of Reasons. To say that a reason is adequate for a position or action is roughly to say that the reason (if true) justifies it, as the proposition that without inoculations we will have a deadly epidemic might justify requiring (minimally risky) inoculations. My sixth point, then, is that adequacy is chiefly a matter of justification. The kind of justification will differ with the kind of issue, for instance political or moral, and I take it that an adequate reason provides enough justification to make it at least minimally reasonable to do (or believe) the thing in question. As the example of an epidemic indicates, technical knowledge may be required to obtain such a reason; but the reason itself need not be difficult to understand. I cannot here propose a complete theory of the adequacy of sociopolitical reasons, but the following seems a plausible element in such a theory. If such a reason is secular, no special religious qualifications are needed to understand it; if it is adequate, any appropriately educated person can understand it; and if it is an adequate reason for a law or public policy, then either it or something it clearly implies will at least normally be intelligible to a normal adult with a good high school education. As this suggests, I do not take it that one has adequate reason only if one can adduce the deepest available ground to support it. We can be well supported by a foundation too deep for us to find and exhibit for skeptical inquiries. This is why one need know little about the technical side of public health to appreciate an adequate reason for inoculations.[9] Even in biochemistry, knowing the danger does not require knowing the cause. One should, however, be willing to say more than simply that a kind of action, say cloning of human beings, is wrong or that another, say imposing high taxes to relieve poverty, is obligatory. It is widely realized that actions are not morally wrong or obligatory for no reason, and forthrightness often requires that we indicate why we consider a type of action wrong when we are using the point to justify important conduct. It is required at least by the spirit of the principle of secular rationale that one be ready to do so. In a sense, to say simply that something is wrong is not to give a reason but to express a commitment to there being one.

Having an Adequate Reason. In allowing that one can have a reason without being able to give the deepest available ground to support it, I am acknowledging not only that we may sometimes properly rely on experts to assure us that there is a justification for a position we take to warrant political action, but that we may also rely more generally on testimony. The conditions for justifiedly doing this are complicated and controversial.[10] The point needed here (my seventh in clarifying the principle of secular rationale) is that we do not qualify as *having* adequate reason for a position or action merely by virtue of accepting a set of propositions that *constitute* one; we must also rationally accept the proposition(s) in question and see the relevance of the proposition(s) to the action or position. If I should see that someone giving me information supporting a public policy is not credible (say because of inconsistencies and gaps in the presentation), and, from the person's testimony, I unjustifiedly accept a reason for adopting the policy, then I do not have adequate reason to support that policy, and I should presumably seek to verify the testimony before acting on it. And, of course, if I do not believe *any* proposition that constitutes a reason for the policy and I could not by reflection arrive at one from what I do believe or from information accessible to me through reflection or memory, I do not have a reason at all, not even a weak and inadequate one. There are, of course, excusable errors, as where one is ill or simply cannot hear the testimony well and must act on it before there is time to reconsider; nor am I suggesting that we must scrupulously check the credibility of everyone who gives us important information. But it is appropriate to a principle expressing an ideal of citizenship to place conditions both on evidential force of a reason and on the citizen's warrant for accepting it.

Prima Facie Obligation. Eighth, I am taking a prima facie obligation to be one that provides a reason for action which is strong enough to justify the action in the absence of conflicting considerations but is also liable to being overridden by one or more such considerations. Among the overriders of the obligation to be willing to offer secular reason are special circumstances in which secrecy is necessary, as where one would be in serious danger if certain people knew what legislation or candidate one was supporting. Under repressive conditions (which, especially in a small community, can exist within a larger liberal democracy) the prima facie obligation to be willing to offer adequate secular reason may also be overridden. As to the obligation to *have* an adequate secular reason, one possible case of overriding would be a kind in which one suddenly finds one must vote, sees that the opposition is voting on a conflicting religious basis, and has confidence that adequate secular reason for one's vote can be found when one explores the issue further. . . .[11]

The Varying Strength of the Obligation. My last point here is that the obligation posited by the principle of secular rationale may be stronger in some kinds of cases than in others, even for the same person, and it tends to be stronger for government officials acting as such than for private citizens. My main interest in this [essay] is ethical standards appropriate to ordinary citizens in a liberal democracy as opposed to government officials therein, but the latter are citizens as well and sometimes act as ordinary citizens. In some such cases, the greater information and social responsibility that go with government positions, or the wide visibility or significant influence of such people as role models, make the prima facie obligation in question stronger for these citizens even when they are not acting in their official capacities. Moreover, even for ordinary citizens, the strength of the obligation varies with circumstances. One must in general be more careful in making a public speech on national television than in a preliminary precinct meeting concerning a primary election. Moreover, the principle of secular rationale applies to officials (in their official conduct) more than to ordinary citizens. Even local officials with little authority are more constrained here; the judiciary, and especially the highest court, are perhaps most constrained.[12]

Returning to the point of view of a religious citizen who wants to live harmoniously in a liberal democracy, consider how one might regard the principle of secular rationale from the perspective of theological assumptions that are standard in Western theism. Might one not think that the principle is one that is religiously acceptable, given God's having created a world in which religious differences are pervasive and secular protections of liberty can be seen to appeal to all normal persons? One might also note that the principle does not preclude appeal to religious considerations, and one might find that often they are harmonious with secular ones. . . .

One might reply, "If people are told that, at least in the absence of adequate secular reasons, they should not rely on religious beliefs to vote for candidates who will protect animals, this is a serious constraint on the free exercise of their religion. As a modern statement of the Presbyterian Church (U.S.A.) puts it, it is a 'denial of faith not to seek its expression in both a personal and a public manner.'"[13] This ignores the point that the obligation expressed in the principle of secular rationale is compatible with a right to do otherwise: a right of "free exercise." But countenancing this right does not imply that every exercise of it is beyond moral criticism. Rights are (in large part) protections against interference. Rights are not a moral license to do everything they forbid others to prevent.

That brings us to a second reply: the objection ignores the point that there are ways to enhance protection of animals without appreciable restrictions of human conduct—nor is the example one in which there is any shortage of good secular reasons for advancing the relevant aim. Thus, the exercise of the right of freedom of action here might be unnecessary as well as criticizable if exercised without appropriate grounds.

Let us, however, pursue the idea that an exercise of a right of freedom of action can be morally criticizable. Suppose that much money must be spent in enforcement of the animal protections in question and that many jobs are lost through the changes in the food sector of the economy, so that human conduct is significantly restricted, even if meat consumption remains legal. Then one might ask the religious voters supporting the protections whether they would accept comparable restrictions of conduct, as well as similar job losses or mandatory changes in their daily work, on the basis of coercive legislation protecting the dandelion as a sacred species or prohibiting miniskirts and brief bathing suits as irreverent. Such examples are perhaps not realistic for Western societies, but they bring out the advantages that the principle of secular rationale offers for a plurality of peoples and faiths. It allows a great deal of expression of faith "in both a personal and a public manner." Its limited constraints on religious expression by some are protections of liberty for others—including the religious. A liberal democracy's restraints of some are liberations for others, and they are intended for the benefit of all.

Another objection is that at least for religious people who do not think in secular terms, the principle would restrict democratic participation. They would, for instance, be unable to engage in public discourse in secular terms.[14] A number of points should be made in reply. One is that there is much democratic participation that does not require advocacy or support of restrictive laws or policies. One can, for instance, query opponents and criticize their objectionable positions; formulate guiding ideals, religious as well as secular; discuss the quality of the records of the people or political parties in question; and arouse concern about the issues in question.

A second point is that the principle of secular rationale does not restrict freedom of speech or the content of one's vocabulary. It does not even treat as prima facie objectionable the kinds of speech needed for the religiously influenced political activities just described; and the requirement of adequate secular reason does not constrain the expression of religious reasons, much less the use of religious language. There are reasons of prudence that often indicate the wisdom of conducting political discussion in secular terms; but these reasons would have force independently of the principle of secular rationale, and nothing in its content accords them exaggerated weight.

Something should also be said about the idea that some people cannot think in secular terms (at least not about weighty matters in human life) or may find it impossible or unduly burdensome to "separate" the secular from the religious in their thinking. The relevant kind of thinking in secular terms does not require suspending one's theism, at least for any kind of theism of major importance in the world today. Even if one thinks of everything as created by God or under God's sovereignty, one will have ways of referring to people and (nonreligious) things without mentioning God, and one can appeal to moral principles—including the ethical imperatives among the Ten Commandments—without depending on religious descriptions. This is entirely compatible with taking those principles to depend on God as much as anything in the creation.

The point here is not that thinking or speaking in secular vocabulary is required by the principle of secular rationale (a restriction I do not endorse for liberal democracy); it is that such vocabulary is available to normal religious people for the sake of conceiving and formulating reasons in a minimally secular fashion. Those reasons can *be* both secular and adequate even if the person having or offering them would not accept them on a secular basis. The only sense in which the principle calls on religious people to separate the religious from the secular is conceptual and, in some cases, verbal. As the Commandments themselves illustrate, one can take a standard having secular content to be theologically grounded without its cogency as providing a secular reason being undermined in the least.

It may still seem that the principle of secular rationale would sometimes have unacceptable consequences. Imagine a person who cannot think of an adequate secular reason for her religiously grounded pacifism and, too quickly to provide time to find a secular reason she can endorse, must vote on whether to go to war. It might seem that my view requires her "to vote against her conscience," since she should vote yes or abstain.[15] This misses the significance of the point that she not only has a *right* to vote no, but also has only a prima facie obligation to abstain from voting. But *given* the importance of her religious convictions to her, and given her intellectual and psychological capacities, voting no may be, from her perspective at least, the rational thing to do. In that case she is not "required" by any moral principle I endorse to vote yes or abstain.

Suppose it *is* rational for the pacifist, on the basis of her overall commitments as a generally rational, religiously committed person, to vote against going to war, but she still lacks an adequate secular reason. We may excuse her voting without it; but we need not for that reason consider it praiseworthy or even best, any more than we need so view someone's breaking a promise on the basis of considerations that, although understandably compelling from the agent's point of view, are objectively mistaken. The case is one in which either her prima facie obligation under the principle of secular rationale is overridden or its nonperformance is at least excusable. What my view requires of conscientious citizens like her who knowingly act against the principle of secular rationale is that they be aware of what they are doing and have conscientious grounds for taking their religious commitments to be overriding or at least excusatory. This is the kind of requirement that is generally implicit in prima facie moral principles (such as the rule requiring the keeping of promises). Here, as in that more general case, morality does not dictate that one never depart from the principle, even if it is in fact true.[16] It does require that one scrutinize departures; but that does not seem too much to ask.

The principle of secular rationale is, then, not unduly burdensome for religious people. Indeed, it may also be expected to have good effects for people *within* a religious tradition, for instance in different denominations, and possibly even in the same denomination, as well as to facilitate good relations *between* different religious traditions and between religious and nonreligious people. Intramural strife can be deadly. History has shown that, and we can surely see it in the contemporary world. It seems less likely to occur where this principle is adopted.

Secular Motivation

Reasons we have for actions or beliefs, reasons we give for them, and reasons we are actually moved by are all important, and in different ways. The second principle I suggest asks citizens to consider not just what they want to do and what reasons they have to do it, but *why* they want to do it. I propose, then, a *principle of secular motivation*, which adds a motivational condition to the rationale principle. It says that one has a (prima facie) obligation to abstain from advocacy or support of a law or public policy that restricts human conduct, unless in advocating or supporting it, one is sufficiently *motivated* by (normatively) adequate secular reason. Sufficiency of motivation here implies that some set of secular reasons is motivationally sufficient, roughly in the sense that (a) this set of reasons explains one's action and (b) one would act on it even if, other things remaining equal, one's other reasons were eliminated. Roughly, the idea is that one should be advocating or supporting the law or policy in question in part *for* some adequate secular reason, where the role of this reason is sufficiently important to explain why one is so acting (even if some other consideration is also sufficient for this). This second principle is less important than the secular-rationale principle to the partial ethics of citizenship I am proposing for liberal democracies, but it is still quite significant. It is also more difficult to interpret and apply. Let us explore it in a concrete case.

To begin with, since an argument can be tacitly religious, say evidentially or motivationally, without being religious in content, we might fail to adhere to at least the secular-motivation principle even when we are offering arguments that on their face are neither religious nor fail to provide an adequate secular reason for their conclusion. Think of the genetic argument for the personhood of the zygote: roughly, the argument that since all the genetic information needed for its development into a person is present at conception, the zygote *is* a person at that point. It might be held that some people who offer this argument are not sufficiently motivated by the secular considerations cited in it, those just mentioned, and (quite apart from whether it is objectively sound) would not find the argument convincing apart from their underlying religious beliefs. They might, for example, think of the zygote as ensouled by God at the moment of its formation or might simply have been brought up to think of all human life as sacred.[17]

There are two cases here. In one, the person realizes that the secular reason does not motivate. I might realize that, for instance, the idea of ensoulment is what really convinces me on the abortion question. Here the secular reason is presented as a rationalization for the position held on a religious basis. In the other case, I do not realize that the secular reason is not motivating. There the presentation of the reason is an unconscious rationalization. A rationalization *can* be good, in that the ground it invokes may actually justify what it is intended to support. But it is quite characteristic of rationalizations to be unsuccessful attempts to provide justification where—as is common in difficult matters or where we are influenced by prejudice—we doubt we have one independently. That the reasons we offer in giving rationalizations do not motivate us may be a sign of their failure to justify. It is at least a sign of their failure to convince us; that is one reason we do not like giving them if we can avoid it, and do not like being given such reasons by others in their attempts to convince *us*.

There is another kind of case in which the principle of secular motivation applies. Suppose I believe that assisted suicide is morally wrong, but my only ground is my religious belief that God giveth life, and only God should take it. That this kind of act is morally wrong is not a religious view, and let us assume for the sake of argument that it can justify a legal prohibition of assisted suicide. But if I am motivated by it essentially on account of my theistic ground, then under the principle of secular motivation I have a prima facie obligation not to support legal coercion on the basis of it. Adherence to that very principle, however—even if the adherence itself is partly religious, as it may be owing to, say, acceptance of the do-unto-others rule—may lead me to seek an adequate secular reason that motivates me in the same direction. If I find it, the fact that my search for it was in part religiously motivated does nothing to prevent my now satisfying the principle.

It may be thought that the principle of secular motivation burdens only the religious, but it in fact applies to those who oppose religion in certain ways. The principle is meant to rule out a certain kind of *anti*religious motivation as proper in coercive sociopolitical action. A free democracy should be wary not only of religious domination, but also of antireligious domination. Imagine a scientific argument aimed at excluding creationism from discussion in public school science courses: the secular considerations it cites might not be motivating, and if the exclusionary policy is proposed on the basis of antireligious motivation of a kind that does not count as secular, then even if it accords with the rationale principle, offering it does not accord with the motivation principle. Its proponent lacks a set of secular reasons that is both evidentially adequate and motivationally sufficient.[18]

Consider, by contrast, a case in which someone argues for a voucher system on the ground that parents, and especially religious ones, should be free to educate their children in academically adequate schools of their choice, including those that teach a particular religious point of view, and so should receive a voucher for each child, which can be used toward the costs of their children's attending *any* accredited school.[19] Here the *content* of the proposed legislation, unlike that of proposed restrictions of abortion, includes a concern with religion and even envisages some likelihood of promoting its practice; but the *ground* given for the legislation is not intrinsically religious: one could support a voucher system on this ground without specially favoring the religious over, say, nonreligious people who are simply dissatisfied with the general quality of public education, just as legislators can take account of the religiously based preferences of their constituents *as* their deep-seated preferences without thereby favoring the religious as such over other constituents. One might support such a system even if there are no church-affiliated schools at the time. This system is less far-reaching than government's directly supporting religious as well as secular schools, as in the Netherlands. That policy probably cannot satisfy the neutrality principle . . . as a voucher system might be argued to do,[20] since the former both directly supports religious institutions as such and, by comparison with a voucher system, would be more likely to create a presumption that there should be religiously affiliated schools. If, however, pressing for a voucher system is to conform to the principle of secular motivation, then some such secular consideration should be both (normatively) adequate and sufficiently motivating. If one's *only* reason for supporting vouchers is to promote the religious devotion of one's children (or of other children), then even if one is expressing a kind of religious virtue, one is not exhibiting civic virtue.[21]

Granted, if there is an *adequate* secular reason for a policy, then no overall harm need be expected from instituting the policy; this is in part why the principle of secular rationale is the more important of the two. In this light, it may be thought that one may offer the reason as justifying one's conduct even if it does not motivate one. One may. But harm can come from the way a policy is instituted even if not directly from the policy itself, and harm certainly may come from habits that allow one to support coercion of others for religious reasons so long as one can find an adequate secular rationale.

Let us also apply the do-unto-others rule to this case: one would not like having a different religious group, with which one deeply disagrees, press for its religiously preferred policies solely for religious reasons of its own, even if a good secular reason could be offered for those policies. It matters greatly to us *why* people do what they do. If we have too little sense of it, we do not know what to expect from them. To be sure, someone who has both motivating and nonmotivating reasons can present both, and this might seem to solve the problem. It does not. Indeed, if, in supporting a law or public policy, we present a set of reasons in the usual way, hence without taking special care to imply that none of them need be motivating, the normal presumption is that they are all motivating. We can say, as a paid advocate might, something like, "Here are the arguments," but if we do this in a way that distances us enough from the reasons to rebut the presumption that they are motivating for us, there is a sense in which we conceal from others in the discussion or debate *who* we are. There is a place for such concealment for instance in criminal trials, but it should be generally avoided in policy discussions in a liberal democracy.

Where one takes it that someone with both secular and religious reasons is not sufficiently motivated by a secular reason offered, one's tendency to disapprove may be modified, if only slightly, where the secular reason motivates to *some* degree but is inessential to determining support for the policies, which would have been promoted in its absence. We are especially likely to be wary of the dominance of religious motivation if, as with illegal euthanasia, the policy or law in question is backed by severe punishments. If we think the law or policy unjustified, we may feel coerced by someone else's religious views; but even if we agree, we may well think that *others* may feel coerced—or we may wonder how we will fare in later legislation. As elsewhere in ethical matters, there can be a wrong way to do the right thing. The right way in cases of coercion must (for additional reasons to be given shortly) incorporate appropriate motivation.

Some Important Aspects of Religious Reasons in Politics

The stress on secular reasons as evidential and motivational elements important in the ethics of citizenship must not be taken to imply that no other constraints on appropriate reasons are required, such as prohibitions of racist grounds for public policy. This is not the place for an account of what makes certain reasons appropriate overall. Religious reasons, conceived (for instance) as reasons for human conduct that are ultimately grounded in God's nature or commands (or, at least from the point of view of religious persons, are rationally believed to be so grounded), are a major subject in their own right. There are some respects in which they are special in relation to liberal democracy even by contrast with other reasons—such as certain "intuitive" deliverances about other people—that are not accessible to any normal adult and are often inadequate though clearly secular.[22] Here are some salient points that help to distinguish religious reasons from certain secular ones, such as a number of moral reasons.

Infallible Supreme Authority. First, the kinds of religious reasons of greatest concern . . . are directly or indirectly viewed as representing an infallible authority, in a sense taken to imply that the propositions expressing them *must* be true.[23] A further implication which many feel in such cases is that not to act on such considerations is a violation of divine command and is seriously wrong or even punishable by damnation. Some who think this do not require that the religiously deficient person need have any *moral* guilt at all in order to merit negative treatment, such as disapproval, rejection, or damnation. If moral guilt is not required, then even coercion of the virtuous might seem warranted—and perhaps reinforced insofar as they may be seen as eminently worth saving. Furthermore, it is not just that one must act in some way to achieve the desired result, say by proselytizing; one must do *any* deed commanded by such a supreme authority.

Condemnatory Tendencies. A second, closely related point is that very commonly those who identify with what they regard as the ultimate divine source of religious reasons believe that anyone who does not identify with it is forsaken, damned, or in some other way fundamentally deficient. This disapproval is often enhanced or even inflamed by others' openly rejecting the relevant command or standard, as is common in, for example, sexual matters. Nor are religious people always consoled by knowledge that the disagreement with their religiously inspired views is respectful; this can be so even if they think those rejecting the views do so on the basis of *their* religious convictions. Following a false God—or misunderstanding the true one—can be even worse than secular error.

The Threat of Religious Domination. Third, religious reasons often dictate practices that are distinctively religious in content (such as prayer) or intent (such as preserving a fetus on the ground that it is a gift from God), and therefore are plausibly seen in some cases as forcing others who are either not religious or differ in religious outlook to observe a religious standard. This applies particularly where a religious consideration is used in favor of a practice for which there are no secular reasons persuasive to most reflective people not antecedently sympathetic on religious grounds, as in the case of most of the currently popular restrictions of abortion. Religious reasons for laws or public policies, then, can threaten, or be widely seen as threatening, not only coercion in general but *religious coercion*: coercion of religious conduct.

Cults and the Specter of Fanaticism. Fourth, for at least many religions—and commonly for cults—rational, relevantly informed outsiders are unable to discern effective checks on certain possible tendencies for clergy (or, in some cases, votaries) to project, whether consciously or otherwise, their own views or preferences into their interpretations of one or another authoritative religious source, including even God.[24] In this case there is, in addition to the possibility of some people's cloaking their prejudices with absolute authority, the possibility that the views and motives of those who follow them lack the minimal autonomy that citizens in a liberal democracy may hope for in one another. Even if at the polling place the rule is one person, one vote, it might be argued that people under the influence of cult leaders or certain other kinds of dominating religious figures may be casting votes that not only fail to be independent but are also even less open to reconsideration than most of the votes unduly influenced by secular figures.

Dangers of an Inflated Sense of Self-Importance. Insofar as the liabilities that go with cults and fanaticism are a serious problem—as they surely have been both historically and in the contemporary world—we can see a fifth point. There is a danger not only of one religion's dominating others or nonreligious people, but also of one person's doing so, or one religiously powerful coterie's doing so, or even of a single individual's doing it, or at least of one or more zealots taking themselves to be important in a way that makes them uncooperative as citizens. This may be in or outside politics. The belief in a supreme God with sovereignty over the world should induce humility, but it need not. Indeed, the better one thinks one represents God—especially when God is being ignored or disobeyed—the more important one may naturally think one is oneself. Who has not heard preachers apparently enthralled by their voices? There is a kind of zeal that, in influential clergy or religiously influential laypeople, can erode citizenship and, sometimes, substitute a personal vision for genuine religious inspiration.

Passionate Concern with Outsiders. Sixth, owing to some of these points (among others), religious people often tend to be, in a way that is rare in secular matters, highly and stubbornly passionate about the importance of everyone's acting in accordance with religious reasons (whether because they are accepted or not), even in private conduct, and nonreligious people often tend to be highly and stubbornly passionate about not being coerced to do so. If many who are religious are vehemently opposed to the sins of a multitude outside their fold, many who are not religious are incensed at the thought of manipulation in the name of someone else's nonexistent deity.

The Centrality and Delicacy of Religious Liberty. Partly because religious liberty is a constitutive foundation (or at least a cogent rationale) for liberal democracy, citizens in such a state are naturally and permissibly resentful about coercion by religious factors (which may lead to restrictions of their specifically religious behavior) in a way in which they are not permissibly resentful concerning coercion by, for instance, considerations of public health. Even the moral errors of others are, for many, easier to abide as supports of coercion than religious convictions having the same result. Perhaps the thought is that one can argue with others concerning their moral or economic or philosophical views in a way one cannot argue with them about their religious convictions. And if religious considerations are not appropriately balanced with secular ones in matters of coercion, there is a special problem: a clash of gods vying for social control. Such uncompromising absolutes easily lead to destruction and death.

Intergenerationality. It is more characteristic of religious commitment than of other kinds of institutional commitment that one tends to want to bring up one's children (if one has any) in the faith. With this desire often comes a sense of alienation or even betrayal if they reject the faith once brought up in it. In the present age, many have learned to live with such alienation, but it remains a source of deep concern, normally more so than counterpart reactions to apostasy in aesthetic, political, and sometimes even ethical matters. In many cases religious people can tolerate what they take to be profound ethical differences with their children, but this may be in part because those differences do not seem profound to them unless they contravene the morality of the religion in question. Many Christian parents, for instance, can live with their children's ethical liberality in sexual matters and departure from church membership largely because they see the children as retaining a commitment to the "social gospel" of love and service.

There may be other kinds of reasons to which each of these eight points (or close counterparts) applies; but if there are any nonreligious reasons to which all of them apply, it is in a different way and is in any event a good prima facie reason to impose similar restrictions on the use of those reasons. Given that I have treated religious reasons as special in important respects, I should add that nothing I have said about them entails that religion is necessarily either "esoteric" or in any way irrational, or even that there cannot be cogent arguments for God's existence from nonreligious premises. One can hold that there are such arguments, and even that they should be compelling to any rational person who properly considers their premises in the light of the data, yet still consider the principles of secular rationale and motivation to be sound commitments in political philosophy.[25]

Virtuous Action versus Merely Permissible Conduct

It might still seem that motivation should not matter if the quality of one's reasons is good enough. This is a very difficult issue. But I would stress that insofar as we are thinking of the advocacy or other public behavior as supposed to be action *from virtue*, we should look not just at what kind of act it is and what can be said for it abstractly, but also at how it is grounded in the agent's *character*.[26] As Kant distinguished acting merely in conformity with duty and acting *from* duty, and Aristotle distinguished—as any virtue theorist should—actions that *express* virtue from those not virtuously performed but merely "in the right state," that is, of the right type, we should distinguish actions that proceed from civic virtue and actions that are merely in conformity with it. I am granting that morally, one may, within one's rights, advocate a coercive course of action without being motivated by an adequate secular reason for that action; my contention is that to do so is not always consonant with virtue.

The principle of secular motivation, then, may be viewed as a *virtue principle*, whereas the principle of secular rationale is better viewed as a (minimum) *justification principle*. Action in accord with the latter, being supportable by adequate reason, may be considered to be at least minimally justified, in the sense that it is permissible even if not obligatory (some alternative may, e.g., be equally warranted). But this does not imply that the action is virtuously performed, or indeed performed for any remotely admirable reason; nor does it imply that the agent is virtuous. Actions in accord with the principle of secular motivation, being sufficiently motivated by adequate reason, may be considered to be (at least to that extent) not only justified but also (civically) virtuous. Even if the agent is not habitually virtuous, the occasion in question is one on which an evidentially adequate set of reasons is also motivationally sufficient, and so produces action that is to this extent virtuously performed.

It is a main contention . . . that justification for sociopolitical action can be readily combined with motivation sufficient to produce such action, and that where this combination does not occur, conscientious citizens—whether religious or not—are prima facie obligated to resist supporting coercive laws or policies even where they feel confident that they have an adequate rationale. Even if one could act virtuously where one's justifying reasons are not motivating, when a rationale that one takes to be adequate does not motivate one, there is a significant chance that this is because it does not deserve to carry one's conviction, either objectively or in the light of one's own best standards.

One may wonder, of course, whether principles weaker than those I have defended may accomplish much the same results. This may turn out to be so, but so far I have not found preferable principles. One might think that in place of adequate secular reason we might mention just plausible secular reason; or one might suggest that it is enough for an adequate secular reason to be necessary (as opposed to sufficient) for motivating the conduct in question. Here it should be remembered that we are formulating a kind of ideal; that, partly for this reason, there is a right to act otherwise; and that nonconformity to the principles may be warranted by overriding considerations or excused. Given these qualifications, the notions of a plausible reason and the weaker motivational condition are too weak to provide good ideals. . . .

SOME PROBLEMS OF APPLICATION

Application of the principles of secular rationale and secular motivation can be complicated because there may be considerable difficulty in determining whether a reason one has for doing or believing something is secular, or constitutes an evidentially adequate ground, as well as in deciding whether it is in fact motivating. These difficulties merit extensive study. Here I simply offer three suggestions.

First, we should be guided by what we can learn from considering paradigms of both kinds of reason, evidential and motivational. There is much to be learned from asking, of what seem our most cogent reasons, why they justify, and, of our most moving reasons, why they influence us. Second, wherever the two kinds of reason (evidential and motivating) diverge on a major issue, we should inquire why. If I think that capital punishment is sometimes morally justified but believe it is wrong on religious grounds, I should ask why, and I may learn much from reflection on the matter. Third—and this suggestion may require one to seek outside help—in borderline cases where the secular status of a reason is in question, we should consider whether it would be taken to be secular by a reflective person who sincerely and comprehendingly claims to be nonreligious and considers it carefully.[27] A religious consideration, viewed from inside a religious tradition to which it belongs, need have no theological identifying marks and easily seems to be second nature, or perhaps a dictate of purely natural law, as heterosexual preference appears to many people to be; but from the outside such an element can sometimes be seen to be rooted in a tradition that the outsider recognizes as religious and may find alienating. Dialogue with other citizens of diverse backgrounds may help greatly in reducing the incidence of such alienation.

The difficulty of determining whether a reason one has is a motivating element in one's sociopolitical conduct is especially likely to occur long before the relevant action or long afterward. But what the motivation principle (beyond the rationale principle) requires of conscientious citizens contemplating support of restrictive laws or policies is making the following three (and perhaps at most these three) manageable efforts.

First, conscientious citizens should try to formulate all the significant reasons they have for each major option—itself often a very useful exercise even apart from determining motivation and especially in assessing the weight of one's overall evidence. We revise, often improve, and commonly unify our views in the process of seeking to ground them in reasons. Until we have a good sense of what reasons we have, we are in a poor position to determine which, if any, is motivating.

Second, where one or more reasons is religious, conscientious citizens facing decisions of the kind in question should consider the motivational weight of each reason taken by itself as well as in the context of the others (if none is religious, the principle does not imply any need to go any further into motivation, though some other principle may). In examining motivational weight, there are a number of questions we can consider. How persuasive does a consideration seem to us? Are we influenced by it through commitment to some authority backing it or by its content, and how important to us is this basis of its persuasiveness? How concerned or upset would we feel if it were challenged or could not be realized in action? How did we acquire it, and does this show anything about the strength of its grip on us?

Third, citizens in the relevant position should attempt to ascertain, by considering hypothetical situations and felt motivational or cognitive impulses or tendencies, whether each reason is motivationally sufficient. We should ask ourselves, for example, what really impresses us as supporting the proposition or action; what occurs to us first (or most spontaneously) on the matter; whether we would believe something if we did not accept a certain premise for it; and whether a given reason taken by itself seems persuasive to us, in the sense of providing a feeling of surety.

In short, my two principles imply that we should ask of our reasons certain evidential, introspective, historical, and hypothetical questions. One must, with any such principles, use practical wisdom in deciding how much effort to expend in a given case of contemplated action. But once inquiry is focused by a commitment to these principles, much can be accomplished in even a few moments of reflection.

Practical wisdom is also crucial in determining how much of one's public discourse should be couched in religious terms. . . . Even if one is scrupulously abiding by the secular motivation principle, one may still have and present religious reasons for one's sociopolitical views. The principles of secular rationale and secular motivation concern advocacy and support of a certain range of laws and public policies; they do not restrict freedom of speech or preclude using religious reasons in major ways. Nor do they imply that religion should be "privatized," as if it had to be kept to oneself, or that it should be marginal in influencing public life.[28] It is not a necessary consequence of adherence to these principles that the religious ideals and efforts of the citizens in question are any less effective in changing society.

The rationale and motivation principles do not even imply that one need hesitate to appeal publicly to religious reasons in support of a widely contested view if it is purely moral, as where abortion is said to be morally wrong because it destroys a gift of God. Neither the crucial premise for this moral conclusion nor the conclusion itself entails that abortion should be *illegal* in a free and democratic society, and stating the premise, even publicly, does not automatically count as supporting a coercive law or public policy. There are, moreover, ways to offer the argument even in public policy contexts (e.g., by taking care to bring these limitations out) that do not imply one's supporting restrictive laws or public policies.[29]

One may, however, easily be wrong in thinking that bringing religious reasons to bear on a moral question or, especially, a public policy issue, will make one more convincing; one may instead polarize the discussion. It can well turn out that advancing religious reasons for a controversial social policy leads the opposition to advance conflicting religious reasons. This, in turn, can lead to suspicions about the motivation or the cogency of even the secular reasons on each side. It is true that people who seek equilibrium between their religious and their secular views may often be prepared to revise the latter as well as the former; but this disposition is not always present, and deadlock may occur where compromise would have been possible.

Fortunately, if the motivation principle is widely accepted by the parties to a dispute—indeed, perhaps even if it is not—and if one is in good communication with people who disagree on the issue at hand, one will likely get substantial help from them in determining what one's motivating reasons in the dispute are. Whenever religious reasons seem to them motivationally too strong, people who disagree on the issue in question should be expected to help one probe one's grounds. Others hear our voices better than we do. They may also think of revealing questions about us that we ourselves overlook or observe words or deeds that teach us something we did not realize about our own thinking or motivation.[30]

It could be that most people are not usually good at forming reasonable judgments regarding even what reasons they have, much less which of these reasons, if any, are motivating.[31] If this is so, the effort to find out may be all the more needed; if, through self-examination, I cannot tell what my reasons for a belief or desire of mine are, I should probably wonder whether I have any normatively adequate reasons for it; and I am likely to make better decisions if I try to find some good reasons for the relevant belief or desires. If, moreover, I cannot tell pretty accurately which reasons motivate me and about how much they do so at least relative to other reasons, I cannot adequately understand myself or reasonably predict my own behavior.

Given the self-examination that, for some people, may be required for conscientious adherence to the rationale and motivation principles, it may appear that they would exclude some religious people from "full participation in political debate and action on some important issues."[32] To assess this, we must distinguish the two quite different cases of debate and (other) action, such as voting for more restrictive abortion laws. We should also distinguish *full* participation in debate from *unrestricted* participation. I can participate fully in political debate—even dominantly—whether or not I use all my arguments or express all my sentiments. To be sure, if I have only religious considerations to bring to such a debate—something that . . . seems unlikely to hold for informed, reflective religious people—then the rationale principle may lead me not to use them in certain ways. I may, for instance, point out their bearing, but I may not advocate coercive legislation on the basis of them. That, however, is a restraint I would wish to be observed by people who, for *their* religious reasons, want to restrict my liberty.

To see the issue in perspective, we have to keep in mind that *any* moral principle applying to sociopolitical conduct will restrict it in some cases. But I can adhere to the rationale and motivation principles and still fully participate in a significant range of political actions even concerning abortion and even aimed at producing its rejection: I can prominently and forcefully support policies, candidates, and parties that seek to *dissuade* people from doing it. What I may not do without adequate secular reason (unless my obligation regarding secular rationale is overridden) is advocate or support *coercive* laws or public policies on this or other matters that concern me. That, too, is a kind of restraint I would wish to be observed by members of other religious groups who would want to coerce my behavior in the direction of their religiously preferred standards.

THE ETHICS OF CITIZENSHIP AND THE ACCOMMODATION OF RELIGION

This is a good place to emphasize a number of further interpretive points about the rationale and motivation principles. Together these points help to show what the principles do not exclude and how large a role they accommodate for religious considerations in the political arena.

Leveraging by Reasons versus Arguing from Reasons

Contrary to appearances, in special cases the principles allow presenting reasons that one is not motivated by—or even does not believe evidentially adequate. I have in mind cases in which one is not arguing *from* those reasons but presenting them as considerations acceptable to one's audience and supporting a position that (typically but not necessarily) one *does* take to be sound. Call this *leveraging*. In the common case in which one accepts the conclusion oneself, it is a way of trying to achieve agreement on something by working from premises to which one's interlocutor is already committed. Here one's point is not that the premises are true (something one may or may not believe), but that the interlocutor already believes them, or should believe them, say, because they are either plainly true or clearly follow from what the interlocutor believes.

There is no question that leveraging occurs and is widely accepted in debate and advocacy. But how can one present reasons that are not one's own in this way without insincerity or "dissembling"?[33] One possibility (which may or may not be combined with leveraging) is simply saying such things as, "Here are two good reasons for this position," where one takes both to be convincing to one's audience but is not oneself moved by them. This case is troubling: we have to imagine the speaker's thinking a reason for a position to be good, yet not having that as a reason for holding the position or even pulling the speaker in the direction of holding it. This is extremely rare in rational persons, especially if they *hold* the position, which normally one will if one is sincerely trying to persuade others of it. If I think the reason I give is good, and if I hold the position that I adduce this reason to support, it will normally be at least in part *for* this reason that I hold the position.

A second possibility is pointing out reasons the audience already has that support the policy, whether one thinks they are good reasons or not. This second case, by contrast, is really not one of offering reasons *for the position*; it is giving reasons *for the audience to hold the position*. This is leveraging: one tries to move an audience to a view by noting one or more reasons there are for it from the audience's point of view.[34] Leveraging is compatible with not holding the position and even with thinking that the reasons do not in fact support it.

A third possibility is to offer reasons one thinks will convince one's audience but does not believe good (this need not be leveraging, since one may be persuading the audience of a new point of view as opposed to appealing to one the audience antecedently holds). At best, this practice manipulates people; it also tends to undermine good reasoning in those who are taken in; and thirdly, it tends to be deceitful, since it is very difficult to present reasons for a view in a convincing way without implying that one takes them to support it.

The first and last objections seem also to apply to presenting good reasons that are not one's own; doing this tends to manipulate others—whom one is in effect asking to accept something on a ground that does not move oneself—and certainly a convincing presentation of the reasons will make it appear (contrary to what is the case) that they are one's own.[35] As to leveraging by appealing to reasons the audience already has, consider a case of a common kind, in which it is done so as to avoid giving the audience warrant to conclude that one is offering reasons one accepts as genuinely supporting the position in question—as we normally do accept reasons we offer in promoting a position we hold. Here it is likely to be evident that it *is* leveraging; for plainly one is pointing out why, from the audience's point of view, the position is worthy. That may or may not undermine one's effectiveness in persuading.

Political Argument, the Public Persona, and the Participant in a Community

Leveraging has an important place in political discourse. But if it is all I do, the audience cannot see *who* I am. I am like a lawyer representing a client in court: my job is to represent the client's point of view within certain limits, and my personal view does not matter. This is not generally a good way to relate to fellow citizens. As communitarians have perceived, I should be an individual who participates in the life of the community, not a political persona identified chiefly with my abstract position. It tends to conceal much of my perspective and so may well fail to promote understanding of me or my view; and it tends to arouse suspicion and so is likely either to undermine my efforts at persuasion or to make me seem an unknown quantity whose future conduct may be unpredictable.

There are, then, good grounds for thinking that in the main the reasons one offers for a position in public should be among one's own reasons for holding it. They may not be *all* of these; but if it tends toward insincerity to offer reasons for a position one holds that are not among one's reasons for holding it—say, because they are believed by one's audience but not oneself—it also tends toward insincerity to offer (without qualification) reasons for it that, though one accepts them in the abstract, are not (motivationally) sufficient for one's holding it. If one successfully adheres to the principles of secular rationale and secular motivation, two good consequences follow: first, one is presenting reasons that are evidentially sufficient and so should tend to be persuasive to a rational audience irrespective of its point of view; and second, one is being sincere and so should not arouse the suspicion that easily arises from offering reasons that are not one's own.

These considerations about the importance of sincerity may illuminate an insightful critical comment that Nicholas Wolterstorff has made about liberalism, notably Rawls' version, but not restricted to that: the liberal "is trying to discover, and to form, the relevant community. He thinks we need a shared political basis . . . I think the attempt is hopeless and misguided. We must learn to live with a politics of multiple communities."[36]

I agree that it is hopeless for a pluralistic society to operate as a single community in the sense in which that implies a shared overall view of the world, including religious and sociopolitical outlook. But suppose we distinguish first- and second-order communities. Why is it not possible to seek a *second-order community* whose members are the different and overlapping religious, ethnic, professional, and other communities of which Wolterstorff speaks? Members of the second-order community will tend to have less in common than those of a first-order one; but a commitment to principles of mutual self-government and civic activity, such as those I have proposed, can do much to nurture understanding and tolerance.

Motivational and Evidential Cooperation of Religious and Secular Reasons

Like the principle of secular rationale, the principle of secular motivation is in one way quite inclusive. It allows that one may have and be motivated by religious reasons *as well as* secular ones. One may indeed believe the former more basic than the secular reasons that motivate one in sociopolitical matters, as in the case of someone who thinks that the most basic reasons for a principle, though not the only adequate reasons for it, are religious (here one might again think of the Ten Commandments). The ideal for religious citizens is a special kind of cooperation between the religious and the secular, not the automatic supremacy of the former over the latter. That cooperation requires that some secular reason play an essential role, but not that the person *regard* that role as primary or *take* the secular to be more important than the religious or even independent of it.

It should also be stressed that my use of such separationist principles by no means presupposes that religious reasons cannot be evidentially adequate. One need have no view on their adequacy to see the grounds for requiring that they be accompanied by adequate secular reason wherever they are used to advocate or support coercive laws or public policies. The principles also allow that religious reasons may be motivationally *sufficient* for a political stance (though not motivationally necessary, since secular reasons could not then be motivationally sufficient—they would be unable to produce belief or action without the cooperation of religious elements).

There is still another role my principles allow religious reasons to play, one that is easily overlooked. These reasons can be *causally sufficient* for producing a secular justification of a law or public policy, in the sense that one's having such reasons can, say through one's thinking about them or about related considerations, lead one to discover an evidentially adequate secular reason. That reason in turn can be motivationally sufficient (even independently of its continuing to receive support from the religious factors leading to its discovery). A bridge initially raised on one set of pillars may or may not continue to rest on them, in whole or in part. In the orders of discovery and motivation, either religious or secular reasons can be primary; and each kind can cooperate evidentially or motivationally with the other.

The rationale and motivation principles not only allow a conscientious citizen's judging the religious reasons in question to be more important than the secular ones, but they also allow being more *strongly* motivated by them; this is perfectly consistent with one's being sufficiently motivated by adequate secular reason. Holding such judgments is also compatible with adhering to the principle of ecclesiastical political neutrality. The principles simply aim at preventing a certain kind of domination by religious reasons in contexts in which citizens should constrain them. Moreover, for both individuals and institutions, adhering to the principles makes it much easier to speak in public in a way that is both intelligible and persuasive to a diverse citizenry.

To be sure, in public advocacy of laws and policies that restrict human conduct, it seems *generally* best to conduct discussion in secular terms; but there may be special contexts in which candor or other considerations require laying out all of one's main reasons.[37] If one does articulate religious reasons in a public debate, it should help to be able to express both commitment to the principle of secular rationale and reasons that accord with it. This would show a respect for a religiously neutral point of view that any rational citizen may share.[38] The principles of secular rationale and secular motivation may, however, be adhered to without being stated or even consciously endorsed. It is the reasons one has and is motivated by that matter most, not what one would say about one's reasons or about the principles those reasons should satisfy.

Although the rationale and motivation principles (and indeed everything I have contended here) are entirely consistent with religious reasons' being evidentially adequate, the evidential adequacy of those reasons is not a presupposition of liberal democracy—nor, of course, is their evidential inadequacy.[39] Indeed, it may be that the absence of both presuppositions is a negative commitment of liberal democracy, a special kind of neutrality regarding religious matters, one that seems to go somewhat beyond neutrality toward religious institutions. This view is supportable, to differing degrees, from the perspective of any of the paths to liberal democracy. . . . Even apart from that, I think it would be inappropriate for a theory of liberal democracy to contain either epistemological claim, just as it would violate the neutrality of a liberal state toward religion to support antireligious practices or institutions as such.[40] This epistemological neutrality perhaps need not be a positive plank in even a fully articulated democratic constitution, but it is an important strand in much liberal-democratic theory.

Ideals, Rights, and Democratic Respect

. . . I want to reiterate that my position as applied to individual conduct is above all one that lays out what we ought to do in something like an ideal case. It describes an aspect of civic virtue . . . not a limitation of civil (or other) rights. I have not claimed, for example, that there is no *right* to base one's votes on a religious ground. But surely we can do better than guide our civic conduct merely within the constraints imposed by our rights. An ethics that directs us merely to live within our rights gives us too minimal a guide for daily life.

One important way in which my position is highly consonant with theistic religion, and in particular with the Hebraic-Christian tradition, is its insistence that morality speaks to the heart and mind, not just to the hand and mouth: our thoughts, attitudes, and feelings can be morally criticizable or praiseworthy, as well as can our words and deeds. And our deeds, however well they can be rationalized by the reasons we can offer for them, *bespeak* the reasons that motivate them. We as agents, as opposed to our deeds, are judged more by the reasons *for* which we act than by the reasons we had for which we *could* have acted. Loving one's neighbors as oneself implies appropriate motives as well as good deeds, and it is far more than just respecting their rights of civic courtesy.

It is also worth reiterating that the domain of application of my principles is primarily contexts of political advocacy and of public policy decision. The principles are addressed especially to citizens as voters and supporters of laws and public policy, to legislators in their official capacities, to judges in making and justifying decisions, and to administrators, especially government officials, laying down and interpreting policies. But the principles apply differently in different contexts: less, for instance, in the classroom than in the statehouse, less in private discussion than in corporate board rooms.

There are, to be sure, proceduralist models of democracy that are less demanding than the conception I endorse. I have been thinking mainly of a constitutional liberal democracy. My claim is that a substantially weaker separation of church and state than I have defended is not fully consonant with the ideals of liberal democracy; and I think that sound ethics itself dictates that, out of respect for others as free individuals with human dignity, we should always have and be sufficiently motivated by adequate secular reason for our positions on those matters of law or public policy in which our decisions will (or might be reasonably expected to) significantly restrict human freedom.

If my fellow citizens are fully rational and are adequately informed concerning the matter at hand—an ideal combination many do not often realize—and I cannot convince them of my view by arguments framed in the concepts we share (or can readily share) as rational beings, then even if mine is the majority view I have a strong prima facie obligation not to coerce them. Perhaps the political system embodies a legal right for the majority to do so; presumably there is even a moral right to do so, at least given a certain mutual understanding of and commitment to majority rule. But the principles I am suggesting still make a plausible and weighty claim on our allegiance. They require, in certain contexts and for certain purposes, partial secularization of our advocacy, argumentation, and decisions. But they do not restrict our ultimate freedom of expression, and they leave us at liberty to fulfill our cherished religious ideals in all the ways compatible with a system in which those with differing ideals are equally free to pursue theirs.

Chapter 4

Liberal Civic Education
and Religious Fundamentalism

The Case of God v. John Rawls?

Stephen Macedo

LIBERALISM AND THE LIMITS OF DIVERSITY

Nowadays it often appears that liberals have been outflanked on the issue
of diversity. Political activists and theorists increasingly insist that greater
weight be given to what distinguishes particular groups from others.
Those who clamor for a "politics of difference" are as likely to be attacking as seeking to extend liberal values and practices.

Iris Marion Young, for example, wants a politics that "attends to rather
than represses difference," in which no group "is stereotyped, silenced, or
marginalized."[1] She dismisses the ideal of impartiality and such notions
as moral universality, human nature, essentialism, and various other
pre-postmodern sins and vices, because all deny the basic significance
of group-based differences: "Groups cannot be socially equal unless
their specific experience, culture, and social contributions are publicly
affirmed and recognized."[2] Young rejects "melting pot ideals of assimilation and unity," not surprisingly, arguing that the "desire for political
unity will suppress difference, and tend to exclude some voices and

perspectives from the public."³ She advocates "bilingual-bicultural maintenance programs" to preserve and affirm group-specific identities.⁴

The notion of a politics that does not "devalue or exclude any particular culture or way of life" is neither plausible nor attractive.⁵ Young's
own stance has only the appearance of all-inclusiveness. She champions
1960s New Left constituencies (blacks, native people, women, gays, the
disabled) and simply leaves aside complaints of Nazis, fundamentalists,
or even the Amish, all of whom could claim to be victims of oppression,
at least as Young describes it.

Fundamentalists, for example, could claim to be victims of stereo-
typing and cultural marginalization. They lack status and respectability
in important centers of cultural power and would certainly join Young in
challenging pretensions to impartiality, especially those of "modern scientific reason." Many fundamentalists undoubtedly consider themselves
oppressed in these ways.⁶

Is solicitude for fundamentalists a fair-minded extension of multicultural concern to the political Right? The idea is not as farfetched as it
may seem. Nomi Stolzenberg has recently defended the plausibility of
the fundamentalist charge that teaching "diverse viewpoints in a tolerant
and objective mode threatens the survival of their culture" and is a liberal
means of assimilation, "that insidious cousin of totalitarianism."⁷

The indiscriminate embrace of difference and diversity should be
resisted. Inevitably, some groups will be marginalized and feel oppressed
by even liberal public policies and the wider culture those policies help
promote. Unfortunate as they are, such feelings may indicate the need
for adjustments not in public policy but in the group. Assimilation is
an inescapable and legitimate object of liberal policy: it all depends
on the justifiability of the values toward which institutions assimilate and
the reasonableness of the means. Liberal diversity is diversity shaped
and managed by political institutions.⁸

The "politics of difference" is unfocused but not entirely misguided.
It could be taken as a useful warning against the aspiration of even
some liberals to a politics that would directly promote ideals (such as
autonomy) in all spheres of life. We should, I want to argue here, heed
the warnings against totalistic liberalisms, not in the name of the politics
of difference, but under the banner of political liberalism and a limited
but tough-minded conception of public educational authority.⁹ I want
to argue for a political liberalism with spine. While we should put aside
matters about which reasonable people disagree, we should also be
resolute in facing up to the fact that no version of liberalism can make

everyone happy. Perhaps, in the end, our politics does come down to a holy war between religious zealots and proponents of science and public reason. Political liberalism, I shall argue, offers the hope of deliverance from both politics as holy war and politics as the embrace of nonjudgmental, unqualified pluralism.[10]

MOZERT V. HAWKINS AND THE FUNDAMENTALIST COMPLAINT

Even the most basic forms of liberal civic education give rise to complaints grounded in religious diversity; we will focus here on one striking example, *Mozert v. Hawkins*, which involved a 1983 complaint by "born again" Christian families against the local school board in Hawkins County, Tennessee.[11] The families charged a primary school reading program with denigrating their religious views, both in its lack of religious "balance" and in the uncommitted, evenhanded nature of the presentations.[12] The complaint was, in part at least, not so much that a particular religious claim was directly advanced by the readings, but that the program taken as a whole exposed the children to a variety of points of view and that this very exposure to diversity interfered with the free exercise of the families' religious beliefs by denigrating the truth of their particular religious views. (Parent Vicki Frost said that "the word of God as found in the Christian Bible 'is the totality of my beliefs.'"[13])This complaint was not the only one offered by the *Mozert* parents, but it was the most reasonable one and is, in any case, the complaint on which I want to focus here.

The families asked that the children be allowed to opt out of the reading program, and that program only, while remaining in the public schools. Some schools at first allowed these students to participate in an alternative reading series, but within a few weeks the County School Board resolved to make the reading program mandatory for all and to suspend children who refused to participate.[14] A number of children were indeed suspended, after which some withdrew and went to Christian schools, others resorted to homeschooling, some transferred out of the county schools, and a few simply returned to their public schools.[15]

Mozert raises fundamental questions in an apparently moderate posture. The families did not seek to impose their ideas on anyone else through the public school curriculum and did not (apparently) challenge the general legitimacy of secular public schooling. They wanted only to opt out of a particular program while remaining in public schools—how much harm could there be in that? And yet, the *Mozert* objections went to the heart of civic education in a liberal polity: how can tolerance be taught without exposing children to diversity and asking them to forbear from asserting the truth of their own particular convictions, at least for political purposes?[16]

Mozert recalls the famous case in which Amish parents objected to sending their children to public high school on the ground that doing so would expose their children to a wide variety of "alternative life styles" and undermine the simplicity and otherworldliness essential to their religious community.[17] In both cases parents effectively claimed that exposing children to different ways of life would prevent their becoming members of their respective faith communities. The Amish case was, in a way, politically easy, since being Amish is not a growth industry: the Amish pose no threat to the health of the wider liberal society.[18] Protestant fundamentalists are far more numerous and powerful and are often highly politicized and hostile to at least some liberal values.

Two issues immediately arise. Can exposure to diversity interfere with the free exercise of religious beliefs? If so, does a liberal state have the authority to condition a benefit such as public schooling on the willingness of parents to have their children exposed to diversity?

First the threshold matter: can exposure to diversity interfere with religious freedom? Judge Lively denied it: "Exposure to something does not constitute teaching, indoctrination, opposition or promotion of the things exposed."[19] The matter would have been quite different were the state directly to inculcate particular religious ideas, or to require particular acts forbidden by the students' religious convictions, or to mandate affirmations or professions of belief.[20]

Other judges conceded that the reading program interfered with the parents' ability to pass along their religious values. The program could be likened, Judge Boggs suggested, to requiring Catholic students to read items on the Catholic Church's official index of prohibited books, under pain of giving up the right to free public schooling.[21] Public schooling is available to these fundamentalists only on condition that they do things they view as at odds with salvation. The children may resort to Christian schools or homeschooling but, Boggs noted, even the modest tuition charged by local Christian schools "amounted to about a doubling of the state and local tax burden of the average resident."[22]

Let us concede that the mandatory reading program interferes with these parents' ability to teach their children their particular religious views. Whether this is a violation of moral rights is another question. To address that question, let us consider the precise nature of the interference and its possible justification.

COMPREHENSIVE VERSUS POLITICAL LIBERALISM

The most straightforward justification of the reading program would be on the basis of a comprehensive liberal ideal of life as a whole centered on autonomy or individuality. Public schools, a comprehensive liberal might say, need not confine themselves to any narrowly defined civic mission but may properly promote, as Amy Gutmann puts it, "rational deliberation among ways of life."[23] To this, of course, the *Mozert* families are fundamentally opposed, and the comprehensive liberal will reply that fundamentalists are simply wrong to deny the importance of critical thinking in all departments of life.

Comprehensive liberal ideals are deeply partisan and not easily defended. They claim too much. Do we really want to premise political authority on the contention that critical thinking is the best way to attain religious truth? Perhaps this can be avoided. An alternative approach would be to put aside such matters as religious truth and the ultimate ideals of human perfection and attempt to justify at least the most basic matters of justice on grounds widely acceptable to reasonable people— and not only to those who share our particular view of the whole truth. Such is the approach suggested by John Rawls' *Political Liberalism*. I want to defend that approach here and display its practical promise. That political liberalism has any practical promise is denied by those who regard it as representing nothing more than the prejudices of "American East Coast liberals."[24] In fact, however, the federal court in *Mozert* rejected reliance on comprehensive ideals of life in favor of a stance resembling political liberalism.

Judge Lively defended the authority of public schools to teach values "essential to a democratic society," including toleration; they may "acquaint students with a multitude of ideas and concepts," so long as they avoid direct "religious or anti-religious messages." Public schools, he said, may teach "civil tolerance," which is the notion that "in a pluralistic society we must 'live and let live.'"[25] Schools may not teach a religious doctrine of toleration, such as one which says, "all religions are merely different roads to God."[26] "No instrument of government" could legitimately "require such a belief or affirmation." Public schools may, in effect, teach that all religions are the same in the eyes of the state, not that they are all the same in the eyes of God. By construing the public doctrine of toleration as strictly civil, Lively accepted fundamentalist parent Vicki Frost's insistence that "we cannot be tolerant in that we accept other religious views on an equal basis with ours."[27]

Notice the similarity with political liberalism, which starts with the conviction that reasonable people disagree deeply and permanently about their religious beliefs and philosophical ideals of life. Political liberalism bids us to acknowledge that, given the difficult matters of judgment involved, people may reasonably disagree about the justifiability of even purportedly liberal ideals of life as a whole, such as Kantian autonomy or Millian individuality. That the good life consists in autonomy is properly regarded as one more sectarian view among others, no more worthy of commanding public authority than other philosophical and religious ideals of life that reasonable people might reject.[28] Political liberalism extends the principle of toleration, as Rawls puts it, from religion to contestable philosophical ideals of life.[29]

People who disagree about their highest ideals and their conceptions of the whole truth might nevertheless agree that public aims such as peace, prosperity, and equal liberty are very important. That is political liberalism's virtue: it focuses our attention on shared political values without requiring or expecting agreement on ultimate ends or a comprehensive set of moral values governing all of our lives.

The basic motive behind political liberalism, it should be emphasized, is not fear of conflict or a desire to exclude religious speech from the public realm but the desire to respect reasonable people. In a free society, many of our fellow citizens hold fundamental moral and religious beliefs that we believe false but which we can also allow are within the bounds of the reasonable for political purposes.[30] What political liberalism asks of us is not to renounce what we believe to be true but to acknowledge the difficulty of publicly establishing any single account of the whole truth.[31] It invites us to put some of our (true) beliefs aside when it comes to laying the groundwork for common political institutions. In accepting this invitation, we are not moved by the power of those with whom we join but by respect for their reasonableness. We do not seek to respect pluralism or diversity as such but reasonable pluralism.[32]

Political liberals do not, as some argue, seek to exclude religious people from the public realm or to curtail their political speech.[33] The aim, rather, is to suggest that the most basic political rights and institutions should be justified in terms of reasons and arguments that can be shared with reasonable people whose religious and other ultimate commitments differ. Religious beliefs are, on this account, regarded as no different than secular ideals of life as a whole. Neither Protestant fundamentalism nor Dewey's secular humanism are proper grounds for determining basic rights and constitutional principles.

Political liberalism does not "silence" people or limit First Amendment rights to free speech. There may be a variety of ways, indeed, in which religious speech can *support* political liberalism by clarifying the depth of one's commitment to liberal principles and the political authority of public reasons.[34] The crux of the matter is not speech at all but the legitimate grounds of coercion. The point of specifying the nature of public reason is to argue that when defining the constitutional basics—the fundamental rights and principles that will limit and direct the fearsome coercive powers of the modern state—we should, at least at the end of the political day, affirm the authority of grounds that we can share with our reasonable fellow citizens. Acknowledging the political authority of public reasons is one mark of a virtuous citizen, but people are entirely within their rights not to be virtuous, here as elsewhere.

The *Mozert* court's notion of civil toleration offers a way to extend political liberalism to public schooling. We focus on shared public principles and leave the religious dimensions of the question aside. The public school curriculum would in this way avoid directly confronting or denying the *Mozert* families' contention that the Bible's authority should be accepted uncritically. "When asked to comment on a reading assignment," Lively said, "a student would be free to give the Biblical interpretation of the material or to interpret it from a different value base." There was "no compulsion to affirm or deny a religious belief" or, presumably, any other comprehensive moral view.[35] By simply leaving aside the religious question as such (at least in the sense of not taking an official position on it), Lively and political liberals leave the school door open to reasonable fundamentalists, that is, to those willing to acknowledge for political purposes the authority of public reasonableness.

Political liberals must walk a tightrope, emphasizing the great weight of shared political aims but, so far as possible, avoiding comment on the wider moral and religious claims. Children should not be chastised for saying in class that God created mankind, though they might also be asked to describe scientific theories and evidence on the issue of human origins. Political liberals might well applaud the concurring opinion of Judge Chambliss, in the Scopes Monkey Trial, who tried to save the Tennessee law at issue by construing it not as a ban on the teaching of evolution but as a ban on the teaching of any theory that positively denies a role for God in the creation of the universe.[36] This Solomonic move could be seen as a political liberal attempt to keep public authority from directly endorsing or disparaging any particular religious view; it defends the place in public schools of widely accepted scientific evidence while not taking a position on the question of how—or whether—God fits into the whole business.[37] Chambliss would have allowed the teaching of theories of evolution on this condition.

It is tempting to say that the only real difference between political and comprehensive liberalisms is that proponents of the latter are simply more candid in admitting that liberal institutions foster an ideal of life as a whole and that "civil" toleration inevitably promotes "religious" toleration. Candor is not, however, the crux of the matter: political liberalism stands for a restraint that would be unnatural for one committed to the political authority of a vision of the good life as a whole informed by autonomy or individuality. Political liberals will reject in principle a public program that teaches a religious doctrine of toleration or one that advances John Dewey's claim that science is the "one sure road of access to truth."[38] Political liberalism aims to open its doors to those who reject the wider moral ideals of Kant, Mill, or Dewey. Comprehensive liberalism stands for values that really are broader and deeper and more stridently partisan than those of political liberalism.

LIBERALISM AS INDIRECT ESTABLISHMENT OF RELIGION?

Political liberalism avoids certain vexing religious and philosophical disputes about which reasonable people have long differed. Nothing in my defense of political liberalism should, however, be taken to suggest that it is nonpartisan, uncontroversial, or equally accommodating of all religious beliefs. The goods promoted by political liberalism (freedom, peace, prosperity) will not be valued equally by people of different faiths. More to the point at hand, promoting core liberal political virtues—such as the importance of a critical attitude toward contending political claims—seems certain to have the effect of promoting critical thinking in general. Liberal political virtues and attitudes will spill over into other spheres of life. Even a suitably circumscribed political liberalism is not really all that circumscribed: it will in various ways promote a way of life as a whole.[39]

Political liberalism is neutral with respect to ideals of life as a whole only in the very limited sense of not relying on the justifiability of any particular comprehensive ideal or view of the whole truth.[40] Political liberal principles are neutral only in being publicly justified independently of religious and other comprehensive claims. Citizens are asked to put aside their comprehensive moral and religious conceptions, in the sense that they should acknowledge the political authority and adequacy of reasons that can be shared by reasonable people who disagree about their ultimate ideals.[41]

It is certainly possible to conceive of far more demanding forms of neutrality or fairness. One might argue that public policies should have neutral effects on the (major?) religions of society, insofar as is possible. Citizens might, under such a scheme, refuse ever to put aside their deepest moral commitments for the sake of public reflection on shared secular aims and interests; they would instead invoke these beliefs in the public realm and use them as a yardstick for measuring the acceptability of basic public principles. Encouraging people to bring their ultimate commitments—religious, philosophical, etc.—directly to bear in politics might reflect a desire to respect and preserve their group-based identities and convictions.[42] In some places—quite apart from what theorists might like—people might simply refuse to put aside religious and ethnic group-based sensitivities. Political liberalism is quite different: it advances an ideal of citizenship according to which we formulate and defend basic principles of justice by relying on public reasons that we can share while disagreeing about our ultimate commitments.

The very aspiration to think about politics from a perspective that is in this way independent of religious views and other controversial comprehensive conceptions is nonneutral: its appeal will vary greatly among people of different faiths. Totalistic faiths (such as Vicki Frost's belief in the Christian Bible as the "whole truth") will be especially resistant to thinking about politics (or anything else) from a perspective that in any way "brackets" the truth of their particular religious views. It does no good to deny that some will find the strictures of liberal public reason burdensome. To refrain from invoking our religious beliefs when exercising public power may come naturally to many who have grown up within a pluralistic liberal order—but let that not obscure the significance of this form of restraint. Niklas Luhmann seems to downplay liberalism's significance by arguing that a liberal society stands for nothing as a whole. Indeed, he suggests, seeking a meaning or point of the modern social order as a whole is fundamentally anachronistic, for ours is a "differentiated society," a fragmented social order divided into distinct spheres of life: economic, political, religious, educational, and so on. Principles apply in particular spheres but not across society as a whole.[43]

The problem is that a differentiated society does stand for something as a whole—several things in fact. Luhmann himself allows that the division of society into many spheres allows individuals facing unwanted constraints in one sphere to flee to another.[44] A differentiated society thus serves the cause of freedom and promotes moral laxity as well as a certain kind of individualism. All this is exactly what fundamentalists object to. In such an environment, Vicki Frost will have a hard time teaching her children that the "totality" of truth is found in the Christian Bible. Many forms of discipline will be hard to sustain in the differentiated society, which indirectly fosters distinctive forms of personality, culture, and even religious beliefs and which is, then, a particular type. We should avoid the common tendency to underdescribe the pattern of life which is liable to be promoted by even a circumscribed political liberalism.

We should also avoid the increasingly popular tendency to exaggerate liberalism's religious partisanship. Nomi Stolzenberg commits this error, I believe, by arguing that when liberals ask people to bracket their religious beliefs for the sake of public reflection on political principles, they take sides in a debate within Protestantism.[45] She points out that fundamentalism was born as a rejection of those modernist and "liberal" strains within American Protestantism that encouraged people to bracket inherited convictions about the truth of scriptures for the sake of historical or critical studies of their meaning. Modernist Protestants often embraced not only the higher criticism, which studies the meaning of the Gospels in light of their original historical context, but also the view that religious views should adjust to the findings of modern science. Fundamentalists resist bracketing the truth of religious claims, Stolzenberg insists, for such a stance lacks religious seriousness. The "essential point" for fundamentalists is that "the objective study of religion, and objective approaches to knowledge in general, are quintessentially secular humanist activities."[46] On Stolzenberg's account, the liberal demand that we not rely upon religious grounds or invoke religious truths in politics gives the *religious* opponents of fundamentalism all that they have sought. Fundamentalists have every reason, therefore, to make holy war against liberalism.

Such a conclusion would be far too hasty, because Stolzenberg's analysis does not apply to political liberalism. The political liberal avoids saying anything about how religion is to be studied; that is left to churches and other private groups. The political liberal can live with the notion that fundamentalism may be the truth in the religious sphere—so long as it does not claim political authority.[47] Political liberals will, moreover, make common cause with moderate fundamentalists to deny political power to any—including secular humanists—who would shape basic rights and principles of justice in light of their view of the whole truth.[48] Room is provided, in this way, for a broad range of religious orientations to converge on a shared political view. Finally, political liberalism asks of fundamentalists only what it asks of others, including proponents of secular ideals, such as Dewey's humanism: to put reasonably contestable comprehensive ideals to one side in the political realm and to focus on values such as peace and freedom that can be shared by reasonable people.[49]

There is, then, a crucial difference between political liberalism's insistence on the political authority of public reasons and the theological controversies between fundamentalists and their opponents. The higher criticism—on Stolzenberg's account—says bracket the truth question (or put aside your belief in inherited truths) for the sake of religious study. The political liberal says recognize that the question of religious truth must be bracketed in order to justify the basic principles that will guide the coercive power we hold together as a political community. We should not sell this concession short, and it is not obvious that fundamentalists (at least moderate fundamentalists) will do so. Political liberalism is, therefore, not as partisan as Stolzenberg suggests.

Stolzenberg is not alone in her hasty leap for the proposition that fundamentalism and liberalism are at war. Stephen Carter proposes "that in its stated zeal to cherish religious belief under the protective mantle of 'neutrality,' liberalism is really derogating religious belief in favor of other, more 'rational' methods of understanding the world. The great risk lying a bit further down this path is that religion, far from being cherished, will be diminished, and that religious belief will ultimately become a kind of hobby: something so private that it is as irrelevant to public life as the building of model airplanes."[50] Another worry might be that religious people will increasingly understand the liberal settlement in Carter's terms and so make holy war against it.

Carter believes that liberalism rests on the authority of a model of reason that is secular, scientific, and at odds with fundamentalist religious communities and biblical hermeneutics. For Carter, liberalism chooses science over religion, and in the name of neutrality tells religion to get lost. In the name of fairness, Carter would broaden political justification to include the religious voice and invite people to enter the political arena with their religious convictions intact and in play.

Political liberalism is not, however, grounded in a comprehensive commitment to science; reasonable people may believe that in some areas science pulls up short, and political liberalism does not settle the

matter of just where or when. Political liberalism seeks to avoid upping
the ante with Carter, and for good reason. Consider what happens
when Stanley Fish embraces Carter's characterization of our public life.
Liberalism claims, he says, to be ultimately tolerant, fair, and dependent
only on reason: a court of appeal above the ideological and sectarian
fray. But, Fish charges, there is no "reason" above the fray, no ultimate
fairness or neutral standpoint. Liberalism places its faith in scientific reason, which has no privileged claim to transcendence, only pretensions
thereto. Since liberalism defines itself by its nonpartisanship, says Fish,
"one can only conclude, and conclude nonparadoxically, that liberalism
doesn't exist."[51]

Political liberalism offers a way to defuse this war of absolutes. It seeks
ground shared by reasonable people and leaves it to citizens individually
to connect political values with their beliefs about the truth as a whole.
As a public matter, we will not share a common account of liberalism's
transcendence because we do not share a common conception of the
whole truth. That does not mean that liberalism is grounded in skepticism or that it is ungrounded in a transcendent view. Each citizen is free
to connect the shared political view with his own view of the whole truth
in his own way. If one of the comprehensive views that supports liberalism is true, then liberalism is grounded in the true transcendent view.
(And in that case, as Rawls says, those political liberals who espouse false
comprehensive views at least have true political views.)[52] This does not
mean that liberalism's justification is uncontroversial or nonpartisan.
Every political theory is both controversial and partisan—noticing that is
no great victory for Fish. Since political liberalism, properly understood,
does not claim to be nonpartisan, Fish would be rash to conclude that it
does not exist (perhaps we should conclude that Fish does not exist?).

Political liberalism is not the only possible response to Carter's
dilemma. Comprehensive liberals could shout "charge!" and rush to
defend science, autonomy, individuality, John Deweyism, or what-have-
you as the paths to the whole truth about the human good. Liberals could
sound a strategic retreat and settle for a modus vivendi or peace treaty
among fundamentally opposed groups who lack shared grounds for principled agreement. These strategies have their eloquent defenders. Political liberalism attempts, instead, to head off the clash of ultimates and to
avoid both liberalism as holy war and liberalism as uneasy peace.

The distinction between religious and civil toleration helps mark off
the space on which to construct a principled but politic liberalism: a
liberalism grounded not in the authority of science per se, but in shared

standards of reason. It is not neutral in its effects, but it at least disallows the use of political power to promote directly anyone's contestable comprehensive ideals. It seeks a reasonable consensus and trust among those who might otherwise be as deeply opposed as Carter suggests, and that is at least worth trying for.

Liberalism is not as directly partisan as Stolzenberg, Carter, and Fish suggest. It does not require that people "bracket" the truth question when studying religion (the *Mozert* contest is over a reading program, not a religion class); it does not endorse secular humanism or the scientific study of religion. A political liberal citizen can hold that in religious matters one should defer to sacred books or higher authorities. Of course, it may not be easy to forbear from asserting one's fundamentalist religious views in the political realm, not as easy as restraining one's Unitarian or Lockian or Millian convictions. But to ask less of people is to renounce the notion that good liberal citizens should justify basic political principles in terms that can be shared with reasonable fellow citizens, and not only with members of one's own sect.

The political liberal offers a bargain to moderates in all comprehensive camps, whether fundamentalist Protestant or autonomy-pursuing liberal: let's put aside our wider convictions when designing commonly authoritative political institutions and focus on principles and aims that pass the tests of public reason. These concessions will not satisfy everyone, but they are significant.

RELIGIOUS ACCOMMODATIONS AND SUBSTANTIVE NEUTRALITY: TOWARD A SECOND STAGE OF PUBLIC JUSTIFICATION?

Political liberalism, I have argued, furnishes good reasons for justifying basic political principles in terms of public aims and values that can be shared by reasonable people. Clearly enough, however, even publicly justifiable principles and programs will have nonneutral effects and impose disparate burdens on adherents of different comprehensive religious and moral views. Fairness might seem to suggest that at some point we should examine the disparate impact of publicly justified policies, especially on groups outside the political and cultural mainstream. These will often be groups whose comprehensive conceptions exist in decided tension with the shared values of the political order. One way to do this is to provide public justification with a second stage: a stage where, having constructed a reasonable public view, we consider pleas for accommodations and exemptions from marginal groups. Let us consider whether public justification should have such a second stage of principled exception making and, if so, whether its aim should be the kind of maximum feasible accommodation that Galston advocates in his ["Two Concepts of Liberalism"].*

A second stage might be a way to grapple with the charge that liberalism deploys merely formal principles of neutrality and fairness. Political liberalism puts conflicting comprehensive views aside; it does not seek a compromise or balance among those wider views; it does not furnish any sort of guide for weighing and assessing the disproportionate effects of various public laws and policies. Those wider effects can be discerned only if we take up the comprehensive normative perspectives of those who dissent from the liberal order. A more substantial ideal of neutrality or fairness would take up these comprehensive perspectives and assess the burdens that liberal policies place on particular groups or persons when viewed from their comprehensive perspectives, to balance these burdens against public aims, and to grant exemptions and accommodations in the name of securing "real" neutrality and fairness.[53]

Solicitude for group-based diversity might well argue for these more substantial notions of fairness and neutrality. Fundamentalists are not powerless, but they are certainly outside the cultural and intellectual mainstream, especially with respect to the educational establishment, and so would seem to deserve a sensitive hearing. Should public justification have a second stage? And should the fundamentalist families be allowed to opt out of the reading program because of its disproportionate impact on their faith community?

If offered as alternatives to political liberalism, the attractions of more substantive conceptions of neutrality and fairness are more apparent than real. Pursuing the mirage of perfect fairness would, first of all, be utterly debilitating: how could we possibly ensure that public policies have neutral effects on the innumerable faiths and worldviews in our regime? Announcing an ideal of perfect fairness or neutrality of effect would, moreover, heighten group consciousness, group-based grievances, and political divisions.[54] "Perfect fairness" is also unappealing: it means being fair to reasonable and unreasonable views, to those who recognize the political authority of public reasons that can be shared by people who disagree and those who do not. Why should we apologize if disparate burdens fall on proponents of totalistic religious or moral views who

*Galston, "Two Concepts of Liberalism," *Ethics* 105, no. 3 (1995): 516–34.
—Ed.

refuse to concede the political authority of public reason? We must not forget how such people would behave if they had political power.

We should avoid a postmodern angst about our inability publicly to establish a comprehensive scheme of human values. Political liberalism accepts the fact of reasonable disagreement over comprehensive moral and religious ideals. That acceptance should do nothing to corrode our confidence in the principles that pass the test of public reason. It is wrong to say that liberalism makes do with mere "formal" neutrality and "formal" fairness when more substantive accounts are available. There is as much substance in political liberalism's conceptions of neutrality and fairness as our shared standards of reasonableness—and respect for reasonable disagreement—allow.

We should not pursue the mirage of perfect fairness, but that does not mean that we should never consider pleas for accommodations and exemptions: where public imperatives are marginal and the burdens on particular groups are very substantial, accommodations will sometimes be justified. We should, however, enter into the process of exception making critically and without aiming at anything so broad as Galston's principle of maximum feasible accommodation of diversity. The particular claims of the fundamentalist families in *Mozert* are, for example, not especially strong. The reading program at stake does indeed impose disproportionate burdens on parents attempting to inculcate fundamentalist religion. But we must remember that the source of the apparent "unfairness," the cause of the "disparate impact" here, is a reasonable attempt to inculcate core liberal values. The state is within the limits of its rightful authority. The bedrock liberal insistence on toleration is a constraint on the range of religious practices that can be tolerated. It is hard to see how schools could fulfill the core liberal civic mission of inculcating toleration and other basic civic virtues without running afoul of complaints about "exposure to diversity." Since "exposure to diversity" is a necessary means for teaching a basic civic virtue, it cannot support a fundamental right to be exempted from an otherwise reasonable educational regime.

Of course, there are uncertainties as to the reading program's efficacy, along with all other efforts to inculcate moral virtues.[55] It would be extremely hard to show that any particular school program is crucial for realizing the core liberal value of toleration. Empirical questions in this area seem intrinsically hard to settle, however, and so judgments about fundamental rights should turn on other grounds. The program stands as a reasonable effort to familiarize students with diversity and teach toleration. The basic question of principle is, Do families have a moral right to opt out of reasonable measures designed to educate children toward very basic liberal virtues because those measures make it harder for parents to pass along their particular religious beliefs? Surely not. To acknowledge the legitimacy of the fundamentalist complaint as a matter of basic principle would overthrow reasonable efforts to inculcate core liberal values. It would provide religious fundamentalists with a right to shield their children from the fact of reasonable pluralism. Liberal civic education is bound to have the effect of favoring some ways of life or religious convictions over others. So be it.

As a matter of basic principle at least, we have good reason to refuse the *Mozert* families' request to opt out. If intransigence here appears to be at odds with religious freedom, it must be remembered that rightful liberty is civil liberty, or liberty that can be guaranteed equally to all. All of us must accept limits on our liberty designed to sustain a system of equal liberty for all. Each of us can reasonably be asked to surrender some control over our own children for the sake of reasonable common efforts to ensure that all future citizens learn the minimal prerequisites of citizenship. There is no right to be exempted from measures reasonably designed to help secure the freedom of all.

We have so far left aside the fact, moreover, that we are dealing with children who are not mere extensions of their parents. The religious liberty of parents does not extend with full force to their children. Adult Christian Scientists might be allowed to refuse medical treatment but not for their children. Insulating children from diversity is less serious than keeping them from needed medicine, but some level of awareness of alternative ways of life is a prerequisite not only of citizenship but of being able to make the most basic life choices. This ground alone might well be adequate to deny the claimed right to opt out.

Some will object to my intransigence, pointing out that we allow people to opt out of public schooling altogether and to go to private schools: to parochial and fundamentalist schools, and even homeschooling.[56] If we concede a right to opt out of public schooling altogether, how can we justify intransigence in *Mozert*? I would concede the right to opt out of public schooling, but that right should be understood to be conditioned by a public authority to regulate private schools to ensure that civic basics are taught. True enough, in most states private schools and homeschooling are only minimally regulated, especially with respect to civic education.[57] That states do not fully exercise their rightful authority, however, does not mean they do not have it. So while there is a (moral and constitutional) right to opt out of public schooling, there is no right to opt selectively out of those basic civic exercises that the state may reasonably require for all children. Concomitantly, private schools have no right to resist reasonable measures to ensure that all children learn basic civic virtues.[58]

Intransigence is in principle justified in *Mozert* because a politically basic purpose—the promotion of toleration—is at stake. Only the most basic public purposes will routinely trump religious complaints and warrant intransigent support. When more marginal political values are at stake—in school or elsewhere—then religious complainants may well have a stronger case. The fundamentalists in *Mozert* might, for example, have objected to aspects of the curriculum far more incidentally or marginally related to the pursuit of basic civic aims—art classes for example; then we would approach their complaints at least somewhat differently.[59]

One can easily imagine religious complaints that should gain a favorable hearing. The fundamentalists might have conceded the legitimacy of the core civic mission of the readers, while mounting an objection based on liberal values themselves. They might have objected (let us suppose) that the purported "diversity" of views in the readers lacks respectful depictions of religious ways of life. They might have charged the readers with combining glowing portrayals of secularist, this-worldly ideals of life and disparaging portrayals of the more conservative forms of religious belief.[60] While it would be unreasonable to insist on perfect "balance" in school readers or other parts of the curriculum, political liberals can sympathize with objections to a reading program so heavily biased toward a particular comprehensive view that it appears designed to advance that view and denigrate alternatives.

Liberals can do more than insist intransigently on core liberal values; we should insist on political respect for fundamentalists who acknowledge the political authority of liberal public principles. Such fundamentalists are reasonable fellow citizens whose religious convictions should not be gratuitously disparaged in readers that profess to expose children to diversity and to teach toleration. The political liberal will hold, after all, that children from religious families are not the only ones who need lessons in tolerance. The children of evangelical atheists and of those who espouse totalistic versions of liberalism also need to learn political respect for fellow citizens who hold other reasonable views.

When complaints are advanced by small and politically weak religious groups, moreover, courts can help ensure that their concerns are taken seriously and that they are treated with equal concern and respect. To leave accommodations and exceptions to the democratic branches is virtually to ensure that complaints advanced by minority religious communities will often be slighted, so the courts must play a role.

My main concern here has been to argue that the *Mozert* families have no moral right to be accommodated, at least on the basis of the principled grounds surveyed here. Besides principled reasons for exception making and accommodation, political liberalism also suggests certain prudential grounds.[61] Political liberals aspire to a society in which people share a public moral order. This aim would suggest that we have prudential grounds to accommodate dissenters when doing so helps draw them into a public moral order that is always coming-into-being. In the case of the *Mozert* families, this points to the relevance of the consideration mentioned earlier: will the refusal to accommodate drive these families out of public schools altogether and into Christian schools?[62] Can we accommodate the families while only minimally compromising our principled concern with teaching toleration? While the *Mozert* families had, therefore, no fundamental moral right to be accommodated (and no judicially enforceable constitutional right, so far as I can see), school administrators who anticipated the withdrawal of these families altogether from the public system may well have had prudential reasons to accommodate them in order to keep the children within the public system.[63]

To say that the practice of prudential accommodation should promote assimilation into liberal political values raises the (seemingly inescapable) question: what about the Amish? Allowing Amish parents to pull their children out of high school (as Galston advocates) does not promote assimilation into liberal values. On the other hand, the Amish were no threat to the larger society; they are "private persons standing in merely private relations to others," as Hegel said of the Quakers and Anabaptists.[64] This makes it much easier to recognize the good qualities promoted by the Amish way of life: the law-abidingness and hard work that so impressed Justice Burger.

We cannot be entirely happy about accommodating the Amish, however. That they are hardworking does not impugn the fact that, as Jeff Spinner argues, they are not in other respects good liberal citizens.[65] Amish society is patriarchal—women are regarded as unequal helpers of men—and Amish children are not prepared for being critically reflective citizens. While the state has no business promoting broad ideals like personal autonomy, moreover, to allow Amish parents to withdraw their children from high school could thwart the children's ability to make adequately informed decisions about how to live their lives.

Spinner points out, however, that Amish communities are not quite as closed-off as some idealized pictures might suggest. The Amish know that there is an outside world and that it will accept them if they choose to join it. Amish teenagers sometimes go to Florida for spring break, and about 20 percent of the Amish leave their communities altogether.[66] There appears to be a real, if constrained, "exit option" from the Amish community, and that should at least soften our anxieties about the Amish high school exemption. If the defection rate were higher, of course, we would probably insist that Amish children be fully prepared for life in the wider society. Spinner sensibly suggests that our attitude toward the Amish should be one of "grudging tolerance": they are not in important respects good liberal citizens, but they do not wholly tyrannize over their children, and they keep to themselves. This stance seems far more appropriate than Galston's puzzling (but not uncommon) romanticization of the Amish (and of diversity in general): perhaps we may tolerate the Amish but we should not (at least in important respects) celebrate them. If we accommodate them (and this remains a difficult matter in the case of *Wisconsin v. Yoder* that I would lean toward deciding in the affirmative) we should do so on narrow grounds that do not necessarily apply to other religious groups.

All this makes it clearer that fundamentalist parents cannot claim the same grounds for exemption as do the Amish. Fundamentalists are not sectarians living apart but are, as noted above, increasingly politicized and hostile to many liberal values and practices.

We may, then, sometimes consider claims for accommodations or exceptions or even adjustments in public policies based on comprehensive grounds. Does this, as some conservatives warn, open the back door to the very comprehensive sources of irresolvable conflict that political liberalism works so hard to push out the front? Does it open the sort of Pandora's box of religious complaints that Justice Scalia and others have warned against?[67] In a sense, of course, it does, but the context is all important. Basic political issues have been settled in accord with the strictures of public reason. Most people affirm liberal principles and accept the vast bulk of public policy without deep conscientious reservations. We do not, moreover, enter into a second stage with the expectation that the political order as a whole will be reexamined for its "substantive" neutrality or fairness. We expect only that some extraordinary burdens on particular groups may be lessened or eliminated without great damage to the basic integrity of the public order.

Liberals need not deny that it is sometimes legitimate to acknowledge comprehensive moral and religious views in politics as grounds for possible accommodations or exceptions. We have a long practice of allowing Quakers exemptions from combat duty even though we regard their sincere and deeply held beliefs as unreasonable in important respects. So long as most people accept political liberal values and strictures with regard to most basic matters of principle, we can safely proceed to consider comprehensively based pleas for exceptions and accommodations, as indeed we do.[68] In other instances, it will sometimes be legitimate to consider the comprehensive views of others in order to check that their public reasons are not mere fronts for their comprehensive moral or religious agenda (are Sunday closing laws, publicly justified on civil grounds as a common day of rest, actually just ways of favoring the dominant Christian community?) and to ensure that religious minorities are being treated as equals. It is neither necessary nor possible to banish completely comprehensive considerations from politics.

There are, then, various public grounds for accommodating dissenters by making exceptions to general, publicly justified rules, but the mere fact of a burden on someone's religious beliefs creates no automatic or general right to be exempted from a public requirement. Political liberalism holds that laws must be based on reasonable public grounds. When faced with dissenters who refuse to recognize the weight or authority of those grounds, we must not cast aside our public standards. We may sometimes accommodate or exempt dissenters when their claims do not challenge core liberal values, but we cannot, at the exception stage, discover or construct some new or higher ground that promises necessarily to reconcile religious dissenters to the political order. We must listen to dissenters, engage them in political conversation, and indeed encourage them to state their objections publicly. We cannot guarantee that we will do more. We must, in the end, be prepared to acknowledge and defend core liberal and democratic values. We should not announce, with Galston, in advance of any examination of specific cases, that we intend to accommodate diversity wherever doing so is not a direct threat to social unity. Such a stance gives too much to diversity and too little to shared liberal purposes.

WHAT GOOD IS POLITICAL LIBERALISM?

That, as I understand it, is political liberalism and its distinctive and illuminating approach to the problem of diversity. In closing, I want to consider a powerful line of criticism, one that would concede political liberalism's coherence but deny its necessity or usefulness.[69]

People should not, according to these critics, be expected to put aside their religious and other comprehensive moral views, even when fashioning basic political principles. Joseph Raz argues that the "epistemic abstinence" on which political liberalism rests is impossible and, anyhow, unnecessary. It is impossible because Rawls must assume some truths, such as that peace and freedom are good. It is unnecessary because even if people participate in politics with all of their moral and religious values engaged and fully in play, worries about chaos and bloody conflict are unconvincing. The comprehensive conceptions widely held in our society prescribe persuasion rather than coercion as the proper approach to nonbelievers. Political stability, in any case, has more to do with affective ties than shared principles.[70]

Unrepentant comprehensive liberals reject the strategy of avoidance in favor of a strategy of engagement: they would invite our deepest disagreements onto the political stage to be grappled with directly. Allowing people to grapple openly with their deepest moral differences is more respectful (or at least respectful in a different way) than telling people they must put aside their deepest convictions when considering the most important political matters, especially since we know this will be much harder for some people than for others. The strategy of avoidance robs our politics of its most profound sources of vigor, excitement, and importance, and it promotes forms of personality unencumbered by deep commitments to communities and ideals and a politics of mere proceduralism. Our deepest disagreements should be dealt with at retail, not moved off the political agenda at wholesale. Dropping political liberalism's strategy of avoidance would, critics say, promote a wider and more profound diversity of political viewpoints, deeper forms of mutual respect, and a more robust political life.

Against these powerful criticisms it must be allowed that political liberalism may not be the best ideal along every conceivable dimension. There are bound to be tradeoffs among competing values, and we must be satisfied if political liberalism seems on balance best able to secure our most basic political aims. With this in mind, let me try to dispatch the critics.

Raz's charge that political liberalism rests on unacknowledged claims to truth appears itself to rest on a misunderstanding.[71] Political liberalism does not leave comprehensive questions altogether aside, but that is not the same as asserting a particular view of the whole truth. Any liberalism assumes a certain range of answers to many ultimate questions, and political liberals assert that the values supporting the liberal settlement override competing sets of values. Asserting the public unacceptability (or even falsehood) of religious imperatives requiring the persecution of heretics—or other illiberal measures—does not depend on a particular account of religious truth. Citizens may adjust their religious convictions to shared political principles in their own way, and in any number of ways.[72] While political liberalism cannot avoid ruling out some accounts of what has ultimate value, it does not rest on a particular comprehensive account of the truth or the good as a whole.

So claims about the truth and the human good as a whole can be largely excluded from the public justification of the constitutional essentials, but why should they be if the major comprehensive views in our society generate from within many of the same limitations on the use of political power as political liberalism? Of course, insofar as the major comprehensive views in a society do generate the same limits as political liberalism, it is hard to see what the disagreement is. Political liberalism is not essentially a claim about the inappropriateness of religious speech. The important thing for political liberalism is that we can share and publicly affirm the authority of public grounds that are adequate to justify the constitutional essentials. If religious people wish to bear witness to the justifiability of political liberalism from the point of view of their religious perspectives, this may be not only appropriate but also helpful on certain occasions. Pointing out that publicly shared grounds gain further support from our (extrapolitical) conceptions of the truth as a whole might, for example, assuage the doubts of those who question the sincerity of our allegiance to political liberalism.[73]

Of course, comprehensive moralities may not generate all of the same limits on the use of state power as does political liberalism. Political liberalism, as we have seen, provides reasons for pulling up short at the comprehensive educational agenda of Deweyite liberalism. Even if comprehensive liberalisms do generate limits on the political pursuit of perfectionism, political liberalism may have the advantage of barring coercive perfectionism in principle and at the very base, and this should help attract the trustful allegiance of people with opposing but still reasonable conceptions of the good.

Indeed, there are other ways that political liberalism seems better able than its competitors to promote trust. First, under political liberalism citizens share not only substantive principles but a public form of reasoning and a common rationale for the basis of their political order as

well. Leaving basic political arrangements dependent on radically different rationales invites division and distrust. Where a political community
shares not only substantive commitments but also publicly available
reasons and evidence, all of this becomes part of its political culture and
should have a broadly educative effect.

Second, political liberalism generates trust from its simplicity: it relies
only on forms of reasoning and evidence that are publicly accessible
and available to citizens generally. Comprehensive liberals, on the other
hand, are prepared to shape public power on the basis of principles subject to deep but reasonable disagreement, so it is hard to see why they
would follow political liberalism's exclusion of complex and subtle forms
of reasoning. Here again, comprehensive liberalisms appear to invite
greater conflict and distrust.[74]

Political liberalism may have one other important advantage: it may
be better able than comprehensive liberalisms to promote the transition
of a modus vivendi (from a condition of mere peace, i.e., backed not by
shared principles but only a balance of power) to a more principled public order. Suppose in a given society people's religious views are deeply
opposed and at odds with liberal principles. And yet, battle fatigue leads
them to establish peace and grudgingly to accept the need for political
cooperation. How might this society move toward a more principled
order?

Rawls suggests that political liberalism may be especially capable of
taking advantage of "a certain looseness" in the comprehensive views
of most people. Some people are bound to have religious or moral convictions that stand in some tension with liberal politics. They may not,
however, have worked out all the connections among their political
and extrapolitical convictions and values. Political liberalism may be
especially able to take advantage of this intellectual loose-jointedness:
"There is lots of slippage, so to speak, many ways for liberal principles of
justice to cohere loosely with those (partially) comprehensive views."[75]
The thought here seems to be that, by avoiding comprehensive claims
to truth, political liberalism does not provoke the kinds of comprehensive reflection about the coherence and compatibility of one's values
as a whole—one's religious and political values, for example—that
might make it harder for some people to live with the liberal political
order. So, "many if not most citizens come to affirm the principles of
justice . . . without seeing any particular connection, one way or the
other, between those principles and their other views."[76] While such
individuals may eventually reflect on the connections and possible

incompatibilities among their political and extrapolitical values, political liberalism's strategy of avoidance makes it more likely that this will occur only after they have lived under liberal arrangements for awhile. Then, when critical reflection does occur, Rawls suggests, prior experience of the great goods of the liberal order should help ensure that any incompatibilities are resolved by adjusting the comprehensive doctrines rather than rejecting political liberalism.[77]

Political liberalism seems capable, therefore, of easing the transition from a modus vivendi to a principled public order. Does political liberalism do this by exploiting a certain false consciousness, by accommodating, if not creating, a lack of broad and deep reflectiveness? A possible rejoinder to political liberalism might assert that if comprehensive liberalisms make transitions to a liberal order more difficult by provoking broader and deeper reflection on the connections among our political lives and other spheres of value, they also in this way help ensure that these transitions are more informed, reflective, and genuinely consensual. Political liberalism appears to exploit an implicit tradeoff between stable allegiances, on the one hand, and principled transparency and critical reflection, on the other. The more provocative comprehensive liberalisms, in contrast, might be viewed as more respectful of our capacity for critical reflectiveness.

Does political liberalism generate certain blessings on the basis of less than fully self-conscious transformations of belief? Does political liberalism depend on pulling the wool over people's eyes? Or, if that is too strong, does it prosper on the basis of not pulling the wool away from people's eyes?

None of these charges is sound. Every institution and practice is educative, after all, and no political order counts solely on self-conscious educative measures. Most important, political liberals are prepared fully and openly to justify the transformative institutions and practices they support, and that is sufficient. While political liberalism may seem to make philosophy take a back seat to the practical imperatives of politics, we must remember that political liberalism views deep but reasonable disagreement about the good life as a permanent consequence of freedom in modern conditions. Political liberalism provides, indeed, a philosophical account of why it is that political justification need not and should not depend on a particular account of the whole truth.

Some comprehensive liberals will continue to respond that all of this is unnecessary or worse: there is widespread agreement on many substantive political principles and procedures. We can afford to allow comprehensive moral and religious opinions to grapple in the political realm, in a way that Europeans of the sixteenth century could not and citizens of the former Yugoslavia or Lebanon cannot. We are amply ballasted by agreement; we may indeed be overly ballasted by commercialism and political life.

The question that these comprehensive liberals fail to address, however, is to what do we owe this political ballast, and what must we do to preserve it? If our political culture is dependent on our political institutions—including the work done by the political avoidance of religious controversy—then encouraging the politicization of the deepest and historically most destructive forms of disagreement could undermine the culture and jettison the ballast.

In any case, the critics of political liberalism seem consistently to miss the essential point: when determining the basic shape of the awful coercive powers of the modern state, should we not try and offer our fellow citizens reasons that they ought to be able to accept without making the absurdly unreasonable demand that they first accept our convictions about the ultimate ends of human life? Political liberalism holds out the hope of politics as a shared moral order without depending on unrealistic expectations of agreement on the most difficult questions of life.[78]

One final advantage of political liberalism can be noted in closing. The very fact that political liberalism lays claim to only a part of the moral realm should help foster political moderation. Even if political liberalism tends to transform extrapolitical commitments in its own image, it also provides real space for reasonably autonomous communities and institutions to develop. Political liberalism bars governments and political actors from making comprehensive claims to value and meaning; it leaves our allegiances divided. Political liberalism discourages total investments of moral capital in the political realm, and that is all to the good.

Diversity is often a great liberal resource, but not always. There are religious and other forms of diversity that we have no reason to embrace or even accommodate. Political liberalism allows us to regard declarations of holy war as premature, but equally important, it should furnish liberals with sufficient spine to stand up for their own core values. It softens but does not eliminate the tension between a this-worldly politics and many religions. That must be good enough. To true believers we pledge ourselves to public justifications and the avoidance of both religious and philosophical ideals of life. We will sometimes accommodate dissenting groups, but we must remind fundamentalists and others that they must pay a price for living in a free pluralistic society.

Chapter 5

Why Dialogue?

Bruce Ackerman

Begin by considering the role of dialogue in the life of a morally reflective person—a person, that is, who seriously asks himself how he should live and tries to live his life according to the answers he finds most plausible. How does talking enter into this exercise in self-definition?

Well, it all depends. Surely Socrates' response remains relevant: compared to the question of the good life, do not all others pale by comparison? And how better to discover the truth than to engage in discussion with anyone and everyone who professes an answer?

And yet I cannot allow Socrates to monopolize my moral vision. His fixation upon his single question threatens to distort the shape of human life—when will I get on with life itself if I am forever hung up on the question of how I ought to live? This is not to say that I should close myself off from moral questioning after adolescence; only that I must walk a tightrope, taking irreversible steps in the moral twilight while retaining the courage to stop and pause later on to peer among the shadows—at the risk of learning that my earlier decisions were worthless or worse.

This reflection leads to second thoughts about the happy image of Socrates roaming the forum in search of the next know-it-all who might be snared into serious conversation. If answering Socrates' question does not amount to the whole of my life, I shall have to be far more selective about my conversation partners. I shall have to listen hard when others tell me that one book is a waste of time, another worth reading; this person a fool, another worth talking to. The need for extreme selectivity engenders, in turn, doubts about the value of the dialogues I actually do conduct. Perhaps there is some Socrates out there who would, if I only spent more time searching for him, help me discover the absurdities in the plausible-sounding-stuff-I am-listening-to?

Such anxieties may lead to the exploration of two very different paths—both of which lead away from a dialogic view of ethics. One path leads to the question of faith: given the fragmentary character of the real-world dialogues I conduct, the real question is whom should I trust in helping me pick appropriate talking partners—which church or school or tradition?

But I need not ask myself this question. Instead of appealing to external authority, I may appeal to myself. "Bruce, don't be too impressed with what Kant said, or your Aunt Selma for that matter. You will have to think for yourself. Talking to others is no substitute. Admittedly, your own moral insight isn't much to write home about; but, in the end, it's all you've got."

For all its hubristic dangers, I subscribe to this individualistic view. For the present, though, I am not interested in defending individualism against the partisans of authority. Instead, I want to emphasize an aspect of moral phenomenology which both sides recognize. As a real-world matter, neither side supposes that talking to others is of supreme importance in moral self-definition. The key decisions are made in silence: Whom to trust? What do I really think? Although talking to others can be useful in thinking things through, a little talk may go a long way; a lot may lead nowhere. The moral value of my life does not merely depend on how I rationalize it in conversation, but upon the intrinsic value of my moral beliefs, and my success in living up to them. Thus, I do not really think less of somebody who refuses the offer of some would-be Socrates: "Stop bothering me, Socrates, I've better things to do with my time than blab with you." Such a response may well be a symptom of some deeper spiritual disease; but it may merely serve as a marker for the mature recognition that there is more to the moral life than mere talk.

All this gives me a real problem when I turn from personal morality to public life. Here I want to reverse field and proclaim dialogue as the first obligation of citizenship. Although a morally reflective person can permissibly cut herself off from real-world dialogue, a responsible citizen cannot with similar propriety cut herself off from political dialogue.

My task is not merely to suggest why this is so, but to confront the asymmetry problem: to explain why dialogue seems so much more fundamental in public than in personal life.

I

But perhaps I am making problems for myself? Perhaps there is no fundamental asymmetry between the status of dialogue in public and personal life?

One way to reestablish symmetry, of course, is to demote political dialogue and deny that it is any more exigent than talk in other domains. A second way is to reassert the ultimately dialogic character of all morality—personal as well as public. I shall start by considering this second, more positive, way of reestablishing symmetry: if, despite appearances, dialogue is more generally important to morality than I have supposed, then maybe I am wrong in thinking I must solve the asymmetry problem to redeem a dialogic view of political life?

To take this line, it is not necessary to ignore the moral phenomenology with which we began. One need only deprive it of foundational importance. Sure, each of us may appropriately shut himself off from moral dialogue on countless occasions in personal life. But real-world exigencies should not blind us to the regulatory role of an ideal speech situation in our search for moral enlightenment. Despite our excusable failure to live up to the discursive ideal, we nevertheless suppose that we *should* be prepared to justify our moral choices if we ever found ourselves in an ideal dialogue with Socrates, Freud, and whomever-else-might-be-around-at-the-time. Indeed, we implicitly claim as much whenever we try to justify our lives to ourselves (or others). To wax ontological: moral truth just is the name we give to those conclusions which would be reached in an ideal speech situation; nothing more and nothing less.[1]

This, transparently, is quite a mouthful; and I am skeptical about its ultimate validity. For the present, though, it is not necessary to explore these doubts with you. Even if we ultimately came to endorse the dialogic ideal of morality, I do not think we will do so in a way that reestablishes symmetry with the dialogic responsibilities of public life. To explain why,

I must emphasize that I am not interested in emphasizing the role of talk in some ideal world we shall never inhabit. I am talking about the very imperfect world in which we live. So long, then, as the partisan of the ideal speech situation excuses the real-world evasion of dialogue when people confront the moral dilemmas of personal life, he is still left with a troublesome asymmetry: Why does a dialogic ideal that allows such easy escape by real-world people in personal life *not* allow such an easy escape when these very same people confront the dilemmas of public life?

This is, I think, quite a hard question to answer—so long, at least, as we continue to look upon dialogue as a tool for the discovery of moral truth. For the world of practical politics does not seem at all close to anybody's idea of an ideal speech situation. Politicians do talk a lot, but it is not unduly cynical to suppose that they mean less of what they say than other folk. Thus, if I were trying to carve out a limited area of practical life where I had an especially strong obligation to participate in the dialogic search for moral truth, politics seems an unlikely place to start. However imperfect a philosophy classroom or church discussion group or psychoanalytic office may seem in comparison with the ideal speech situation, surely they are better bets than the public forum? If we do not think we are morally required to talk in one or another of these more private places, why should the search for moral truth require us to take talk seriously in politics?

The Athenians killed Socrates after all; and the modern state has hardly been more hospitable to the spirit of moral philosophy.

II

Such reflections naturally lead me to question the asymmetry thesis from the other side. If practical political life seems such an unlikely forum for the dialogic search for moral truth, why insist that dialogue is especially central to politics?

Because there are other important things to talk about than the moral truth: in particular, how people who disagree about the moral truth might nonetheless reasonably solve their ongoing problem of living together. This is, at any rate, how liberals characteristically formulate the problem of political order;[2] and it is from this vantage point that I wish to vindicate the asymmetry thesis. That is, I do not propose to base my case for public dialogue on some assertedly general feature of the moral life but upon the distinctive way liberals conceive of the problem of public order. This means, of course, that my argument will not convince people who reject the underlying liberal problematic. The most I can do here is to set up the problem in a way that makes rejection difficult.

Consider then a simple model of a liberal polity, consisting of N primary groups. Each primary group consists of one or more people who have combined faith and reason in an effort to search out the moral truth. Members of the same primary group have come up with the same answer to Socrates' question; members of different groups, different answers. Despite their ongoing disagreements, all groups find themselves on the same planet, in potential conflict over the planet's scarce resources. Hence the problem of liberal politics: how are the different groups to resolve their problem of mutual coexistence in a reasonable way?

Assume the position of P, a morally reflective member of one or another primary group, and you can begin to see why dialogue seems especially important for the successful solution of *this* problem. After all, if P could be confident that people outside her group, the not-Ps, had reached the same conclusions as she did in their search for moral truth, then talking to them about the problem of coexistence might not be so important. Instead, each individual group could unilaterally declare its moral truths "to be self-evident" and authorize governmental officials to resolve all conflicts by consulting these self-evident truths. Since, on this hypothesis, each group's truths are identical to the others, there would be no need for the groups to talk *to one another* in order to come to terms about the aims of legitimate government. It is, however, precisely because P has reason to know that the not-Ps have not reached the same moral conclusions that talk seems especially exigent. Whereas there may only be one moral truth, there are surely an infinite number of paths to moral error. Precisely because P believes that she has got closest to the truth, all she knows about the not-Ps is that each has taken one of an infinite number of wrong turns on the path to truth. But which wrong turn?

The answer will be critical in the solution of the liberal problem of coexistence. Perhaps the moral "errors" of the not-Ps will prove so serious to P that she will be unable to work out reasonable terms of coexistence with her fellow earthlings; but perhaps not. It all depends upon the particular moral mistakes made by the not-Ps and how these "errors" relate to the disputes that P and the not-Ps must resolve before they can live together on the same planet. There is, moreover, only one way for P to find out how matters stand. And that is to talk to the not-Ps about it.

In undertaking this exercise in liberal conversation, P is not to try to convince the not-Ps to change their minds and see, at long last, the compelling truth of P. Instead, the conversation has a more pragmatic intention. It recognizes that, for the moment at least, neither P nor not-P is going to win the moral argument to the other's satisfaction and proceeds to consider the way they might live together despite this ongoing disagreement. P's refusal to talk to the not-Ps about this pragmatic question simply disqualifies her from the liberal project. She cannot think of herself as a participant in a *liberal* state unless she is willing to participate (in one way or another) in this ongoing conversation with the not-Ps. In contrast, P can think of herself as a participant in the search for moral truth without ever talking about this subject to the not-Ps (or to her fellow Ps for that matter).

It is this simple difference which motivates the asymmetry thesis: the liberal citizen must recognize a dialogic obligation of a categorically different, and more imperative, kind than he does in his personal pursuit of the moral truth. To put my point paradoxically, it is precisely because the liberal state does *not* aim for moral truth that its citizens must recognize themselves under such peremptory dialogic obligations. Let us call this the *supreme pragmatic imperative*: if you and I disagree about the moral truth, the only way we stand half a chance of solving our problems in coexistence in a way both of us find reasonable is by talking to one another about them.

III

But is the pragmatic imperative really supreme? Granted, dialogue may be one way of reasonably solving the liberal's problem of coexistence, but is it the only way? If not, why should we prefer dialogue over its competitors?

These questions motivate the centuries-long liberal fascination with the marketplace as an alternative to more dialogic forms of dispute resolution. Here I am, needing some bricks to complete my cathedral; there you are, needing some beer to complete a wonderful Sunday afternoon at the football game. Do we really have to talk to one another to resolve our problem in mutual coexistence? Why do I not just trade some of my beer for some of your bricks at a mutually satisfactory rate of exchange? Why is trading not a perfectly reasonable way of sidestepping our moral disagreement over the relative merits of our Sunday activities? What does dialogue have to do with it?

My answer is that dialogue has a lot to do with it, and it is question-begging to pretend otherwise. The point is hardly novel but bears repeating, given the ease with which modern philosophical marketeers manage to evade it. It is the old question of *meum* and *tuum*. Of course, once I agree that those bricks over there are rightfully called "yours," and you agree that this beer over here is rightfully "mine," we may then sidestep our moral disagreements by trading away to our hearts' content.[3] But why does the marketeer suppose that both of us are so ready to indulge his complacent assumptions? After all, the question of distributive justice has not just arisen in the history of Western civilization.

Moreover, something special happens to the marketeer's pretensions to sweet reasonableness once I respond to his eager offer to sell me some bricks for my cathedral by denying that the bricks are rightfully his to sell in the first place. As I move toward the bricks with appropriative intent, our marketeer has but two choices. One is to use brute force to repel my assertion of superior right; the other is to engage me in a conversation that seeks to persuade me that, despite our disagreement over the ulti-mate value of cathedrals and football stadiums, it is reasonable for me to recognize the legitimacy of his superior claim to the bricks. In making this claim, the "brick owner" may try to link up his assertion of right to the liberal virtues of a market system. Moreover, depending on the exist-ing distribution of property rights, he might well convince me.

But this in no way defeats my point. We are not now trying to locate the place of the market within a discursive theory of political justifica-tion. We are considering whether market forms of coordination can plausibly allow liberals to deny dialogue the fundamental place accorded it by the supreme pragmatic imperative. The answer is "no" so long as the marketeer is prepared to concede that we may appropriately ques-tion each other's entitlements to the bargaining chips we bring to the bargaining table.

This seems worth emphasizing at a time when some of the best known free-market tracts ostentatiously fail to satisfy the pragmatic imperative's demand for dialogic legitimation. Robert Nozick, for example, does not deny that a satisfactory defense of market relations requires a theory of justice that defines the conditions under which one person might rightfully appropriate something his competitors also desire. Remark-ably enough, he does not even try to come up with such a theory in his well-known *Anarchy, State, and Utopia*,[4] charmingly suggesting that it would be a mistake to hold off publication until perfection were reached (xiii–xiv). Perhaps this was good enough for a young man writing in the early 1970s; fifteen years later, I begin to grow suspicious about his con-tinuing silence: Does Nozick simply suppose the question of distributive justice will go away because he refuses to answer it? Why should others take his defense of markets seriously when he does not even try to answer the most obvious question about them?[5]

IV

But how to discharge the dialogic burden of liberalism? How to talk to people who disagree with you about the moral truth? One thing is clear. Somehow or other, citizens of a liberal state must learn to talk to one another in a way that enables each of them to avoid condemning their own personal morality as evil or false. Otherwise, the conversation's pragmatic point becomes pointless.

This has hardly been lost upon the great spokesmen for the liberal tradition from Hobbes to the present. Indeed, the history of liberal thought can be read as a series of efforts to provide conversational models that would enable political participants to talk to one another in an appropriately neutral way. Rather than sustain self-confident liberal dialogue, however, these efforts have helped generate widespread skepticism about the conceptual possibility of neutrality. This skepticism poses an even greater threat to the pragmatic imperative than does a question-begging faith in the market. Whatever reasons Kant may have had for his great maxim, surely liberal pragmatists will not question the wisdom of "Ought implies can." If we cannot find a way to talk to one another neutrally, we do not seem to have much choice but to give up on the pragmatic imperative and return to the age-old effort to base political life on the truth, the whole truth, and nothing but the truth about the moral life.

To make matters grimmer, I can hardly deny that the history of liberal thought gives substance to this skeptical suggestion. Although many have sought to blaze a path to neutrality, the goal has proven disturbingly elusive. Given centuries of failure, perhaps I am naively optimistic to suppose that we should continue the quest. Naive or not, this is what I do suppose. Simple prudence, however, suggests the wisdom of studying the mistakes of the past before trying to formulate a more defensible conception of a worthwhile neutrality. Although I can hardly present a comprehensive catalog of liberal error, it will be useful to isolate three recurring false moves before trying to break out of the impasse.

The first false move tries to isolate a single value that all people consider most important despite their transparent disagreements over other values. By focusing upon the political implications of this supreme value, perhaps all of us may talk our way to a solution to our problems of coexistence in a way that we all find reasonable?

For this conversational maneuver to succeed, all groups must identify the same value as supreme. The most promising candidate, as Hobbes saw early on, is the fear of death. What is equally clear, to me at least, is that neither the fear of death nor anything else has the moral resolving power Hobbes hoped for it. As a sometime resident of New York City, I have cultivated a healthy appreciation of life's evanescent quality. Yet I am happy to report that I have not promoted self-preservation to the supreme place in my moral scheme. Indeed, I would despise a person who was not willing to sacrifice his life for more important things on suitable occasions. Thus, I would refuse to participate in a political conversation that began: "However much you and I disagree on other matters, we both accept the supreme importance of self-preservation." Rather than provide me with a neutral starting point, a Hobbesian political conversation would constantly oblige me to say things I found morally demeaning, despicable, false. If the point of liberal conversation is to enable me to talk to you without affirming moral propositions I think are false, the Hobbesian line goes nowhere.

So does a second well-worn path to neutrality. Here I am not called upon to affirm the existence of a single supreme value that trumps all our lesser moral disagreements. Instead, I am invited to translate my disagreements into a specially sanitized evaluative framework that promises to purge them of their nonneutral aspect. The classic example is Jeremy Bentham's felicific calculus, based on the neutral-seeming principle that "pushpin is as good as poetry." Once citizens of a Benthamite polity learn to translate their disputes into the common denominator of utility, they are promised a discourse that will enable them to discuss their conflicts in a technocratic way that requires none of them to say anything inconsistent with their primary moral beliefs.

The trouble comes, however, when we inquire about the manual that assesses the value of each human activity in terms of its "utility." My point is not the "standard" epistemological objection—whatever it may be—to interpersonal comparisons of utility. Of course, if it proves impossible to make interpersonal comparisons, the utilitarian can hardly make good on his promised translation manual, and we have reached a dead end very quickly. Since I believe that this objection is overblown,[6] I do not want to rest my case against the translation strategy on epistemological grounds.

Instead, I shall suppose that my utilitarian has emerged triumphant over his epistemological critics, producing a manual that plausibly compares the "utility" produced by pushpin, poetry, and much more besides.

It is at this stage that I want to enter my neutrality objection. However much one might admire the manual as a work in technocratic translation, it is quite another thing for the utilitarian to insist that his sanitized language must be used by the rest of us in talking about our political problems. Instead, his demand that all of us use his manual will provoke the very kind of unneutral dialogue that he wished to avoid in the first place: why does my desire for pushpin merit two utility points while your desire for poetry merits four? If *this* is what utility means, I refuse to speak a political language that obliges me to falsify my primary moral beliefs in such a systematic fashion!

So much, then, for two wrong turns down the path toward neutrality. Let us consolidate our ground by calling one the *trumping strategy*: here the liberal seeks to trump primary moral disagreement by positing a supreme moral value we all putatively share as the basis of neutral political dialogue. Call the second the *translation strategy*: here we are invited to translate our moral categories into some allegedly uncontroversial framework of political assessment. Since neither strategy looks at all promising, we can now give the skeptic's question about neutrality a sharper edge: is there a liberal way of responding to primary moral disagreement without trying to trump it or to translate it?

V

Well, I suppose we can try to transcend it. Thus Rawls, especially in his Kantian phase, seemed[7] to be inviting us to gain perspective on our primary moral disagreements by trying to strip away all the particular life experiences that make them seem so important to us. If we might only think our way to the astonishing ignorance of the inhabitants of the "Original Position," perhaps we could solve our problems in political coexistence by talking to one another in a neutral way?

Rawls' proposal is only the last in a long line of liberal exercises in transcendence. Many a utilitarian, for example, has urged us onward and upward to a perspective that, when compared to Rawls', seems downright attractive. At least we are not obliged to think of ourselves as ignorant ciphers whose principal slogan is "more-for-me"; we are instead to talk to one another as if we were knowledgeable and benevolent ideal observers[8] of the ongoing political struggle, concerned only to maximize the group's welfare. The formidable differences between ignorant contractor and benevolent observer should not, however, blind us to a basic flaw they have in common. Partisans of both modes of transcendence seek to charge us an admission ticket, as it were, before we may participate in political conversation. We can only join the dialogue if we can manage to speak in the accents of the approved transcendent being without falsifying our primary moral commitments. If this is the price of admission, it is perfectly reasonable to refuse to pay it: "You so-called liberals say you'll only allow me to participate in political dialogue if I address our mutual problems from the vantage point of your favorite transcendent being. But it is precisely this affirmation of your recipe for transcendence that I find morally objectionable."

Since Rawls' construction now dominates liberal thought, this complaint currently takes the form of eloquent attacks on the deracinating conception of the self presupposed by his thought experiment. A generation ago, when liberals took ideal observing more seriously, the complaint had to do with the extraordinary kind of self-immolation required in thinking myself into a position where the personal involvements of Bruce Ackerman counted no more (if no less) than those of Joe Shmoe.[9] Although I am sympathetic to these particular complaints, it is more important to generalize them. The root of the problem is the wrongfulness involved in requiring citizens to affirm the value of *any* particular exercise in transcendence as a necessary condition for discursive participation. Any such demand will predictably require some citizens to talk about themselves in morally demeaning and falsifying ways; and it is precisely this demand that makes the pragmatic imperative pointless. Trying to transcend our moral disagreements seems, in short, no more promising than translating or trumping them. Once again, we have reached an impasse: is there a way out?

VI

Yes, I think there is. It is the path of conversational restraint. The basic idea is very simple. When you and I learn that we disagree about one or another dimension of the moral truth, we should not search for some common value that will trump this disagreement; nor should we try to translate it into some putatively neutral framework; nor should we seek to transcend it by talking about how some unearthly creature might resolve it. We should simply say *nothing at all* about this disagreement and put the moral ideals that divide us off the conversational agenda of the liberal state. In restraining ourselves in this way, we need not lose the chance to talk to one another about our deepest moral disagreements in countless other, more private, contexts. We simply recognize that, while these ongoing debates continue, we will gain nothing of value by falsely asserting that the political community is of one mind on deeply contested matters. Doubtless the exercise of conversational restraint will prove extremely frustrating— for it will prevent each of us from justifying our political actions by appealing to many of the things we hold to be among the deepest and most revealing truths known to humanity. Nonetheless, our mutual act of conversational restraint allows all of us to win a priceless advantage: none of us will be obliged to say something in liberal conversation that seems *affirmatively false*. Having constrained the conversation in this way, we may instead use dialogue for pragmatically productive purposes: to identify normative premises all political participants find reasonable (or, at least, not unreasonable).

To refine this simple idea, begin by clarifying its intended domain of application. In calling for conversational constraint, I am not trying to stifle the voices of those who wish to challenge one or another aspect of their ongoing power relationship with others. To the contrary, a liberal polity must allow any person to raise any question she wants to if its dialogic project is to succeed: if the point of liberal politics is to come up with solutions that all participants find reasonable, how could this possibly be accomplished if citizens are not even allowed to place all their questions on the discursive agenda?

My principle of conversational restraint does not apply to the questions citizens may ask, but to the answers they may legitimately give to each other's questions:[10] whenever one citizen is confronted by another's question, he cannot suppress the questioner, nor can he respond by appealing to (his understanding of) the moral truth; he must instead be prepared, in principle,[11] to engage in a restrained dialogic effort to locate normative premises that both sides find reasonable.

The substantive outcome of this liberal dialogue will, of course, depend upon our primary moral commitments. Nonetheless, we can say something pretty general about the formal relationship between liberal political conversation and the talk going on in other places in liberal society. To make the formal points simple, suppose that there were only two primary groups in our liberal society and that their efforts at constrained conversation have succeeded in isolating some common evaluative ground. The overall shape of normative conversation, then, will look something like this:

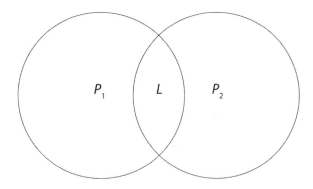

P_1 and P_2 represent the set of moral propositions each primary group affirms in conversations among members of the same group. In intergroup conversation, however, participants only make use of the L-propositions for purposes of conflict resolution. For it is only these propositions that will not be condemned as false by members of either group (though the reasons P_1 and P_2 will give to justify any particular L-proposition may, of course, be quite different).

While I hope you find this formalism clarifying, I should emphasize that it only describes the first, and more negative, stage of the liberal dialectic— the stage where liberal citizens, through the exercise of conversational restraint, identify L-propositions that might function as public value premises in a liberal political argument. Even if such a purging operation were completely carried out,[12] it remains for the liberal citizenry to fashion affirmative arguments out of the available public premises—arguments sufficiently incisive to resolve the citizenry's ongoing disputes. Obviously, this affirmative operation can be a creative business. Depending on the L-set, there may be a host of discursive possibilities available.

For present purposes, the important thing to notice is the distinctive character of these arguments. On the one hand, none of the participants condemn any of their normative premises as morally false; on the other hand, the argumentative aim is not to discover the ultimate moral truth. Instead, it is to provide citizens with something different—a way of reasonably responding to their continuing moral disagreement. As a consequence, the ongoing political dialogue looks very different from the kinds of conversation idealized by critical theorists like Jürgen Habermas. Most importantly, liberal citizens do not feel free to introduce any and all moral arguments into the conversational field. Instead of looking to ultimate conversational victory in some far-distant ideal speech situation, their energies are focused on the formidable task of governing *this* world through a political dialogue that does not require participants to renounce publicly their deepest moral beliefs. However humble the liberal's dialogic ambitions may seem from the unreachable heights of the ideal speech situation, my principal aim has been to convince you that even such a limited dialogic objective is not necessarily an impossible dream; that you and I may strive to govern this world through dialogue, albeit dialogue of a special kind.

VII

But, I hear you ask, is this fourth path toward neutrality really different from the first three? Does not it, too, demand something from people that they may not be morally prepared to give?

Yes, but the sacrifice is of a different kind. Rather than require people to say things they believe are false, I am asking them to make a special kind of emotional sacrifice. At least on those occasions when liberal citizens meet with one another to reason their way to legally authoritative resolutions of their disputes, each must try to repress his desire to say many things which he believes are true but which will divert the group's energy away from the elaboration of the pragmatic implications of the *L*-set.

This kind of selective repression is, I think, a familiar feature of social life. It is continually required by the ongoing exercise that sociologists call role-playing. Each social role can be understood as a set of conventional constraints upon acceptable symbolic behavior. When acting as a lawyer, I operate under constraints different from those delimiting my conduct as a teacher, which are different, in turn, from those involved in working on a construction project. Some role definitions allow for a broader range of symbolic behavior than others; but all roles are constraining, placing vast domains of conversation off the agenda so long as the participants are acting within a particular role framework.[13]

Truth is not necessarily a defense for stepping out of role. Thus, when I go into a class on political philosophy, I must restrain any impulse I might have to talk about the calculus of variations—even though my remarks on the calculus may be truer than anything I have to offer about politics. To be a competent social actor, I must constantly engage in a process of selective repression—restraining the impulse to speak the truth on a vast number of role-irrelevant matters so as to get on with the particular form of life in which I am presently engaged. Just as you and I try to stick to the point when we are building a car or worshipping God, so, too, liberal citizens must exercise a similar kind of self-control when engaging in liberal politics—joining together neither to build a better Buick nor to save men's souls, but to solve the conflicts of social life on terms that all participants may find reasonable. Thus, in calling upon people to exercise conversational self-restraint in public life, I am asking them to exercise a fundamental competence that all socialized human beings possess (to one or another degree).

But, of course, this is hardly enough to make my demand morally uncontroversial: the idea of conversational constraint is, at best, a part of a satisfactory political philosophy, not the whole of it. Most obviously, my proposal will be opposed by the partisans of an ethic of radical spontaneity, who look upon all roles as if they were merely fetters on the human spirit and call upon us to smash any role as soon as we begin to perform it competently.[14] On this level, the defense of the conversational restraints of liberal citizenship is simply a special case of a more general affirmation of the value of role-playing in social life. Such a defense need not deny the reality of spiritual constraint which the romantic critic finds so confining, nor the importance of working with others to create new role relations that better express the different aspects of our being. (Indeed, my proposal to develop more fully the role of liberal citizen falls precisely under this second heading.) Instead, a defender of liberal role-playing should argue that the romantic critic has chosen the wrong way to ease the sense of role constriction that threatens to strangle him. Rather than assault the very idea of role-playing, it seems wiser to seek relief in the marvelous human capacity to shift role engagements over time. I can be a lawyer, teacher, construction worker, father, baseball coach—as well as a liberal citizen. Although each of these roles imposes its own constraints, the value of my life is hardly exhausted by the way I confront the challenges of any particular one; it depends as well on how I shift from role to role over time and build up a meaningful whole out of these temporally limited parts. This seems a better response to the inadequacies of any individual role than a romantic effort to repudiate role-playing entirely.

Even if so much were conceded, the defense of liberal restraint must proceed to a second stage. After all, I am not arguing for any system of roles, but a system that gives the role of liberal citizenship a central place. What is so good about trying to solve disputes through a neutrally constrained dialogue?

VIII

There are many ways to answer this question. Some will seek to elaborate the intrinsic virtues of liberal citizenship—the distinctive value of the liberal's relentless effort to weave a web of intelligibility that can link parties together despite their many moral differences from one another, the moral value of allowing all of us to participate in politics without falsifying our deepest convictions. Others will pursue more consequentialist paths—emphasizing the value of the open society that it is the aim of liberal citizenship to produce.

My aim here, however, has not been to convince you of the ultimate value of liberal citizenship. It has been to suggest its distinctive character. I have tried to explain the liberal grounds for the dialogic imperative in politics and defend this pragmatic imperative against two relatively obvious objections—one raised by the free-marketeer, the other by the neutrality skeptic. Although the question-begging character of the free-marketeer's objection is pretty obvious,[15] I have only begun to take the skeptic seriously. At best, I have suggested why the admitted failures of the past need not discourage us from blazing a new trail toward the liberal state—one through which, by the resolute exercise of conversational restraint, you and I may talk to one another in ways that neither of us condemns as morally unreasonable.

I have not even tried to establish affirmatively that the path of conversational restraint will not finally lead liberals to a fourth dead end. As you and I discover that we disagree about more and more things, perhaps we will find that the exercise of conversational restraint leaves us nothing to say to one another about our basic problems of coexistence. In terms of our simple Venn diagram, perhaps the L-set will turn out to be empty. This seems especially likely since the typical Western society contains many primary groups, whereas our simple picture only schematizes the L-set of a two-group society. As we increase the number of circles in our diagram, the conversational space described by the intersecting L-set will get progressively smaller and smaller. Under modern conditions, does it shrink to zero?

This is the question I asked myself in *Social Justice in the Liberal State*.[16] Rather than rehearse my own answer, it has seemed more important to encourage you to think the question worth asking—by cautioning you against a superficial diagnosis of the liberal aspiration. Liberalism does not depend upon a question-begging faith in markets. Nor need it demand an alienating form of self-presentation that requires us to repudiate publicly our deepest moral convictions. Instead, it calls upon us to reflect upon the pragmatic imperative to talk to strangers as well as soul mates; and to consider whether, despite the strangers' strangeness, we might still have something reasonable to say to one another about our efforts to coexist on this puzzling planet.

Chapter 6

Religion as Conversation-Stopper

Richard Rorty

These days intellectuals divide up into those who think that something new and important called "the postmodern" is happening and those who, like Habermas, think we are (or should be) still plugging away at the familiar tasks set for us by the Enlightenment. The ones who, like me, agree with Habermas typically see the secularization of public life as the Enlightenment's central achievement and see our job as the same as our predecessors': getting our fellow citizens to rely less on tradition and to be more willing to experiment with new customs and institutions.

Our skepticism about the postmodern may incline us to be skeptical also about the modern and, more specifically, about Virginia Woolf's Foucault-like claim that human nature changed around 1910. But something crucially important to the progress of secularization did happen around then. To remind ourselves of what it was, it helps to reread [Tennyson's] *In Memoriam A. H. H.* One of the striking things about the poem is the poet's need, and ability, to believe in the immortality of the soul. One of the striking things about the biographies of Tennyson is the biographers' agreement that Tennyson and Hallam never went to bed together. Two young men who loved each other that much would, nowadays, be quite likely to do so. But the same religious beliefs that let Tennyson hope so fervently to see his friend in heaven also kept him out of Hallam's arms.

The big change in the outlook of the intellectuals—as opposed to a change in human nature—that happened around 1910 was that they began to be confident that human beings had only bodies, and no souls. The resulting this-worldliness made them receptive to the idea that one's sexual behavior did not have much to do with one's moral worth, an idea that the Enlightenment-minded author of "Locksley Hall" still found impossible to accept. It is hard to disentangle the idea that I have an immortal soul from the belief that this soul can be stained by the commission of certain sexual acts. For sex is the first thing that comes to mind when we think about the human body as something located down there, underneath the human soul. So when we started thinking that we might have only complicated, accomplished, vulnerable bodies, and no souls, the word *impurity* began to lose both sexual overtones and moral resonance.

For these reasons, the biggest gap between the typical intellectual and the typical nonintellectual is that the former does not use *impurity* as a moral term and does not find religion what James called a "live, forced and momentous option." She thinks of religion as, at its best, Whitehead's "what we do with our solitude," rather than something people do together in churches. Such an intellectual is bound to be puzzled or annoyed by Stephen L. Carter's *The Culture of Disbelief: How American Law and Politics Trivialize Religious Devotion* (New York: Basic Books, 1994). For Carter puts in question what, to atheists like me, seems the happy, Jeffersonian compromise that the Enlightenment reached with the religious. This compromise consists in privatizing religion, keeping it out of what Carter calls "the public square," making it seem bad taste to bring religion into discussions of public policy. Whereas many religiously inclined intellectuals stick to what he calls an "individual metaphysic," Carter, an Episcopalian, defines religion as "a tradition of group worship."

We atheists, doing our best to enforce Jefferson's compromise, think it bad enough that we cannot run for public office without being disingenuous about our disbelief in God; despite the compromise, no uncloseted atheist is likely to get elected anywhere in the country. We also resent the suggestion that you have to be religious to have a conscience—a suggestion implicit in the fact that only *religious* conscientious objectors to military service go unpunished. Such facts suggest to us that the claims of religion need, if anything, to be pushed back still further, and that religious believers have no business asking for more public respect than they now receive. Carter, however, thinks that privatizing religion trivializes it. He says that "the legal culture that guards the public square still seems most comfortable thinking of religion as a hobby, something done in privacy, something that mature, public-spirited adults do not use as the basis for politics."

Carter's inference from privatization to trivialization is invalid unless supplemented with the premise that the nonpolitical is always trivial. But this premise seems false. Our family or love lives are private, nonpolitical, and nontrivial. The poems we atheists write, like the prayers our religious friends raise, are private, nonpolitical, and nontrivial. Writing poems is, for many people, no mere hobby, even though they never show those poems to any save their intimates. The same goes for reading poems and for lots of other private pursuits that both give meaning to individual human lives and are such that mature, public-spirited adults are quite right in not attempting to use them as a basis for politics. The search for private perfection, pursued by theists and atheists alike, is neither trivial nor, in a pluralistic democracy, relevant to public policy.

Carter criticizes

> the effort by the contemporary liberal philosophers to create a conversational space in which individuals of very different viewpoints can join dialogic battle, in accord with a set of dialogic conventions that all can accept. The philosophical idea is that even though all of us have differing personal backgrounds and biases, we nevertheless share certain moral premises in common.*

Carter here gives a good description of both of the least common denominators of the positions of Rawls and Habermas, the two most prominent social thinkers of the present day, and of the central secularizing message of the Enlightenment. He is quite right to say that "all these efforts to limit the conversation to premises held in common would exclude religion from the mix."† But he thinks that such exclusion is unjust.

Such exclusion, however, is at the heart of the Jeffersonian compromise, and it is hard to see what more just arrangement Carter thinks might take the place of that compromise. Contemporary liberal philosophers think that

---

* Stephen Carter, *The Culture of Disbelief: How American Law and Politics Trivializes Religious Devotion* (New York: Doubleday, 1993), 55.—Ed.
    † Carter, *Culture of Disbelief,* 55.—Ed.

we shall not be able to keep a democratic political community going unless the religious believers remain willing to trade privatization for a guarantee of religious liberty, and Carter gives us no reason to think they are wrong.

The main reason religion needs to be privatized is that, in political discussion with those outside the relevant religious community, it is a conversation-stopper. Carter is right when he says:

> One good way to end a conversation—or to start an argument—is to tell a group of well-educated professionals that you hold a political position (preferably a controversial one, such as being against abortion or pornography) because it is required by your understanding of God's will.‡

Saying this is far more likely to end a conversation than to start an argument. The same goes for telling the group, "I would never have an abortion," or, "Reading pornography is about the only pleasure I get out of life these days." In these examples, as in Carter's, the ensuing silence masks the group's inclination to say, "So what? We weren't discussing your private life; we were discussing public policy. Don't bother us with matters that are not our concern."

This would be my own inclination in such a situation. Carter clearly thinks such a reaction inappropriate, but it is hard to figure out what he thinks would be an appropriate response by nonreligious interlocutors to the claim that abortion is required (or forbidden) by the will of God. He does not think it good enough to say: "OK, but since I don't think there is such a thing as the will of God, and since I doubt that we'll get anywhere arguing theism vs. atheism, let's see if we have some shared premises on the basis of which to continue our argument about abortion." He thinks such a reply would be condescending and trivializing. But are we atheist interlocutors supposed to try to keep the conversation going by saying, "Gee! I'm impressed. You must have a really deep, sincere faith"? Suppose we try that. What happens then? What can either party do for an encore?

Carter says that he wants "a public square that does not restrict its access to citizens willing to speak in a purely secular language, but instead is equally open to religious and nonreligious argument." This may mean simply that he wants us atheists to stop screaming "keep religion out of politics!" when the clergy say that abortion is against God's will while nodding approvingly when they say that gay bashing is [God's will]. If so, I entirely agree with him. The best parts of his very thoughtful, and often persuasive, book are those in which he points up the inconsistency of our behavior, and the hypocrisy

‡ Carter, *Culture of Disbelief*, 23.—Ed.

involved in saying that believers somehow have no right to base their political views on their religious faith, whereas we atheists have every right to base ours on Enlightenment philosophy. The claim that in doing so we are appealing to reason, whereas the religious are being irrational, is hokum. Carter is quite right to debunk it.

Carter is also right to say that liberal theory has not shown that "the will of any of the brilliant philosophers of the liberal tradition, or, for that matter, the will of the Supreme Court of the United States, is more relevant to moral decisions than the will of God." But he is wrong in suggesting that it has to show this. All liberal theory has to show is that moral decisions that are to be enforced by a pluralist and democratic state's monopoly of violence are best made by public discussion in which voices claiming to be God's, or reason's, or science's, are put on a par with everybody else's.

It is one thing to say that religious beliefs, or the lack of them, will influence political convictions. Of course they will. It is another thing to say, as Carter says, that the public square should be open to "religious argument," or that liberalism should "develop a politics that accepts whatever form of dialogue a member of the public offers." What is a specifically religious "form of dialogue" except perhaps a dialogue in which some members cite religious sources for their beliefs? What could a specifically religious argument be except an argument whose premises are accepted by some people because they believe that these premises express the will of God? I may accept those same premises for purely secular reasons—for example, reasons having to do with maximizing human happiness. Does that make my argument a nonreligious one? Even if it is exactly the argument made by my religious fellow citizen? Surely the fact that one of us gets his premises in church and the other in the library is, and should be, of no interest to our audience in the public square. The arguments that take place there, political arguments, are best thought of as neither religious nor nonreligious.

Carter frequently speaks of religion as a "source of moral knowledge" rather than as a "source of moral beliefs." Of course, if we knew that religion were a source of moral knowledge, we should be foolish to shove it to the outskirts of the square. But part of the moral of Rawls' and Habermas' work—and especially of Habermas' replacement of "subject-centered" with "communicative" reason—is that we should be suspicious of the very idea of a "source of moral knowledge." It is reasonable to call a physics textbook or teacher a source of knowledge. Knowledge is justified true belief. Since physics is a relatively noncontroversial area, what such teachers and textbooks say is usually both justified and (as far as anybody now knows) true. When it comes to morals rather than science, however, every textbook, Scripture, and teacher is offset by a competing textbook, Scripture, or teacher. That is why, in the public square of a pluralistic democracy, justification is always up for grabs, and why the term "source of moral knowledge" will always be out of place.

I take the point of Rawls and Habermas, as of Dewey and Peirce, to be that the epistemology suitable for such a democracy is one in which the only test of a political proposal is its ability to gain assent from people who retain radically diverse ideas about the point and meaning of human life, about the path to private perfection. The more such consensus becomes the test of a belief, the less important is the belief's source. So when Carter complains that religious citizens are forced "to restructure their arguments in purely secular terms before they can be presented," I should reply that "restructuring the arguments in purely secular terms" just means "dropping reference to the source of the premises of the arguments," and that this omission seems a reasonable price to pay for religious liberty.

Carter thinks that "contemporary liberal philosophers . . . make demands on [the religion's] moral conscience to reformulate that con-science—to destroy a vital aspect of the self—in order to gain the right to participate in the dialogue alongside other citizens." But this require-ment is no harsher, and no more a demand for self-destruction, than the requirement that we atheists, when we present our arguments, should claim no authority for our premises save the assent we hope they will gain from our audience. Carter seems to think that religious believers' moral convictions are somehow more deeply interwoven with their self-identity than those of atheists with theirs. He seems unwilling to admit that the role of Enlightenment ideology in giving meaning to the lives of atheists is just as great as Christianity's role in giving meaning to his own life. Occasionally he suggests that we contemporary liberal ideologues suffer from the same spiritual shallowness that American law attributes to the nonreligious pacifist. Even if this were the case, however, Carter would still need to tell us why a speaker's depth of spirituality is more relevant to her participation in public debate than her hobby or her hair color.

Part II

INTEGRATIONIST VIEWS

Chapter 7

The Role of Religion
in Decision and Discussion
of Political Issues

Nicholas Wolterstorff

THE ROLE OF CITIZEN AND ITS ETHIC

A most unusual form of state emerged in the early modern period in the West: liberal democracy. Nothing of the sort was known before. Though such states are now sufficiently common to be familiar to all who read these words, they are still far from universal.

Characteristic of liberal democracies, though not peculiar to them, is that they have *citizens*, not merely *subjects*. My principal topic in the following pages is the role of citizen in a liberal democracy: how that role should be performed. I will not by any means have the entirety of that role in mind, however. All my attention will be concentrated on one rather narrow, but important and intensely controversial, aspect of what goes into being a good citizen of a liberal democracy. It will be liberal democracy as we find it in the present-day United States that I will mainly have in view. Though some aspects of the role of citizen in a liberal democracy remain constant across all liberal democracies at all stages in their history, I wish to attend not only to such constants, but also to how the role is best performed here and now.

I assume that there is such a social role as that of citizen in a liberal democracy. Each of us is, as it were, a player in an evolving drama. In that drama, we each play many social roles, and many of us play the same role. Connected with each such role—so, too, then with the role of citizen—are rights and duties and mutual expectations. And beyond rights and duties, there are better and worse ways of playing the role—including, again, that of citizen. These roles are social artifacts; our knowing how to play them is the consequence of social learning. We are neither born with this knowledge, nor is it the automatic consequence of arriving at a certain level of biological maturity. In the course of our learning to play some such role, we learn the rights and duties pertaining thereto and some of the better and worse ways of playing the role—though we also learn, along the way, that at many points there is dispute rather than agreement as to what those duties are and the better and worse ways of carrying them out.

Though it is always possible to repudiate some social role, or deliberately to play it very badly, for many roles it is not a mere matter of choice whether one will or will not play them. It is expected that one will. Often it is not merely expected; it is regarded as obligatory that one do so. For example, if one becomes a father, then, other things being equal, it is not only expected that one will play the role of father; it is generally viewed as a matter of obligation that one do so. Naturally, one may choose to play the role of father in a new and different way, not as it has customarily been done, but that is a different matter. More radically, one may refuse to play the role of father not out of laxness but on the ground that somehow it would be wrong of one to do so, or, more moderately, on the ground that biological fatherhood carries with it no obligation to play the social role of father.

No doubt there are some people who, though citizens of liberal democracies, want as little as possible to do with playing the role of citizen. Usually indifference will be the cause. But it may well be that some people have moral scruples against playing the role any more than absolutely necessary. I will have relatively little to say about the extent to which citizens of liberal democracies are obligated to play the role of citizen; my attention will be focused almost entirely on that role itself. It is natural to wonder whether this sort of abstraction is possible—and if possible, desirable. I think it is both. It is quite possible to consider, say, the role of bishop in the Orthodox church of the thirteenth century without asking whether it was good that this or that person—or indeed, any person—played that role; for certain purposes it is not only possible but helpful to consider that role abstractly.

A common theme in the writings of those who have theorized about liberal democracy, going back into the late seventeenth century when liberal democracies were just beginning to emerge, is that a good citizen (and functionary) of a liberal democracy will impose certain *epistemological* restraints on the manner in which he decides and/or debates political issues; in his deciding and/or debating, he will refrain from letting reasons of a certain sort be determinative. Specifically, a common theme has been that a good citizen of a liberal democracy will refrain from allowing religious reasons to be determinative when deciding and/or debating political issues of certain sorts—or perhaps of any sort whatsoever, unless, perchance, those religious reasons are themselves held for reasons of the acceptable sort. Obviously, there will be other restraints as well on the decisions and discourse of the good citizen in a liberal democracy, restraints of content, for example. The good citizen of a liberal democracy (whose citizenry is religiously diverse) will refrain from advocating that only Presbyterians be permitted to hold office. My topic in the pages that follow is that proposed epistemological restraint. Is it indeed a requirement of being a good citizen in a liberal democracy that one's religion not be determinative of one's decisions on political issues, and/or that it not be determinative of the case one makes to others in favor of one's decision?

WHAT IS A LIBERAL DEMOCRACY?

I had better take a moment to explain what I mean by liberal democracy. Though it is entirely possible for liberal democracy to be the form of governance in a society all of whose members share the same religion, much—though by no means all—of the point of liberal democracy would be missing in such a situation. Liberal democracy is in good measure a mode of governance relevant to those societies in which different religions are represented—and not only different religions, but different comprehensive perspectives on reality, the good life, and human destiny. Indeed, liberal democracy originated as a solution to the religious conflicts ravaging English society in the seventeenth century.

Liberal democracy is that mode of governance that grants to all people within the territory of its governance equal protection under law, that grants to its citizens *equal freedom* in law to live out their lives as they see fit, and that requires of the state that it be neutral as among all the religions and comprehensive perspectives represented in society. *Equal protection* under law for all people, *equal freedom* in law for all citizens, and *neutrality* on the part of the state with respect to the diversity of religions and comprehensive perspectives—those are the core ideas. Along with them is one immensely important addition: the governance of society is ultimately vested in the normal law-abiding adult citizens of society, and at the point of ultimate vesting, each such citizen has equal voice. Normally this voice is exercised by voting for office bearers and for options in referenda.

Liberal democracy, so defined, is an ideal type. For one thing, exemplification of the type requires decisions at a multitude of different points, and often it is not clear exactly what the decisions ought to be concerning the arrangements and practices necessary for equal protection, equal freedom, equal voice, and state neutrality. Thus it is that even among those who embrace the type, there is a great deal of controversy. But second, it is also an ideal type because, even on matters where the implications are clear, nowhere is it fully exemplified; exemplification of the type in any particular society is never anything more than approximate. No society is anything more than *more or less* a liberal democracy.

This can be seen from two distinct angles. Full exemplification is at certain points regarded as undesirable, even among those who embrace the type. Suppose that all normal law-abiding adult citizens in the state of New York have equal voice in the selection of their U.S. senators, and that all such citizens in the state of Rhode Island likewise have equal voice in the selection of their U.S. senators. Nonetheless, the extreme disparity of population in these two states results in an obvious inequality of voice of a certain sort when the senators of these two states take their seats in Congress. The composers of the U.S. Constitution regarded such disparity of voice as desirable; probably most citizens of the United States continue to do so. Second, countries such as the United States have been on a historical trajectory toward exemplifying more and more fully the ideal of liberal democracy, without yet being anywhere near doing so fully. For a long time, only white adult males—initially, white male *landholders*—enjoyed equal protection, freedom, and voice. Next, it was white adult males and females, then adults generally. The point is that the liberal-democratic ideal has had to win its way slowly in societies that were already structured along other lines, and against countervailing ideals and convictions.

Someone might question whether the Idea of liberal democracy really has *functioned as an ideal*—as those last words of mine suggest. As to history, it might be said that nothing more has been at work than the struggle of various groups to achieve their interests. And as to argumentation, it might be said that the controversies that have characterized liberal democracies have not been controversies over how to embody in history those big ideas of equal protection, equal freedom, equal voice, and state neutrality, but detailed disputes over how to legislate and adjudicate in particular cases. The parties to such disputes may well have tossed in references to "big ideas" such as liberty and equality, but that was mere rhetoric, sincere or insincere as the case may be. What was actually involved was nothing else than the attempt to secure one's interests.

This objection is onto something; otherwise it would not have the plausibility that undoubtedly it does have. Nonetheless, I do not concede the main point. In my judgment, many of our controversies in the United States really have been controversies over the attempt to think through what would constitute equal protection, freedom, and voice in particular cases. And present in the mix of the many factors that motivate us, individually and collectively, has been the ideal of achieving a society of equal protection, freedom, and voice. That ideal has had to compete with other considerations; often it has lost, and often it continues to lose, the competition. But it is and has been a member of the competition, and sometimes it wins. Sometimes we have acted as we have so as to bring the ideal closer to earth.

It may help if we dwell for a moment on how remarkable this Idea of liberal democracy is and how even more remarkable it is that certain societies should come rather close to embodying the Idea. Nobody who is at all reflective believes that all religions and comprehensive perspectives in contemporary American society are equally correct and beneficial. How could they be, since on many points they flagrantly contradict each other? And should anyone say that correctness is not at issue when it comes to religions and comprehensive perspectives, that claim itself contradicts all those religions and perspectives that incorporate the conviction that correctness is at issue. But if we each believe that there are religions and perspectives present in society that are false and deleterious, it is remarkable that we should nonetheless advocate granting equal freedom to all, and remarkable likewise that we should insist that the state be neutral as among all these competing religions. Almost always in the past, societies have coped with religious diversity by granting hegemony to one among the many religions, confining members of the other religions to millets, ghettos, and so forth. It is also remarkable that we should consent to place ultimate political power in the hands of "the people," and that we should be willing to let "the people" exercise that power by granting to all normal adult law-abiding citizens equal voice within voting schemes judged more or less fair. Obviously, some people are much wiser on political matters than others; why give the foolish as much voice as the wise?

THE LIBERAL POSITION

A society in which all people are accorded equal protection under the law, in which all citizens are granted equal freedom in law to live their lives as they see fit, in which all normal adults are accorded equal voice within fair voting schemes, and in which the state is neutral as among the religions and comprehensive perspectives present in society—such a society needs a set of laws to govern the interactions among its members. Arriving at such laws will typically be a multistage process: citizens voting for legislators, citizens speaking out in public for and against proposed laws, legislators passing laws, judges applying laws, citizens voting on referenda, and so forth. At every stage, the question arises: on what basis are decisions to be made and debates to be conducted, whether by citizens or officials? What I shall call "the liberal position" is one among several competing answers to this question. I do, I readily admit, court confusion in speaking both about *liberal democratic society*, and about the *liberal position*. But the term *liberal* is so well established in both uses that innovation seems misguided.

One answer to our question—not the liberal position, let me say at once—is that the basis for all such decisions and debates on the part of citizens is simply perceived self-interest. Citizens make up their minds on the basis of perceived self-interest, they debate with their fellow citizens on that basis, and they act politically on that basis. They vote their perceived self-interest, and they do what they can—in conformity with the laws, of course—to get the legislators to vote their way. The legislators then settle on such trade-offs as they anticipate will win them election next time around. On this view, liberal politics is, through and through, competition among interests—a historically novel arrangement for satisfying the ever-shifting majority. On this view, the role of citizen in a liberal democracy really does not come to much with respect to the obligations attaching thereto.

That, as I say, is not the liberal position. The liberal position is that the proper goal of political action in a liberal democratic society, on the part of citizens and officials alike, is *justice*. The end at which the good citizen aims in her deliberations, decisions, actions, and debates on political issues is that the rules governing our social interaction secure justice.

And what is the appropriate source of the factual and moral convictions on the basis of which determinations of justice are to be made? That, for the person who embraces the liberal position, is the central question. Definitive of the position is a negation at this point: citizens (and officials) *are not* to base their decisions and/or debates concerning political issues on their religious convictions. When it comes to such activities, they are to allow their religious convictions to idle. They are to base their political decisions and their political debate in the public space on the principles yielded by some source *independent* of any and all of the religious perspectives to be found in society. To this, the liberal adds one important qualification and one important addendum. The qualification is this: should the independent source itself yield convictions that are appropriately classified as "religious," these may be used in decision and debate. The point is that no "positive" religion is to be used thus. The addendum is this: the source must be such that it is *fair* to insist that everybody base his or her political decisions, as well as public political debates, on the principles yielded by that source. This addendum eliminates what would otherwise be obvious candidates for the political basis. A good many of the nationalisms of the contemporary world are rich and thick enough to serve as the basis of the political decisions and debates of the members of society; in addition, they are often relatively independent of the religions to be found in the society. But rarely if ever will it be fair to insist that the life of the polity be based on some nationalism, because it is no longer ever true that all the citizens of a single polity belong to the same nation, the same "people."

Given this understanding of what I have called "the liberal position," it turns out that what is in view here is not one position, but a *family* of positions, with the members of the family differing along a number of distinct strands of similarity and difference. This must be kept in mind in all that follows; my phrase "the liberal position" is only a convenient name for the *family* of liberal positions.

What leaps to mind at once is that, since the family is picked out with a negation, it is possible for different members of the family to go beyond the shared negation with different positive suggestions as to the nature of the independent source. This possibility has in fact been actualized. Some have argued that the basis should be "publicly accessible reasons"; others have argued that it should be "secular reasons"; yet others have argued that it should be reasons derived from the shared political culture of one's liberal democracy. Furthermore, it is possible to expand or contract the negation itself, thereby gaining yet additional members of the family. As to expansion: one might hold that it is not only out of order to base one's political decisions and debates on one's *religion*; it is equally out of order, for those who are not religious, to base their decisions and debates on their nonreligious comprehensive perspectives. And as to contraction: one might hold that it is acceptable to base one's political decisions and debates on religious reasons if those reasons satisfy some qualification in addition to the one already mentioned—if, for example, those religious reasons are nonsectarian.

It will prove important to have in view some of the other axes along which members of that family which constitutes the liberal position resemble and differ from each other. Whereas some members of the family impose the same restraint on personal decision and public debate alike, others allow a person to decide issues for himself as he wishes and impose the restraint only on the reasons one offers in public debate. Again, the restraints that some propose are meant for all political issues, whereas others, such as Rawls, intend their restraints only for "constitutional issues" and "matters of basic justice." And yet again, the proposals differ with respect to how one's nonreligious reasons for or against some political position are to be related to one's religious reasons, should one have religious reasons. Some say that it is acceptable for one's religious reasons to motivate one's decision or action, provided that one also has a nonreligious reason that would be sufficient, by itself, as motive; others insist that whatever religious reasons one may have ought not to play any motivating role at all. Some insist that one should never use religious reasons in public debate; others hold that it is acceptable to do so, provided one is both able and ready to offer nonreligious reasons. Lastly, there is, as one would expect, considerable divergence among the members of the family as to how religious reasons are to be identified, with the consequence that a reason that is disallowed as religious on one proposal is permitted as nonreligious on another.

What unites this buzzing variety of positions into one family of liberal positions is that they all propose a restraint on the use of religious reasons in deciding and/or debating political issues. That is the heart of the matter. The positions of interest to us here are those that propose a *significant* restraint. In principle, a proposed restraint on religious reasons might be so narrow in its application that it almost never applies to anybody. Such a position would be of no interest to us here—given the presence of so many big fish in the pond. In a specific practical situation, it might be not only interesting but desperately important.

Though I am taking the *religious-reason restraint* to be, by itself, definitive of what I mean by "the liberal position," it should be noted that it is typical of those who propose significant versions of this restraint also to embrace a certain understanding of the neutrality that the state in a liberal democracy is supposed to exercise with respect to the religions present in that society. We may call it the *separation* interpretation. It is possible to interpret the neutrality proviso as requiring that government and its agents treat all religions *impartially*. That is not the interpretation that those who hold a significant version of the liberal position typically adopt. The position that the liberal typically adopts is rather that government is to do nothing to advance or hinder any religion. The difference between these two interpretations, the *impartiality* interpretation and the *separation* interpretation, can most easily be seen by taking note of the difference in result on the issue of state aid to schools with a religious orientation. The impartiality position says that if the state aids any school, it must aid all schools, and aid them all equitably—no matter what their religious orientation, if any. The separation position says that the state is to aid no school whose orientation is religious. The First Amendment in the United States Bill of Rights specifies that the government shall neither establish any religion, nor infringe on the free exercise of any. That formulation is ambiguous as between the impartiality and the separation positions. The U.S. Supreme Court, in its decisions over the past fifty years, has nonetheless consistently interpreted the amendment as an affirmation of the separation position. It has ruled as if Jefferson's *wall of separation* metaphor had been incorporated into the Constitution. Possibly the recent *Virginia v. Rosenberger* decision indicates a change in direction.

THE ETHIC OF THE CITIZEN AND RESTRAINTS ON REASONS

It is easy to see why and how the role of citizen in a liberal democracy imposes restraints on the legislation that one advocates. There are probably some evangelical Christians who believe that American society would be better off if only evangelical Christians were allowed to vote and hold office. But such an arrangement would be flamboyantly out of accord with the Idea of liberal democracy. Of course, such a person might also be of the view that liberal democracy should be abolished. But our topic, let us be reminded, is not whether American society, or any other, should be liberal democratic in form, nor whether it is a good thing that citizens of this or any other liberal democracy play the role of citizen. Our topic is instead the contours of that role of citizen.

Once again, then, it is obvious that the role of citizen involves restraints on the legislation advocated. But what is the rationale for *epistemological* restraints on the decisions and debates of citizens? That is, why should epistemological restraints be laid on a person *when the legislation advocated by that person does not violate the restraints on content*? What difference does it make what reasons citizens use in making their decisions and conducting their debates, if the positions they advocate do not violate the Idea of liberal democracy? And in particular, why should *religious* reasons (which are not derived from the independent source) be singled out for exclusion?

Not only is it not at once evident what rationale there might be for proposing such a restraint, but on the face of it, there is something pro-foundly paradoxical about the suggestion that the role of citizen in a liberal democracy includes this restraint. The restraint appears, on the face of it, to violate the equal freedom component within the Idea of liberal democracy. On the face of it, the Idea of liberal democracy implies the *absence* of any such restraint. A significant part of how some citizens exercise their religion is that their decisions and debates on political issues are in good measure based on their religious convictions. Using their religious convictions in making their decisions and conducting their debates on political issues is part of what constitutes conducting their lives as they see fit. What is going on here? The liberal position—restraint on religious reasons—appears to be in flagrant conflict with the Idea of liberal democracy.

Is it perhaps the liberal position that at this point it is best not to exemplify the Idea of liberal democracy? If so, then, speaking strictly, the liberal position is not that this epistemological restraint belongs to the role of citizen in a liberal democracy, but that at this point the subjects of the state should not play that role. At this point, it is best that the society not exemplify the Idea of liberal democracy. Or is the clue, perhaps, to be found in the "equal" of the phrase, "equal freedom to live one's life as one sees fit"? Though the restraint appears to be imposed nonequitably, singling out, as it does, *religious* reasons, when only some citizens would ever use such reasons, does it prove, on scru-tiny, to preserve equality of freedom?

ARE RELIGIOUS REASONS TOO DANGEROUS TO PERMIT?

One reason regularly cited, more in the past than now, for insisting that citizens not use religious reasons for their decisions and/or debates on political issues (and for adopting the separation rather than the impartiality interpretation of state neutrality) is that it is simply too dangerous, in a situation of religious pluralism, to allow religion to intrude into politics in this way. Religion stirs up too many passions. The amity of society will be endangered and, thereby, the stability and endurance of the state. By analogy: many of us have found ourselves in family situations where the only way to preserve peace in the family was for everyone to agree not to bring up certain religious issues—or certain political issues! So too: best that all citizens refrain from citing religious reasons in public debate on political issues—that instead they make use exclusively of reasons derived from some equitable independent source.

And what about using religious reasons to make up one's own mind on political issues? Picture the situation if that is permitted and practiced, while the use of religious reasons in public discussion is prohibited. Many citizens would arrive at their views on political issues by reasoning from their religious convictions. Then, however, when they get together in discussion and debate, they conceal that these are their reasons; instead they offer reasons derived from the independent source.

Social peace would admittedly not be endangered by this sort of practice. But for one thing, it is patently unrealistic as a proposal. Most people who reasoned from their religion in making up their minds on political issues would lack the intellectual imagination required for reasoning to the same position from premises derived from the independent source. Probably in many cases it just could not be done: in the absence of detailed information about the religion, on the one hand, and about the independent source, on the other, we do not actually know. But even if it could be done, it is appropriate to hesitate over the massive dissembling that would take place. Many members of society would hold their political views for religious reasons; then, in public, they would conceal this fact about themselves and offer quite distinct reasons.

In short, the most reasonable position in the region would seem to be that citizens should hold their political views for reasons derived from the independent source. Should some of the views thus held also be held for religious reasons, that would be acceptable; it would be a case of harmless overdetermination.

Let us be clear on the relation of this particular version of the liberal position to the Idea of liberal democracy. No attempt is made to *derive* this version of the position from the Idea; indeed, none is even made to show that the version is *compatible* with the Idea. Whether or not it is compatible, the argument is that citizens ought not to hold their views and conduct their debates concerning political issues on the basis of religious reasons. Should some citizen think otherwise, then, in this regard, he ought not to live out his life as he sees fit. Nobody has ever proposed enforcing this obligation by criminalizing such behavior; it would be enforced by social disapproval. And should it be the case that the restraint in question is imposed unequally, then this clear-and-present-danger argument proves in fact to be an argument for not exemplifying the Idea of liberal democracy at this point.

What about the argument itself: is it cogent? Of course, without a suggestion as to what the independent source is to be, we do not yet have a definite version of the liberal position. But let us consider all by itself this particular argument against the use of religious reasons in decisions and discussions on political issues.

Whether the argument is or is not cogent all depends, it seems to me, on the particular society one has in mind and the particular stage in the history of that society. For seventeenth-century England, it quite clearly was cogent: social peace did depend on getting citizens to stop invoking God, canonical Scriptures, and religious authorities when discussing politics in public—to confine such invocations to discussions within their own confessional circles.

American society at the end of the twentieth century is a different matter. We now have behind us a long history of religious tolerance. There is plenty of passion in the politics of the present-day United States, but those passions are, for the most part, not attached to such religious reasons as people might have for their political positions, but to those political positions themselves: passionate feelings pro and con the so-called welfare state, for example. More generally: the slaughter, torture, and generalized brutality of [the twentieth] century has mainly been conducted in the name of one or another secular cause—nationalisms of many sorts, communism, fascism, patriotisms of various kinds, economic hegemony. In seventeenth-century Europe, human beings cared deeply about religion. In [the twentieth] century, most have cared more deeply about various secular causes. It would be dangerously myopic to focus one's attention on the danger that religion poses to the polity while ignoring the equal or greater danger posed by secular causes.

The other side of the matter is also worth mentioning. Many of the social movements in the modern world that have moved societies in the direction of liberal democracy have been deeply and explicitly religious in their orientation: the abolitionist movement in nineteenth-century America, the civil rights movement in twentieth-century America, the resistance movements in fascist Germany, in communist Eastern Europe, in apartheid South Africa. These movements are often analyzed by Western academics and intellectuals as if religion were nowhere in the picture. The assumption, presumably, is that religion plays no explanatory role in human affairs and thus does not require mentioning. It is only an epiphenomenon. The people in Leipzig assembled in a meeting space that just happened to be a church to listen to inspiring speeches that just happened to resemble sermons; they were led out into the streets in protest marches by leaders who just happened to be pastors.[1] Black people in Cape Town were led on protest marches from the black shantytowns into the center of the city by men named Tutu and Boesak—who just happened to be bishop and pastor, respectively, and who just happened to use religious talk in their fiery speeches. Thus does ideology conceal reality and distort scholarship! Even the free-and-equal doctrine, which lies at the very heart of liberal democracy, had religious roots—in Protestant dissent of the seventeenth century.

LOCKE'S VERSION OF THE LIBERAL POSITION

When we now move on to consider other arguments that have been offered for the view that the role of citizen in a liberal democracy includes a restraint on the use of religious reasons, we shall want at the same time to consider what is being proposed as the independent source of principles to serve as basis for decisions and discussions on political issues. Should that independent source be inadequately identified, prove incapable of doing the work asked of it, or be of such a nature that it would be unfair to ask of all citizens that they use it in their decisions and discussions on political issues, then the version as a whole will be unacceptable, no matter how cogent the argument against the use of religious reasons might be, considered alone. Of course, a version might also founder on one and another detail; for example, it might refuse to allow the use of religious reasons in making decisions even when they do nothing more than overdetermine the decision, whereas, given the fundamental rationale of the version, such use of religious reasons ought to be allowed. On this occasion I will skip lightly over such details, focusing on the rationale offered for the restraint on religious reasons, and on the independent basis proposed as replacement.

Let me now be explicit—the view that I will be defending is that the liberal position is unacceptable in all its versions. It is unacceptable not because none of the extant versions happens to get all the details right, but unacceptable because no rationale offered for the restraint is cogent, and no independent source meets the demands.

Let me make clear that it is not the Idea of liberal democracy that I oppose; to the contrary, I firmly embrace it. What I oppose is *the liberal position*: the thesis that the role of citizen in a liberal democracy includes a restraint on the use of reasons, derived from one's religion, for one's decisions and discussions on political issues, and a requirement that citizens instead use an independent source. In due course I will explain and defend my alternative to the liberal position, which I will be calling the *consocial* position. I contend that the consocial position is fully harmonious with the Idea of liberal democracy.

We have no option but to make a choice from among the multiplicity of different versions of the liberal position. I propose confining myself to the most influential of the traditional versions, that of John Locke, and to the most influential of the contemporary versions, that of John Rawls. All the important options and issues concerning rationale and independent sources will come up.[2]

John Locke was one of the first, and remains one of the greatest, theorists of liberal democracy. Locke did not explicitly distinguish between the use of religious reasons in deciding political issues for oneself and the use of such reasons in discussing political issues in public. His attention was focused entirely on the proper basis for the formation of political convictions; it never occurred to him that anything different, or even additional, had to be said about reasons that one offers in the public space. Even the distinction between public and private, which for a long time now has played a fundamental role in almost all versions of the liberal position, plays no role whatsoever in Locke's discussion. What Locke had to say about the proper source of principles to serve as a basis for political opinions was pretty much a straightforward implication of his general epistemology; it is that epistemology, then, that we must spend most of our time trying to get in hand.[3]

Though Locke had a good deal to say about knowledge, the focus of his attention was not on that but on *belief*. This contrast—*not knowledge, but belief*—will be puzzling to students of contemporary epistemology in the analytic tradition, since knowledge is standardly treated there not as something *other* than belief but as a species of belief: knowledge is that species of belief whose propositional content is true, whose status is justification (or warrant), and so forth. But that is not how Locke was thinking of knowledge—nor indeed how most of the tradition before him thought of knowledge. Whereas Locke described belief as *taking some proposition to be true*, he understood knowledge as consisting in *awareness* of some entity or fact—"perception," as he regularly called it. He acknowledged that awareness of some fact regularly evokes belief of the corresponding proposition, but it was the former, not the latter, that he identified as knowledge.

What mainly drew Locke's attention, when reflecting on belief, was that our beliefs are often false; from there he moved on, with never a hesitation in his skip, to affirm that we are all under obligation to govern and regulate our belief-forming faculties with the aim of improving the proportion of truth to falsehood in their output.

It will be worth taking a moment to set Locke's thought here within a somewhat broader context. In everyday life we all take for granted that beliefs have merits and defects, and that these merits and defects are of various sorts. One of the most important distinctions is between those merits and defects that have nothing to do with truth, and those that are what one might call "truth-relevant." The merit of *making one feel happy* is an example of the former. Perhaps the belief that you passed the exam is what has put you in a happy mood; its doing so had nothing at all to do with its truth. As to truth-relevant merits: the most obvious example—all too obvious—is truth itself. What is especially important to notice, however, is the multiplicity and diversity of truth-relevant merits and defects. In addition to "truth," writers on these matters have used the following adjectives, assuming that they were thereby picking out truth-relevant merits in beliefs: "justified," "warranted," "rational," "reliably formed," "scientific," "self-evident," and—to cut the list short—"certain." I said that writers on these matters have used these adjectives *assuming* that they were picking out truth-relevant merits; I did not say that they were in fact picking out such merits. My reason for caution is my conviction that some adjectives on the list—"justified" and "rational" in particular—are incurably vague, and that all too often it is impossible to know what merit the writer was picking out with the adjective because there really was not any one that he was picking out. Debates about *the nature of justification* and *the nature of rationality* have usually, for that reason, been utterly futile. But that beliefs do come with a variety of truth-relevant merits, and that often we do pick out one or another of them—of this there can be no doubt.

Among such merits is what I shall call *entitlement*. Entitled beliefs are permitted beliefs. "You should have known better than to assume that half an hour was enough to allow for changing planes in O'Hare." "You should never have believed what he told you without also checking it out with his wife." We use such sentences to charge each other with holding beliefs that we are not entitled to hold, not permitted. Rather often, in recent academic writing on these matters the adjective "rational" is used as a synonym for "entitled": a belief that one is entitled to hold is said to be a belief that it is rational for one to hold. For the reason indicated above, however, when speaking in my own voice, I shall almost always abjure the use of the word *rational*.

Locke, as I mentioned, was more interested in belief than in knowledge. Since knowledge, in his words, is "short and scanty," and would never be anything but that, mainly it fell on us human beings to regulate our belief-forming faculties, and to regulate them with the aim of believing what is true and of not believing what is false. Not only is it desirable that we do so; we have obligations to do so. It is on account of such obligations that the merit of entitlement enters the picture, and the demerit of nonentitlement. Not being entitled to some belief is grounded in the fact that one has failed at some point to fulfill one's obligations concerning the regulation of one's belief-forming faculties.

Locke set out then to formulate a criterion for entitlement in beliefs— or what in essentials comes to the same thing: he set out to formulate the deontological rules that hold for the governance of our belief-forming faculties. Not a *general* criterion for entitlement, however. Though much of Locke's rhetoric is universalistic, a number of passages, both in the *Essay Concerning Human Understanding* and in the *Conduct of the Understanding*, make clear that he had no interest whatsoever in offering a criterion of entitlement applicable to all beliefs. He was concerned exclusively with situations of maximal concernment—"concernment" being his word. That is, he was concerned exclusively with situations in which one is obligated to do the best to find out the truth of the matter, and to believe in accord with the results of one's endeavor. His strategy was to articulate a practice of inquiry whose competent employment constitutes, in his judgment, doing the best: the *optimal* practice of inquiry. It follows that, on matters of maximal concernment, one is entitled to one's belief (or nonbelief) if and only if one has competently employed the optimal practice and believes or refrains from believing in a manner appropriate to the results of the employment.

Locke sometimes describes this (supposedly) optimal practice as "listening to the voice of Reason." At other times he describes it as "getting to the things themselves." The point of the latter formulation is that, by employing the practice, one gets to the things themselves *instead of resting content with what people tell one about the things*. One circumvents tradition.

The essential elements of the practice are easily described. We can think of it as having three stages. With some proposition in mind concerning the matter in question, one first collects evidence concerning the truth or falsehood of the proposition, this evidence to consist of a nonskewed and sufficiently ample set of beliefs that are certain for one because their propositional content corresponds directly to facts of which one is (or remembers having been) aware. Second, by the exercise of one's reason, one determines the probability of the proposition on that evidence. And last, one adopts a level of confidence in the proposition corresponding to its probability on that evidence. To competently employ this practice, says Locke, is to do the human best.

Whether or not a matter is of maximal concernment to a person is a function of the whole contour of that person's obligations—the consequence of which is that what matters are of maximal concernment varies from person to person. Locke insisted on an extremely important limitation on this principle of variation, however. Matters of religion and morality are of maximal concernment to everybody. Nobody is entitled to hold his religious or moral convictions on the unverified say-so of someone else. Accordingly, everybody is obligated to employ the optimal practice on such matters.

Locke believed that by employing the practice, we could arrive at a very substantial body of moral truths. This is the *natural law*, which functions so pivotally in his *Second Treatise of Government*. Natural law, for Locke, simply is those moral truths that are accessible to human reason, unaided by divine revelation. And what he means by "human reason," in this context, is that optimal practice of inquiry, described above. Locke also believed that by employing the optimal practice, we could arrive at a substantial set of beliefs about God and could establish the reliability of the New Testament. Thereby we would gain a second mode of access to moral truth, because the teachings of Jesus include the fundamental tenets of natural law—and much more besides.

Locke was thus most definitely not a proponent of secularism. His thought was rather that when it comes to matters of morality and religion, it is the obligation of all of us to employ the optimal practice, thus to arrive at a "rational" morality and a "rational" religion. Rather than appealing to the moral and religious traditions into which we have been inducted, it is our obligation, by employing the optimal practice, to appeal solely to the deliverances of our generic human nature applied directly to the things themselves.

It follows that, when deciding and discussing political matters, we are not entitled to appeal to our own particular religious tradition. It would be wrong to do so. It would be wrong to appeal to one's own religious tradition whether or not the matter under consideration was political. That is not to say that everything we have come to believe, by virtue of being inducted into some religious and moral tradition, is off-limits in political debate. If, by employing that optimal practice, in which one supposedly makes use only of one's generically human capacities applied directly to the things themselves, one succeeds in arriving at some of the content of one's tradition, then one is entitled to appeal to that content in one's political decisions and discussions. But one is entitled to do so *only because* those religious and moral propositions are part of the yield of that optimal practice. Religious reasons *as such* are not excluded from decision and discussion, only those that are what I shall call "uncertified."

Locke's rationale for the restraint he proposes on the use of uncertified religious beliefs as reasons in decision and discussion on political issues is now eminently clear: we should not use uncertified religious beliefs in that manner because we should not even have such beliefs. We are not entitled to them. And if we should not even *have* them, then we should certainly not *use* them as reasons. Only beliefs that one is permitted to have are beliefs that one is permitted to use as reasons. Furthermore, the restraint is indubitably equitable; religion is not being subjected to an invidious classification. Though Locke certainly had his eye on the destructive consequences of using religion to argue about politics in the public square, the classification that is actually operative in the restraint he proposes is not that of religious versus nonreligious beliefs, but that of entitled versus nonentitled beliefs. As it turns out, most of the religious beliefs that people actually hold are not entitled. But the same is true for most of the moral beliefs that people hold—whether or not those moral beliefs are intertwined with religion. Locke's fundamental thought is that the role of citizen in a liberal democracy incorporates the requirement that the beliefs one uses as reasons, in deciding and discussing political issues, be beliefs to which one is entitled. To this he adds a thesis about entitlement: one is only entitled to those moral and religious beliefs that are the output of one's adequate employment of the (supposedly) optimal practice.

The elegance of Locke's version of the liberal position is undeniable, and the explicitness of the underlying epistemology, admirable. All versions of the liberal position, with the exception of the clear-and-present-danger version, make crucial use of epistemological assumptions in what they say about acceptable versus nonacceptable reasons. Yet seldom is the epistemology brought up front and developed articulately. John Locke is one of the great and noble exceptions to this generalization.

But elegant and admirable though it be, Locke's version of the liberal position will not do—fundamentally because its underlying epistemology, though admirably articulated, is nonetheless untenable. Since almost no one today would contest that claim, my critique will be brief.[4]

In the first place, the rationale Locke offers for restraint on the use of religious reasons is defective. Locke holds that only if one holds one's religious beliefs for reasons of that highly specific sort that he specifies is one entitled to those beliefs. The development in recent years, at the intersection of philosophy of religion and epistemology, of what has come to be known as "Reformed epistemology," is a powerful attack on that claim.[5] *Decisive*, even—though I say this as one who has participated in the development. Not only is it not the case that one must hold one's religious beliefs for reasons of the Lockean sort to be entitled to them; it is not, in general, necessary that one hold them for any reasons at all. Something about the belief, the person, and the situation brings it about that the person is entitled to the belief. But that need not be another belief whose propositional content functions as reason for the religious belief. Entitlement simply does not effect the winnowing that Locke thought it would.

Second, the independent source that Locke proposed comes nowhere near yielding the beliefs necessary for making our political decisions and conducting our political discussions. That source, remember, was the practice that Locke thought to be optimal. Not only did Locke hold that moral truths, sufficient for our personal and communal lives, would be yielded by the recommended practice. He held that a *scientia* of morality was possible, comparable, so he held, to the already-extant *scientia* of mathematics. That is to say: he thought that it was possible, beginning with certitudes, to construct a deductive system of moral truths. Probability calculations need not enter the picture. And in Locke's system, let us recall, one is certain of a proposition on account of being aware of (or remembering having been aware of) the corresponding fact. Locke was heavily pressed, in his own day, to validate his bold claim by actually developing a science of morality. He conceded that he was incapable of doing so—though there is no evidence, in my judgment, that that concession was based on doubts about the possibility of the project. He simply thought that, elderly as he then was, he wasn't "up to" it. The skepticism of the critics has by now been amply borne out, however: no one has ever developed a *scientia* of morality. Indeed, no one has ever succeeded in developing a system of morality by using the somewhat less demanding procedures of Locke's optimal practice. (Less demanding, in that probabilistic inferences are allowed in addition to deductive inferences.)

A third point of critique is worth adding, since the issues posed will prove relevant later in our discussion. Fundamental to Locke's strategy and vision was his conviction that communal traditions and individual say-so are endlessly productive of error. At points of "concernment" that are maximal, we must all set aside all that we believe on the say-so of others and apply our generically human hard-wiring directly to "the things themselves." In his eyes, what made the practice of inquiry, which he recommended, optimal was that by employing it, we did exactly that. We got at "the things themselves" by employing only our generically human hard-wiring.

In the penultimate chapter of the *Essay*, however, Locke offers a devastating critique of this visionary hope, apparently without realizing how devastating it is. The critique consists of a counterexample. Imagine, says Locke, a child reared in Roman Catholicism, who comes to accept as indubitable truth the doctrine of transubstantiation. Now, in fact, that doctrine, says Locke, is not only false, but self-evidently false. Nonetheless, the person reared in Catholicism does not believe that the doctrine is false, even when he grasps it as firmly as does Locke. Both he and Locke are aware of the proposition in question—in Locke's terminology, both he and Locke "perceive" the proposition. In Locke's case, that perception immediately evokes disbelief of the proposition. In the case of the Catholic believer, it does not.

Why the difference? The answer, obviously, is that the Catholic person has been programmed in such a way that disbelief is not forthcoming even though he has the requisite "perception." That, anyway, is how Locke would describe the situation, had the terms *hard-wiring* and *programming* been available to him for metaphorical use. The Catholic person would of course return the favor and say that *Locke* had been programmed in such a way that the "perception" did not evoke the belief. The picture with which Locke operated, in the main body of his *Essay*, was that we all come hard-wired with belief-forming dispositions. These dispositions then get activated by certain experiences, the output being beliefs; these beliefs, unless they are simply forgotten, are then stored in memory. Among the experiences that evoke beliefs in us are people telling us things; we have a disposition to believe what people tell us. But since so much of what people tell us is false, when we are confronted with an issue of maximal concernment, best to ignore what they tell us and simply make use of those belief-forming dispositions of ours that are activated by direct awareness of facts.

That, I say, is the picture with which Locke operated in the body of his work. In that penultimate chapter, a quite different picture puts in its appearance. The beliefs that we already have, however acquired, are not merely stored inertly in memory, waiting to be lifted out should the occasion arise. They become components in our programming. What determines whether I will believe the doctrine of transubstantiation, upon grasping it, is the beliefs that I bring with me to the enterprise. In forming beliefs in response to experience, I do not and cannot operate as a generic human being; I operate as a person with such-and-such a contour of beliefs, such-and-such a contour of affections, such-and-such a contour of habits and skills of attention—and so forth. What I come to believe is a function of my experience plus what I already believe. It is not just a function of my experience. The traditions into which we have been inducted cannot just be set on the shelf, cannot be circumvented. They have become components of ourselves as belief-forming agents: components of our programming. We live *inside* our traditions, not *alongside*.

Let me close my discussion of Locke by remarking that as long as the Lockean practice, or something like it, was widely thought to yield a substantial "rational" religion, along with "rational" evidence for the reliability of the Christian Scriptures, American religious leaders were relatively content with the liberal position. That was the situation throughout the nineteenth century. It was when skepticism on those scores became widespread—impelled especially, in my judgment, by the emergence of Darwinian evolutionary theory and the rise of biblical criticism—that tensions began to mount between religious believers and defenders of the liberal position. That tension has in recent years become acute.

RAWLS' VERSION OF THE LIBERAL POSITION

As was the case for Locke, the principal questions we want to answer in our exposition of John Rawls are these: What rationale does he offer for the restraint he proposes on religious reasons? What does he propose as the independent source? Is that source effectively identified, will it do the work asked of it, and is it fair to demand of religious people that they use this source, rather than their religion, as the basis of their decisions and discussions on political matters?

One way of interpreting Locke is to see him as urging the formation of a *new* comprehensive perspective on matters of religion, morality, and science—a properly grounded perspective, in competition with all those ungrounded perspectives that get handed down in tradition or devised by fancy. It is this new comprehensive perspective that is to serve as basis for our political decisions and discussions. Well aware of this classic liberal strategy, Rawls, in his *Political Liberalism*,[6] makes no bones about his conviction that "the question the dominant tradition has tried to answer has no answer; no comprehensive doctrine is appropriate as a political conception" (135). Not at least for a liberal democracy. In such a society, no one of the comprehensive doctrines can "secure the basis of social unity, nor can it provide the content of public reason on fundamental political questions" (134). One of the great merits of Rawls' discussion is that, under "comprehensive doctrines," he includes not only religions but comprehensive philosophies. In a liberal democracy, no comprehensive perspective—be it religious or not, be it of God and the good, or only of the good, be it an extant perspective or one newly devised—no comprehensive perspective can properly serve as the basis of decisions and discussions on fundamental political questions, nor would social unity be secured by allowing any one to function thus.

Much of what lies behind this claim on Rawls' part is chastened epistemology. Political liberalism, he says, must concede the existence in liberal democracies of a plurality of religions with adherents who are entitled to their adherence. And not just religions: "It must concede that there are many conflicting reasonable comprehensive doctrines with their conceptions of the good" (135). The test of entitlement does not pick out one from the diversity; neither can it serve as a guide for devising a new "rational" religion, or some "rational" secular perspective, which will then be the sole entitled member of the mix. "The political culture of a democratic society," says Rawls, "is always marked by a diversity of opposing and irreconcilable religious, philosophical, and moral doctrines. Some of these are perfectly reasonable, and this diversity among reasonable doctrines political liberalism sees as the inevitable long-run result of the powers of human reason at work within the background of enduring free institutions" (3–4). I acknowledge that Rawls' reasonableness is not identical with my entitlement. But in the course of his discussion it becomes clear, so I judge, that if "reasonable" in the above passage is interpreted as entitled, Rawls would happily affirm that too.

We seem stymied. A number of the distinct perspectives on reality and the good life present in our society are "rational," "reasonable"; the people who embrace them are entitled to do so. The test of entitlement does not single out any one member from the totality. But neither is there any other feature, possessed by only one among the totality of comprehensive perspectives, which would justify us in granting to the perspective possessing that feature hegemony in political decision and discussion. That is Rawls' unspoken assumption. What then can function as the basis of decision and discussion on political matters?

The answer Rawls offers is, if nothing else, provocative. Though he himself does not use the term "*consensus populi*," his suggestion, at bottom, is that, in a liberal democracy, the *consensus populi* ought to be used to form the political basis of the discussions and decisions of the citizens. The situation of Locke, in the late seventeenth century, with respect to liberal democracy, was that of having to argue for the institution of this form of political organization. We, now, are in the fortunate situation of living within established liberal democracies, some of them now several centuries old.

For any political structure that is not merely imposed on a populace, there is a shared political culture that undergirds that structure. The subjects understand themselves and their relationships in a certain way, and that communal self-understanding comes to expression in the political structure—with all due allowance for distorting factors. So, too, with liberal democracy. There is a political culture of which the political structure is an expression. Specifically, citizens of liberal democracies understand themselves as free and equal; they take themselves to be—they regard themselves as being—free and equal.

At this point our political theorists are to enter the picture. Let the political theorists among us analyze the political culture—the political "mind"—of our liberal democracies, with the aim of identifying the fundamental organizing ideas of that culture. To say that the citizens of such societies regard themselves as free and equal is an important first stab at that analysis, but it is much too general, much too ambiguous, much too vague. What we need is a much more careful and detailed analysis. That done, let our theorists then "elaborate" or "unfold" (27) those ideas into principles of justice—principles "specifying the fair terms of social cooperation between citizens regarded as free and equal" (4).

It goes almost without saying that the identification by our theorists of the constituent ideas of our political culture, and the elaboration of those ideas into principles of justice, must not be whimsical, arbitrary, or ideological. The principles that our theorists arrive at must be ones that it is reasonable for them to expect all citizens of liberal democracies to endorse *who use the light of our common human reason*. The principles must "win [their] support by addressing each citizen's reason" (143). In due course we will see why Rawls thinks that this is the appropriate stipulation to place on the analysis and elaboration.

It is the principles of justice thus arrived at that are to function as the *basis* of decisions and discussions on political matters. The independent source that Rawls proposes is that two-stage procedure, performed by our theorists, of analyzing the political culture of one's liberal democracy into its constituent ideas, and then elaborating those ideas into principles specifying the fair terms of social cooperation between citizens regarded as free and equal. The principles that are to function as the political basis in our liberal democracy are to be extracted from the shared political culture of that liberal democracy.

Notice, says Rawls, that the principles of justice thus arrived at will be "freestanding" (10) with respect to all the comprehensive perspectives present in society. They will not have been derived from any one of those perspectives—not even from the overlap among them. They will have been derived instead from the shared political culture of the society.

However, if the society is to be at all stable and enduring, the comprehensive perspectives present within the society—or at least the reasonable ones among them—must each find the proposed principles of justice acceptable from its own standpoint.[7] Citizens must "within their comprehensive doctrines regard the political conception of justice as true, or as reasonable, whatever their view allows" (151). "Thus, political liberalism looks for a political conception of justice that we hope can gain the support of an overlapping consensus of reasonable religious, philosophical, and moral doctrines in a society regulated by it" (10). Given that in a liberal democracy no one comprehensive perspective is to enjoy a hegemony that stifles opposition by coercion and persuasion, such an "overlapping consensus" is necessary for the stability and endurance of the society. Yet the source of the principles that are to function as the political basis is independent of one and all comprehensive doctrines. The principles are to be *arrived at*—to repeat—by theoretical reflection on the shared political culture of one's liberal democracy.

And why does the role of citizen in a liberal democracy incorporate the requirement that we base our political decisions and discussions on the yield of the *consensus populi*, rather than on our own religious and philosophical perspectives? Rawls freely acknowledges that there is something paradoxical about the liberal restraint on the use of religious reasons. Speaking on behalf of the objector, he asks:

> why should citizens in discussing and voting on the most fundamental political questions honor the limits of public reason? How can it be either reasonable or rational, when basic matters are at stake, for citizens to appeal only to a public conception

of justice and not to the whole truth as they see it? Surely, the most fundamental questions should be settled by appealing to the most important truths, yet these may far transcend public reason! (216)

No doubt the liberal position is paradoxical for the reason Rawls cites. It is even more paradoxical for another reason. This is a point I made earlier: given that it is of the very essence of liberal democracy that citizens enjoy equal freedom in law to live out their lives as they see fit, how can it be compatible with liberal democracy for its citizens to be *morally restrained* from deciding and discussing political issues as they see fit?

The novelty of Rawls' strategy is that, just as those principles of justice which are to serve as the political basis are to be extracted from the *consensus populi* of one's liberal democracy, so, too, the rationale for the restraint is to be extracted from that same *consensus populi*. Let me first state what I take to be the core idea and then introduce the details.

The core idea is this: in a liberal democracy, "political power, which is always coercive power, is the power of the public, that is, of free and equal citizens as a collective body" (216). Citizens in a liberal democracy are free and equal co-holders of political voice. Now suppose that I form my opinion concerning some proposed policy, law, or constitutional provision on the basis of reasons that I know you do not accept and conduct my discussion with you on the same basis. In acting thus, I am not giving your view on the matter equal weight with mine; I am not treating your voice as equal to mine. Were I to give your view equal weight with my own, I would not plunge ahead and decide and debate as I do—namely, on grounds that I know you do not accept.[8]

Now for the details. This is what Rawls says by way of rationale for his proposal:

When may citizens by their vote properly exercise their coercive political power over one another when fundamental questions are at stake? Or in the light of what principles and ideals must we exercise that power if our doing so is to be justifiable to others as free and equal? To this question political liberalism replies: our exercise of political power is proper and hence justifiable only when it is exercised in accordance with a constitution the essentials of which all citizens may reasonably be expected to endorse in the light of principles and ideals acceptable to them as reasonable and rational. This is the liberal principle of legitimacy. And since the exercise of political power itself must be legitimate, the ideal of citizenship imposes a moral, not a legal, duty—the duty

of civility—to be able to explain to one another on those fundamental questions how the principles and policies they advocate
and vote for can be supported by the political values of public
reason. This duty also involves a willingness to listen to others
and a fair-mindedness in deciding when accommodations to
their views should reasonably be made. (217)

The thought, I take it, is this: it would be absurd to require of us that
we never choose or advocate a policy unless everybody agrees with us on
that policy. Rather, it is the *reasons* for our decisions and advocacies that
we must attend to, not the policies chosen and advocated on the basis
of those reasons. As to those reasons, it would again be asking too much
to require that we use only those reasons that everybody *in fact* accepts,
or only those that we know everybody accepts. It is asking too much in
two distinct respects. In the first place, all that can be required is that
we confine ourselves to reasons *that it is reasonable of us to believe* would
be generally accepted. *Would* be accepted, *if* what? If those reasons were
presented to our fellow citizens, presumably. And second, it cannot be *all
one's fellow citizens* whose acceptance is critical. There will be some among
them who are not reasonable on the issue in question and some whose
views on the issue are not rational. If it were the requirement that one
must only use reasons that it is reasonable for one to believe that *everybody*
would accept—the unreasonable people along with the reasonable, those
whose view on the matter is not rational as well as those whose is—the
requirement would seldom if ever be satisfied.

In short, the reasons that one must use in deciding and discussing political issues are reasons about which it is reasonable for one to believe that
they would be accepted by all those of one's fellow citizens who are reasonable on the issue, and whose thought about the matter is rational. One may
know that a number of one's reasonable and rational fellow citizens draw
different conclusions from those reasons; that is to be expected. But at least
all of us are now deciding and discussing on the same shared basis.[9]

One final detail. Citizens need not, of course, always undertake to
explain in public why they decide as they do. The requirement, in that
regard, is that they "be able to explain" (217, 243); and not only able,
but "ready" (218, 226).

Let us pull things together by having before us another statement by
Rawls of the rationale. Democracy, he says,

implies . . . an equal share in the coercive political power that
citizens exercise over one another by voting and in other ways.

As reasonable and rational, and knowing that they affirm a diversity of reasonable religious and philosophical doctrines, they should be ready to explain the basis of their actions to one another in terms each could reasonably expect that others might endorse as consistent with their freedom and equality. Trying to meet this condition is one of the tests that this ideal of democratic politics asks of us. Understanding how to conduct oneself as a democratic citizen includes understanding an ideal of public reason. (217–18)

RAWLS' ATTEMPT TO IDENTIFY
THE INDEPENDENT SOURCE

Let me begin my critique of Rawls' theory with some comments about his attempt to identify an independent source of principles of justice, to be used as the basis of political decisions and discussions. Here a considerable number of substantial difficulties arise. Let us remind ourselves that Rawls' aim at this point is to find a source that will yield principles of justice that it is reasonable to expect all one's reasonable and rational fellow citizens to share. The source Rawls proposes is itself something shared—not those principles themselves, but the shared political culture of an extant liberal democracy.

Rawls assumes that the *shared political culture* of certain extant societies is what I have been calling *the Idea of liberal democracy*. I see no reason whatsoever to suppose that that assumption is true. Earlier I made the point that no actual society is anything more than *more or less* a liberal democracy in its political structure; the counterpart point here is that no actual society has a political mentality that is anything more than *more or less* liberal in its constituent ideas. The *actual* political culture of a country such as the United States, for example, is a mélange of conflicting ideas. Among those ideas are the various strands that go to make up the Idea of liberal democracy. But those are far from universally embraced. A Tocquevillian *description* of the actual political mind—the political "Idea," in the Hegelian sense—of American society, would bring to the surface a number of conflicting strands. Current controversies about the rights of practicing homosexuals and about the propriety and legitimacy of prayers in the public schools are illustrative examples. On these particular issues, the Idea of liberal democracy yields clear conclusions: homosexuals should enjoy equal freedom under law to live their lives as they see fit, and state-sponsored schools should not include prayers as an official part of the school program.

Yet large numbers of Americans see otherwise. They do not accept the Idea of liberal democracy at these points. Rawls works with an extraordinarily idealized picture of the American political mind. One can see why: if the Idea of liberal democracy is not identical with the shared political culture of American society, then the prospect of extracting from that political culture principles of justice that are both shared and *appropriate to a liberal democracy* is hopeless.

"We start," says Rawls, "by looking to the public culture itself as the shared fund of implicitly recognized basic ideas and principles. We hope to formulate these ideas and principles clearly enough to be combined into a political conception of justice congenial to our most firmly held convictions. We express this by saying that a political conception of justice, to be acceptable, must accord with our considered convictions, at all levels of generality, or in what I have called elsewhere 'reflective equilibrium'" (8). I submit that only if we look at the political culture of American society through the rose-tinted glasses of the Idea of liberal democracy, viewing inconsistencies with that Idea as mere "deviations" from the regnant "mind," will we fail to see that on many issues a good many Americans are firmly opposed to the Idea of liberal democracy. The Idea of liberal democracy does not capture their "considered convictions."

But suppose it were the case that the totality of the fundamental ideas constituting the political culture of American society was identical with the Idea of liberal democracy. The work that Rawls assigns to political theorists raises additional problems with his theory. Our political theorists are to analyze our political mentality into its constituent ideas; that done, they are then to elaborate those ideas into principles of justice. These principles are to be ones that one can reasonably expect the reasonable and rational among one's fellow citizens to embrace. To arrive at such principles is the goal of the task assigned to our theorists.

It would take a good deal of exegetic industry to figure out what Rawls means by "reasonable," and even more to figure out what he means by "rational." In spite of the fact that epistemological concepts and claims are at the very center of his theory, his inarticulateness on matters of epistemology, when contrasted with Locke, for example, is striking.

Some phrases lead one to prick up one's ears in suspicion that the Enlightenment understanding of how reason works is still operative. Rawls has, of course, given up the hope that we can arrive at principles of justice by employing something like the Lockean practice. Rather than supposing that we can get at the moral facts themselves by the employment of our generically human hard-wiring, he unabashedly starts with a certain tradition: an ongoing political culture. He does not attempt to dig beneath that to "the things themselves." What he does say, though, is that the principles proposed must "win [their] support by addressing each citizen's reason" (143), and that they must be ones that one can reasonably expect all citizens to endorse *who use the light of our common human reason*. But our common human reason is always a programmed human reason; what we come to believe by the use of our reason (whatever Rawls might have in mind by that) is a function, in part, of what we already believe. And we differ in our beliefs—differ in particular, now, in our comprehensive perspectives.

In short, Rawls is still working with that same picture of the "understanding" with which Locke worked, before that penultimate deconstructionist chapter of the *Essay*. The idea is that it is possible for our theorists to remove their comprehensive perspectives from their programming, to deposit them in memory, and then, using only the light of our common human reason, to analyze the ideas of our political culture and elaborate those ideas into principles of justice. It is possible for laypersons to do the same when, handed some proposed principles by the theorists, they consider whether to endorse them. Presumably it is that Enlightenment understanding of the workings of our belief-forming dispositions, including, then, our reason, that accounts for the hope, if not confidence, which Rawls has, that our political theorists will be able to accomplish the task set to them: that they will be able, working in the recommended fashion, to arrive at principles of justice that they can reasonably expect their reasonable and rational fellow citizens to endorse.

The truth of the matter seems to me exactly the opposite. No matter what principles of justice a particular political theorist may propose, the reasonable thing for her to expect, given any plausible understanding whatsoever of "reasonable and rational," is *not* that all reasonable and rational citizens would accept those principles, but rather that *not all* of them would do so. It would be utterly *unreasonable* for her to expect all of them to accept them. It would be unreasonable of her even to expect all her reasonable and rational fellow theorists to accept them; the contested fate of Rawls' own proposed principles of justice is illustrative.[10] What is reasonable for her to expect is that her proposals will stir up controversy and dissent not only at the point of transition from the academy to general society, but within the academy.

In short, there is no more hope that reasonable and rational citizens will come to agreement, in the way Rawls recommends, on principles of justice, than that they will come to agreement, in the foreseeable future, on some comprehensive philosophical or religious doctrine. It is odd of Rawls to have thought otherwise; he must have been thinking, as I have suggested, that analysis and elaboration of a shared culture is an enterprise that can be insulated against the effects of our perspectival disagreements.

In one interesting passage (226–27), Rawls concedes the point that I have been making. "Keep in mind," he says, "that political liberalism is a *kind* [my italics] of view." Members of the liberal family differ from each other not only on "the substantive principles" of justice that they propose, but also on "the guidelines of inquiry" that they propose for arriving at those. What nonetheless unites them into members of the *liberal* family is, in the first place, their agreement on "an idea of public reason." Which is to say, their agreement that our political decisions and discussions are to be based on principles yielded by what I have called an "independent source." And what unites them, secondly, is that the "substantive principles of justice . . . are liberal"—that is, appropriate to the agreement "that citizens share in political power as free and equal." This second point amounts to an affirmation of the liberal principle of political legitimacy: for a constitution and laws to be legitimate, they must express, or if not express, then at least be consistent with, the agreement that citizens share in political power as free and equal.

Rawls then adds that "accepting the idea of public reason and [the liberal] principle of legitimacy emphatically does not mean . . . accepting a particular liberal conception of justice down to the last details of the principles defining its content." In fact, it does not even mean accepting principles as general as those that Rawls proposes. "The view I have called 'justice as fairness'," says Rawls, "is but one example of a liberal political conception; its specific content is not definitive of such a view."

> The point of the ideal of public reason is that citizens are to conduct their fundamental discussions within the framework of what each regards as a political conception of justice based on values that the others can reasonably be expected to endorse and each is, in good faith, prepared to defend that conception so understood. This means that each of us must have, and be ready to explain, a criterion of what principles and guidelines we think other citizens (who are also free and equal) may reasonably be expected to endorse along with us. [226–27]

In short, all that is required is that we agree on the idea of public reason, that we agree on the liberal principle of legitimacy, and that we each have a criterion, which our fellow citizens find reasonable, for testing proposed principles of justice against those two nonnegotiable points of agreement.

We may find, says Rawls, "that actually others fail to endorse the principles and guidelines our criterion selects." "That is to be expected," he adds. It is even to be expected that they will not endorse the criterion itself. Though they find it reasonable, they do not endorse it; "many will prefer another criterion." But "we must have such a criterion," says Rawls.

Why is that? Because this requirement

> imposes very considerable discipline on public discussion. Not any value is reasonably said to meet this test, or to be a political value; and not any balance of political values is reasonable. It is inevitable and often desirable that citizens have different views as to the most appropriate political conception [of justice]; for the public political culture is bound to contain different fundamental ideas that can be developed in different ways. An orderly contest between them over time is a reliable way to find which one, if any, is most reasonable. [227]

This is remarkable. Public reason does not have, and does not have to have, any substantive content—any positive principles of justice. The independent source does not, and need not, yield such principles. We can live without them. We do not need, for political life in a liberal democracy, principles endorsed by all reasonable and rational citizens. We do not need such principles for our political decisions and discussions. The debates that take place within a liberal democracy can be about everything political, except for just two things: the liberal principle of legitimacy and the idea of public reason. Those must be taken for granted.

It turns out, then, that the idea of public reason is *an ideal*—Rawls himself calls it that—and may never be anything more. We debate with each other with the goal in mind of discovering principles of justice that are faithful to the liberal principle of legitimacy and that we can reasonably expect all our reasonable and rational fellow citizens to endorse. We may never find them. That is acceptable. We can live with the fact that the independent source that we have identified does not, and may never, actually yield principles of the sort we thought we needed. It may be that at most what it does is eliminate certain principles. And, to repeat the point made earlier, some of the principles eliminated by the Idea of liberal democracy will not be eliminated by the political culture of an actual society such as the United States, for no actual society, in mind and practice, is more than *more or less* a liberal democracy.

DOES THE SOURCE YIELD THE PRINCIPLES NEEDED?

I have not thus far mentioned the scope of the restraint that Rawls lays on reasons derived from comprehensive religious and philosophical perspectives. That may have led the reader to assume that the restraint holds for *all* political decisions and discussions. Not so. The restraint holds only for *constitutional essentials* and *matters of basic justice*. Or to look at the situation from the other side: it is only for such issues that the citizens of a liberal democracy are obligated to appeal to public reason. Only on such issues, by and large, will assistance be forthcoming from that source. Certainly it is desirable that the yield of public reason be richer than this, but as long as it is not, we will have to be content with this limited utility, while acknowledging that this "is already of enormous importance":

> If a political conception of justice covers the constitutional essentials and matters of basic justice—for the present this is all we aim for—it is already of enormous importance even if it has little to say about many economic and social issues that legislative bodies must regularly consider. To resolve these more particular and detailed issues it is often more reasonable to go beyond the political conception and the values its principles express, and to invoke nonpolitical values that such a view does not include. (230)

Kent Greenawalt, in two important books, *Religious Convictions and Political Choice*[11] and *Private Consciences and Public Reasons*,[12] has cogently argued that none of the independent sources proposed by those contemporaries who embrace the liberal position is capable of resolving for us some of the most important and contentious political issues that we face today. Worse yet: on some of these issues, those independent sources are simply irrelevant; they have nothing to say. From the above passage (and plenty of others) it is clear that Rawls concedes that many political issues lie beyond the reach of the independent source that he proposes; hence the qualification, "constitutional essentials and matters of basic justice." He appears relatively content with this limitation, quite clearly because he thinks that public reason, whatever its limitations, is capable of dealing with the most important political issues confronting us. Some of the cases that Greenawalt develops shatter that assumption; the thought unavoidably comes to mind that, rather than spending huge quantities of intellectual imagination and energy on developing the liberal position, perhaps we ought to be considering how to deal with the cases not covered. Let me briefly consider just two of the examples that Greenawalt discusses and then refer the reader to his books for a full treatment of these, and other, examples.

First, the issue of welfare assistance. On this issue we are faced, in our society, with positions along a continuum that goes all the way from those which hold that government should have nothing to do with welfare, limiting its activities to protecting people against force and fraud, to those which hold that the government is responsible for the distribution of social resources. Now suppose one holds the latter and then adds—thereby honoring the liberal principle of legitimacy—that the government, in carrying out its responsibility, ought to treat all persons as free and equal. It turns out that this allows for a number of significantly distinct distributive formulas. Let me quote Greenawalt:

> Among the most familiar are the Marxist formula, "From each according to his abilities, to each according to his needs," the utilitarian principle of maximizing average or total welfare, and the suggestion of Rawls that distribution should be equal except as inequality will increase goods even for representative members of the least advantaged economic group. In different respects each of these views treats all citizens as equal. For Marx, each's needs count equally; for the utilitarian, each's capacity for happiness (or some surrogate) counts equally in the search for maximum overall welfare; for Rawls, each's entitlement to resources in a fundamental sense is equal and inequalities are allowed only if everyone is made better off. (*Religious Convictions and Political Choice*, 174)

Greenawalt observes that "a choice among these and other distributive approaches will depend on some initial premise about proper notions of human equality and upon complex judgments about human nature and actual or potential social relations" (174). That seems definitely correct. But consider the notion of human equality. What these disputes over the appropriate distributive formula reveal is that though all who embrace the Idea of liberal democracy agree in the affirmation that citizens are to be treated as free and equal, there are significantly different understandings of what we are affirming when we affirm that. Analysis of the constituent ideas of liberal democracy will not *resolve* our disagreement; if it truly is an analysis, it will *lay bare* our disagreement. If that which is presented as an analysis resolves the dispute among competing distributive formulae, then it is something more, or other, than an analysis. For resolution of the disagreement, convictions derived from somewhere else than our shared political culture will have to be utilized.

That was a case in which Rawls' own preferred principles of justice give definite guidance for the resolution of an important and contentious political issue; the difficulty was that the mere Idea of liberal democracy does not enable us to choose between those principles and various competitors. Several of the other issues that Greenawalt develops are ones to which the Idea of liberal democracy is just irrelevant. I have in mind various issues that hinge crucially on who has "standing." One component of the Idea of liberal democracy is that all persons who come within the jurisdiction of the state are to be granted equal protection under law. But that does not tell us who is a person. And one of the crucial issues in our raging dispute over abortion is whether the fetus is a person. To this question, the Idea of liberal democracy has nothing at all to contribute. Indeed, it is compatible with the Idea of liberal democracy to concede that the fetus is not a person and then to go on to argue that the equal protection under law which the Idea of liberal democracy accords to persons ought to be accorded to certain nonpersons as well—specifically, human fetuses.

IS IT FAIR TO ASK EVERYONE TO USE THE SOURCE?

Those were issues pertaining to the independent source that Rawls proposes for the principles that are to serve as basis of decisions and discussions on constitutional essentials and matters of basic justice: Has the source been adequately identified? Does it yield the principles wanted? A final question concerning the source is this: is it equitable to ask of everyone that, in deciding and discussing political issues, they refrain from using their comprehensive perspectives and appeal instead to the yield of the independent source?

In two regards, it seems to me not equitable. One is a point to which I called attention near the beginning of our discussion. It belongs to the *religious convictions* of a good many religious people in our society that *they ought to base* their decisions concerning fundamental issues of justice *on* their religious convictions. They do not view it as an option whether or not to do so. It is their conviction that they ought to strive for wholeness, integrity, integration, in their lives: that they ought to allow the Word of God, the teachings of the Torah, the command and example of Jesus, or whatever, to shape their existence as a whole, including, then, their social and political existence. Their religion is not, for them, about *something other* than their social and political existence; it is *also* about their social and political existence. Accordingly, to require of them that they not base their decisions and discussions concerning political issues on their religion is to infringe, inequitably, on the free exercise of their religion. If they have to make a choice, they will make their decisions about constitutional essentials and matters of basic justice on the basis of their religious convictions and make their decisions on more peripheral matters on other grounds—exactly the opposite of what Rawls lays down in his version of the restraint.

The second inequity is a kind of unfairness that pertains more to practice than theory. Much if not most of the time we will be able to spot religious reasons from a mile away: references to God, to Jesus Christ, to the Torah, to the Christian Bible, or to the Koran are unmistakably religious. Typically, however, comprehensive secular perspectives will go undetected. How am I to tell whether the utilitarianism or the nationalism of the person who argues his case along utilitarian or nationalist lines is or is not part of his comprehensive perspective?

RAWLS' RATIONALE

What remains to consider is the rationale that Rawls offers. The claim is that if I make my decision concerning some political issue for reasons that I know certain of my reasonable and rational fellow citizens do not accept, and if I furthermore explain to them my reasons for my decision, knowing they do not accept them, then I am not treating them as free and equal with myself. In particular, I am not according them equal political voice with myself. Is this true?

Its truth is certainly not self-evident. Start with a few points that, though important, are nonetheless not quite central. In the first place, if my fellow citizen's agreeing or not agreeing with me has *something* to do with my according him equal political voice, then why is not my *conclusion* the relevant thing rather than my reason? The assumption seems to be that if I use reasons you do not accept, then you are right in thinking that I am not treating you as my equal; whereas if I hold to a conclusion that you do not accept for reasons that you do accept, then you would not be right in thinking that I am not treating you as my equal. I fail to see it. After all, it is, in the last resort, the *conclusions* people come to that lead them to support whatever laws and policies they do support.

Second, if my using reasons that I know you do not endorse really does constitute my not treating you as equal, then it constitutes that whether or not the issue is constitutional essentials or matters of basic justice. Is my moral failure perhaps the greater, the more important the issue? I fail to see that it is. Given Rawls' concession that public reason does not yield much in the way of generally accepted principles of justice, his rationale for his restraint on religious reasons, if it were cogent, would have the consequence that even those who most firmly embrace the Idea of liberal democracy would regularly and unavoidably be violating one of the fundamental principles of that Idea.

Third, there is something very much like a fallacy of composition in Rawls' reasoning at this point. To see this, let us separate the reasons I have for my acceptance of a certain policy from the reasons that I offer in public for that policy. There is no reason, in general, why these should be the same. Of course, if I say or suggest that my reason was such-and-such, when in fact it was not, that would be dissembling. But there is an eminently honorable reason for discrepancy between the reason one offers in public discussion for a certain policy and one's own reason for accepting that policy; namely, one wants to persuade one's discussion partner to accept the policy, and one knows or suspects that different reasons will attract her from those that attracted oneself. Given this fact of honorable discrepancy, it is a good question to which of these two uses of reasons Rawls' rationale ought to be applied. To the latter, I would think. If I can defend a policy I accept with reasons that you find cogent, what difference does it make to you whether those were also for me the determinative reasons?

So suppose it is true that, when conversing with Ryan, I must, to honor his freedom and equality, offer reasons for the policy I accept which I can reasonably expect him to endorse; and suppose it is true, likewise, that, when conversing with Wendy, I must, to honor her freedom and equality, offer reasons for the policy I accept which I can reasonably expect *her* to endorse. It does not follow that the reasons I offer to Ryan must be the same as those I offer to Wendy. To Ryan, I offer reasons that I hope he will find persuasive; to Wendy, I offer reasons that I hope she will find persuasive. Why must they be the same reasons? They need not even be reasons that I accept—let alone reasons that for me personally were determinative. Ad hoc reasons, tailor-made for one's addressee, seem entirely adequate. And if Wendy listens in on my reasoning with Ryan, and Ryan, on my reasoning with Wendy, what difference does that make? In short, one's reasons do not have to be reasons for all comers.

But what about the claim itself? None of these points speaks directly to that. Is it true that if I decide to accept a proposed policy, law, or constitutional provision on the basis of reasons that I know some of my reasonable and rational fellow citizens do not accept, I am thereby not treating them as free citizens possessing equal political voice with myself? And is it true that if I defend a proposed policy, law, or constitutional provision on the basis of such reasons, then, too, I am not treating them as free and equal citizens? Let us state the issue more sharply. Suppose the policy I decide to accept is such that I know there are some reasonable and rational fellow citizens to whom I cannot defend it with reasons that they accept. Am I violating their freedom and equality in making my decision for those reasons?

I think the answer to that question is: yes, there is a sense of "freedom and equality" such that I am violating their freedom and equality, *so understood*. Rather than withholding decision on the ground that, of two opinions of equal weight, one says No and the other says Yes, I embrace my own view of the matter. In doing so, I perforce do not treat the opinions as being of equal weight. And notice that it does not matter whether coercion is in view. Whether the issue at hand is a law to be backed up with coercive force, a rule governing cooperation, or a philosophical issue, it makes no difference: if my opinion is Yes and yours is No, and if rather than abstaining from decision, I embrace the Yes, then I am not treating your opinion as equal to mine.

The question, though, is whether *this* sense of equality is relevant to liberal democracy. It seems to me about as clear as anything can be that it is not relevant. In a democracy, we discuss and debate, with the aim of reaching agreement. We do not just mount the platform to tell our fellow citizens how we see things. We listen and try to persuade. Typically our attempts at persuasion are on an ad hoc basis: offering to Republicans reasons that we think might appeal to them, if we can find such, to Democrats reasons that we think might appeal to them, if we can find such, to Christians reasons that we think might appeal to them, if we can find such, to America-firsters reasons that we think might appeal to them, if we can find such. And so forth. Seldom, even on unimportant issues, do we succeed in reaching consensus, not even among reasonable and rational citizens of these different stripes. But we try.

Then, finally, we vote. It cannot be the case that in voting under these circumstances, we are violating those concepts of freedom and equality that are ingredient in the Idea of liberal democracy, since almost the first thing that happens when societies move toward becoming liberal democracies is that they begin taking votes on various matters and living with the will of the majority—subject to provisos specifying rights of minorities.

The concept of equal voice that is relevant to liberal democracy is that we shall deal with our diverse opinions by establishing fair voting procedures, and then, within [those procedures], give everybody's opinion equal weight. Everybody's voice on the matter being voted on is to count as equal with everyone else's. The judges on the U.S. Supreme Court argue and debate with each other, trying to reach consensus. Most of the time they fail; often their failure is not simply a failure to reach consensus on results, but a failure to reach consensus on how the issue should be approached, what line of reasoning should be determinative. Eventually they vote. In that vote, each judge's vote carries equal weight: a paradigm of treating each other as free and equal.

What is striking about our contemporary proponents of the liberal position is that they are still looking for a politics that is the politics of a community with shared perspective. They see that that perspective cannot, in our societies, be a comprehensive perspective; and that that community cannot be a community which is the social embodiment of a comprehensive perspective. So they propose scaling down our expectations. Take a society that is more or less a liberal democracy, and then consider a single aspect of that society, a single dimension: the political. Think of that, if you will, as constituting an *aspectual* community, a *dimensional* community. The perspective which it embodies will be the shared political culture of the society. That perspective will not be comprehensive; all in all, it will be more like a shared perspective on social justice than a shared perspective on the good life in general and more like a shared perspective on the nature of the political person than a shared perspective on human nature in general. But that limited perspective and that dimensional community will be sufficient for the purposes at hand.

So-called communitarians regularly accuse proponents of the liberal position of being against community. One can see what they are getting at. Nonetheless, this way of putting it seems to me imperceptive of what, at bottom, is going on. The liberal is not willing to live with a politics of multiple communities. He still wants communitarian politics. He is trying to discover, and to form, the relevant community. He thinks we need a shared political basis; he is trying to discover and nourish that basis. For the reasons given, I think that the attempt is hopeless and misguided. We must learn to live with a politics of multiple communities.

WHAT DOES RESPECT REQUIRE?

A final point must be made about the Rawlsian rationale for restraint on the use of reasons derived from one's comprehensive perspective. Rawls' argument is that treating a fellow citizen as free and equal requires not using reasons for political decisions and discussions that one could not reasonably expect one's fellow citizens to endorse. Now the person who embraces liberal democracy does not see himself as participating in an arbitrary resolution at this point. To the contrary: he sees our treating each other as free and equal as a way of paying due respect to what we are—to our status. Not to pay respect, in these ways and others, to what we are is morally wrong. In *Political Liberalism* Rawls does not call much attention to this phenomenon of morally required respect. He does not think he has to. He thinks the citizens of liberal democracies already recognize that they ought to treat each other as free and equal, so he starts with that communal recognition and argues that failure to impose on ourselves the restraint on religious reasons that he recommends would be *inconsistent* with that recognition. Nonetheless, he himself does not regard the recognition as free-floating but as grounded in what one might call "the morality of respect."[13]

Up to this point we have followed Rawls in his practice of looking at the giving of reasons derived from one's comprehensive perspective exclusively from the standpoint of the speaker. We have asked whether the speaker, in offering reasons from his own perspective to someone whose perspective is different, is or is not paying due respect to the freedom and equality of the other person. Suppose that we now look at the same phenomenon from the opposite end, from the standpoint of the addressee. Suppose that you offer to me reasons derived from your comprehensive standpoint; and that I, fully persuaded of the moral impropriety of such behavior by the advocates of the liberal position, brush your remarks aside with the comment that in offering me such reasons, you are not paying due respect to my status as free and equal. Only if you offer me reasons derived from the independent source will you be paying me due respect. To offer me such reasons is to demean me; I will not listen.

Such a response would be profoundly disrespectful in its own way. It would pay no respect to your particularity—to you *in* your particularity. It would treat your particularity, and you *in* your particularity, as of no account. Can that be right? Is there not something about the person who embraces, say, the Jewish religion, that I, a Christian, should honor? Should I not honor her not only as someone who is free and equal, but *as* someone who embraces the Jewish religion? Is she not worth honoring not only in her similarity to me, as free and equal, but *in* her particular difference from me—in her embrace of Judaism?[14] Of course, I mean Judaism to be taken here as but one example among many. Are persons not often worth honoring *in* their religious particularities, in their national particularities, in their class particularities, in their gender particularities? Does such honoring not require that I invite them to tell me how politics looks from their perspective—and does it not require that I genuinely listen to what they say? We need a politics that not only honors us in our similarity as free and equal, but in our particularities. For our particularities—some of them—are constitutive of who we are, constitutive of our narrative identities.

In addition: does not the presence of embodied Judaism in our midst enrich our common life? Cannot the understanding of politics by those of us who do not embrace Judaism be enriched by Judaism's understanding of politics? But how could such enrichment ever take place if in the public square, we do our best to silence all appeals to our diverse perspectives, regarding the felt need to appeal to them here and there as simply a lamentable deficiency in the scope and power of public reason—a deficiency whose overcoming we hope for?

NO RESTRAINT ON RELIGIOUS REASONS

We have looked at the most influential of the traditional liberal positions and at the most influential of the contemporary. In both cases, we have found that the rationale offered for restraint on the use of religious reasons in deciding and discussing political issues was far from persuasive and that the proposal made for an independent source was seriously deficient. Our attention was focused on the heart of the matter, not on fine-mesh details of rationales and proposals. Had the latter been the case, the proponent of the liberal position might reasonably have hoped to repair the damage. In fact, I see no way of doing so. The liberal position looks hopeless. I see no reason to suppose that the ethic of the citizen in a liberal democracy includes a restraint on the use of religious reasons in deciding and discussing political issues. Let citizens use whatever reasons they find appropriate—including, then, religious reasons.

Recently a group of Christians, organized as the Christian Environment Council, appeared in Washington, D.C. Addressing the national media and the congressional leadership, they spoke up in support of endangered species, declaring themselves opposed to "any Congressional action that would weaken, hamper, reduce or end the protection, recovery, and preservation of God's creatures, including their habitats, especially as accomplished under the Endangered Species Act." The heart of the reason they offered was that "according to the Scriptures, the earth is the Lord's and all that dwells within it (Psalm 24:12), and the Lord shows concern for every creature (Matthew 6:26)." I fail to see that those Christians, in offering, in the public square, those reasons for their position, were violating the ethic of the citizen in a liberal democracy. Let it be added that if they want to persuade those who do not accept the Hebrew or Christian Bible as authoritative, they will of course have to find and offer other, additional reasons for their position. Whether or not a reason for a position is *appropriate* depends not only on the position but on one's purpose. Reasons are used for doing different things.

When I say, "Let citizens use whatever reasons they find appropriate," I do not by any means want to be understood as implying that no restraints whatsoever are appropriate on a person's reasoning from his or her religion. Restraints of three sorts pertain to the citizen of a liberal democracy.

In the first place, restraints are needed on the manner of discussion and debate in the public square. In our manner of argumentation, we ought to show respect for the other person. Our discussions ought to be conducted with *civility*. The virtues of civility belong to the ethic of the citizen.

There will be disputes as to what those virtues are. What does respect for the freedom and equality of the other person require by way of *manner* of discussion and debate? What does respect for that which is of worth in the particularity of the other person require? My own view is that those virtues prove considerably thicker than the word *civility* would naturally suggest. They require listening to the other person with a willingness to learn and to let one's mind be changed. In some cases they require repentance and forgiveness.

Second, the debates, except for extreme circumstances, are to be conducted and resolved in accord with the rules provided by the laws of the land and the provisions of the Constitution. It is certainly not out of place to argue for changes in those laws and in those provisions, but, except for extreme circumstances, that argumentation is itself to be conducted in accord with the extant laws and provisions.

Third, there is a restraint on the overall goal of the debates and discussions. The goal is political justice, not the achievement of one's own interests. Here I side with the liberal position, against the competition-of-interests position.

On what basis do I claim that these restraints belong to the ethic of the citizen in a liberal democracy? Are they grounded in the Idea of liberal democracy? Can they, accordingly, somehow be extracted from that Idea? Not without controversy. The view that the proper goal of political discourse is satisfaction of interests is seen by some as just as compatible with the Idea of liberal democracy as the view of the liberal position, which says that the proper goal is political justice; so, too, the view I espouse, that political discourse at its best is governed, among other things, by respect for certain of the peculiarities of one's fellow citizens, is seen by me and others as just as compatible with the Idea of liberal democracy as the view of the liberal position, which holds that it is governed only by respect for the freedom and equality of citizens.

In short: in some measure, at least, it is my own moral and religious perspective that leads me to articulate the ethic of the citizen in a *liberal* democracy as I do. Even at this point of articulating the ethical component of the role of citizen, we cannot leap out of our perspectives. And even if we could, there is nothing firm that we could leap on to: no adequate independent source. The ethic of the citizen is itself up for debate in constitutional democracies of a by and large liberal character.

DO WE NEED CONSENSUS?

The question that arises at this point is this: do we not *need* what the representatives of the liberal position call a *political basis*? Do we not need an abiding set of agreed-on principles to which all of us, from day to day and year to year, can appeal in deciding and discussing political issues—at least the most important among them, those that deal with "constitutional essentials and matters of basic justice"?[15]

Apparently not. None of our contemporary defenders of the liberal position believes that any extant society actually has such a basis. I think they are right on that. They see themselves not as describing the basis some society already has, but as offering proposals for obtaining such a basis. They think liberal democracies *should have* such a basis; often they speak of such societies as *needing* such a basis. Yet many of our contemporary societies manage to be ongoing constitutional democracies of a relatively liberal character. Apparently, such a basis is not necessary.

We aim at agreement in our discussions with each other. But we do not for the most part aim at achieving agreement concerning a political basis; rather, we aim at agreement concerning the particular policy, law, or constitutional provision under consideration. Our agreement on some policy need not be based on some set of principles *agreed on* by all present and future citizens and *rich enough* to settle all important political issues. Sufficient if each citizen, for his or her own reasons, agrees on the policy today and tomorrow—not for all time. It need not even be the case that each and every citizen agrees to the policy. Sufficient if the agreement be the fairly gained and fairly executed agreement of the majority.

That is the nature of political decision and discussion in constitutional democracies that are relatively liberal in character and whose citizens embody a diversity of comprehensive perspectives: ad hoc, full of compromise, tolerant of losing the vote, focused on the specific, and on the here and now and the near future. Something so jerry-built may not long endure. But the risk is worth taking, and not only because the alternatives are all worse. There is something about each of us that merits respect by each treating each as free and equal.

THE CONSOCIAL POSITION

Early in my discussion, I called the position I would be defending the *consocial* position. The consocial position agrees with the liberal position and opposes the competition-of-interests position concerning the goal of political discussions, decisions, and actions: the goal is political justice. But it departs from the liberal position on two defining issues. First, it repudiates the quest for an independent source and imposes no moral restraint on the use of religious reasons. And second, it interprets the neutrality requirement, that the state be neutral with respect to the religious and other comprehensive perspectives present in society, as requiring *impartiality* rather than *separation*. What unites these two themes is that, at both points, the person embracing the consocial position wishes to grant citizens, no matter what their religion or irreligion, as much liberty as possible to live out their lives as they see fit. On the two issues mentioned, he sees the person embracing the liberal position as recommending policies incompatible with the Idea of liberal democracy. We have already noted how the liberal position's recommendation of restraint on religious reasons infringes on the free exercise of religion. Let me now briefly call attention to how the liberal's embrace of the separation interpretation does the same.

The state, in all contemporary constitutional democracies, funds a large part of the educational system. One can imagine a constitutional democracy in which that is not the case; in the contemporary world, however, it always is the case. Given such state funding, the separation interpretation specifies that the state must not in any significant way aid any religion—nor any comprehensive nonreligious perspective.

Now suppose there are parents present in society for whom it is a matter of religious conviction that their children receive a religiously integrated education—of a particular sort. Such parents are in fact present in contemporary American society. Were the state to fund an educational program in accord with the religious convictions of any of those parents, it would, obviously, be aiding their religion and thereby violating the separation principle. But conversely, if the state funds other schools but refuses to fund schools satisfactory to those parents who want a religiously integrated education (of a particular sort) for their children, then those parents, in a perfectly obvious way, are discriminated against. If those parents are forbidden by law to establish and patronize schools that teach in accord with their religious convictions, then the discrimination is embodied in law. If they are not legally forbidden to establish and patronize such schools, then the discrimination is embodied in economics. Were those parents to establish and patronize schools that teach in accord with their convictions, they would have to pay for those schools out of their own pockets, while still contributing to the general tax fund for the other schools. Obviously the free exercise of their religion is thereby infringed on—in a way in which that of others is not. They do not enjoy equal freedom, in this regard, to live out their lives as they see fit.

The situation poses an inescapable dilemma for the separation interpretation. Given that interpretation, there is nothing that can be done that does not either violate the separation principle or inequitably infringe on the free exercise of someone's religion or irreligion. The only escape from the dilemma is to give up the separation interpretation and adopt the impartiality interpretation: let the state fund equitably all schools that meet minimum educational requirements.

There is a common pattern to the impression of the person who embraces the liberal position that his insistence on an independent source deals fairly with religion, and to his impression that his insistence on the separation interpretation deals fairly with religion. The common pattern is this: the liberal assumes that requiring religious people to debate and act politically for reasons other than religious reasons is not in violation of their *religious* convictions; likewise he assumes that an educational program that makes no reference to religion is not in violation of any parent's *religious* convictions. He assumes, in other words, that though religious people may not be in the habit of dividing their lives into a religious component and a nonreligious component, and though some might not be happy doing so, nonetheless, their doing so would in no case be in violation of their religion. But he is wrong about this. It is when we bring into the picture people for whom it is a matter of religious conviction that they ought to strive for a religiously integrated existence—then especially, though not only then, does the unfairness of the liberal position to religion come to light.

APPLICATION TO PUBLIC OFFICIALS

My attention has been focused on the ethic of the citizen in a liberal democracy, that is, on the ethical requirements embedded in the *role* of citizen: does that ethic include a restraint on the use of religious reasons for political decisions and discussions? Let me conclude with some brief comments on the use of religious reasons by officials: legislators, executives, and judges.

Legislators lie on one side of a divide that is important for this question, and executives and judges, on the other. That divide is this: legislators play a pivotal role in the normal process whereby a democratic society reaches its decisions about the laws that shall govern the interactions of its citizens; executives and judges exercise their roles after the society has reached its decision.

The executive is handed the laws and constitutional provisions, with instructions to administer their implementation and enforcement; the judge is likewise handed the laws and constitutional provisions, with instructions to adjudicate disputes in the light of them. Both are acting on behalf of the community, implementing the community's will. The community has chosen its laws and constitution; now it commissions executives to administer and enforce the law, and judges to adjudicate by reference to the law. Accordingly, when people are functioning in the role of executive or judge, the question of whether they personally approve the laws and provisions never arises; a person is never asked, when functioning in either of those roles, for his personal opinion on the matter. Thus also the question of offering reasons from his religion for or against the legislation or constitution never arises. The role of executive is only to administer and enforce, of judge, to adjudicate. If anyone in the role has moral or religious scruples against doing so, then, depending on how serious the scruples, he or she must get out of the role.

Administration and adjudication are not mechanical procedures; both activities require interpretation. And beyond a doubt the comprehensive perspectives, be they religious or otherwise, of executives and judges, play a role in the processes through which executives and judges arrive at interpretations; it could not be otherwise. Nonetheless the fact remains that both executives and judges are acting on behalf of the community; the community has made up its mind on the law and now wants that law administered, enforced, and used in adjudication. Musical performance also incorporates interpretation. But the musical performer is not interpreting on behalf of anyone. It is open to her to give a totally astonishing, unexpected, even whimsical, interpretation. If she is not thereby irresponsibly shattering expectations, what difference does it make? Not so for executives and judges: they have been duly commissioned to administer and adjudicate, and therefore to interpret, on behalf of the community. Thus the question arises: which interpretations, in the light of which perspectives, are permissible?

The answer in a democratic society is that the citizens themselves eventually answer that question—on the basis of whatever reasons individual citizens find cogent. In effect, society says to its executives and judges: go ahead, interpret; we will eventually tell you, by elections, recalls, referenda, protest movements, and so forth, whether we think you have strayed from what is permissible.

The role of the legislator is different. Laws, as he deals with them, are still prospective. Accordingly, reasons for and against their enactment are very much in the picture. The question definitely does arise for the legislator: is it acceptable to make his decision, and then to argue the case, on personal religious grounds?

Though not commissioned to implement society's decision, playing a crucial role, instead, in society's arriving at its decision, the legislator is nonetheless also not a private citizen. He is a representative. But what is it to be a representative? Is it to do what he can to discover the will of the majority of his constituents—or the most powerful among them, or the most vocal—and then vote accordingly? Or is it to decide as he personally judges best—taking into account, as he makes his decision, whatever considerations his constituents may call to his attention? The issue has never been resolved in our societies; some of us hold one view; some, another. On the former construal of the role of representative, whatever reasons the person who is representative may personally have, religious or not, for or against the proposed legislation, do not enter the picture. On the latter construal, they very well may. Indeed, on the latter construal of the role of representative, no general restraint on the use of religious reasons seems relevant or appropriate. The representative must decide as she judges best—after gleaning what wisdom she can from her constituents, and anyone else. Her decision will have to be in the light of all that she believes, including her religion or irreligion, as the case may be. She runs the risk of being removed from office next time around. But that is the risk any representative takes who sees her role not as one who follows political polls but as one who exercises political wisdom.[16]

Chapter 8

What Respect Requires—
And What It Does Not

Christopher J. Eberle

CENTRAL THESIS

My central thesis is that a citizen is morally permitted to support (or oppose) a coercive law even if she enjoys only a religious rationale for that law. As I see the matter, a citizen need not be morally criticizable in any respect just in virtue of her willingness to support her favored coercive laws only on religious grounds. I want to make clear at the outset, however, that I do *not* endorse the position that a responsible citizen may support (or oppose) a coercive law without *concern* for whether she enjoys a plausible nonreligious rationale for that law, without even *attempting* to articulate some rationale that will be convincing to her compatriots. After all, the claim that a citizen is in no respect morally criticizable for supporting (or opposing) a coercive law solely on religious grounds is entirely consistent with the claim that she has an obligation to do what she can to avoid putting herself in such a condition. And I will argue that a responsible citizen has that obligation: each citizen ought sincerely and conscientiously to attempt to articulate a plausible nonreligious rationale for any coercive law she supports. So, to put my central thesis in summary fashion: a citizen has an obligation sincerely and conscientiously to pursue a plausible nonreligious rationale for her favored coercive laws, but she does not have an obligation to withhold support from a coercive law for which she lacks a plausible nonreligious rationale.

I have no illusions regarding the popularity of this thesis. Defending it puts me at loggerheads with a number of prominent theorists, including John Rawls, Charles Larmore, Bruce Ackerman, Robert Audi, Amy Gutmann, Thomas Nagel, Lawrence Solum, and Gerald Gaus (among many others). Although each of these thinkers differs in significant respects, each adheres to his or her own blend of what I shall call *justificatory liberalism*.[1] And it is in virtue of their adherence to the claims constitutive of justificatory liberalism that Rawls, Larmore, et al., are committed to rejecting my central thesis. As a consequence, I will attempt to establish my central thesis by articulating and evaluating the central arguments put forward in support of the claims constitutive of justificatory liberalism.

Which claims constitute justificatory liberalism? A brief characterization will have to do. Justificatory liberals are, of course, committed to liberal principles and practices. So, for example, they believe that the power of the state over citizens should be severely constrained; that each citizen should enjoy certain familiar rights: freedom of religion, freedom of conscience, freedom of association, the right to own private property, etc.; that laws should be publicly promulgated prior to the state's enforcing those laws; that citizens should be tried in independent courts and accorded "due process" when defending themselves; that each citizen may participate in selecting her political representatives and thus have some modicum of influence over the laws to which she is subject; and so on. Adherence to a suitable menu of such substantive liberal claims is a necessary condition of adherence to justificatory liberalism (hence, the moniker justificatory *liberalism*).

But a commitment to liberal practices and principles is not sufficient for commitment to justificatory liberalism; adherence to such substantive liberal commitments as mentioned above does not distinguish justificatory liberalism from other species of liberalism.[2] The following claim, however, does make such a distinction: that each citizen ought to provide a *public justification* for her favored coercive laws.[3] According to justificatory liberals, each citizen ought to support only those coercive laws that she sincerely takes to be justifiable to each of her rational, reasonable, and adequately informed compatriots—to each member of the public (hence, the moniker *justificatory* liberalism).

As a consequence of her commitment to public justification, the justificatory liberal must provide citizens with guidance as to the sorts of grounds that are appropriate for them to employ as a basis for their favored laws. In order to provide that guidance, the justificatory liberal must articulate a defensible conception of public justification, viz., a conception that specifies both "the reasons that should inform political debate in a [liberal] democracy" and the reasons that should *not* inform political decision making and advocacy in a liberal democracy.[4]

Although there is considerable disagreement among justificatory liberals regarding the sorts of grounds that a citizen may and may not employ as a basis for supporting or rejecting a given coercive law, that disagreement does not extend to grounds of every sort. Justificatory liberals *unanimously* agree that a responsible citizen in a liberal democracy ought not support (or reject) a coercive law on the basis of her religious convictions alone.[5] In addition to unanimous agreement on that point, justificatory liberals typically regard a citizen who supports a favored coercive law for which she lacks a nonreligious rationale as exemplifying in a *paradigmatic* way the sort of behavior they intend to discourage.

The justificatory liberal, then, assents to the claim that a citizen ought not support (or reject) a coercive law on the basis of her religious convictions alone. That claim is a nonnegotiable, constitutive feature of justificatory liberalism—of her commitment to public justification. I believe that a citizen may support (or reject) a coercive law on the basis of her religious convictions alone. That is the crux of the issue between us.

Before I rashly set about showing that my position on this issue is the correct one, it will be helpful to try to focus more clearly on just what that issue is. And in order to do that, I'll mark two distinctions of central importance, viz., between mere and justificatory liberalism and between pursuing public justification and exercising restraint.

Mere versus Justificatory Liberalism

The distinguishing feature of justificatory liberalism is a commitment to a constraint on the sort of *rationale* a citizen should enjoy for her favored coercive laws. Since what distinguishes the justificatory liberal from other species of liberals is a matter of the sort of justification required for proposed laws, not the proposed laws themselves, it is possible to reject justificatory liberalism without thereby rejecting any of the substantive commitments characteristically associated with a liberal polity (e.g., freedom of religion, freedom of association, etc.). It is possible, in short, to adhere to mere liberalism (where a sufficient condition of a citizen's being committed to mere liberalism is that she is committed to characteristic liberal policies) without also being committed to justificatory liberalism.[6] Thus, for example, Elijah can affirm the claim that each citizen ought to enjoy a fundamental and inviolable right to religious freedom; Elijah can enjoy only a religious rationale for that claim, and he can deny that he should refrain from attempting to encode the right to religious freedom into law if he cannot provide a public justification for that right. In that case, Elijah adheres to a fundamental liberal commitment—to religious freedom—but eschews justificatory liberalism. He is, we may assume, a mere, but not a justificatory, liberal.

Two brief notes about this distinction between mere and justificatory liberalism. First, the justificatory liberal differs from the mere liberal with respect to the specific sort of justification that we may reasonably require of citizens: the justificatory liberal requires public justification, and the mere liberal rejects that requirement. But those who reject justificatory liberalism are not thereby committed to denying that they have *any* justification for substantive liberal commitments. To the contrary, mere liberals are free to believe that they have powerful arguments for the characteristic liberal commitments to freedom of conscience, due process, etc. How can one believe that one has powerful arguments for liberal commitments and yet deny that one enjoys a public justification for those commitments? Because of the special sort of constraint associated with *public* justification, Elijah can have what he takes to be, and what in fact are, compelling religious reasons to assent to the claim that, e.g., each citizen has a right to freedom of religion and, at the same time, believe that other reasonable and conscientious citizens can have, from their respective points of view, good reason to reject his rationale for that claim. In that case, Elijah's rationale does not count as a public justification: his rationale, though compelling from *his* own point of view, does not articulate in the appropriate way with his *compatriots'* respective points of view. Having adequate grounds for a given policy is one thing; having grounds that one's compatriots will (or can) take to be adequate is another matter altogether.

Second, the justificatory liberal differs from the mere liberal in affirming a *particular* constraint on the bases on which it is appropriate for a citizen to support her favored coercive laws. But it is not the case that those who reject justificatory liberalism are thereby committed to rejecting *all* constraints on the reasons properly employed as a basis for proposed laws. Thus, for example, although I deny that each citizen must be publicly justified in adhering to her favored coercive laws, I believe that each citizen ought to be *rationally* justified in adhering to each law she supports. So, mere liberals and justificatory liberals differ, not necessarily with respect to *whether* there are constraints on political decision making and advocacy associated with the role of citizen in a liberal democracy, but with respect to *what* those constraints are: the justificatory liberal requires public justification, whereas the mere liberal rejects that constraint.

My central thesis is consistent with mere liberalism and is inconsistent with justificatory liberalism. Consequently, the dispute in this essay has *nothing* to do with the specific policies a responsible citizen ought to support and *everything* to do with the sorts of reasons a citizen may and may not employ as a basis for her favored coercive laws.

Public Justification versus Restraint

As I understand the position, the defining feature of justificatory liberalism is its commitment to public justification. A close analysis of that commitment reveals that the justificatory liberal typically has in mind two distinct claims, viz., (1) that a citizen should pursue public justification for her favored coercive laws and (2) that a citizen should not support any coercive law for which she lacks a public justification. That is, the core appeal to public justification is often an appeal to two distinct theses: the *norm of public justification* and the *doctrine of restraint*. It is essential to my position in this essay that we clearly distinguish between these theses.

In order to distinguish between the norm of public justification and the doctrine of restraint, it will be helpful to consider a passage that fails to observe that distinction. Consider the following argument pressed by Robert Audi:

> A liberal democracy by its very nature resists using coercion, and prefers persuasion, as a means to achieve cooperation. What we are persuaded to do, by being offered reasons for it, we tend to do autonomously and to identify with; what we are compelled to do we tend to resent doing. [1] Thus, when there must be coercion, liberal democracies try to justify it in terms of considerations—such as public safety—that any rational adult citizen will find persuasive and can identify with. [2] This is one reason why religious grounds alone are not properly considered a sufficient basis of coercion even if they happen to be shared by virtually all citizens. If fully rational citizens in possession of the relevant facts cannot be persuaded of the necessity of the coercion—as is common where that coercion is based on an

injunction grounded in someone else's religious scripture or revelation—then from the point of view of liberal democracy, the coercion lacks an adequate basis.[7]

The statement I have marked as [1] is a claim about public justification, about the sorts of claims—"those that any rational adult citizen will find persuasive"—by appeal to which a responsible citizen *tries* to justify her favored policies. Claim [2], by contrast, is a claim about restraint, about a sort of reason—"religious beliefs alone"—by relying on which a citizen should *not* support a given policy. In the passage cited, Audi seems to claim that [1] provides reason to adopt [2]; in my idiolect, he seems to claim that the norm of public justification constitutes good reason for the doctrine of restraint. If I am correct, however, the fact that responsible citizens in liberal democracies should attempt to articulate grounds for their favored policies acceptable to "any rational adult citizen" is not a reason *at all* for the claim that they should not support coercive policies on religious grounds alone. More generally, the claim that a citizen should pursue public justification is not a reason *at all* for the claim that a citizen ought to exercise restraint. Why?

The doctrine of restraint lays down a constraint on the coercive laws a citizen is permitted to support: a citizen is permitted to support a coercive law, *L, only if* L is publicly justified. The "only if" provides the doctrine of restraint with its critical edge: a citizen who lacks public justification for *L should not* support L. The norm of public justification, by contrast, enjoins a citizen to do what she can to ensure that each of her fellow citizens has adequate reason to accept her favored policies; as Audi says, "liberal democracies try to justify [laws on the basis] of considerations . . . that any rational adult citizen will find persuasive."[8] It seems entirely possible that a citizen can do everything that can reasonably be expected of her by way of attempting to discern a public justification, and thus have satisfied her obligation to pursue public justification, without being successful in the attempt. Pursuits can fail; we try but do not invariably succeed in our efforts. That a citizen has an obligation to pursue public justification for a given policy provides her with no guidance at all as to what she should do in that case: that she ought to pursue public justification, pretty obviously, provides her with no guidance in answering the question, "what should I do in the event that, *having pursued public justification*, I nevertheless find myself without the desired justification?" The justificatory liberal claims that she should cease and desist from supporting that policy.[9] That is as it may be, but that claim is distinct from the claim that a citizen ought to pursue public justification, and thus requires additional argumentation.[10]

It might be the case that, although distinct, the norm of public justification *entails* the doctrine of restraint, so that a citizen who has an obligation to adhere to the norm of public justification ought thereby to adhere to the doctrine of restraint. And since, as I will argue later, there is more than adequate reason to accept the norm of public justification, the distinction I am attempting to draw might seem purely academic. But this line of argument is not promising. In fact, I think, this line of argument gets the relations between restraint and public justification exactly backward.

It is plausible to suppose that a citizen who ought to exercise restraint ought also to pursue public justification. If a citizen should do her best not to support a coercive law *L* for which she lacks a public justification, then she *should* seek out public justification for *L*. Why? If a citizen can discharge some obligation only by pursuing a given course of action, then she is likewise obliged to pursue that course of action. If parents can discharge their obligation to satisfy a child's needs only by holding down a job, then their obligation to provide for that child implies an obligation to pursue gainful employment. As a matter of realistic fact, citizens can discharge their obligation to exercise restraint only by actively seeking out public justification for their favored policies.[11] Pursuit of public justification is an unavoidable means to the end of discharging the obligation to exercise restraint. So the obligation to exercise restraint implies an obligation to pursue public justification.

But an obligation to pursue public justification does not imply an obligation to exercise restraint. A citizen can be obliged to pursue public justification for her favored coercive laws without also being committed to withholding support from those laws if public justification is not in the offering. Why is that the case? A citizen can discharge her obligation to pursue public justification without also exercising restraint. The latter is not related as means to the former end in the way that the former is related to the latter. That a citizen ought to pursue public justification does not require that she withhold support from policies for which she lacks public justification any more than a citizen who has an obligation to seek gainful employment thereby incurs an obligation to support her children. She might have the latter obligation, but she does not have it in virtue of having the obligation to seek employment.

So, then, not only are the obligations to pursue public justification and to exercise restraint distinct, and not only does the obligation to exercise restraint imply an obligation to pursue public justification, but, more importantly, an obligation to pursue public justification does not imply an obligation to exercise restraint. Thus, it is false that, as Gerald Gaus claims, "the reverse side of our commitment to justify imposing our norms on others is a commitment to refrain from imposing norms that cannot be justified."[12]

I want to emphasize the importance of the distinction between pursuing public justification and exercising restraint for my argument. Since, as I will argue later, each citizen has an obligation to pursue public justification for her favored policies, and since, as I also will argue later, a responsible citizen does not have an obligation to exercise restraint, it is essential to my argument that the norm of public justification does not entail the doctrine of restraint. I also want to emphasize the importance to the justificatory liberal of *failing* to distinguish between public justification and restraint. As I see the matter, there are powerful arguments in support of the claim that a citizen ought to pursue public justification for her favored laws, but there are no comparably powerful arguments in support of the claim that a citizen ought to exercise restraint. So long as we do not distinguish between pursuing public justification and exercising restraint, a successful argument in support of the former appears to establish the latter. As a consequence, the plausibility of justificatory liberalism, understood as a commitment to both the norm of public justification and the doctrine of restraint, depends upon blurring the distinction between public justification and restraint.

Given the centrality of this distinction to my argument, I formulate two theses that will (hopefully) encourage us to bear that distinction in mind for the duration. The *norm of public justification* is as follows:

> Each citizen morally ought to pursue a public justification for each coercive law that she decides to support or that she advocates that others support.

The *doctrine of restraint* is as follows:

> Each citizen morally ought to refrain from supporting, or advocating that others support, any coercive law for which she lacks a public justification.

With this distinction in mind, we are in a position to further clarify the central issue at stake in this essay. My central thesis is in no way inconsistent with the norm of public justification. Indeed, as I shall show shortly, since each citizen ought to respect her compatriots as persons, each citizen ought to pursue public justification for her favored coercive laws. But my central thesis is inconsistent with the doctrine of restraint. Given that a rationale that depends essentially on religious premises does not constitute a public justification, and given that, according to the doctrine of restraint, a citizen ought not support any coercive law for which she lacks a public justification, it follows that, according to the doctrine of restraint, a citizen ought not support any coercive law solely on the basis of a religious rationale. So the focus of the ensuing discussion will rest squarely on the doctrine of restraint.

WHAT RESPECT REQUIRES

One of the fundamental intuitions animating justificatory liberalism strikes me as compelling: that "respect for persons" imposes important constraints on the reasons a citizen may employ as a basis for her favored coercive laws. More particularly, the justificatory liberal correctly argues that, since each citizen has an obligation to respect her compatriots, she has an obligation to pursue public justification for each of the coercive laws she supports. But that is not all. A citizen's obligation to respect her compatriots imposes a variety of additional constraints on the reasons she properly employs as a basis for her favored coercive laws. The burden of this section is to identify those constraints and to show why each is required by the norm of respect.[13] These constraints combine to form an ideal of conscientious engagement which each citizen should obey in her political deliberations and advocacy.

Respect for Persons?

I begin by explicating the conception of respect implicit in my understanding of respect for persons. I do not have in mind what Stephen Darwall has called *appraisal respect*, that is, the sort of respect that consists of a positive assessment of a person's character or some aspect thereof.[14] The conception of appraisal respect will not do the work I require of it. Why? One of the defining features of appraisal respect is that not every person deserves it. Since appraisal respect is a "positive appraisal of an individual made with regard to those features which are excellences of persons . . . it is not owed to everyone, for it may or may not be merited."[15] This is an obvious point. Since Mother Teresa manifests certain virtues in an exemplary way, we evaluate her character positively, whereas Joseph Stalin, who was beset with a large quantity of despicable character traits, does not command our admiration. But the sort of respect I am interested in must apply to *each* of a citizen's compatriots, whether virtuous or vicious, weak or powerful, wise or foolish, greedy or giving. Why? Because the central component of the ideal of conscientious engagement I intend to articulate in this [essay], viz., the obligation to pursue public justification, extends to each and every one of her compatriots.[16] The "public" for whom a citizen ought to attempt to articulate a public justification includes, I believe, each of her compatriots, not just those she likes, or who share her convictions, or who are morally upright, or who are cooperative. Since an argument from appraisal respect to public justification can support only the conclusion that a citizen ought to address a public justification to those compatriots who merit esteem, and, since the target conclusion is that a citizen ought to try to justify her favored coercive laws to each of her compatriots, a persuasive argument from respect to public justification will not employ the notion of appraisal respect.[17]

If we are to show that a citizen has an obligation to respect each of her compatriots, we are going to have to employ a different conception of respect than that of appraisal respect. A more promising candidate is what Darwall calls *recognition* respect. A citizen has recognition respect for her compatriots as persons just in case she accords due moral weight in her deliberations to the fact that her compatriots are persons. What does it mean for a citizen to accord due moral weight in her deliberations to the fact that her compatriots are persons? At the very least, it is "to regard that fact as itself placing restrictions on what it is [morally] permissible for [her] to do."[18] What is it to allow some fact (such as that one's compatriots are persons) to place restrictions on what it is morally permissible to do? At the very least, it is to recognize that that fact ought to *make a difference* as to the way one acts: to accord due weight to some fact is to allow one's understanding of what one ought to do to be *sensitive* to that fact. Thus, for example, to have recognition respect for the fact that Nathaniel is my son is to recognize that his being my son makes a moral difference—other things being equal, the fact that Nathaniel is my son obliges me to treat him differently from other persons: I ought to feed and clothe him but not, *ceteris paribus*, another person's son. If I deny that I ought to treat Nathaniel differently than any other person, then I fail to accord due weight to the fact that he is my son, and thus lack recognition respect for the fact that he is my son.

In order to respect some fact (such as that one's compatriots are persons) in the recognitional sense, one has to accord *due* weight to that fact. But how does one determine what weight some fact ought to have in one's deliberations? In order to identify the moral constraints imposed on me by the fact that Nathaniel is my son, I must determine which moral truths bear on the fact that Nathaniel is my son. So I must have recourse to moral truths about how parents ought to treat their children, how obligations to persons with whom I have a special relationship articulate with obligations I have toward people in general, etc. In short, having respect for the fact that Nathaniel is my son forbids me simply to ignore that fact in my deliberations and requires that I advert to whatever moral commitments bear on that fact to determine what weight Nathaniel's being my son ought to have regarding how I ought to act.

On the conception of respect I will employ in articulating the ideal of conscientious engagement, a citizen respects her compatriots as persons only if she accords due moral weight to the fact that her compatriots are persons, which, in turn, requires that the fact that a citizen's compatriots are persons makes a moral difference to the way she acts. I will argue, of course, that the fact that a citizen's compatriots are persons ought to make a difference as to the manner in which she supports her favored coercive laws. But we can determine what difference respect for persons should make for a citizen's behavior only if we know what a person is. So, what feature of a citizen's compatriots is picked out by the fact that they are persons?[19]

We can begin to answer that question by contrasting persons with inanimate objects. A crucially important difference between a (properly functioning) person and an inanimate object is that a person cares about what happens to her, whereas an inanimate object does not. *Mattering* suffices to distinguish a person from, say, a rock. A rock is indifferent (not to say unmoved) as to whether it is crushed to pieces, dropped over a cliff, run over by a truck, or used to landscape a lawn. A person, typically, is not. What accounts for this difference between persons and inanimate objects? In normal cases, a person has a set of concerns and commitments that can be either fulfilled or frustrated. Different outcomes count as better or worse (from her perspective), more or less desirable (from her perspective), as a consequence of whether those outcomes consummate or frustrate her cares and concerns. A rock, by contrast, lacks a set of concerns and commitments that can be either frustrated or fulfilled. Because a rock lacks cares and concerns, it cannot rank outcomes as better or worse, and so nothing that happens matters to it.

Mattering matters. The fact that other persons care about the outcomes of our actions makes a moral difference: the fact that other people care about what happens to them, but that rocks do not care about what happens to them, obliges us to treat people differently from rocks.[20] As a consequence, at least one of the facts to which a citizen ought to accord due weight in her deliberations regarding coercive laws is that those laws matter to her compatriots. More particularly, the fact that a citizen's compatriots care about the coercive laws she supports imposes moral constraints on the bases on which she supports her favored laws. The crucial question is, of course, what those constraints are, a topic I will broach in short order.

Mattering does not, however, identify precisely enough the feature of persons to which I will appeal in articulating the ideal of conscientious engagement. After all, although the phenomenon of mattering distinguishes persons from inanimate objects, it does not distinguish persons from mere animals. Animals, like persons, have a set of cares and concerns in virtue of which different outcomes rank as better and worse, and that can be frustrated, and thus that matter to them. However, persons differ from animals in respects that oblige a citizen to treat animals differently from how she treats persons. What is that relevant difference? A crucial part of that answer is: *reflective* mattering.[21] Here is one way (not the only way) to cash out the notion of reflective mattering. In addition to having a set of cares and commitments in virtue of which things matter to her, a person is also capable of reflecting on her cares and commitments—she can form "higher level" desires, beliefs, cares, and commitments regarding her "lower level" desires, beliefs, cares, and commitments. Thus, Elijah can form the higher-level desire that he no longer desires fatty food and can form the higher-level belief that he should believe that fatty foods are unhealthy. In this respect, humans are different from animals: Elijah's dog can desire fatty foods but cannot form desires about that desire or commit itself to changing that desire.[22]

A person's capacity to form higher-level cares and commitments has an important consequence: that capacity enables her to exercise some degree of reflective influence over her lower-level cares and commitments. For example, Elijah can come to believe that his uncritical reliance on the testimony of others is misguided and, as a consequence, form the higher-level commitment to be much more reluctant to believe other people just on their say-so. By contrast, Elijah's dog lacks such a capacity to alter, modify, and correct its (lower-level) commitments and desires.

So a person not only has a perspective on the world in virtue of which things matter to her, but she has some degree of reflective control over that perspective: she can modify, alter, and correct it if appropriate. A responsible citizen ought to pay due regard to that fact about her compatriots. If she does, I will argue, she ought to adhere to at least six distinct constraints on the manner in which she decides to support her favored coercive policies.

Respect and Rational Justification

There is a distinction between rational and public justification. To boil a highly contentious matter down to bare essentials, I stipulate the following: rational belief formation is centrally a matter of the way a citizen forms her beliefs, e.g., whether she pursues evidence in the appropriate manner, is appropriately reflective about the issues at hand, considers a sufficiently wide array of objections, etc. Of course, that a citizen forms her beliefs in the appropriate way does not ensure that she will arrive at any particular conclusions: the beliefs she rationally arrives at are a function of her starting point, the evidence available to her in her cognitive environment, the authorities on which she relies, etc. In short, whether a citizen is rationally justified in assenting to a particular claim depends on two factors: the way she forms her beliefs and the fund of beliefs and experiences on which she relies in evaluating that claim. A citizen is rationally justified in regarding some coercive law as morally appropriate only if she arrives at that conclusion in the appropriate manner (e.g., by discharging the various epistemic obligations that properly govern belief-formation in a given case) and only if, as judged from the perspective provided by her other beliefs and experiences—her *evidential set*—she enjoys adequate reason to believe that that law is morally appropriate.[23] By contrast, a citizen is publicly justified in supporting some coercive law only if she enjoys a rationale for that law that articulates, in the appropriate way, with the points of view of *other* citizens (where the propriety in question can be explicated in various ways). Although I am concerned primarily with the claim that a citizen has an obligation to refrain from supporting any coercive law for which she cannot discern a public justification, the comparable claim regarding rational justification is of considerable importance to my central thesis. So in this section, I will address the topic of the relation between respect and rational justification: I articulate an argument in support of the claims that a citizen who respects her compatriots as persons ought to pursue a high degree of rational justification for any coercive law she supports and ought to withhold her support from any coercive law for which she lacks a high degree of rational justification. Here is that argument.

> (1) If a citizen ought to respect her compatriots as persons, then she ought to accord due weight, not just to the fact that various states of affair matter to her compatriots, but also to what matters to her compatriots.

Suppose that, when deliberating about how to treat Jill, Jack intends to accord due weight to the fact that Jill has a set of cares and concerns in virtue of which his actions matter to her. But suppose that Jack knows almost nothing about the specific content of Jill's cares and concerns: he has no idea what, in particular, matters to her. So, for example, Jack surmises that Jill cares about money, but he does not know whether she wants to accumulate it or give it away. In that case, the fact that Jill cares about money will be deliberatively "inert": since he does not know whether she wants more money or less money, Jack has no idea whether to give her money or take money away from her. Jack's ignorance of the content of Jill's concerns about money renders him incapable of reliably guiding his action by reference to her concerns. Of course, there is nothing special about Jill's concerns about money, and so we may generalize the point: the fact that Jill has cares and concerns in virtue of which various states of affairs matter to her will be deliberatively inert unless Jack takes due notice of the content of those cares and concerns. So, since Jack ought to accord due weight to the fact that Jill has cares and concerns in virtue of which his actions matter to her, and since he can discharge that obligation only if he accords due weight to the content of her cares and concerns, Jack ought to accord due weight to what Jill cares about.

> (2) If a citizen ought to accord due weight to what matters to her compatriots, then she ought to accord due weight to the fact that her compatriots are legitimately averse to being coerced.

Coercion, I stipulate, is a matter of actual punishment or of the threat of punishment; the state coerces a citizen, for example, when it incarcerates her for committing some crime and when it threatens to incarcerate her if she commits some crime. We—adult citizens in (more, rather than less) full possession of our faculties—typically care deeply about coercion; it matters a great deal to us either that we are punished, or that we are threatened with punishment, for our actions. More precisely, we have a profound *aversion* to coercion. We typically resent being forcibly forbidden to act in ways that we wish to act or believe that we ought to act. (This claim is an empirical judgment about what matters to us, and so might be false, but I assume that it will resonate sufficiently with the reader to render argument superfluous.)

Of course, the mere fact that a citizen is deeply averse to some state of affairs imposes no constraints on how we may act: if that citizen's aversion to some course of action is completely unreasonable, then the fact that she is averse to that course of action might make no difference at all regarding the moral propriety of that course of action. But I will assume that our aversion to coercion is typically legitimate: as Robert Adams argues, we are legitimately averse to coercion because coercion tends to violate our agency.[24] I will make short work of this step in the argument, then, by assuming the following: because coercion tends to violate our agency, we regard the aversion that most feel toward being coerced as entirely legitimate and, therefore, as a fact that imposes powerful constraints on the way we may properly treat our compatriots.

> (3) If a citizen ought to accord due weight to the fact that her compatriots are legitimately averse to being coerced, then she ought to recognize that she has a prima facie moral obligation not to coerce her compatriots.

As I noted in my explication of the concept of recognition respect, we can determine what sort of weight we ought to accord some fact only if we have recourse to moral truths that bear on that fact. So, in order to determine what follows from a citizen's obligation to accord due weight to the fact that her compatriots are legitimately averse to being coerced, we must have recourse to whatever moral considerations bear on that moral fact.

With this in mind, there are certain moral platitudes we can expect any morally decent person to obey, each of which expresses a *presumption*: in almost every circumstance, lying is wrong; in the vast majority of cases, we should not torture others; typically, we ought not steal. There is another claim that, although more abstract than the aforementioned, is no less platitudinous, viz., when my actions affect another person and that person legitimately resents my actions, then that person's legitimate aversion counts as a presumption against the moral propriety of that course of action. Alternatively put, when some course of action affects another person and that person legitimately resents that course of action, then I have a *prima facie* obligation not to pursue that course of action.

The last platitude has a direct bearing on (3). A citizen who accepts the platitude that we have a prima facie obligation not to pursue any course of action that affects others in ways that they legitimately and deeply resent, and who wants to accord due weight to the fact that people are legitimately and deeply averse to coercion, will conclude that there is a (moral) presumption against coercion. The fact that citizens are legitimately and deeply averse to some course of action should have the weight of a presumptive moral veto on that course of action. And since, of course, a citizen who supports a coercive law engages in an indirect kind of coercion, she ought to recognize that there is a moral presumption against her support of that law.

> (4) If a citizen ought to recognize that she has a prima facie obligation not to coerce her compatriots, then she ought not coerce them unless coercing them is morally appropriate, all things considered.

The platitude that we ought not lie (or steal or torture) expresses *only* a presumption: there are exceptional circumstances in which we ought to lie (or steal or torture). This is undoubtedly the case with respect to the presumptive moral impropriety of pursuing a course of action to which the affected persons are legitimately and deeply averse. And, of course, the prima facie prohibition on coercion is also defeasible: as Michael Perry has argued, "that various considerations counsel against pursuit of coercive political strategies, and that we should therefore be wary, as a general matter, about pursuing such strategies, is not to say that no such strategy should ever be pursued. That position—radical tolerance—would be extreme and extremely silly."[25] If other considerations outweigh or undermine the presumption against coercion, then it is appropriate, all things considered, for me to pursue a coercive course of action. So, even though respect for other persons requires that I recognize a prima facie obligation not to coerce them, that prima facie obligation can be overridden by countervailing considerations.

> (5) If a citizen should not coerce her compatriots unless coercing them is morally appropriate, all things considered, then she ought to pursue rational justification for the claim that her coercive actions are morally appropriate, all things considered.

Suppose that Elijah is committed to supporting only those laws that are morally appropriate, all things considered. In order for Elijah to make good on that commitment, he must employ the appropriate *means* in pursuing that commitment. One of the things he has to do is determine whether, in a given case, a coercive law really is morally appropriate. It is no mean task to determine whether, in the case of a given law, the presumption against coercion is overridden. We do not, unfortunately, enjoy cognitive capacities that enable us to intuit, just on considering the matter, whether the presumption against coercion is overridden in a given case; such matters are often opaque on first, and even second and third, reflection. Given the way that human beings are put together, we have a realistic prospect of resolving such moral conundrums only if we attempt to resolve them in a rational manner. Hence, Elijah will collect what he takes to be relevant evidence; he will weigh the moral propriety of alternative courses of action; he will rely on those he takes to be trustworthy authorities; he will consult with his compatriots as to the soundness of his arguments for and against alternative courses of action, etc. And at the end of the process, he will decide whether he ought to support a given law on the basis of all the reliable evidence he takes to be relevant to the moral propriety of that law. He will, in short, employ his cognitive capacities in accord with the canons of rationality in order to determine whether the coercive laws he supports are morally appropriate, all things considered.

Consider, by contrast, a citizen who employs a game of chance to determine whether he ought to support some coercive law. Suppose that Brutus realizes that a law that criminalizes polygamy will authorize the state to employ force to hinder citizens from engaging in polygamy: the state will be authorized to incarcerate recalcitrant polygamists, remove children from the care of their polygamous parents, and the like. And suppose that Brutus resolves that question by the "rock, paper, scissors" method. So long as he realizes that his decision-making method does not afford him a reliable basis for discerning moral truths, Brutus' basis for resolving his indecision manifests his *disrespect* for his polygamous compatriots. His decision-making "method"—his failure to obey the canons of rationality—manifests a callous indifference to the fact that his compatriots are deeply averse to being forcibly prohibited from pursuing their polygamous lifestyle, and thus that they may be coerced only if coercion is morally appropriate, and, therefore, that Brutus should pursue rational justification for the claim that coercion is morally appropriate in this case.

> (6) Hence, if a citizen supports a coercive law, she ought to pursue rational justification for the claim that that law is morally appropriate, all things considered.

Claim (6) follows from (1)–(5) and so is in no need of further justification. Claim (6) is, however, in need of further explication. Although I have no brief and illuminating way to explicate the intuition that some claims enjoy "more" or a "higher degree" of rational justification than others, it is clear that that intuition is accurate: my belief that some proof is valid enjoys a higher degree of rational justification, *ceteris paribus*, when based on an exhaustive analysis of the steps involved than it would were it based on a vague recollection about how that proof goes. Although I will not attempt to explicate the notion of degrees of rational justification, (6) should be read as requiring a *high degree* of rational justification, not just a minimal degree of rational justification. Why?

The more important a decision we face, the more concerned we should be to ensure that our decision is correct. That we should be more concerned to decide important decisions correctly than to decide trivial decisions correctly has epistemic implications: we should do what we can to ensure that, when faced with an important decision, we make that decision on the basis of the best grounds available to us. If I am entrusted to invest my child's college funds, I should base my investment decision on my best analysis of the market and not on a whim or guesswork. We do not have similar expectations for the bases on which we make trivial decisions: that I pick a brand of beer for the evening barbecue without accumulating evidence about my guest's preferences generates no cries of condemnation. In short, we should proportion our epistemic expectations for a given decision to the importance of that decision: the more important a decision, the higher our epistemic standards should be for the rationale on the basis of which we make that decision.

The fact that, in many cases, her compatriots are deeply averse to being coerced, rather than, say, that they are mildly irritated by coercion, renders a citizen's decision to coerce her compatriots particularly important. Given that a responsible citizen should attempt to ensure that very important decisions are decided on highly reliable grounds, and given that a decision to coerce another person is extremely important, it follows that a respectful citizen should pursue a high degree of rational justification for any coercive policy she supports.

It is, of course, possible that a citizen who pursues rational justification for the overall moral propriety of a coercive law will fail to acquire a sufficiently powerful justification for that law. What then? She ought to be unwilling to support that law. Why? Given the argument up to this point, I can address this question with brevity. As I indicated above in (4), a citizen who respects her compatriots ought not to coerce them unless the presumption against coercion is overridden. Suppose that Elijah, having pursued rational justification for a given law, L, cannot acquire any—so far as he can tell, there is nothing to be said in favor of the moral propriety of L. In that case, Elijah lacks good reason to believe that L is morally appropriate. If Elijah lacks good reason to believe that L is morally appropriate, then all Elijah has to go on in determining whether L is morally appropriate is *guesswork*. But guesswork is no more reliable a way to discern his moral obligations than is the "rock, paper, scissors" method. Since, then, Elijah is committed to supporting only those coercive laws that are morally appropriate, and since he cannot effectively pursue that commitment if he lacks good reason to believe that a given coercive law is morally appropriate, then Elijah ought to withhold support from any coercive law for which he cannot acquire a sufficiently high degree of rational justification.[26]

So the obligation to support only those coercive laws that are morally appropriate, all things considered, imposes on each citizen two distinct obligations: both to pursue rational justification for the claim that a given coercive law is morally appropriate, all things considered, and to withhold support from any coercive law for which she cannot discern the appropriate rational justification. Note that I do not claim that the obligation to withhold support from a given law absent a sufficiently high degree of rational justification *follows from* the obligation to pursue a high degree of rational justification. Rather, there is independent reason to believe both conclusions: both courses of action are essential means to the end of supporting only those coercive laws that are morally appropriate, all things considered.[27]

Respect and Public Justification

The argument I articulated in support of the claim that a citizen ought to pursue rational justification for her favored coercive laws depends on the premise that respect for her compatriots requires her to accord due weight to what *matters* to her compatriots. However, as I noted in my explication of the concept of respect for persons, a person typically has not only a set of cares and concerns in virtue of which things matter to her, but also the ability to *reflect* upon and *revise* her cares and concerns and thus to *alter* what matters to her. A citizen who respects her compatriots will take into account that fact when deliberating about how she may treat her compatriots. My intention in this section is to identify the constraints that that further fact imposes on the manner in which a responsible citizen supports her favored coercive policies. In particular, I argue (a) that a citizen ought to communicate to her compatriots her reasons for coercing them, and (b) that a citizen ought to attempt to articulate a rationale for the coercive laws she supports that will be convincing to her compatriots.

Regarding (a): A citizen's obligation to respect her compatriots imposes on her an obligation to do her best to *address* her compatriots; that is, a citizen who coerces her compatriots ought to *inform* them about her reasons for coercing them. Why? Suppose that Elijah recognizes that some coercive law *L*—a law that criminalizes polygamous marriages and authorizes the state forcibly to remove children from their polygamous parents' custody—is deeply troubling to some of his compatriots. And suppose that, because he realizes how deeply *L* matters to polygamous parents, Elijah commits himself to pursuing rational justification for *L*. Also stipulate that he has acquired a high degree of rational justification for the claim that *L* is morally appropriate—he concludes, in good conscience, and after adhering to the appropriate canons of rationality, that the Bible portrays polygamy as unnatural and thus as destructive to self and others. By hypothesis, then, Elijah pursues and achieves rational justification for the claim that *L* is morally appropriate; moreover, he does so out of respect for his compatriots as persons. And suppose that Elijah decides to support *L* on that basis. But suppose that Elijah refuses to address his compatriots, not because he is incapable of doing so, nor because he thinks it will do no good, but because he has no desire to address his compatriots.

In that case, Elijah fails to respect his compatriots as persons; he treats his compatriots, not necessarily as objects, but as nonpersons. He does not treat them merely as objects since, by hypothesis, he has been motivated to pursue rational justification for the claim that *L* is morally appropriate by his recognition that his compatriots are deeply averse to being coerced. Clearly, he regards his compatriots very differently than he would if he thought his compatriots had the moral status of a piece of lint, as if his compatriots were mere things to whom his actions do not matter, and thus who may be manipulated at will.

But Elijah treats his compatriots as if they lacked the second component of personhood I mentioned earlier; that is, he treats them as if they were mattering but unreflective beings. Otherwise put, Elijah treats his compatriots as if they were merely animals. Why? On the one hand, consider that, if Elijah is to accord due weight to the fact that his dog, Fido, has cares and concerns in virtue of which things matter to it, he must ensure that he does not frustrate its cares and concerns in a morally inappropriate manner—for example, he ought not beat it without adequate moral justification. On the other hand, if it is morally appropriate for Elijah to punish Fido in some situation, he has no obligation to address Fido—Fido's inability to follow a line of argument, and its consequent indifference to Elijah's providing it with a line of argument, absolves Elijah of any obligation to inform Fido of his reasons for coercing it. With respect both to his dog and his compatriots, Elijah is willing to ensure that his coercive laws are rationally justified but does not communicate his justifying rationale to those on the receiving end of his coercive ways.

But Elijah's compatriots differ from Fido in such a way that they merit differential treatment: Elijah's compatriots have the ability to understand, reflect upon, and evaluate Elijah's reasons for coercing them. And the fact that Elijah's compatriots have that capacity imposes on Elijah the obligation to inform his compatriots of his reasons for coercing them. Why? Why ought Elijah exit his interiority in order to address the other? There are (at least) two reasons.

First, one of the most valuable features of our compatriots is that they are independent centers of action—each inhabits a perspective on the world that is distinct to each person and that provides each with her own reasons to act as she sees fit. If Elijah is to respect his compatriots as persons, then he must accord due weight to the fact that each of his compatriots has the capacity to inhabit a distinctive point of view and, since the fact that each of his compatriots inhabits a distinctive point of view is particularly valuable, he ought to act accordingly. How should we treat those who have a valuable capacity? We encourage them to exercise that capacity and to develop and refine it insofar as doing so is feasible. We refrain from undermining it or destroying it, insofar as that is possible and appropriate. Thus, for example, if Elijah's child has a special knack for portraiture and has the desire to develop her incipient talent, then Elijah ought, *ceteris paribus*, to enable her to develop that capacity. At the very least, Elijah ought not unnecessarily thwart her development.

Exactly the same relation obtains between the way Elijah ought to treat his compatriots and the significant value of his compatriots' capacity to construct a distinctive perspective on the world. He should encourage his compatriots to exercise that capacity and, as a consequence, should resist circumventing their exercise of that capacity. But for Elijah to coerce his fellow citizens without even attempting to communicate to his compatriots his reasons for coercing them—although he could easily do so—is unnecessarily to circumvent their capacity to understand the world from their respective points of view and, thus, is to disrespect them.

Second, Elijah's support for a given coercive law plays a role in bringing distress to his compatriots. Since he plays a role in bringing distress to his compatriots, then he ought to do what he feasibly can to ameliorate that distress. He can ameliorate the distress he visits upon his compatriots by attempting to communicate his reasons for coercing them. How so? Elijah's willingness to address his compatriots manifests his recognition that each has her own distinctive point of view and that it is of sufficient value that he is compelled to explain himself to them. By recognizing that his compatriots have their own points of view and by allowing his recognition of that fact to motivate him to address his compatriots, he communicates to them that he recognizes the very great significance of their ability to form their own opinions regarding his actions—in spite of the fact that he happens to disagree with them in this case—and, thus, mitigates to some degree the distress generated by his coercive ways.[28] So doing what he can to communicate his reasons for coercing his compatriots not only encourages his compatriots to develop capacities that have great value, but conveys the high regard in which he holds his compatriots' agency and so ameliorates the distress he causes by coercing them.

Regarding (b): I take it, then, that a citizen who respects his compatriots as persons will accord due weight to their ability to reflect on his actions from their distinctive points of view and will, as a consequence, attempt to address his compatriots. But what form ought that address take? In particular, does Elijah's obligation to respect his compatriots oblige him to pursue public justification for his favored coercive laws? Should Elijah attempt to inhabit the mindset of his compatriots in order to articulate, not just a rationale for a favored law that *he* finds convincing, but also one which, he hopes, will be convincing to his compatriots? Some deny that he does. Consider William Galston's widely discussed criticism of the argument from respect:

> While the (general) concept of equal respect may be relatively uncontroversial, the (specific) conception surely is not. To treat an individual as person rather than object is to offer him an explanation. Fine; but *what kind* of explanation? Larmore seems to suggest that a properly respectful explanation must appeal to beliefs already held by one's interlocutors. . . . This seems arbitrary and implausible. I would suggest, rather, that we show others respect when we offer them, as explanation, what we take to be our true and best reasons for acting as we do.[29]

If Galston is correct, a citizen who respects her compatriots need not attempt to articulate a public justification for her favored laws (where Galston has in mind a conception of public justification according to which a public justification consists only of premises to which all citizens actually adhere). Rather, a citizen who respects her compatriots offers them her true and best reasons for some policy, where "true" and "best" are a function of that citizen's particular point of view—reasons that she takes to be true given her evidential set and that she takes to be superlative given her evidential set.

Galston's proposal is vulnerable to an initial objection that requires emendation. It is possible that Elijah's true and best reasons are miserably inadequate and that he realizes that they are. It might be the case that Elijah's mother demanded that he support a coercive law L that criminalizes polygamy and that the appeal to his mother's demand is his best reason for supporting L, but that reason does not render him rationally justified in supporting L, much less rationally justified to a sufficiently high degree. If Elijah realizes that his true and best reasons fall short of the required degree of rational justification, and nevertheless insists on supporting L—perhaps he doesn't want to disappoint "Mother"—then he disrespects his compatriots: as I argued earlier, any decision to coerce another person is so important that that decision must pass a fairly high epistemic threshold.

We need to amend Galston's proposal as follows: a citizen discharges her obligation to respect her compatriots by articulating her best reasons for a favored coercive law, where her best reasons constitute a high degree of rational justification for the claim that that law is morally appropriate. I take it that Galston's proposal, as amended, is tantamount to the claim that a citizen who achieves a high degree of rational justification for the claim that a favored coercive law is morally appropriate, and who communicates that rationale to her compatriots, thereby discharges her obligation to respect her compatriots, and, consequently, has no obligation to do anything more by way of providing a rationale for her favored laws.

Even as amended, however, Galston's proposal strikes me as inadequate. Why? If Galston is correct, a citizen can satisfy her obligation to respect her compatriots without being concerned to articulate a rationale for a favored coercive law that her compatriots will find even remotely convincing. That is, a citizen can articulate her best reasons for a favored coercive law, and thus satisfy Galston's proposal, all the while realizing that her best reasons will be utterly unconvincing to her compatriots. But

I believe that a citizen who respects her compatriots should attempt to provide her compatriots with reasons they will find convincing.

Why? If, as we have seen, Elijah has a prima facie obligation to avoid coercing his compatriots by, say, supporting a law L that criminalizes polygamy, and if the reason he has the prima facie obligation to avoid supporting L is that he has a prima facie obligation to avoid treating his compatriots in ways to which they are deeply averse, then he surely has a prima facie obligation to do what he can to ameliorate the distress caused by his supporting L. If Elijah has a prima facie obligation not to *cause* his compatriots distress, then he must also have a prima obligation to *minimize* any distress he causes in cases when that prima facie obligation is overridden.

But there is a simple way for Elijah to ameliorate his compatriots' aversion to L. He can try to convince them that L is morally defensible. Of course, he will not be able to convince his compatriots to support L by appealing to his true and best reasons; by hypothesis, those reasons will not be convincing to his compatriots. He has to search for some other rationale. If he is to succeed in convincing his compatriots that they should support L, Elijah is going to have to articulate some rationale for L that will be plausible to people with very different evidential sets than his—for example, he will have to articulate a rationale for criminalizing polygamy that does not include the premise that the Bible is divinely inspired. He will have to step out of his worldview; he must inhabit the points of view of his compatriots in order to determine what would convince them. And then he should endeavor to articulate a rationale for a ban on polygamy that will be convincing to them. In short, Elijah ought to pursue public justification for L. Since Galston's position is consistent with Elijah's being utterly indifferent to trying to make sense of L from his compatriots' respective points of view, Galston's position is therefore inadequate.

Three brief notes about this conclusion. First, while there appears to be a stable core to the concept of public justification, there is considerable controversy among justificatory liberals as to the appropriate conception of public justification—although a public justification is a rationale that "articulates appropriately" with the distinctive points of view of a diversely committed citizenry, it is unclear just in what respects a prospective public justification must articulate. The argument I have presented in support of the claim that respect requires public justification does not, so far as I can tell, require that we adopt any particular conception of public justification. Nevertheless, the argument I have presented for the claim that a citizen ought to pursue public justification seems to be better satisfied by some conceptions than by others.

In particular, the argument I have articulated seems to articulate best with a "populist" conception of public justification, that is, one according to which a rationale counts as a public justification just in case each member of the public finds that rationale convincing, given her actual epistemic condition. Ideally, I suppose, Elijah would be able to articulate a classically foundationalist argument in support of a ban on polygamy—that is, in the best of all possible worlds, he would be able to identify certain indubitable premises from which it deductively follows that polygamy ought to be criminalized. Since that sort of argument is never available for interesting political claims, Elijah is going to have to lower his expectations: perhaps he ought to pursue a rationale that draws on premises that his compatriots already accept or that draws on premises that comport with his compatriots' actual evidential sets. Or, perhaps, given that that sort of argument is also typically unavailable for interesting political commitments, he will have to lower his expectations even further: he will have to be satisfied with pursuing some rationale constituted by premises that are *in principle accessible* to his compatriots. Alternatively, Elijah can satisfy his obligation to pursue public justification by articulating a rationale that is constituted solely by premises that are amenable of *external criticism*: even if he can't articulate a rationale that will convince his compatriots that a ban on polygamy is appropriate, he can at least give his compatriots the opportunity to "play the spoiler" by presenting them with an argument that they have a realistic chance of convincing him is unsound. The point is that Elijah's obligation to pursue public justification can be satisfied by his pursuit of arguments that articulate with his compatriots' respective points of view in a variety of quite disparate respects. Of course, at some point, Elijah might have to conclude that he cannot articulate an argument that connects in any meaningful way with his compatriots' points of view and thus that his pursuit of public justification has ended in failure.

Second, in order for Elijah to satisfy his obligation to pursue a public justification for his favored coercive laws, he must articulate a rationale that articulates appropriately with the distinctive points of view of *each* of his compatriots. But nothing I have argued supports the conclusion that he must articulate one argument that articulates appropriately with the distinctive points of view of each of his compatriots. Given that Elijah's goal is to ameliorate the distress inevitably generated by the ban on polygamy that he supports, and given that Elijah can ameliorate that distress by presenting different arguments to different citizens, Elijah discharges his obligation to ameliorate his compatriots' distress by attempting to articulate a selection of arguments for the ban on polygamy, such that each citizen finds, within that selection, at least one rationale that articulates in the appropriate way with her distinctive point of view.[30] That said, it seems preferable that Elijah articulates at most a small selection of widely convincing arguments; as a practical matter, that is the only way he'll be able to articulate a rationale that stands a realistic chance of convincing the large number of diversely committed citizens who inhabit a modern liberal democracy.

Third, my argument in support of the claim that a citizen ought to pursue a public justification for her favored coercive laws does not require that she pursue a rationale that *she* finds convincing. After all, her goal is to ameliorate the distress she causes to her compatriots as a consequence of her support for coercive laws they find objectionable, and she can ameliorate her compatriots' distress by articulating a rationale that *they* find convincing. As with the prior point, there is a difference between what the argument for public justification requires and what is preferable: it strikes me as preferable that Elijah finds convincing the argument(s) for polygamy he addresses to his compatriots, since it will then be clear that he is not attempting to *manipulate* his compatriots. So Elijah should strive to articulate a small selection of arguments for his favored coercive laws that both he and his compatriots regard as providing adequate reason to believe that those coercive laws are morally appropriate.

Respect and Mutual Criticism

Up to this point, my analysis of what respect requires focuses too narrowly on what a citizen should do *for* her compatriots. In attempting to determine what respect requires regarding the bases on which a citizen supports *her* favored coercive laws, I have focused almost entirely on her grounds for supporting her favored coercive laws and on the reasons she ought to try to *provide* for her compatriots. But a citizen who fully respects her compatriots ought to be open to movement in the opposite direction. A citizen who respects her compatriots ought to be willing to learn from her compatriots, with a willingness that requires her to subject her political commitments to her compatriots' scrutiny and to change her commitments if shown sufficient reason to so do. A citizen who respects her compatriots as persons attempts, not just to ensure that her own noetic house is in order, and not just to show her compatriots that they should think as she does, but also to submit her political commitments to her compatriots' scrutiny. She doesn't just teach her compatriots the moral truth; she is also willing to learn from them regarding the various possible respects in which her point of view is occluded by self-interest, ideology, prejudice, self-deception, etc.

Why does a citizen's obligation to respect her compatriots require from her a willingness to learn from her compatriots? Any minimally reflective citizen will recognize the possibility that a coercive policy she supports is morally inappropriate. Although she ought to withhold support from any coercive law for which she lacks an appropriately high degree of rational justification, and thus will take herself to enjoy a high degree of rational justification for any coercive law she persists in supporting, she will nevertheless be a fallibilist about her political commitments and, in particular, about her conviction that a given coercive policy is morally appropriate.

In a large-scale polity constituted by millions of diversely committed persons, each citizen will be situated in an environment populated by many persons whose judgments regarding her favored policies merit her admiration. For her to ignore those compatriots, and for her to refuse to make use of their capacity to enlighten her about the moral propriety of her favored policies, is to fail to manifest respect for the fact that her compatriots are persons. Why? Given that her compatriots are deeply averse to coercion, a citizen should do what is feasibly in her power to ensure that the coercive policies she supports are morally appropriate. Given the availability of fellow citizens whose positions on her favored coercive laws merit her admiration, it is certainly within her power to rely on those citizens in order to ferret out coercive laws she mistakenly believes merit her support. She should therefore do so. In short, given that respect requires that a citizen ought to do what is within her power to withhold support from morally inappropriate coercive laws, given that a citizen might be wrong about the moral propriety of her favored laws, and given the availability of compatriots who have the capacity to *enlighten* her about the moral impropriety of her favored coercive laws, a citizen ought to be willing to allow her compatriots to aid her in exposing laws she falsely believes are morally appropriate.

Note that I interpret the scope of this fallibility requirement *narrowly*: as applying to a citizen's political commitments and to the grounds that directly bear on her political commitments. A citizen's obligation to respect her compatriots does *not* commit her to fallibilism regarding all of her convictions, or even to all of those convictions that bear on her political commitments. Some of the former are sufficiently "remote" from her political commitments to obviate the need to subject them to the criticism of her compatriots.[31] To take a silly example; although Descartes' conviction that he exists clearly has *some* bearing on his political commitments, Descartes need not take seriously the possibility that that conviction is false. To take an example closer to the topic at hand, although Elijah's commitment to the claim that God exists is obviously relevant to his political commitments, Elijah need not take seriously the possibility that that conviction is false. It seems to me far too onerous a burden to impose on citizens the expectation that they ought to take seriously the possibility that the convictions that define their respective *moral* identities might be false (whether those commitments are basic moral claims, such as that torture is prima facie morally wrong, or *theological* claims, such as that God exists). What Elijah needs to do is to take seriously the possibility that political commitments he accepts on the basis of his theistic commitments might be false or misguided.

Respect and Human Dignity

The norm of respect for others imposes on a citizen at least one more constraint. It seems clear that the norm of respect imposes at least some minimal *substantive* constraints on the reasons a citizen employs as a basis for her favored laws. In particular, a citizen who respects her compatriots ought not support a coercive law on the basis of any reasons that deny the personhood of her compatriots. To take an obvious example, the Nazi who supports a law that obliges Jewish people to live only in ghettos on the basis of the claim that Jewish people are "bacilli" and thus must be quarantined from the rest of humanity *thereby* disrespects her Jewish compatriots. Indeed, she disrespects her compatriots even if she is a "good Nazi" who fulfills each of the constraints to which I have argued respect requires her to adhere: she pursues and achieves rational justification for the claim that Jewish people are bacilli, she attempts to provide a public justification for the claim that Jewish people are bacilli, and she is willing to submit her commitment to the claim that Jewish people are subhuman to the critical scrutiny of her compatriots. Commenting on William Galston's criticism of the argument from respect, Michael Perry writes:

> It is never to show respect for a human being for one person to offer to another—for example, for a Nazi to offer to a Jew—a reason to the effect that "You are not truly or fully human" even if the Nazi sincerely takes that to be his best reason for acting as he does.[32]

A responsible citizen in a liberal democracy will refuse to support a coercive law on the basis of any claim that denies the personhood and dignity of her compatriots, no matter how conscientiously and rationally she arrives at those claims.

The Ideal of Conscientious Engagement

As I noted at the outset of this section, justificatory liberals are correct that reflection on the norm of respect indicates the constraints we may legitimately expect each citizen to satisfy regarding the manner in which she supports her favored coercive laws. In fact, I believe that a citizen who adheres to the norm of respect will adhere to at least six constraints on the reasons she employs in political decision making and advocacy.

(1) She will pursue a high degree of rational justification for the claim that that policy is morally appropriate.

(2) She will withhold support from a given coercive policy if she cannot acquire a sufficiently high degree of rational justification for the claim that that policy is morally appropriate.

(3) She will attempt to communicate to her compatriots her reasons for coercing them.

(4) She will pursue public justification for her favored coercive policies.

(5) She will listen to her compatriots' evaluation of her reasons for her favored coercive policies with the intention of learning from them about the moral (im)propriety of those policies.

(6) She will not support any policy on the basis of a rationale that denies the dignity of her compatriots.

These six constraints constitute an *ideal of conscientious engagement* that ought, I believe, to govern the way a citizen in a liberal democracy supports her favored coercive laws. As I see the matter, a citizen who satisfies that ideal supports her favored coercive laws in a morally exemplary manner and is, insofar as she satisfies that ideal, free from reasonable moral criticism; correlatively, a citizen who fails to satisfy that ideal is, *ceteris paribus*, the object of reasonable moral criticism.

Adopting a label for the six constraints that, I have argued, follow from the norm of respect for persons gives us a convenient way to refer to those constraints. But I have not adopted that label solely in the interests of convenience. Referring to the six constraints that follow from the norm of respect as an ideal of conscientious engagement indicates that the constraints each citizen should strive to satisfy fall under two categories.

First, each citizen ought to arrive at conclusions of conscience in a *conscientious* manner. A citizen who respects her compatriots will not be satisfied with supporting coercive laws that she merely takes to be morally appropriate. She will do her level best to ensure that the coercive laws she supports *really are* morally appropriate. She can best determine whether a given coercive law is morally appropriate by obeying her epistemic obligations insofar as they bear on her belief that a given coercive law is morally appropriate. Thus, she ought to obey (1): she ought to evaluate her favored political commitments in accord with the canons of rational belief-formation. And she ought to obey (2) as well: if she concludes, after she has discharged the relevant epistemic obligations, that some coercive law she supports lacks moral legitimacy, then she ought to withdraw her support from that law. In short, epistemic conscientiousness in the way a citizen supports her favored coercive laws is essential to her arriving at conclusions of conscience that manifest her respect for her compatriots.

But a citizen who conscientiously arrives at conclusions of conscience by no means satisfies her obligation to respect her compatriots; she must supplement her conscientious pursuit of rational justification with a commitment to *engaging* her compatriots. The sort of engagement we can legitimately expect of a citizen requires, as I have noted above, a movement in two different directions. First, she must articulate her rationale for her favored coercive laws to her compatriots and, in so doing, put her compatriots in a position to object to that rationale—claims (3) and (5). In so doing, she puts her compatriots in a position to change her mind as to the soundness of her rationale for her favored coercive laws. And this is as it should be: a citizen who coerces her compatriots engages in too serious a matter to do so without due regard for her fallibility and thus without the benefit of her compatriots' critical insights. Second, assuming that her compatriots are *unable* to convince her to withdraw her support from her favored coercive laws, and assuming that a citizen is rationally justified in *persisting* in her belief that some coercive law is morally appropriate, she ought to do what is within her power to identify some rationale for her favored coercive laws that is, or stands a reasonable chance of being, convincing to her compatriots. So each citizen must engage her compatriots in the sense that she must exit her own parochial point of view and attempt to inhabit the points of view of her compatriots in order to put herself in a position to provide them with reasons for her favored coercive laws that they regard as compelling—claim (4). In short, deliberative and persuasive engagement with her compatriots regarding the coercive laws a citizen supports is essential to a citizen manifesting the appropriate respect for her compatriots.

A final point about the internal structure of the ideal of conscientious engagement. Referring to the six constraints as a unified ideal indicates that those constraints bear some important relation to one another. Most fundamentally, claim (6) constitutes that unifying role: a responsible citizen will adhere to each of the components of the ideal of conscientious engagement out of respect for the dignity of her compatriots.

The ideal of conscientious engagement, it seems to me, provides citizens with the sort of guidance they need in order to do their part to ameliorate the social disharmony generated by the application of power in a pluralistic society. For it seems clear that if citizens genuinely and sincerely adhere to the normative constraints on political decision making and advocacy that follow from the norm of respect, they considerably ameliorate the resentment and disharmony that naturally results from being subject to coercive laws one rejects. After all, if each citizen adheres to the ideal of conscientious engagement and makes it clear that she does so out of respect for her compatriots as persons, it seems obvious that when citizens are coerced on the basis of laws they reject, they need not feel disrespected and thus will find it easier to acquiesce to those laws.

This last point merits further reflection. Nicholas Rescher has argued that we ought to take due notice of the distinction between *consensus* and *acquiescence*. Consensus regarding some coercive law denotes a collective agreement regarding the propriety of that law. If each citizen subject to a given coercive law affirms the propriety of that law, then there exists consensus regarding that law. "Consensus by its very nature is a condition of intellectual uniformity, a homogeneity of thought and opinion."[33] Acquiescence denotes a collective willingness to endure certain objectionable conditions. Although many citizens subject to some law might reject the claim that that law is morally appropriate, they need not thereby find it so objectionable as to be unwilling to act in accord with it. Acquiescence "is not a matter of *approbation* but rather one of a mutual restraint, which, even when disapproving and disagreeing, is willing (no doubt reluctantly) to 'let things be,' because the alternative—actual conflict or warfare—will lead to a situation that is still worse."[34]

There is no doubt that consensus regarding coercive laws is desirable; no morally responsible citizen *wants* to support coercive laws that her compatriots find deeply objectionable. But consensus on coercive laws is seldom *achievable*: each citizen must be willing to acquiesce to many coercive laws that she regards as morally inappropriate. The fact that each of us must be willing to acquiesce to coercive laws that we regard as morally objectionable renders particularly important the constraints on reasons I have argued that the norm of respect imposes on each citizen in a liberal democracy. For, it seems obvious to me, we will be much more willing to acquiesce to coercive laws we regard as morally objectionable if the imposition of those laws is achieved in such a way as to affirm our value and in full recognition of the burden placed on us. If our concerns are simply discounted, if we are not consulted, if our compatriots impose their will on us in whimsical fashion, if our compatriots do not even attempt to discern some rationale that might convince us that some coercive law is morally appropriate, then we will find it much more difficult to acquiesce than if our compatriots hear our concerns, consider our objections on their merits, make a good faith effort to explain why that coercive law is in fact morally defensible, and, throughout the process, make clear that they are willing to abide by such constraints out of respect for our dignity as persons. So long as our compatriots affirm our dignity as persons and manifest that affirmation by committing themselves to the ideal of conscientious engagement, then they have done all we can reasonably ask of them to ameliorate the tensions and frustrations inevitably generated by our disagreement regarding the coercive laws to which we are subject.

WHAT RESPECT DOES NOT REQUIRE

If the line of thought I pursued in the prior section is convincing, justificatory liberals correctly focus on the norm of respect in order to identify (at least some of) the constraints a responsible citizen obeys in deciding whether to support a given coercive law and in advocating that others support that law. Since a citizen ought to respect her compatriots, she ought to adhere to the ideal of conscientious engagement. But the justificatory liberal wants to show a great deal more than that a citizen ought to adhere to that ideal. She also wants to show that respect for persons requires a citizen to adhere to the doctrine of restraint. And her commitment to the doctrine of restraint is, arguably, her central commitment. So the question I address in this section is as follows: given that a citizen ought to respect her compatriots, does she have an obligation, not only to adhere to the ideal of conscientious engagement, but also to the doctrine of restraint?

The Intuitive Plausibility of the Claim that Respect Requires Restraint

It is not uncommon for a claim, *C*, to grip us, to strike us as having the "ring of truth," independently of our ability explicitly to articulate reasons to accept *C*. Indeed, it is not uncommon for our intuitive conviction that *C* is true to motivate us to pursue a rationale for *C* so that our attempt to substantiate *C* is a *consequence*, not a *cause*, of our conviction that *C* is true. In that case, the arguments we present for *C* reinforce our commitment to *C*, a commitment that might persist even if we realize that any explicitly articulated arguments we might have for *C* are unsound. The intuitive attractiveness of *C* can operate, then, at a deeper and arguably more important level than our ability to construct arguments for *C*.

I believe that the claim that respect requires restraint strikes many justificatory liberals as deeply plausible in that way. The *intuition* that respect requires restraint drives the various attempts to articulate *arguments* in support of that claim and persists even when one or another of those arguments is shown to be fallacious.[35] But I think that the intuitive plausibility of that claim is illusory; more particularly, I think that its initial plausibility is a consequence of the *rhetoric* that often accompanies affirmations of the doctrine of restraint rather than the inherent plausibility of the claim that respect requires restraint. Once we pierce through the rhetoric, I am hopeful that the claim that respect requires restraint will lose its intuitive luster.

The justificatory liberal's characterization of those who refuse to exercise restraint is a crucial component of the rhetorical aspect of the case for restraint. In fact, I believe that the regular and consistent practice among justificatory liberals of exemplifying the refusal to exercise restraint by reference to bogeymen, such as Jerry Falwell or Pat Robertson, plays a crucial role in eliciting the intuitive feeling that the doctrine of restraint is true. For concreteness' sake, let's consider a particular case. Some years ago, Bill McCartney, then head coach of the University of Colorado–Boulder football team and subsequent founder of Promise Keepers, asserted that homosexual lifestyles are an "abomination of almighty God" and, on that basis, urged his fellow Coloradans to support Amendment 2, which would have repealed laws in Denver, Boulder, and Aspen prohibiting work and housing-related discrimination against homosexual citizens and would have forbidden the passage of any comparable law elsewhere in the state.[36] So long as McCartney constitutes a paradigm of the sort of citizen who refuses to exercise restraint, it will be quite natural for us to take a refusal to exercise restraint as a manifestation of disrespect and, correlatively, it will be natural to take advocacy of restraint as a necessary and effective means of discouraging other citizens from emulating McCartney's behavior. But it is not at all clear that it is McCartney's refusal to exercise restraint that merits the judgment that he disrespects his compatriots.

There are various other possibilities. Our sense that McCartney disrespects his compatriots might be evoked by a number of factors that are distinct from, but easily confused with, his refusal to exercise restraint. I list three, although there are no doubt more. First, McCartney's support for Amendment 2 involves an emotionally charged issue—homosexuality—about which many feel deeply and have strongly held convictions. Since it is easy for revulsion at the *substantive injustice* of Amendment 2 to elide into revulsion at McCartney's refusal to exercise restraint regarding Amendment 2, it will be easy for us to attribute our sense that McCartney disrespects his compatriots, not to its proper object—the injustice of Amendment 2—but to his refusal to exercise restraint. The same elision is a danger when the justificatory liberal exemplifies the refusal to exercise restraint by reference to citizens who advocate laws that criminalize abortion, ban or severely restrict the dissemination of pornography, ban or restrict the dissemination of birth control, etc.

Second, McCartney belongs to a group that is very unpopular among academics—evangelicals—about which those familiar with the literature on restraint—academics—are likely to harbor invidious stereotypes. If an evangelical, particularly one who fulminates about abominations of God, constitutes our paradigm of the refusal to exercise restraint, it is no wonder that we have an allergic reaction to the refusal to exercise restraint—it is very easy for a distaste for *those who refuse to exercise restraint* to elide into a distaste for their refusal to exercise restraint. I do not think it an exaggeration to claim that the evangelical or fundamentalist, particularly one who advocates policies that are unpopular among academics, serves as the most common whipping boy for the justificatory liberal. And I surmise that a great deal of the intuitive plausibility of the doctrine of restraint is a consequence of the subterranean association of religious "fanatics," such as McCartney, with the refusal to exercise restraint.

Third, the most likely confusion that elicits our sense that McCartney's refusal to exercise restraint is *ipso facto* disrespectful is an elision from his refusal to exercise restraint to his refusal to adhere to the constraints constitutive of the ideal of conscientious engagement—most particularly, the obligation to pursue public justification. As we have seen in the previous section, a citizen who refuses to pursue public justification exhibits a callous indifference to the fact that her compatriots are deeply averse to coercion. As a consequence, we have legitimate grounds for imputing disrespect to McCartney if, as I assume is the case, he refuses to pursue public justification for his commitment to Amendment 2. But if we fail to distinguish between public justification and restraint, then we will naturally impute to those who refuse to exercise restraint the sort of indifference we legitimately impute to those who refuse to pursue public justification. How would we react if presented with a citizen who assiduously pursues public justification for her favored coercive laws (and who satisfies the various other constraints constitutive of the ideal of conscientious engagement) yet refuses to exercise restraint? So far as I am aware, justificatory liberals don't consider that possibility.

In order to avoid being misled by the rhetorical device of exemplifying the refusal to exercise restraint by reference to citizens who are distasteful in a variety of irrelevant respects, it will be helpful to test the intuitive judgment that respect requires restraint by portraying a citizen who refuses to exercise restraint but who is admirable in other respects—she supports the "right" policies, she doesn't belong to a religious group about whom we are likely to have a variety of invidious stereotypes, she strives to fulfill the ideal of conscientious engagement. If, once we have bracketed extraneous factors, the citizen we portray does not evoke in us the sense that she disrespects her compatriots, then we ought to conclude that the intuitive appeal of the claim that respect requires restraint is due to the rhetoric that accompanies admonitions to exercise restraint, rather than the actual propriety of the doctrine of restraint.

With this is mind, consider the following portrait. Elijah believes that the wide and ever widening disparities in wealth between rich and poor, both within his country and between rich countries and poor countries, is morally repugnant. As a consequence, Elijah advocates quite a radical redistribution of wealth. Although Elijah's condemnation of the disparity between rich and poor is based partly on moral commitments he believes his fellow citizens have good reason to accept from their respective points of view, the radicalism of his proposed redistribution has a peculiarly religious rationale. Elijah has acquainted himself with liberation theology, has come to believe that God has a "preference for the poor," and has concluded that God's preference for the poor obligates us to take quite drastic measures in narrowing the disparities in life opportunities between rich and poor. Stipulate that, given his evidential set, Elijah enjoys a high degree of rational justification for the claim that radical measures to redistribute wealth are morally obligatory.

Given his conviction that existing disparities between rich and poor are morally repugnant, Elijah rationally regards himself as morally obliged to support a whole bevy of proposed laws that will, he believes, effect the desired radical redistribution. But Elijah wants to avoid cramming his favored laws down his compatriots' respective throats. So Elijah pursues public justification for his favored policies out of recognition for the fact that many of his compatriots will find his favored policies misguided or even morally offensive. Unfortunately, even though Elijah is fully committed to public justification and articulates such nonparochial arguments as he can find, he takes his pursuit of public justification to have ended in failure. His radicalism turns out to be uneliminably dependent on his theological commitments—commitments many of his compatriots have no good reason to accept (given their evidential sets). He comes to this conclusion as a consequence of long hours of serious deliberation and vigorous argument with his compatriots, in which it becomes clear that many of them have, given their respective evidential sets, no good reason to accord the needs of the poor—particularly those who live in distant lands—the weight that he believes their needs deserve.

Given the importance of the issues involved, however, Elijah persists in supporting the drastic measures he believes will alleviate the conditions of the poor, even though he cannot convince his compatriots that he is correct. He regards his situation as *tragic*—doubly so. First, the destitute are in desperate need of aid, and his compatriots' refusal to redistribute wealth costs lives, perpetuates suffering, and sustains injustice. Second, he is conscience-bound to impose his religiously grounded norms on citizens who, he realizes, nonculpably lack what they take to be compelling reason to accept those norms.

Does Elijah disrespect his compatriots? I cannot see that he does. He takes no joy in imposing his conviction that God has a preference for the poor on his compatriots; his support for a radical redistribution of wealth is motivated, not by a gleeful imposition of power, and not by indifference to his compatriots' cares and concerns, but by his commitment to act in accord with moral obligations for which he has, by hypothesis, a high degree of rational justification. In short, he acts in accord with the dictates of his conscience, dictates he has arrived at in a fully conscientious manner. Moreover, he has done what is within his power, by virtue of his genuine and sincere pursuit of public justification and his willingness to engage in long hours of sustained dialogue with his compatriots, to avoid simply imposing his religiously grounded moral norms on his compatriots. In short, Elijah does not desire to support his favored policies on the basis of his religious convictions alone; he has done what is within his power to avoid doing that, but he is conscience-bound to act in accord with what he rationally believes to be the dictates of justice.

I see no basis for imputing disrespect to Elijah. Indeed, I see no basis for criticizing Elijah in any respect whatsoever. Our reaction to Elijah, however, in all likelihood differs from our reaction to McCartney. Many will regard McCartney's advocacy of Amendment 2 as obviously disrespectful, and many others will regard it as deeply problematic. What accounts for that difference (assuming that there is one)? Each of the factors I mentioned above might have a role to play. Part of the explanation for our different evaluation of Elijah and McCartney is, perhaps, a consequence of the differential attractiveness of their respective political commitments—at least among academics, it is much more popular to advocate for the poor than to militate against the homosexual. Part of the explanation is, perhaps, that Elijah belongs to a religious group about which we lack invidious stereotypes. Academics are much more likely to warm to the liberation theologian than to the evangelical. Part of the explanation is, perhaps, that McCartney's manner of advocacy is gratuitously inflammatory and thus offensive, whereas Elijah's is cooperative and deliberative. Who can deny that, at the subterranean level at which we make our judgments of intuitive plausibility, those sorts of factors, rather than McCartney's refusal to exercise restraint, generates the intuition that McCartney acts disrespectfully?

I surmise, however, that the most important factor in explaining why McCartney strikes us as disrespectful whereas Elijah does not is that, unlike McCartney, Elijah is attuned to the distinctiveness of his compatriots' points of view and desires to communicate with his compatriots so that they have reason to see that they should support his favored laws. Elijah *pursues* public justification for his favored policies and *thereby* exhibits respect for his compatriots. In this, he is crucially different from citizens such as McCartney who are not interested in public justification at all. Such citizens, I think, disrespect their compatriots. But not Elijah.

The contrast I have drawn between McCartney and Elijah should attune us to the critical distinction between pursuing public justification and exercising restraint. So long as we fail to abide by that distinction, we will be inclined to assimilate Elijah into the ranks of those who, quite obviously, are not interested in communicating at all with their compatriots. Since Elijah refuses to exercise restraint, he *must* refuse to pursue public justification, and since Elijah refuses to pursue public justification, he *ipso facto* disrespects his compatriots. But when we make the required distinction, it should be clear that we lack adequate reason to impute disrespect to those who, like Elijah, refuse to exercise restraint but pursue public justification. Not only, then, does distinguishing between public justification and restraint enable us to arrive at a nuanced evaluation of Elijah's manner of political deliberation and advocacy, but it gives us insight into why we might have been inclined to accuse him of disrespect in the first place.

Arguments for Restraint

Once we remove the rhetorical clutter that accompanies many discussions of the doctrine of restraint, I believe that it is quite implausible to impute disrespect to a citizen just on account of her unwillingness to exercise restraint. Such judgments of plausibility are, of course, irreducibly subjective and person-relative; what we take to have the "ring of truth" varies as a consequence of our interests, background commitments, individual experience, etc. So it is entirely possible that I have accomplished little by way of injecting doubt into the claim that respect requires restraint; perhaps that claim will persist in appearing intuitively obvious to the reader. That is as it may be. Given this clash between intuitions, it seems that the only way to resolve the issue is to determine whether there are any *arguments* that settle the matter. If the justificatory liberal can construct some argument in support of the claim that respect requires restraint, then it does not matter very much that that claim seems highly implausible— plenty of initially implausible claims turn out to be true. And it is to an analysis and critique of one such argument I now turn. (There are many other extant arguments that purport to vindicate the doctrine of restraint, but I'll save an analysis of such arguments for another occasion.)

Robert Audi has presented an argument that it is plausible to construe as moving from the claim that a citizen ought to respect her compatriots to the claim that a citizen ought to exercise restraint. That argument begins with the claim that a citizen ought to respect her compatriots as her equal, moves to the claim that she ought to be willing to reverse roles with them, and concludes with the claim that she ought not support any coercive policy on the basis of her religious convictions alone.

According to Audi, each citizen ought to adhere to what he calls *the principle of secular rationale*: "A citizen has a prima facie obligation not to advocate or support any law or public policy that restricts human conduct, unless [she] has, and is willing to offer, adequate secular reason for this advocacy or support (say for [her] vote)."[37] Pretty obviously, the principle of secular rationale is a very specific formulation of the doctrine of restraint. It is a version of the doctrine of restraint that applies specifically to religious convictions.

What argument does Audi present in support of the claim that a citizen ought to adhere to the principle of secular rationale? Here is an argument inspired by some of the things Audi says in his discussion of the principle of secular rationale.

> (1) Jack cannot respect Jill and also adhere to a policy of deciding which coercive laws merit his support if he would resent Jill's adhering to a relevantly similar policy in deciding which policies merit her support.
>
> (2) Jack's supporting coercive laws whose justification relies solely on a religious rationale would be to adhere to a policy he would resent were Jill to adhere to a relevantly similar policy.
>
> (3) Therefore, Jack ought not support those laws whose justification relies solely on a religious rationale.

Regarding (1): One of a citizen's fundamental moral obligations is to treat her compatriots as persons who enjoy a dignity and value that is *equal to* her dignity and value. A necessary condition of a citizen's treating other persons as equally valuable is that she is willing to *reverse roles* with them. Because Jack and Jill have equal value as persons, it is inappropriate for Jack to pursue practices he is unwilling to allow Jill to pursue as well. This constraint ought to govern, not just the coercive laws Jack supports, but also Jack's reasons for supporting his favored coercive laws. Most importantly, for our purposes, the role-reversal constraint applies to Jack's practice of supporting his favored coercive policies on the basis of his religious convictions alone. Thus, Audi writes: "If the only reasons that move me are religious, and if I would not want to be coerced on the basis of religious reasons playing a like role in someone with a conflicting religious perspective, I would want to abstain from coercion."[38]

Regarding (2): Audi is confident that religious citizens will be unwilling to generalize the policy of supporting coercive laws solely on the basis of their religious convictions. If Audi is correct, nearly everyone regards as reprehensible the prospect of being coerced solely on religious grounds:

> There is something repugnant about being convicted (or having one's liberty restricted) on the basis of someone else's religious attitudes or views, even if they are only a significant part and not

the whole of the ground of the . . . coercer's . . . case; or at least this is a feeling that tends to be shared both by those who are religious—especially if they are in a religious minority in their society—and those who simply respect liberty, whether or not they are religious.[39]

If Audi is correct about the intuitive repugnance most citizens feel toward the prospect of being coerced on another citizen's religious grounds, it would seem that such citizens would be unwilling to accept a generalized policy permitting *any* citizen to support her favored coercive laws solely on religious grounds. In short, rejection of Audi's principle of secular rationale does not pass the role-reversal test. (And insofar as unwillingness to obey only those principles that pass a role-reversal test is indicative of a citizen's having respect for her compatriots as her equals, then a citizen who rejects the principle of secular rationale seems to disrespect her compatriots.)

Audi's argument is most convincing, it seems to me, when formulated concretely. Audi confronts the religious adherent who considers rejecting his principle of secular rationale with a specific law that depends solely on religious grounds for its justification and asks whether she would be willing to allow others to violate his principle of secular rationale in that case. Addressing a hypothetical citizen who decides solely on religious grounds to support a law that restricts meat consumption, Audi writes:

> Suppose . . . that much money must be spent in enforcement and that many jobs are lost through the changes in the food sector of the economy, so that human conduct is significantly restricted, even if meat consumption remains legal. Then one might ask the religious voters in question whether they would accept comparable restrictions of their conduct, as well as similar job losses or mandatory shifts, on the basis of coercive legislation protecting the dandelion as a sacred species or prohibiting miniskirts and brief bathing suits as irreverent.[40]

According to Audi, any citizen who decides to support, on the basis of her religious convictions alone, a coercive law that restricts the consumption of animal meat must be willing for her compatriots to adhere to a relevantly similar policy: she must be willing to allow her compatriots to support, solely on the basis of *their* (religious) conviction that the dandelion is sacred, a coercive law that forbids her to engage in the wanton destruction of dandelions and thus to mow her lawn. If, of course, she is unwilling for others to do so, then she ought to be unwilling to support any coercive law on the basis of *her* religious convictions alone.

What should we make of Audi's case for (his version of) the doctrine of restraint? Audi's argument hinges on the bet that his audience will balk at the prospect of being coerced on the basis of religious convictions they reject. Thus, for example, Audi is confident that the members of his audience will resent being forbidden to mow their respective lawns solely on the ground that dandelions are sacred. I think that Audi's confidence is well justified. Or perhaps I should speak only for myself: I would resent such a law. But what follows from that? In order to answer that question, it is essential to specify exactly *why* I would resent being subject to a law that forbids me to kill dandelions. Only if we can identify my reasons for that reaction is it possible to determine the respects in which I am and the respects in which I am not willing to reverse roles with my compatriots. (It is to reasons for reactions, rather than reactions, that the role-reversal test applies.)

As I introspect on Audi's scenario, I find that the following is the case: I find it hard to believe that a citizen who genuinely and sincerely pursues *rational* justification for the claim that dandelions are sacred would conclude that dandelions are in fact sacred and, furthermore, would be willing to coerce me on that basis. The claim that dandelions are sacred, and thus that killing them is morally objectionable, is so absurd that it is hard to imagine that a rational citizen could, in good conscience, support a coercive law on its basis. But as I argued in the previous section, I have a legitimate expectation that my compatriots will withhold their support from any coercive law that lacks, from the perspective of their respective evidential sets, the requisite rational justification. If my compatriots persist in supporting a coercive law that lacks the requisite rational justification, then I may legitimately resent their support for that law.

It seems to me that we can explain my resentment at being subject to a law that forbids me to kill dandelions, not by reference to the fact that my compatriots have only a religious reason for that law, but by reference to the fact that (I naturally assume that) they lack the requisite rational justification for that law. Since it is unlikely that my compatriots are rationally justified in believing that dandelions are sacred, it is plausible to suppose that my resentment is a consequence of the fact that I reasonably believe that my compatriots either have failed to pursue rational justification or that they are willing to coerce me without having achieved the requisite rational justification. Consequently, the resentment I feel *need not* be attributable to my compatriots' willingness to support that law on the basis of their religious beliefs alone.

Of course, I do not deny that it is possible for my compatriots to be rationally justified in believing that dandelions are sacred. So it is easy to reformulate Audi's scenario. Without taking the time to fill out all of the details, assume that a majority of citizens have genuinely and sincerely pursued rational justification for the claim that dandelions are sacred; assume further that they are willing to withhold their support from the law that prohibits massacring dandelions if they lack adequate reason to support that law; and suppose that they take themselves to have acquired that requisite rational justification. Suppose finally that each member of the majority has satisfied each of the other constraints that constitute the ideal of conscientious engagement.

How do I react to Audi's scenario thus reconstructed? Would I resent being coerced by a law that forbids me to kill dandelions if my compatriots are rationally justified in believing that the dandelion is sacred, and having attempted publicly to justify that law, are willing to accommodate me, taking seriously my objections to that law, etc.? It is hard to tell, since the possible world we are now discussing is not particularly close to the actual one (and as R. M. Hare has persuasively argued, our "intuitive" reactions and emotional responses are designed to provide accurate moral guidance in the actual world and nearby possible worlds and might very well be highly unreliable moral guides in distant possible worlds).[41] Nevertheless, it seems worthwhile to make the effort. So here is my best estimate of the situation.

Although it is less clear to me that I would resent being subject to a law that forbids me to kill dandelions in that case, it seems, on introspection, that I nevertheless would experience some degree of resentment. At the very least, I would experience frustration and anger at being subject to that law. I very much want to mow my lawn and would do so were I not discouraged from doing so by the state. The fact that I am forcibly inhibited from achieving my aims is a natural source of frustration, anger, and perhaps even resentment.[42]

Does this provide the advocate of restraint with the opening necessary to drive home the essential point? I do not believe that it does. The frustration, anger, and resentment I would feel if subject to a law that forbids me to kill dandelions seems to me a consequence, not of the fact that my compatriots support that law on the basis of their religious convictions alone but of the *content* of that law. It is the law itself that frustrates and infuriates me, not the religious content of my compatriots' reasons for supporting that law. The imposition of that law inhibits me from attaining ends I very much want to pursue; as a consequence, it is entirely natural and appropriate for me to feel frustration and anger at being so constrained. But I do not see that my reaction has anything in particular to do with my compatriots' reasons for supporting that law.

Whatever their reasons for supporting that law, then, so long as I persist in my desire to mow my lawn and thus to kill dandelions, that law would frustrate my desires and thus lead to the anger and frustration I feel at being subject to that law.

We can see that the religious basis of a law forbidding the killing of dandelions has nothing do with the frustration I feel at being subject to that law by replacing that religious basis with a secular basis. Suppose that an environmentalist group has successfully lobbied to have a law enacted that forbids me to mow my lawn on the basis that dandelions are an endangered species. Suppose, however, that I reject that rationale—I do not believe that dandelions are endangered. (At the very least, they seem to be thriving in my corner of reality.) Keeping my desire to mow my lawn constant, I see no reason to believe that I would feel any less resentment or frustration at being subject to that law given that it has an entirely secular basis than I would feel were it to enjoy an entirely religious basis. So long as the content of the law is sufficiently objectionable, my allergic reaction to that law persists whatever its rationale. Thus, the cause of my resentment is not that the law has only a religious rationale. But in that case, I will have no problem reversing roles with those who support their favored coercive laws solely on religious grounds.

The strength of the argument under discussion is that it provides a simple and straightforward way to get at the heart of the issue of the proper role of religious convictions in political decision making and advocacy: are those who reject the doctrine of restraint, as I do, prepared to apply their refusal to exercise restraint impartially, such that they are willing to permit each citizen to decide whether a coercive law merits her support on the basis of her religious convictions alone? The weakness of this version of the argument is that it depends entirely on what the audience is willing to allow others to do.[43] And I find that I have no hesitation allowing others to decide whether a coercive law merits their support on the basis of their religious convictions alone. More precisely, I have no hesitation allowing my compatriots to decide whether a coercive law merits their support on the basis of their religious convictions alone, *so long as* each of my fellow citizens adheres to the constraints constitutive

of the ideal of conscientious engagement. Indeed, I cannot imagine discouraging others from supporting whatever coercive laws that they take
in good conscience to be morally obligatory, whatever the content of
their reasons (with one important exception: so long as those reasons do
not deny my dignity as a person).

CONCLUDING COMMENTS ON THE ARGUMENT
FROM RESPECT

I mentioned at the outset that the distinction between pursuing public
justification and exercising restraint is critical to my argument. I trust
that the subsequent discussion has borne that judgment out. The justificatory liberal's valorization of public justification is most plausible, even
platitudinous, when she advocates pursuing public justification: who
really disagrees, for example, with the claim that it is worth striving for
a "reasonable consensus and trust among those who might otherwise be
. . . deeply opposed"[?][44] Who would object to trying to resolve political
disagreements by focusing "on values such as peace and freedom that
can be shared by reasonable people"[?][45] If such constraints on political
decision making and advocacy exhausted the justificatory liberal's creed,
then there would be precious little with which to disagree.[46] All would
be sweetness and light. But, of course, the justificatory liberal wants to
press for much more than such platitudes; she also wants to make a
claim about what a citizen should do when she has made the necessary
effort to support some favored coercive law on the basis of appeals to
"peace and freedom" but that effort fails. If she enjoys only a religious
rationale for that coercive law, according to the justificatory liberal, then
she should withhold her support from that coercive law. It is that latter
claim that is highly contentious, that many religious citizens find quite
burdensome, and for which they will require some compelling rationale.
And as I see the matter, the justificatory liberal has not provided that
compelling rationale. Although each citizen ought to adhere to the various constraints constitutive of the ideal of conscientious agreement, and
in particular the norm of public justification, I know of no compelling
argument in support of the claim that she ought also adhere to the doctrine of restraint. Indeed, it seems to me that imposing the doctrine of
restraint on religious citizens is itself a violation of the norm of respect,
given that it constitutes an imposition that would require of most citizens
a willingness to violate their most fundamental commitments. But that
stronger claim is, as with so many others, a topic for another day.

Chapter 9

The Principles

Paul J. Weithman

The principles I shall defend are:

(5.1) Citizens of a liberal democracy may base their votes on reasons drawn from their comprehensive moral views, including their religious views, without having other reasons which are sufficient for their vote—provided they sincerely believe that their government would be justified in adopting the measures they vote for.

(5.2) Citizens of a liberal democracy may offer arguments in public political debate that depend upon reasons drawn from their comprehensive moral views, including their religious views, without making them good by appeal to other arguments—provided they believe that their government would be justified in adopting the measures they favor and are prepared to indicate what they think would justify the adoption of the measures.

. . . These principles put me at odds with what I call the "standard approach" to questions about religion and political decision making.

Unlike proponents of the standard approach, I distinguish voting from advocacy in public political debate and impose a higher standard on the latter than the former. According to (5.1) and (5.2), someone offering a religious political argument in public must be prepared to indicate what she thinks would justify enactment of the measure she favors. Someone voting for a measure must believe that enacting it would be justified, but she need not be prepared to indicate what the justification is. More important, these principles allow citizens to vote on the basis of their religious views and to offer religious political arguments in public, without having or being prepared to offer accessible reasons. The person who argues in public for a measure must be prepared to say what she thinks would justify the government in enacting it, but the justification she is prepared to offer may depend upon claims, including religious claims, which proponents of the standard approach would deem inaccessible.

The arguments of this [essay] constitute only a partial defense of the principles. For reasons I shall mention in the conclusion of this [essay], completing the defense requires confronting the standard approach in its most nuanced and plausible forms. . . . Before I defend (5.1) and (5.2), I want to address a number of questions these principles raise.

SOME PRELIMINARY CLARIFICATIONS

(5.1) says that citizens may base their votes on their comprehensive moral views, including their religious views. I shall say more about comprehensive moral views in a moment. For now, note that in this context, "views" are systematically ordered sets of propositions. A moral view is a systematically ordered set of propositions that concern right or good conduct and, usually, that concern what makes conduct right or good. Religious moral views are moral views that use religious propositions to support their ethical or metaethical claims. . . . I am operating with the concept of religion implicit in the educated common sense of most Americans. Thus religious propositions include propositions that presuppose the existence of God, propositions about the sacredness of texts, about the holiness of persons and ways of life, about the worship of God and about other devotional practices. They also include certain propositions about believing and acting, including the beliefs that some persons are authoritative interpreters of sacred texts, that some persons are authorities about dogma, worship, or the way to holiness, and the proposition that the sacredness of some text provides grounds for accepting its authority.

(5.2) says that citizens may make arguments that depend upon reasons drawn from their religious views. But what is "dependence"? I am concerned with what people may do intentionally or what they may reasonably be taken to have done intentionally, not what they may do accidentally or unwittingly. The dependence I have in mind is therefore dependence as seen from the point of view of the person offering the argument or from what others reasonably suppose that point of view to be. Thus the principle allows citizens to offer arguments that seem sound to them only because they accept a religious conviction or that others reasonably believe seem sound to them only because they accept a religious conviction. It also allows them to offer arguments that seem valid to them only because they accept such a belief.

Consider an example. Suppose someone argues that the genetic uniqueness of the fetus implies its personality and that personality implies worthiness of legal protection. Suppose further that someone in his audience takes these inferences to be self-evidently valid in this sense: he thinks the inferences are valid and that any propositions adduced to support their validity would be no better warranted than the inferences themselves. For the sake of illustration, we may even suppose that the auditor is right. Still, if the person who offered the argument thinks it would be a mistake to accept the inferences unless one also accepts the supporting pronouncements of someone she regards as reliable because religiously authoritative, then she has offered an argument that depends upon her religious view. If she seems to think this, then she may reasonably be taken to have offered an argument that depends upon her religious view.

The term *comprehensive view* is, of course, adapted from John Rawls. Rawls speaks of "comprehensive doctrine" and refers to some moral conceptions as "comprehensive." He distinguishes moral conceptions that are "fully comprehensive" from those that are "partially" so. Thus Rawls says that a moral conception

> is comprehensive when it includes conceptions of what is of value in human life, and ideals of personal character, as well as ideals of friendship and of familial and associational relationships, and much else that is to inform our conduct, and in the limit to our life as a whole. A conception is fully articulated if it covers all recognized values and virtues within one rather precisely articulated system; whereas a conception is only partially comprehensive

> when it comprises a number of, but by no means all, nonpolitical values and virtues and is rather loosely articulated.[1]

The phrase "comprehensive conception" as Rawls uses it is therefore very inclusive. Indeed it is so inclusive that it is most usefully thought of as a contrast term. The contrast is with what Rawls calls "political conceptions." These . . . are moral conceptions that are developed from ideas implicit in political culture, that apply primarily to what Rawls calls "the basic structure of society"[2] and only derivatively to other subjects and that can be presented independent of comprehensive conceptions. I use the term *moral view* to denote what Rawls denotes by the phrase "moral conception." When I speak of "comprehensive moral views," I am referring to comprehensive moral conceptions in the Rawlsian sense, including both fully and partially comprehensive conceptions. Like Rawls, I use the term *comprehensive moral view* as a contrast term. The relevant contrast is with political conceptions as he understands them.

(5.1) says that citizens who vote for a measure must believe government would be justified in adopting it; (5.2) says that citizens who advocate a measure in public political debate must be ready to indicate what they think would justify government's adoption of it. What is it to believe that government would be justified in adopting a measure? Are there any constraints on the sort of justification citizens must believe is available?

According to the standard approach, government must justify laws and policies to those affected by them by offering reasons for their enactment. Proponents of this approach then isolate the kinds of reasons capable of justifying government action. Reasons of this kind are "justifying reasons." They then argue that citizens must have and be prepared to offer one another justifying reasons for the measures they favor, at least when their most important interests are at stake. If my view were a version of the standard approach, then (5.1) would require that citizens who vote for a measure believe there are justifying reasons of sufficient strength for it. (5.2) would require that they be ready to indicate what those reasons are. But (5.1) and (5.2) do not constitute a version of the standard approach. My argument against that approach does not depend upon denying either that it is possible to isolate a set of justifying reasons, or that it is possible to specify properties justifying reasons must have, though as I shall show, I have doubts about the property of accessibility. What I do deny is that citizens are obligated to have or be ready to offer one another justifying reasons.

Government is justified in adopting some measure only if there are good reasons for government to adopt it given its legitimate ends and the moral constraints within which it must operate. When someone believes government would be justified in adopting a measure, what she believes is that there are good reasons for government to adopt it given what she takes its legitimate ends to be and the moral constraints within which she thinks it must operate. (5.1) and (5.2) refer to liberal democratic governments. If these principles are to express role-specific duties of democratic citizenship, the ends citizens impute to government and the constraints under which they believe government must operate must be aims of and constraints on liberal democratic government.

What are those ends and constraints? . . . Democratic states are committed to treating their citizens as equals. More specifically, democracies regard all their citizens as equally possessed of fundamental interests that government must respect when it pursues its legitimate aims. Furthermore, the aim of liberal democratic government is to serve the common interest rather than the interest of any one class or any one section of the economy. In order for (5.1) and (5.2) to express obligations of liberal democratic citizenship, citizens asking themselves whether their government would be justified in adopting the measure they favor must understand their government to satisfy these conditions. That is, they must impute to government what might be called a "common interest view of its aims." They must ask whether a government whose purpose is the promotion of the common good would have good reason to adopt the measure in question. Moreover, they must ask themselves whether adoption or enforcement of the measure would entail violating the requirement that government equally respect the essential interests of all its citizens. A plausible common interest view for liberal democratic government will require respect for the rights and liberties traditionally associated with liberal democracy. Perhaps a common interest view of governmental aims is best spelled out using the notions of participation and full participation . . . but about this there will be reasonable disagreement. Thus while citizens may agree about some of the ends government must or may pursue to promote the common good, about some fundamental interests, constraints on government power, and justifying reasons for government action, they may disagree about others. They may also disagree about how various considerations are to be weighted and balanced when a decision must be made. As I shall argue, these disagreements are reasonable in some circumstances. It is because they are reasonable in those circumstances that (5.1) and (5.2) allow citizens to rely on a wide range of reasons, including religious reasons.

Why do the principles require that citizens believe *their* government, rather than liberal democratic governments more generally, would be justified in adopting the measures they favor? I assume that different constitutional arrangements can be appropriate for different liberal democracies because of their histories, traditions, and cultures, that citizens are generally at least somewhat aware of major differences between their own political systems and others, and that this awareness generally leads them to recognize that they may have to make different arguments for some political arrangements than citizens of a different democracy might have to make.

These legitimate differences in constitutional arrangements are not confined to differences in governmental structure, such as the differences between the presidential and Westminster systems. They extend to differences that may affect basic liberties. In Germany, for example, some liberties are entrenched, and while freedom of expression is permitted, it is a crime to deny the Holocaust. The United Kingdom has an established church. The United States, by contrast, has no entrenchment and no established church. Because of these differences, there are differences in what measures liberal democratic governments can justifiably enact. The British government, I am supposing, may justifiably impose taxes to support a church while the American government may not. Suppose the principles allowed citizens to advocate measures provided they sincerely believed liberal democratic government—rather than their liberal democratic government—would be justified in enacting them and were prepared to indicate why. Then someone could argue that the United States government should establish a church because he sincerely believes and is prepared to indicate why the British government is justified in establishing one. This seems unacceptable. An American who wants to argue for an established church in the United States must be prepared to make the case that his government would be justified in establishing one. That case would be a more difficult one to make in the United States because tradition has created a widely held and strong expectation that there shall be no establishment.

Finally, (5.2) is clearly more demanding than (5.1). While (5.1) requires citizens who vote for a measure to believe that government is justified in adopting it, it does not require that they be able to say what the justification is. (5.2), by contrast, requires that citizens who advocate a measure in public political debate be able to produce a justification. They must be able to indicate what would justify government's adoption of the measure they favor. Why impose a more stringent requirement on advocacy than on voting?

The answer is that there is a difference in the way reasons for voting and reasons adduced in advocacy are typically elicited and received. Advocacy is and is generally taken to be an exercise in persuasion in which someone volunteers considerations in support of her position. When she offers those considerations, the people she is addressing can reasonably take those considerations as reasons addressed to them. The person advocating the outcome, they can suppose, offers those considerations because she thinks others should regard those considerations as good reasons *for them* to support the outcome. By contrast, voting in large liberal democracies is usually secret. We do not usually know how others vote or why. When someone does give his reasons for voting, the reasons he gives are offered and received as reasons that were supposed to be good reasons for *him*.

To see the significance of these differences for present purposes, consider some examples.

Suppose that I read an editorial arguing for a legal ban on physician-assisted suicide. I find the editorial cogently argued. It persuades me both that legalizing PAS would have dire implications for women and minorities and that these concerns outweigh the liberty interests at stake. I decide to vote against a referendum legalizing PAS on the basis of the editorial's arguments. By election day, I know that I want to vote against the referendum even though I have forgotten why I once believed the liberty interests at stake are outweighed by other considerations. But I also know that my memory is reliable and that if I seem to remember having once been persuaded of things on grounds I then found compelling, I in fact was once persuaded of those things on grounds that I then found compelling. Moreover I believe that I have not since found grounds to believe that the reasoning I once found compelling was faulty. In this case, it seems to me, my vote against the referendum was responsible even though I do not suppose that my memory and my belief in its reliability provide others with good reasons to vote as I did.

Now suppose I am asked to vote on a ballot referendum imposing a new tax on industries that dump effluents into the water supply. The polluting industries insist that the taxes will drive them to a state with less strict environmental regulation and that the cost to the local economy of their departure will outweigh the value of the environmental gains realized when the polluters cease production. Proponents of the tax argue otherwise. They maintain that relocation costs are too high for the industries to bear and that their profits are such that they can easily afford the tax. The economic calculations may be too complex for me to perform and I may not have ready access to the requisite information. The proponents of the tax are, however, experts in environmental and industrial economics whom I trust because of their impartial position. I can, it seems to me, take their word over that of the industrial representatives and responsibly vote for the referendum.

The point of these examples is to illustrate how memory and testimony can function when someone decides how to vote. They can ground a voter's beliefs that there are good reasons for the measure the voter favors and that government would be justified in adopting that measure. But now consider someone who advocates a ban on PAS at hearings that are supposed to air views on the referendum and help citizens make an informed decision. She does so on the grounds that she once read an open letter on the subject that she found persuasive, but she cannot recall any of the reasoning. Her memory may furnish a good reason *for her* to think that the ban is a good idea and that government would be justified in enforcing it. She cannot assume that it provides *her audience* good reason to believe the same things, since she cannot assume they know the reliability of her memory. She must be ready to make good her appeal to her memory by indicating what she takes to be the reasons for the ban and for the claim that government would be justified in enforcing it. Why?

As I noted earlier, advocacy is an exercise in persuasion. The pragmatics of this exercise create certain expectations. Those who are addressed by someone trying to persuade them expect to be offered considerations that the speaker takes to be good reasons for them, reasons they should find rationally compelling. They may expect even more. They may, for example, also expect to be offered reasons that the advocate takes to be good ones for her—reasons she would find rationally compelling, reasons she recognizes as good ones, or reasons that in fact move her. I leave these stronger expectations aside here. . . . What matters for present purposes is the minimal requirement. If someone offers what she should know cannot be good reasons for others, those she addresses may feel insulted, condescended to, or patronized. It may seem arrogant to suppose that others should regard one's own uncorroborated and impressionistic memories as a good reason to decide so important a political outcome. The resentment or mistrust engendered by the perceptions of arrogance and condescension may not always be justified. There are times when others overreact or are too ready to take offense in political debate. But I am assuming that resentment is justified when, as in this case, the advocate should have known better. If, as I also assume, citizens are obliged to avoid engendering justified resentment, then they should be prepared to offer what they evidently take to be adequate reasons for the outcomes they favor.

This conclusion gains further support when we turn our attention to what it is advocates try to persuade their audience to do. When someone advocates a measure banning PAS in public political debate, she tries to persuade her audience to support the ban—typically by voting for it. If they are to vote responsibly, then by (5.1) they must believe there are adequate reasons for the ban. It would surely be wrong for someone to urge others to vote for the ban while being unable to provide them with the grounds they would have to have to vote for it responsibly. It would, that is, be wrong to urge others to vote for a ban on PAS while not being prepared to show them what the reasons for it are. Therefore someone who advocates an outcome thereby incurs the stronger duty expressed by (5.2).

(5.1) does not require that citizens be ready to indicate what they think justifies government in adopting the measures they favor. It allows them to vote responsibly while relying on testimony about what political outcomes are good ones and what candidates endorse the best measures. Reliance of this kind is inevitable in elections in which a large number of important issues are at stake and in which issues are sufficiently complicated. But I do not deny that it is good for citizens to be informed about issues and candidates, to know why some measures are better solutions to political problems than others, and to know which candidates are better suited to hold office. I do not deny that it is good for citizens to know the reasons for their own political positions rather than to take those positions on trust from others. I merely deny that this is a duty of responsible citizenship. I therefore think that

> (5.3) It is an excellence of citizenship to be able to offer reasons one thinks would justify government in enacting the measures one favors.

Of course this is not an excellence everyone has time to pursue. Other activities or other duties may keep them from learning enough about issues to realize the excellence singled out in (5.3). So, too, may other role-specific excellences include other excellences of citizenship. Someone may, for example, be engaged in a kind of public service that allows her to satisfy her other duties but is too time-consuming to allow her to study political questions. By engaging in such demanding public service, she realizes a different excellence of citizenship that competes with the excellence of (5.3).

THE PRINCIPLES: THEIR DEPARTURE FROM THE
STANDARD APPROACH

(5.1) and (5.2) are controversial principles. To bring out how controversial they are, let me give some examples of their implications.

> Mark's state has posed a referendum that would legalize physician-assisted suicide. While trying to decide how to vote on the referendum, Mark reads the open letter Cardinal Joseph Bernardin of Chicago wrote to the United States Supreme Court, urging the justices not to find a right to PAS in the Constitution. Were it not for the letter, Mark would be unsure whether the values Bernardin cites outweigh citizens' liberty interest in determining the time and manner of their deaths. After reading the letter, Mark concludes that they do because the author is a religious authority whom he believes to be reliable on difficult moral questions. Because he thinks that Cardinal Bernardin is correct about there being no right to PAS, he votes against the referendum. His vote is based on the deliverance of a religious authority. (5.1) implies that this is morally permissible.

> . . . It is common for American presidential candidates to make campaign stops at African American churches. Imagine that Sarah reads of such a visit in the paper or is present when a candidate visits her congregation. She believes that the candidate has the correct position on the issues, or at least the most important issues, of the campaign. She thinks this because she thinks that the candidate has the endorsement of her pastor and that the pastor, as a religious authority, has greater insight into the difficult moral questions at issue in the campaign. (5.1) implies that she may vote for the candidate on this basis.

Mary must decide between two candidates for office, each of whom takes some positions she finds attractive. In order to make her decision, Mary must decide which issues—hence which positions—are most important. She believes on religious grounds that the poor have the most urgent claim on the nation's conscience and resources. She therefore decides that a candidate's stand on issues that bear most directly on the poor should be decisive. Mary may vote for the candidate whose stand on these issues she favors.

Anne thinks targeting the innocent populations of other countries with nuclear weapons is offensive to God. To think that the nation-state is worth protecting in this way betrays, she thinks, an idolatrous

nationalism and treats God's children as mere pawns in a geopoliti-
cal game. She therefore thinks it would be wrong for government
to pursue policies of nuclear deterrence that depend upon aiming
land-based missiles at civilian populations. (5.2) implies that she
may present this argument at a public meeting about the federal
government's construction of missile silos in her county, even if she
has no other argument to offer.

Jerry believes that the flourishing of his country and its vigor depend
upon parts of its legislation conforming with the precepts of natural
law that bear on the common good. He believes, for example, that
legislation should strengthen traditional families. Not only does Jerry
believe that legislation should conform to natural law, but his beliefs
about the precepts of natural law depend upon his comprehensive
view, a view elucidated by religious authorities. (5.1) implies that
Jerry may vote for candidates because they would try to bring about
the conformity Jerry favors, provided he thinks government would
be justified in enacting the measures in question. (5.2) implies
that Jerry may argue publicly for such candidates on the grounds that
they would try to bring about the conformity he favors, even if he has
no other argument to offer, provided he thinks government would
be justified in adopting the measures in question and is prepared to
say what would justify the adoption.

As I indicated, these examples are intended to show the controversial
implications of (5.1) and (5.2). The riders to these principles may,
however, make the view defended here seem like a version of what I
have been calling "the standard approach." According to proponents
of the standard approach, citizens should be prepared to offer one
another justifying reasons for the measures they vote for and advocate.
As the examples make explicit, (5.1) requires that someone who bases
her vote on her comprehensive doctrine believe government would
be justified in adopting the measures she favors. (5.2) requires that
someone whose contributions to public political debate depend upon
her comprehensive doctrine believe government would be justified in
adopting the measures she favors and be prepared to indicate what she
thinks would justify their enactment. Thus both (5.1) and (5.2) seem
to make responsible voting and advocacy parasitic on the availability of
justifying reasons. (5.1) seems to require that citizens believe there are
justifying reasons for the measures they favor. (5.2) seems to require
that citizens believe there are justifying reasons and that they be ready

to offer them. I seem to have departed from the standard approach only by proposing a more demanding principle for advocacy than for voting. This seems a relatively insignificant difference.

(5.1) and (5.2) do bear some similarity to principles associated with the standard approach, but that similarity masks deep differences. One important difference between (5.1) and (5.2) on the one hand, and principles associated with the standard approach on the other, is that the standard approach requires that citizens be ready to offer one another justifying reasons. (5.1) and (5.2) impose no such requirements. (5.1) says that citizens must believe government would be justified in enacting the measures for which they vote. It therefore implies that they must believe there is a justification. It does not, however, require that those reasons be of the kind that *actually would justify* government's enactment of the measures in question. Someone satisfies (5.1) if he sincerely but mistakenly believes that there is a justification for those measures. (5.2) imposes the additional requirement that citizens who advocate a policy be ready to say what they think would justify the government's enactment of it. Like (5.1), (5.2) can be satisfied by someone who is mistaken about what would justify governmental enactment of the measure she favors.

A more significant difference is that according to the standard approach, justifying reasons must be accessible reasons. The standard approach therefore implies that citizens must have and be ready to offer one another accessible reasons for the policies they favor. As will become apparent, I am deeply skeptical of the notion of "accessibility." There may be many considerations—from the promotion of public health, economic growth, and environmental quality to the demands of basic human rights—that everyone agrees can be justifying reasons and that seem, intuitively, to be accessible. But if we are to decide whether religious reasons and other reasons drawn from comprehensive views are accessible, it will be necessary to go beyond these clear cases and develop conditions of accessibility. If accessible reasons are to play the role that they are assigned by the standard approach, ensuring the right forms of mutual trust and civility, then the criteria of accessibility will have to be widely even if tacitly shared. This, in turn, will require that citizens identify with a certain specification of their citizenship. Citizens will have to think of themselves, perhaps implicitly, as persons who are owed reasons that satisfy those criteria.

The problem is that there is pervasive and reasonable disagreement about what kinds of reasons can be justifying reasons, about what reasons are accessible, about what reasons citizens owe to each other, and hence about the specification of citizenship with which citizens should identify. It is because of these problems that (5.1) and (5.2) do not require that citizens must have or be ready to offer accessible reasons. The principles can be satisfied by someone who believes government action can be justified by reasons that proponents of the standard approach deem inaccessible. To return to some of the examples, Mark may believe that human law should promote the common good and that the violation of some precepts of natural law impedes that good. He may believe that clerics have insight into the requirements of the natural law and the common good that he does not. He may therefore believe that government would be justified in enforcing a ban on PAS because PAS goes against a precept of natural law the violation of which impedes realization of the common good. Anne may think that government actions ought not be repugnant to God. She might think that government would be justified in imposing a moratorium on the construction of missile silos because, of the available courses of action—moratorium or continued construction—the moratorium is the one that satisfies that condition. Neither Mark nor Anne would satisfy the requirements of the standard approach, yet they satisfy the principles defended here.

(5.1) and (5.2) allow religion to play a much more prominent role in political decision making than the standard approach does. As a consequence, these principles allow votes and advocacy that proponents of the standard approach would regard as violations of the duties of citizenship. It may be that the principles permit votes and political arguments we do not like for measures that we hope will lose. This is not a possibility that I deny. I merely maintain that these votes and arguments do not violate citizens' role-specific duties. Acknowledging that they do not is consistent with working hard to ensure the electoral defeat of those who cast or offer them.

The standard approach does point toward an important truth about responsible citizenship. To see this, consider the requirement that citizens be ready to offer one another reasons for law and policy that are of the same kind as government must offer citizens. This requirement lies at the heart of the standard approach. . . . Robert Audi moves directly from a claim about the reasons government must offer to a claim about the kinds of reasons citizens must be prepared to offer. Rawls is somewhat more expansive. He urges citizens to test the arguments they intend to offer by imagining that they are public officials who must justify government action to citizens generally.[3] This exercise of the imagination is supposed to help citizens identify the arguments they must be prepared to offer one another. Why do proponents of the standard approach move from the reasons government must offer to the reasons citizens must be prepared to offer?

Though they do not say so, I believe proponents of the standard approach think

> (5.4) It would be irresponsible for a citizen to vote for or publicly advocate a measure if she does not reasonably think government would be justified in enacting it should her side win the political contest.

I believe they also think that if the issue at stake is important enough, citizens are obliged to behave responsibly. According to this line of thought, they are therefore obliged to argue and vote only for measures that they reasonably think government would be justified in enacting. To ensure mutual trust and civility, they should be ready to show others that they are voting and debating responsibly. They should therefore be prepared to adduce reasons they reasonably think are justifying reasons for the laws and policies they vote for and advocate. And, I believe proponents of the standard approach think, there are some kinds of reasons that all reasonable citizens can recognize as justifying reasons and that are sufficient to settle political questions or the most important political questions.

There may, as I have stressed, be significant overlap in the sets of reasons reasonable citizens take to be justifying. There are, however, considerations that fall outside the overlap. These are considerations that some citizens take to be justifying but that others do not. In light of reasonable disagreement about whether these reasons are justifying, the standard approach's claim about responsible citizenship is too strong. Rather than requiring that citizens advocate and vote only for measures that can be defended by reasons of the relevant kind if enacted, I am arguing that responsible citizenship requires that citizens advocate and vote only for measures that they *sincerely believe* would be justified. The subtlety of this important difference explains the superficial similarity between my view and the standard approach.

It may be that the citizen who satisfies the demands of the standard approach realizes some good of citizenship that is not realized by those who merely satisfy (5.1) and (5.2). It may be, that is, that

> (5.5) It is an excellence of citizenship to be able to offer reasons of the sort that justify government in adopting the measures one favors.

It may also be an excellence of citizenship to strive to bring about a coincidence between the reasons that one thinks justify governmental adoption of some measure and the reasons that really do justify it. It may, that is, be an excellence of citizenship to try to bring it about that one realizes the excellence mentioned in (5.5) or to do one's part to bring about a society in which everyone realizes that excellence. Unfortunately I cannot pursue these suggestions here.

THE PRINCIPLES: A DEFENSE

(5.1) and (5.2) require that citizens who vote for a measure bearing on their own and others' fundamental interests believe that the government's adoption of the measure they vote for can be justified. (5.2) requires that citizens who advocate such a measure be prepared to indicate what a justification is. Yet the principles do not imply that citizens who satisfy them share a view of what justifies government action. Instead they are premised on the supposition that people disagree about what interests are fundamental and what justifies the government's adoption of a law or policy. They require only that citizens invoke the standards of justification that they sincerely believe to be correct. As a consequence, the principles depart significantly from the standard approach, allowing citizens to vote on grounds, and to offer arguments, that many philosophers would deem inaccessible and to do so in favor of political outcomes that many may not like. What tells in favor of the principles?

Principles governing voting and public political advocacy are supposed to be principles the general observation of which maintains civility among citizens or, to use a phrase I have employed elsewhere, keeps relations among citizens on their proper footing. To determine what the proper footing is, some philosophers begin by trying to determine what justifications or reasons citizens are obliged to offer one another. They then argue that the world in which the obligation to offer those reasons is generally honored sets the benchmark of civility. Others begin with intuitions about civility and argue that observing the obligations they defend seems to promote civility as they understand it. It is, however, a mistake to suppose either that civility can simply be defined in terms of principles that are defended on an independent basis or that our intuitions about civility can be taken at face value. . . . Voting and advocacy are collective undertakings. We cannot determine what responsible participation in those undertakings requires or what relations among citizens should be like without knowing what arguments they can reasonably expect others to offer them, on what basis they can reasonably expect others to vote, and how they can reasonably expect to be treated.

What expectations are reasonable depends in turn on how it is reasonable for citizens to think of their role and on what citizens can reasonably expect others to believe about the reasons they owe each other. If there are reasonable disagreements about what kinds of reasons are accessible and about what ends government must serve, then it would be unreasonable for some citizens to expect others to offer them reasons they regard as accessible. In that case they may resent being offered reasons they regard as inaccessible, but it would be a mistake to cite their resentment as evidence that those who offered them the inaccessible reasons have violated some moral obligation. Then the claim that the duty of civility requires offering or being prepared to offer others accessible reasons for one's political position would be too strong. Rather than defining civility as what results from compliance with voting and advocacy principles or beginning with a notion of civility and arguing that only the readiness to provide accessible reasons can bring it about, it is better to ask what sorts of reasons it is reasonable for citizens to expect and frame our account of civility accordingly.

The religious arguments citizens offer one another, the reasons on which they rely when they vote, the interests or some of the interests they regard as fundamental, their views about what justifies government action, and hence the specification of citizenship with which they identify, all may result from their exposure to the political arguments and activities of churches. Thus the political argument and activity of churches can lead to citizens holding different opinions on these matters. Of course it does not follow immediately that we should regard this disagreement as reasonable. Nor does it follow that the right accounts of civility and of citizens' reasonable expectations of one another should make allowances for those who rely exclusively on religious reasons and arguments. These conclusions depend upon what disagreements political philosophy should regard as reasonable and upon empirical data about the societies in question. The result is that different principles of responsible voting and advocacy may be appropriate for different societies. I want to argue that there is reasonable disagreement about what specification of liberal democratic citizenship is the right one, about what kinds of reasons justify government action, and about what kinds of reasons citizens may rely on when they vote or publicly advocate political outcomes. Since I have said that the reasonability of such disagreement depends upon social circumstance, I shall be concerned with the United

States and, by implication, with other societies in which religion makes similarly valuable contributions to liberal democracy.

There is reasonable disagreement about some subject when reasonable people reasonably endorse different conclusions about it. Whether people reasonably endorse different conclusions on some subject depends upon how they arrived at those conclusions. Thus whether a disagreement is reasonable depends upon whether some parties to the disagreement satisfy plausible standards of reasonability and whether they had adequate evidence available to them, whether they took adequate account of the evidence or whether their reasoning was in some way faulty or corrupted, and, most important, what explains their divergent opinions if their evidence and reasoning are adequate. Note that Rawls' claim that disagreement about the good is reasonable depends upon just such considerations. Reasonable people, for these purposes, are people who are willing to cooperate with others on fair terms. Rawls thinks disagreement about the good is natural even among people who are reasonable in this sense and who live under free institutions, for human beings who reason adequately and have access to adequate information still labor under what he calls "the burdens of judgment."[4] Thus he says that reasonable pluralism about the good is "the natural outcome of the activities of human reason under enduring free institutions."[5]

Now let us turn to the disagreement with which I am concerned. The parties to this disagreement in whom I am most interested are, for obvious reasons, those who think they may rely exclusively on religious reasons and who effectively identify with a specification of citizenship that permits this. Consider those who fit this description and who, in addition, impute a common-interest conception of legitimate aims to their liberal democratic government, think that government must respect the usual rights and liberties, think government should be responsive to the will of the people, and who, when deliberating about what measures to advocate and vote for, are guided by what they think liberal democratic government may justifiably do. Such people seem to satisfy an intuitively plausible standard of reasonability. I am supposing that their views about their own citizenship and about the reasons on which citizens may rely when making political decisions result, at least in part, from the political activity of churches. This activity, I am supposing, explains or helps to explain the disagreements with which I am concerned. Does this, together with the claim that some parties to the disagreement are reasonable, establish that the disagreement is reasonable? To show that it does, it is necessary to advert to the empirical data.

One line of argument seizes on Rawls' claim that pluralism about the good is a *natural* outcome and maintains that the disagreement in which I am interested is no less natural. According to this line of thought, religiously inspired political movements in the United States, religiously motivated political behavior, and the use of explicitly religious political arguments are due in part to the political engagement of churches. While these institutions are not primarily political in their aims, the ways in which they pursue their institutional missions are influenced by their perception of the needs of their congregants and their society. They intervene in public political debate and civic argument because there are arguments they think need to be made and points of view that need to be represented. They attempt to promote realized citizenship because they think that otherwise their congregants would not be integrated into political life. They may succeed in these attempts because of a peculiarity of American political life: the absence or weakness of other institutions that might have been expected to mobilize those who now become politically involved through their religion. Thus, according to this line of thought, the political engagement of churches in the United States is the result, in part, of their having adapted to fulfill a function in American politics: the function of enabling certain segments of the population to participate in the political process. This is a function that other institutions of civil society might well have fulfilled if churches had not and that they do fulfill elsewhere. This is because, under conditions of freedom, it is natural for secondary associations to flourish. It is also natural for them to play the role of integrating citizens into political life. . . . Indeed, it might be said, a working liberal democracy depends on this. But it is also natural for free secondary associations that are politically involved—and not just churches—to develop and transmit differing views about citizenship and its duties, just as it is natural for some free secondary associations to develop and transmit differing views about the human good. Disagreement of the former kind among reasonable citizens is therefore just as natural as disagreement of the latter kind.

This line of thought can be supplemented by another that makes do without claims about what is natural. Secondary associations—according to the data I have adduced, churches—provide the only mechanism by which some citizens realize their citizenship. If the operation of these mechanisms results in disagreement about citizenship and its duties, this disagreement is reasonable in this sense: it would be unreasonable to expect the disagreement to vanish. This is because it would be asking too much of the citizens with whom I am concerned to expect them not to have the views about citizenship that they do, since the alternative entails disengagement from politics. In societies in which churches fulfill the political functions I have highlighted, the disagreement that interests me is reasonable disagreement.

What difference does it make if disagreement is reasonable? Some reasonable disagreement may be easily and unproblematically eliminated. Where elimination is not unproblematic, the features of disagreement that make it reasonable explain what is wrong with eliminating it. Thus Rawls says that disagreement about the good can be eliminated only by the oppressive use of state power. What would make the use of power to eliminate such disagreement oppressive is that it would be an objectionable infringement on the free exercise of practical reason by reasonable people. As we saw, it is because disagreement about the good is the natural result of the free exercise of reason by reasonable people that the disagreement is a reasonable one. Thus the reasons the disagreement is reasonable show why it would be objectionable to eliminate it. It may be that disagreement about citizenship and the reasons on which citizens may rely can also be eliminated only by the use of state power. Such use of state power would be oppressive for similar reasons.

But even if we are to imagine that it can be eliminated because churches ceased to engage in the activity that fosters religious political argument, religiously inspired political activity and the identification with the associated specifications of citizenship, the disagreement cannot be eliminated *ceteris paribus* without cost. To show the cost of eliminating it, it will be useful briefly to recall the contributions churches make to democracy. . . . These contributions are of two sorts. Churches contribute to civic argument and to public political debate by circulating their teaching in civil society, by lobbying, by bringing about the satisfaction of conditions—especially the *minimally democratic agenda* and *adequate representation conditions*—on debate in governmental fora, and by oppositional advocacy. These contributions . . . enrich debate about economic justice, the environment, defense policy and international relations, immigration policy, assisted suicide, and capital punishment. Part of what makes them valuable . . . is their employment of distinctive moral concepts to challenge accepted understandings of liberal democratic values.

The other contribution churches make is to widespread identification with citizenship, and thus to the realization of citizenship, especially by the poor and minorities. Churches serve as venues of political discussion. They also serve as places where people learn about issues and candidates, acquire organizational and parliamentary skills that can be transferred to politics, acquire a sense of self-worth that seems to be correlated with political participation, and acquire a sense of themselves as persons who can join with others to hold public officials accountable. Effecting people's realization of their citizenship makes large-scale participation in collective debate and decision making possible. Indeed . . . the ability to participate in and to recognize debate as *public* debate depends upon identifying with one's citizenship. Furthermore, the realization of citizenship should be reckoned one of the components of subjective well-being. Thus effecting the realization of citizenship is an enormous social achievement. It is, or should be, one of the goals of liberal democracy. The contributions churches make to it, like the contributions they make to civic argument and public political debate, are too important to be lost. There may, of course, be costs involved in allowing exclusive reliance on religious arguments and religious reasons in politics. Doing so may result in the advocacy of policies that strike us as unjust and that cannot be defended on nonreligious grounds. But the greater cost to liberal democracy would be the political marginalization of those whom churches integrate into political life, most notably the poor and minorities.

It is because churches perform the valuable functions I have discussed that disagreements among reasonable citizens to which they give rise are reasonable. Showing that a disagreement is reasonable does more than show why its elimination or disappearance may be problematic. It also shows what citizens may reasonably expect of each other. Rawls would maintain that, given the burdens of judgment, it would be unreasonable for citizens to expect agreement on the good. Given the causes of the disagreement in which I am interested, it would be unreasonable for citizens to expect agreement on a specification of citizenship and on the kinds of reasons on which citizens may properly rely. Norms of voting and political argument, the general observance of which requires such agreement, require too much.

I have said that the disagreements on which I have focused—and the seemingly problematic arguments and votes that result—will be eliminated only if churches stop making these contributions. This is a social scientific conjecture. It cannot be proven definitively. The best I can do to defend it is to argue that what appears to be an alternative that allows churches to make these contributions without producing arguments and votes that seem problematic would not, in fact, allow churches to make the contributions I have highlighted. That alternative, which initially seems promising, is that churches draw some clear distinctions in their own theory and practice, distinctions that would be important in a fully developed version of the standard approach. The relevant distinctions are between contributions to public political debate and civic argument, and between grounds for voting and reasons for political action that does not contribute to a binding decision. Once they have drawn these distinctions, churches can make thoroughly theological contributions to civic argument. They can use those contributions to develop the social teachings of their tradition and challenge dominant social values. When they enter public political debate, however, churches must have and be ready to offer accessible reasons for their political positions and must encourage their members to do the same. They should encourage their members to participate in politics, provide them with political information, and help them to develop civic skills. They should also encourage them to find accessible grounds for their votes and to be ready to offer those reasons to justify their votes, at least on fundamental issues. Thus according to this alternative, political discussion and political action will be governed by two sets of norms. Public political debate and voting will be governed by some version of the standard approach. Civic argument and other political action will be governed by (5.1) and (5.2) or by other, weaker principles. By teaching and example, churches should ensure that these two sets of norms are honored.

This alternative, if feasible, would allow churches to make many of the contributions I have highlighted without producing the arguments and votes that proponents of the standard approach find problematic. Unfortunately, the alternative is not feasible. The problem is that the norms that govern public political debate tend, as a sociological matter, to be taken as norms for other discourse as well. Those who think they should be ready to produce accessible reasons in public political debate tend to insist on them in civic argument as well. One result is that the distinctive moral argument that was to be among churches' contributions to democracy is eliminated even from discussions in which it is ostensibly permissible. Such self-censorship is not something for which I can produce rigorous empirical evidence, but there is, I believe, ample anecdotal evidence to support it.[6]

The claim of self-censorship gains additional plausibility once we see why it is natural for people to apply norms from public political debate to civic argument as well. The disposition to comply with norms requiring accessible reasons in public political debate requires those who have other, nonaccessible reasons for their position to recognize that not all interlocutors regard their nonaccessible reasons as good ones for the political outcomes they favor. Only if they recognize this will those with nonaccessible reasons be prepared to supplement their arguments and explain their votes with accessible reasons. As a matter of psychological fact, it is easy to slide from the belief that not everyone regards nonaccessible reasons as good reasons for political outcomes to the belief that nonaccessible reasons are bad reasons for those outcomes. Once someone sees some kinds of reasons as bad reasons, he is more likely to refrain from using them, and to insist that others refrain from using them, whether engaged in public political debate or in civic argument. If this slide is widely made—if large numbers of people mistake the claim that nonaccessible reasons need to be supplemented for the claim that nonaccessible reasons are bad reasons that should not be offered—then the alternative will not be feasible.[7]

If, as I have argued, citizens' disagreements about what reasons can justify government action are reasonable disagreements—if the parties to this disagreement are reasonable and if the disagreement can be eliminated only at an unacceptably high cost—then the disagreement is one that voting and advocacy principles must accommodate. They must do so by allowing citizens to rely on their religious convictions when they cast their votes and to adduce religious arguments for their political positions even when they have no other reasons to which they can appeal. This is exactly what (5.1) and (5.2) allow.

Those who worry that religion is often used to support extreme political positions and that this causes resentment and incivility have, paradoxically, an additional reason to accept (5.1) and (5.2). It is often said that compliance with principles of the standard approach is necessary to keep relations among citizens on their proper footing. But it may be that compliance with these principles is less effective at producing civility in the long run than compliance with (5.1) and (5.2). Allegedly extreme political positions may be altered precisely because the religious groups that back them in the public forum on religious grounds cannot win adequate political support for their positions. Not all religious groups modify their positions in response to political or cultural reversals; some thrive on the sense that they are embattled minorities and become more strongly oppositional.[8] Even churches and religious citizens who do modify their views may do so over the course of several election cycles rather than immediately. There is, however, evidence that conscious moderation takes place, at least in the United States.[9] Such moderation may, over time, reduce the polarization caused by the earlier adoption of positions that were regarded as extreme. The force of public opinion and the responsiveness of politically active organizations to it are among the moderating and equilibrating forces of liberal democracy. They are among the forces that, over the longer run, counteract forces of polarization and encourage social unity.[10] It would be very odd if those who fear religious extremism and incivility in liberal democracy argued that citizens violate a role-specific duty when they engage in conduct that is the first step to their adoption of more moderate views.

. . . I have relied on the data to show that disagreements about citizenship and the reasons on which citizens may rely are reasonable and result from contributions to democracy that are too valuable to be lost.[11] At this point it may be objected that I have drawn the wrong conclusions from the empirical data I have adduced about the contributions churches make to democracy. Those data do not help us uncover what the prima facie obligations of citizenship are. Those obligations are to be determined philosophically from the value commitments of liberal democracy. Empirical data help us determine whether the prima facie obligations of citizenship are overridden because of the prevalence of special circumstances or nonstandard conditions.

The problem with this line of thought is that obligations, even prima facie obligations, are supposed to have normative force. They are supposed to guide our conduct and inform our critical judgment. If the normal conditions of human life were such that putative obligations were regularly overridden or evacuated of their force, it would be questionable whether the norms really were *obligations* at all. They might retain some normative force, but it would arguably be the force possessed by ideals rather than duties. Anyone proposing even prima facie obligations must therefore make some assumptions about standard conditions. This is especially so if the obligations are to be defended on consequentialist grounds, as voting and advocacy principles sometimes are. For then the claim that some norm expresses an obligation depends upon claims about the normal consequences of violating it. But what are standard conditions for present purposes? And what is special or nonstandard about actual conditions?

The objector may maintain that our target is a set of principles that express the prima facie obligations of the citizens of liberal democracies as such. Principles as general as that must presuppose a description of standard conditions that abstracts away from the conditions of particular liberal democracies like the United States. The proper description must include only those conditions that are true of liberal democracies as such or, perhaps, conditions common to all and only liberal democracies. In these conditions, acts of ecclesiastical political involvement will not have the features or consequences to which I have pointed in this [essay]; these are features, it might be said, that these acts have only in the United States. In light of their society's circumstances, citizens of and churches in this or that liberal democracy may be excused from the prima facie obligations the principles express. But the features that certain acts may have in those special circumstances should not be taken into account in determining what prima facie obligations there are in the first place.

The problem with this argument is that it is far from clear if any description could be given of the conditions common to all and only liberal democratic societies. Or at any rate it is not clear that one could be given that is both detailed enough to show the characteristic features of ecclesiastical involvement in politics and general enough that it is not merely an abstract description of some one society. Even if such a description could be given, liberal democracies surely change over time so that what was true of all of them at one time may not be true of all of them at another. Therefore some argument must be given for designating the conditions common to liberal democracies at one time rather than another as the standard ones for purposes of determining prima facie obligations. It is, however, hard to see why prima facie obligations should be based upon the features certain acts have at a given time in the history of liberal democracy rather than on the features they have in one or another liberal democracy. An attempt to describe the conditions characteristic of liberal democracies "as such" will fare no better.

Alternatively it might be said that the conditions of an ideally just liberal democracy are the ones relevant to determining the prima facie obligations of citizens. This thought will be especially appealing to someone interested in determining what prima facie obligations citizens have in virtue of their commitment to just liberal democracy. For in a liberal democracy that is ideally just, it might be thought, citizens act from their commitment to liberal democracy. They would willingly satisfy the obligations this commitment entails. Ideal conditions might therefore seem to afford a clear and uncluttered view of the actions citizens would perform when they are moved by their liberal democratic commitments. An ideally just liberal democracy would also be one without unjustifiable economic and political inequality for churches to combat, nor would it be one in which the poor need churches to help them realize their citizenship. Once ideal conditions are taken as standard, the data to which I have referred are seen to be irrelevant to citizens' prima facie obligations.

This line of thought assumes that in an ideal liberal democracy churches would not need to endorse some economic policies as more just than others because such a society would be economically just, or very nearly so. It therefore overlooks that possibility that church involvement in politics could be among the ways an ideal liberal democracy might maintain economic justice. A more serious problem with the reply is that an ideally just liberal democracy does *not* afford a clear view of citizens' actions when they are moved by the relevant commitments. If anything, it affords a view of the morally significant features such actions have when citizens are moved by those commitments, when each person's willingness to act on her commitments is mutually recognized and when institutions are designed so that action on these commitments results in economic and political justice. It is hard to see how the morally significant features that certain acts have in such ideal conditions bear on the prima facie obligations citizens are under in actual ones, where there is deep disagreement about what justice demands and when social institutions quite conspicuously fail to produce just outcomes. It is therefore hard to see that our prima facie political obligations could depend only upon the morally significant features our political acts would have under ideal conditions, remote as they are from our own experience.[12]

It still might be maintained that I have focused on the actual circumstances of one society—the United States. While some set of actual conditions may be standard for purposes of determining the duties of liberal democratic citizenship, those so clearly peculiar to a particular society cannot be. The answer to this objection is that it is not at all obvious that the conditions I have discussed are peculiar to one society. . . . It could well be that in other countries churches make the same contributions to democracy that they do in the United States. Even if they do not, it may be that other organizations in civil society—such as ideologically oriented labor unions—do and that they convey comprehensive views. It is precisely because this possibility cannot be foreclosed that (5.1) and (5.2) apply to comprehensive views generally, and not just to religion.

Finally, to return to the main line of argument, note that religious contributions to public political debate can be appreciated by citizens who are not of the same denomination as the advocate and by those who are not religious at all. Whether or not they are religious, they can see that a religious argument draws on claims that are, from the advocate's point of view, moral claims. This will be evident from the fact that the advocate regards them as categorical claims that preempt the claims of self-interest. They may also be able to feel the force of religious discourse by sympathetically recasting it so that it refers to experiences with which they are familiar, claims that they can accept or aspirations they share. That is what many Americans presumably did and continue to do with the religious arguments of Martin Luther King Jr. King's biographer, Taylor Branch, wrote that King thought "religion and democratic politics are united in their purest essences and yearnings."[13] The possibility that citizens will sympathetically interpret one another casts some doubt on the claims that religious reasons are inherently inaccessible or that their use in politics inevitably leads to resentment and the erosion of mutual trust.

Whether citizens are willing or able sympathetically to interpret one another no doubt depends upon the prevalence of certain conditions. It depends, for example, on citizens' sharing background knowledge about the religious views appealed to in public political debate, so that they can understand and sympathetically interpret the premises that are relied upon, the stories and imagery that are used, and the rhetorical devices that are employed. It may be that increasing pluralism makes the requisite background knowledge harder to maintain, though perhaps this problem could be addressed with an aggressive program of multi-cultural education. Citizens' readiness to interpret others sympathetically may also depend upon the moral authority of or respect for those who advocate on religious grounds. Alan Wolfe once wrote of Martin Luther King Jr. that he

> managed to build upon America's religious and moral founda-
> tions to uphold the dignity of the individual . . . he said of civil
> rights demonstrators, "The patter of their feet as they walked
> through the Jim Crow barriers in the great stride toward freedom
> is the thunder of the marching men of Joshua. And the world
> rocks beneath their tread. My people, my people, listen, listen,
> the battle is in our hands." In the aftermath of the Birmingham
> bombing, King spoke not of retribution but of redemption. . . .
> Words like this are rarely heard in American politics these days,
> because so few have the moral stature to utter them.[14]

Such respect can easily be lost. It would be prudent for churches and religious citizens to conduct themselves in ways that do not squander the respect and moral authority on which a sympathetic reception of their religious advocacy depends. This may require limiting their explicitly religious interventions in politics or making good those interventions with nonreligious arguments. What matters for present purposes is that the imperative to do so is one of prudence rather than of moral obligation.

CONCLUSION

. . . The defense of the role I allow religion in political decision making falls into two parts. The first part of the defense consists of the arguments found in this [essay]. Those arguments leave some important questions unanswered and some important claims to be vindicated. . . . The standard approach gains considerable plausibility from the claims that citizens have a fundamental interest in their liberty or its essential use and that it is most important for citizens to qualify their reliance on religious considerations when deciding on political outcomes that bear on those interests. I noted that proponents of the standard approach claim citizens' general willingness to offer one another accessible reasons keeps their relations on the proper footing. But, I said, it is not possible to isolate kinds of reasons that do for relations among citizens what accessible reasons are supposed to do when citizens' liberty interests are at stake.

Chapter 10

Religious Reasons
in Political Argument

Jeffrey Stout

Religious diversity, like racial diversity, has been a source of discord throughout American history. Most Americans claim to be religious, but their convictions are hardly cut from the same cloth. Given that some of these convictions are thought to have highly important political implications, we should not be surprised to hear them expressed when citizens are exchanging reasons for their respective political views. Secular liberals find the resulting cacophony deeply disturbing. Some of them have strongly urged people to restrain themselves from bringing their religious commitments with them into the political sphere. Many religious people have grown frustrated at the unwillingness of the liberal elite to hear them out on their own terms and have recently had much to say against the hypocrisies and biases of secularism. Freedom of religion now strikes some prominent theologians as a secularist ruse designed to reduce religion to insignificance. . . .

Freedom of religion consists first of all in the right to make up one's own mind when answering religious questions. These include, but are not limited to, such questions as whether God exists, how God should be conceived, and what responsibilities, if any, human beings have in response to God's actions with regard to them. Freedom of religion also consists in the right to act in ways that seem appropriate, given one's answers to religious questions—provided that one does not cause harm to other people or interfere with their rights. Among the expressive acts obviously protected by this right are rituals and other devotional practices performed in solitude, in the context of one's family, or in association with others similarly disposed. More controversial, however, is a class of acts that express religious commitments in another way, namely, by employing them as reasons when taking a public stand on political issues. What role, if any, should religious premises play in the reasoning citizens engage in when they make and defend political decisions?

The free expression of religious premises is morally underwritten not only by the value we assign to the freedom of religion, but also by the value we assign to free expression generally. All citizens of a constitutional democracy possess not only the right to make up their minds as they see fit, but also the right to express their reasoning freely, whatever that reasoning may be. It is plausible to suppose that the right to free expression of religious commitments is especially weighty in contexts where political issues are being discussed, for this is where rulers and elites might be most inclined to enforce restraint. Any citizen who chooses to express religious reasons for a political conclusion would seem, then, to enjoy the protection of two rights in doing so: freedom of religion and freedom of expression. And these rights not only have the legal status of basic constitutional provisions, but also hold a prominent place in the broader political culture. Otherwise, the framers of the U.S. Constitution would not have had reason to affirm them explicitly in the Bill of Rights.

I have no doubt that the expression of religious reasons should be protected in these ways. Indeed, I would encourage religiously committed citizens to make use of their basic freedoms by expressing their premises in as much depth and detail as they see fit when trading reasons with the rest of us on issues of concern to the body politic. If they are discouraged from speaking up in this way, we will remain ignorant of the real reasons that many of our fellow citizens have for reaching some of the ethical and political conclusions they do. We will also deprive them of the central democratic good of expressing themselves to the rest of us on matters about which they care deeply. If they do not have this opportunity, we will lose the chance to learn from, and to critically examine, what they say. And they will have good reason to doubt that they are being shown the respect that all of us owe to our fellow citizens as the individuals they are.

Of course, having a right does not necessarily mean that one would be justified in exercising it. Clearly, there are circumstances in which it would be imprudent or disrespectful for someone to reason solely from religious premises when defending a political proposal. But some philosophers hold, more controversially, that such circumstances are more the exception than the rule. Richard Rorty, the most important contemporary pragmatist, has claimed that reasoning from religious premises to political conclusions is nowadays either imprudent, improper, or both. The late John Rawls, the most distinguished political philosopher of our time, at first defended a similarly restrictive view. He later made a concession to free expression by qualifying that policy somewhat but still considered it improper to introduce religious reasons into public discussion of matters of basic justice unless those reasons are redeemed in the long run by reasons of a different kind. In this [essay], turning first to Rawls and then to Rorty, I will explain why their arguments for these positions fail to persuade me. The point is not to refute them, but to provide a rationale for approaching the topic differently.

RELIGION AND PUBLIC REASON

In a religiously plural society, it will often be rhetorically ineffective to argue from religious premises to political conclusions. When citizens are deeply divided over the relevant religious questions, arguing in this way is rarely likely to increase support for one's conclusions. Sometimes such reasoning not only fails to win support, but also causes offence. Reasoning from religious premises to political conclusions can imply disrespect for those who do not accept those premises. For example, such reasoning can be calculated to convey the undemocratic message that one must accept a particular set of religious premises to participate in political debate at all. In the United States, such a message is now often reserved for atheists and Muslims, but Jews and Catholics can still occasionally sense it in the air. Therefore, there are moral as well as strategic reasons for self-restraint. Fairness and respectful treatment of others are central moral concerns.

Rawls begins with such concerns, arguing as follows. Political policies, when enacted in law, are backed by the coercive power of the state. To be recognized as a free and equal citizen of such a state is to be treated as someone to whom reasons must be offered, on request, when political policies are under consideration. The reasons that are demanded are not just any reasons. Each citizen may rightfully demand reasons why *he or she* should view the proposed policy as legitimate. It does not suffice in this context to be told why other people, on the basis of their idiosyncratic premises and collateral commitments, have reached this conclusion. It is not enough for a speaker to show that he or she is entitled to consider a proposal legitimate. The question on each concerned citizen's mind will rightly be, "Why should *I* accept this?" Fairness and respect require an honest effort, on the part of any citizen advocating a policy, to justify it to other reasonable citizens who may be approaching the issue from different points of view.

So far, so good. Proper treatment of one's fellow citizens does seem to require an honest justificatory effort of this sort. When proposing a political policy, one should do one's best to supply reasons for it that people occupying other points of view could reasonably accept. I wholeheartedly embrace this ideal when it is phrased in this (relatively weak) way. But Rawls goes much further than this.

He argues that citizens should aspire to fulfill a much more demanding ideal of public reason. The unqualified version of this ideal, put forward in the original clothbound edition of *Political Liberalism*, held that our reasoning in the public forum should appeal strictly to ideals and principles that no reasonable person could reasonably reject.[1] By agreeing to abide by such principles and to rely solely on them when reasoning in the public forum, citizens enter a social contract. The contract specifies the fair terms of social cooperation in the form of justice as fairness. According to this conception of justice, the principles of the social contract are those we would select as a basis for social cooperation if we were behind a "veil of ignorance." Behind the veil, we would not know such facts about ourselves as our race, gender, medical condition, intellectual capacities, religious commitments, or comprehensive moral outlook. In ignorance of these facts, but still looking out in a reasonable way for our interests in the resulting system of social cooperation, we would be bound to select fair principles. Political liberalism does not put forward this conception of justice as a component of a comprehensive moral outlook, whether religious or secular. This conception of justice is not premised on a doctrine of what our true good ultimately consists in, on a view of the meaning of life, or even on the full-fledged Kantian liberalism Rawls had defended in *A Theory of Justice*. It is a "free-standing political conception," put forward in the hope that it can become and remain the object of a stable "overlapping consensus" among reasonable persons holding conflicting comprehensive doctrines. As such, it gives priority to the rightness of fair social cooperation, insofar as this might conflict with some idea of the good.

Many of Rawls' religious readers have been prepared to grant that some version of the veil of ignorance would be useful in fleshing out a defensible notion of fairness. A principle designed to regulate economic life, for example, should be chosen from a point of view in which we don't know whether we will end up being among the least well-off. A principle regulating discrimination in hiring should be chosen from a point of view in which we feign ignorance of our gender and racial identities. Fair enough. But Rawls' critics have long expressed doubts about similarly excluding knowledge of one's comprehensive religious and philosophical commitments. Rawls allows those behind the veil of ignorance to have access to a "thin" conception of the good, but his critics hold that in drawing the line between a thin conception and their own comprehensive doctrines, he is begging the question in favor of his own liberal views. For this is the move that underwrites two key components of Rawlsian liberalism: the priority of the right over the good and the conception of public reason with which we are concerned here. The critics protest that neither of these key ideas can meet the high standard Rawls proposes for judging such matters: these are both notions that a reasonable person could reasonably reject.

Public reason, Rawls says, "is public in three ways: as the reason of citizens as such, it is the reason of the public; its subject is the good of the public and matters of fundamental justice; and its nature and content is public, being given by the ideals and principles expressed by society's conception of political justice, and conducted open to view on that basis" (PL, 213). The limits of public reason are meant to apply to deliberation on essential constitutional provisions and matters of basic justice, not to political deliberation on lesser matters (PL, 214). The ideal of circumspection pertains not only to the reasoning of legislators and other officials, but also to the reasons citizens use when arguing for candidates for public office and when deciding how to vote "when con-stitutional essentials and matters of basic justice are at stake" (PL, 215). These are the sorts of contexts Rawls has in mind when he refers to the public forum. He classifies reasoning expressed in other contexts, such as a university or church colloquium, as private (PL, 220). All of these points are essential from Rawls' point of view. Neglecting any of them makes the ideal of public reason seem much more restrictive than he intends it to be.

Now consider the crucial notion of ideals and principles that no rea-sonable person could reasonably reject. What is a "reasonable person"? As Rawls sees it, "knowing that people are reasonable where others are concerned, we know that they are willing to govern their conduct by a principle from which they and others can reason in common" (PL, 49 n. 1). What public reason requires of citizens is that they be reasonable in the Rawlsian sense. And this means being willing to accept a common basis for reasoning that others, similarly motivated, could not reasonably reject. In short, to be reasonable is to accept the need for a social contract and to be willing to reason on the basis of it, at least when deliberating in the public forum on basic constitutional and political matters. This definition implicitly imputes *unreasonableness* to everyone who opts out of the contractarian project, regardless of the *reasons* they might have for doing so. "Persons are reasonable in one basic aspect when, among equals say, they are ready to propose principles and standards as fair terms of cooperation and to abide by them willingly, given the assurance that others will likewise do so. Those norms they view *as reasonable for everyone to accept and therefore as justifiable to them*" (PL, 49; emphasis added). "By contrast, people are unreasonable in the same basic aspect when they plan to engage in cooperative schemes but are unwilling to honor, or even to propose . . . any general principles or standards for specifying fair terms of cooperation" (PL, 50). It is clear from the context that the general principles or standards at issue in the last quoted passage are those that meet the requirement I have italicized in the previous one. Notice that someone can count as unreasonable on this definition even if he or she is epistemically entitled, on the basis of sound or compelling reasons, to consider the quest for a *common* justificatory basis morally unnecessary and epistemologically dubious. To count as reasonable, in the sense of "socially cooperative," Rawls assumes that one must find his contractarian quest for a common justificatory basis plausible. My problem is that I don't find this quest plausible. Or more mildly: I am not persuaded that it is going to meet with success. For this reason, I want to explore the possibility that a person can be a reasonable (socially cooperative) citizen without believing in or appealing to a freestanding conception of justice.

Rawls is quick to move from imagining the basis on which citizens "can reason in common" to concluding that *only* by conducting our most important political reasoning on this basis can we redeem the promise of treating our fellow citizens fairly in matters pertaining to the use of coercive power. And this conclusion leads, in turn, to a restrictive view of the role religious reasons can play in the public forum. It is clear that, in our society, religious premises cannot be part of the basis on which citizens can reason in common, because not all citizens share the same religious commitments, and nobody knows how to bring about agreement on such matters by rational means. Religion is a topic on which citizens are epistemically (as well as morally and legally) entitled to disagree. If so, it follows from the considerations just mentioned that using religious premises in our reasoning on basic political issues conflicts with the ideal of public reason as originally stated by Rawls. If the point of the social contract is to establish a basis on which citizens can reason in common, and religious premises are not part of that basis, then introducing such premises in the public forum automatically fails to secure the legitimacy of whatever proposal this basis was meant to support.

This conclusion strikes me as extremely counterintuitive, given that it seems so contrary to the spirit of free expression that breathes life into democratic culture. As Nicholas Wolterstorff says, "given that it is of the very essence of liberal democracy that citizens enjoy equal freedom in law to live out their lives as they see fit, how can it be compatible with liberal democracy for its citizens to be *morally restrained* from deciding and discussing political issues as they see fit?"[2] Rawls seems to be saying that while the right to express our religious commitments freely is guaranteed twice over in the Bill of Rights, this is not a right of which we ought make essential use in the center of the political arena, where the most important questions are decided. Is it always wrong for citizens in the public forum to reason solely on the basis of religious premises, at least when considering matters of basic justice and constitutional essentials?

Rawls implied as much in the first, clothbound edition of *Political Liberalism*, but amended his position in the "Introduction to the Paperback Edition" in 1996 and in his paper, "The Idea of Public Reason Revisited."[3] His amended view is that reasonable comprehensive doctrines, including religious doctrines, "may be introduced in public reason at any time, provided that in due course public reasons, given by a reasonable political conception, are presented sufficient to support whatever the comprehensive doctrines are introduced to support" (PL, li–lii). According to this "proviso," a citizen may offer religious reasons for a political conclusion, but only if he or she eventually supplements those reasons by producing arguments based in the social contract. The amended Rawlsian view is that religious reasons are to IOUs as contractarian reasons are to legal tender. You have not fulfilled your justificatory obligations until you have handed over real cash. I find this version of the position slightly more plausible than the original, simply because it is less restrictive. It makes a bit more room for such instances of exemplary democratic reasoning as the religiously based oratory of the abolitionists and of Martin Luther

King Jr. But Rawls confesses that he does not know whether these orators "ever fulfilled the proviso" by eventually offering reasons of his officially approved sort (PL, lii n. 27). So, strictly speaking, from a Rawlsian point of view the jury is still out on these cases.

I see it as a strong count against Rawls' current position that these particular speakers will barely squeak by on his criteria, if they manage to do so at all. The alleged need to satisfy the proviso in such cases suggests to me that something remains seriously wrong with the entire approach Rawls is taking. Two main types of reason-giving are to be found in the relevant speeches, but Rawls classifies both of them as private, because they do not appeal to the common justificatory basis. In the first type, which Rawls calls "declaration" (CP, 594), the speakers express their own religious reasons for adopting some political proposal. In the second type, which Rawls calls "conjecture" (CP, 594), the speakers engage in immanent criticism of their opponents' views. As immanent critics, they either try to show that their opponents' religious views are incoherent, or they try to argue positively from their opponents' religious premises to the conclusion that the proposal is acceptable. What they do not do is argue from a purportedly common basis of reasons in Rawls' sense. Rawls does not examine these forms of reason-giving in any detail. He merely classifies them as private and moves on. He does not show why a speaker who combines them when addressing fellow citizens on constitutional essentials, like the right to own slaves and who gets to vote, needs eventually to offer argument of some other kind.

Rawls is similarly ambivalent and therefore unpersuasive on Lincoln's Second Inaugural Address, perhaps the highest ethical achievement of any political speaker in U.S. history. What gets Lincoln barely off the hook is that "what he says has no implications bearing on constitutional essentials or matters of basic justice" (PL, 254). I am not certain that this is true. The speech is about the question of how a nation at war with itself over slavery can remain a union. Lincoln's answer, in effect, is that it can do so only if, at the moment when one side wins the war, the people and the state representing them behave "with malice toward none; with charity for all." This includes behavior intended to "achieve and cherish a just and lasting peace," which in Lincoln's view obviously includes taking the right stand on constitutional essentials and matters of basic justice. In any event, suppose he had addressed such matters directly and at greater length, continuing the theme, introduced earlier in the speech, of two parties that both read the same Bible and pray to the same God, whom they believe to be a just judge of wrongdoers. Suppose he had spelled out his immanent criticisms of the self-righteous religious views, the moralistic dualisms, that both sides were then preparing to enact politically. Would the religious content in Lincoln's speech then have been improper? Would he be engaged in private speech, despite speaking as the president to the people on a very public occasion? Something is deeply wrong here. The speeches of King and Lincoln represent high accomplishments in our public political culture. They are paradigms of discursive excellence. The speeches of the abolitionists taught their compatriots how to use the terms *slavery* and *justice* as we now use them. It is hard to credit any theory that treats their arguments as placeholders for reasons to be named later.

I do not intend to go very far into the details of the debate between Rawls and his critics.[4] My purpose in this section and the next is rather to determine what it is in his contractarian starting point that leads Rawls and others to say such counterintuitive things. If my diagnosis is correct, then the amended version of his position, while it is less paradoxical than the original, does not overcome the basic difficulties in his approach to the topic. My conclusion will be that we ought to reframe the question of religion's role in political discussion in quite different terms.

The trouble is at least partly a matter of epistemology. I suspect that Rawls has overestimated what can be resolved in terms of the imagined common basis of justifiable principles and has done so because at this one point in constructing his theory he has drastically underestimated the range of things that socially cooperative individuals can reasonably reject. He has underestimated what a person can reasonably reject, I suspect, because he has underestimated the role of a person's collateral commitments in determining what he or she can reasonably reject when deciding basic political questions. What I can reasonably reject depends in part on what collateral commitments I have and which of these I am entitled to have. But these commitments vary a good deal from person to person, not least of all insofar as they involve answers to religious questions and judgments about the relative importance of highly important values. It is naive to expect that the full range of political issues that require public deliberation—issues on which we need *some* policy—will turn out to be untouched by such variation. Rawls would grant this. Indeed, it may be part of his reason for viewing "the diversity of reasonable comprehensive religious, philosophical, and moral doctrines found in modern democratic societies" as a central problem for political liberalism to address (PL, 36). The question is why constitutional essentials and matters of basic justice are not also affected, for it is reasonable to suppose, when discussing such elemental issues, that the relative importance of highly important values—a matter on which religious traditions have much to say—is a relevant consideration. Rawls might wish to deny this on the basis of his doctrine of the priority of the right over the good, but this doctrine also strikes me as the sort of thing over which epistemically responsible people have good reason to disagree.

I am tempted to put the point by saying that this doctrine is the sort of thing *reasonable* people would be *entitled* to disagree over. For the moment, let me use the term "reasonable" in a way that departs from Rawls' definition. In this sense, a person is reasonable in accepting or rejecting a commitment if he or she is "epistemically entitled" to do so, and reasonable people are those who comport themselves in accord with their epistemic responsibilities.[5] I do not see how the same epistemology can consistently (a) declare the people holding various comprehensive views to be reasonable in this sense, and (b) declare the people who dissent from the social contract not to be reasonable in the same sense. To make (a) turn out to be correct, one would need to assume a relatively permissive standard of reasonableness. But if one then applies the same permissive standard of reasonableness to those who dissent from the social contract, (b) is going to be very hard to defend. According to my epistemology the more permissive standard seems to be the right one to apply in both instances. But if we link the term "reasonable" to epistemic entitlement and apply the term in a relatively permissive way, it will be very hard to make those who reject the contractarian project *on epistemological grounds* qualify as unreasonable.

This appears to be why Rawls has a stake in introducing his definition of reasonableness. The point of doing so is to guarantee that a reasonable person will be committed to the contractarian project of trying to find, and abide by, a common basis of principles. But this move only begs the question of why the contractarian project of establishing a common basis is itself something no one can reasonably reject in the sense of epistemic entitlement. We still need an answer to this question. There appear to be sound *epistemological* reasons for rejecting the quest for a common basis, reasons rooted in the permissive notion of epistemic entitlement that lends plausibility to the doctrine of reasonable pluralism in the first place.

Rawls gave an interview to *Commonweal*, a liberal Catholic journal, in 1998 (reprinted in CP, 6, 16–22). In it he asks how we are to avoid religious civil wars like those of the sixteenth century without adopting his position. "See, what I should do is to turn around and say, what's the better suggestion, what's your solution to it? And I can't see any other solution." He continues: "People can make arguments from the Bible if they want to. But I want them to see that they should also give arguments that all reasonable citizens might agree to. Again, what's the alternative?" (CP, 620). Let us see whether we can find one.

Rawls' amended position entails that it would be inherently unfair, when speaking in the public forum on questions of basic justice, to rely solely on religious premises. This would hold, presumably, even in a case where my epistemological suspicions were realized and it proved impracticable to reason on the basis of a principle that all reasonable citizens could reasonably accept. But suppose this did turn out to be impracticable—for the simple reason that some epistemically responsible people who desire social cooperation have reason for rejecting each candidate principle. Must we then not consider the matter at all? Must we remain silent when it comes up for discussion? How could a requirement of silence in such a case be deemed *reasonable*—that is to say, justified?

For that matter, how could it be deemed *fair* in a society committed to freedom of religion and freedom of expression? I do not see how it could be. As Wolterstorff argues:

> It belongs to the *religious convictions* of a good many religious people in our society that *they ought to base* their decisions concerning fundamental issues of justice *on* their religious convictions. They do not view as an option whether or not to do so. It is their conviction that they ought to strive for wholeness, integrity, integration, in their lives; that they ought to allow the Word of God, the teachings of the Torah, the command and example of Jesus, or whatever, to shape their existence as a whole, including, then, their social and political existence. Their religion is not, for them, about *something other* than their social and political existence; it is *also* about their social and political existence. Accordingly, to require of them that they not base their decisions and discussions concerning political issues on their religion is to infringe, inequitably, on the free exercise of their religion.[6]

It might be thought that offering religious reasons, without supplementing them by appeal to the social contract, is inherently disrespectful. But why need this be a sign of disrespect at all? Suppose I tell you honestly why I favor a given policy, citing religious reasons. I then draw you into a Socratic conversation on the matter, take seriously the objections you raise against my premises, and make a concerted attempt to show you how *your* idiosyncratic premises give *you* reason to accept my conclusions. All the while,

I take care to be sincere and avoid manipulating you (CP, 594). Now, I do not see why this would qualify as a form of disrespect. Yet it does not involve basing my reasoning on principles that no reasonable citizen could reasonably reject.

The conception of respect assumed in the objection seems flawed. It neglects the ways in which one can show respect for another person in his or her particularity.[7] The reason Rawls neglects these ways is that he focuses exclusively on the sort of respect one shows to another individual by appealing to reasons that *anyone* who is both properly motivated and epistemically responsible would find acceptable. Why would I be failing to show respect for X if I offered reasons to X that X ought to be moved by from X's point of view?[8] Why would it matter that there might be other people, Y and Z, who could reasonably reject those reasons? Suppose Y and Z are also part of my audience. If I am speaking *as* a citizen *to* fellow citizens, unconstrained by expectations of confidentiality, they might well be. This is all I would mean by "speaking in public." Does my immanent criticism of X then show disrespect to Y and Z? No, because I can go on to show respect for them in the same way, by offering *different* reasons to them, reasons relevant *from their point of view*. Socratic questioning is a principal tool of justificatory discourse as well as a way of expressing respect for one's interlocutor as a (potential) lover of justice and sound thinking. But it does not proceed from an already-agreed-on, common basis.

It appears that Rawls is too caught up in theorizing about an idealized form of reasoning to notice how much work candid expression and immanent criticism—declaration and conjecture—perform in real democratic exchange. Immanent criticism is both one of the most widely used forms of reasoning in what I would call public political discourse and one of the most effective ways of showing respect for fellow citizens who hold differing points of view. Any speaker is free to request reasons from any other. If I have access to the right forum, I can tell the entire community what reasons move me to accept a given conclusion, thus showing my fellow citizens respect as requesters of my reasons. But to explain to them why *they* might have reason to agree with me, given their different collateral premises, I might well have to proceed piecemeal, addressing one individual (or one type of perspective) at a time. Real respect for others takes seriously the distinctive point of view *each* other occupies. It is respect for individuality, for difference.

Rawls builds strong assumptions about the nature of discursive sociality into his conception of a "reasonable person." Such a person is by definition someone who is prepared to play by the discursive rules of the imagined common basis on all essential matters. But why not view the person who takes each competing perspective on its own terms, expressing his own views openly and practicing immanent criticism on the views of others, as a reasonable (i.e., socially cooperative, respectful, reason-giving) person? Why limit oneself in the Rawlsian way to the quest for a *common* basis, given the possibility that a common basis will not cover all essential matters? I do not see any convincing answers to these questions in Rawls' writings or in the works of other contractarian theorists. These questions reveal, I think, that the social contract is essentially a substitute for communitarian agreement on a single comprehensive normative vision—a poor man's communitarianism. Contractarianism feels compelled to reify a sort of all-purpose, abstract fairness or respect for others because it cannot imagine ethical or political discourse *dialogically.*[9] Its view of the epistemological and sociological dimensions of discursive practices is essentially blinkered.

Wolterstorff puts the point in a slightly different way:

> So-called "communitarians" regularly accuse proponents of the liberal position of being against community. One can see what they are getting at. Nonetheless, this way of putting it seems to me imperceptive of what, at bottom, is going on. The liberal is not willing to live with a politics of multiple communities. He still wants communitarian politics. He is trying to discover, and to form, the relevant community. He thinks we need a shared political basis; he is trying to discover and nourish that basis . . . I think that the attempt is hopeless and misguided. We must learn to live with a politics of multiple communities.[10]

My qualm about this way of putting the point I want to make is that it concedes too much to group thinking. We do have multiple communities in the sense that the points of view many citizens occupy fall into recognizable types. And some of these communities work hard, for legitimate reasons, at reaching consensus on topics that matter deeply to them. But the differences that set off one such community from another are not the only differences that make a difference in political debate. There are also differences that set off individuals from the communities in which they were raised or with which at some point they became affiliated. Respect for individuals involves sensitivity to the ways in which they can resist conformity to type. Wolterstorff calls for a "consocial" model of discursive sociality for a democratic society. By envisioning a multitude of discursive communities exchanging reasons both within and across their own boundaries, such a model advances well beyond the social-contract model Rawls employs. But we need another layer of complication to make the picture fully realistic.

On my model, each individual starts off with a cultural inheritance that might well come from many sources. In my case, these sources included the training I received in Bible school, the traditional stories my grandmother told on Sunday afternoons, and the example of a pastor committed passionately to civil rights. But they also included an early exposure to Emerson, Whitman, and Thoreau; the art, novels, and music brought into my home by my bohemian older brother; and countless other bits of free-floating cultural material that are not the property of any group. And they included interactions with hundreds of other people whose racial and religious backgrounds differed from mine. It would simply be inaccurate to describe my point of view as that of my family, my co-religionists, or my race. One would fail to show me respect as an individual if one assimilated my point of view to some form of group thinking. The consocial model still fails to do justice to the kinds of individuality and alienation that modern democracies can promote.

Rawls derives his idea of public reason from conceptions of fairness and respect that are in fact to be found in the political culture of modern democracy. But he develops this idea in a way that brings it into tension with conceptions of free expression and basic rights that also belong to the same culture. It is not clear why this tension should be resolved by adopting a Rawlsian conception of public reason.[11] It seems more reasonable to suppose that one should try to argue from universally justifiable premises, whenever this seems both wise and possible, while feeling free nonetheless to pursue other argumentative strategies when they seem wise. This would be to treat the idea of public reason as a vague ideal, instead of reifying it moralistically into a set of fixed rules for public discussion. The truth in the contractarian argument for restraint is that it would indeed be *ideal* if we could resolve any given political controversy on the basis of reasons that none of us could reasonably reject. But it has not been demonstrated that all important controversies can be resolved on this sort of basis, so it seems unwise to treat the idea of public reason as if it entailed an all-purpose principle of restraint. The irony here is that the contractarian interpretation of the idea of public reason is itself something that many epistemically and morally responsible citizens would be entitled, on the basis of their own collateral beliefs, to reject.

The contractarian position has a descriptive component and a normative component. The descriptive component is an account of what the norms of democratic political culture involve. It distills a rigorist interpretation of the idea of public reason out of various commitments that are found in that culture. The normative component endorses a principle of restraint as a consequence of that interpretation. I worry that religious individuals who accept the descriptive component of contractarianism as a faithful reconstruction of what the norms of democratic political culture involve will, understandably, view this as a reason for withdrawing from that culture. Why should one identify with the democratic process of reason-exchange if the norms implicit in that process are what the contractarians say they are? I believe this thought is in fact one of the main reasons that antiliberal traditionalists like Stanley Hauerwas, Alasdair MacIntyre, and John Milbank have largely displaced Reinhold Niebuhr, Paul Tillich, and the liberation theologians as intellectual authorities in the seminaries, divinity schools, and church-affiliated colleges of the wealthier democracies.

We are about to reap the social consequences of a traditionalist backlash against contractarian liberalism. The more thoroughly Rawlsian our law schools and ethics centers become, the more radically Hauerwasian the theological schools become. Because most of the Rawlsians do not read theology or pay scholarly attention to the religious life of the people, they have no idea what contractarian liberalism has come to mean outside the fields of legal and political theory. (There are a few Rawlsians in religious studies, but they are now on the defensive and vastly outnumbered.) One message being preached nowadays in many of the institutions where future preachers are being trained is that liberal democracy is essentially hypocritical when it purports to value free religious expression. Liberalism, according to Hauerwas, is a secularist ideology that masks a discriminatory program for policing what religious people can say in public. The appropriate response, he sometimes implies, is to condemn freedom and the democratic struggle for justice as "bad ideas" for the church.[12] Over the next several decades this message will be preached in countless sermons throughout the heartland of the nation.

Rawls found it frustrating that Hauerwas and his allies tend to ignore the careful distinctions he draws between liberalism as a comprehensive moral doctrine and the strictly *political* liberalism he had been trying to perfect in his later years. His *Commonweal* interviewer asked whether he denied that he was "making a veiled argument for secularism." He responded by saying, "Yes, I emphatically deny it. Suppose I said that it is not a veiled argument for secularism any more than it is a veiled argument for religion. Consider: there are two kinds of comprehensive doctrines, religious and secular. Those of religious faith will say I give a veiled argument for secularism, and the latter will say I give a veiled argument for religion. I deny both" (CP, 619). But nobody is charging Rawls with giving a veiled argument for religion. The charge being made by his secular and religious critics alike is that he is wrong to expect everybody to argue in the same terms, which just happen to be a slightly adjusted version of the same terms dictated by his comprehensive secular liberalism. The critics doubt the need for the kind of decorum the liberal professor wants to impose on the discussion. And they doubt that a reluctance to adopt justice as fairness as a common basis for discussion makes someone unreasonable. These suspicions would not subside, it seems to me, even if Rawls' critics took full measure of all the distinctions and qualifications he has added to his theory. From the vantage of the religious critics, in particular, the complications would still seem both ad hoc and excessively restrictive.[13]

* * * *

I have heard that Hauerwas expressed the religious reasons for his criticisms of U.S. militarism in public, before a religiously mixed gathering of citizens in the nation's capital, not long after September 11, 2001. In my view, it was good that he did, regardless of whether he intends to satisfy Rawls' proviso. Hauerwas' audience on this occasion presumably included people who were concerned about such basic questions as whether states have a right to fight wars of self-defense and whether the constitutional provision requiring Congress to declare war continues to apply. These citizens were anxious to hear the arguments of a highly influential pacifist and also to hear those arguments subjected to public criticism from other points of view. Democracy would not have been better served, it seems to me, if these reasons had been circulated only behind the closed doors of churches and religiously affiliated schools, where they would be somewhat less likely to face skeptical objections. Especially given that Hauerwas now enjoys wide influence among American Christians, he ought to be encouraged to speak in public so that the citizenry as a whole can inform itself about the content and strength of his arguments.[14] And if he someday chooses to address a congressional committee or speak on behalf of political candidates, so much the better.

One factor to keep in mind when considering the new traditionalism is that Hauerwas and his allies accept the descriptive component of contractarian liberalism. That is, they take this form of liberalism at face value as an accurate account of what the ethical life of modern democracy involves. It is because they view it as a faithful reflection of our political culture that they are so quick to recommend wholesale rejection of that culture. I hold that the contractarians have distorted what this culture involves by wrongly taking a sensible, widely shared, vague ideal to be a clear, fixed, deontological requirement built into the common basis of our reasoning. If I am right about this, the new traditionalists are wrong to reject that culture as implicitly committed to the contractarian program of restraint—what Hauerwas calls "the democratic policing of Christianity."[15] Rejecting what contractarianism and the new traditionalism have in common will permit us, I hope, to reopen the entire question of the role of religious reasoning in public life.

BETWEEN KANT AND HEGEL

The contemporary contractarian version of the question is, "What moral constraints on the use of religious premises in political reasoning are implied by the common basis of reasoning affirmed in the social contract?" The sought-for principles might not turn out to be Kant's exactly, but the requirement that they be conceived in terms of a common justificatory basis on the model of a social contract is recognizably Kantian in lineage, self-consciously so in Rawls' formulation. Rawls does depart from Kant in a number of ways, and at some points appears to be conscious of his debts to the expressivism of both Hegel and Dewey. These latter debts are most obvious in his theoretical aspiration to make explicit the central elements of the shared political culture and in his closely related doctrine of reflective equilibrium. On both of these points, Rawls is borrowing ideas from the expressivist tradition in an attempt to transform "Kantian constructivism" into a "political constructivism" tailored to the needs of political liberalism. The theoretical aspiration is a version of Hegel's notion that the task of philosophy is to comprehend its own age in thought. The doctrine of reflective equilibrium articulates a Hegelian conception of dialectical reasonableness. But in his commitment to the metaphor of the social contract and in the definition of the "reasonable person" he uses to explicate that metaphor, Rawls remains a Kantian. From an expressivist point of view, his departures from Kant improve on the work of his distinguished predecessor, but they leave him in an untenable position—in effect, halfway between the coherent alternatives of Kant and Hegel.

Norms, according to an expressivist conception, are creatures of the social process in which members of a community achieve mutual recognition as subjects answerable for their actions and commitments. It is the business of reflective practices to make norms explicit in the form of rules and ideals and to achieve reflective equilibrium between them and our other commitments at all levels of generality. The social process in which norms come to be and come to be made explicit is dialectical. It involves movement back and forth between action and reflection as well as interaction among individuals with differing points of view. Because this process takes place in the dimension of time and history, the beliefs and actions one is entitled to depend in large part on what has already transpired within the dialectical process itself. Hegel considered Kant's preoccupation with universally valid principles epistemologically naive and was suspicious of the adequacy of the social contract when construed in expressivist terms as a model of rational commitments implicit in the shared political culture. Rawls briefly discusses Hegel's criticisms of social-contract theories (PL, 285–88), claiming that while these criticisms might be effective against some versions of the social contract, they do not tell against his. I am not persuaded, however, that Rawls takes Hegel's full measure in this response, for he focuses too narrowly on Hegel's explicit commentary on the social contract, without exploring the implications of Hegel's philosophy, taken as a whole. Rawls discusses Hegel at greater length in *Lectures on the History of Moral Philosophy*. But in focusing primarily on Hegel's *Philosophy of Right* and in his understandable attempt to steer clear of Hegel's metaphysical doctrines, he ends up paying too little attention to Hegel's epistemology and his account of concepts, both of which figure heavily in his critique of Kant.[16]

Consider any art, science, or sport you please.[17] It should be clear that the norms of the practice at a given time constrain the behavior of those who participate in it by supplying them with reasons not to do certain things they are physically able to do. Behavior within the social practice is open to criticism in terms of the norms as they have come to be. But conformity to the norms opens up the possibility of novel performances, which have the dialectical potential to transform the practice, thus changing its norms. In the possibility of novel, practice-transforming performances one catches sight of what Brandom calls "the paradigm of a new kind of freedom, *expressive* freedom."[18] By foregrounding the dialectical process in which social practices, and the norms implicit in them, evolve over time, Hegel was both borrowing from Kant and moving beyond him. Kant had drawn the crucial contrast between constraint by norms, which he calls freedom, and constraint by causes. Hegel was able to extend the Kantian conception of freedom as constraint by norms by setting it within his dialectical account of norms. For if norms are creatures of social practices, then the sorts of free expression made possible through constraint by norms will vary in accordance with the social practices under consideration and with the dialectic of normative constraint and novel performance unfolding in time.

Once this point is fully understood, it is no longer clear why we need to tether our social and political theory to the search for a common basis of reasoning in principles that all "reasonable" citizens have reason to accept. The principles that one might have reason to reject will depend on one's dialectical location—on the social practices one has been able to participate in and on the actual history of norm transformation they have undergone so far. Among these practices will be religious practices, which carry with them their own styles of reasoning, their own vocabularies, and their own possibilities of expressive freedom. If the thoroughly dialectical view of epistemic entitlement is correct, why expect all socially cooperative, respectful persons to have reason to accept the same set of explicitly formulated norms, regardless of dialectical location? It is of course possible that they will, and they may indeed do so for a time, but the substance of a common ethical life, according to Hegel, does not reside in the explicitly formulated abstract norms that arise from the dialectical process in which we strive for reflective equilibrium. It resides in the myriad observations, material inferences, actions, and mutually recognitive reactions that constitute the dialectical process itself. This changes at least a bit with every discursive move that is made by every interlocutor. The abstract norms are often misleading or inadequate attempts to make explicit what is implicit in the ethical life of the people. Moreover, they are typically a full step behind the dialectical process—because the Owl of Minerva takes flight at dusk.

We can get at this from another angle by considering the two quite different paradigms of the reasonable person that one finds in the Kantian and expressivist traditions. The Kantian paradigm of the reasonable person is the individual who is prepared to agree to rules that everyone else, acting on the same motivation, would have compelling reason to accept. The Hegelian paradigm is rather the individual who is prepared to engage in discursive exchange with any point of view that he or she can recognize as responsibly held. As the expressivist sees it, the series of exchanges need not operate on a single common basis, tailored to all, but might well involve improvisational expression of one's own point of view and ad hoc immanent criticism of one's interlocutors. The expectation is that different improvisations and different immanent criticisms—indeed, different vocabularies—might well be called for in response to each interlocutor. The one thing upon which a reasonable person can more or less count is the need to transcend whatever set of rules and concepts a distinguished philosopher has described as demanded by our common use of reason.

The point of the contractarian program of restraint was to provide us with security against illegitimate forms of coercive interference on the part of rulers and fellow citizens. This is a matter of *negative* freedom, freedom *from* something. We still have ample reason to concern ourselves with this sort of freedom when assessing the political arrangements that are open to us. But there is also another sort of freedom to nurture and protect, namely, expressive freedom. And this ought to make us hesitant to embark on a Rawlsian program of restraint. Expressive freedom is *positive*, the freedom *to* transform both oneself and one's social practices through a dialectical progression of novel performances and their consequences. To take expressive freedom seriously is to see our capacity to engage in reasoning, including ethical and political reasoning, as something that cannot be captured definitively in the mere application of rules that no reasonable person could reasonably reject. For a reasonable person, in the Hegelian sense, is someone who is always in the process of transforming the inferential significance of the normative concepts at his or her disposal by applying them to new situations and problems.

The social-contract metaphor is too static to serve as an apt model for this process. What contractarianism seems to be looking for is a way of identifying the norms of social cooperation that fixes their inferential significance in advance, so that discursive exchange can be conceptually (and socially) stable. The norms are then taken to be settled and in need only of application in the approved procedures of deliberative discourse. This approach is analogous to what Hegel, in his critique of Kant's theoretical philosophy, calls the faculty of the understanding (*Verstand*), whereas Hegel prefers the more flexible, pragmatic, improvisational faculty of reason (*Vernunft*), which he plausibly associates with the concept of spirit (*Geist*). Brandom develops the contrast between Verstand and Vernunft as follows:

> Understanding concepts in terms of the categories of the understanding is treating them as fixed and static. It allows progress only in the sorting *of judgments* into true and false, that is, in the *selection* from a repertoire fixed in advance of the correct concepts to apply in a particular instance. But Hegel wants to insist that if one ignores the process by which concepts *develop*—what other concepts they develop out of, and the forces implicit in

them, in concert with their fellows, that lead to their alteration (what Hegel calls their "negativity")—then the sort of content they have is bound to remain unintelligible.[19]

I am saying that this idea is also at work in Hegel's worries about Kantian practical and political philosophy. Social-contract theory is an attempt to tame the concepts of ethical and political discourse in the interest of stabilizing the social order. It hopes to settle the basic question of the fair terms of social cooperation so that deliberative discourse can proceed within a stable "contractual" framework. It imagines itself as an alternative to two threats: the communitarian threat to individual autonomy, which achieves stability but in the wrong way, and the anarchic threat of a war of all against all, which does not achieve stability at all. Social stability is to be achieved by fixing the *terms* of social cooperation, the conceptual framework implicit in the notion of the reasonable person. The practical expression of social-contract theory is, unsurprisingly, a program of social control, an attempt to enforce moral *restraint* on discursive exchange by counting only those who want to reason on the basis of a common set of fixed rules as *reasonable*. It is no wonder that the result sits uneasily with the aspirations of expressive freedom. Hegel wants to avoid this outcome by redefining "reasonable" in terms of the dialectic of expressive freedom.

It should now be clear why a democratic expressivist would never be tempted to discount abolitionist oratory, Lincoln's Second Inaugural Address, and King's sermons as mere IOUs. For such an expressivist sees democratic discourse as an unfolding dialectic in which the paradigmatic instances of "reasonableness" involve either dramatically significant innovations in the application of an entrenched normative vocabulary or especially memorable exemplifications of discursive virtue. They are paradigmatic because they move "reasonableness" forward, thus exercising some (defeasible) authority over future applications of the relevant concepts.[20] For this reason, we cannot tell the story of the unfolding dialectic without giving them a prominent place in it. Any view that makes them appear marginal or something less than paradigmatic instances of "reasonableness," simply because they do not conform to an abstract account of discursive propriety, deserves rejection.

According to Brandom, "Kant tells a *two-phase* story; according to which one sort of activity *institutes* conceptual norms, and then another sort of activity *applies* those concepts. First, a reflective judgment (somehow) makes or finds the determinate rule that articulates [a] concept.

Then, and only then, can that concept be applied in the determinate judgments and maxims that are the ultimate subjects of the first two Critiques."[21] It is this two-phase story that Hegel rejects, and he rejects it when it appears in Kant's account of empirical concepts, in his moral philosophy, and in his social-contract theory. Hegel's alternative, dialectical story implies that contractarianism is incorrect in thinking that something like the social contract is *needed* as the basis of social cooperation. Our normative concepts are not instituted at the contractual level and then applied on the basis of the constitutive contract. They are instituted in the process of mutual recognition in which individuals hold one another responsible and implicitly impute to others the authority to keep normative track of one another's attitudes. This process does not *need* the social contract to get going or to get along.[22] The process of exchanging reasons is already a system of social cooperation; it needs no help from the formal structure of the social contract to become one. But if the social contract is unnecessary, if our norms are instituted in a different way, then why define a "reasonable person" as someone who is motivated to forge and live by the principles of the social contract? Why not count anyone as a "reasonable person" who participates responsibly in the process of discursive exchange that has reflective equilibrium as its ever-evolving end? Why not see this process as the way in which democratic citizens strive, at least in their better moments, to become a more perfect union of responsible, socially cooperative selves?

There are at least three commitments that a pragmatist sensitive to these Hegelian concerns would want to bring together in an acceptable self-understanding of democratic practices. Implicit in our way of treating one another is a conception of ourselves as citizens who (a) ought to enjoy *equal standing* in political discourse; (b) deserve respect *as individuals* keeping track of the discussion from their own distinctive points of view; and (c) have a personal and perhaps religious stake in the exercise of *expressive freedom*. Given (a) and (b), we have reason to accept an ideal according to which it would be appropriate, much of the time, to reason from widely justifiable premises in the political arena. But given the emphasis in (b) on the distinctive points of view from which individuals keep track of the discussion, a pragmatist will not be tempted to construe this ideal as an absolute requirement to reason only from a common basis of principles. If we then interpret (c) in terms of the dialectic of normative constraint and novel performance, it seems reasonable to expect that various sorts of hard decisions will have to be made *as the dialectic unfolds*. By applying normative concepts, participants in the process of reason-exchange effectively decide which social and political constraints to accept in the hope of enhancing, among other things, the expressive religious freedom of the citizenry.

Pragmatic expressivists accept the Kantian insight that there need to be constraints if there is to be freedom. But they reject the two-step procedure of social-contract theory—that is, the notion that to have any constraints, we must first *fix* the terms of social cooperation contractually and then simply abide by the agreed-upon rules. They also see the central problem to be addressed in social and political deliberation as the question of which forms of expressive freedom we, as individuals and as a group, wish to promote and enjoy. There are infinitely many possible forms of expressive freedom. We opt for some over others not by signing a social contract but rather by promoting some social practices at the expense of others, both through our direct participation in them and the institutional arrangements we make for them. But as Brandom says, the expressivist way of framing the central problem of social and political deliberation does not "even begin to settle questions about the trade-offs between different varieties of negative and positive freedom."[23] For this reason, expressivism has been the preferred idiom of starkly incompatible forms of resistance to contractarian liberalism. On the all-important questions of which social practices to promote and how to promote them, expressivists divide sharply, with Emersonians at one end of the spectrum and traditionalists at the other. Emersonians, who place high value on the possibilities of novel expression, are inclined to use the freedoms afforded by the First Amendment as an institutional framework for promoting nonstandard social practices and the forms of spirited individuality they foster. Traditionalists, however, have argued on expressivist grounds for a much less permissive vision of social life. They have claimed that the higher forms of ethical and religious self-cultivation are possible only within the normative constraints of a relatively strict regimen of established communal practices. Expressivists of this sort have sometimes been willing to impose fairly severe restrictions on the expression of religious dissent in order to reap the rewards of expressive freedom and spiritual excellence they take to be possible only within a religiously unified community.

In the United States, such proposals have not made much headway, but milder versions of them, which involve shrinking the divide between church and state instead of eliminating it entirely, are gaining ground. One thing counting against traditionalist proposals in the American context is that relatively strict church-state separation and ample freedom of religious expression comport well with a political culture that was shaped in large part by immigrants in flight from restrictive religious orthodoxies. Another count against traditionalism is the sheer extent of religious diversity in this society. Members of minority traditions—including those who join me in seeing Emerson, Whitman, and Thoreau as among the greatest spiritual exemplars of expressive freedom yet produced by America—have every reason to oppose restrictions on the public expression of religious dissent against majority views. One can hope that they will do so successfully for the foreseeable future.

My version of pragmatism endorses major themes from Hegel's critique of Kant. It then combines Hegel's dialectical normative expressivism with the Emersonian conviction that the most substantial spiritual benefits of expressive freedom are to be found in a form of social life that celebrates democratic individuality as a positive good. One can see this combination of ideas initially come together, I believe, in Whitman and Dewey.

The Hegelian component of my pragmatism has a number of things in common with the most plausible forms of the new traditionalism. These include an emphasis on the importance of self-cultivation as an exercise of expressive freedom and an understanding of the dialectically social basis of norms. On Hegelian grounds, I sympathize with the traditionalist's distaste for the contractarian liberal's program of restraint. But I do not see resentment of contractarians as a reason for alienating myself from democratic hopes and freedoms. The traditionalist story that a particular religious tradition in fact functions as a community of virtue over against the sinfulness of the surrounding social world strikes me as extremely dubious as well as exceedingly prideful. I do not propose to replace the contractarian program of restraint with its traditionalist counterpart—a different set of restrictions, typically designed to maintain a patriarchal orthodoxy, instead of a liberal professor's idea of discursive decorum.

Finally, I oppose the contractarians and the new traditionalists on the most important point they share. For they both hold, as I do not, that the political culture of our democracy implicitly requires the policing or self-censorship of religious expression in the political arena. If Rawls is right, contractarian theory may require this. But the descriptive component of his contractarianism is only one competing account of what the ethical life of democracy involves. If its picture of our culture is distorted, then we are not already implicitly committed to the social contract featured in that picture. The picture neither supports the contractarian argument for restraint, nor provides a reason for the traditionalist to reject the political culture it depicts. In this one respect, our political culture is a nobler thing than its leading theoretical defenders and detractors make it out to be. Judging by how the members of our society behave, they are more deeply committed to freedom, and to a more substantive, positive kind of freedom, than the theorists suspect. For historically they have not restrained themselves in the way contractarians have proposed. That is why Rawls has trouble corralling his historical examples. The abolitionists did not restrain themselves in this way. Abraham Lincoln did not. Martin Luther King Jr., did not. Dorothy Day did not. Rosemary Radford Ruether does not. Wendell Berry does not. Furthermore, many members of our society would resist with considerable fury any traditionalist attempt to establish an orthodox alternative to freewheeling democratic exchange. More power to them.

Let me now sum up how I would want to construe our implicitly recognized norms for employing religious premises in political reasoning. First, I would insist that the ideal of respect for one's fellow citizens does not in every case require us to argue from a common justificatory basis of principles that no one properly motivated could reasonably reject. Second, I would recommend the mixed rhetorical strategy of expressing one's own (perhaps idiosyncratic) reasons for a political policy while also directing fair-minded, nonmanipulative, sincere immanent criticism against one's opponent's reasons. Arguing in this way is not only extremely common, but also easily recognizable as a form of respect.

Third, I would refer, as the new traditionalists do (and as a liberal like Stephen Macedo also does), to the importance of virtues in guiding a citizen through the process of discursive exchange and political decision making. There are people who lack civility, or the ability to listen with an open mind, or the will to pursue justice where it leads, or the temperance to avoid taking and causing offense needlessly, or the practical wisdom to discern the subtleties of a discursive situation. There are also people who lack the courage to speak candidly, or the tact to avoid sanctimonious cant, or the poise to respond to unexpected arguments, or the humility to ask forgiveness from those who have been wronged. Such people are unlikely to express their reasons appropriately, whatever those reasons may be. When it comes to expressing religious reasons, it can take a citizen of considerable virtue to avoid even the most obvious pitfalls. I know of no set of rules for getting such matters right. My advice, therefore, is to cultivate the virtues of democratic speech, love justice, and say what you please.[24]

IS RELIGION A CONVERSATION-STOPPER?

The contractarian program of restraint is a moralistic one. Richard Rorty's argument for restraint in "Religion as Conversation-Stopper" is pragmatic.[25] He claims that the public expression of religious premises is likely to bring a potentially productive democratic conversation grinding to a halt. "The main reason religion needs to be privatized is that, in political discussion with those outside the relevant religious community, it is a conversation-stopper." When someone does introduce a religious premise into a political discussion, Rorty says, "the ensuing silence masks the group's inclination to say, 'So what? We weren't discussing your private life; we were discussing public policy. Don't bother us with matters that are not our concern'" (PSH, 171). Assuming that we want to keep the conversation going, we have good reason for excluding the expression of religious premises from public political discussion.

Rorty sounds a bit like a contractarian when he endorses what he calls the "Jeffersonian compromise that the Enlightenment reached with the religious" (PSH, 169) and an epistemology he associates not only with Dewey and C. S. Peirce, but also with Rawls and Habermas (PSH, 173). The content of the Jeffersonian compromise, he says, is that we should limit conversation to premises held in common, thereby excluding the expression of religious premises. But he does not go on to theorize about universally valid principles, about which he has expressed doubts on other occasions. So the Jeffersonian compromise implies the same program of restraint that the social contract does without having the same purported epistemic status and without being expressed in the same moralistic tone. Why Rawls and Habermas emerge as model epistemologists in this context remains unclear. Rorty does not say that employing religious premises in public conversation violates a universally justifiable principle of respect; he says that doing so is in "bad taste" (PSH, 169).

This argument is hardly Rorty's most rigorously developed contribution to public life, but it is, I think, a more accurate reflection of our political culture than is the Rawlsian argument. There are in fact many situations in which the introduction of religious premises into a political argument seems a sign of bad taste or imprudence on the part of a speaker. This is what I was getting at near the end of the previous section when I referred to the need for practical wisdom and tact. The reason that relying on religious premises is often imprudent when debating matters of public policy is not, however, that it violates a compromise supposedly reached between "the Enlightenment" and "the religious." It is rather that, in a setting as religiously divided as ours is, one is unlikely to win support for one's political proposals on most issues simply by appealing to religious considerations.

Is it true that religion is essentially a conversation-stopper? I would have thought that the pragmatic line should be that religion is not *essentially* anything, that the conversational utility of employing religious premises in political arguments depends on the situation. There is one sort of religious premise that does have the tendency to stop a conversation, at least momentarily—namely, faith-claims. We can understand why faith-claims have this tendency if we describe them in the way Brandom does. A faith-claim, according to Brandom, avows a cognitive commitment without claiming entitlement to that commitment.[26] In the context of discursive exchange, if I make a faith-claim, I am authorizing others to attribute the commitment to me and perhaps giving them a better understanding of why I have undertaken certain other cognitive or practical commitments. I am also making the claim available to others as a premise they might wish to employ in their reasoning. But I am not accepting the responsibility of demonstrating my entitlement to it. If pressed for such a demonstration, I might say simply that it is a matter of faith. In other words, "Don't ask me for reasons. I don't have any."

It should be clear how this common sort of discursive move tends to put a crimp in the exchange of reasons. If, at a crucial point in an argument, one avows a cognitive commitment without claiming entitlement to that commitment and then refuses to give additional reasons for accepting the claim in question, then the exchange of reasons has indeed come grinding to a halt. But there are two things to keep in mind here. First, a claim can be religious without being a faith-claim. It is possible to assert a premise that is religious in content and stand ready to demonstrate one's entitlement to it. Many people are prepared to argue at great length in support of their religious claims. So we need to distinguish between discursive problems that arise because religious premises are not widely shared and those that arise because the people who avow such premises are not prepared to argue for them.

Second, as Brandom points out, faith is not "by any means the exclusive province of religion" (AR, 105). Everyone holds some beliefs on nonreligious topics without claiming to know that they are true. To express such a belief in the form of a reason is to make what I have been calling a faith-claim. One would expect such claims to be fairly common in discussions of especially intractable political questions. When questions of this kind get discussed, there are typically hard-liners on both sides who not only propose answers, but also claim to know that their answers are right. Yet there is typically a group of people in the middle who are prepared to take a stand, if need be, but would never claim they knew that they were right. The abortion debate is like this, and so is the debate over the problem of dirty hands in the fight against terrorism. In fact, the phenomenon of nonreligious faith-claims is quite common in political discourse, because policy making often requires us to take some stand when we cannot honestly claim to know that our stand is correct. That is just the way politics is.

It is important in this context to recall the distinction between being entitled to a belief and being able to justify that belief to someone else. Even in cases where individuals do plausibly claim to be epistemically entitled to religious premises, they might still be unable to produce an argument that would give their interlocutors reason to accept those premises. To assert such a premise would not qualify as a faith-claim in the strict sense that I have just defined, but it would create a potential impasse in conversation. Yet here again, the same sort of difficulty arises for all of us, not only for religious believers, when we are asked to defend our most deeply engrained commitments, especially those that we acquired through acculturation instead of through reasoning. We are normally entitled to hold onto commitments of this kind unless they prove problematical in some way—for example, by turning out to be either internally incoherent or too hard to square with newly acquired commitments that strike us as highly credible. If the reason for excluding the expression of religious commitments is that they create this type of discursive impasse, then the only fair way to proceed is to exclude the expression of many nonreligious commitments as well. But if we go in this direction, Rorty's view will require silence on many of the most important issues on the political agenda.

As Rorty grants, many citizens in fact affirm political conclusions that are influenced in some way by their religious commitments. Such commitments typically have a bearing on how one ranks highly important moral concerns. When President Truman was deciding what strategy to pursue in bringing World War II to an end, for example, he had to come to terms with two conflicting moral concerns. One of these had to do with his hope to minimize the number of deaths resulting from his strategy. The other had to do with his qualms about dropping atomic weapons and firebombs on civilian targets. When the question arises of how we should instruct our future leaders to act when they face a similar conflict, citizens are free to speak their minds. If a group of citizens deems the latter concern more important than the former, or vice versa, they should feel free to say so. But when they do, they are likely to be pressed for reasons. Suppose their actual motivating reasons are religious ones not widely shared among their fellow citizens, and it is clear that some citizens, employing their own reasonably held collateral commitments as premises, would be entitled to reject them. In that case, there appear to be three options: (1) to remain silent; (2) to give justifying arguments based strictly on principles already commonly accepted; and (3) to express their actual (religious) reasons for supporting the policy they favor while also engaging in immanent criticism of their opponents' views.

I see nothing in principle wrong with option (3), especially in circumstances that tend to rule out option (2). It could be, for example, that option (2) is difficult or impossible to pursue because the principles that supposedly belong to the Jeffersonian compromise, when conjoined with factual information accessible to the citizenry as a whole, do not entail a resolution of the issue. It is plausible to suppose that the problem of dirty hands has been hard to resolve precisely because some reasonable citizens are justified in rejecting one solution of the problem, while other reasonable citizens are justified in rejecting the opposite solution. But even if this is not granted, it is clear that there are other issues that cannot be resolved solely on the basis of commonly accepted principles. Kent Greenawalt argues persuasively that the debates over welfare assistance, punishment, military policy, abortion, euthanasia, and environmental policy all fall into this category.[27] It appears, then, to be a consequence of Rorty's argument for restraint that we should leave a long list of important political issues both unresolved and, even more implausibly, unaddressed.

In *Contingency, Irony, and Solidarity*, Rorty has this to say:

> All human beings carry about a set of words which they employ to justify their actions, their beliefs, and their lives. These are the words in which we formulate praise of our friends and contempt for our enemies, our long-term projects, our deepest self-doubts and our highest hopes. They are the words in which we tell, sometimes prospectively and sometimes retrospectively, the story of our lives. I shall call these words a person's "final vocabulary."[28]

Rorty then explains this term as follows: "It is 'final' in the sense that if doubt is cast on the worth of these words, their user has no noncircular argumentative recourse. Those words are as far as he can go with language; beyond them there is only helpless passivity or a resort to force."

What Rorty is describing here is the sort of discursive commitment one can be entitled to even though one would not know how to defend it. I can imagine no way of banning the use of final vocabularies, in this sense, from political discussion, even if it were a desirable thing to do, which it plainly is not. What makes some people religious is that the vocabularies in which they tell the stories of their lives—including their stories of our common political life—have religious content. Like Rorty, they tend to be speechless when pressed for linear reasons for adopting their final vocabularies. But unless those vocabularies become severely problematical, what reason would they have for abandoning them?

Rorty grants that there is "hypocrisy involved in saying that believers somehow have no right to base their political views on their religious faith, whereas we atheists have every right to base ours on Enlightenment philosophy. The claim that in doing so we are appealing to reason, whereas the religious are being irrational, is hokum." He is also realistic enough to admit that "religious beliefs, or the lack of them, will influence political convictions. Of course they will" (PSH, 172). So his point in endorsing the Jeffersonian compromise appears to be simply that it is always wise, pragmatically speaking, to confine the premises of our political arguments to commitments held in common. Religious premises are to be excluded not because they involve faith-claims and not because they involve vocabularies that cannot be defended without circularity, but rather because they are not held in common. He seems to mean *actually held in common*; he is not referring, as the contractarians do, to what all *reasonable* persons *would* accept. But the problem remains the same. Reasons actually held in common do not get us far enough toward answers to enough of our political questions. The proposed policy of restraint, if adopted, would cause too much silence at precisely the points where more discussion is most badly needed. The policy would itself be a conversation-stopper.

Suppose you are debating an issue of the type Greenawalt highlights, and you are still trying to argue your case solely by reference to commonly accepted principles and generally accessible information. Imagine that one of your interlocutors, sensing that you are not fully disclosing your own premises, says, "But what's your actual reason? What really moves you to accept this conclusion?" Now you must either dissemble or choose between options (1) and (3). But why not choose (3)? There are many circumstances in which candor requires full articulation of one's actual reasons. Even if it does lead to a momentary impasse, there is no reason to view this result as fatal to the discussion. One can always back up a few paces and begin again, now with a broader conversational objective. It is precisely when we find ourselves in an impasse of this kind that it becomes most advisable for citizens representing various points of view to express their actual reasons in greater detail. For this is the only way we can pursue the objectives of understanding one another's perspectives, learning from one another through open-minded listening, and subjecting each other's premises to fair-minded immanent criticism.

Like the contractarians, when Rorty discusses the role of religion in politics, he completely neglects the potential benefits of ad hoc immanent criticism in overcoming momentary impasses. But he does, in other contexts, recognize the value of carrying on a discussion at this level. His name for such discourse in *Philosophy and the Mirror of Nature* was "conversation."[29] There Rorty suggested that "*conversation* [be seen] as the ultimate context within which knowledge is to be understood."[30] What he meant by conversation was a kind of discursive exchange in which "our focus shifts . . . to the relation between alternative standards of justification, and from there to the actual changes in those standards which make up intellectual history."[31] The role of edifying philosophy, as Rorty presented it in that book, is to keep discursive exchange going at those very points where "normal" discourse—that is, discourse on the basis of commonly accepted standards—cannot straightforwardly adjudicate between competing claims. Conversation is a good name for what is needed at those points where people employing different final vocabularies reach a momentary impasse. But if we do use the term *conversation* in this way, we shall have to conclude that conversation is the very thing that is not stopped when religious premises are introduced in a political argument. It is only the normal discourse of straightforward argument on the basis of commonly held premises that is stopped. The political discourse of a pluralistic democracy, as it turns out, needs to be a mixture of normal discourse and conversational improvisation.[32] In the discussion of some issues, straightforward argument on the basis of commonly held standards carries us only so far. Beyond that, we must be either silent or conversational. But we can be conversational, in the spirit of Rorty's most edifying philosophical work, only by rejecting the policy of restraint he endorses.

I came of age ethically, politically, and spiritually in the civil rights movement, where I acquired my democratic commitments from prophetic ministers. In college, when I moved rapidly down the path that leads from Schleiermacher to Feuerbach, Emerson, and beyond, I found myself collaborating mainly with dissenting Protestants, secular Jews, and members of the radical Catholic underground in the struggle against U.S. involvement in the Vietnam War. I have known since then that it is possible to build democratic coalitions including people who differ religiously and to explore those differences deeply and respectfully without losing one's integrity as a critical intellect. This [essay] is offered in the hope that similarly diverse coalitions and equally full expression of differences remain possible in democratic culture today, if we can only summon the will to form them.

Chapter 11

The Crisis of Christian Identity in America

Cornel West

Our solutions and decisions are relative, because they are related to the fragmentary and frail measure of our faith. We have not found and shall not find—until Christ comes again—a Christian in history whose faith so ruled his life that every thought was brought into subjection to it and every moment and place was for him in the kingdom of God. Each one has encountered the mountain he could not move, the demon he could not exorcise. . . . All our faith is fragmentary, though we do not all have the same fragments of faith.
—H. Richard Niebuhr, *Christ and Culture* (1951)

I must take the responsibility for how, mark my word, *how* I react to the forces that impinge upon my life, forces that are not responsive to my will, my desire, my ambition, my dream, my hope—forces that don't know that I'm here. But I know I'm here. And I decide whether I will say yes, or no, and make it hold. This indeed is the free man, and this is anticipated in the genius of the dogma of freedom as a manifestation of the soul of America, born in what to me is one of the greatest of the great experiments in human relations.
—Howard Thurman, *America in Search of a Soul* (1976)

The religious threats to democratic practices abroad are much easier to talk about than those at home. Just as demagogic and antidemocratic fundamentalisms have gained too much prominence in both Israel and the Islamic world, so too has a fundamentalist strain of Christianity gained far too much power in our political system, and in the hearts and minds of citizens. This Christian fundamentalism is exercising an undue influence over our government policies, both in the Middle East crisis and in the domestic sphere, and is violating fundamental principles enshrined in the Constitution; it is also providing support and "cover" for the imperialist aims of empire. The three dogmas that are leading to the imperial devouring of democracy in America—free-market fundamentalism, aggressive militarism, and escalating authoritarianism—are often justified by the religious rhetoric of this Christian fundamentalism. And perhaps most ironically— and sadly—this fundamentalism is subverting the most profound, seminal teachings of Christianity, those being that we should live with humility, love our neighbors, and do unto others as we would have them do unto us. Therefore, even as we turn a critical eye on the fundamentalisms at play in the Middle East, the genuine democrats and democratic Christians among us must unite in opposition to this hypocritical, antidemocratic fundamentalism at home. The battle for the soul of American democracy is, in large part, a battle for the soul of American Christianity, because the dominant forms of Christian fundamentalism are a threat to the tolerance and openness necessary for sustaining any democracy. Yet the best of American Christianity has contributed greatly to preserving and expanding American democracy. The basic distinction between Constantinian Christianity and prophetic Christianity is crucial for the future of American democracy.

Surveys have shown that 80 percent of Americans call themselves Christians, 72 percent expect the Second Coming of Christ, and 40 percent say they speak to the Christian God on intimate terms at least twice a week. America is undeniably a highly religious country, and the dominant religion by far is Christianity, and much of American Christianity is a form of Constantinian Christianity. In American Christendom, the fundamental battle between democracy and empire is echoed in the struggle between this Constantinian Christianity and prophetic Christianity.

This battle between prophetic Christians and Constantinian Christians goes back to the first centuries of the Christian movement that emerged out of Judaism. The Roman emperor Constantine's incorporation of Christianity within the empire gave Christianity legitimacy and respectability but robbed it of the prophetic fervor of Jesus and the apocalyptic fire of that other Jew turned Christian named Paul. Until Constantine converted to Christianity in AD 312 and decriminalized it with the Edict of Milan in 313, and his successor Theodosius I made Christianity the official religion of the empire, the Christian movement had been viciously persecuted by the imperial Romans, primarily because the growing popularity of the Christian message of humility, and of equality among men, was understood as a threat to Roman imperial rule.

Jesus was so brutally executed by the Roman empire—crucifixion being the empire's most horrific and terrifying tactic of punishing offenders to its rule—precisely because his preaching of the coming of the kingdom of God was seen by the Romans as dangerously subversive of the authoritarianism and militarism of the Roman state. Ironically, Jesus' message of love and justice promoted a separation of his prophetic witness from Caesar's authority—"render unto Caesar what is Caesar's," Christ said. Yet the nihilistic imperialism of the Romans was so power-hungry that it couldn't tolerate the growing popularity of the Christian sects. When the growth of the religion couldn't be stopped, the Roman empire co-opted it. With Constantine's conversion, a terrible co-joining of church and state was institutionalized from which the religion and many of its victims, especially Jews, have suffered ever since. Constantinian Christianity has always been at odds with the prophetic legacy of Jesus Christ. Constantine himself seems to have converted to Christianity partly out of political strategy and imperial exigency, and then proceeded to use the cloak of Christianity for his own purposes of maintaining power.

As the Christian church became increasingly corrupted by state power, religious rhetoric was often used to justify imperial aims and conceal the prophetic heritage of Christianity. Immediately after his conversion, Constantine targeted numerous Christian sects for annihilation—such as the Gnostics and other groups that questioned the books of the Old Testament—as he consolidated power by creating one imperial version of Christianity. The corruption of a faith fundamentally based on tolerance and compassion by the strong arm of imperial authoritarianism invested Christianity with an insidious schizophrenia with which it has been battling ever since. This terrible merger of church and state has been behind so many of the church's worst violations of Christian love and justice—from the barbaric crusades against Jews and Muslims, to the horrors of the Inquisition and the ugly bigotry against women, people of color, and gays and lesbians.

This same religious schizophrenia has been a constant feature of American Christianity. The early American branch of the Christian movement—the Puritans—consisted of persecuted victims of the British empire in search of liberty and security. On the one hand, they laid the foundations for America's noble anti-imperialist struggle against the British empire. On the other hand, they enacted the imperialist subordination of Amerindians. Their democratic sensibilities were intertwined with their authoritarian sentiments. The American democratic experiment would have been inconceivable without the fervor of Christians, yet strains of Constantinianism were woven into the fabric of America's Christian identity from the start. Constantinian strains of American Christianity have been on the wrong side of so many of our social troubles, such as the dogmatic justification of slavery and the parochial defense of women's inequality. It has been the prophetic Christian tradition, by contrast, that has so often pushed for social justice.

When conservative Christians argue today for state-sponsored religious schools, when they throw their tacit or more overt support behind antiabortion zealots or homophobic crusaders who preach hatred (a few have even killed in the name of their belief), they are being Constantinian Christians. These Constantinian Christians fail to appreciate their violation of Christian love and justice because Constantinian Christianity in America places such a strong emphasis on personal conversion, individual piety, and philanthropic service and has lost its fervor for the suspicion of worldly authorities and for doing justice in the service of the most vulnerable among us, which are central to the faith. These energies are rendered marginal to their Christian identity.

Most American Constantinian Christians are unaware of their imperialistic identity because they do not see the parallel between the Roman empire that put Jesus to death and the American empire that they celebrate. As long as they can worship freely and pursue the American dream, they see the American government as a force for good and American imperialism as a desirable force for spreading that good. They proudly profess their allegiance to the flag and the cross not realizing that just as the cross was a bloody indictment of the Roman empire, it is a powerful critique of the American empire, and they fail to acknowledge that the cozy relation between their Christian leaders and imperial American rulers may mirror the intimate ties between the religious leaders and imperial Roman rulers who crucified their Savior.

I have no doubt that most of these American Constantinian Christians are sincere in their faith and pious in their actions. But they are relatively ignorant of the crucial role they play in sponsoring American imperial ends. Their understanding of American history is thin and their grasp of Christian history is spotty, which leaves them vulnerable to manipulation by Christian leaders and misinformation by imperial rulers. The Constantinian Christian support of the pervasive disinvestment in urban centers and cutbacks in public education and health care, as well as their emphatic defense of the hard-line policies of the Israeli government, has much to do with the cozy alliance of Constantinian Christian leaders with the political elites beholden to corporate interests who provide shelter for cronyism. In short, they sell their precious souls for a mess of imperial pottage based on the false belief that they are simply being true to the flag and the cross. The very notion that the prophetic legacy of the grand victim of the Roman empire—Jesus Christ—requires critique of and resistance to American imperial power hardly occurs to them.

These American Constantinian Christians must ask themselves, Does not the vast concentration of so much power and might breed arrogance and hubris? Do not the Old Testament prophets and teachings of Jesus suggest, at the least, a suspicion of such unrivaled and unaccountable wealth and status? Are not empires the occasion of idolatry run amok? Most Christians, including Constantinian ones, are appalled by the ugly AIDS epidemic in Africa—thirty million now—and around the world (forty million). Why has the response of the American empire to this crisis been abysmal? Doesn't the interest of drug companies and their influence on the U.S. government hamper our ability to discover or make available cheap drugs for our ailing fellow human beings? Is it not obvious that the U.S. response would be much different if AIDS victims were white heterosexual upper-middle-class men in Europe or America? Must Christians respond solely through private charities in this disastrous emergency? The response to the AIDS crisis is but one example of the moral callousness of imperial rulers that should upset any Christian. Were not subjugated Jews and later persecuted Christians in the early Roman empire treated in such inhumane and unacceptable ways? In criticizing the Constantinianism in American Christianity, however, we must not lose sight of the crucial role of prophetic Christianity as a force for democratic good in our history. The values engendered by Christian belief were crucial in fueling first the democratic energy out of which the early religious settlers founded nascent democratic projects and then the indignation with the abuses of the British empire that drove the American Revolution. And the Founders took great pains to establish guarantees of religious freedom in the Constitution out of a deep conviction about the indispensable role of religion in civic life. The most influential social movements for justice in America have been led by prophetic Christians: the abolitionist, women's suffrage, and trade-union movements in the nineteenth century and the civil rights movement in the twentieth century. Though the Constantinian Christianity that has gained so much influence today is undermining the fundamental principles of our democracy regarding the proper role of religion in the public life of a democracy, the prophetic strains in American Christianity have done battle with imperialism and social injustice all along and represent the democratic ideal of religion in public life. This prophetic Christianity adds a moral fervor to our democracy that is a very good thing. It also holds that we must embrace those outside of the Christian faith and act with empathy toward them. This prophetic Christianity is an ecumenical force for good, and if we are to revitalize the democratic energies of the country, we must reassert the vital legitimacy of this prophetic Christianity in our public life, such as the principles of public service, care for the poor, and separation of church and state that this Christianity demands. And we must oppose the intrusions of the fundamentalist Christianity that has so flagrantly violated those same democratic principles.

Most American Christians have little knowledge of many of the most powerful voices in the rich prophetic tradition in American Christianity. They are unfamiliar with the theologian Walter Rauschenbusch, who in his *Christianity and the Social Crisis* (1907) and numerous other influential books was the primary voice of the Social Gospel movement at the turn of the last century. As the industrial engines of the American empire ramped up, leading to the excesses of the Gilded Age, this theological movement perceived that industrial capitalism and its attendant urbanization brought with them inherent social injustices. Its adherents spoke out against the abuse of workers by managements that were not sufficiently constrained by either morality or government regulation. As Rauschenbusch eloquently wrote:

> Individual sympathy and understanding has been our chief reliance in the past for overcoming the differences between the social classes. The feelings and principles implanted by Christianity have been a powerful aid in that direction. But if this sympathy diminishes by the widening of the social chasm, what hope have we?*

With the flourishing of American industrialism, our society was becoming corrupted by capitalist greed, Rauschenbusch warned, and Christians had a duty to combat the consequent injustices.

* Walter Rauschenbusch, *Christianity and the Social Crisis* (New York: Macmillan, 1907), 252.—Ed.

Most American Christians have forgotten or have never learned about the pioneering work of Dorothy Day and the Catholic Worker Movement, which she founded in 1933 during the Great Depression to bring relief to the homeless and the poor. Day set up a House of Hospitality in the slums of New York City and founded the newspaper *Catholic Worker* because she believed that

> by fighting for better conditions, by crying out unceasingly for the rights of the workers, of the poor, of the destitute—the rights of the worthy and the unworthy poor . . . we can to a certain extent change the world; we can work for the oasis, the little cell of joy and peace in a harried world.†

Some of these prophetic Christians have been branded radicals and faced criminal prosecution. During the national trauma of the Vietnam War, the Jesuit priests and brothers Philip and Daniel Berrigan led antiwar activities, with Daniel founding the group Clergy and Laity Concerned about Vietnam. The brothers organized sit-ins and teach-ins against the war and led many protests, notoriously breaking into Selective Service offices twice to remove draft records, the second time dowsing them with napalm and lighting them on fire. "The burning of paper, instead of children," Daniel wrote in explanation of their action, "when will you say no to this war?" Both brothers served time in prison for those break-ins but went on to engage in civil disobedience protests against later U.S. military interventions and the nuclear arms race.

After a lifetime of eloquent Christian activism, the Reverend William Sloan Coffin should be better known to Americans today. Chaplain of Yale University during the Vietnam War, he spoke out strongly and early against the injustice of that incursion and went on to become president of SANE/FREEZE, the largest peace and justice organization in the United States, and minister of Riverside Church in Manhattan. The author of many powerful books, including *The Courage to Love* and *A Passion for the Possible*, he once said in an interview:

> I wonder if we Americans don't also have something that we should contribute, as it were, to the burial grounds of the world, something that would make the world a safer place. I think there is something in us. It is an attitude more than an idea. It lives less in the American mind than under the American skin. That

† Dorothy Day, "Love Is the Measure," editorial in *The Catholic Worker* (June 1946).—Ed.

is the notion that we are not only the most powerful nation in the world, which we certainly are, but that we are also the most virtuous. I think this pride is our bane and I think it is so deep seated that it is going to take the sword of Christ's truth to do the surgical operation.

He also presciently said, "No nation, ours or any other, is well served by illusions of righteousness. All nations make decisions based on self-interest and then defend them in the name of morality."

Although Martin Luther King Jr. is well known, he is often viewed as an isolated icon on a moral pedestal rather than as one grand wave in an ocean of black prophetic Christians who constitute the long tradition that gave birth to him. There is David Walker, the free-born antislavery protester, who in 1829 published his famous *Appeal*, a blistering call for justice in which, as a devout Christian, he writes:

> I call upon the professing Christians, I call upon the philanthropist, I call upon the very tyrant himself, to show me a page of history, either sacred or profane, on which a verse can be found, which maintains, that the Egyptians heaped the *insupportable insult* upon the children of Israel, by telling them that they were not of the *human family*. Can the whites deny this charge? Have they not, after having reduced us to the deplorable condition of slaves under the feet, held us up as descending originally from the tribes of Monkeys or Orang-Outangs? O! my God! I appeal to every man of feeling—is not this insupportable? Is it not heaping the most gross insult upon our miseries, because they have got us under their feet and we cannot help ourselves? Oh! Pity us we pray thee, Lord Jesus, Master.

There is the deeply religious Ida B. Wells-Barnett, the anti-lynching activist who wrote shockingly of the gruesome truths of that peculiarly American form of terrorism in her pamphlet *A Red Record*, and who went on to found the women's club movement, the first civic activist organization for African American women. More Americans should remember Benjamin E. Mays. Ordained into the Baptist ministry, he served as the dean of the School of Religion at Howard University and held the presidency of Morehouse College for twenty-five years, where he inspired Martin Luther King Jr. Mays helped launch the civil rights movement by participating in sit-ins in restaurants in Atlanta and was a leader in the fight against segregated education. There is the towering theologian Howard

Thurman, also ordained into the Baptist ministry, dean of Rankin Chapel at Howard University and pastor of the first major U.S. interracial congregation in San Francisco, who traveled to India and met with Mahatma Gandhi and whose book *Jesus and the Disinherited* provided some of the philosophical foundation for the nonviolent civil rights movement.

The righteous fervor of this black prophetic Christian tradition is rich with ironies. When African slaves creatively appropriated the Christian movement under circumstances in which it was illegal to read, write, or worship freely, the schizophrenia of American Christianity was intensified. Some prophetic white Christians became founders of the abolitionist movement in partnership with ex-slaves, while other white Christians resorted to a Constantinian justification of the perpetuation of slavery. One's stand on slavery became a crucial litmus test to measure prophetic and Constantinian Christianity in America. The sad fact is that on this most glaring hypocrisy within American Christianity and democracy, most white Christians—and their beloved churches—were colossal failures based on prophetic criteria.

The vast majority of white American Christians supported the evil of slavery—and they did so often in the name of Jesus. When Abraham Lincoln declared in his profound Second Inaugural Address that both sides in the Civil War prayed to the same God—"Neither party expected for the war, the magnitude, or the duration, which it has already attained. . . . Both read the same Bible, and pray to the same God; and each invokes His aid against the other"—he captured the horrible irony of this religious schizophrenia for the nation.

Black prophetic Christians—from Frederick Douglass to Martin Luther King Jr.—have eloquently reminded us of the radical fissure between prophetic and Constantinian Christianity, and King's stirring Christian conviction and prophetic rhetoric fueled the democratizing movement that at last confronted the insidious intransigence of the color line. In fact, much of prophetic Christianity in America stems from the prophetic black church tradition. The Socratic questioning of the dogma of white supremacy, the prophetic witness of love and justice, and the hard-earned hope that sustains long-term commitment to the freedom struggle are the rich legacy of the prophetic black church. Yet Constantinian Christianity is so forceful that it is even making inroads into this fervent black prophetic Christianity. The sad truth is that the black church is losing its prophetic fervor in the age of the American empire. The power of the Constantinian Christian coalition must not be underestimated.

The rewards and respectability of the American empire that tempt Christians of all colors cannot be overlooked. The free-market fundamentalism that makes an idol of money and a fetish of wealth seduces too many Christians. And when the major example of prophetic Christianity—the black church tradition—succumbs to this temptation and seduction, the very future of American democracy is in peril. The crisis of Christian identity in America is central to democracy matters.

The separation of church and state is a pillar for any genuine democratic regime. All non-Christian citizens must have the same rights and liberties under the law as Christian citizens. But religion will always play a fundamental role in the shaping of the culture and politics in a democracy. All citizens must be free to speak out of their respective traditions with a sense of tolerance—and even respect—for other traditions. And in a society where Christians are the vast majority, we Christians must never promote a tyranny of this majority over an outnumbered minority in the name of Jesus. Ironically, Jesus was persecuted by a tyrannical majority (Roman imperial rulers in alliance with subjugated Jewish elites) as a prophetic threat to the status quo. Are not our nihilistic imperial rulers and their Constantinian Christian followers leading us on a similar path—the suffocating of prophetic voices and viewpoints that challenge their status quo?

The battle against Constantinianism cannot be won without a reempowerment of the prophetic Christian movement, because the political might and rhetorical fervor of the Constantinians are too threatening; a purely secular fight *won't* be won. As my Princeton colleague Jeffrey Stout has argued in his magisterial book *Democracy and Tradition* (2003), in order to make the world safe for King's legacy and reinvigorate the democratic tradition, we must question not only the dogmatic assumptions of the Constantinians but also those of many secular liberals who would banish religious discourse entirely from the public square and admonish disillusioned prophetic Christians not to allow their voices and viewpoints to spill over into the public square. The liberalism of influential philosopher John Rawls and the secularism of philosopher Richard Rorty—the major influences prevailing today in our courts and law schools—are so fearful of Christian tainting that they call for only secular public discourse on democracy matters. This radical secularism puts up a wall to prevent religious language in the public square, to police religious-based arguments and permit only secular ones. They see religious strife leading to social chaos and authoritarianism.

For John Rawls, religious language in public discourse is divisive and dangerous. It deploys claims of religious faith that can never be settled by appeals to reason. It fuels disagreements that can never be overcome by rational persuasion. So he calls for a public dialogue on fundamental issues that limits our appeals to constitutional and civic ideals that cut across religious and secular Americans and unite us in our loyalty to American democratic practices. There is great wisdom in his proposal but it fails to acknowledge how our loyalty to constitutional and civic ideals may have religious motivations. For prophetic Christians like Martin Luther King Jr., his appeal to democratic ideals was grounded in his Christian convictions. Should he—or we—remain silent about these convictions when we argue for our political views? Does not personal integrity require that we put our cards on the table when we argue for a more free and democratic America? In this way, Rawls's fear of religion—given its ugly past in dividing citizens—asks the impossible of us. Yet his concern is a crucial warning.

For Richard Rorty religious appeals are a conversation stopper. They trump critical dialogue. They foreclose political debate. He wants to do away with any appeal to God in public life, especially since most appeals to God fuel the religious Right. He is a full-fledged secularist who sees little or no common good or public interest in the role of religion in civic discourse. Like Rawls, he supports the rights and liberties of religious citizens, but he wants to limit their public language to secular terms like democracy, equality, and liberty. His secular vision is motivated by a deep fear of the dogmatism and authoritarianism of the religious Right. There is much to learn from his view and many of his fears are warranted. But his secular policing of public life is too rigid and his secular faith is too pure. Ought we not to be concerned with the forms of dogmatism and authoritarianism in secular garb that trump dialogue and foreclose debate? Democratic practices—dialogue and debate in public discourse—are always messy and impure. And secular policing can be as arrogant and coercive as religious policing.

Prominent religious thinkers have also made impassioned arguments for the distancing of religion from American public discourse. Theologian Stanley Hauerwas's prophetic ecclesiasticism and John Milbank's radical orthodoxy—the major influences in seminaries and divinity schools—are so fearful of the tainting of the American empire that they call for a religious flight from the public square. For Hauerwas, Christians should be "resident aliens" in a corrupt American empire whose secular public discourse is but a thin cover for its robust nihilism. His aim is to preserve the integrity of the prophetic church by exposing the idolatry of Constantinian Christianity and bearing witness to the gospel of love and peace. His deep commitment to a prophetic church of compassion and pacifism in a world of cruelty and violence leads him to reject the secular policing of Rawls and Rorty and to highlight the captivity of Constantinian Christians to imperial America. But he finds solace only in a prophetic ecclesiastical refuge that prefigures the coming kingdom of God. His prophetic sensibilities resonate with me and I agree with his critique of Constantinian Christianity and imperial America. Yet he unduly downplays the prophetic Christian commitment to justice and our role as citizens to make America more free and democratic. For him, the pursuit of social justice is a bad idea for Christians because it lures them toward the idols of secular discourse and robs them of their distinctive Christian identity. My defense of King's legacy requires that we accent justice as a Christian ideal and become even more active as citizens to change America without succumbing to secular idols or imperial fetishes. To be a prophetic Christian is not to be against the world in the name of church purity; it is to be in the world but not of the world's nihilism, in the name of a loving Christ who proclaims the this-worldly justice of a kingdom to come.

Hauerwas's radical imperative of world-denial motivates Milbank's popular Christian orthodoxy that pits the culprits of commodification and secularism against Christian socialism. His sophisticated wholesale attack on secular liberalism and modern capitalism is a fresh reminder of just how marginal prophetic Christianity has become in the age of the American empire. But, like Hauerwas, he fails to appreciate the moral progress, political breakthroughs, and spiritual freedoms forged by the heroic efforts of modern citizens of religious and secular traditions. It is just as dangerous to overlook the gains of modernity procured by prophetic religious and progressive secular citizens as it is to overlook the blindness of Constantinian Christians and imperial secularists. And these gains cannot be preserved and deepened by reverting to ecclesiastical refuges or sectarian orthodoxies. Instead they require candor about our religious integrity and democratic identity that leads us to critique and resist Constantinian Christianity and imperial America.

All four towering figures—Rawls, Rorty, Hauerwas, and Milbank—have much to teach us and are forces for good in many ways. Yet they preclude a robust democratic Christian identity that builds on the legacy of prophetic Christian-led social movements. Jeffrey Stout—himself the most religiously musical, theologically learned, and philosophically subtle of all secular writers in America today—has, by contrast, argued that American democrats must join forces with the legacy of Christian protest exemplified by Martin Luther King Jr. He knows that the future of the American democratic experiment may depend on revitalizing this legacy. The legacies of prophetic Christianity put a premium on the kind of human being one chooses to be rather than the amount of commodities one possesses. They thereby constitute a wholesale onslaught against nihilism—in all of its forms—and strike a blow for decency and integrity. They marshal religious energies for democratic aims, yet are suspicious of all forms of idolatry, including democracy itself as an idol. They preserve their Christian identity and its democratic commitments, without coercing others and conflating church and state spheres.

There can be a new democratic Christian identity in America only if imperial realities are acknowledged and prophetic legacies are revitalized. And despite the enormous resources of imperial elites to fan and fuel Constantinian Christianity, the underfunded and unpopular efforts of democrats and prophetic Christians must become more visible and vocal. The organizations of prophetic Christianity, such as the World Council of Churches, the civic action group Sojourners, and the black prophetic churches, must fight their way back into prominence in our public discourse. They must recognize that they have been under a kind of siege by the Constantinians and have not lost their dominance by accident.

Ironically, the powerful political presence of imperial Christians today is inspired by the success of the democratic Christian-led movement of Martin Luther King Jr. The worldly engagement of King's civil rights movement encouraged Constantinian Christians to become more organized and to partner with the power elites of the American empire. The politicization of Christian fundamentalism was a direct response to King's prophetic Christian legacy. It began as a white backlash against King's heritage in American public life, and it has always had a racist undercurrent—as with Bob Jones University, which until recently barred interracial dating.

The rise of Constantinian Christianity in America went hand in hand with the Republican Party's realignment of American politics—with their use of racially coded issues (busing, crime, affirmative action, welfare) to appeal to southern conservatives and urban white centrists. This political shift coincided with appeals to influential Jewish neoconservatives primarily concerned with the fragile security and international isolation of the state of Israel. In particular, the sense of Jewish desperation during the Yom Kippur War of 1973—fully understandable given the threat of Jewish annihilation only thirty years after the vicious holocaust in

Europe—drove the unholy alliance of American Republicans, Christian evangelicals, and Jewish neoconservatives.

On the domestic front, the fierce battle over admissions and employment slots produced a formidable backlash led by Jewish neoconservatives and white conservatives against affirmative action. The right-wing coalition of Constantinian Christians and Jewish neoconservatives helped elect Ronald Reagan in 1980. The fact that 35 percent of the most liberal nonwhite group—American Jews—voted for Reagan was a prescient sign of what was to come. When the Reverend Jerry Falwell of the Moral Majority received the Jabotinsky Award in 1981 in Israel, Constantinian Christianity had arrived on the international stage, with Jewish conservatism as its supporter. Imperial elites—including corporate ones with huge financial resources—here and abroad recognized just how useful organized Constantinian Christians could be for their nihilistic aims.

The rise of Constantinian Christian power in our democracy has progressed in stages. First, ecumenical groups like the World Council of Churches, the National Council of Churches, and liberal mainline denominations (Episcopalians, Presbyterians, Lutherans, and Congregationalists)—who spoke out in defense of the rights of people of color, workers, women, gays, and lesbians—were targeted. The Christian fundamentalists (with big money behind them) lashed out with vicious attacks against the prophetic Christian voices, who were branded "liberal," and worked to discredit the voices of moderation. In McCarthyist fashion, they equated the liberation theology movement, which put a limelight on the plight of the poor, with Soviet Communism. They cast liberal seminaries (especially my beloved Union Theological Seminary in New York City) as sinful havens of freaks, gays, lesbians, black radicals, and guilty white wimps. Such slanderous tactics have largely cowed the Christian Left, nearly erasing it off the public map.

The Christian fundamentalists have also tried to recruit Constantinian Christians of color in order to present a more diverse menagerie of faces to the imperial elites in the White House, Congress, state houses, and city halls, and on TV. The manipulative elites of the movement knew that this integrated alliance would attract even more financial support from big business to sustain a grassroots organizing campaign in imperial churches across the country. The veneer of diversity is required for the legitimacy of imperial rule today.

The last stage in the rise of the Constantinians was their consolidation of power by throwing their weight around with well-organized political action groups, most notably the Christian Coalition and the Moral Majority. With this political coordination they gained clout, power, legitimacy, and respectability within the golden gates of the American empire—they were acknowledged as mighty movers, shakers, and brokers who had to be reckoned with in the private meetings of the plutocrats and their politicians. Imperial elites recognized just how useful the Constantinian Christians could be for their nihilistic aims. The journey for Constantinian Christians from Ronald Reagan's election in 1980 to George W. Bush's selection in 2000 has been a roaring success—based on the world's nihilistic standards.

Never before in the history of the American Republic has a group of organized Christians risen to such prominence in the American empire. And this worldly success—a bit odd for a fundamentalist group with such otherworldly aspirations—has sent huge ripples across American Christendom. Power, might, size, status, and material possessions—all paraphernalia of the nihilism of the American empire—became major themes of American Christianity. It now sometimes seems that all Christians speak in one voice when in fact it is only that the loudness of the Constantinian element of American Christianity has so totally drowned out the prophetic voices. Imperial Christianity, market spirituality, money-obsessed churches, gospels of prosperity, prayers of let's make-a-deal with God or help me turn my wheel of fortune have become the prevailing voice of American Christianity. In this version of Christianity the precious blood at the foot of the cross becomes mere Kool-Aid to refresh eager upwardly mobile aspirants in the nihilistic American game of power and might. And there is hardly a mumbling word heard about social justice, resistance to institutional evil, or courage to confront the powers that be—with the glaring exception of abortion.

Needless to say, the commodification of Christianity is an old phenomenon—and a central one in American life past and present. Yet the frightening scope and depth of this commercialization of Christianity is new. There is no doubt that the churches reflect and refract the larger market-driven nihilism of our society and world. Yet it is the nearly wholesale eclipse of nonmarket values and visions—of love, justice, compassion, and kindness to strangers—that is terrifying. Where are the Christian voices outraged at the greed of corporate elites while millions of children live in poverty? Do American Christians even know that the three richest men in the world have more wealth than the combined gross domestic product of the bottom forty-eight countries or that the personal wealth of the richest individuals is equal to the annual income of the poorest 47 percent of the entire world's population? Philanthropy is fine, but what of justice, institutional fairness, and structural accountability?

There are, however, groups of prophetic Christians who are taking up the challenge of confronting the rise of the Christian Right and have realized the necessity of countering those powerful organizations with their own. There is Jim Wallis, who leads the activist group Sojourners; the Reverend James Forbes of Riverside Church in New York City; Sujay Johnson Cork of the Hampton Preachers' Conference; the Reverend Charles Adams of Hartford Memorial Church in Detroit; the Reverend Jeremiah Wright of Trinity Church in Chicago; Bishop Charles E. Blake of West Angeles Church of God in Christ; the Reverend I. Alfred Smith of Allen Temple in Oakland; and Father Michael Pfleger of Faith Community of Saint Sabina in Chicago. And there are quite a few more.

Yet it is undeniable that the challenge of keeping the prophetic Christian movement vital and vibrant in the age of the American empire is largely unmet as of yet. The pervasive sleepwalking in American churches in regard to social justice is frightening. The movement led by Martin Luther King Jr.—the legacy of which has been hijacked by imperial Christians—forged the most subtle and significant democratic Christian identity of modern times. And it now lies in ruins. Can prophetic Christians make its dry bones live again?

The Constantinian Christianity of the Bush administration—especially of President Bush, Attorney General John Ashcroft, and Congressman Tom DeLay—whatever authentic pietistic dimensions it may have, must not be the model of American Christian identity. Its nihilistic policies and quests for power and might supersede any personal confessions of humility and compassion. Even the most seemingly pious can inflict great harm. Constantine himself flouted his piety even as he continued to dominate and conquer peoples. Yet a purely secular effort against the religious zealotry will never be powerful enough to prevail; it is only with a coalition of the prophetic Christians of all colors, the prophetic Jews and Muslims and Buddhists, and the democratic secularists that we can preserve the American democratic experiment.

The recent controversy over Mel Gibson's *The Passion of the Christ* reveals the nihilistic undercurrents of the conservative coalition and potential rifts within it. The vicious Christian anti-Judaism and anti-Semitism over the past eighteen centuries stem primarily from the wedding of biblical narratives of Jesus' Crucifixion that highlight Jewish responsibility and Roman innocence to Constantine's incorporation of Christianity into imperial power. As long as the early Christians—themselves largely Jewish—were a persecuted minority in the Roman empire, their biblical claims about Jewish culpability and Roman indifference regarding the murder of Jesus were a relatively harmless intra-Jewish debate in the first century AD about a prophetic Jew who challenged the Jewish colonial elites and Roman imperial authorities. For example, when the phrase "the Jews" is used sixteen times in Mark, Luke, and Matthew and seventy-one times in John, these writers of the synoptic Gospels—themselves Jews—were engaged in an intramural debate between themselves and non-Christian Jews. Both groups were persecuted by imperial Roman authorities. And all knew of the thuggery of such authorities—including that of Pontius Pilate fifty years before. With the Roman destruction of the Jewish temple in AD 70, rabbinical Judaism emerged alongside the Jewish-led Christian movement. The Christian and Judaic struggle for the souls of Jews in imperial Rome was intense, yet under oppressive conditions for both groups.

With the adoption of Christianity as the official religion of the Roman empire in the fourth century AD—and the persecution of all other religions—the intramural debate became lethal. And the phrase "the Jews" in the Gospels became the basis of a vicious Christian anti-Judaism and pernicious imperial policy that blamed, attacked, maimed, and murdered Jews of Judaic faith. With the injection of race, Christian anti-Judaism (a religious bigotry) became Christian anti-Semitism (a racist bigotry). Jews who converted to Christianity could avoid the former, but all Jews suffered the latter. And the history of both bigotries is a crime against humanity—then and now.

Mel Gibson's gory film of Jesus' murder, which verges on a pornography of violence, resonates deeply with the ignorance and innocence of sincere Constantinian Christians in the American empire, whose grasp of the source of anti-Semitism is weak and whose complicity with imperial arrogance is ignored. His portrayal of Jewish responsibility and Roman innocence fits the centuries-long pattern of Christian anti-Semitism—in its effect, not in his intention.

Ironically, those Jews who eagerly aligned themselves with Constantinian Christians to defend imperial America and the colonial policies of the Israeli state now see the deep anti-Semitism of their Christian fundamentalist allies. And they are right. But these same Jewish conservatives—Constantinian Jews—fail to see their own complicity with imperial American elites who support and condone colonial policies and racist anti-Arab sentiments of Israeli conservative elites. Democracy matters promoted by prophetic Christians, Jews, Muslims, Buddhists and secular progressives—require moral consistency and ethical integrity. We all fall short yet we must never fail to fight all forms of bigotry, especially when racist propaganda is conjoined to nihilistic quests for power and might. Will the deep dimensions of Christian anti-Semitism shatter the conservative coalition in imperial America? Will Jewish elites in Hollywood begin to question the racist stereotypes of other groups they've condoned now that this controversy has turned against them?

I speak as a Christian—one whose commitment to democracy is very deep but whose Christian convictions are even deeper. Democracy is not my faith. And American democracy is not my idol. To see the Gospel of Jesus Christ bastardized by imperial Christians and pulverized by Constantinian believers and then exploited by nihilistic elites of the American empire makes my blood boil. To be a Christian—a follower of Jesus Christ—is to love wisdom, love justice, and love freedom. This is the radical love in Christian freedom and the radical freedom in Christian love that embraces Socratic questioning, prophetic witness, and tragicomic hope. If Christians do not exemplify this love and freedom, then we side with the nihilists of the Roman empire (cowardly elite Romans and subjugated Jews) who put Jesus to a humiliating death. Instead of receiving his love in freedom as a life-enhancing gift of grace, we end up believing in the idols of the empire that nailed him to the cross. I do not want to be numbered among those who sold their souls for a mess of pottage—who surrendered their democratic Christian identity for a comfortable place at the table of the American empire while, like Lazarus, the least of these cried out and I was too intoxicated with worldly power and might to hear, beckon, and heed their cries. To be a Christian is to live dangerously, honestly, freely—to step in the name of love as if you may land on nothing, yet to keep stepping because the something that sustains you no empire can give you and no empire can take away. This is the kind of vision and courage required to enable the renewal of prophetic, democratic Christian identity in the age of the American empire.

Chapter 12

Why Political Reliance on Religiously Grounded Morality Is Not Illegitimate in a Liberal Democracy

Michael J. Perry

INTRODUCTION

. . . The two main questions I address in this [essay] are these:

Do citizens or their political representatives contravene the morality of liberal democracy by relying on religiously grounded moral belief in public discussions about whether to outlaw or otherwise disfavor conduct (abortion, for example, or same-sex unions)?

Do legislators or other policymakers contravene the morality of liberal democracy by outlawing or otherwise disfavoring conduct on the basis of religiously grounded moral belief?

Assume that . . . government officials do not violate the nonestablishment norm by disfavoring conduct on the basis of religiously grounded moral belief. This leaves open the possibility that government officials nonetheless betray the morality of liberal democracy by doing so. In my judgment, however . . . the morality of liberal democracy does not forbid legislators or other policymakers to disfavor conduct on the basis of religiously grounded

311

moral belief. . . . Nor does the morality of liberal democracy forbid citizens or their political representatives to rely on religiously grounded moral belief in public discussions about whether to disfavor conduct.

THE MORALITY OF LIBERAL DEMOCRACY

What is the morality—what are the moral commitments—of liberal democracy? The foundational moral commitment of liberal democracy is to the true and full humanity of *every* person—and, therefore, to the inviolability of *every* person[1]—without regard to race, sex, religion, and so on. This commitment is axiomatic for liberal democracy.

> Perhaps the litmus test of whether the reader is in any sense a liberal or not is Gladstone's foreign-policy speeches. In [one such speech,] taken from the late 1870s, around the time of the Midlothian campaign, [Gladstone] reminded his listeners that "the sanctity of life in the hill villages of Afghanistan among the winter snows is as inviolable in the eye of almighty God as can be your own . . . that the law of mutual love is not limited by the shores of this island, is not limited by the boundaries of Christian civilization; that it passes over the whole surface of the earth and embraces the meanest along with the greatest in its unmeasured scope." By all means smile at the oratory. But anyone who sneers at the underlying message is not a liberal in any sense of that word worth preserving.[2]

Moreover, this foundational commitment to the inviolability of every person is a principal ground of liberal democracy's further commitment to certain basic human freedoms. As Charles Larmore has put the point: "The familiar constitutional rights of free-expression, property, and political participation, though no doubt serving to promote the goal of democratic self-rule, also have an independent rationale. They draw upon that most fundamental of individual rights, which is the right [of every person] to equal respect."[3] Indeed, these two allied commitments— to the humanity/inviolability of every person and to certain basic human freedoms—are constitutive of liberal democracy; they are what make a democracy a "liberal" democracy. *These two commitments are the heart of the morality of liberal democracy.*

A conference at which I spoke in May 1999 was titled Political Thought after Liberalism.[4] This was, I thought, a puzzling title. We citizens of the United States, and of other liberal democracies, do not now live in a time that is "after liberalism." We Americans are all liberals now. (There is only slight rhetorical excess here: we Americans are, *almost* all of us, liberals now.) That is, we are all not merely democrats (small *d*) but *liberal* democrats. We are all committed both to the true and full humanity of every person and, therefore, to certain basic human freedoms (liberties). Indeed, we have come to cherish these freedoms, and to trumpet them to the world, as human rights. In the United States, the moral arguments and the related political arguments about such matters as same-sex unions, physician-assisted suicide, the death penalty, and abortion are not, in the main, arguments between liberals on the one side and nonliberals on the other. Rather, these arguments are, in the main, arguments among liberals. They are arguments among citizens all of whom are committed to the true and full humanity of every person and to the basic human freedoms characteristic of—indeed, constitutive of—early-twenty-first-century liberal democracies.

This is not to deny that there are important differences among liberals.

> Some liberals are religious believers; others are not. Some liberals give a religious justification for their liberalism—for their commitment both to the true and full humanity of every person and to the basic human freedoms constitutive of liberal democracy; others give a nonreligious justification. (It is not the character of the justification that one gives for one's commitment to the true and full humanity of every person that, in part, makes one a liberal; it is the commitment itself.)

> Some liberals are moral conservatives, reluctant to abandon moral orthodoxies in favor of dissenting moral positions (e.g., about homosexuality); others are not conservative, or are less so.

> Some liberals are pessimistic about the capacity of government, especially centralized national government, to accomplish much good in the world, so they are wary about relying on government to make the world a better place, either the world at home or the world abroad; others are not pessimistic, or are less so.

And so on. But notwithstanding these and other important differences, we Americans are (almost) all liberals now. I know that this thought does not go down easily. We live in a time when demagogues, polemicists, and pundits have largely succeeded in turning the word "liberal" into an epithet—a dirty word. Let us reclaim our discourse. We Americans are all liberals now, because we affirm the true and full humanity of every person, without regard to race, sex, religion, and so on, and we also affirm, therefore, certain basic human freedoms (e.g., the freedoms of speech, press, and religion). It is this twofold affirmation that makes a democracy a "liberal" democracy, a political morality a "liberal" political morality, and a person a "liberal." No understanding or interpretation of the term *liberal* is *less* tendentious than this. We're (almost) all liberals now.

But, again, this doesn't mean that we liberals can't or don't disagree among ourselves—sometimes passionately and deeply—about many things. One of the things we disagree about: the legitimacy of political reliance on religiously grounded morality.

RELYING ON RELIGIOUSLY GROUNDED MORAL BELIEF IN PUBLIC POLITICAL ARGUMENT

In the United States, there is no constitutional impediment to religious believers' (citizens, legislators, policymakers)[5] introducing religiously grounded belief that conduct is immoral into public political argument, including argument of the sort with which I am principally concerned here: argument about whether or not to disfavor the conduct. (There are, however, substantial constitutional impediments to government's disallowing the introduction of such belief into public political argument: the constitutional norms that protect the freedoms of speech and press and the free exercise of religion.)[6] But this does not mean that religious believers *may* introduce religiously grounded moral belief into public political argument. That one is constitutionally free to do something—for example, utter a racial epithet—does not entail that one is also morally free to do it. In a liberal democracy, may religious believers introduce religiously grounded moral belief into public political argument; is it morally permissible, in a liberal democracy, for them to do so? This is a not question about political strategy but about political morality—the morality of liberal democracy. "The distinction between principle and prudence should be emphasized. The fundamental question is not whether, as a matter of prudent judgment in a religiously pluralist society, those who hold particular religious views ought to cast their arguments in secular terms. Even an outsider can say that the answer to that question is clearly, 'Yes, most of the time,' for only such a course is likely to be successful overall."[7]

Again, the two constitutive commitments of liberal democracy—the two commitments that make a democracy "liberal"—are (1) the commitment to the true and full humanity of *every* person, without regard to race, sex, religion, and so on, and (2) the allied commitment to certain basic human freedoms. Nothing in the morality of liberal democracy—nothing in either of liberal democracy's two constitutive commitments—supports the claim that it is illegitimate for religious believers to introduce religiously grounded moral belief into public political argument. Introducing such belief into public political argument does not, in and of itself, betray either of liberal democracy's two constitutive commitments.

Nonetheless, some persons want to keep religiously grounded moral belief out of public political argument as much as possible. The American philosopher Richard Rorty, for example, has written approvingly of "privatizing religion—keeping it out of . . . 'the public square,' making it seem bad taste to bring religion into discussions of public policy."[8] However, a powerful practical consideration opposes Rorty's position—a powerful practical reason why even nonbelievers should want religious believers, when they participate in public political argument, to articulate the religiously grounded moral belief that moves them to defend the position they do.

Imagine that it is proposed to make, or to maintain, a political choice disfavoring conduct that many citizens believe to be immoral—the political choice, for example, not to extend the benefit of law to same-sex unions. Imagine, too, that a widely accepted religiously grounded belief holds that the conduct is immoral—for example, the biblically grounded belief that homosexual sexual conduct is, always and everywhere, immoral. It is inevitable, in the United States, that some citizens and legislators will support the political choice at least partly on the ground of the religiously (biblically) grounded belief. It is also inevitable that some citizens and legislators, because they accept the religiously grounded belief, will take more seriously than they otherwise would, and perhaps accept, a secular (i.e., nonreligious) belief that supports the political choice—for example, the belief that homosexuality, like alcoholism, is a pathology that ought not to be indulged,[9] or the belief that legalizing same-sex unions would subvert the institution of heterosexual marriage. Because of the role that religiously grounded moral belief inevitably plays in the political process, then, it is important that such beliefs, no less than secular moral beliefs, be presented in public political argument *so that they can be tested there*.

Indeed, sometimes it is appropriate and even important that religiously grounded moral belief be tested, in the to-and-fro of public political argument, on its own terms. Consider, in that regard, scriptural scholar Luke Timothy Johnson's admonition:

> If liberal Christians committed to sexual equality and religious
> tolerance abandon these texts as useless, they also abandon the
> field of Christian hermeneutics to those whose fearful and—it
> must be said—sometimes hate-filled apprehension of Christianity

will lead them to exploit and emphasize just those elements of the tradition that have proved harmful to humans. If what Phyllis Trible has perceptively termed "texts of terror" within the Bible are not encountered publicly and engaged intellectually by a hermeneutics that is at once faithful and critical, then they will continue to exercise their potential for harm among those who, without challenge, can claim scriptural authority for their own dark impulses.[10]

It is easy to anticipate the dismissive reply that public political argument is simply too debased to serve as a context for serious critical discussion of religiously grounded moral belief. My response is twofold. First, if public political debate is too debased to serve as a context for serious critical discussion of religiously grounded moral belief, then it is too debased to serve as a context for serious critical discussion of secular moral belief as well—and of much else, too. Second, the issue that engages me here is the proper role of religiously grounded morality, not in a politics too debased for serious critical discussion of moral belief, but in a politics at least *sometimes* and in *some* places—in *some* fora—fit for such discussion. Is it naive to think that American politics fits that profile? It is useful to recall here that public political discussion takes place in op-ed pieces and magazine articles, for example, as well as in television ads and on bumper stickers; indeed, it takes place much more seriously in the former fora than in the latter.

Still, some persons, such as Rorty, want to privatize religion; they want to keep religiously grounded moral belief out of "the public square" as much as possible. Why? Because religiously grounded arguments about controversial political issues can be quite divisive? American history does not suggest that religiously grounded arguments about controversial moral/political issues—racial discrimination, for example, or war—are invariably, or even usually, more divisive than secular arguments about those issues.[11] Some issues are so controversial that arguments about them are inevitably divisive without regard to whether the arguments are religiously grounded.[12]

To be sure, religious discourse in public—whether in public political argument or in other parts of our public culture—is sometimes quite sectarian and therefore divisive. But religiously grounded moral discourse is not necessarily more sectarian than secular moral discourse. It can be much less sectarian. After all, certain basic moral premises common to the Jewish and Christian traditions, in conjunction with the supporting religious premises, still constitute the fundamental moral horizon of most Americans—much more than do Kantian (or neo-Kantian) premises, or Millian premises, or Nietzschean premises (and so forth). According to Jesuit sociologist John Coleman, "the tradition of biblical religion is arguably the most powerful and pervasive symbolic resource" for public ethics in the United States today. "Our tradition of religious ethics seems . . . to enjoy a more obvious public vigor and availability as a resource for renewal in American culture than either the tradition of classic republican theory or the American tradition of public philosophy." Coleman reminds us that "the strongest American voices for a compassionate just community always appealed in public to religious imagery and sentiments, from Winthrop and Sam Adams, Melville and the Lincoln of the Second Inaugural Address, to Walter Rauschenbusch and Reinhold Niebuhr and Frederick Douglass and Martin Luther King." As Coleman explains, "The American religious ethic and rhetoric contain rich, polyvalent symbolic power to command sentiments of emotional depth, when compared to 'secular' language, . . . [which] remains exceedingly 'thin' as a symbol system." Coleman emphasizes that "when used as a public discourse, the language of biblical religion is beyond the control of any particular, denominational theology. It represents a common American cultural patrimony. . . . American public theology or religious ethics . . . cannot be purely sectarian. The biblical language belongs to no one church, denomination, or sect." In Coleman's view,

> The genius of public American theology . . . is that it has transcended denominations, been espoused by people as diverse as Abraham Lincoln and Robert Bellah who neither were professional theologians nor belonged to any specific church and, even in the work of specifically trained professional theologians, such as Reinhold Niebuhr, has appealed less to revelational warrant for its authority within public policy discussions than to the ability of biblical insights and symbols to convey a deeper human wisdom. . . . Biblical imagery . . . lies at the heart of the American self-understanding. It is neither parochial nor extrinsic.[13]

Another reason for wanting to fence religiously grounded moral belief out of public political argument focuses on the inability of some believers to achieve a critical distance from their religious belief—the kind of critical distance essential to truly deliberative argument. But in the United States and in other liberal democracies, many believers *are* able to achieve a critical distance from many if not all of their religious beliefs;[14] they are certainly as able to do so as they and others are able to gain a critical distance from other fundamental beliefs.[15] Undeniably, some believers are unable to achieve much if any critical distance from their fundamental religious beliefs. As so much in the twentieth century attests, however, one need not be a religious believer to adhere to one's fundamental beliefs with closed-minded or even fanatical tenacity.

Although no one who has lived through recent American history should believe that religious contributions to the public discussion of controversial moral issues are invariably deliberative rather than dogmatic, there is no reason to believe that religious contributions are never deliberative. Religious discourse about the difficult moral issues that engage and divide us citizens of liberal democratic societies is not necessarily more monologic (or otherwise problematic) than resolutely secular discourse about those issues. Because of the religious illiteracy—and, alas, even prejudice—rampant among many nonreligious intellectuals,[16] we probably need reminding that, at its best, religious discourse in public culture is not less dialogic—not less open-minded, not less deliberative—than is, at its best, secular discourse in public culture. (Nor, at its worst, is religious discourse more monologic—more closed-minded and dogmatic—than is, at its worst, secular discourse.)[17] The Jesuit theologian David Hollenbach has developed this important point:

> Much discussion of the public role of religion in recent political thought presupposes that religion is more likely to fan the flames of discord than contribute to social concord. This is certainly true of some forms of religious belief, but hardly of all. Many religious communities recognize that their traditions are dynamic and that their understandings of God are not identical with the reality of God. Such communities have in the past and can in the future engage in the religious equivalent of intellectual solidarity, often called ecumenical or interreligious dialogue.[18]

A central feature of Hollenbach's work is his argument, which I accept, that the proper role of "public" religious discourse in a society as religiously pluralistic as the United States is a role to be played, in the main, much more in public culture—in particular, "in those components of civil society that are the primary bearers of cultural meaning and value—universities, religious communities, the world of the arts, and serious journalism"—than in public argument specifically about political issues.[19] He writes: "The domains of government and policy-formation are not generally the appropriate ones in which to argue controverted theological and philosophical issues."[20] But, as Hollenbach goes on to acknowledge, "it is nevertheless neither possible nor desirable to construct an airtight barrier between politics and culture."[21]

There is, then, this additional reason for not discouraging the introduction of religiously grounded moral belief into public political argument: in a society as overwhelmingly religious as the United States,[22] we do present and discuss—and we should present and discuss—religiously grounded moral belief in our public culture. ("We can freely and intelligently exercise our freedom of choice on fundamental matters having to do with our own individual ideals and conceptions of the good only if we have access to an unconstrained discussion in which the merits of competing moral, religious, aesthetic, and philosophical values are given a fair opportunity for hearing.")[23] Rather than try to do the impossible—maintain a wall of separation ("an airtight barrier") between the religiously grounded moral discourse that inevitably and properly takes place in public culture ("universities, religious communities, the world of the arts, and serious journalism") on the one side, and the discourse that takes place in public political argument ("the domains of government and policy-formation") on the other side—we should simply welcome the presentation of religiously grounded moral belief in *all* areas of our public culture, *including* public argument specifically about contested political choices.[24] Indeed, we should not merely welcome but *encourage* the presentation of such belief in public political argument—so that we can test it there.

But we can and should do more than test religiously grounded moral belief in public political argument. We should also, in the course of testing such beliefs, let ourselves be tested by them. In a political community that aspires to be not merely democratic but *deliberatively* democratic, there is surely virtue in allowing ourselves to be tested by positions with which, at the outset, we disagree. [Some] years ago, in my book *Morality, Politics, and Law,* I wrote:

> If one can participate in politics and law—if one can use or resist power—only as a partisan of particular moral/religious convictions about the human, and if politics is and must be in part about the credibility of such convictions, then we who want to participate, whether as theorists or activists or both, must examine our own convictions self-critically. We must be willing to let our convictions be tested in ecumenical dialogue with others who do not share them. We must let ourselves be tested, in ecumenical dialogue, by convictions we do not share. We must, in short, resist the temptations of infallibilism.[25]

Richard Rorty no doubt speaks for many secular intellectuals in suggesting that we act to "privatiz[e] religion—[to] keep it out of . . . 'the public square,' making it seem bad taste to bring religion into discussions of public policy."[26] But Rorty is wrong. We should make it seem bad taste to sneer when people bring their religious convictions to bear in public discussions of controversial moral/political issues, such as homosexuality and abortion. It is not *that* religious convictions are brought to bear in public political argument that should worry us, but *how* they are sometimes brought to bear (e.g., dogmatically). But we should be no less worried about how fundamental secular convictions are sometimes brought to bear in public political debate.

Rorty and others to the contrary notwithstanding, we Americans—nonbelievers no less than believers—should welcome and even encourage the forthright presentation of religiously grounded moral belief in public political argument. Let me recapitulate the points I have featured here:

> Given the influential role that some religiously grounded moral beliefs play in our politics, it is important that we test such beliefs in public political argument. Moreover, our political culture cannot be truly deliberative unless we let ourselves be tested by religiously grounded moral beliefs. It is important, therefore, that we "public-ize" religion, not privatize it.

> In the United States, religiously grounded moral belief in public political argument is not necessarily more sectarian or divisive than secular moral belief. Nor are those who rely on religiously grounded moral belief in public political argument necessarily less deliberative than those who rely only on secular moral belief.

> It is quixotic, in any event, to attempt to construct an airtight barrier between religiously grounded moral discourse in public culture—which discourse is not merely legitimate but important—and such discourse in public political argument.

OUTLAWING OR OTHERWISE DISFAVORING CONDUCT ON THE BASIS OF RELIGIOUSLY GROUNDED MORAL BELIEF

* * * *

I said that in the United States there is no constitutional impediment to religious believers' introducing religiously grounded belief about the (im)morality of conduct into public argument about whether to disfavor the conduct. . . . But that there is no constitutional impediment does not entail that there is no moral impediment. Does the morality of liberal democracy forbid religious believers, especially legislators and other policymakers, to disfavor conduct on the basis of religiously grounded moral belief? This question has broader relevance than the question of whether the nonestablishment norm forbids them to do so: not every liberal democracy has a constitutional requirement that government not establish religion. Nor need every liberal democracy have such a requirement; as I have explained elsewhere, if a constitution vigorously protects the free exercise of religion, then the fact that it does not forbid government to establish religion does not imperil anyone's human rights.[27]

Just as nothing in the morality of liberal democracy forbids citizens or their political representatives to introduce religiously grounded moral belief into public political argument, nothing in the morality of liberal democracy forbids legislators or other policymakers to disfavor conduct on the basis of religiously grounded belief that the conduct is immoral. Disfavoring conduct on the basis of religiously grounded moral belief does not, in and of itself, betray either of liberal democracy's two constitutive commitments. Nothing either in the commitment to the true and full humanity of every person or in the allied commitment to certain basic human freedoms forbids legislators or other policymakers to disfavor conduct on the basis of a religiously grounded moral belief just *in virtue of the fact that the belief is religiously grounded.* (. . . If the weaker claim cannot be sustained—the claim that, according to the morality of liberal democracy, one may not make a political choice disfavoring conduct on the basis of religiously grounded belief that the conduct is immoral—then it is unnecessary to focus on the stronger claim that in making the choice one may not rely on such belief at all.) Nicholas Wolterstorff is right that the morality of liberal democracy, properly understood, forbids no such thing.[28]

> The ethic of the citizen in a liberal democracy imposes no restrictions on the reasons people offer in their discussion of political issues in the public square, and likewise imposes none of the reasons they have for their political decisions and actions. If the position adopted, and the manner in which it is acted upon, are compatible with the concept of liberal democracy, and if the discussion concerning the issue is conducted with civility, then citizens are free to offer and act on whatever reasons they find compelling. I regard it as an important implication of the concept of liberal democracy that citizens should have this freedom—that in this regard they should be allowed to act as they

see fit. Liberal democracy implies, as I see it, that there should be no censorship in this regard.[29]

We can all agree, of course, that the morality of liberal democracy—not to mention the First Amendment's protection of the freedoms of speech and press and the free exercise of religion—tolerates no formal (i.e., legal) censorship; Wolterstorff is right to insist that the morality of liberal democracy tolerates no informal (moral) censorship either.

Why, then, might one be inclined to conclude that government—in particular, legislators and other policymakers, acting collectively—should not disfavor conduct on the basis of religiously grounded moral belief? Two main reasons—two main arguments—come to mind: the argument from respect and the argument from divisiveness.

The argument from respect can be understood as an argument based on the morality of liberal democracy, which is committed to the true and full humanity of every person and therefore grounds "the right [of every person] to equal respect."[30] According to the argument from respect, for government to outlaw or otherwise disfavor conduct on the basis of religiously grounded moral belief is for government to act on the basis of a moral belief that some persons subject to the ban or regulation reasonably reject, and for government to do *that* is for it to deny to those persons the respect that is their due as persons—or, as John Rawls has put it, as "free and equal" persons.[31] (Although this claim could be directed at political reliance on religiously grounded moral belief, it is typically directed at political reliance on controversial moral belief, whether or not religiously grounded.) This claim frequently appears, in one guise or another, in essays purporting to present the "liberal" position on the issue of morality's proper role in politics. For example, Stephen Macedo has written that "the liberal claim is that it is wrong to seek to coerce people on grounds that they cannot share without converting to one's faith."[32] Notwithstanding the frequency of its appearance, this "liberal" claim is deeply problematic.

Consider William Galston's response to the claim (as he understands the claim):

> [Charles] Larmore (and Ronald Dworkin before him) may well be right that the norm of equal respect for persons is close to the core of contemporary liberalism. But while the (general) concept of equal respect may be relatively uncontroversial, the (specific) conception surely is not. To treat an individual as person rather than object is to offer him an explanation. Fine; but *what kind of*

explanation? Larmore seems to suggest that a properly respectful explanation must appeal to beliefs already held by one's
interlocutors; hence the need for neutral dialogue. This seems
arbitrary and implausible. I would suggest, rather, that we show
others respect when we offer them, as explanation, what we take
to be our best reasons for acting as we do.[33]

Galston's response needs to be both corrected and amended. First, the
correction: Galston misconceives Larmore's position, which is that political
"justification must appeal, not simply to the beliefs that the other happens
to have, but to the beliefs he has on the assumption (perhaps counterfactual) that he affirms the norm of equal respect [for persons]."[34] Larmore
[later] affirmed this aspect of his position: "The terms of political association are to be judged by reference to what citizens would accept, were they
reasonable *and committed to the principle of equal respect for persons.*"[35]

Now, two crucial but friendly amendments to Galston's response:
First, it is never for one to show respect for another for him to offer to
her—for example, for a Nazi to offer to a Jew—an explanation to the
effect that "You are not truly or fully human," even if the Nazi sincerely
takes that to be his best reason for acting as he does. Second, respect
counsels not only that we offer others, as explanation, what we take to be
our best reasons for acting as we do, but also that we try to discern and
then communicate to them whatever reason or reasons *they* might have
for supporting—or, at least, for being less hostile to—the law or policy at
issue. Chris Eberle has developed and defended this important point. As
Eberle emphasizes, however, respect requires that we try to discern and
then communicate such reasons. It does not require that if we fail in the
effort, we restrain ourselves from acting as—from supporting the law or
policy that—we otherwise would.[36]

Robert Audi has been one of the most important contributors to the
literature about the proper role of religion in politics.[37] In his variation
on the "liberal" position, Audi writes: "If you are fully rational and I cannot convince you of my view by arguments framed in the concepts we
share as rational beings, then even if mine is the majority view, I should
not coerce you."[38] But *why?* I concur in Gerald Dworkin's observation:
"There is a gap between a premise which requires the state to show equal
concern and respect for all its citizens and a conclusion which rules out
as legitimate grounds for coercion the fact that a majority believes that
conduct is immoral, wicked, or wrong. That gap has yet to be closed."[39]
Indeed, it is doubtful that the gap *can* be closed. It is altogether obscure
why we do not show others the respect that is their due, first, "when we

offer them, as explanation, what we take to be our best reasons for acting as we do" (so long as our reasons do not assert, presuppose, or entail
the inferior humanity of those to whom the explanation is offered) and,
second, when we try (even if in the end we fail) to discern and communicate other reasons that might win their consent, or at least diminish their
hostility, to the law or policy at issue.[40]

The argument from divisiveness provides a second main reason why
one might be inclined to conclude that government should not outlaw
or otherwise disfavor conduct on the basis of religiously grounded
moral belief: the social costs—costs mainly in the form of divisiveness
and ensuing social instability—are too high. Let me put the argument
from divisiveness, as we may call it, in context: in the United States
and in kindred liberal democracies, freedom of religion enjoys vigorous
constitutional protection; therefore, the set of moral beliefs on which
government may base a political choice is limited. For example, government may not base a political choice on the belief that Roman Catholicism is a morally corrupt religion. In thinking about the argument from
divisiveness, then, let's focus not on moral beliefs on which government
constitutionally may *not* base a political choice—least of all a coercive
political choice—but on moral beliefs on which it constitutionally *may*
base a political choice.

It is implausible that in a liberal democracy such as the United States,
basing a political choice on a constitutionally optional but nonetheless
controversial moral belief—such as the belief that same-sex unions are
immoral—will usually be *more* divisive if there is only a religious ground
for the belief than if there is a secular ground (whether or not there is also
a religious ground). As American history makes clear, some issues are so
controversial that any political resolution of the issue is destined to be quite
divisive without regard to whether the basis of the resolution is solely religious or solely secular or partly religious and partly secular.[41] Even if it be
granted that some imaginable instances of political reliance on religiously
grounded moral belief might, along with other factors, precipitate social
instability, the fact remains that "conditions in modern democracies may
be so far from the conditions that gave rise to the religious wars of the sixteenth century that we no longer need worry about religious divisiveness
as a source of substantial social conflict."[42] John Courtney Murray warned
against "project[ing] into the future of the Republic the nightmares, real or
fancied, of the past."[43] As Murray's comment suggests, a rapprochement
between religion and politics forged in the crucible of a time or place very
different from our own is not necessarily the best arrangement for our

time and place. "What principles of restraint, if any, are appropriate may depend on time and place, on a sense of the present makeup of a society, of its history, and of its likely evolution."[44]

In my judgment, neither the argument from respect nor the argument from divisiveness bears the weight of the proposition that government should not disfavor conduct on the basis of religiously grounded moral belief. (Not that there are no other arguments in support of that proposition, but the argument from respect and the argument from divisiveness are the two main arguments.)[45] Neither argument bears the weight even of the weaker proposition that government should not disfavor conduct on the basis of religiously grounded moral belief if there is no plausible, independent secular grounding for belief.

I said that nothing in the morality of liberal democracy forbids legislators or other policymakers to disfavor conduct on the basis of a religiously grounded moral belief just in virtue of the fact that the belief is religiously grounded. But an even stronger claim commands our assent: one particular religiously grounded belief—one fundamental religiously grounded moral claim—is not only a legitimate ground of political choice in a liberal democracy but a most fitting ground.

"Moral" argument, as I have explained elsewhere,[46] is often—and most fundamentally—about this: Which human beings ought we to care about—which ones, that is, besides those we already happen to care about, those we already happen to be emotionally or sentimentally attached to: ourselves, our families, our tribes, and so on? Which human beings ought to be the beneficiaries of our respect; the welfare, the well-being, of which human beings ought to be the object of our concern? Which human beings are inviolable; which are subjects of justice? All human beings, or just some? As I noted earlier . . . one of the two constitutive commitments of liberal democracy—one of the two commitments that make a democracy "liberal"—is the commitment to the true and full humanity of *every* person, without regard to race, sex, religion, and so on.[47] (The second constitutive commitment, grounded in part on the first, is to certain basic human freedoms.) The commitment is responsive to the "which human beings ought we to care about" inquiry: it is axiomatic, for liberal democracy, that every person is inviolable. Of course, the proposition that every person is inviolable is embraced by many who do not count themselves religious believers, but, as I have explained elsewhere,[48] it is obscure *on what basis* one who is not a religious believer, one who is an agnostic or even an atheist, can claim (indeed, can believe) that every person is inviolable: Why is it the case—*in virtue of what* is it the case—that every person is "not to be violated; not liable or allowed to suffer violence; to be kept sacredly free from profanation, infraction, or assault"?[49] As Jeff McMahan has emphasized, "understanding the basis of our alleged inviolability is crucial both for determining whether it is plausible to regard ourselves as inviolable, and for fixing the boundaries of the class of inviolable beings."[50] In any event, that every person is inviolable is, for many religious believers, a religiously embedded tenet. And, in a liberal democracy, it is altogether fitting—it is altogether "liberal"—for religious believers to make political choices, including *coercive* choices—choices to ban or require conduct—on the ground of what is, for them, a religious claim: that each and every person is sacred, that all persons are subjects of justice.[51]

* * * *

Chapter 13

The Vulnerability
of the Naked Public Square

Richard John Neuhaus

Martin Luther King Jr. and Jerry Falwell. Friends of both would likely be offended by the suggestion that they are in any way similar. And yet they are, I believe. Of course they are also strikingly different figures, with quite different analyses of what is wrong with America and what ought to be done about it. They were on opposite sides of the civil rights struggle in the fifties and sixties. (Without going so far as to say that King was right, the Falwells regularly acknowledge that they were wrong on race.) There is the sharpest contrast between King's enprincipled non-violence and Falwell's advocacy of bellicose toughness in dealing with the Communists. Numerous other differences, political and theological, could be itemized. But in this they are similar: both Martin Luther King and Jerry Falwell disrupt the business of secular America by an appeal to religiously based public values.

Although in quite different ways, both are profoundly patriotic figures. Dr. King's dream was of America as an exemplar of racial and social justice, an anticipation of that "beloved community" promised by God. The patriotic fervor with which Dr. King invoked an American promise is often forgotten. But the March on Washington, for instance, can never be forgotten by those who were there, nor, one hopes, by the millions who have watched its replay on television documentaries. On that oppressively hot Wednesday afternoon of August 28, 1963, before the Lincoln Memorial, a baritone trumpet sought to recall America to its better self. "Five score years ago, a great American, in whose symbolic shadow we stand, signed the Emancipation Proclamation," Dr. King began. He then described the ways in which the promise had not been kept and rhetorically etched the shape of its fulfillment. "This will be the day when all God's children will be able to sing with new meaning 'My country 'tis of thee, sweet land of liberty, of thee I sing. Land where my fathers died, land of the pilgrim's pride, from every mountain side, let freedom ring.'" Lest we succumb to the prejudice that patriotic rhetoric is by definition ignoble, the peroration deserves to be committed to memory:

> When we let freedom ring, when we let it ring from every village and every hamlet, from every state and every city, we will be able to speed up that day when all God's children, black men and white men, Jews and Gentiles, Protestants and Catholics, will be able to join hands and sing in the words of that old Negro spiritual, "Free at last! Free at last! Thank God almighty, we are free at last!"

A biographer of King, who had learned in the school of economic determinism that moral appeals are but the instrumental disguise of class conflict, says of the March on Washington speech: "This was rhetoric almost without content, but this was, after all, a day of heroic fantasy."[1] Such a comment suggests that the impingement of religious vision upon the public square can be permitted from time to time—if it is employed in the right causes, and if it is not taken too seriously. Thus also today's discharge of religious language in public space is assumed to hide narrow partisan interests. Although immeasurably less eloquent or persuasive than Dr. King's, contemporary religious rhetoric of populist patriotism deserves to be treated as seriously. To treat it seriously does not, of course, mean that one agrees. But when today's political preachers lift up a vision of a morally rejuvenated America serving as the base for global evangelism and as the defense against atheistic totalitarianism, there is no good reason to doubt that they are—to use that much overworked word—sincere. That is, it is not necessarily suspect language, language employed to advance some purpose other than the purpose indicated by the language itself.

To be sure, activists in whatever cause employ—and even, in the negative sense of the term, exploit—language in order to conceal loyalties and heighten emotional commitment. Activism is inescapably concerned not for disinterested truth but for *effective* truth, truth that is effective in advancing the purpose at hand. From this reality derives the pervasive mendacity that distorts all political engagement, to a greater or lesser degree. That being said, it remains important to note which rhetoric is chosen to advance the cause. Few leaders are so false to the core as to choose a rhetoric for its manipulative effect alone. As skeptical as we may rightly be about appeals to moral ideals, it is reasonable to believe that the ideals by which leaders would call others to judgment are the ideals by which, at least in their more reflective moments, they believe they are themselves judged. This observation is not invalidated by La Rochefoucauld's famous maxim, "Hypocrisy is the homage that vice pays to virtue." The truth of the maxim does not allow even the greatest cynic to be dismissive about moral ideals in public discourse. On the contrary, the hypocrisies by which we know ourselves to fail are of decisive importance. Be they hypocrisies or be they truths nobly adhered to, they are the moral points of reference by which communities are called to accountability. My point is not to suggest that either Dr. King or current political preachers are hypocritical. It is to emphasize that they are alike in proposing a vision of public virtue, and that that vision is religiously based.

The assertion that binds together otherwise different causes is the claim that only a transcendent, a religious, vision can turn this society from certain disaster and toward the fulfillment of its destiny. In this connection "destiny" is but another word for purpose. From whatever point on the political spectrum such an assertion is made, it challenges the conventional wisdom that America is a secular society. In recent decades we have become accustomed to believe that of course America is a secular society. That, in the minds of many, is what is meant by the separation of church and state. But this way of thinking is of relatively recent vintage. As late as 1931 the Supreme Court could assert without fear of contradiction, "We are a Christian people, according to one another the equal right of religious freedom, and acknowledging with reverence the duty of obedience to the will of God." The 1931 case had to do with whether a conscientious objector to war could become a citizen. After the above statement about obedience to God, the Court concluded, "But, also, we are a nation with the duty to survive." Citizenship was denied (*U.S. v. Macintosh*).

In 1952, in a dispute over students getting off from public schools in released time for religious instruction, Justice Douglas, hardly a religiously observant man, wrote, "We are a religious people whose institutions presuppose a Supreme Being" (*Zorach v. Clauson*). As time went on, however, the Court's references to religion had less and less to do with what is usually meant by religion. That is, religion no longer referred to those communal traditions of ultimate beliefs and practices ordinarily called religion. Religion, in the court's meaning, became radically individualized and privatized. Religion became a synonym for conscience. For instance, in cases again related to conscientious objection, exemption from the military draft was to be allowed on the "registrant's moral, ethical, or religious beliefs about what is right and wrong [provided] those beliefs be held with the strength of traditional religious convictions" (*Welsh v. U.S.*, 1970). Thus religion is no longer a matter of content but of sincerity. It is no longer a matter of communal values but of individual conviction. In short, it is no longer a public reality and therefore cannot interfere with public business.

Such a religious evacuation of the public square cannot be sustained, either in concept or in practice. When religion in any traditional or recognizable form is excluded from the public square, it does not mean that the public square is in fact naked. This is the other side of the "naked public square" metaphor. When recognizable religion is excluded, the vacuum will be filled by *ersatz* religion, by religion bootlegged into public space under other names. [T]o paraphrase Spinoza: transcendence abhors a vacuum. The reason why the naked public square cannot, in fact, remain naked is in the very nature of law and laws. If law and laws are not seen to be coherently related to basic presuppositions about right and wrong, good and evil, they will be condemned as illegitimate. After having excluded traditional religion, then, the legal and political trick is to address questions of right and wrong in a way that is not "contaminated" by the label "religious." This relatively new sleight-of-hand results in what many have called "civil religion." It places a burden upon the law to act religiously without being suspected of committing religion. While social theorists might talk about "civil religion," the courts dare not do so, for that too would be an unconstitutional "establishment" of religion.

Admittedly, it is all very confusing. The late Alexander Bickel of Yale recognized more clearly than most that law inevitably engages ultimate beliefs about right and wrong. If law is to be viewed as legitimate, it must be backed by moral judgment. But, it is argued, in a society where moral judgments differ in source and conclusion, the final grounding of moral judgment must be disguised so as not to give democratic offense. It must be grounded so *generally* so as to obscure the particularities of religious disagreement in a pluralistic society. Bickel proposes a way in which this might be done:

> The function of the Justices . . . is to immerse themselves in the tradition of our society and of kindred societies that have gone before, in history and in the sediment of history which is law, and in the thought and the vision of the philosophers and the poets. The Justices will then be fit to extract "fundamental presuppositions" from their deepest selves, but in fact from the evolving morality of our tradition. . . . The search for the deepest controlling sources, for the precise "how" and the final "whence" of the judgment may, after all, end in the attempt to express the inexpressible. This is not to say that the duty to judge the judgment might as well be abandoned. The inexpressible can be recognized, even though one is unable to parse it.[2]

This is an elegantly convoluted way of thinking about right and wrong in a democratic society that in fact understands its morality to be derived from the Judeo-Christian tradition. Bickel's proposal is for a semi-sanitized public square, for a legal process that is religious in function but dares not speak the name of religion. ("Philosophers and poets" are admitted, be it noted, but not prophets or religious ethicists and teachers.) The tortured reasoning required by the exclusion of identifiable religion is surely a puzzle to many, perhaps most, Americans. It may be that they are puzzled because they do not understand the requirements of a pluralistic society. Or they may be puzzled because they are more impressed by the claim that this is a democratic society. In a democratic society, presumably, the public business is carried on in conversation with the actual values of people who are the society. In a survey of North Carolinians in the 1970s, 74 percent agree with the statement: "Human rights come from God and not merely from laws." Seventy-eight percent claim the U.S. flag is "sacred." And, despite Vietnam and all that, a third assent to the proposition "America is God's chosen nation today."[3] North Carolinians may be more "traditional" than other Americans on these scores, although there is no reason to assume that. One suspects, rather, that there is among Americans a deep and widespread uneasiness about the denial of the obvious. The obvious is that, in some significant sense, this is, as the Supreme Court said in 1931, a Christian [nation]. The popular intuition is that this fact ought, somehow, to make a difference. It is not an embarrassment to be denied or disguised. It is an inescapable part of what Bickel calls the "tradition of our society and of kindred societies that have gone before." Not only is it tradition in the sense of historic past; it is demonstrably the present source of moral vitalities by which we measure our virtues and hypocrisies.

The notion that this is a secular society is relatively new. It might be proposed that, while the society is incorrigibly religious, the state is secular. But such a disjunction between society and state is a formula for governmental delegitimation. In a democratic society, state and society must draw from the same moral well. In addition, because transcendence abhors a vacuum, the state that styles itself as secular will almost certainly succumb to secularism. Because government cannot help but make moral judgments of an ultimate nature, it must, if it has in principle excluded identifiable religion, make those judgments by "secular" reasoning that is given the force of religion. Because this process is already advanced in the spheres of law and public education, there is a measure of justice in the complaints about "secular humanism." Secular humanism, in this case, is simply the term unhappily chosen for *ersatz* religion.

More than that, the notion of the secular state can become the prelude to totalitarianism. That is, once religion is reduced to nothing more than privatized conscience, the public square has only two actors in it—the state and the individual. Religion as a mediating structure—a community that generates and transmits moral values—is no longer available as a countervailing force to the ambitions of the state. Whether in Hitler's Third Reich or in today's sundry states professing Marxist-Leninism, the chief attack is not upon individual religious belief. Individual religious belief can be dismissed scornfully as superstition, for it finally poses little threat to the power of the state. No, the chief attack is upon the *institutions* that bear and promulgate belief in a transcendent reality by which the state can be called to judgment. Such institutions threaten the totalitarian proposition that everything is to be within the state, nothing is to be outside the state.

It is to be expected that the move in this discussion from the naked public square to the dangers of totalitarianism will be resisted by some readers. It may seem too abrupt and even extreme. We will be coming back to the subject in order to fill in some of the intermediate steps. At the moment, suffice it to register a degree of sympathy with those who resist talk about the dangers of totalitarianism. They object, quite rightly, that many discussions of the threat of totalitarianism are only thinly veiled attacks upon Communism. A one-sided attack upon Communism, they protest, tends to overlook the many forms of authoritarian government that also violate our understandings of democratic freedom.

Authoritarian, sometimes brutally authoritarian, regimes with which the United States is allied end up being tolerated or even lauded in order to maintain a common front against the Communist adversary. There is considerable merit to this critique, unfortunately. Anti-Communism is a necessary but hardly a sufficient basis for understanding the perils of our day. In this light, then, one can sympathize with those who resist much contemporary talk about the threat of totalitarianism.

A less admirable component in that resistance, however, is the naive notion that "it can't happen here." Those who subscribe to this notion are too often oblivious of the novelty and fragility of liberal democracy as a political system. They are inadequately sensitive to the distinctly minority status of such an order in our world. It is thought that liberal democracy and the freedoms associated with it are somehow "normal," part of the "establishment." The new and exciting thing, in this view, is the proposal of alternatives to liberal democracy. In the longer reaches of history, however, liberal democracy appears as a curious exception to the various tyrannies under which human beings have suffered. Of the 160 member nations of the United Nations, probably less than thirty qualify as democracies in the sense that we tend to take for granted. This historical and contemporary perspective is essential. Without such a perspective, it is impossible to understand what Americans from Jefferson to Lincoln to John F. Kennedy intended when they spoke of America as an "experiment" launched and sustained in defiance of the "normal" course of history.

Those who think all talk about a totalitarian threat to be exaggerated also evidence an insouciance, sometimes a willful ignorance, with respect to the fact that liberal democracy does have declared adversaries. There are adversaries such as the authoritarian regimes of South America, South Africa, and the Philippines. In a significant way, however, these authoritarian regimes are not adversaries. That is, they do not claim to be adversaries, they do not oppose liberal democracy in principle; rather, they often claim to aspire to liberal democracy, asserting that their denial of democratic freedoms is only a temporary expedient on the way to that goal. And in fact we are not without recent examples of authoritarian societies that have been moved toward democracy; Spain, Portugal, and Nigeria are cases in point. In both the long and short term, the more ominous adversaries of liberal democracy are those forces that are totalitarian in principle. The only global, systematic movement of this kind today is Marxist-Leninism. In the 1930s, Mussolini's Fascism and Hitler's National Socialism represented another such movement. After World War II, and despite loose talk that equates any repressive regime with "fascism," only

Marxist-Leninism is left as a theoretically comprehensive and, to many, morally compelling global adversary of liberal democracy.

In such a world it is not extreme but elementary common sense to be concerned about the threat of totalitarianism. "It can't happen here" is but a form of whistling in the dark. It is strange that among the foremost whistlers are some civil libertarians who are otherwise always reminding us of how precarious are the constitutional freedoms that we are too inclined to take for granted. The threat of totalitarianism is not posed chiefly by the prospect of defeat as a result of nuclear war. Nor is the main anxiety that the Soviet Union will launch a victorious march across Alaska and down through Canada. The chief threat comes from a collapse of the idea of freedom and of the social arrangements necessary to sustaining liberal democracy. Crucial to such a democratic order is a public square in which there are many actors. The state is one actor among others. Indispensable to this arrangement are the institutional actors, such as the institutions of religion, that make claims of ultimate or transcendent meaning. The several actors in the public square—government, corporations, education, communications, religion—are there to challenge, check, and compete with one another. They also cooperate with one another, or sometimes one will cooperate with an other in competition with the others. In a democracy the role of cooperation is not to be deemed morally superior to the roles of checking and competing. Giving consistent priority to the virtue of cooperation, as some Christians do, is the formula for the death of democracy.

There is an inherent and necessary relationship between democracy and pluralism. Pluralism, in this connection, does not mean simply that there are many different kinds of people and institutions in societal play. More radically than that, it means that there are contenders striving with one another to define what the play is about—what are the rules and what the goal. The democratic soul is steeled to resist the allure of a "cooperation" that would bring that contention to a premature closure. Indeed, within the bond of civility, the democratic soul exults in that contention. He exults not because contention is a good in itself, although there is a legitimate joy in contending, but because it is a necessary provisional good short of the coming of the kingdom of God. He strives to sustain the contention within the bond of civility, also, because he recognizes the totalitarianism that is the presently available alternative to such democratic contention.

John Courtney Murray, the great Jesuit analyst of American democracy, understood the nature of the contest in which we are engaged. For many years his work was viewed as suspect by church authorities, but he was soundly vindicated by Vatican Council II. Christian thinkers such as Murray and Reinhold Niebuhr are frequently discounted today as old hat. Such mindless dismissal results in part from a desire to espouse the latest thing. It is a bias of the superficially educated that books written thirty years ago, not to say three hundred years ago, are passé. In Christian circles this dismissal takes the curious twist of being conducted in the name of the most current version of "true Christianity," based upon biblical books written two thousand and more years ago. Murray, a deeply educated man, understood that epochs are not demarcated by publishers' seasons. The test of our epoch, he understood, is to sustain the democratic "proposition" in the face of the human yearning for monism. Monism is another word for totalitarianism, and Murray described it this way:

> [The] cardinal assertion is a thorough-going monism, political, social, juridical, religious: there is only one Sovereign, one society, one law, one faith. And the cardinal denial is of the Christian dualism of powers, societies, and laws—spiritual and temporal, divine and human. Upon this denial follows the absorption of the Church in the community, the absorption of the community in the state, the absorption of the state in the party, and the assertion that the party-state is the supreme spiritual and moral, as well as political authority and reality. It has its own absolutely autonomous ideological substance and its own absolutely independent purpose: it is the ultimate bearer of human destiny. Outside of this One Sovereign there is nothing. Or rather, what presumes to stand outside is "the enemy."[4]

The prelude to this totalitarian monism is the notion that society can be ordered according to secular technological reason without reference to religious grounded meaning. Murray again:

> And if this country is to be overthrown from within or from without, I would suggest that it will not be overthrown by Communism. It will be overthrown because it will have made an impossible experiment. It will have undertaken to establish a technological order of most marvelous intricacy, which will have been constructed and will operate without relations to true political ends; and this technological order will hang, as it were, suspended over a moral confusion; and this moral confusion will itself be suspended over a spiritual vacuum. This would be the real danger resulting from a type of fallacious, fictitious, fragile unity that could be created among us.[5]

This "vacuum" with respect to political and spiritual truth is the naked public square. If we are "overthrown," the root cause of the defeat would lie in the "impossible" effort to sustain that vacuum. Murray is right: not Communism, but the effort to establish and maintain the naked public square would be the source of the collapse. Totalitarian monism would be the consequence of such a collapse. Because it is the only totalitarian ideology in play today, the consequence would likely be Marxist-Leninist; which is to say it would be, in one form or another, Communism. The probability that it would be a distinctively American form of Communism will not vindicate those who now say "It can't happen here." Americans may, with a little help from their adversaries, find their own distinctive way to terminate the democratic experiment to which they gave birth. The fact that democracy's demise bears the marking "Made in America" will console only national chauvinists. It will be little comfort to those whose devotion to America was derived from their devotion to the democratic idea.

The naked public square is, as Murray suggests, an "impossible" project. That, however, does not deter people from attempting it. In the minds of some secularists the naked public square is a desirable goal. They subscribe to the dogma of the secular Enlightenment that, as people become more enlightened (educated), religion will wither away; or, if it does not wither away, it can be safely sealed off from public consideration, reduced to a private eccentricity. Our argument is that the naked public square is not desirable, even if it were possible. It is not desirable in the view of believers because they are inescapably entangled in the belief that the moral truths of religion have a universal and public validity. The Ten Commandments, to take an obvious example, have a normative status. They are not, as it has been said, Ten Suggestions or Ten Significant Moral Insights to be more or less appreciated according to one's subjective disposition. Even if one is not a believer, the divorce of public business from the moral vitalities of the society is not desirable if one is committed to the democratic idea. In addition to not being desirable, however, we have argued that the naked public square is not possible. It is an illusion, for the public square cannot and does not remain naked. When particularist religious values and the institutions that bear them are excluded, the inescapable need to make public moral judgments will result in an elite construction of a normative morality from sources and principles not democratically recognized by the society.

The truly naked public square is at best a transitional phenomenon. It is a vacuum begging to be filled. When the democratically affirmed institutions that generate and transmit values are excluded, the vacuum will be filled by the agent left in control of the public square, the state. In this manner, a perverse notion of the disestablishment of religion leads to the establishment of the state as church. Not without reason, religion is viewed by some as a repressive imposition upon the public square. They would cast out the devil of particularist religion and thus put the public square in proper secular order. Having cast out the one devil, as noted earlier, they unavoidably invite the entrance of seven devils worse than the first.

The totalitarian alternative edges in from the wings, waiting impatiently for the stage to be cleared of competing actors. Most important is that the stage be cleared of those religious actors that presume to assert absolute values and thus pose such a troublesome check upon the pretensions of the state. The state is not waiting with a set of absolute values of its own or with a ready-made religion. Far from waiting with a package of absolutes, in a society where the remnants of procedural democracy survive, the state may be absolutely committed only to the relativization of all values. In that instance, however, the relativity of all things becomes the absolute. Without the counterclaims of "meaning-bestowing" institutions of religion, there is not an absence of religion but, rather, the triumph of the religion of relativity. It is a religion that must in principle deny that it is religious. It is the religion that dare not speak its name. In its triumph there is no contender that can, in Peter Berger's phrase, "relativize the relativizers."[6]

The entrance of the seven devils that take over the cleansed public square is not an alarmist scenario. Conceptually there is no alternative to it, unless of course one believes that a society can get along without a normative ethic. Admittedly, there are those who do believe this. They are, as Alasdair MacIntyre contends, the barbarians. "This time," writes MacIntyre, "the barbarians are not waiting beyond the frontiers; they have already been governing us for quite some time."[7] That the barbarians are composed of the most sophisticated and educated elites of our society makes them no less barbarian. The barbarians are those who in principle refuse to recognize a normative ethic or the reality of public virtue.

The barbarians are the party of emancipation from the truths civilized people consider self-evident. The founding fathers of the American experiment declared certain truths to be self-evident and moved on from that premise. It is a measure of our decline into what may be the new dark ages that today we are compelled to produce evidence for the self-evident. Not that it does much good to produce such evidence, however, for such evidences are ruled to be inadmissible since, again in principle, it is asserted that every moral judgment is simply an instance of emotivism, a statement of subjective preference that cannot be "imposed" upon others. MacIntyre's dismal reading of our times is no doubt an accurate description of the *logic* of contemporary philosophical, moral, and legal reasoning. Fortunately, the real world is not terribly logical. The vitalities of democracy protest that dour logic. Populist resentment against the logic of the naked public square is a source of hope. That resentment is premised upon an alternative vision that calls for a new articulation. When it finds its voice, it will likely sound very much like the voice of Christian America. That voice will not be heard and thus will not prevail in the public square, however, unless it is a voice that aims to reassure those who dissent from the vision.

We have said that conceptually there is no alternative to a *de facto* state religion once traditional religion is driven from the public square. Even if some were to argue that an alternative could be hypothetically conceived, we must attend to actual historical experience. We have witnessed again and again the entrance of the seven devils worse than the first. In every instance except that of the Third Reich, in [the twentieth] century they have entered under the banner of Communism. We who embrace the liberal tradition have suffered from a debilitating obtuseness on this score. It has too often been left to conservatives and reactionaries to point out that the emperor carries a very nasty club. Afraid to be thought anti-Communist, a species of liberalism has degenerated to fevered anti-anti-Communism.

This is the unpopular truth underscored by Susan Sontag in the dramatic 1982 confrontation at Town Hall in New York City. The meeting, the reader will recall, was for the purpose of expressing solidarity with Solidarity, the Polish labor movement that had been brutally repressed under martial law. The meeting was sponsored in part by the *Nation*, a magazine of self-consciously liberal orthodoxy. An impressive lineup of literary and entertainment celebrities were expected to say nice things about the revolutionary proletariat in Poland and the dangers of fascist repression in the United States. Ms. Sontag went beyond expectations. She pointed out that the repression in Poland was not an aberration but inherent in the theory and practice of Marxist-Leninism. She noted that the left routinely railed against the threat of fascism.

> We had identified the enemy as fascism. We heard the demonic language of fascism. We believed in, or at least applied a double standard to, the angelic language of communism. . . . The émigrés from communist countries we didn't listen to, who found it far easier to get published in the *Reader's Digest* than in the *Nation*

or the *New Statesman*, were telling the truth. Now we hear them. Why didn't we hear them before? . . . The result was that many of us, and I include myself, did not understand the nature of the communist tyranny. . . . What the recent Polish events illustrate is a truth that we should have understood a very long time ago: that communism is fascism. . . . Not only is fascism the probable destiny of all communist societies, but communism is in itself a variant of fascism. Fascism with a human face.[8]

The conclusion to be drawn is not that the *Reader's Digest* is the oracle of truth. Anti-Communism combined with American boosterism is not a sufficient political philosophy. But, as Ms. Sontag would argue, neither is anti-anti-Communism sufficient. Alexander Solzhenitsyn comes closer to being an oracle on these questions. Commenting on the Polish developments following the emergence of Solidarity in 1981, he notes the ways in which sundry socialists of a Marxist bent attempt to dissociate themselves from what is happening in that tortured land, or even try to claim Solidarity as a representative of "true socialism" in protest against socialism's Communist distortion. "It is the Communist ideology that, with its heavy steps, is crushing Poland," writes Solzhenitsyn, "and let us admit it is not entirely alien to the socialists, though they are protesting vehemently: The ideology of any communism is based on the coercive power of the state. Let's not be mistaken: Solidarity inspired itself not by socialism but by Christianity."[9] Beyond reasonable doubt, it is the presence of the Catholic Church in the Polish public square that prevents the regime from realizing its ambition for total control.

A literal example of the consistently denuded public square is, of course, Red Square in Moscow. Because it is in the nature of public squares not to remain naked, there is the sacred shrine of Lenin's tomb where thousands are transported each day to stand in line, waiting their turn to pay homage. Within this circumscribed space the maxim "All within the state, nothing outside the state" is fulfilled. On several occasions in the early eighties a few bold Soviet citizens attempted to unfold banners appealing for peace and disarmament. They were promptly arrested and hustled off to psychiatric clinics. As Murray tried to help us understand, in such a society opposition to the will of the party is by definition a sign of insanity, or worse. *Tass*, the official newspaper (there being, of course, no other kind), described the dissident "Committee to Establish Trust Between the U.S.S.R. and the U.S.A." as an "act of provocation of Western secret services." According to the *New York Times* report, the protestors were condemned as "anti-Sovieteers, renegades and criminals . . . a handful of swindlers who do not represent anyone in the Soviet Union."[10]

In our society the proponents of the naked public square do not describe themselves as proponents of the naked public square. Some are technocratic liberals, some are secular pragmatists, some are libertarians of either the leftist or rightist sort. Some are socialists who insist that we need to establish "rational control" of political, economic, and cultural forces in order to forge something like a national purpose and plan. Whatever the rationale or intention, however, the presupposition is the naked public square, the exclusion of particularist religious and moral belief from public discourse. And whatever the intention, because the naked square cannot remain naked, the direction is toward the state-as-church, toward totalitarianism. And again, the available form of totalitarianism—an aggressively available form, so to speak—is Marxist-Leninism.

In one of his less felicitous statements, President Carter in a major foreign-policy address cautioned against our "inordinate fear of Communism." He did not make clear what measure of fear might be ordinate. Similarly, those who now underscore the dangers of Communism caution us against an inordinate fear of McCarthyism. Presumably, in this respect too there is a measure of fear that is ordinate. The present argument suggests that both fears are legitimate and necessary. Of the two, McCarthyism as a form of what Richard Hofstadter called "the paranoid style" in American politics is the more immediate possibility. We have been through that and the scars are still touchable. In the longer term— say, the next twenty to sixty years—totalitarianism is the more ominous prospect. This does not mean we should risk "just a little" McCarthyism in order to ward off that prospect. It does mean that we should stop calling a sensible anxiety about that prospect "McCarthyism." It does mean we should stop telling ourselves and others that the choice is between McCarthyism, which truncates liberal democracy, and totalitarianism, which terminates liberal democracy. An open-eyed awareness of the fragility of liberal democracy, and of the alternatives to it, is the best insurance against being reduced to such a dismal choice. As that awareness is heightened, we will as a society be more resistant both to the totalitarian temptation and to the illusion that democracy can be saved by becoming less democratic.

In 1981 the Institute on Religion and Democracy was established in Washington, D.C. Its declared purpose was to lift up the public significance of religion in the democratic process, to promote democratic ideals within the religious communities, and, as a necessary correlate of that, to oppose those dynamics in the churches that seem inclined toward the totalitarian temptation. "Christianity and Democracy" is the Institute's manifesto-like assertion of what it means by democracy:

> Democratic government is limited government. It is limited in the claims it makes and in the power it seeks to exercise. Democratic government understands itself to be accountable to values and to truth which transcend any regime or party. Thus in the United States of America we declare ours to be a nation "under God," which means, first of all, a nation under judgment. In addition, limited government means that a clear distinction is made between the state and the society. The state is not the whole of the society, but is one important actor in the society. Other institutions—notably the family, the Church, educational, economic and cultural enterprises—are at least equally important actors in the society. They do not exist or act by sufferance of the state. Rather, these spheres have their own peculiar sovereignty which must be respected by the state.[11]

The statement goes on to affirm the importance of participation, equality, and fairness in a democratic society. Without dwelling on the point, it notes that "as a matter of historical fact democratic governance exists only where the free market plays a large part in a society's economy." The statement and the Institute received widespread (some would say inordinate) attention in the general media and in the churches. They were the object of a formal debate sponsored by the National Council of Churches and of numerous critiques by theologians and social philosophers on all points of the political spectrum.[12]

The debate produced around groups such as the Institute on Religion and Democracy gives some reason to believe that this decade could be remembered as a time of reinvigorated appreciation of the democratic idea among Christians in America. The intuition of the connection between democracy and religion was until recently part of the foundational consensus supporting what Murray called "the American proposition." It was a constitutive element of the vital center in American thought. The vital center, it will be recalled, was the title Arthur M. Schlesinger Jr., chose for his 1949 manifesto in favor of democratic freedom. *The Vital Center* is in the tradition of Walter Lippmann's "public philosophy" and John Dewey's "common faith." If one did not know that *The Vital Center* was written [in 1962], she would suspect it was written by one of those who today are called neo-conservative. It is a curiosity of our time that the mainstream liberalism of a few decades ago—and nobody has more assiduously attended to his credentials as a mainstream liberal than Arthur M. Schlesinger Jr.—is the neo-conservatism of today. The mainstream liberal argument then was, quite rightly, viewed as a radical proposition on the screen of world-historical change. Schlesinger wrote:

> Our problem is not resources or leadership. It is primarily one of faith and time: faith in the value of our own freedoms, and time to do the necessary things to save them. To achieve the fullness of faith, we must renew the traditional sources of American radicalism and seek out ways to maintain our belief at a high pitch of vibration. To achieve a sufficiency of time, we must ward off the totalitarian threat to free society—and do so without permitting ourselves to become the slaves of Stalinism, as any man may become the slave of the things he hates.[13]

Schlesinger and those like him then viewed with approval, indeed the highest hope, the role of the "affirmative" or "positive" state. They knew there were dangers in the self-aggrandizement of the state, but the acknowledgment of the importance of other public actors is almost an aside:

> In the short run, the failure of voluntary initiative invites the spread of state power. In the long run, the disappearance of voluntary association paves the way for the pulverization of the social structure essential to totalitarianism. By the revitalization of voluntary associations, we can siphon off emotions which might otherwise be driven to the solutions of despair. We can create strong bulwarks against the totalitarianization of society.[14]

But this nod to what we have called the mediating structures of society is almost cancelled out by the emphasis upon state power. To be sure, Schlesinger observed then, "We have strayed too far from the insights of Burke and de Maistre; we have forgotten that constitutions work only as they reflect an actual sense of community."[15] He also warned against "arrogant forms of individualism." "It is only so far as . . . individualism derives freely from community, that democracy will be immune to the virus of totalitarianism."[16] The reiterated "we" in Schlesinger's writing, however, is finally the "we" of the total society, the "we" of the state. This is because, in his view, the great domestic threat is the antidemocratic influence of the corporation, of "the business plutocracy." "The corporation began to impersonalize the economic order," wrote Schlesinger.

Impersonality produced an irresponsibility which was chilling the lifeblood of society. The state consequently had to expand its authority in order to preserve the ties which hold society together. The history of governmental intervention has been the history of the growing ineffectiveness of the private conscience as a means of social control. The only alternative is the growth of the public conscience, whose natural expression is the democratic government.[17]

There, in succinct form, is the nub of the dispute. The choice, we would contend, is not between the private conscience and the public conscience expressed by the state. The private conscience, as Schlesinger also wanted to say in part, is not private in the sense of being deracinated, torn from its roots. It is not "arrogantly" individualistic. Private conscience too is communal; it is shaped by the myriad communities from which we learn to "put the world together" in an order that is responsive to our understanding of right and wrong. As for "the public conscience," it is a categorical fallacy. It harks back to Rousseau's mythology of a "general will" of which the state is the expression. "The Public" does not have a conscience. "The People" does not have a conscience. Only persons and persons-in-community have consciences.

Schlesinger's enthusiasm for the triumph of "the affirmative state" is not widely shared today, neither on the right nor on the left. It is not merely that there is a groundswell of opposition to "big government" or an antimodernist passion for decentralization in obedience to the axiom that "small is beautiful." It is all that, but it is not merely that. It is rather that there is a growing awareness of the limits of the political, a recognition that most of the things that matter most are attended to in communities that are not government and should not be governmentalized. This awareness is what some critics describe as a "retribalization" or "reprivatization" of American life. But "tribe" used in this way is simply a pejorative for community. And, far from this being a process of reprivatization, it is an expansion of our understanding of what is public. We are no longer content to let "public" be synonymous with "government." Thus, for example, in education the distinction is not between public schools and private schools. It is rather between government schools and voluntary schools, or "schools of choice."[18] All schools that advance a public interest and meet the needs of their relevant publics are public schools.

Jefferson, Jackson, Lippmann, Dewey, Schlesinger, and a host of others strove to articulate democracy as a creedal cause. The last chapter of *The Vital Center* is titled "Freedom: A Fighting Faith." But finally it is a faith in which freedom is the end as well as the means. It is a faith devoid of transcendent purpose that can speak to the question of what freedom is for. This is, of necessity, a religious question. The truly "positive" state that presumes to address this question becomes the state-as-church. The Marxists are right: the political freedom of liberal democracy is essentially a "negative" freedom (freedom from). If we are not to succumb to totalitarianism, the positive meaning of freedom must be addressed in a manner, and through institutions, beyond the competence of what is ordinarily meant by politics or the government. The public square is the stage of many actors, not all of whom are following the same script. It is very confusing. It is democratic.

Historically, the churches in America have been leading actors in voicing the positive side of freedom's question. The purpose of Christianity in America, it is said somewhat scornfully, was to establish "The Righteous Empire."[19] In the nineteenth century there was the hope to construct "a complete Christian commonwealth." The mainline churches, as they are called, have retired such rhetoric in recent decades. Many of their members, joined by today's moral majoritarians, want to pick it up again. Those who retired the idea tended to share the liberal assumption that the tasks of moral definition could and should be taken over by "the public conscience" expressed through the state. In the frequently uncritical affirmation of "the secular city," it was thought a triumph that the churches could step back from what had been a transitional role in the public square. Now it is recognized, however, that man has not "come of age" in the way that many thought. We still need, we more urgently need, the critical tutelage of traditions that refuse to leave "man on his own."

Negative freedom is dangerous to ourselves and others if it is negative freedom alone. As Murray argued, it is not only dangerous but it is "impossible." It is most dangerous *because* it is impossible. That is, its very attempt invites the termination of the democratic freedom in the name of which the attempt is made. The question is not *whether* the questions of positive freedom will be addressed. The question is *by whom*—by what reasonings, what traditions, what institutions, what authorities—they will be addressed. If they are to be addressed democratically in a way that gives reasonable assurance of a democratic future, we must work toward an understanding of the public square that is both more comprehensive and more complex. Along the way to such an understanding, we must listen with critical sympathy to those who are speaking the very new-old language of Christian America.

Chapter 14

The Public Philosophy of Contemporary Liberalism

Michael J. Sandel

Times of trouble prompt us to recall the ideals by which we live. But in America today, this is not an easy thing to do. At a time when democratic ideals seem ascendant abroad, there is reason to wonder whether we have lost possession of them at home. Our public life is rife with discontent. Americans do not believe they have much say in how they are governed and do not trust government to do the right thing.[1] Despite the achievements of American life in the last half [of the twentieth] century—victory in World War II, unprecedented affluence, greater social justice for women and minorities, the end of the Cold War—our politics is beset with anxiety and frustration.

The political parties, meanwhile, are unable to make sense of our condition. The main topics of national debate—the proper scope of the welfare state, the extent of rights and entitlements, the proper degree of government regulation—take their shape from the arguments of an earlier day. These are not unimportant topics; but they do not reach the two concerns that lie at the heart of democracy's discontent. One is the fear that, individually and collectively, we are losing control of the forces that govern our lives. The other is the sense that, from family to neighborhood to nation, the moral fabric of community is unraveling around us. These two fears— for the loss of self-government and the erosion of community—together define the anxiety of the age. It is an anxiety that the prevailing political agenda has failed to answer or even address.

Why is American politics ill equipped to allay the discontent that now engulfs it? The answer lies beyond the political arguments of our day, in the public philosophy that animates them. By public philosophy, I mean the political theory implicit in our practice, the assumptions about citizenship and freedom that inform our public life. The inability of contemporary American politics to speak convincingly about self-government and community has something to do with the public philosophy by which we live.

A public philosophy is an elusive thing, for it is constantly before our eyes. It forms the often unreflective background to our political discourse and pursuits. In ordinary times, the public philosophy can easily escape the notice of those who live by it. But anxious times compel a certain clarity. They force first principles to the surface and offer an occasion for critical reflection.

LIBERAL AND REPUBLICAN FREEDOM

The political philosophy by which we live is a certain version of liberal political theory. Its central idea is that government should be neutral toward the moral and religious views its citizens espouse. Since people disagree about the best way to live, government should not affirm in law any particular vision of the good life. Instead, it should provide a framework of rights that respects persons as free and independent selves, capable of choosing their own values and ends.[2] Since this liberalism asserts the priority of fair procedures over particular ends, the public life it informs might be called the procedural republic.[3]

In describing the prevailing political philosophy as a version of liberal political theory, it is important to distinguish two different meanings of liberalism. In the common parlance of American politics, liberalism is the opposite of conservatism; it is the outlook of those who favor a more generous welfare state and a greater measure of social and economic equality.[4] In the history of political theory, however, liberalism has a different, broader meaning. In this historical sense, liberalism describes a tradition of thought that emphasizes toleration and respect for individual rights and that runs from John Locke, Immanuel Kant, and John Stuart Mill to John Rawls. The public philosophy of contemporary American politics is a version of this liberal tradition of thought, and most of our debates proceed within its terms.

The idea that freedom consists in our capacity to choose our ends finds prominent expression in our politics and law. Its province is not limited to those known as liberals rather than conservatives in American politics; it can be found across the political spectrum. Republicans sometimes argue, for example, that taxing the rich to pay for welfare programs is a form of coerced charity that violates people's freedom to choose what to do with their own money. Democrats sometimes argue that government should assure all citizens a decent level of income, housing, and health, on the grounds that those who are crushed by economic necessity are not truly free to exercise choice in other domains. Although the two sides disagree about how government should act to respect individual choice, both assume that freedom consists in the capacity of persons to choose their values and ends.

So familiar is this vision of freedom that it seems a permanent feature of the American political and constitutional tradition. But Americans have not always understood freedom in this way. As a reigning public philosophy, the version of liberalism that informs our present debates is a recent arrival, a development of the last forty or fifty years. Its distinctive character can best be seen by contrast with a rival public philosophy that it gradually displaced. This rival public philosophy is a version of republican political theory.

Central to republican theory is the idea that liberty depends on sharing in self-government. This idea is not by itself inconsistent with liberal freedom. Participating in politics can be one among the ways in which people choose to pursue their ends. According to republican political theory, however, sharing in self-rule involves something more. It means deliberating with fellow citizens about the common good and helping to shape the destiny of the political community. But to deliberate well about the common good requires more than the capacity to choose one's ends and to respect others' rights to do the same. It requires a knowledge of public affairs and also a sense of belonging, a concern for the whole, a moral bond with the community whose fate is at stake. To share in self-rule therefore requires that citizens possess, or come to acquire, certain qualities of character, or civic virtues. But this means that republican politics cannot be neutral toward the values and ends its citizens espouse. The republican conception of freedom, unlike the liberal conception, requires a formative politics, a politics that cultivates in citizens the qualities of character self-government requires.

Both the liberal and republican conceptions of freedom have been present throughout our political experience, but in shifting measure and relative importance. Broadly speaking, republicanism predominated earlier in American history, liberalism later. In recent decades, the civic or formative aspect of our politics has largely given way to the liberalism that conceives persons as free and independent selves, unencumbered by moral or civic ties they have not chosen.

This shift sheds light on our present political predicament. For despite its appeal, the liberal vision of freedom lacks the civic resources to sustain self-government. This defect ill-equips it to address the sense of disempowerment that afflicts our public life. The public philosophy by which we live cannot secure the liberty it promises, because it cannot inspire the sense of community and civic engagement that liberty requires.

How the liberal conception of citizenship and freedom gradually crowded out the republican conception involves two intersecting tales. One traces the advent of the procedural republic from the first stirrings of American constitutionalism to recent debates about religious liberty, free speech, and privacy rights. Another traces the decline of the civic strand of American political discourse from Thomas Jefferson's day to the present.[5]

These stories, taken together, bring to clarity the self-image that animates—and sometimes debilitates—our public life. They do not reveal a golden age when all was right with American democracy. The republican tradition coexisted with slavery, with the exclusion of women from the public realm, with property qualifications for voting, with nativist hostility to immigrants; indeed it sometimes provided the terms within which these practices were defended.

And yet, for all its episodes of darkness, the republican tradition, with its emphasis on community and self-government, may offer a corrective to our impoverished civic life. Recalling the republican conception of freedom as self-rule may prompt us to pose questions we have forgotten how to ask: What economic arrangements are hospitable to self-government? How might our political discourse engage rather than avoid the moral and religious convictions people bring to the public realm? And how might the public life of a pluralist society cultivate in citizens the expansive self-understandings that civic engagement requires? If the public philosophy of our day leaves little room for civic considerations, it may help to recall how earlier generations of Americans debated such questions, before the procedural republic took hold. But in order to identify the relevant strands of the story, we need to specify more fully the version of liberalism that informs our present politics.

THE ASPIRATION TO NEUTRALITY

The idea that government should be neutral on the question of the good life is distinctive to modern political thought. Ancient political theory held that the purpose of politics was to cultivate the virtue, or moral excellence, of citizens. All associations aim at some good, Aristotle wrote, and the polis, or political association, aims at the highest, most comprehensive good: "any polis which is truly so called, and is not merely one in name, must devote itself to the end of encouraging goodness. Otherwise, a political association sinks into a mere alliance, which only differs in space from other forms of alliance where the members live at a distance from one another. Otherwise, too, law becomes a mere covenant—or (in the phrase of the Sophist Lycophron) 'a guarantor of men's rights against one another'—instead of being, as it should be, a rule of life such as will make the members of a polis good and just."[6]

According to Aristotle, political community is more than "an association for residence on a common site, or for the sake of preventing mutual injustice and easing exchange." Although these are necessary conditions for political community, they are not its purpose or ultimate justification. "The end and purpose of a polis is the good life, and the institutions of social life are means to that end." It is only as participants in political association that we can realize our nature and fulfill our highest ends.[7]

Unlike the ancient conception, liberal political theory does not see political life as concerned with the highest human ends or with the moral excellence of its citizens. Rather than promote a particular conception of the good life, liberal political theory insists on toleration, fair procedures, and respect for individual rights—values that respect people's freedom to choose their own values. But this raises a difficult question. If liberal ideals cannot be defended in the name of the highest human good, then in what does their moral basis consist?

It is sometimes thought that liberal principles can be justified by a simple version of moral relativism. Government should not "legislate morality," because all morality is merely subjective, a matter of personal preference not open to argument or rational debate. "Who is to say what is literature and what is filth? That is a value judgment, and whose values should decide?" Relativism usually appears less as a claim than as a question: "Who is to judge?" But the same question can be asked of the values that liberals defend. Toleration and freedom and fairness are values too, and they can hardly be defended by the claim that no values can be defended. So it is a mistake to affirm liberal values by arguing that all values are merely subjective. The relativist defense of liberalism is no defense at all.

UTILITARIANISM VERSUS KANTIAN LIBERALISM

What, then, is the case for the neutrality the liberal invokes? Recent political philosophy has offered two main alternatives—one utilitarian, the other Kantian.[8] The utilitarian view, following John Stuart Mill, defends liberal principles in the name of maximizing the general welfare. The state should not impose on its citizens a preferred way of life, even for their own good, because doing so will reduce the sum of human happiness, at least in the long run. It is better that people choose for themselves, even if, on occasion, they get it wrong.

"The only freedom which deserves the name," writes Mill in *On Liberty*, "is that of pursuing our own good in our own way, so long as we do not attempt to deprive others of theirs, or impede their efforts to obtain it." He adds that his argument does not depend on any notion of abstract right, only on the principle of the greatest good for the greatest number. "I regard utility as the ultimate appeal on all ethical questions; but it must be utility in the largest sense, grounded on the permanent interests of man as a progressive being."[9]

Many objections have been raised against utilitarianism as a general doctrine of moral philosophy. Some have questioned the concept of utility and the assumption that all human goods are in principle commensurable. Others have objected that by reducing all values to preferences and desires, utilitarians are unable to admit qualitative distinctions of worth, unable to distinguish noble desires from base ones. But most recent debate has focused on whether utilitarianism offers a convincing basis for liberal principle, including respect for individual rights.[10]

At first glance, utilitarianism seems well suited to liberal purposes. Seeking to maximize overall happiness does not require judging people's values, only aggregating them. And the willingness to aggregate preferences without judging them suggests a tolerant spirit, even a democratic one. When people go to the polls, we count their votes, whatever they are.

But the utilitarian calculus is not always as liberal as it first appears. If enough cheering Romans pack the Colosseum to watch the lion devour the Christian, the collective pleasure of the Romans will surely outweigh the pain of the Christian, intense though it be. Or if a big majority abhors a small religion and wants it banned, the balance of preferences will favor oppression, not toleration. Utilitarians sometimes defend individual rights on the grounds that respecting them now will serve utility in the long run. But this calculation is precarious and contingent. It hardly secures the liberal promise not to impose on some the values of others.

The case against utilitarianism was made most powerfully by Immanuel Kant. He argued that empirical principles such as utility were unfit to serve as a basis for morality. A wholly instrumental defense of freedom and rights not only leaves rights vulnerable but fails to respect the inherent dignity of persons. The utilitarian calculus treats people as means to the happiness of others, not as ends in themselves, worthy of respect.[11]

Contemporary liberals extend Kant's argument with the claim that utilitarianism fails to take seriously the distinction between persons. In seeking above all to maximize the general welfare, the utilitarian treats society as a whole as if it were a single person; it conflates our many, diverse desires into a single system of desires. It is indifferent to the distribution of satisfactions among persons, except insofar as this may affect the overall sum. But this fails to respect our plurality and distinctness. It uses some as means to the happiness of all and so fails to respect each as an end in himself or herself.

In the view of modern-day Kantians, certain rights are so fundamental that even the general welfare cannot override them. As John Rawls writes in *A Theory of Justice*, "Each person possesses an inviolability founded on justice that even the welfare of society as a whole cannot override. . . . The rights secured by justice are not subject to political bargaining or to the calculus of social interests."[12]

So Kantian liberals need an account of rights that does not depend on utilitarian considerations. More than this, they need an account that does not depend on any particular conception of the good, that does not presuppose the superiority of one way of life over others. Only a justification neutral among ends could preserve the liberal resolve not to favor any particular ends or to impose on its citizens a preferred way of life. But what sort of justification could this be? How is it possible to affirm certain liberties and rights as fundamental without embracing some vision of the good life, without endorsing some ends over others?

The solution proposed by Kantian liberals is to draw a distinction between the "right" and the "good"—between a framework of basic rights and liberties, and the conceptions of the good that people may choose to pursue within the framework. It is one thing for the state to support a fair framework, they argue; something else to affirm some particular ends. For example, it is one thing to defend the right to free speech so that people may be free to form their own opinions and choose their own ends, but something else to support it on grounds that a life of political discussion is inherently worthier than a life unconcerned with public affairs, or on the grounds that free speech will increase the general welfare. Only the first defense is available on the Kantian view, resting as it does on the ideal of a neutral framework.

Now the commitment to a framework neutral with respect to ends can be seen as a kind of value—in this sense the Kantian liberal is no relativist—but its value consists precisely in its refusal to affirm a preferred way of life or conception of the good. For Kantian liberals, then, the right is prior to the good, and in two senses. First, individual rights cannot be sacrificed for the sake of the general good; and second, the principles of justice that specify these rights cannot be premised on any particular vision of the good life. What justifies the rights is not that they maximize the general welfare or otherwise promote the good, but rather that they constitute a fair framework within which individuals and groups can choose their own values and ends, consistent with a similar liberty for others.

The claim for the priority of the right over the good connects the ideal of neutrality with the primacy of individual rights. For Kantian liberals, rights "function as trump cards held by individuals." They protect individuals from policies, even democratically enacted ones, that would impose a preferred conception of the good and so fail to respect people's freedom to choose their own conceptions.[13]

Of course, proponents of the liberal ethic notoriously disagree about what rights are fundamental and what political arrangements the ideal of the neutral framework requires. Egalitarian liberals support the welfare state and favor a scheme of civil liberties together with certain social and economic rights—rights to welfare, education, health care, and so on. They argue that respecting the capacity of persons to pursue their own goods requires government to assure the minimal prerequisites of a dignified life. Libertarian liberals (usually called conservatives in contemporary politics) defend the market economy and claim that redistributive policies violate people's rights. They argue that respect for persons requires assuring to each the fruits of his or her own labor, and so favor a scheme of civil liberties combined with a strict regime of private property rights. Whether egalitarian or libertarian, Kantian liberalism begins with the claim that we are separate, individual persons, each with our own aims, interests, and conceptions of the good life. It seeks a framework of rights that will enable us to realize our capacity as free moral agents, consistent with a similar liberty for others.

THE LIBERAL SELF

The Kantian case against utilitarianism derives much of its force from its contrasting conception of the person, its view of what it means to be a moral agent. Where utilitarians conflate our many desires into a single system of desire, Kantian liberals insist on the separateness of persons. Where the utilitarian self is simply defined as the sum of its desires, the Kantian self is a choosing self, independent of the desires and ends it may have at any moment. Kant expressed this idea by attributing to human beings the capacity to act with an autonomous will. Contemporary liberals rely on the similar notion of a self given prior to and independent of its purposes and ends.

The claim for the priority of the right over the good, and the conception of the person that attends it, oppose Kantian liberalism not only to utilitarianism but also to any view that regards us as obligated to fulfill ends we have not chosen—ends given by nature or God, for example, or by our identities as members of families, peoples, cultures, or traditions. Encumbered identities such as these are at odds with the liberal conception of persons as free and independent selves, unbound by prior moral ties, capable of choosing our ends for ourselves. This is the conception that finds expression in the ideal of the state as a neutral framework. For Kantian liberals, it is precisely because we are freely choosing, independent selves that we need a neutral framework, a framework of rights that refuses to choose among competing values and ends. For the liberal self, what matters above all, what is most essential to our personhood, is not the ends we choose but our capacity to choose them. "It is not our aims that primarily reveal our nature," but rather the framework of rights we would agree to if we could abstract from our aims. "For the self is prior to the ends which are affirmed by it; even a dominant end must be chosen from among numerous possibilities."[14]

The liberal ethic derives much of its moral force from the appeal of the self-image that animates it. This appeal has at least two sources. First, the image of the self as free and independent, unencumbered by aims and attachments it does not choose for itself, offers a powerful liberating vision. Freed from the sanctions of custom and tradition and inherited status, unbound by moral ties antecedent to choice, the liberal self is installed as sovereign, cast as the author of the only obligations that constrain. More than the simple sum of circumstance, we become capable of the dignity that consists in being persons of our "own creating, making, choosing."[15] We are agents and not just instruments of the purposes we pursue. We are "self-originating sources of valid claims."[16]

A second appeal of the liberal self-image consists in the case it implies for equal respect. The idea that there is more to a person than the roles he plays or the customs she keeps or the faith he affirms suggests a basis for respect independent of life's contingencies. Liberal justice is blind to such differences between persons as race, religion, ethnicity, and gender, for in the liberal self-image, these features do not really define our identity in the first place. They are not constituents but merely attributes of the self, the sort of things the state should look beyond. "Our social position and class, our sex and race should not influence deliberations made from a moral point of view."[17] Once these contingencies are seen as products of our situation rather than as aspects of our person, they cease to supply the familiar grounds for prejudice and discrimination. Nor does it matter, from the standpoint of liberal justice, what virtues display or what values we espouse. "That we have one conception of good rather than another is not relevant from a moral standpoint. In acquiring it we are influenced by the same sort of contingencies that lead to rule out a knowledge of our sex and class."[18] Despite their many differences, libertarian and egalitarian liberals agree that people's entitlements should not be based on their merit or virtue or moral desert, for the qualities that make people virtuous or morally deserving depend on factors "arbitrary from a moral point of view."[19] The liberal state therefore does not discriminate; none of its policies or laws may presuppose that any person or way of life is intrinsically more virtuous than any other. It respects persons as persons and secures their equal right to live the lives they choose.

CRITIQUE OF KANTIAN LIBERALISM

Kantian liberals thus avoid affirming a conception of the good by affirming instead the priority of the right, which depends in turn on a picture of the self given prior to its ends. But how plausible is this self-conception? Despite its powerful appeal, the image of the unencumbered self is flawed. It cannot make sense of our moral experience, because it cannot account for certain moral and political obligations that we commonly recognize, even prize. These include obligations of solidarity, religious duties, and other moral ties that may claim us for reasons unrelated to a choice. Such obligations are difficult to account for if we understand ourselves as free and independent selves, unbound by moral ties we have not chosen. Unless we think of ourselves as encumbered selves, already claimed by certain projects and commitments, we cannot make sense of these indispensable aspects of our moral and political experience. Consider the limited scope of obligation on the liberal view. According to Rawls, obligations can arise in only one of two ways, as "natural duties" we owe to human beings as such or as voluntary obligations we incur by consent. The natural duties are those we owe persons *qua* persons—to do justice, to avoid cruelty, and so on. All other obligations, the ones we owe to particular others, are founded in consent and arise only in virtue of agreements we make, be they tacit or explicit.[20]

Conceived as unencumbered selves, we must respect the dignity of all persons, but beyond this, we owe only what we agree to owe. Liberal justice requires that we respect people's rights (as defined by the neutral framework), not that we advance their good. Whether we must concern ourselves with other people's good depends on whether, and with whom, and on what terms, we have agreed to do so.

One striking consequence of this view is that "there is no political obligation, strictly speaking, for citizens generally." Although those who run for office voluntarily incur a political obligation (that is, to serve their country if elected), the ordinary citizen does not. "It is not clear what is the requisite binding action or who has performed it."[21] The average citizen is therefore without any special obligations to his or her fellow citizens, apart from the universal, natural duty not to commit injustice.

The liberal attempt to construe all obligation in terms of duties universally owed or obligations voluntarily incurred makes it difficult to account for civic obligations and other moral and political ties that we commonly recognize. It fails to capture those loyalties and responsibilities whose moral force consists partly in the fact that living by them is inseparable from understanding ourselves as the particular persons we are—as members of this family or city or nation or people, as bearers of that history, as citizens of this republic. Loyalties such as these can be more than values I happen to have, and to hold, at a certain distance. The moral responsibilities they entail may go beyond the obligations I voluntarily incur and the "natural duties" I owe to human beings as such.[22]

Some of the special responsibilities that flow from the particular communities I inhabit I may owe to fellow members, such as obligations of solidarity. Others I may owe to members of those communities with which my own community has some morally relevant history, such as the morally burdened relations of Germans to Jews, of American whites to American blacks, or of England and France to their former colonies.[23] Whether they look inward or outward, obligations of membership presuppose that we are capable of moral ties antecedent to choice. To the extent that we are, the meaning of our membership resists redescription in contractarian terms.

It is sometimes argued, in defense of the liberal view, that loyalties and allegiances not grounded in consent, however psychologically compelling, are matters of sentiment, not of morality, and so do not suggest an obligation unavailable to unencumbered selves. But it is difficult to make sense of certain familiar moral and political dilemmas without acknowledging obligations of solidarity and the thickly constituted, encumbered selves that they imply.

Consider the case of Robert E. Lee on the eve of the Civil War. Lee, then an officer in the Union army, opposed secession, in fact regarded it as treason. And yet when war loomed, Lee concluded that his obligation to Virginia outweighed his obligation to the Union and also his reported opposition to slavery. "With all my devotion to the Union," he wrote, "I have not been able to make up my mind to raise my hand against my relatives, my children, my home. . . . If the Union is dissolved, and the Government disrupted, I shall return to my native State and share the miseries of my people. Save in her defense, I will draw my sword no more."[24]

One can appreciate the poignance of Lee's predicament without necessarily approving of the choice he made. But one cannot make sense of his dilemma as a *moral* dilemma without acknowledging that the call to stand with his people, even to lead them in a cause he opposed, was a claim of moral and not merely sentimental import, capable at least of weighing in the balance against other duties and obligations. Otherwise, Lee's predicament was not really a moral dilemma at all, but simply a conflict between morality on the one hand and mere sentiment or prejudice on the other.

A merely psychological reading of Lee's predicament misses the fact that we not only sympathize with people such as Lee but often admire them, not necessarily for the choices they make but for the quality of character their deliberation reflects. The quality at stake is the disposition to see and bear one's life circumstance as a reflectively situated being— claimed by the history that implicates me in a particular life, but self-conscious of its particularity, and so alive to other ways, wider horizons.

But this is precisely the quality that is lacking in those who would think of themselves as unencumbered selves, bound only by the obligations they choose to incur.

As the Lee example illustrates, the liberal conception of the person is too thin to account for the full range of moral and political obligations we commonly recognize, such as obligations of solidarity. This counts against its plausibility generally. But it may even be too weak to support the less strenuous communal obligations expected of citizens in the modern welfare state. Some stronger conception of community may be required, not only to make sense of tragic-heroic dilemmas such as Lee's, but even to sustain the rights that many liberals defend.

While libertarian liberals ask little of citizens, more generous expressions of the liberal ethic support various policies of public provision and redistribution. Egalitarian liberals defend social and economic rights as well as civil and political rights, and so demand of their fellow citizens a high measure of mutual engagement. They insist on the "plurality and distinctness" of individuals but also require that we "share one another's fate" and regard the distribution of natural talents as "a common asset."[25]

Liberalism as an ethic of sharing emphasizes the arbitrariness of fortune and the importance of certain material prerequisites for the meaningful exercise of equal liberties. Since "necessitous men are not free men," and since in any case the distribution of assets and endowments that make for success is "arbitrary from a moral point of view," egalitarian liberals would tax the rich to help the poor secure the prerequisites of a dignified life. Thus the liberal case for the welfare state depends not on a theory of the common good or on some strong notion of communal obligation, but instead on the rights we would agree to respect if we could abstract from our interests and ends.

The liberal case for public provision seems well suited to conditions in which strong communal ties cannot be relied on, and this is one source of its appeal. But it lies vulnerable nonetheless to the libertarian objection that redistributive policies use some people as means to others' ends, and so offend the "plurality and distinctness" of individuals that liberalism seeks above all to secure.[26] In the contractual vision of community alone, it is unclear how the libertarian objection can be met. If those whose fate I am required to share really are, morally speaking, *others*, rather than fellow participants in a way of life with which my identity is bound, then liberalism as an ethic of sharing seems open to the same objections as utilitarianism. Its claim on me is not the claim of a community with which I identify, but rather the claim of an arbitrarily defined collectivity whose aims I may or may not share.

If the egalitarian replies that social and economic rights are required as a matter of equal respect for persons, the question remains why *these* persons, the ones who happen to live in my country, have a claim on my concern that others do not. Tying the mutual responsibilities of citizenship to the idea of respect for persons *qua* persons puts the moral case for welfare on a par with the case for foreign aid—a duty we owe strangers with whom we share a common humanity but possibly little else. Given its conception of the person, it is unclear how liberalism can defend the particular boundaries of concern its own ethic of sharing must presuppose.

What egalitarian liberalism requires, but cannot within its own terms provide, is some way of defining the relevant community of sharing, some way of seeing the participants as mutually indebted and morally engaged to begin with. It needs a way of answering Emerson's challenge to the man who solicited his contribution to the poor—"Are they *my* poor?"[27] Since liberal social and economic rights cannot be justified as expressing or advancing a common life of shared pursuits, the basis and bounds of communal concern become difficult to defend. For as we have seen, the strong notion of community or membership that would save and situate the sharing is precisely the one denied to the liberal self. The moral encumbrances and antecedent obligations it implies would undercut the priority of right.

MINIMALIST LIBERALISM

If we are not the freely choosing, unencumbered selves that Kantian liberals imagine us to be, does it follow that government need not be neutral, that politics should cultivate the virtue of its citizens after all? Some political philosophers argue that the case for neutrality can be detached from the Kantian conception of the person. The case for liberalism, they argue, is political, not philosophical or metaphysical, and so does not depend on controversial claims about the nature of the self. The priority of the right over the good is not the application to politics of Kantian moral philosophy, but a practical response to the familiar fact that people in modern democratic societies typically disagree about the good. Since this defense of neutrality does not depend on a Kantian conception of the person but instead "stays on the surface, philosophically speaking," it might be described as minimalist liberalism.[28]

Minimalist liberals acknowledge that we may sometimes be claimed by moral or religious obligations unrelated to a choice. But they insist that we set these obligations aside when we enter the public realm, that we bracket our moral and religious convictions when deliberating about politics and law. In our personal lives, we may regard it as unthinkable to view ourselves "apart from certain religious, philosophical, and moral convictions, or from certain enduring attachments and loyalties." But we should draw a distinction between our personal and our political identities. However encumbered we may be in private, however claimed by moral or religious convictions, we should bracket our encumbrances in public and regard ourselves, *qua* public selves, as independent of any particular loyalties or conceptions of the good.[29]

The insistence that we separate our identity as citizens from our identity as persons gives rise to an obvious challenge. Why should our political identities not express the moral and religious convictions we affirm in our personal lives? Why, in deliberating about justice and rights, must we set aside the moral judgments that inform the rest of our lives? Minimalist liberals reply that separating our identity as citizens from our identity as persons honors an important fact about modern democratic life. In traditional societies, people sought to shape political life in the image of their own moral and religious ideals. But modern democratic societies are marked by a plurality of moral and religious ideals. Moreover, this pluralism is reasonable; it reflects the fact that, even after reasoned reflection, decent, intelligent people will come to different conceptions about the nature of the good life. Given the fact of reasonable pluralism, we should try to decide questions of justice and rights without affirming one conception of the good over others. Only in this way can we affirm the political value of social cooperation based on mutual respect.[30]

Minimalist liberalism seeks to detach liberal principles from political controversy, including debates about the nature of the self. It presents itself "not as a conception of justice that is true," but as one that can serve as a basis for political agreement in a democratic society. It asserts "the priority of democracy over philosophy." It offers a political conception of justice, not a metaphysical or philosophical one.[31]

The minimalist case for liberalism depends on the plausibility of separating politics from philosophy, of bracketing moral and religious questions where politics is concerned. But this raises the question why the practical interest in securing social cooperation and mutual respect is always so compelling as to defeat any competing moral interest that could arise from within a substantive moral or religious view. One way of assuring the priority of the practical is to deny that any of the moral or religious conceptions it brackets could be true. But this is precisely the sort of controversial metaphysical claim the minimalist liberal wants to avoid. If the liberal must therefore allow that some such conceptions might be true, then the question remains: what guarantees that no moral or religious doctrine can generate interests sufficiently compelling to burst the brackets, so to speak, and morally outweigh the practical interest in social cooperation?

CRITIQUE OF MINIMALIST LIBERALISM

Minimalist liberalism lacks a convincing answer to this question. For notwithstanding the importance of political values such as toleration, social cooperation, and mutual respect, it is not always reasonable to set aside competing values that may arise from substantive moral and religious doctrines. At least where grave moral questions are concerned, whether it is reasonable to bracket moral and religious controversies for the sake of political agreement partly depends on which of the contending moral or religious doctrines is true. Minimalist liberalism wants to separate the case for toleration from any judgment about the moral worth of the practices being tolerated. But this separation is not always defensible. We cannot determine whether toleration is justified in any given case without passing moral judgment on the practice in question.

This difficulty is illustrated by two political controversies that bear on grave moral and religious questions. One is the contemporary debate about abortion rights. The other is the famous debate in 1858 between Abraham Lincoln and Stephen Douglas over popular sovereignty and slavery.[32]

The Abortion Debate

Given the intense disagreement over the moral permissibility of abortion, the case for seeking a political solution that brackets the moral and religious issues—that is neutral with respect to them—would seem especially strong. But whether it is reasonable to bracket, for political purposes, the moral and religious doctrines at stake depends largely on which of those doctrines is true. If the doctrine of the Catholic Church is true, if human life in the relevant moral sense really does begin at conception, then bracketing the moral-theological question of when human life begins is far less reasonable than it would be on rival moral and religious assumptions. The more confident we are that fetuses are, in the relevant moral sense, *different* from babies, the more confident we can be in affirming a political conception of justice that sets aside the controversy about the moral status of fetuses.

As the contemporary debate over abortion reflects, even a political conception of justice presupposes a certain view of the controversies it would bracket. For the debate about abortion is not only a debate about when human life begins, but also a debate about how reasonable it is to abstract from that question for political purposes. Opponents of abortion resist the translation from moral to political terms because they know that more of their view will be lost in the translation; the neutral territory offered by minimalist liberalism is likely to be less hospitable to their religious convictions than to those of their opponents. For defenders of abortion, little comparable is at stake; there is little difference between believing that abortion is morally permissible and agreeing that, as a political matter, women should be free to decide the moral question for themselves. The moral price of political agreement is far higher if abortion is wrong than if it is permissible. How reasonable it is to bracket the contending moral and religious views depends partly on which of those views is more plausible.

The minimalist liberal might reply that the political values of toleration and equal citizenship for women are sufficient grounds for concluding that women should be free to choose for themselves whether to have an abortion; government should not take sides on the moral and religious controversy over when human life begins. But if the Catholic Church is right about the moral status of the fetus, if abortion is morally tantamount to murder, then it is not clear why the political values of toleration and women's equality, important though they are, should prevail. If the Catholic doctrine is true, then the minimalist liberal's case for the priority of political values must become an instance of just-war theory; he or she would have to show why these values should prevail even at the cost of some 1.5 million civilian deaths each year.

Of course, to suggest the impossibility of bracketing the moral-theological question of when human life begins is not to argue against a right to abortion. It is simply to show that the case for abortion rights cannot be neutral with respect to the underlying moral and religious controversy. It must engage rather than avoid the substantive moral and religious doctrines at stake. Liberals often resist this engagement because it violates the priority of the right over the good. But the abortion debate shows that this priority cannot be sustained. The case for respecting a woman's right to decide for herself whether to have an abortion depends on showing that there is a relevant moral difference between aborting a fetus at a relatively early stage of development and killing a child.

The Lincoln-Douglas Debates

Perhaps the most famous case for bracketing a controversial moral question for the sake of political agreement was made by Stephen Douglas in his debates with Abraham Lincoln. Since people were bound to disagree about the morality of slavery, Douglas argued, national policy should be neutral on that question. The doctrine of popular sovereignty he defended did not judge slavery right or wrong but left the people of the territories free to make their own judgments. "To throw the weight of federal power into the scale, either in favor of the free or the slave states," would violate the fundamental principles of the Constitution and run the risk of civil war. The only hope of holding the country together, he argued, was to agree to disagree, to bracket the moral controversy over slavery and respect "the right of each state and each territory to decide these questions for themselves."[33]

Lincoln argued against Douglas' case for a political conception of justice. Policy should express rather than avoid a substantive moral judgment about slavery, he maintained. Although Lincoln was not an abolitionist, he believed that government should treat slavery as the moral wrong it was and prohibit its extension to the territories. "The real issue in this controversy—pressing upon every mind—is the sentiment on the part of one class that looks upon the institution of slavery as a wrong, and of another class that does not look upon it as a wrong." Lincoln and the Republican Party viewed slavery as a wrong and insisted that it "be treated as a wrong, and one of the methods of treating it as a wrong is to make provision that it shall grow no larger."[34]

Whatever his personal moral views, Douglas claimed that, for political purposes at least, he was agnostic on the question of slavery; he did not care whether slavery was "voted up or voted down." Lincoln replied that it was reasonable to bracket the question of the morality of slavery only on the assumption that it was not the moral evil he regarded it to be. Any man can advocate political neutrality "who does not see anything wrong in slavery, but no man can logically say it who does see a wrong in it; because no man can logically say he don't care whether a wrong is voted up or voted down."[35]

The debate between Lincoln and Douglas was not primarily about the morality of slavery, but about whether to bracket a moral controversy for the sake of political agreement. In this respect, their debate over popular sovereignty is analogous to the contemporary debate over abortion rights. As some contemporary liberals argue that government should not take a stand one way or another on the morality of abortion, but let each woman decide the question for herself, so Douglas argued that national policy should not take a stand one way or the other on the morality of slavery, but let each territory decide the question for itself. There is of course the difference that in the case of abortion rights, those who would bracket the substantive moral question typically leave the choice to the individual, while in the case of slavery, Douglas' way of bracketing was to leave the choice to the territories.

But Lincoln's argument against Douglas was an argument about bracketing as such, at least where grave moral questions are at stake. Lincoln's point was that the political conception of justice defended by Douglas depended for its plausibility on a particular answer to the substantive moral question it sought to bracket. Even in the face of so dire a threat to social cooperation as the prospect of civil war, it made neither moral nor political sense to aspire to political neutrality. As Lincoln concluded in his final debate with Douglas, "Is it not a false statesmanship that undertakes to build up a system of policy upon the basis of caring nothing about the very thing that every body does care the most about?"[36]

Present-day liberals will surely resist the company of Douglas and want national policy to oppose slavery, presumably on the grounds that slavery violates people's rights. But it is doubtful that liberalism conceived as a political conception of justice can make this claim without violating its own strictures against appeals to comprehensive moral ideals. For example, a Kantian liberal can oppose slavery as a failure to treat persons as ends in themselves, worthy of respect. But this argument, resting as it does on a Kantian conception of the person, is unavailable to minimalist liberalism. So, too, are the antislavery arguments of many American abolitionists in the 1830s and 1840s, who emphasized the sin of slavery and made their case in religious terms.

The debates over abortion and slavery show that a political conception of justice must sometimes presuppose an answer to the moral and religious questions it purports to bracket. At least where grave moral questions are at stake, it is not possible to detach politics and law from substantive moral judgment. But even in cases where it is possible to conduct political debate without reference to our moral and religious convictions, it may not always be desirable. The effort to banish moral and religious argument from the public realm for the sake of political agreement may end by impoverishing political discourse and eroding the moral and civic resources necessary to self-government.

This tendency can be seen in our present public life. With a few notable exceptions, such as the civil rights movement of the 1950s and 1960s, our political discourse in recent decades has come to reflect the liberal resolve that government be neutral on moral and religious questions, that matters of policy and law be debated and decided without reference to any particular conception of the good life. But we are beginning to find that a politics that brackets morality and religion too completely soon generates its own disenchantment. A procedural republic cannot contain the moral energies of a vital democratic life. It creates a moral void that opens the way for narrow, intolerant moralisms. And it fails to cultivate the qualities of character that equip citizens to share in self-rule.

In [*Democracy's Discontent*], I try to show that the liberalism of the procedural republic provides the public philosophy by which we live. Despite its philosophical failings, it is the theory most thoroughly embodied in our practices and institutions. Now it might be thought that the very existence of the procedural republic as a sustained practice puts to rest the philosophical objections raised against it. If the neutral state succeeds in securing a scheme of rights without appealing to a sense of community beyond the social contract, if its members can exercise their agency as free citizens without seeing themselves as claimed by civic obligations beyond consent, then abstract worries about community and self-government, toleration and moral judgment, would seem at best beside the point. Either those objections are mistaken, or liberal politics is sufficiently autonomous of theory to proceed unimpaired by philosophical infirmity.

But its prevalence as practice is no proof against its poverty as theory. To the contrary, what goes wrong with the philosophy shows up in the practice. The predicament of liberal democracy in contemporary America recapitulates the tensions that inhabit its ideals. Far from proving the autonomy of liberal politics, its practice confirms what its philosophy foretells: the procedural republic cannot secure the liberty it promises, because it cannot sustain the kind of political community and civic engagement that liberty requires.

Chapter 15

Democratic Deliberation *after* Religious Gag Rules

J. Caleb Clanton

Surveys indicate that nearly half of all Americans claim that their political behavior is affected in some way by their religious convictions.[1] According to a Gallup poll, some 64 percent of registered voters said their personal religious beliefs and faith would be a factor when deciding how to vote in the 2004 presidential election.[2] And according to other more recent polls, 28 percent of Americans asked think that religious leaders should advise government officials when it comes to drafting policy,[3] and 46 percent think the Bible must be a source of legislation.[4] These data suggest that many, if not most, Americans think it is acceptable for religious commitments to inform the activities of the democratic public square—from public deliberation about policy to voting.

Naturally, political theorists have heavily debated whether citizens are wrong to form their political views and choose how to vote on the basis of religious convictions not shared by all citizens. A prevailing view among many liberal theorists is that citizens should bracket their religious convictions in the public square.[5] Critics have sharply disagreed.[6] Now, many people think this issue is unresolved, and they certainly are not unreasonable for thinking this. Moreover, if they are right, then what we need is simply more debate on this issue. I think, though, that the critics are largely right, for reasons I will mention just briefly in a moment. And, if the *critics* are right, then a question stands in need of more attention: *how and to what extent* should religious reasoning figure into our model of the democratic public square? In response to that question, what I will argue here is that citizens should feel free to advance their relevant religious views but in a manner that is open to truth-seeking inquiry and the possibility of deliberative defeat.

I

The debate concerning whether religion should influence the activities of the public square mostly centers on the intuition that the coercive power of the state ought to be justified on the basis of reasons that are recognized by citizens of all walks of life. This sort of intuition, for instance, is at the heart of a recent ruling of the Colorado Supreme Court. In March of 2005, the court threw out a death penalty in a gruesome rape-and-murder case precisely because several of the jurors had distributed and discussed Bible passages such as "eye for eye, tooth for tooth" while deliberating the sentence.[7] Of course, these judges are hardly alone in thinking that jurors step out of bounds in basing their decisions on Levitical law. John Rawls, for example, addresses the issue concerning religion's proper role in a pluralistic democracy by fleshing out the implications of his liberal principle of legitimacy, which states that the exercise of political power "is only proper when we sincerely believe that the reasons we offer for our political action may reasonably be accepted by other citizens as a justification of those actions."[8] This principle requires citizens to give reasons for their political views and votes in terms that are acceptable to *all* parties involved so that the exercise of power can be justified—at least in principle—to "every last individual," as Jeremy Waldron says.[9] In order for citizens to be able to meet this demand, liberals argue that citizens should practice "conversational restraint"[10] and observe "gag rules"[11] with respect to their deepest comprehensive moral, religious, and philosophical doctrines when deliberating and voting on important political matters. Only by appealing to public reasons that remain neutral with respect to these comprehensive doctrines can citizens express respect for fellow citizens as free and equal, thereby meeting the demands entailed by the liberal principle of legitimacy.

Of course, the fact that Rawls added the now infamous proviso in 1996 suggests that he saw some problems facing his initial articulation of public reason and the strictly separatist strategy implied therein. In an effort to widen his view of public reason (and presumably make it more inclusive), Rawls comes to allow reasons drawn from a comprehensive doctrine to be voiced in public deliberation, "provided that in due course public reasons . . . are presented sufficient to support whatever the comprehensive doctrines are introduced to support."[12] And while this wider view of public reason may suggest that the public square can allow religious reasoning, the fact remains that Rawls' wide view only permits religious *language* in the public square. For the proviso requirement still implies that reasons drawn from a citizen's comprehensive doctrine cannot do any actual justificatory work—that's why they must be attached to a promissory note of sorts.[13] And if those reasons cannot do any justification, they cannot provide the basis for the justification of a citizen's political views and votes in the public square.[14] Consequently, this IOU allowance does not significantly dilute Rawls' religious-political separatism.

However intuitive liberal separatism may seem to us—and indeed, it is intuitive—it is not without some serious flaws. I will simply mention three of them, though I should stress that my task *here* is not to argue that they cannot be resolved[15]—I'm just going to suppose for the purposes of this essay that they cannot, or at least, that they have not been resolved. Note that the standard Rawlsian liberal view of deliberation and voting expects citizens to bracket their religious reasoning and identity upon entering the public square. The problem with this expectation, as Michael Sandel has shown,[16] is that it presupposes and affirms a particular nonneutral—albeit *decidedly* liberal and Kantian—conception of the self as detachable from its commitments and obligations. Consequently, the separatist strategy implicit within liberalism is hypocritical: whereas religious citizens are expected to refrain from appealing to their comprehensive religious doctrines, Rawlsian liberalism presupposes its own comprehensive doctrine according to which such restraints can be motivated. And, even by Rawls' own standards, a liberalism that is rooted in *any* particular comprehensive doctrine—even a decidedly nonreligious liberal doctrine—will *ipso facto* not be sufficiently liberal.

What's more, there remains an important question that liberals have yet to answer satisfactorily: where is the source of *truly* public reasons, i.e., reasons that are actually common to all citizens and neutral among all comprehensive doctrines? Supposedly, these neutral reasons are to be drawn from our shared political culture. But it seems that, just as there is disagreement at the level of our deepest comprehensive doctrines, there is also disagreement at the level of our shared political culture. So, as Nicholas Wolterstorff aptly puts it: "the prospect of extracting, from that political culture, principles of justice that are both shared and appropriate to a liberal democracy is hopeless."[17] If we cannot locate a shared fund of neutral public reasons in the way Rawls would like, then liberal separatists cannot justify (let alone motivate) a politics of omission wherein religious citizens are expected to practice conversational constraint.

But even if liberals suggest that the neutrality requirement of public reason is simply a regulative ideal, the standard liberal model of public reasoning still faces a serious problem. The problem with this neutrality requirement as a regulative is that it is politically dangerous. For if religious gag rules discourage citizens from discussing their political views in a manner that reflects the deeper comprehensive doctrines that animate them, then they will likely resort to some form of deliberation with others of like mind who *will* allow them to bring their views to the table. Resorting to such enclave deliberation can severely limit the argument pool and the range of views to which citizens are exposed. Considerable social scientific research (especially that of Cass Sunstein[18]) suggests that such enclave deliberation will likely result in the polarization of a control group's viewpoints. And this sort of polarization can pose very practical threats to political stability, peaceable deliberation, and social tolerance within a democracy.[19] Ironically, this seems to be the antithesis of what Rawls' separatism was designed to accomplish.

II

If these criticisms are on target and if it is indeed true that the separatist restrictions and gag rules imposed on religious reasoning in the public square are out of order, then it makes sense for us to start thinking about how and to what extent religious reasoning should figure into our model of the democratic public square. To that end, I ask: what might a democratic public square that is open to religious reasoning look like?

The model of the democratic public square I want to propose says that religious citizens are free to employ whatever reasons they see fit to advance in the course of public deliberation. Likewise, the secularist is free to do the same. Of course, simply because citizens are free to advance arguments that are informed by religious reasons does not mean that their arguments will win (i.e., prove to be the best argument) in the course of deliberation. In fact, the religiously informed argument may be defeated. It might be shown, for instance, that the religious argument advanced is internally incoherent or contradictory; that it commits the religious citizen to other things to which she is unwilling to commit; that it does not present adequate evidence for the conclusion or one of the premises; that the conclusion does not follow from the premises; or that the consequences entailed by the conclusion are themselves undesirable or in conflict with one another. In any case, when a religious citizen employs her religious reasons in the course of public deliberation, she implicitly takes a certain risk: her religious line of reasoning may actually be defeated.

For example, a religious citizen may have her religious reasons regarding some particular political matter, M, engaged in immanent criticism (as Stout aptly explains[20]) by one of her secularist interlocutors. The secularist immanent critic might then point out to the religious citizen that her view is inconsistent from within the perspective of her own religious doctrine. And this may cause the religious citizen to abandon or refine her previous line of reasoning concerning M. Of course, it might very well be the religious citizen who engages the secularist in immanent criticism. The risk of defeat, then, cuts both ways. Prior to deliberation there is no way of knowing for sure which side will win out over the other; hence the *risk* implicit in the participation in public deliberation.

Admittedly, it is no easy task to determine when, in fact, an argument or line of reasoning in the course of public deliberation has been definitively defeated, i.e., when *deliberative defeat* has occurred. This is a point to which I will return (in section VI). For the moment, though, let us ask: what should happen if and when, in the course of deliberation concerning M, a particular religious argument/line of reasoning, R, is defeated? If R is defeated in public deliberation, the citizen has basically two options: to pursue either what I will call an *ex post* separatist strategy or what I will call an *ex post* reconstructivist strategy. First, let me explain the *ex post* separatist strategy. One variation of this *ex post* separatist strategy available to the religious citizen is simply to abandon the particular element of her religious system of belief that pertains to the expression of R, meanwhile leaving other elements of her religious system of belief intact. Another type of *ex post* separatist strategy available to the religious citizen is to adopt what Rorty calls "Jefferson's compromise"[21] and simply privatize the particular element of her religious system of belief pertaining to R (thus only abandon it within the public sphere) for the purposes of pursuing "private perfection."[22] Or it might mean that the religious citizen remains privately motivated by R (even though it has met deliberative defeat) to hold the same view concerning M. However, in such a case, this religious citizen advances only nonreligious reasons in the public square for the same view concerning M. For example, a religious citizen might be privately motivated to oppose abortion for religious reasons, yet voice only nonreligious reasons for banning abortion when involved in public deliberation. Whether the religious citizen abandons or merely privatizes R, pursuing an *ex post* separatist strategy will lead the religious citizen—in light of the fact that R with respect to M has been defeated—to bracket R in the public square and employ only nonreligious reasons for her public-policy proposals regarding M, with the understanding that she might be able to refine R such that it becomes assertable in future deliberation.[23] In the meantime presumably, she should not allow R to be the determining factor when voting with respect to M, given the deliberative defeat of R.

Another option available to religious citizens in the face of deliberative defeat is to try to resuscitate R (in the light of its defeat) by pursuing some variation of an *ex post* reconstructivist strategy. One variation of this strategy will lead the religious citizen to reinterpret and recast semantically those elements of her religious system of beliefs that pertain to and inform R so that R_r (where R_r means R after sufficient semantic reconstruction) can be advanced in a way that is no longer open to defeat. This means that the language and terms used in the expression of R (such that R_r could be achieved) would be interpreted metaphorically or symbolically. For instance, let us imagine a religious citizen who advocates a certain foreign-aid policy on the basis of a religious line of reasoning— say, "because Jesus tells us to do so"—which somehow gets defeated. This religious citizen may opt for semantically reinterpreting the phrase "because Jesus tells us to do so" to mean roughly "because it serves our human goals to do so." Here the language of Jesus is simply advanced, at least within the public square, as motivationally potent metaphor.

Another variation of the *ex post* reconstructivist strategy would be simply to adjust one's theology/religion itself such that it systematically expresses an altogether different line of reasoning (i.e., an altogether different R) with respect to M. In either case, the *ex post* reconstructivist strategy is pursued by the religious citizen with the understanding that the presently defeated R might be further refined such that it is no longer defeated, thereby suspending the need for a continued pursuit of an *ex post* reconstructivist strategy.

I do not mean here to be advocating any one of these strategies over and above another. I simply mean to sketch these as *potential* options (among others, perhaps) for the religious citizen in the face of deliberative defeat. Which option or variation is pursued will, in large part, depend upon the particular situation. In any case, it is crucial to notice that in both of these post-defeat scenarios the separatist and reconstructivist strategies would be *pursued* by the citizens themselves. That is, the *ex post* separatist and reconstructivist strategies I have sketched are not *imposed* upon religious citizens prior to entering the public square. If an *ex post* separatist or reconstructivist strategy is pursued by a religious citizen within the public square, it is pursued as a conscientious response to a forum of deliberation that has heard and engaged the religious citizen's R. On this model of the public square, inclusion acts as the default; exclusion or modification of religion comes as a result of deliberative defeat. Whereas *ex ante* separatist and reconstructivist strategies seek to impose *ex ante* gag rules and constraints that are not justified to religious citizens, *ex post* separatist and reconstructivist strategies in fact do offer reasons and justification to religious citizens for the restraint and reconstructivism to be pursued. In short, religious citizens should pursue these strategies precisely because, as a result of deliberation, the religious reasons offered have been defeated.

III

Such an open model of the public square, then, does not require religious citizens to bracket their religious doctrines *prior* to entering the public square. Rather, citizens are invited to participate in public deliberation with whatever reasons they see fit to bring, with the understanding that further deliberation may defeat the line of reasoning they initially bring to the public domain. As such, citizens are allowed to *engage* one another at the most fundamental level within the political sphere. This level of deep engagement is prohibited by the restrictive model of the public square advanced by *ex ante* separatists. Yet, only when the public square is open to citizens as they choose to come can those citizens actually engage one another deeply and thereby participate in the "kind of public deliberation necessary to test the plausibility of contending comprehensive moralities—to persuade others of the merits of our moral ideals, to be persuaded by others of the merits of theirs."[24] I think of this model as being "Socratic" because it positions Socrates as an exemplar of one participating in public discourse. Throughout most of Plato's dialogues,

Socrates is presented as being committed to engaging his interlocutors as they come—i.e., complete with their commitments and convictions—with the hope of involving those interlocutors in truth-seeking inquiry. Participation in this sort of inquiry, Socrates understands, opens him up to the possibility of not only refuting his interlocutors but also being refuted by them.[25]

Interestingly, it can be said that Socrates expresses toward his engaged interlocutor an attitude of respect, one which is distinctively at odds with the conception endorsed by Rawls. On the neutralist liberal view, citizens respect one another by justifying their political positions according to reasons that are not drawn from their own comprehensive doctrines. Thus, under this Rawlsian view, showing respect for others requires that a citizen not only bracket her own deep comprehensive doctrinal convictions but also ignore those held by her interlocutors, at least as far as *justification* of fundamental political matters is concerned. As such, the liberal conception of respect expresses itself as a process of leaving others alone and refusing to engage them as they come. Gag rules and conversational restraints imposed upon religious citizens, the liberal suggests, help us achieve this form of respect in the public square by forcing us to offer public reasons. But, for Socrates, ignoring an interlocutor (by means of ignoring his deeply held convictions) is precisely a form of *disrespect*. Consider, for instance, the manner in which Socrates uncharacteristically disengages (by means of silence) some of Plato's dramatic characters like Cleitophon in the *Cleitophon* and the Eleatic Stranger in the *Sophist*. Socrates does not try to engage these individuals, and hence refuses to show them respect, precisely because they willingly refuse to allow for the possibility of actual engagement. In the *Cleitophon* (as in the *Republic*), Socrates has nothing to say to Cleitophon who, as seen in the *Republic*, rejects the distinction between truth and falsity.[26] In the *Sophist*, Socrates refuses to participate in discussion with the Eleatic Stranger who seeks to "lay unfilial hands upon that pronouncement" (242b) of Parmenides concerning the law of noncontradiction, thereby putting such a law "to a mild degree of torture" (237b).[27] In both cases, Socrates refuses to engage those interlocutors who choose to undermine the necessary logical conditions for truth-seeking inquiry. Involving others in inquiry for Socrates is the greatest manifestation of respect precisely because doing so takes that interlocutor seriously and implicitly accepts the risks of doing so: the interlocutor might be right, and thus Socrates might be refuted. It is only when others would prevent that inquiry from taking place by undermining or rejecting the logical conditions for inquiry that Socrates writes them off and does not engage them. In this manner, the Socratic conception of respect is consistent with the "deliberative mode of respect" advocated by Michael Sandel.

> We respect our fellow citizen's moral and religious convictions by engaging, or attending to, them—sometimes by challenging and contesting them, sometimes by listening and learning from them—especially when those convictions bear on important political questions. There is no guarantee that a deliberative mode of respect will lead in any given case to agreement with, or even appreciation of, the moral and religious convictions of others. It is always possible that learning more about a moral or religious doctrine will lead us to like it less. But the respect of deliberation and engagement afford a more spacious public reason than liberalism allows. It is also a more suitable ideal for a pluralist society. To the extent that our moral and religious disagreements reflect the ultimate plurality of human goods, a deliberative mode of respect will better enable us to appreciate the distinctive goods our different lives express.[28]

Not only does this open model of the public square facilitate this Socratic conception of respect, but it also facilitates the level of Socratic engagement necessary to prevent the doxastic polarization effect affiliated with enclave deliberative groups. Separatist models of public discourse tell religious citizens that their most deeply held religious convictions have no place in the public forum. This restriction poses a serious practical threat to the stability of our democracy precisely because if citizens are told that they cannot discuss their most deeply held convictions in the public square, they will likely turn to enclave deliberative groups wherein they are free to do so. The polarization resulting from these sorts of enclaves threatens the sort of extremism, hatred, intolerance, and violence democratic societies should hope to avoid. The Socratic engagement possible within an open public square may do much to diffuse this political threat of instability associated with group polarization.

IV

Such an open model of the public square, then, invites citizens to bring their religious convictions into public deliberation and thereby accept the risks of doing so. As implied above, a fair amount pivots upon our understanding of what constitutes the deliberative defeat of a line of reasoning. And, to be sure, explaining what constitutes deliberative defeat is not easy. Perhaps it will be useful, then, to proceed by first saying a little about what does *not* necessarily constitute deliberative defeat.

Simply because a religious citizen's line of reasoning in public deliberation falls short of *convincing* his fellow interlocutors does *not* entail that her argument has been somehow defeated in the relevant sense. Imagine a case where, in the course of deliberation, a religious line of reasoning concerning M does not win anyone over. There may be, for instance, a counterbalancing set of secular reasons. However, it might very well be the case that neither line of reasoning definitively defeats the other (nor is either line defeated by any other set of reasons). What then?

In cases where a religious line of reasoning proves unconvincing but stands undefeated, that line of religious reasoning may be useful for democratic deliberation nonetheless. One of the main difficulties facing Stout's view of public reason is that it seems to advocate prudential constraints on religious reasoning on the grounds that (as Stout sees it) religious reasons are mostly unconvincing in our otherwise very secular, public discourse.[29] Thus, it is an act of prudence for religious citizens to employ nonreligious modes of discourse in order to avoid resentment of religious pluralism and the consequent secularized public discourse. Of course, such prudential constraints are only prudent if the aim within deliberation is simply to convince interlocutors. But this may not be the goal after all; hence, Stout's prudential constraints seem insufficiently motivated.[30] So, the question arises: what function(s) might an unconvincing and yet undefeated religious line of reasoning serve? Religious reasoning may very well be useful in *interrupting* the dominant forum of deliberation in such a way as to *challenge* and call into question that forum of deliberation itself. Consequently, religious reasoning takes on the distinctively Socratic function of confounding one's interlocutors. Like the broad torpedo-fish to which Socrates is likened in Plato's *Meno*,[31] religious reasoning might numb the current framework of discussion and bring its participants to a critical state of *aporia*, or perplexity, with respect to the values, terms, topics, and assumptions implicit within the current framework of discourse. And, operating as a sort of gadfly,[32] religious reasoning might thus stimulate a second-order inquiry into the appropriateness of the status quo implicit within the first-order deliberation. This second-order inquiry may act to disambiguate the values, terms, topics, and assumptions implicit in the first-order deliberation. Or, in virtue of the challenge posed by the religious reasoning, the result of this second-order inquiry might be the reconsideration, reinterpretation, or redefinition of those values, terms, topics, and assumptions such that deliberation at the first-order level can be entertained differently in the future. This may mean that the religious line of reasoning is no longer unconvincing at the first-order level. Or it may just mean that the values, terms, topics, and assumptions implicit in the first-order deliberation stand unchanged but are now made *explicit* as a result of the second-order inquiry prompted by the religious contestation. Making terms explicit may be a good in its own right precisely because doing so effectively abandons any overly ambitious claim that the current framework of discussion is "neutral" in some Rawlsian sense. This pushes the forum of deliberation beyond the politics of hypocrisy toward a politics of honesty. In any case, the second-order deliberation brings about inquiry concerning not only *how* to deliberate at the first order but also *what* to deliberate about at the first order. Thus, religious reasoning may be useful in the following respect: religious reasoning might pose a Socratic challenge to the current framework of discussion, which leads to *aporia*, which prompts further inquiry and deliberation, thus promoting the politics of open engagement and honesty. In short, religious reasoning may serve democratic deliberative forums well simply by allowing, facilitating, and sometimes forcing the road to inquiry to remain open, as C. S. Peirce would have it.[33]

Perhaps one of the most important and telling historical examples of this sort of gadfly-function of religious reasoning and participation in the public square comes to us from Martin Luther King Jr. during the civil rights movement of the 1960s. King advanced overtly religious arguments and advocated religiously motivated nonviolent protests in order to create what he referred to as "constructive, nonviolent tension" in the city of Birmingham, Alabama. Yet, as King explains, the goal was not simply to create turmoil for the sake of turmoil or retaliation against an unjust government. Rather, as he writes in the "Letter from a Birmingham Jail,"

> Just as Socrates felt that it was necessary to create a tension in the mind so that individuals could rise from the bondage of myths and half-truths to the unfettered realm of creative analysis and objective appraisal, so must we see the need for nonviolent gadflies to create the kind of tension in society that will help men rise from the dark depths of prejudice and racism to the majestic heights of understanding and brotherhood. The purpose of our direct-action program is to create a situation so crisis-packed that *it will inevitably open the door to negotiation.*[34]

King's use of religious reasoning and religiously motivated direct-action campaigns were aimed at prompting second-order deliberations about how deliberations and negotiations at the first order (concerning race relations in Birmingham) were being conducted. It was hoped that this inevitable second-order deliberation would ultimately expose the values, principles, flaws, biases, and limitations of the deliberations taking place at the first order—namely, that African Americans were being systematically excluded from good-faith negotiations with city leaders. And, so King suggests, it was necessary to prompt this second-order deliberation (by means of this constructive tension) so that negotiations at the first order could take place properly and in a way that was democratically inclusive of African Americans.

V

Let us imagine for a moment that religious reasoning executes within a particular forum of deliberation this Socratic torpedo-fish/gadfly function outlined above. In other words, let us assume that the nondefeated yet unconvincing (at the first order) line of religious reasoning provokes enough contestation of the current framework of deliberation to prompt a second-order inquiry. Let us imagine further that the religious line of reasoning is unable to resolve/determine the second-order inquiry and thus remains unconvincing at the first order. Despite the fact that the religious line of reasoning remains unconvincing, the end result may be the disambiguation, clarification, and explicit articulation of the values, terms, etc. previously implicit within the first-order forum of deliberation. Now, in addition to the fact that the religious line of reasoning remains unconvincing, let us imagine that it still has not been definitively defeated. There is no clear-cut winner or loser in this forum of deliberation, even though many of the values, terms, assumptions, etc. have been clarified through second-order inquiry. I will call this scenario *deliberative stalemate*. What should we do in the face of such deliberative stalemate?

One way of trying to answer this question is by first getting clear on exactly what our goals might be at this point. At this juncture, liberals would have us simply accept this present state of disagreement as an inevitable fact of reality. Rawls might have us cite the present state of deliberative stalemate as evidence for what he calls "the fact of reasonable pluralism."[35] However, simply because there is a stalemate at this particular juncture in deliberation does not entail that there will be stalemate tomorrow or the next day. The truth is: we simply do not know what the future of deliberation holds. As Sandel reminds us, contra Rawls, "Whether it is possible to reason our way to agreement on any given moral or political controversy [and thus overcome deliberative stalemate] is not something we can know until we try."[36] Thus, one of our goals at this juncture should be to preserve the possibility of further inquiry on the matter at hand such that a deliberative stalemate could be overcome in the future. This is to say, with Peirce, that we should not block the road to further inquiry in pursuit of the truth. Perhaps some religious line of reasoning is right; perhaps it is wrong. In any case, we need to preserve the notion that deliberative defeat is possible on either side of an issue. And this means that inquiry and deliberation needs to persist so we can determine if one or more parties in the deliberation can be eventually defeated. Thus, one of our goals in the face of deliberative stalemate should be to promote the conditions for the possibility of further deliberation and inquiry.

Unfortunately, though, the nature of politics is at times such that some decisions *must* be made and be made in a timely fashion. Crudely put, we do not always have the luxury to wait public inquiry out with respect to certain issues. Some political issues are so time-indexed, severe, and salient that they demand that we *do* something even as we wait out further deliberation and inquiry on the matter. Thus, in the face of deliberative stalemate, one of our goals will surely be that we, in fact, enable ourselves to make certain sorts of political decisions, even though we would rather wait until deliberation and inquiry definitively tell us what we should do.

Hence, we have these two goals in the face of deliberative stalemate: (1) to preserve the possibility of further deliberation and inquiry such that defeat (and ultimately victory) can be established, and (2) to preserve our capacity to make certain sorts of decisions when situations demand us to do so. So our question becomes roughly this: how do we devise a politics that is attuned to the preservation and furthering of public deliberation that is nonetheless capable of addressing important and timely political matters? Obviously, there is no easy answer to this difficult question. However, I will try to sketch out a response below that takes into account these two goals.

Let us imagine a deliberative stalemate concerning M. If it is the case that the political situation around which M revolves does not require immediate and timely action, then it is safe to say that deliberation should simply continue until all defeatable lines of argument are eliminated and the victorious line is identified. However, if the situation *does* require immediate and timely action such that a decision cannot wait out the trajectory of further deliberation and inquiry, we have a

different situation on our hands. Let us call these cases *act-now deliberative stalemate situations*.[37] In these cases, perhaps the best we can do is
pause deliberation momentarily and, in a manner of speaking, hash out
a *temporary modus vivendi* with respect to M. That is, we might simply
try to come up with some sort of second-best compromise to which
all parties can agree until such time as deliberation is able to decide
otherwise, whenever that may be. Of course, this means that concerning M no one deliberative party will get exactly what it might desire.
This sort of *modus vivendi* will be at best a bargaining of interests and a
carving out of policy and public strategies of action in accordance with
that bargaining process.

How might this temporary *modus vivendi* be reached? We might take
a vote, whether that is a vote of the relevant legislature or a referendum.
But that, too, might be outside the range of feasibility given the timely
nature of the situation. In such cases, then, the courts will likely need to
conduct the *modus vivendi* formation. In any case, the goal will be to assess
the disagreement at hand within the act-now deliberative stalemate as it
currently stands concerning M, weigh the competing interests involved
on all deliberative sides, and try to gerrymander some sort of policy that
is maximally sensitive to as many interests as possible. Presumably, this
gerrymandered policy will be one that makes certain sorts of concessions
to involved parties. So, for instance, the *modus vivendi* policy will attempt
to make as many concessions as possible to the undefeated and unconvincing religious line of reasoning in the act-now deliberative stalemate
situation. This pushes to the surface a distinctly different nondelibera-
tive—albeit *expressive*—function of religious reasoning within the public
square: to *express* the deeply held convictions of religious citizens such
that they can be taken into account in the formulation of a temporary
modus vivendi. Because religious citizens are afforded the space within the
public square to voice their religious convictions and reasons, we have
not only a way to assess what their interests are in forming the *modus
vivendi* but also some indication of the fervor with which those interests are held. Making these sorts of assessments will better enable us to
understand how and to what degree to tilt the distribution of privileges
and obligations of the *modus vivendi* agreement.

It is important to note, however, that hashing out a temporary *modus
vivendi* policy needs to take place within a constitutional framework.
Such a framework acts as de facto guide when deciding what sorts of
concessions can be made and to what extent. Such a framework will
institutionally prevent us from making horribly regrettable mistakes in

the formation of *modus vivendi* policy. So, for instance, we might be able to make certain sorts of concessions to the religious parties involved in an act-now deliberative stalemate concerning M, but we would not be willing to make the sorts of concessions that would violate the schedule of rights ensured within a constitutional framework. Of course, this constitutional framework will systematically tend to bias the nature of the *modus vivendi* agreement in a fairly liberal direction. However, this is not to say that the constitutional framework within which these agreements are made is itself closed to revision. It may be the case that deliberation ultimately defeats some tenet of that framework such that future *modus vivendi* agreements should be formulated differently. This, of course, will be a difficult feat—but not impossible.

Another significant task of hashing out a temporary *modus vivendi* in the case of an act-now deliberative stalemate will be to come up not only with certain legal policies with respect to M but also with certain public strategies of action aimed at designing institutions that could prevent, or at least diminish, the need for such legal policy in the first place. For example, it may very well be the case that we are currently in an act-now deliberative stalemate with respect to euthanasia in this country. However, hashing out certain temporary *modus vivendi* legal policy with respect to euthanasia may prove less helpful than coming up with ways to avoid the *need* for euthanasia altogether. We can at least start to diminish the demand for euthanasia greatly by implementing certain practical strategies of action aimed at improving palliative care and strengthening the bonds between the elderly and their families and communities. Similarly, with respect to the abortion issue, we might pursue a public strategy of action aimed at encouraging and facilitating a culture of adoption so as to lessen the demand for the abortion of unwanted pregnancies. By diminishing the demand for euthanasia and abortion, we can take at least some practical steps toward making certain nonlegislative/nonpolicy concessions (by means of these strategies of action) to those who oppose euthanasia and abortion with undefeated and unconvincing reasons within the act-now deliberative stalemate situation. Effectively, these strategies of action are aimed at lessening the extent to which legal policy would even be relevant with respect to M. The hope is to dissolve the conflict in some sense prior to the need for policy. Again the expressive function of religion in the public square emerges: the expression of deeply held religious convictions within the public square will help tilt the table when it comes to deciding what strategies of action to pursue and how to pursue them.

I call this *modus vivendi* "temporary" for an important reason. This *modus vivendi* is not a compromise made at the terminus of all possible inquiry concerning M. It is simply one that is hashed out with the concomitant understanding that deliberation concerning M will continue in hopes of overcoming the present status of stalemate. Given that the fact of disagreement present within a stalemate situation does not entail that the stalemate will persist, it may be the case that continued deliberation can inform us as to the truth concerning M. If this is the case, the *modus vivendi* agreement concerning M is abandoned and a new policy coined in accordance with the outcome of deliberation takes its place. Or it may be the case that continued deliberation and inquiry only inform us (at any given moment) that certain positions with respect to M have been defeated. In such cases, the *modus vivendi* is revised: we adjust the sorts of concessions made and the distribution of privileges and obligations present within the *modus vivendi* agreement accordingly. In either case, continued deliberation is crucial to the maintenance of the temporary *modus vivendi* agreements. This is to say, then, that a temporary *modus vivendi* with respect to M is only as permanent as, and thus contingent upon, the conditions of the deliberative stalemate concerning M.

As mentioned above, given the constitutional framework within which a temporary *modus vivendi* is to be hashed out, it will likely be the case that any given temporary *modus vivendi* will be roughly liberal. But notice that this is not tantamount to liberalism as such. Insofar as the *modus vivendi* agreement is temporary to the degree that it (along with the constitutional framework itself) is contingent upon the trajectory of further deliberation and inquiry, a defining feature of liberalism is abandoned. Effectively, the fact that open deliberation and inquiry constantly checks the *modus vivendi* (and even the constitutional framework within which this occurs) means that the right is thought to be not prior to the good in the manner suggested, for instance, by Rawls.[38] In theory, we can adjust the schedule of rights operative both within a *modus vivendi* and the constitutional framework in accordance with the outcomes of deliberation.

VI

Admittedly, this open model of the public square hinges on the idea that deliberative defeat is a possibility within the course of public deliberation. It is therefore necessary to say something about what deliberative defeat might look like. As we have already seen, deliberative defeat does not mean simply that a line of reasoning concerning M is unconvincing. For it may be the case that the unconvincing line of reasoning is, in fact, unconvincing precisely because the framework of discussion is itself systematically biased against the conditions under which such reasoning would be persuasive in the first place. This does not, however, rule out the possibility that such a line of reasoning is in fact correct.

Most clearly, an argument would be defeated in the course of deliberation if it could be shown that it is invalid, i.e., that there is some incoherence, contradiction, *non sequitur*, or other fallacy in the reasoning from the premise(s) to the conclusion(s) of the argument. Of course, it is possible that competent deliberators will have already ironed out any such inconsistencies, contradictions, *non sequiturs*, and other fallacies prior to advancing their lines of reasoning in the course of public deliberation. If that is true, it might be unlikely that there will be any problems pertaining to the validity of the argument to expose such that deliberative defeat can be established.

Another avenue to establishing deliberative defeat would be to show one's interlocutor that his line of reasoning commits him to other things which would be unpalatable. Given that these collateral commitments are, in fact, unacceptable to him, he is prompted to abandon the initial line of reasoning advanced. However, it is at least possible, if not entirely probable, that a deliberator might simply bite the bullet and own up to those collateral commitments, so as to avoid admitting deliberative defeat.

Deliberative defeat might come about by showing that there is either too little or too weak evidence in support of either the premises or conclusion of a deliberator's line of reasoning. Of course, the assessment of evidence is a tricky thing. Exactly what constitutes evidence for premises or conclusions (such that evidential sufficiency is either attained or not) is itself open to legitimate contestation at times. Religious citizens may feel that some aspect of their experience or revelation should count as sufficient evidence for religious premises, while atheists might reject the same as insufficient. Thus, given the difficulties of evidential assessment, it may be quite difficult in some cases to demonstrate deliberative defeat along these lines.

It may be the case that deliberative defeat is demonstrated by pointing out that the consequences of a deliberator's line of reasoning are themselves undesirable. So, for instance, we might try to point out that the consequences of a policy proposed by a religious line of reasoning are negative and hence that the line of reasoning is defeated. Of course, it may very well be the case that the advocate of a particular policy may again bite the bullet and simply deny that the consequences are, in fact,

382 J. Caleb Clanton

negative as his interlocutor claims. As such, consequentialist assessments will be a difficult way to demonstrate deliberative defeat.

But this is all just to say the obvious: that deliberative defeat is, indeed, *difficult* at times to demonstrate within the public square—not that deliberative defeat is itself impossible. It may turn out, for instance, that the doctrine of ensoulment can be shown to be true and hence that it should inform our decisions about abortion policy. Of course, that same doctrine might prove to be false. Right now, we might not yet know definitively. However, it may be the case that, in the course of deliberation, we can definitively conclude that the doctrine of ensoulment is, indeed, false. In such a case, then, this doctrine will have faced deliberative defeat.

Of course, there remains this problem: what if the course of deliberation and inquiry has definitely established a religious line of reasoning, *R*, to be false and, meanwhile, advocates of *R* remain unmoved and continue to hold *R*? Can there be deliberative defeat even when all parties are not convinced that defeat has occurred with respect to *R*? Here, perhaps a distinction between *objective* and *subjective* deliberative defeat is helpful. On the one hand, if deliberation and inquiry has definitely demonstrated *R* to be false, *R* has faced *objective* deliberative defeat. But, just because objective defeat of *R* has occurred does not mean that proponents of *R* will in fact abandon *R*, i.e., acknowledge that *R* has been objectively defeated. (And, conversely, just because *R* has been abandoned by a proponent does not entail that *R* has in fact been objectively defeated.) To acknowledge that the *R* which one has advanced has been objectively defeated is for *R* to be *subjectively* defeated. In any case, the practical question lingers: what do we do when *R* has been objectively defeated but not subjectively defeated, abandoned, or otherwise appropriately altered by its proponents? There is, of course, no easy solution to such a problem.

In any case, the concept of objective deliberative defeat outlined above will no doubt leave some wanting and waiting to hear more. For instance, one might wonder how we can establish with confidence (and hence without reasonable contestation) if and when a position has been definitively defeated in the course of public deliberation. In order to answer this sort of question fully, though, one would need to spell out a criterion or set of criteria in the light of which some position could be definitively falsified. Of course, the difficulty here is that such falsification criteria would be contingent on some underlying conception of truth. And given that there is still considerable debate among epistemologists concerning competing theories of truth, what gets to count as *the* criteria for deliberative defeat is indeed a matter for further investigation and deliberation, particularly for epistemologists. That being said, whatever criteria of objective defeat we might eventually wish to adopt—and whether they are established by community agreement or by some heavenly Platonic form or rooted in a pragmatist, coherence, correspondence, or some other theory of truth—it is not necessary that we solve these obviously important epistemological problems before we make use of the concept of deliberative defeat as a placeholder of sorts within a normative model of public deliberation. That there remain unsettled epistemological problems need not be an indictment of my model of public deliberation. For whatever criteria of deliberative defeat we might find appropriate to adopt, we still stand in need of having some workable concept of deliberative defeat in place for any model of public deliberation to proceed. In fact, that my model of deliberation remains uncommitted to any robust philosophical and epistemological theories can be seen as one of its strengths, for the function of deliberative defeat as a place-holder concept within my model of deliberation can accommodate any number of epistemological accounts.

VII

In any case, perhaps the most significant problem for any potential deliberative scenario is that a citizen—religious or nonreligious—*is simply not open* to the possibility of acknowledging the defeat of the position she advances in the public square. That is, perhaps a citizen holds R with respect to M in such a way that is closed to any further inquiry. Still in other words, perhaps a citizen holds R with respect to M so tenaciously that she does not (and will not) entertain the possibility that R could be refuted in any way, thereby refusing to acknowledge the possibility of both objective and subjective deliberative defeat. Ought religious citizens who hold their religious beliefs in this manner introduce them into the public square with respect to M?

I think not. If it is the case that a religious citizen holds her belief with respect to M in an utterly nonfallibilistic manner—she is unable to acknowledge or own up to the objective deliberative defeat of that belief (if and when it occurs)—then that religious citizen ought not to introduce her religious belief into public deliberation regarding M. For public deliberation presupposes the possibility of deliberative defeat. Therefore, if a religious citizen denies the possibility of the defeat of her religious belief with respect to M, then that religious citizen effectively denies the possibility of her religious belief participating in deliberation and inquiry with respect to M. Consequently, the religious citizen in this case should not advance her position with respect to M into a forum of public deliberation precisely because she refuses to accept the risk of defeat implicit in doing so. She refuses both to be engaged as an interlocutor participating in public deliberation concerning M and to engage others concerning M. In refusing to engage others, she refuses to show respect for others, at least with respect to deliberation of M. Thus, for this religious citizen to advance her religious belief with respect to M in the public forum, even though she refuses to engage in actual deliberation concerning M (and thus to show respect for others in the public forum), is for her to fail at democratic citizenship, at least with regard to M.

This view above commits me therefore to saying that the civic duties of good democratic citizenship presuppose what I will call a *fallible-inquiry requirement* incumbent on religious (as well as secularist) citizens in the public square. If a religious citizen wishes to participate in the public square concerning M, she should be willing to participate in inquiry with other citizens not only with respect to the truth of other viewpoints concerning M, but also with respect to the truth of her own religious view as it pertains to M. This means, then, that the religious citizen must be willing to hold her religious line of reasoning with respect to M in a fallible manner when entering the public square, implying that she acknowledges the possibility (and the risk) that her belief might be defeated. If it is the case that a religious citizen is able and willing to hold her religious belief with respect to M in a manner that is open to the possibility of defeat and thus in compliance with this fallible-inquiry requirement, then that religious citizen does not violate the terms of good citizenship simply by introducing her religious lines of argument with respect to M in the public square. For that religious citizen is attempting to participate in deliberation and thus to engage and to be engaged, to show respect for and to be respected by her interlocutors.

But what exactly justifies this fallible-inquiry requirement? Clearly, meeting this requirement positions a citizen such that she is open to deliberation with others. But what justifies the requirement that one be open to deliberation in the first place? Some political theorists, like Amy Gutmann and Dennis Thompson, argue that citizens have some sort of deliberation-independent moral duty to give and exchange reasons with others.[39] But, note that this sort of argument assumes that we *already* agree that liberal values like reciprocity and accountability to one's fellow citizens should trump other values that one might have.[40]

When trying to justify something like the fallible-inquiry requirement, Cheryl Misak is right:

> We can't simply rest on the appealing thought that deliberation, conversation, and taking seriously the views of others is the right way to proceed. We must not beg the question in favor of the liberal democratic values [such as reciprocity or openness to inquiry] we may hold dear.[41]

So, what then justifies this fallible-inquiry requirement? Misak's Peircean theory of deliberative democracy is helpful here.[42] As she points out, there is an organic connection between holding a belief and the obligation to participate in inquiry with others. For one to say that she believes (or for her to assert) *p* is for her to hold that *p* is true. And, for one to hold that *p* is true is for her to hold that *p* cannot be further refined and could henceforth meet the challenges brought forward. For one to maintain all of that is for her to be engaged in the process of justifying her held belief to others—to giving and exchanging reasons concerning *p*. Thus, when someone says that she believes *p*, she is thereby committed "to defending *p*—to arguing that [one is], and others are, warranted in believing *p*."[43] Of course, in order to defend *p*, she must be *willing* to entertain challenges to *p*, such that her belief *p* is "responsive to or answerable to reasons and evidence."[44] And this means, of course, that a believer of any variety is tacitly committed to participating in deliberation and thereby owning up to the risk of deliberative defeat. This, of course, does *not* entail that all citizens will actually meet the justificatory demands to which they are committed in virtue of such embedded epistemic norms. Yet, it does entail that the fallible-inquiry requirement for proper participation in the democratic public square is itself justified, given the connection between holding beliefs and the tacit commitment to being responsive to reasons in a deliberative forum.

I should pause here to emphasize what makes my view distinct from the defense of religious participation in politics advanced by Christopher Eberle. Unlike Rawlsian liberals, Eberle seeks to accommodate religious participation in the public square by easing the public justificatory requirements of liberalism. While Rawlsian liberals claim that citizens should show respect to their fellow citizens (as free and equal) by successfully offering public reasons sufficient to justify their coercive policies, Eberle argues that respect for fellow citizens simply requires that citizens *sincerely attempt* to offer convincing secular reasons.[45] Thus, for Eberle, even if one fails to produce this corroborating secular rationale in support of her position, she has met the duties of good citizenship if she *pursues* it.[46] The implication of his view, of course, is that religious reasoning is perfectly acceptable in the public square, as long as the citizen puts forth an earnest effort to provide nonreligious reasons to others by "conscientiously engaging" her compatriots in such a way as to hear objections and, potentially, to change her mind.

On the surface, it might appear that my own view above is quite close to Eberle's in that we are both permissive of religious reasoning, as long as citizens meet minimal justificatory responsibilities to engage in deliberation with other citizens. That being said, there are at least two key differences that are worth mentioning here. First, whereas Eberle permits religious reasoning, he thinks that it is necessary for citizens to pursue some distinctly nonreligious rationale, even if it is not found. Given the suspicions expressed earlier concerning the possibility of neutral public reasons, I want to avoid making this demand. Rather, my model of the public square simply asks citizens to be willing to hold their religious lines of reasoning in a certain manner—i.e., in such a way that is open to the possibility of objective deliberative defeat and hence the exchange of reasons. Second, my view is distinct from Eberle's insofar as it provides a nonquestion-begging answer to the following: why engage in truth-seeking inquiry with others in the first place? It seems to me that Eberle's view relies too much on the happy coincidence that any particular religious view will or can countenance his "ideal of conscientious engagement." For instance, we can imagine a religious citizen asking the following question of Eberle: why should I be interested in respecting others by even attempting to offer *any* rationale for the positions I advocate? Here, like other liberals mentioned above, Eberle seems committed to begging the question about what justifies the requirement of fallible engagement in inquiry; my Peircean view above provides an epistemic argument as to why they should.

Now, of course, someone might find this Peircean argument suspicious and want to object to it by claiming that there are cases where a citizen could believe *p* to be true and yet *legitimately* refuse to hold *p* fallibly and in a manner that positions her to meet the justificatory responsibilities of exchanging reasons with others. For instance, one might say that there are certain beliefs that no reasonable person could possibly call into question. Take, for example, the belief, *S*, "that sexual abuse of young children is morally bad." No one in her right mind, so it seems, would say that sexual abuse of young children is morally unobjectionable. However, when someone asserts *S*, she may very well be confronted with an interlocutor who calls S into question by objecting to the assumed definition of sexual abuse implicit in the expression of S. It might be asked, for example, if any physical contact below the shoulders counts as sexual abuse. Now, the proponent of S is put in a situation where she needs to consider what her definition of sexual abuse ought to be. And it is precisely at this point that she needs to be prepared to offer reasons in support of her favored definition—and hence her belief S, as she interprets it—when objections are leveled. And in order to consider reasons when faced with an objection, she needs to be willing to recognize that her definition of sexual abuse might be wrong. Note, of course, that the same could be said of any belief that we might otherwise think to be beyond the scope of reasonable objection. Once we are challenged to flesh out the details of what we mean by this or that belief, there emerges room for reasonable objections and hence the need to answer them through the exchange of reasons.

Another sort of objection to the Peircean argument for the fallible-inquiry requirement might run as follows: there are certain social contexts wherein one might take *p* to be true and yet not have a duty to hold *p* in such a manner that it is open to deliberative defeat and hence the free exchange of reasons precisely because doing so would make her especially vulnerable to either ridicule, manipulation, or some other form of mistreatment. Thus, in such a context, the interest in avoiding ridicule or mistreatment would overrule the responsibilities of holding *p* fallibly and exchanging reasons in light of objections. For example, consider someone who believes G, "that the state should legalize same-sex marriage." We can imagine a situation wherein if she voices her actual reasons for holding G, she might face extreme opposition in the form of chastisement and dismissal due to the unpopularity of some of her views concerning homosexuality. In this case, the fear of alienation or harsh treatment by her interlocutors might motivate her to conceal her actual reasons for believing G and, hence, not to offer them for critique or objection. But, clearly, this sort of case represents a situation wherein one's interlocutors are acting in bad faith as far as inquiry is concerned, for their aim may be nothing more than to poke fun at or to twist words of or simply to hurt persons with whom they disagree. And this case is not a properly deliberative scenario. Consequently, one's civic obligations under these conditions may change. There may be some need for what David Estlund calls "countervailing deviation" from ideal deliberation in order to achieve a situation wherein constructive deliberation can occur.[47] For instance, there may be a need for some from of activism.[48]

But my Peircean argument above simply demonstrates that believers are tacitly committed to participating in actual inquiry when and where it is available. In other words, my view is a normative view that applies to citizens within the scope of properly deliberative circumstances.

VIII

In many ways, the discussion in this essay has been leading back to the fundamental question I asked at the outset: *how and to what extent* should religious reasoning figure into our model of the democratic public square? My view is essentially a conditional integrationism. If a religious citizen is able and willing to hold her religious belief with respect to M in such a way that meets the fallible-inquiry requirement outlined above, then I can see no reason why we should ask that citizen to bracket her religion upon entering the public square. A religious citizen who meets this requirement with respect to the beliefs she holds concerning M does not violate the terms of good democratic citizenship when she employs her religious reasoning in public deliberation concerning M, at least until the point of deliberative defeat, if and when that occurs. Likewise, a citizen who meets the fallible-inquiry requirement with respect to the religious lines of reasoning she holds concerning M does not violate the duties of democratic citizenship when she votes on the basis of that undefeated religious line of reasoning with respect to M. If a religious citizen is not able or willing to meet this fallible-inquiry requirement with respect to her religious beliefs held concerning M, then she violates the terms of democratic citizenship when she introduces her religious beliefs in the public deliberation of M. Whether or not this same religious citizen (who refuses to meet the fallible-inquiry requirement) can vote on the basis of her religious beliefs with respect to M is indeed a trickier question. If her religious belief has met objective deliberative defeat, although not subjective deliberative defeat (precisely because she refuses to acknowledge objective defeat), I think we would want to say that she acts as a bad citizen when she votes in accordance with an objectively defeated line of reasoning. Of course, in her eyes, she is not doing anything wrong precisely because her position, so she thinks, has not been defeated. As such, the practical problem remains: how do we convince this citizen to meet her obligations as a democratic citizen? In cases where both the fallible-inquiry requirement has not been met and where defeat of the same belief has not occurred, the issue gets a bit cloudier. My inclination is to suppose that she violates the same duties of citizenship when she votes according to a noninquiry-ready yet undefeated religious belief. But that judgment may be too quick. For although this citizen holds her religious belief with respect to M in a nonfallibilistic manner, her belief might nevertheless be correct. If so, it seems that we have a case of true but unjustified (and unjustifiable, at least as far as the religious citizen in question is concerned) belief. Should we commit to saying that a citizen who holds a true belief, though in the wrong way, stands in violation of the duties of good democratic citizenship when she votes on the basis of that true belief? Here, it is just not clear to me what to say.

In any case, I should note the potential danger involved with my conditional integrationist view as presented above. An objection might run something like this: does meeting the fallible-inquiry requirement of the public square require religious citizens to reconstruct their religion *prior* to entering the public square? The fear represented by this sort of question is that the manner in which someone holds a particular belief (i.e., either in a nonfallible or fallible manner) bears upon the content of the belief held. So one might object: to ask a religious citizen to hold her belief with respect to M such that the fallible-inquiry requirement is satisfied is to ask her to reconstruct the content of the religious belief actually held with respect to M. If this objection is correct, then to claim that the religious beliefs *actually held* by citizens are being accommodated within my model of the public square is at best misleading. For, so the objection might run, it is not the actually held religious beliefs that are being allowed into public discourse but sufficiently reconstructed religious beliefs.

If this objection above is correct, then my model of the public square will not have room enough to accommodate those religious citizens it was designed to include. For it might be the case that a number of religious citizens find that they do not and cannot hold any of their religious beliefs in a fallibilistic manner (such that the fallible-inquiry requirement could be met) without compromising the beliefs actually held. If this is the case, it will indeed be difficult to find room for religion in the public square on my model. Of course, it must be added that the same sorts of exclusions obtain with respect to secularist citizens as well. If secularists are unable to hold their views and convictions in a fallibilistic manner in such a way as to meet the fallible-inquiry requirement, then they will be likewise excluded from my model of the public square. What this means then, in the end (if this objection is correct), is that my model of the public square will be able to accommodate perhaps only a small circle of deliberators who find that they can meet the fallible-inquiry requirement without having to reconstruct (and thus compromise) the views and convictions that they really hold concerning M. And this narrowness may be a problem in its own right.

But I think this sort of objection to my model of the public square jumps the gun. It may be true that any number of the beliefs held by a religious citizen are held in a nonfallibilistic manner such that meeting the fallible-inquiry requirement with respect to those beliefs would require the reconstruction of those beliefs prior to entering the public square (which would mean that *that* citizen's religion has no room in the public square). But perhaps this is not as frequent as some might suppose. Perhaps it would behoove us to slow down and work on a case-by-case basis when making these sorts of determinations. It might be true, for instance, that many of a religious citizen's religious beliefs as they pertain to relevant political matters are held in a properly fallible manner such that meeting the fallible-inquiry requirement would not require reconstruction of her religious beliefs. Perhaps with respect to any particular M, a religious citizen finds herself fully committed to some R but is still in principle open to the idea that R might be wrong concerning M. We should not simply assume that this religious citizen is unwilling to exchange reasons about the views that she holds. How would we find this out? I suggest that we start by asking her. For instance, it may appear to us that a religious citizen holds her belief that abortion is wrong in a nonfallibilistic manner when she says she holds that belief on the basis of a Bible passage such as Psalm 139:13-16 or Jeremiah 1:5, which she considers to be God's infallible Word on the matter. But is it really the case that the religious citizen in question holds her belief concerning *abortion policy* in a nonfallibilistic manner? Might we not simply ask her the following: Is there any conceivable way that you might have misinterpreted these scriptural passages on this matter? Would you be open to the possibility of what Stout calls immanent criticism? It may very well turn out that this religious citizen thinks that, in fact, she has the correct interpretation of God's Word, but she might still be open to the idea that she is wrong. If this is the case, she holds her relevant religious belief, *at least with respect to the issue at hand*, in a manner that meets the fallible-inquiry requirement. As such, no reconstruction of her religious conviction is required *prior* to entering the public square and the above objection is quelled.

Now, some might want to push me a bit further by claiming that religious believers commonly hold to certain *core* religious claims about which they either are or should be unwilling or unable to admit defeat.[49]

Could a typical Christian, for instance, hold the claim that "all men and women are created in the image of God" fallibly? Could she meet the fallibility requirement with respect to claims about the lordship of Jesus Christ or other such claims? Of course, the concern raised by these sorts of questions is whether my model of the public square is, at the end of the day, simply too restrictive in what it requires for responsible democratic citizenship. It may seem that my fallible-inquiry requirement is asking religious citizens to be wishy-washy, unconvicted, or unfaithful, and hence to choose democracy over one's religion.

But I think the concern here is, again, off base. The fallible-inquiry requirement does not necessarily require religious believers to hold core religious claims fallibly or to call into question what they take to be their religious source(s) of normative authority. For instance, a religious citizen might properly stand firm and say that she takes Scripture to be absolutely infallible when it states that persons are created in the image of God. However, when a citizen brings that claim into the public square— i.e., when that claim is used in the justification of policy with respect, say, to civil rights or slavery or whatever—she is now, of course, interpreting, contextualizing, and applying that core religious claim to M. The fallible-inquiry requirement can be met in this case if she simply considers the move from the religious conception (i.e., core religious claims and the source of normative authority) itself to the particular political entailment— that intermediate space of reasoning, so to speak—and holds *that* fallibly and in a manner attuned to the justificatory responsibilities of exchanging reasons.[50] Even if it turns out that she is unwilling or unable to entertain the possibility that she could be wrong about a central, core religious claim like, say, "Jesus is Lord," that claim *alone*—that is, minus interpretation, contextualization, and application—does not generally entail a particular view concerning this or that public policy.

But what if there were some situation where a citizen's core religious belief—say, "Jesus is Lord"—somehow *itself* lands on the table of democratic discussion concerning M? What happens if the religious believer absolutely refused to acknowledge the possibility that such a belief could be defeated in an argument? What should we say about that? Indeed, this is a difficult case. As implied above, I think that a religious believer could probably find some room in which to remain a fallibilist. But if not, what then? In such a case, it looks like we may have—in that particular case—a situation where this citizen has to make a choice between being a good religious believer (as she sees it) or being a good democratic citizen with respect to M. The choice, in this *particular* case, is either religion *or* democracy. And with respect to this particular case, the citizen might very well go either way to say, "So much the worse for democracy!" or "So much the worse for religion!" But, to be sure, I do not think things need to come to this. In most cases—probably every actual case—one can be a fallibilist about the political implications of one's religious beliefs without even raising the question about whether we could be fallibilists concerning what might be an otherwise unassailable core religious belief.

In any case, it may be true that my model of the public square will still leave out some, perhaps many, religious persons at particular moments with respect to particular issues. However lamentable this may be, this is not necessarily an indictment of my model of the public square. My model is not necessarily aimed at including *all* religious persons, *no matter what*. Rather, I am merely trying to imagine a model of the democratic public square which does not exclude those religious persons who may already find (or in the future come to find) themselves minimally predisposed to deliberative democratic participation. That is, my model of the public square, unlike the *ex ante* separatist proposals, seeks to bring into the fold those democratically predisposed religious persons who wish to be included. It is my suspicion at the end of the day that there are more democratically predisposed religious citizens than some would have us believe. And my model of the public square is merely geared toward erring on the side that attempts to include those religious citizens who are.

Of course, the case-by-case approach advocated by my model of the public square requires that all citizens be willing to practice the deliberative virtue of charity within the public square—i.e., that we be willing to hear the religious citizen out and consider the possibility that, with respect to any given M, this religious citizen is holding her relevant line of reasoning in compliance with the fallible-inquiry requirement. How do we find out if this is actually the case? We ask her questions and try to engage her in inquiry. And, by doing so, we extend to her the first sign of respect. Then we see what happens from there.[51]

Notes

Introduction

1   See Jean Bethke Elshtain, "Religion and American Democracy," in *Public Morality, Civic Virtue, and the Problem of Modern Liberalism*, ed. William Boxx and Gary Quinlivan (Grand Rapids: Eerdmans, 2000), 14. See also the *U.S. Religious Landscape Survey* conducted by the Pew Forum on Religion & Public Life, which reports that 92 percent of Americans hold belief in God or some higher power, http://religions.pewforum.org/pdf/report2religious-landscape-study-key-findings.pdf (accessed July 17, 2008).

2   Sections I and II of this introduction draw heavily from portions of chapter 1 of my *Religion and Democratic Citizenship: Inquiry and Conviction in the American Public Square* (Lanham, Md.: Lexington, 2008), 1–8. Reprinted with permission of Lexington Books.

3   September 2000 Harris Poll. Data provided by the Roper Center for Public Opinion Research, University of Connecticut, http://www.roperweb.ropercenter.uconn.edu/cgi-bin/hsrun.exe/Roperweb/iPoll (accessed September 6, 2004).

4   September 2003 Time/CNN/Harris Interactive Poll. Data provided by the Roper Center for Public Opinion Research, University of Connecticut, http://www.roperweb.ropercenter.uconn.edu/cgi-bin/hsrun.exe/Roperweb/iPoll (accessed September 6, 2004).

5   June 2003 Religion and Public Life Survey by Pew Research, Pew Forum on Religion and Public Life. Data provided by the Roper Center for

Public Opinion Research, University of Connecticut, http://www.roperweb.
ropercenter.uconn.edu/cgi-bin/hsrun.exe/Roperweb/iPoll (accessed September 6, 2004).

6   November 2003 Gallup Poll. Data provided by the Roper Center for Public Opinion Research, University of Connecticut, http://www.roperweb.
ropercenter.uconn.edu/cgi-bin/hsrun.exe/Roperweb/iPoll (accessed September 6, 2004).

7   The U.S. Supreme Court effectively upheld this decision when they refused to hear the case in October of 2005.

8   By "public philosophy" I mean roughly what Michael Sandel means by the term. He defines it as "the political theory implicit in our practice, the assumptions about citizenship and freedom that inform our public life" in his *Democracy's Discontent* (Cambridge, Mass.: Harvard University Press, 1996), 4. Commenting upon this definition, Sandel claims that "a public philosophy is an elusive thing, for it is constantly before our eyes. It forms the often unreflective background to our political discourse and pursuits. In ordinary times, the public philosophy can easily escape the notice of those who live by it. But anxious times compel a certain clarity. They force first principles to the surface and offer an occasion for critical reflection" (Sandel, *Democracy's Discontent*, 4). Sandel is right about this point. My contention here is that we face a tension in our public philosophy that prompts our need to revisit basic questions concerning the role of religion in public life.

9   There are, of course, several different senses of the term *liberal*. Here, I mean to be referring to the sense of liberal that is associated with the dominant version of liberalism currently afloat in contemporary political theory, which may be characterized as "right-over-the-good" liberalism. See Sandel, "A Response to Rawls' Political Liberalism," appendix to the 2nd ed., *Liberalism and the Limits of Justice* (New York: Cambridge University Press, 1998).

10   John Stuart Mill, *On Liberty*, in *Classics of Modern Political Theory*, ed. Steven Cahn (New York: Oxford University Press, 1997), 933.

11   Mill, *On Liberty*, 937.

12   Jeremy Waldron, *Liberal Rights* (New York: Cambridge University Press, 1993), 37.

13   Pointing out the tension between liberal and democratic elements in American culture is a common way of discussing contemporary public philosophy. See, for instance, Benjamin Barber, *A Passion for Democracy* (Princeton: Princeton University Press, 1999); Robert Dahl, *On Democracy* (New Haven: Yale University Press, 1998); John Dryzek, *Democracy in Capitalist Times* (New York: Oxford University Press, 1996); C. B. MacPherson, *The Real World of Democracy* (New York: Oxford University Press, 1965); Jane Mansbridge, *Beyond Adversary Democracy* (Chicago: University of Chicago Press, 1983). While I set up the issue a bit differently, in part I take cues from Chantal Mouffe, who identifies the tension present in liberal democracies as a tension between universalist tendencies of our liberal aims and particularist tendencies of our democratic aspirations. See Mouffe, *The Democratic Paradox* (New York: Verso, 2000).

Chapter 1

1   Leading contemporary examples of philosophical liberalism are: John Rawls, *A Theory of Justice* (Cambridge, Mass.: Harvard University Press,

1971); Ronald Dworkin, "Liberalism," in *Public and Private Morality*, ed. Stuart Hampshire (New York: Cambridge University Press, 1978); Bruce Ackerman, *Social Justice in the Liberal State* (New Haven: Yale University Press, 1980); T. M. Scanlon, "Contractualism and Utilitarianism," in *Utilitarianism and Beyond*, ed. Amartya Sen and Bernard Williams (New York: Cambridge University Press, 1982).

2 See T. M. Scanlon, "Preference and Urgency," *Journal of Philosophy* 72 (1975): 655–69—an essay to which I am much indebted.

3 I am thinking of utilitarianism in a modern version, associated with Sidgwick. In Bentham and Mill, the motives that lead to compliance with the principle of utility are various and not related to its truth.

4 Rawls, *Theory of Justice*, 176.

5 This observation comes from Scanlon, "Contractualism and Utilitarianism," 126. Another interpretation has been suggested to me, however, by Warren Quinn. Perhaps the strains of commitment are simply strains it is unfair to impose on people, and this is shown by our unwillingness, in the Original Position, to choose principles that carry the risk of subjecting us to those strains. This would restore Rawls to the common standpoint category.

6 John Rawls, "Justice as Fairness: Political not Metaphysical," *Philosophy & Public Affairs* 14, no. 3 (1985): 246.

7 Rawls himself treats these issues from a somewhat different point of view in the article just mentioned and in his H. L. A. Hart Lecture, "The Idea of an Overlapping Consensus," *Oxford Journal of Legal Studies* 7, no. 1 (1987): 1–25. I shall not try to compare our approaches here, except to say that mine seems to depend less on actual consensus and seeks an independent moral argument that can be offered to those holding widely divergent values.

8 This would be implied, on one reading, by the second formulation of Kant's categorical imperative—that one should treat humanity never merely as a means, but always also as an end. If you force someone to serve an end that he cannot share, you are treating him as a mere means—even if the end is his own good, as you see it (*Foundations of the Metaphysics of Morals*, Prussian Academy edition, 429–30). See Onora O'Neill, "Between Consenting Adults," *Philosophy & Public Affairs* 14, no. 3 (1985): 261–63; and Christine M. Korsgaard, "The Right to Lie: Kant on Dealing with Evil," *Philosophy & Public Affairs* 15, no. 4 (1986): 330–34.

9 "He would want," in these examples, is not a conditional prediction of what his desires would be in those circumstances; rather, it refers to what he now wants to happen should those counterfactual circumstances obtain—as in the statement "I would want to be restrained if I tried to drink lye during a psychotic episode." The "want" goes outside rather than inside the conditional.

10 See Scanlon, "Preference and Urgency."

11 Gerald Dworkin, "Non-neutral Principles," *Journal of Philosophy* 71 (1974): 492.

12 Dworkin, "Non-neutral Principles," 505.

13 Dworkin, "Non-neutral Principles," 503–4.

14 Rawls, *Theory of Justice*, 214–15.

15 Rawls, *Theory of Justice*, 217–18.

16 Rawls, "Justice as Fairness," 231.

17 Conscientious objection is another matter: its legal acceptance can probably be explained by the liberal principle I am defending.

18   This resembles the conception of "free public reason" that Rawls introduces in section II of "The Idea of an Overlapping Consensus."

19   It may be that further development of this idea would also exclude disagreements based on exceptionally subtle and difficult forms of reasoning, whose results are not testable in any other way. But I shall not try to pursue the suggestion here.

20   See T. Nagel, *The View from Nowhere* (New York: Oxford University Press, 1986), 188, 206–7.

Chapter 2

Emeritus Professor of Philosophy, Harvard University. This essay is a revision of a lecture given at The University of Chicago Law School in November 1993. I should like to thank Joshua Cohen, Erin Kelly, Percy Lehning, Michael Perry, Margaret Rawls, and T. M. Scanlon for their great help and advice in writing this paper. Throughout they have given me numerous suggestions, which I have gladly accepted. Above all, to Burton Dreben I am especially indebted: as so often before, he has been generous beyond measure in his efforts; in every section he has helped me reorganize and reshape the text, giving it a clarity and simplicity it would not otherwise have had. Without their constant advice and encouragement, and that of others mentioned below, I never could have completed the revisions of my original lecture.

1   See John Rawls, *Political Liberalism*, lecture VI, § 8.5 (New York: Columbia University Press, paperback ed., 1996). References to *Political Liberalism* are given by lecture and section; page numbers are also provided unless the reference refers to an entire lecture, section, or subsection. Note that the 1996 paperback edition of *Political Liberalism* contains a new second introduction which, among other things, tries to make clearer certain aspects of political liberalism. Section 5 of this introduction, at l–lvii, discusses the idea of public reason and sketches several changes I now make in affirming this idea. These are all followed and elaborated in what is presented here and are important to a complete understanding of the argument. Note also that the pagination of the paperback edition is the same as the original.

2   I shall use the term *doctrine* for comprehensive views of all kinds and the term *conception* for a political conception and its component parts, such as the conception of the person as citizen. The term *idea* is used as a general term and may refer to either as the context determines.

3   Of course, every society also contains numerous unreasonable doctrines. Yet in this essay I am concerned with an ideal normative conception of democratic government, that is, with the conduct of its reasonable citizens and the principles they follow, assuming them to be dominant and controlling. How far unreasonable doctrines are active and tolerated is to be determined by the principles of justice and the kinds of actions they permit. See Rawls, *Political Liberalism*, § 7.2.

4   See Rawls, *Political Liberalism*, lecture VI, § 6.2.

5   See Rawls, *Political Liberalism*, lecture VI, § 1.2.

6   See Rawls, *Political Liberalism*, lecture VI, text accompanying notes 12–15.

7   These questions are described in Rawls, *Political Liberalism*, lecture VI, § 5, pp. 227–30. Constitutional essentials concern questions about what political rights and liberties, say, may reasonably be included in a written constitution, when assuming the constitution may be interpreted by a supreme

court, or some similar body. Matters of basic justice relate to the basic structure of society and so would concern questions of basic economic and social justice and other things not covered by a constitution.

8   There is no settled meaning of this term. The one I use is not, I think, peculiar.

9   Here we face the question of where to draw the line between candidates and those who manage their campaigns and other politically engaged citizens generally. We settle this matter by making candidates and those who run their campaigns responsible for what is said and done on the candidates' behalf.

10   Often writers on this topic use terms that do not distinguish the parts of public discussion, for example, such terms as *the public square*, *the public forum*, and the like. I follow Kent Greenawalt in thinking a finer division is necessary. See Kent Greenawalt, *Religious Convictions and Political Choice* (New York: Oxford University Press, 1988), 226–27 (describing, for example, the differences between a religious leader's preaching or promoting a pro-life organization and leading a major political movement or running for political office).

11   See Rawls, *Political Liberalism*, lecture VI, § 4.

12   Rawls, *Political Liberalism*, lecture I, § 2.3, p. 14.

13   The background culture includes, then, the culture of churches and associations of all kinds, and institutions of learning at all levels, especially universities and professional schools, scientific and other societies. In addition, the nonpublic political culture mediates between the public political culture and the background culture. This comprises media— properly so named—of all kinds: newspapers, reviews and magazines, TV and radio, and much else. Compare these divisions with Habermas' account of the public sphere. See Rawls, *Political Liberalism*, lecture IX, § 1.3, p. 382 n. 13.

14   See Rawls, *Political Liberalism*, lecture VI, § 3, pp. 220–22.

15   See David Hollenbach, SJ, "Civil Society: Beyond the Public-Private Dichotomy," *The Responsive Community* 15 (1994/95): 5. For example, he says:

> Conversation and argument about the common good will not occur initially in the legislature or in the political sphere (narrowly conceived as the domain in which interests and power are adjudicated). Rather it will develop freely in those components of civil society that are the primary bearers of cultural meaning and value—universities, religious communities, the world of the arts, and serious journalism. It can occur wherever thoughtful men and women bring their beliefs on the meaning of the good life into intelligent and critical encounter with understandings of this good held by other peoples with other traditions. In short, it occurs wherever education about and serious inquiry into the meaning of the good life takes place. (Hollenbach, *Civil Society*, 22)

16   There is some resemblance between this criterion and Kant's principle of the original contract. See Immanuel Kant, *The Metaphysics of Morals: Metaphysical First Principles of the Doctrine of Right*, trans. and ed. Mary Gregor (New York: Cambridge University Press, 1996), §§ 47–49, pp. 92–95 (AK 6:315–18); Immanuel Kant, *On the Common Saying: "This May Be True in Theory, But It Does Not Apply in Practice,"* Part II, in *Kant: Political Writings*, ed. Hans Reiss, trans. H. G. Nisbet (New York: Cambridge University Press, 2nd ed., 1991), 73–87 (AK 8:289–306).

17   See also Rawls, *Political Liberalism*, lecture VI, § 4.2.
18   Rawls, *Political Liberalism*, lecture I, § 2.1, p. 12. For concerns about exiting only by death, see Rawls, *Political Liberalism*, lecture IV, § 1.2, p. 136 n. 4.
19   The idea of reciprocity has an important place in Amy Gutmann and Dennis Thompson, *Democracy and Disagreement* chaps. 1–2 and passim (Cambridge, Mass.: Belknap Press of Harvard University Press, 1996). However, the meaning and setting of our views are not the same. Public reason in political liberalism is purely political, although political values are intrinsically moral, whereas Gutmann and Thompson's account is more general and seems to work from a comprehensive doctrine.
20   For a useful historical survey, see David Held, *Models of Democracy*, 2nd ed. (Stanford, Calif.: Stanford University Press, 1997). Held's numerous models cover the period from the ancient polis to the present time, and he concludes by asking what democracy should mean today. In between he considers the several forms of classical republicanism and classical liberalism, as well as Schumpeter's conception of competitive elite democracy. Some figures discussed include Plato and Aristotle; Marsilius of Padua and Machiavelli; Hobbes and Madison; Bentham, James Mill, and J. S. Mill; Marx with socialism and communism. These are paired with schematized models of the characteristic institutions and their roles.
21   Deliberative democracy limits the reasons citizens may give in supporting their political opinions to reasons consistent with their seeing other citizens as equals. See Joshua Cohen, "Deliberation and Democratic Legitimacy," in *The Good Polity: Normative Analysis of the State*, ed. Alan Hamlin and Philip Pettit (Oxford: Blackwell, 1989), 17, 21, 24; "Review Symposium on Democracy and Its Critics," *Journal of Politics* 53 (1991): 215, 223–24 (comments of Joshua Cohen); Joshua Cohen, "Democracy and Liberty," 13–17 (manuscript on file with *University of Chicago Law Review*), in *Deliberative Democracy*, ed. Jon Elster (New York: Cambridge University Press, 1998).
22   Ronald Dworkin, "The Curse of American Politics," *New York Review of Books* 19 (October 17, 1996) (describing why "money is the biggest threat to the democratic process"). Dworkin also argues forcefully against the grave error of the Supreme Court in *Buckley v. Valeo*, 424 US 1 (1976), Dworkin, 21–24. See also Rawls, *Political Liberalism*, lecture VIII, § 12, pp. 359–63. (*Buckley* is "dismaying" and raises the risk of "repeating the mistake of the Lochner era.").
23   Paul Krugman, "Demographics and Destiny," *New York Times Book Review* 12 (October 20, 1996), reviewing and describing proposals in Peter G. Peterson, *Will America Grow Up Before It Grows Old? How the Coming Social Security Crisis Threatens You, Your Family, and Your Country* (New York: Random House, 1996), and Charles R. Morris, *The AARP: America's Most Powerful Lobby and the Clash of Generations* (New York: Times Books, 1996).
24   Rawls, *Political Liberalism*, lecture I, § 4, pp. 22–28.
25   Here I follow the definition in Rawls, *Political Liberalism*, lecture I, § 1.2, p. 6; lecture IV, § 5.3, pp. 156–57.
26   Some may think the fact of reasonable pluralism means the only forms of fair adjudication between comprehensive doctrines must be only procedural and not substantive. This view is forcefully argued by Stuart Hampshire in *Innocence and Experience* (Cambridge, Mass.: Harvard University Press, 1989). In the text above, however, I assume the several forms of liberalism are each substantive conceptions. For a thorough treatment of these

issues, see the discussion in Joshua Cohen, "Pluralism and Proceduralism," *Chicago-Kent Law Review* 69 (1994): 589.

27   I do think that justice as fairness has a certain special place in the family of political conceptions, as I suggest in Rawls, *Political Liberalism*, lecture IV, § 7.4. But this opinion of mine is not basic to the ideas of political liberalism and public reason.

28   See Jürgen Habermas, *Between Facts and Norms: Contributions to a Discourse Theory of Law and Democracy*, trans. William Rehg (Cambridge, Mass.: MIT Press, 1996), 107–9 (defining the discourse principle). Seyla Benhabib in her discussion of models of public space in *Situating the Self: Gender, Community and Postmodernism in Contemporary Ethics* (New York: Routledge, 1992), says that: "The discourse model is the only one which is compatible both with the general social trends of our societies and with the emancipatory aspirations of new social movements like the women's movement" (113). She has previously considered Arendt's agonistic conception, as Benhabib calls it, and that of political liberalism. But I find it hard to distinguish her view from that of a form of political liberalism and public reason, since it turns out that she means by the public sphere what Habermas does, namely what *Political Liberalism* calls the background culture of civil society in which the ideal of public reason does not apply. Hence political liberalism is not limiting in the way she thinks. Also, Benhabib does not try to show, so far as I can see, that certain principles of right and justice belonging to the content of public reason could not be interpreted to deal with the problems raised by the women's movement. I doubt that this can be done. The same holds for Benhabib's earlier remarks in Seyla Benhabib, "Liberal Dialogue Versus a Critical Theory of Discursive Legitimation," in *Liberalism and the Moral Life*, ed. Nancy L. Rosenblum (Cambridge, Mass: Harvard University Press, 1989), 143, 154–56, in which the problems of the women's movement were discussed in a similar way.

29   Deriving from Aristotle and St. Thomas, the idea of the common good is essential to much of Catholic moral and political thought. See, for example, John Finnis, *Natural Law and Natural Rights* (Oxford: Clarendon, 1980), 153–56, 160; Jacques Maritain, *Man and the State* (Chicago: University of Chicago Press, 1951), 108–14. (Finnis is especially clear, while Aquinas is occasionally ambiguous.)

30   Thus, Jeremy Waldron's criticism of political liberalism as not allowing new and changing conceptions of political justice is incorrect. See Jeremy Waldron, "Religious Contributions in Public Deliberation," *San Diego Law Review* 30 (1993): 817, 837–38. See the reply to Waldron's criticisms in Lawrence B. Solum, "Novel Public Reasons," *Loyola of Los Angeles Law Review* 29 (1996): 1459, 1460 ("General acceptance of a liberal ideal of public reason would permit the robust evolution of political discourse").

31   See note 2 for my definition of *doctrine*.

32   See Rawls, *Political Liberalism*, lecture VI, § 4.

33   Here see Rawls, *Political Liberalism*, lecture IX, § 1.1, pp. 374–75.

34   This thought I owe to Peter de Marneffe.

35   Note here that different political conceptions of justice will represent different interpretations of the constitutional essentials and matters of basic justice. There are also different interpretations of the same conception, since its concepts and values may be taken in different ways. There is not, then, a sharp line between where a political conception ends and its interpretation begins, nor need there be. All the same, a conception greatly

limits its possible interpretations, otherwise discussion and argument could not proceed. For example, a constitution declaring the freedom of religion, including the freedom to affirm no religion, along with the separation of church and state, may appear to leave open the question whether church schools may receive public funds, and if so, in what way. The difference here might be seen as how to interpret the same political conception, one interpretation allowing public funds, the other not; or alternatively, as the difference between two political conceptions. In the absence of particulars, it does not matter which we call it. The important point is that since the content of public reason is a family of political conceptions, that content admits the interpretations we may need. It is not as if we were stuck with a fixed conception, much less with one interpretation of it. This is a comment on Kent Greenawalt, *Private Consciences and Public Reasons* (New York: Oxford University Press, 1995), 113–20, where *Political Liberalism* is said to have difficulty dealing with the problem of determining the interpretation of political conceptions.

36   John Stuart Mill, *On Liberty*, in *Collected Works of John Stuart Mill*, ed. John M. Robson (Toronto: University of Toronto Press, 1977), 18:260–75.

37   See Rawls, *Political Liberalism*, lecture VI, § 4.1 on the proviso and the example of citing the gospel story. For a detailed consideration of the wide view of public political culture, see generally § 4.

38   Of course, I don't here attempt to decide the question, since we are concerned only with the kinds of reasons and considerations that public reasoning involves.

39   See Rawls, *Political Liberalism*, lecture VI, § 2.2.

40   See Robert Audi, "The Place of Religious Argument in a Free and Democratic Society," *San Diego Law Review* 30 (1993): 677. Here Audi defines a secular reason as follows: "A secular reason is roughly one whose normative force does not evidentially depend on the existence of God or on theological considerations, or on the pronouncements of a person or institution qua religious authority," Audi, 692. This definition is ambiguous between secular reasons in the sense of a nonreligious comprehensive doctrine and in the sense of a purely political conception within the content of public reason. Depending on which is meant, Audi's view that secular reasons must also be given along with religious reasons might have a role similar to what I call *the proviso* in Rawls, *Political Liberalism*, lecture VI, § 4.1.

41   See the discussion by Michael Perry of John Finnis' argument, which denies that such relations are compatible with human good. *Religion in Politics: Constitutional and Moral Perspectives* (New York: Oxford University Press, 1997), 85–86.

42   Here I follow T. M. Scanlon's view in "The Difficulty of Tolerance," in *Toleration: An Elusive Virtue*, ed. David Heyd (Princeton: Princeton University Press, 1996), 226. While the whole is instructive, § 3, pp. 230–33 is especially relevant here.

43   See Rawls, *Political Liberalism*, lecture IV, § 3.4, p. 148.

44   See Kent Greenawalt's example of the society of Diverse Fervent Believers in Greenawalt, *Private Consciences and Public Reasons*, 16–18, 21–22.

45   See Rawls, *Political Liberalism*, lecture V, § 6, pp. 195–200.

46   An example of how a religion may do this is the following. Abdullahi Ahmed An-Naʻim, in his book *Toward an Islamic Reformation: Civil Liberties, Human Rights, and International Law* (Syracuse: Syracuse University Press, 1990), 52–57, introduces the idea of reconsidering the traditional interpre-

tation of Shari'ah, which for Muslims is divine law. For his interpretation to be accepted by Muslims, it must be presented as the correct and superior interpretation of Shari'ah. The basic idea of An-Na'im's interpretation, following the late Sudanese author Ustadh Mahmoud Mohamed Taha, is that the traditional understanding of Shari'ah has been based on the teachings of the later Medina period of Muhammad, whereas the teachings of the earlier Mecca period of Muhammad are the eternal and fundamental message of Islam. An-Na'im claims that the superior Mecca teachings and principles were rejected in favor of the more realistic and practical (in a seventh-century historical context) Medina teachings because society was not yet ready for their implementation. Now that historical conditions have changed, An-Na'im believes that Muslims should follow the earlier Mecca period in interpreting Shari'ah. So interpreted, he says that Shari'ah supports constitutional democracy (An-Na'im, 69–100).

In particular, the earlier Mecca interpretation of Shari'ah supports equality of men and women, and complete freedom of choice in matters of faith and religion, both of which are in accordance with the constitutional principle of equality before the law. An-Na'im writes:

> The Qur'an does not mention constitutionalism, but human rational thinking and experience have shown that constitutionalism is necessary for realizing the just and good society prescribed by the Qur'an.

> An Islamic justification and support for constitutionalism is important and relevant for Muslims. Non-Muslims may have their own secular or other justifications. As long as all are agreed on the principle and specific rules of constitutionalism, including complete equality and nondiscrimination on grounds of gender or religion, each may have his or her own reasons for coming to that agreement. (An-Na'im, 100)

(This is a perfect example of overlapping consensus.) I thank Akeel Bilgrami for informing me of An-Na'im's work. I also owe thanks to Roy Mottahedeh for valuable discussion.

47   See Rawls, *Political Liberalism*, lecture VI, § 4.3.
48   Rawls, *Political Liberalism*, lecture I, § 2.3, pp. 13–14 (contrasting public political culture with background culture).
49   I am indebted here to valuable discussion with Dennis Thompson.
50   Greenawalt discusses Franklin Gamwell and Michael Perry, who do evidently impose such constraints on how religion is to be presented. See Greenawalt, *Private Consciences and Public Reasons*, 85–95.
51   Again, as always, in distinction from the background culture, where I emphasize there are no restrictions.
52   Political liberalism is sometimes criticized for not itself developing accounts of these social roots of democracy and setting out the formation of its religious and other supports. Yet political liberalism does recognize these social roots and stresses their importance. Obviously the political conceptions of toleration and freedom of religion would be impossible in a society in which religious freedom was not honored and cherished. Thus, political liberalism agrees with David Hollenbach, SJ, when he writes:

> Not the least important of [the transformations brought about by Aquinas] was his insistence that the political life of a people is not the highest realization of the good of which they are capable—an

insight that lies at the root of constitutional theories of limited government. And though the Church resisted the liberal discovery of modern freedoms through much of the modern period, liberalism has been transforming Catholicism once again through the last half of our own century. The memory of these events in social and intellectual history as well as the experience of the Catholic Church since the Second Vatican Council leads me to hope that communities holding different visions of the good life can get somewhere if they are willing to risk conversation and argument about these visions.

David Hollenbach, SJ, "Contexts of the Political Role of Religion: Civil Society and Culture," *San Diego Law Review* 30 (1993): 877, 891. While a conception of public reason must recognize the significance of these social roots of constitutional democracy and note how they strengthen its vital institutions, it need not itself undertake a study of these matters. For the need to consider this point I am indebted to Paul Weithman.

53   See Rawls, *Political Liberalism*, lecture VI, § 8.2, pp. 248–49.

54   See Rawls, *Political Liberalism*, lecture VI, § 8.3, pp. 249–51. I do not know whether the abolitionists and King thought of themselves as fulfilling the purpose of the proviso. But whether they did or not, they could have. And had they known and accepted the idea of public reason, they would have. I thank Paul Weithman for this point.

55   Luke 10:29-37. It is easy to see how the gospel story could be used to support the imperfect moral duty of mutual aid, as found, say, in Kant's fourth example in the *Grundlegung*. See Immanuel Kant, *Groundwork for the Metaphysics of Morals*, AK 4:423, in Mary Gregor, trans, *Practical Philosophy* (New York: Cambridge University Press, 1996). To formulate a suitable example in terms of political values only, consider a variant of the difference principle or of some other analogous idea. The principle could be seen as giving a special concern for the poor, as in the Catholic social doctrine. See John Rawls, *A Theory of Justice* § 13 (Cambridge, Mass.: Belknap Press of Harvard University Press, 1971) (defining the difference principle).

56   For the relevance of this form of discourse I am indebted to discussion with Charles Larmore.

57   I will mention another form of discourse that I call witnessing: it typically occurs in an ideal, politically well-ordered, and fully just society in which all votes are the result of citizens' voting in accordance with their most reasonable conception of political justice. Nevertheless, it may happen that some citizens feel they must express their principled dissent from existing institutions, policies, or enacted legislation. I assume that Quakers accept constitutional democracy and abide by its legitimate law, yet at the same time may reasonably express the religious basis of their pacifism. (The parallel case of Catholic opposition to abortion is mentioned in Rawls, *Political Liberalism*, lecture VI, § 6.1.) Yet witnessing differs from civil disobedience in that it does not appeal to principles and values of a (liberal) political conception of justice. While on the whole these citizens endorse reasonable political conceptions of justice supporting a constitutional democratic society, in this case they nevertheless feel they must not only let other citizens know the deep basis of their strong opposition but must also bear witness to their faith by doing so. At the same time, those bearing witness accept the idea of public reason. While they may think the outcome of a vote on which all reasonable citizens have conscientiously followed public reason

to be incorrect or not true, they nevertheless recognize it as legitimate law and accept the obligation not to violate it. In such a society there is strictly speaking no case for civil disobedience and conscientious refusal. The latter requires what I have called a nearly just, but not fully just, society. See Rawls, *Theory of Justice*, § 55.

58   I have thought that J. S. Mill's landmark *The Subjection of Women*, in *Collected Works of John Stuart Mill*, 21:259, made clear that a decent liberal conception of justice (including what I called justice as fairness) implied equal justice for women as well as men. Admittedly, *A Theory of Justice* should have been more explicit about this, but that was a fault of mine and not of political liberalism itself. I have been encouraged to think that a liberal account of equal justice for women is viable by Susan Moller Okin, *Justice, Gender, and the Family* (New York: Basic Books, 1989); Linda C. McClain, "'Atomistic Man' Revisited: Liberalism, Connection, and Feminist Jurisprudence," *Southern California Law Review* 65 (1992): 1171; Martha Nussbaum, *Sex and Social Justice* (New York: Oxford University Press, 1998) (a collection of her essays from 1990 to 1996, including "The Feminist Critique of Liberalism," her Oxford Amnesty Lecture for 1996); and Sharon A. Lloyd, "Situating a Feminist Criticism of John Rawls' *Political Liberalism*," *Loyola Los Angeles Law Review* 28 (1995): 1319. I have gained greatly from their writings.

59   Rawls, *Theory of Justice*, § 70–76 (discussing the stages of moral development and their relevance to justice as fairness).

60   However, no particular form of the family (monogamous, heterosexual, or otherwise) is required by a political conception of justice so long as the family is arranged to fulfill these tasks effectively and doesn't run afoul of other political values. Note that this observation sets the way in which justice as fairness deals with the question of gay and lesbian rights and duties, and how they affect the family. If these rights and duties are consistent with orderly family life and the education of children, they are, *ceteris paribus*, fully admissible.

61   See Okin, *Justice, Gender, and the Family*, 90–93.

62   The difference principle is defined in Rawls, *Theory of Justice*, § 13.

63   I borrow this thought from Joshua Cohen, "Okin on Justice, Gender, and Family," *Canadian Journal of Philosophy* 22 (1992): 263, 278.

64   Michael Sandel supposes the two principles of justice as fairness to hold generally for associations, including families. See Michael J. Sandel, *Liberalism and the Limits of Justice* (New York: Cambridge University Press, 1982), 30–34.

65   Mill, *Subjection of Women*, 283–98.

66   Rawls, *Theory of Justice*, § 16, p. 99.

67   This is Okin's term. See Okin, *Justice, Gender, and the Family*, 6, 14, 170.

68   On this point, see Rawls, *Political Liberalism*, lecture VI, § 3.2, pp. 221–22. Whether it is properly voluntary, and if so, under what conditions, is a disputed question. Briefly, the question involves the distinction between the reasonable and the rational explained thus: an action is voluntary in one sense, but it may not be voluntary in another. It may be voluntary in the sense of rational: doing the rational thing in the circumstances even when these involve unfair conditions; or an action may be voluntary in the sense of reasonable: doing the rational thing when all the surrounding conditions are also fair. Clearly the text interprets "voluntary" in the second sense: affirming one's religion is voluntary when all of the surrounding conditions are reasonable, or fair. In these remarks I have assumed that the subjective

conditions of voluntariness (whatever they may be) are present and have only noted the objective ones. A full discussion would lead us far afield.

69   See Victor R. Fuchs, *Women's Quest for Economic Equality* (Cambridge, Mass.: Harvard University Press, 1988). Chapters 3 and 4 summarize the evidence for saying the main cause is not, as it is often said, employer discrimination, while chapters 7 and 8 propose what is to be done.

70   See Rawls, *Political Liberalism*, lecture VI, § 2.3.

71   See Thomas J. Curry, *The First Freedoms: Church and State in America to the Passage of the First Amendment* (New York: Oxford University Press, 1986), 139–48. The quoted language, which appears in Curry, 140, is from the preamble to the proposed "Bill Establishing a Provision for Teachers of the Christian Religion" (1784). Note that the popular Patrick Henry also provided the most serious opposition to Jefferson's "Bill for Establishing Religious Freedom" (1779), which won out when reintroduced in the Virginia Assembly in 1786. Curry, 146.

72   For a discussion of these virtues, see Rawls, *Political Liberalism*, lecture V, § 5.4, pp. 194–95.

73   See James Madison, "Memorial and Remonstrance," in *The Mind of the Founder*, ed. Marvin Meyers (Indianapolis: Bobbs-Merrill, 1973), 8–16. Paragraph 6 refers to the vigor of early Christianity in opposition to the empire, while paragraphs 7 and 11 refer to the mutually corrupting influence of past establishments on both state and religion. In the correspondence between Madison and William Bradford of Pennsylvania, whom he met at Princeton (College of New Jersey), the freedom and prosperity of Pennsylvania without an establishment is praised and celebrated. See William T. Hutchinson and William M. E. Rachal, eds., *The Papers of James Madison*, vol. 1 (Chicago: University of Chicago Press, 1962). See especially Madison's letters of December 1, 1773 (100–101); January 24, 1774 (104–6); and April 1, 1774 (111–13). A letter of Bradford's to Madison, March 4, 1774, refers to liberty as the genius of Pennsylvania (109). Madison's arguments were similar to those of Tocqueville I mention below. See also Curry, *First Freedoms*, 142–48.

74   It does this by protecting the freedom to change one's faith. Heresy and apostasy are not crimes.

75   What I refer to here is the fact that from the early days of the Emperor Constantine in the fourth century, Christianity punished heresy and tried to stamp out by persecution and religious wars what it regarded as false doctrine (for example, the crusade against the Albigenses led by Innocent III in the thirteenth century). To do this required the coercive powers of the state. Instituted by Pope Gregory IX, the Inquisition was active throughout the Wars of Religion in the sixteenth and seventeenth centuries. While most of the American Colonies had known establishments of some kind (Congregationalist in New England, Episcopalian in the South), the United States, thanks to the plurality of its religious sects and the First Amendment which they endorsed, never did. A persecuting zeal has been the great curse of the Christian religion. It was shared by Luther and Calvin and the Protestant Reformers, and it was not radically changed in the Catholic Church until Vatican II. In the Council's Declaration on Religious Freedom—*Dignitatis Humanae*—the Catholic Church committed itself to the principle of religious freedom as found in a constitutional democratic regime. It declared the ethical doctrine of religious freedom resting on the dignity of the human person; a political doctrine with respect to the limits

of government in religious matters; a theological doctrine of the freedom of the Church in its relations to the political and social world. All persons, whatever their faith, have the right of religious liberty on the same terms. "Declaration on Religious Freedom (*Dignitatis Humanae*): On the Right of the Person and of Communities to Social and Civil Freedom in Matters Religious," in *The Documents of Vatican II*, ed. Walter Abbott, SJ (London: Geoffrey Chapman, 1966), 675, 692–96. As John Courtney Murray, SJ, said: "A long-standing ambiguity had finally been cleared up. The Church does not deal with the secular order in terms of a double standard— freedom for the Church when Catholics are in the minority, privilege for the Church and intolerance for others when Catholics are a majority." John Courtney Murray, SJ, "Religious Freedom," in *Documents of Vatican II*, ed. Abbott, 672–73. See also the instructive discussion by Paul E. Sigmund, "Catholicism and Liberal Democracy," in *Catholicism and Liberalism: Contributions to American Public Philosophy*, ed. R. Bruce Douglas and David Hollenbach, SJ (New York: Cambridge University Press, 1994), esp. 233–39.

76   Alexis de Tocqueville, *Democracy in America*, ed. J. P. Mayer, trans. George Lawrence (New York: Harper Perennial, 1988) 1:294–301. In discussing "The Main Causes That Make Religion Powerful in America," Tocqueville says the Catholic priests "all thought that the main reason for the quiet sway of religion over their country was the complete separation of church and state. I have no hesitation in stating that throughout my stay in America I met nobody, lay or cleric, who did not agree about that" (295). He continues:

> There have been religions intimately linked to earthly governments, dominating men's souls both by terror and by faith; but when a religion makes such an alliance, I am not afraid to say that it makes the same mistake as any man might; it sacrifices the future for the present, and by gaining a power to which it has no claim, it risks its legitimate authority. . . .

> Hence religion cannot share the material strength of the rulers without being burdened with some of the animosity roused against them. (297)

He remarks that these observations apply all the more to a democratic country, for in that case when religion seeks political power, it will attach itself to a particular party and be burdened by hostility to it (298). Referring to the cause of the decline of religion in Europe, he concludes, "I am profoundly convinced that this accidental and particular cause is the close union of politics and religion. . . . European Christianity has allowed itself to be intimately united with the powers of this world" (300–301). Political liberalism accepts Tocqueville's view and sees it as explaining, so far as possible, the basis of peace among comprehensive doctrines both religious and secular.

77   In this it agrees with Locke, Montesquieu, and Constant; Kant, Hegel, and Mill.

78   I take the term from Philip Quinn. The idea appears in Rawls, *Political Liberalism*, lecture VI, § 7.1–2, pp. 240–41.

79   I use the term *grounding reasons* since many who might appeal to these reasons view them as the proper grounds, or the true basis—religious, philosophical, or moral—of the ideals and principles of public reasons and political conceptions of justice.

80   Some have quite naturally read the footnote in Rawls, *Political Liberalism*, lecture VI, § 7.2, pp. 243–44, as an argument for the right to abortion in the first trimester. I do not intend it to be one. (It does express my opinion, but my opinion is not an argument.) I was in error in leaving it in doubt whether the aim of the footnote was only to illustrate and confirm the following statement in the text to which the footnote is attached: "The only comprehensive doctrines that run afoul of public reason are those that cannot support a reasonable balance [or ordering] of political values [on the issue]." To try to explain what I meant, I used three political values (of course, there are more) for the troubled issue of the right to abortion to which it might seem improbable that political values could apply at all. I believe a more detailed interpretation of those values may, when properly developed in public reason, yield a reasonable argument. I don't say the most reasonable or decisive argument; I don't know what that would be, or even if it exists. (For an example of such a more detailed interpretation, see Judith Jarvis Thomson, "Abortion," *Boston Review* 20 (1995): 11, though I would want to add several addenda to it.) Suppose now, for purposes of illustration, that there is a reasonable argument in public reason for the right to abortion but there is no equally reasonable balance, or ordering, of the political values in public reason that argues for the denial of that right. Then in this kind of case, but only in this kind of case, does a comprehensive doctrine denying the right to abortion run afoul of public reason. However, if it can satisfy the proviso of the wide public reason better, or at least as well as other views, it has made its case in public reason. Of course, a comprehensive doctrine can be unreasonable on one or several issues without being simply unreasonable.

81   Rawls, *Political Liberalism*, lecture VI, § 7.1, pp. 240–41.

82   For such an argument, see Cardinal Joseph Bernardin, "The Consistent Ethic: What Sort of Framework?" *Origins* 16 (October 30, 1986): 345, 347–50. The idea of public order the cardinal presents includes these three political values: public peace, essential protections of human rights, and the commonly accepted standards of moral behavior in a community of law. Further, he grants that not all moral imperatives are to be translated into prohibitive civil statutes and thinks it essential to the political and social order to protect human life and basic human rights. The denial of the right to abortion he hopes to justify on the basis of those three values. I don't of course assess his argument here, except to say it is clearly cast in some form of public reason. Whether it is itself reasonable or not, or more reasonable than the arguments on the other side, is another matter. As with any form of reasoning in public reason, the reasoning may be fallacious or mistaken.

83   As far as I can see, this view is similar to Father John Courtney Murray's position about the stand the church should take in regard to contraception in *We Hold These Truths: Catholic Reflections on the American Proposition* (New York: Sheed & Ward, 1960), 157–58. See also Mario Cuomo's lecture on abortion in his Notre Dame Lecture of 1984, in *More Than Words: The Speeches of Mario Cuomo* (New York: St. Martin's, 1993), 32–51. I am indebted to Leslie Griffin and Paul Weithman for discussion and clarification about points involved in this and the preceding note and for acquainting me with Father Murray's view.

84   These two powers, the capacity for a conception of justice and the capacity for a conception of the good, are discussed in Rawls, *Political Liberalism*. See

especially lecture I, § 3.2, p. 19; lecture II, § 7.1, p. 81; lecture III, § 3.3, pp. 103–4; and lecture III, § 4.1, p. 108.

85 Rawls, *Political Liberalism*, lecture VI, § 4, pp. 223–27.

86 Sometimes the term *normalize* is used in this connection. For example, persons have certain fundamental interests of a religious or philosophical kind, or else certain basic needs of a natural kind. Again, they may have a certain typical pattern of self-realization. A Thomist will say that we always desire above all else, even if unknown to ourselves, the *Visio Dei*; a Platonist will say we strive for a vision of the good; a Marxist will say we aim for self-realization as species-beings.

87 The idea of such a consensus is discussed at various places in Rawls, *Political Liberalism*. See especially lecture IV, and consult the index.

88 Rawls, *Political Liberalism*, lecture IV, xviii (paperback edition).

89 See Rawls, *Political Liberalism*, lecture IV, § 3.2. It is sometimes asked why political liberalism puts such a high value on political values, as if one could only do that by assessing those values in comparison with transcendent values. But this comparison political liberalism does not make, nor does it need to make, as is observed in the text.

90 On this, see Michael J. Sandel's review of *Political Liberalism*, by John Rawls, *Harvard Law Review* 107 (1994): 1765, 1778–82, and Michael J. Sandel, *Democracy's Discontent: America in Search of a Public Philosophy* (Cambridge, Mass.: Belknap Press of Harvard University Press, 1996), 21–23.

91 Perhaps some think that a political conception is not a matter of (moral) right and wrong. If so, that is a mistake and is simply false. Political conceptions of justice are themselves intrinsically moral ideas, as I have stressed from the outset. As such, they are a kind of normative value. On the other hand, some may think that the relevant political conceptions are determined by how a people actually establish their existing institutions—the political given, as it were, by politics. Viewed in this light, the prevalence of slavery in 1858 implies that Lincoln's criticisms of it were moral, a matter of right and wrong, and certainly not a matter of politics. To say that the political is determined by a people's politics may be a possible use of the term *political*. But then it ceases to be a normative idea and it is no longer part of public reason. We must hold fast to the idea of the political as a fundamental category and covering political conceptions of justice as intrinsic moral values.

92 See Rawls, *Political Liberalism*, lecture VI, § 3.2.

93 See Rawls, *Political Liberalism*, lecture II, § 3.2–4, pp. 60–62. The main points can be set out in summary fashion as follows: (1) Reasonable persons do not all affirm the same comprehensive doctrine. This is said to be a consequence of the burdens of judgment. See note 95. (2) Many reasonable doctrines are affirmed, not all of which can be true or right (as judged from within a comprehensive doctrine). (3) It is not unreasonable to affirm any one of the reasonable comprehensive doctrines. (4) Others who affirm reasonable doctrines different from ours are, we grant, reasonable also, and certainly not for that reason unreasonable. (5) In going beyond recognizing the reasonableness of a doctrine and affirming our belief in it, we are not being unreasonable. (6) Reasonable persons think it unreasonable to use political power, should they possess it, to repress other doctrines that are reasonable yet different from their own.

94 See Rawls, *Political Liberalism*, lecture VI, § 6.3.

95   These burdens are discussed in Rawls, *Political Liberalism*, lecture II, § 2. Roughly, they are sources or causes of reasonable disagreement between reasonable and rational persons. They involve balancing the weight of different kinds of evidence and kinds of values and the like, and they affect both theoretical and practical judgments.

96   Rawls, *Political Liberalism*, lecture II, xviii.

97   Rawls, *Political Liberalism*, lecture II, § 1.1, pp. 49–50.

98   Rawls, *Political Liberalism*, lecture II, § 2–3.4, pp. 54–62.

99   Rawls, *Political Liberalism*, lecture IV, § 1.2–3, pp. 135–37.

100   Rawls, *Political Liberalism*, lecture IX, § 2.1, p. 393.

101   Observe that neither the religious objection to democracy nor the autocratic one could be made by public reasoning.

102   See note 3.

103   See Rawls, *Theory of Justice* § 35 (on toleration of the intolerant); Rawls, *Political Liberalism*, lecture V, § 6.2, pp. 197–99.

Chapter 3

1   A good case for a view of this sort is made by Nicholas Wolterstorff in his contributions to Robert Audi and Nicholas Wolterstorff, *Religion in the Public Square: The Place of Religious Convictions in Political Debate* (Lanham, Md.: Rowman & Littlefield, 1997). Kent Greenawalt's position is less permissive but is a good foil for both mine and Wolterstorff's. Greenawalt's *Private Consciences and Public Reasons* (New York: Oxford University Press, 1995) contains much explication of the rationale for a range of positions on this issue before us.

2   Calling the kinds of obligations in question *religious* is not meant to presuppose the truth of theism. If it is objected that apart from God's existence there are no religious obligations (at least for those who conceive them as ordained by God), we could simply speak of *presumptively religious* obligations, referring to the kind reasonably taken to be incumbent on votaries of a particular religion as such, and proceed: the kinds of church-state issues under discussion would be largely unaffected.

3   It is interesting to note that Paul J. Weithman, in discussing John Courtney Murray, suggests that Murray may have held a view implying that one *cannot* violate an obligation so long as one is acting within one's rights: "If someone has a moral right to do something, then she violates no obligation by doing it." See "The Privatization of Religion," *Journal of Religious Ethics* 22 (1994): 15. Weithman does not himself note the possibility that concerns me here—a possibility illustrated by, say, a case in which an instructor has a right to criticize a student for certain errors but ought not to do so because under the circumstances it is better to leave the matter to a colleague closer to the student.

4   I do not say "*an* adequate secular reason"; we should leave open the possibility of a set of reasons for a position or action that are each short of adequacy but that might together give one overall reason. In some cases they might be drawn together into a single reason, but doing this is not strictly necessary for having adequate reason—a point that applies in nonnormative matters as well as here. Requiring such unification of one's several grounds would make my principle more restrictive.

5   See Robert Audi, "The Separation of Church and State and the Obligations of Citizenship," *Philosophy & Public Affairs* 18, no. 3 (1989): 259–96.

The principle applies with different degrees of force in different contexts. Moreover, the adequacy requirement rules out some nonreligious reasons, e.g., those that are ill-grounded; but my concern is with the specifically religious in relation to the political. I might add that the principle is not meant to require that an adequate reason be objectively correct, in a sense implying that it is equivalent to a true proposition. A false proposition that is sufficiently well justified can count as an adequate reason. My paper just cited spoke of an adequate reason for something as one "whose truth is sufficient to justify" that, and at least one careful commentator on the paper has read this conjunctively rather than conditionally; i.e., as implying both truth and justificatory sufficiency, rather than (as intended) on the model of, e.g., "You need a witness whose testimony for your side is sufficient to sway those in doubt," which does not imply that either the witness or the testimony is actual. An alternative wording is "a reason which, if it should be true, justifies . . . ." See Philip L. Quinn, "Political Liberalisms and Their Exclusions of the Religious," *Proceedings and Addresses of the American Philosophical Association* 69, no. 2 (1995): 35–56, esp. 38–39.

6   It does not, e.g., imply the possibility of existing apart from divine creation. In case taking a reason to be evidentially independent of God seems somehow irreverent, note that the most famous arguments for the existence of God are supposed to have premises with just this status: if they did not, they would fail of their purpose, which is roughly to provide evidential ground for believing God exists, on the basis of considerations not dependent on one's already having that ground.

7   Moral skepticism is not easily refuted, but I have attacked some of its most plausible forms in "Skepticism in Theory and Practice: Justification and Truth, Rationality and Goodness," chap. 3 in my *Moral Knowledge and Ethical Character* (New York: Oxford University Press, 1997). (A positive nonskeptical moral epistemology is developed in chaps. 2, 4, 5, and 11.)

8   For a recent treatment of public reason in contrast to what I call secular reason, see John Rawls, "The Idea of Public Reason Revisited," *University of Chicago Law Review* 64, no. 3 (1997): 765–807. In commenting on my characterization of a secular reason, he says, "This definition is ambiguous between secular reasons in the sense of a nonreligious comprehensive doctrine and in the sense of a purely political conception within the content of public reason" (n. 40). In fact my characterization cannot *mean* either of these but is broad enough to encompass both. Rawls is perhaps influenced here by his own neutralist determination to contrast the purely political with what would normally be called secular, even if it does embody a comprehensive concept of the good, and to argue that the latter kind of secular reason cannot in general be an adequate basis of coercion (he allows a major exception in a proviso).

9   To be sure, probabilities and other complexities may enter in, as with fluoridation of water. But even here a poorly educated person might be able to see that, e.g., we are better off with fluoridation than without it. This point, in any case, is neutral with respect to differences between my view and alternative positions on the adequacy of sociopolitical reasons.

10   I offer a detailed account of the nature of testimony and the conditions under which it confers justification in "The Place of Testimony in the Fabric of Justification and Knowledge," *American Philosophical Quarterly* 34, no. 4 (1997): 404–22.

11   Perhaps the most influential treatment of prima facie reasons is W. D. Ross' in *The Right and the Good* (Oxford: Oxford University Press, 1930). I discuss his conception in detail, clarify it, and bring out how knowledge of major moral principles can have a basis in secular reason in "Intuitionism, Pluralism, and the Foundations of Ethics," in my *Moral Knowledge*.

12   Kent Greenawalt has written instructively on this general topic, particularly the appropriate range of considerations for judges. See *Private Consciences and Public Reasons*, esp. 141–50.

13   See Greenawalt's *Private Consciences and Public Reasons*, 67.

14   This objection is made by (among others) Jeff Jordan in attacking the principle of secular rationale. He says, e.g., "Despite the initial appeal of the idea that one should *couch public discourse* in terms of public reasons, there are at least two reasons to think that adopting the PSR [principle of secular rationale] is ill-advised . . . the PSR carries an unpalatable epistemic consequence . . . [and] would hinder political participation." See Jeff Jordan, "Religious Reasons and Public Reasons," *Public Affairs Quarterly* 11, no. 3 (1997): 248 (italics added). As noted in the text, the principle says nothing about the vocabulary in which public discourse is to be couched; it allows prudence to settle that. As to the epistemic consequence, Jordan claims "the PSR could mandate that one assert a secular and weak reason for a policy and ignore a religious, yet evidentiary [*sic*] stronger, reason for an incompatible policy" (248). First, the requirement that one have and be willing to offer *adequate* secular reason should *not* lead one to assert a reason one takes to conflict with one that is evidentially stronger—nor does the principle even preclude there *being* religious reasons that are evidentially cogent and indeed evidentially stronger than some secular reasons (Jordan's note 15 on page 254 suggests he has not noticed this point in a work of mine he cites). One should regard a reason as *inadequate* if it conflicts with what one considers an evidentially stronger one. Second, the objection again assumes the issue is what to say, as opposed to what kind of reason one should have for advocacy or support of laws and public policies.

15   This case is presented by Peter Smith in "Civility as a Christian Virtue, Part One: Robert Audi's Rules of Secular Rationale and Motivation." He suggests that my view requires her "to vote against her conscience" since she should "vote yes or abstain" (11).

16   Indeed, it is by no means self-evident, and I do not assume, that rationality always requires us even to fulfill a moral obligation on balance, in which case we would *not* have a moral right to do otherwise. This is too large an issue to pursue here.

17   It has been claimed otherwise, e.g., by Vern Sima, in a letter to the *Lincoln Journal Star* (23 October 1993): "I belong to a church that teaches abortion is murder. I am open-minded enough to accept the church's unbounded wisdom. But what ultimately convinced me was scientific evidence and observation. What we have here is science confirming religious truths, not religious truths standing alone, even though that would be enough." I doubt this claim because, for one thing, I cannot see why one must be open-minded to accept what one conceives as "unbounded wisdom" or why, if one thinks that the church's view manifests it, one would not be convinced *before* discovering the scientific evidence. The question is especially urgent given that the writer says the religious truth "would be enough," apparently meaning that the church's view would be acceptable *without* scientific confirmation. Compare the claim

that "There is no longer any serious scientific dispute that the unborn child is a human creature who dies violently in the act of abortion. This brute fact is the root of our national distress over the abortion license." See "The America We Seek: A Statement of Pro-Life Principle and Concern," signed by Michael Novak and Ralph Reed among dozens of others, *First Things* 63 (May 1996): 40. This statement treats the claim following "dispute" as scientific. But if being a child entails, as it ordinarily does, being a person, or if being a creature entails being created by God, then the claim is apparently not scientific but theological or philosophical or both. If, on the other hand, a creature is just a living thing, and a child is a genetically human entity in *any* stage of development from that of zygote on, then the supposed brute fact does not appear to sustain the antiabortion conclusions it is used to support. . . . We might ponder the question whether so many conscientious people would let this kind of ambiguity go unremarked apart from religious motivation to establish their conclusion regarding abortion. And might the attempt to establish that conclusion scientifically bespeak a sense that secular rationale is needed for justified coercion and perhaps that secular innovation is needed for the conscientious imposition of that coercion?

18   Not just any antireligious motivation would fail to count as secular, e.g., where the desire is simply to weaken a religious group enough to prevent its dominating a society. But for purposes of taking the motivation principle to be an element in civic virtue, it is reasonable to construe a desire to destroy a religion or to discredit its deity as nonsecular.

19   The accrediting may take account of certain factors that are not purely academic. It is one thing to give vouchers to support free parental choice, including religious choice; it is another to allow them where racial discrimination is practiced. It is a difficult question when criteria of admission are objectionable in a way that warrants differential governmental treatment.

20   The government in the Netherlands funds both public and sectarian schools, compensating, in part, for any advantages this gives to the latter over the former by requiring national examinations keyed to a core curriculum constituting 80 percent of what students study in the secondary school years. For a brief description of the system, see the article by Laurel Shaper Walters in the *Christian Science Monitor* for December 12, 1992.

21   One may wonder how a religious person who seeks to do everything in fulfillment of God's will can abide by the principle of secular motivation. It would seem that such a person can without irreverence be motivated by the sense of just conduct as dictated by the dignity of persons, at least if the property of being thus dictated is equivalent to the property of being commanded by God. The same point surely holds where the person justifiedly *believes* this equivalence to hold (and perhaps even in certain cases in which the belief is not justified). Even if, in addition, such a person is not sufficiently motivated by any secular consideration *without* thinking of it as religiously acceptable, on a liberal reading of the principle of secular motivation—more liberal than I gave it in "Separation of Church and State"—the person can still be sufficiently motivated by that consideration. If the person is motivated by the consideration and not just by the thought that God commands the action it supports, this would be a case of being motivated *by a secular consideration*, without being (purely) *secularly motivated*. It would not be a pure instance of *civic* virtue . . . since the motivation in question depends on the belief that the consideration in question

is religiously acceptable, but this consideration would at least not be a mere rationalization and would, in addition, be a candidate to satisfy the principle of secular rationale. I am not here endorsing the suggested liberal reading of the principle of secular motivation, but as stated, the principle can bear that reading.

22   Accessibility in the relevant sense is no simple matter: ordinary sensory data of the kind needed to use a ruler or a gauge are clearly accessible, and a clairvoyant sense of the future is clearly not. But it might be argued that anyone who is open-minded, considers natural theology, and attends certain religious services in a good-faith effort to find God thereby has access to good theistic reasons for a certain view of the world. Many people who reluctantly or ambivalently leave their faith would claim to be counterexamples to this; but even if that judgment is accepted, the notion of accessibility is not precise and will remain controversial.

23   Such a position does not imply that these propositions are necessarily true simpliciter but that it is impossible that they be *both* endorsed or accepted by God and false. Thus, one may presumably be as certain of their truth as one is that they are divinely endorsed or accepted. For many people this is a very high degree of certainty.

24   Stephen Carter vividly voices a related point: "I have always been deeply offended by politicians, whether on the left or on the right, who are ready to seize on the language and symbols of religion in order to grub for votes." *The Culture of Disbelief* (New York: Basic Books, 1994), 47.

25   I should add that to Unitarianism—particularly the more common nontheistic forms—my points concerning what is special about religious reasons apply far less than to many other religions. There may indeed be forms of Unitarianism and other broadly religious outlooks that are not plausibly considered religions—though they would be *religious*, in the sense John Dewey noted, in which appropriate attitudes, e.g., of reverence, can mark a perspective as religious even if it is not part of a *religion*. Dewey's distinction among the notions of religion, the religious, and a religion is a major topic of definition that I cannot address directly [here].

26   In "Acting from Virtue," in *Moral Knowledge*, I provide an account of such action, which supports the conception of it employed here.

27   The determination of evidential adequacy is also a difficult matter but is not peculiar to my position on religion and politics; any plausible political philosophy must employ some such notion. It is perhaps some help to say that standard deductive and inductive logic are highly relevant, as is whatever logic of moral discourse there may be that goes beyond them.

28   A number of writers have commented on this, including Carter, *Culture of Disbelief*; and Quinn, "Political Liberalisms." For discussion of the putative "marginalization" and "privatization" of religion in the United States, see Theodore Y. Blumoff, "The New Religionists' Social Gospel: On the Rhetoric and Reality of Religion's 'Marginalization' in Public Life," forthcoming.

29   Here one can be conscientiously mistaken: one can falsely but excusably believe a reason to be secular.

30   Paul J. Weithman, in "The Separation of Church and State: Some Questions for Professor Audi," *Philosophy & Public Affairs* 20, no. 1 (1991): 62–65, and others have questioned how feasible it is to try to follow the principle of secular rationale. See also Lawrence B. Solum, "Faith and Justice," *De Paul University Law Review* 39, no. 4 (1990): 1083–1106, esp. 1089–92. Also

relevant is Weithman's "Rawlsian Liberalism and the Privatization of Religion: Three Theological Objections Considered," *Journal of Religious Ethics* 22, no. 1 (1994): 3–28. The above is only the beginning of a reply to such worries. For another pertinent discussion see Jonathan Jacobs, "Theism and Moral Objectivity," *American Catholic Philosophical Quarterly* 66, no. 4 (1992); and for more recent discussion of related issues by Weithman, see his valuable collection, *Religion and Contemporary Liberalism* (Notre Dame: University of Notre Dame Press, 1997). Some of the authors represented are discussed or cited elsewhere. Regarding the others, the papers by John A. Coleman, SJ (264–90), J. L. A. Garcia (218–53), and Sanford Levinson (7–92) are pertinent to this [essay]. . . .

31   One might think that a person must have *some* motivating reason for any belief or action. But this is not so, if we distinguish reasons from causes or, more subtly, *reasons for which* one believes or acts from mere (explanatory) *reasons why* one does: wishful thinking is a nonrational source of beliefs, and actions not performed intentionally need not be done for a reason, as where one quite unwittingly offends someone.

32   This result is suggested to be implicit in my view in Quinn's "Political Liberalisms," 36.

33   Cf. Wolterstorff's remark that "there is an eminently honorable reason for discrepancy between the reason one offers in public discussion for a certain policy and one's own reason for accepting that policy; namely, one wants to persuade one's discussion partner to accept the policy, and one knows or suspects that different reasons will attract her," though "if I say or suggest that my reason was such-and-such, when in fact it was not, that would be dissembling." Audi and Wolterstorff, 106–7.

34   A reason offered in leveraging may be evidentially good; but in leveraging one is not offering it as such, but relative to the point of view one is in a sense taking. Detailed discussion of leveraging and of the question of the need for sincerity in giving reasons is found in my "The Ethics of Advocacy," *Legal Theory* 1, no. 3 (1995): 251–81.

35   I have defended this point about manipulation in "Ethics of Advocacy" and in "Separation of Church and State."

36   Audi and Wolterstorff, 109.

37   There are many issues here. Some are discussed above, and Kent Greenawalt discusses the issues in both *Religious Convictions and Political Choice* (New York: Oxford University Press, 1988) and *Private Consciences and Public Reasons*.

38   The notion of neutrality is also informatively discussed by Rawls, "Idea of Public Reasons," and Carter, *Culture of Disbelief*. See also Robert van Wyk, "Liberalism, Religion, and Politics," *Public Affairs Quarterly* 1, no. 3 (1987): 59–76, and "Liberalism, Religion, and Politics Again: A Reply to Gordon Graham," *Journal of Social Philosophy* 25, no. 3 (1994): 153–64. (Some of van Wyk's criticism of my view is at least implicitly answered in this [essay].)

39   The Declaration of Independence is one famous document supporting liberal democracy that seems to imply otherwise; but I am not certain that it must be so read, nor do I take it to be as authoritative on this matter as the work of, say, John Stuart Mill.

40   This point (among many others relevant to this [essay]) is brought out by Greenawalt in *Private Consciences and Public Reasons*.

Chapter 4

My thanks for helpful comments on earlier versions to Gerald Gaus, Tyll van Geel, Kent Greenawalt, Abner Greene, Amy Gutmann, Will Kymlicka, Glyn Morgan, Wayne Norman, Michael Sandel, Rogers Smith, Nomi Stolzenberg, and Leif Wenar. Versions of this argument were presented at the College of William and Mary, the University of Ottawa, Tulane University, Princeton University, the Yale Legal Theory Workshop, and a Harvard graduate seminar; my thanks to the participants and to organizers Bruce Ackerman, Own Fiss, George Kateb, Ron Rapaport, David Ross, and Rich Teichgraeber. Thanks also to the Earhart Foundation and the Princeton University Center for Human Values for giving me the time and the perfect setting in which to complete it.

1   Iris Marion Young, *Justice and the Politics of Difference* (Princeton: Princeton University Press, 1990), 7, 95.
2   Young, 174, and see 10, 100–107, 112–15.
3   Young, 88, 118.
4   Young, 181.
5   Young, 37.
6   Fundamentalists could also claim—as Young says of other oppressed groups such as women, blacks, and gays—to be identified with the body and regarded as "ugly, fearful, and loathsome"—i.e., as rednecks, sweaty hicks, and country bumpkins (see Young's account, 124), and the "five faces of oppression" (Young, 48–63), esp. "marginalization" and "cultural Imperialism" (Young, 53–61).
7   Nomi Maya Stolzenberg, "'He Drew a Circle That Shut Me Out': Assimilation, Indoctrination, and the Paradox of Liberal Education," *Harvard Law Review* 106 (1993): 581–667, 583, 582. Stolzenberg's provocative and searching article—to which my own argument is in many ways a response—is mainly concerned to highlight the seriousness of fundamentalist complaints, though she also evinces a good deal of sympathy for those complaints. Like Stolzenberg, Sanford Levinson emphasizes the moral costs to people with totalistic faiths of the liberal "privatization" of religion, giving too much weight to religious objections (see "The Confrontation of Religious Faith and Civil Religion: Catholics Becoming Justices," *DePaul Law Review* 39 [1990]: 1047–81, and "Religious Language and the Public Square," review of *Love and Power: The Role of Religion and Morality in American Politics*, by Michael Perry, *Harvard Law Review* 105 [1992]: 2061–79).
8   And because indiscriminate talk of difference and diversity is all too popular in the academy, William A. Galston seems to me to go well beyond giving "diversity its due" when he advances an interpretation of liberalism as the "Diversity State," a state that affords "maximum feasible space for the enactment of individual and group differences, constrained only by the requirement of liberal social unity" ("Two Concepts of Liberalism," *Ethics* 105, no. 3 [1995]: 524).
9   Political liberalism is potentially tough-minded—I want to develop that potential here.
10 John Rawls, *Political Liberalism* (New York: Columbia University Press, 1993).
11 *Mozert v. Hawkins County Bd. of Education*, 827 F.2d at 1058 (6th Cir. 1987).
12 It was noted in *Mozert*, e.g., "that of 47 stories referring to, or growing out of, religions (including Islam, Buddhism, American Indian religion and

nature worship), only 3 were Christian, and none Protestant" (Danny J. Boggs, Circuit Judge, concurring in *Mozert*, 827 F.2d at 1080–81, n. 13).

13   Opinion of Judge Lively in *Mozert*, 827 F.2d at 1061, quoting the testimony of Vicki Frost.

14   For an excellent account of the political struggle behind the *Mozert* litigation, see Stephen Bates, *Battleground: One Mother's Crusade, the Religious Right, and the Struggle for Control of Our Classrooms* (New York: Simon & Schuster, 1993).

15   See *Mozert*, 827 F.2d at 1059–60. A district court at first overturned the school board's decision, but the board was later upheld by a federal appeals court, which included Judges Lively (writing for the court) and Boggs (concurring).

16   See the helpful discussion in George W. Dent Jr., "Religious Children, Secular Schools," *Southern California Law Review* 61 (1988): 863–941, from which I have learned much. Dent points out that states often excuse religious children by statute from particular parts of the curriculum; some localities allow children to be excused from sex education classes on religious grounds (Dent, 924, n. 337).

17   *Wisconsin v. Yoder*, 406 U.S. 205 (1971).

18   They are what Jeff Spinner calls "partial citizens" in his important book, *The Boundaries of Citizenship: Race, Ethnicity, and Nationality in the Liberal State* (Baltimore: Johns Hopkins University Press, 1994).

19   *Mozert*, 827 F.2d at 1063; some school officials likewise denied that any values at all were being taught. County Superintendent Snodgrass said that the schools do not teach "any particular value" and that they "teach and promote reading, not values" (quoted in *Mozert*, 827 F.2d, at 1077, opinion of Judge Boggs).

20   *Mozert*, 827 F.2d at 1064.

21   *Mozert*, 827 F.2d at 1075–76.

22   *Mozert*, 827 F.2d at 1080. These points are forcefully developed in Stolzenberg, 599–611.

23   Amy Gutmann, *Democratic Education* (Princeton: Princeton University Press, 1987), 30–31. John Dewey insisted that there is "one sure road of access to truth" in all spheres of life: the scientific method (*A Common Faith* [New Haven: Yale University Press, 1934], 32).

24   John Gray, "Can We Agree to Disagree?" *New York Times Book Review*, May 16, 1993, 35.

25   *Mozert*, 827 F.2d at 1069 and 1068, quoting *Bethel School District No. 403 v. Fraser*, 106 S. Ct. 3159, 3164 (1986).

26   *Mozert*, 827 F.2d at 1069.

27   Quoted in *Mozert*, 827 F.2d at 1069.

28   Rawls, *Political Liberalism*, 77–78.

29   Rawls, *Political Liberalism*, 154.

30   As in: "Your Catholicism absurdly defers to the authority of the Bishop of Rome, but I welcome you as a fellow citizen whose public reasonableness is shown by the fact that you do not seek to impose your religious beliefs on me by political means, but instead join with me in acknowledging the political authority of reasons we can share."

31   See Rawls' account of the "burdens of judgment" (Rawls, *Political Liberalism*, 54–58).

32   See Joshua Cohen's helpful discussion, "Moral Pluralism and Political Consensus," in *The Idea of Democracy*, ed. David Copp, Jean Hampton, and John Roemer (New York: Cambridge University Press, 1993).

33   For a popular version of this charge—directed at American liberalism in general rather than political liberalism in particular—see Stephen L. Carter's *Culture of Disbelief: How Law and Politics Trivialize Religious Devotion* (New York: Basic Books, 1993).

34   Rawls clarifies this in "The Idea of Public Reason: Further Considerations" (December 18, 1993, unpublished).

35   *Mozert*, 827 F.2d at 1069.

36   *Scopes v. State*, 289 S.W. 363 (1927), pp. 368–69.

37   Students on this account might be allowed to describe and defend their religious views in class in certain ways, and so, as Kent Greenawalt properly suggested to me, religion will not necessarily be kept altogether out of the public schools. There may of course be good reasons (fears of peer pressure on children with minority religious views) to frown on student professions of religious beliefs in schools, but these are matters I need not settle here.

38   Dewey, *A Common Faith*, 32.

39   In this way, I would continue to hold to what I have said in previous works (such as *Liberal Virtues* [Oxford: Clarendon, 1990]) about liberalism as a way of life or regime. I would now more clearly circumscribe the direct authority of the state, allowing it to promote autonomy and critical thinking in politics but not in, e.g., religion.

40   See Rawls, *Political Liberalism*, 191–94.

41   Of course, those shared public reasons—adequate in themselves for justifying basic principles of justice—will for each citizen be situated within a larger universe of moral value and a view of the whole truth, religious or otherwise. Those wider, extrapolitical beliefs will not be shared by all of our reasonable fellow citizens. Political liberalism never asks citizens to deny that their religious or philosophical beliefs are the ultimate grounds of their political convictions. These ultimate grounds generally need not be invoked in a political context and are, after all, the very things about which we differ reasonably. These ultimate beliefs need not be bracketed in the sense of being denied, but they should be bracketed in the sense of not being invoked or relied upon as the public ground of decision for matters of basic justice. I rely here on Rawls' unpublished paper, "The Idea of Public Reason: Further Considerations."

42   It might be a way of protecting and preserving their "constitutive" commitments, as Michael Sandel would say (see *Liberalism and the Limits of Justice* [New York: Cambridge University Press, 1982]).

43   "In highly complex societies none of the central functions of the societal system can be assumed by a unified organization" (Niklas Luhmann, *The Differentiation of Society*, trans. Stephen Holmes and Charles Larmore [New York: Columbia University Press, 1982], 80, and see chap. 4 generally, and the useful introduction by Holmes and Larmore, ix–xxxvi).

44   "Organizational plans and directives are evaded, distorted, redefined, or intentionally derailed at the level of interaction. The slack relation between official Church dogma and ordinary confessional practice . . . offers a good example of this process of routine deviation" (Luhmann, 79).

45   See Stolzenberg's excellent account, 616–34.

46   Stolzenberg, 614. As Vincent P. Branick puts it on behalf of fundamentalists, "To the degree that the historical-critical method requires that I distance myself and my life decisions from the matter at hand, to the degree the method renders me a detached observer of the Bible 'out there,' it

becomes a game. Such playfulness fails to do justice to the seriousness of scripture" ("The Attractiveness of Fundamentalism," in *What Makes Fundamentalism So Attractive?* ed. Marla Selvidge [Elgin, Ill.: Brethren, 1984], quoted in Stolzenberg, 626).

47   It is not true, then, that liberalism is based on religious uncertainty or value subjectivism, as Stolzenberg suggests (587, 647–65).

48   This is an important concession in the context of *Mozert*, 827 F.2d, since some of the most influential shapers of American public schooling have advocated comprehensive liberalisms diametrically opposed to fundamentalism (see Dewey).

49   As Thomas Nagel argues: "The true liberal . . . is committed to refusing to use the power of the state to impose paternalistically on its citizens a good life individualistically conceived" (*Equality and Partiality* [New York: Oxford University Press, 1991], 165).

50   Stephen L. Carter, "Evolutionism, Creationism, and Treating Religion as a Hobby," *Duke Law Journal* 1987 (1987): 977–96, 978. I am indebted to Glyn Morgan for calling this article to my attention; its argument is consistent with Carter's [subsequent] *Culture of Disbelief.*

51   Stanley Fish, "Liberalism Doesn't Exist," *Duke Law Journal* 1987 (1987): 997–1001, 1001.

52   Rawls, *Political Liberalism*, 127–29.

53   Douglas Laycock distinguishes formal and substantive notions of neutrality or liberty in "Summary and Synthesis: The Crisis in Religious Liberty," *George Washington Law Review* 60 (1992): 841–56, 848–49. Formal neutrality requires only that religious associations not be singled out for especially harsh treatment, but it is satisfied if religious groups receive the same treatment as other groups in society, or if general rules and restrictions are applied evenhandedly to religious associations along with all others. On Laycock's view, formal neutrality is not enough to satisfy the "free exercise" clause of the Constitution. See also the instructive paper by Abner S. Greene, "The Political Balance of the Religion Clauses," *Yale Law Journal* 102 (1993): 1619–44.

54   The Constitution of India contains a guarantee of state "equidistance" from religions, which seems to stand for a guarantee of neutrality of effect (see Rina Verma, "Secularism and Communal Violence in Indian Politics" [thesis prospectus presented to the Department of Government, Harvard University, May 20, 1992]). Verma observes that "equidistance produces communalism by producing insecurity and disequilibrium among religious communities. Instead of remaining at an equal distance from the different religions, the state progressively becomes entangled in trying to please 'all of the communities all of the time.' If it grants one concession to one group, it must grant one to another group, and so on. The process, instead of making all groups feel secure about their position, actually never reaches an equilibrium, increases the burden on the state, and ends up antagonizing all groups involved" (10).

55   See the very skeptical account of political socialization through schooling in Tyll van Geel, "The Search for Constitutional Limits on Governmental Authority to Inculcate Youth," *Texas Law Review* 62 (1983): 197–297, esp. 262–92.

56   In *Pierce v. Society of Sisters*, 268 U.S. 510 (1925), the Supreme Court sustained a challenge by the operators of parochial and private schools to a law

requiring attendance at public schools. I owe this objection to Jon Fullerton and Sanford Levinson.

57   See Neal Devins, "State Regulation of Christian Schools," *Journal of Legislation* 10 (1983): 351–81, esp. 359–63; and Dent, 909–12.

58   I would advance this principle as a corollary to *Pierce*.

59   It will not always be easy to say what is central and what is not, but the ability to read is certainly a basic skill, and, likewise, knowledge of the diversity that constitutes our history and the importance of tolerance are clearly among the core civic aims. Science classes are not as centrally important to the civic mission of schools as any of these.

60   See the account by Paul C. Vitz, *Censorship: Evidence of Bias in Our Children's Textbooks* (Ann Arbor, Mich.: Servant Books, 1986).

61   Again, I leave aside the question of whether courts should examine these additional grounds.

62   This is indebted to conversation with Lief Wenar.

63   Of course there may have been countervailing prudential reasons—an avalanche of requests for exceptions?—pushing in the opposite direction.

64   Hegel, *Philosophy of Right*, trans. T. M. Knox (New York: Oxford University Press, 1967), 168, para. 270.

65   Spinner, 88–92.

66   Spinner, 101–2; most of those who leave the Amish community become Mennonites, not ballet dancers and astronauts, as Justice Douglas seemed to hope.

67   See Justice Scalia's opinion in *Employment Division, Department of Human Resources of Oregon et al. v. Smith*, 110 Sup. Ct. 1595 (1990), esp. 1605; and see Walter Berns, "Religion and the Supreme Court," in *The First Amendment and the Future of American Democracy* (New York: Basic, 1970), 33–79, both of whom overemphasize the fragility of the rule of law.

68   Rawls (*Political Liberalism*, 11) describes the strictures on public reason as applying to the most basic political questions (the "basic structure"). He does not say whether these strictures should govern political questions more broadly, though it would seem strange if normal politics were radically discontinuous with more basic matters of principle, partly because the two are often hard to separate. I do not believe that I need to settle this matter, since the questions of concern in this [essay] are closely linked to basic matters of principle.

69   See Carter's remark, quoted above, 480; see Levinson's concluding remarks, "Religious Language," 2077–79; and Kent Greenawalt, *Religious Convictions and Political Choice* (New York: Oxford, 1988), 12, 35, and passim, though Greenawalt construes the demands of public reasonableness very stringently, perhaps too stringently (see Greenawalt, 153–56, and Rawls' discussion, *Political Liberalism*, lecture 6, § 7); and see Amy Gutmann and Dennis Thompson, "Moral Conflict and Political Consensus," *Ethics* 101 (1990): 64–88. This section is indebted to discussions with Lief Wenar and Michael Sandel.

70   Joseph Raz, "Facing Diversity: The Case of Epistemic Abstinence," *Philosophy and Public Affairs* 19 (1990): 3–47.

71   Which, I should add, is perfectly understandable given that Raz' judgment was rendered well before *Political Liberalism* appeared.

72   See Rawls' discussion, *Political Liberalism*, 209–11; the constraints generated by the political conception "do not refer to, although they limit, the substantive content of comprehensive conceptions of the good."

73   Again, Rawls' "The Idea of Public Reason: Further Considerations" has been very helpful to me here.
74   All this is based on Rawls' discussion, *Political Liberalism*, 162.
75   Rawls, *Political Liberalism*, 160.
76   Rawls, *Political Liberalism*, 160.
77   Rawls, *Political Liberalism*, last paragraph of 160, and also 208.
78   Sandel tries to suggest that there is just as much reasonable disagreement about issues of basic justice as there is about religious truth and other ultimate questions (see his review of *Political Liberalism*, by John Rawls, *Harvard Law Review* 107 [1994]: 1765–94, esp. 1789–94). This seems to me wrong. There does not seem to be any reasonable disagreement about the core meaning of the constitutional basics: the good of basic democratic procedures and core civil liberties. Questions of distributive justice (aside from the existence of a basic safety net) are more difficult and should for that reason not be regarded as among the constitutional essentials (as indeed they are not at present).

Chapter 5

1   This theme has been developed at great length, and from different angles, by Jürgen Habermas throughout his career. Compare his *Knowledge and Human Interests*, trans. Jeremy J. Shapiro (Boston: Beacon, 1971) with *Legitimation Crisis*, trans. Thomas A. McCarthy (Boston: Beacon, 1975) with *The Theory of Communicative Action*, trans. Thomas A. McCarthy (Boston: Beacon, vol. 1: 1984; vol. 2: 1987).
2   Compare T. M. Scanlon, "Contractarianism and Utilitarianism," in *Utilitarianism and Beyond*, ed. Amartya Sen and Bernard Williams (New York: Cambridge University Press, 1982), 103–28, esp. 110–19; Thomas Nagel, "Moral Conflict and Political Legitimacy," *Philosophy and Public Affairs* 16, no. 3 (1987): 215–40.
3   So long, at least, as our trades do not adversely affect others (a big proviso).
4   Robert Nozick, *Anarchy, State, and Utopia* (New York: Basic Books, 1974), cf. 150.
5   Among modern free marketeers, only Friedrich Hayek has sought to challenge the supreme pragmatic imperative outright. Unlike Nozick, Hayek does not merely fail to answer the question of initial entitlements; he tries to cure us of the Enlightenment disease that leads us to think the question is worth asking. Against the Enlightenment, Hayek emphasizes the pathetically limited capacity of individuals to understand their environment. On his view, men and women simply are not built to make the kinds of global judgments about social conditions of the kind propounded by theorists of distributive justice, liberal or otherwise. Instead of such blundering efforts "to correct" the market, the thoughtful person should stand in awed appreciation of the way markets allow imperfect humans to exchange far more information than any one of them could possibly process on his own. Rather than destroy this delicate evolutionary organism, we should root out the Enlightenment fantasy that men and women could, through public dialogue, improve upon the invisible hand of the market. This hubristic conversation about social justice will only empower remote bureaucrats to aggrandize themselves at everybody's expense. So let us just stop asking the question of justice and limit ourselves to bargaining with whatever bargaining chips the market is gracious enough to give us. See Hayek, *Law*,

Legislation, and Liberty: The Mirage of Social Justice (Chicago: University Press, 1976), esp. 62–101.

I am thoroughly unconvinced by Hayek's critique. Not that I wish to minimize the importance of markets. They are a key tool by which people with radically different ideals may coordinate their activities to mutual advantage. It is only Hayek's effort to treat the market as some quasidivine adaptation to the human condition that I find mystifying. Rather than an organic development, the modern market system is the product of an unending series of highly self-conscious decisions by politicians, lawyers, and policemen. Despite their mental limitations, most people are perfectly aware of this, and are quite capable of considering whether the market might operate more fairly if the relevant politicians, lawyers, and policemen were given rather different operating instructions. The point of this note, however, is hardly to deal with Hayek's arguments with the care they deserve, but to point out that they proceed on a level that is more fundamental than most.

6   For some of the reasons suggested by Donald Davidson in "Judging Interpersonal Interests," in *Foundations of Social Choice Theory*, ed. Jon Elster and Aanund Hylland (New York: Cambridge University Press, 1986), 195–211.

7   Despite Rawls' subsequent disavowal of this interpretation, ("Justice as Fairness: Political not Metaphysical," *Philosophy and Public Affairs* 14, no. 3 [1985]: 223–51), I do not believe that critics were simply engaged in tea-leaf reading in finding this theme (uneasily coexisting with many others) in Rawls' major works. See Michael J. Sandel, *Liberalism and the Limits of Justice* (New York: Cambridge University Press, 1982).

8   See Roderick Firth, "Ethical Absolutism and the Ideal Observer," *Philosophy and Phenomenological Research* 12, no. 3 (1952): 317–45.

9   The development of this line of criticism over the last generation can be usefully approached through the work of Bernard Williams. Compare his *Ethics and the Limits of Philosophy* (Cambridge, Mass.: Harvard University Press, 1985) with J. J. C. Smart and Bernard Williams, *Utilitarianism: For and Against* (New York: Cambridge University Press, 1973), 77–155.

10 The simple distinction between questions and answers helps clarify a Rawlsian project with which I am very sympathetic. In ["The Idea of an Overlapping Consensus,"] Rawls is concerned to distinguish a liberal political life from one that is based on a "mere modus vivendi" (*Oxford Journal of Legal Studies* 7, no. 1 [1987]: 1–25, esp. 10–15). For me, this dismissive label describes a regime that extends the principle of conversational restraint beyond its proper bounds to deny citizens the unrestricted right to insist on a liberal answer to any aspect of their power relationship that they wish to question by placing it on the political agenda. Consider, for example, a polity that threatens to punish anyone who tries to precipitate serious political debate about the existing distribution of property rights or gender roles. Although the political agenda is left open to questions on other matters, each person is told that she will simply have "to live with" the status quo so far as this particular dimension of power is concerned. Such a restriction on political freedom, to my mind, categorically deprives the regime of liberal legitimacy, and reduces it to the status of a "mere modus vivendi."

I cannot deny, however, that a "mere modus vivendi" may be the best liberals can realistically hope for under one or another extreme set of conditions—where allowing the serious political consideration of the power that comes from property or whatever will tear the place apart and lead only to the destruction of a polity that might otherwise have generated productive political dialogue on other issues. Even as a temporary expedient, however, the use of such "gag rules" is fraught with danger. Nonetheless, the world being the place that it is, I cannot say that such a drastic step is absolutely unthinkable. See Steven Holmes, "Gag Rules or the Politics of Omission," in *Constitutionalism and Democracy*, ed. Jon Elster and Rune Slagstad (New York: Cambridge University Press, 1988), 19–58.

11   Of course, practical steps must be taken to organize the agenda so as to make it manageable for real-world debate and decision. But this practical task cannot be made the pretext for the infinite deferral of a part of the agenda which some powerful participants do not wish to consider. See note 10.

12   In real life, there will usually be no practical need for a sharp separation of the two phases of the liberal dialectic described in this paragraph.

13   For a brilliant analysis of this aspect of role relations, see Erving Goffman, *Frame Analysis: An Essay on the Organization of Experience* (Cambridge, Mass.: Harvard University Press, 1974).

14   Roberto Unger comes remarkably close to this position in his *Passion* (New York: Free Press, 1984); idem, *Social Theory: Its Situation and Its Task* (New York: Cambridge University Press, 1987); idem, *False Necessity* (New York: Cambridge University Press, 1987).

15   But recall my inadequate treatment of Hayek in note 5.

16   Bruce Ackerman, *Social Justice in the Liberal State* (New Haven: Yale University Press, 1980).

Chapter 7

1   I have in mind here chapter 1 of Jean Cohen and Andrew Arato, *Civil Society and Political Theory* (Cambridge, Mass.: MIT Press, 1992), which manages to analyze the resistance movement in East Germany of the late 1980s without mentioning that churches and pastors were involved!

2   I will reserve my reflections on the views of my discussion partner, Robert Audi, for my rejoinder [in Robert Audi and Nicholas Wolterstorff, *Religion in the Public Square* (Lanham, Md.: Rowman & Littlefield, 1997)].

3   The matters that follow are discussed much more fully in my *John Locke and the Ethics of Belief* (New York: Cambridge University Press, 1996).

4   I might add that I have developed a much more extended critique in my *John Locke and the Ethics of Belief*.

5   See especially the essays in Alvin Plantinga and Nicholas Wolterstorff, eds., *Faith and Rationality* (Notre Dame: University of Notre Dame Press, 1982).

6   John Rawls, *Political Liberalism* (New York: Columbia University Press, 1993). [Subsequent references will be given by in-text citations.]

7   The qualification, that the principles of justice must be acceptable to the *reasonable* perspectives if the society is to be stable and enduring, is understandable but nonetheless questionable. By and large it is the *unreasonable* perspectives that constitute a threat to liberal democracies!

8   In an unpublished essay, Paul Weithman treats Rawls' thought as a species of what he calls "the liberalism of reasoned respect" and traces this liberalism to Kant's notion of respect for each other as rational agents. Certainly he is right to see Rawls as working in the Kantian tradition. But I read Rawls, in *Political Liberalism*, as not only more epistemologically chaste than Locke, but also as more epistemologically chaste than Kant. He wants to avoid appealing to any independent notion of *respect for rational agency*. His argument is that the Idea of liberal democracy itself *implies* restraint on the use of reasons derived from comprehensive religious or philosophical perspectives. The notion of *respect*, though it no doubt underlies Rawls' thought, plays no role in the argument itself.

9   Of course, something has to be said about the reasoning as well as about the reasons, lest thoroughly exotic, and even offensive, conclusions be drawn from eminently acceptable reasons. This is what Rawls says: "on matters of constitutional essentials and basic justice, the basic structure and its public policies are to be justifiable to all citizens, as the principle of political legitimacy requires. We add to this that in making these justifications we are to appeal only to presently accepted general beliefs and forms of reasoning found in common sense, and the methods and conclusions of science when these are not controversial. The liberal principle of legitimacy makes this the most appropriate, if not the only, way to specify the guidelines of public inquiry. What other guidelines and criteria have we for this case?" (Rawls, 224).

10   For those unfamiliar with Rawls' thought on this point, those principles are these two:

> a. Each person has an equal claim to a fully adequate scheme of equal basic rights and liberties, which scheme is compatible with the same scheme for all; and in this scheme the equal political liberties, and only those liberties, are to be guaranteed their fair value.

> b. Social and economic inequalities are to satisfy two conditions: first, they are to be attached to positions and offices open to all under conditions of fair equality of opportunity, and second, they are to be to the greatest benefit of the least advantaged members of society (Rawls, 5–6).

11   Kent Greenawalt, *Religious Convictions and Political Choice* (New York: Oxford University Press, 1988).

12   Kent Greenawalt, *Private Consciences and Public Reasons* (New York: Oxford University Press, 1995).

13   See Rawls, 19: "The basic idea is that in virtue of their two moral powers (a capacity for a sense of justice and for a conception of the good) and the powers of reason (of judgment, thought, and inference connected with these powers), persons are free. Their having these powers to the requisite minimum degree to be fully cooperating members of society makes persons equal."

14   I am thinking here of Charles Taylor's defense of what he calls "the politics of recognition." See "The Politics of Recognition" in the collection of his essays, *Philosophical Arguments* (Cambridge, Mass.: Harvard University Press, 1995).

15   An excellent discussion of this issue, far more expansive than I can intro-
      duce here, is to be found in Nicholas Rescher, *Pluralism* (Oxford: Claren-
      don, 1993), especially chapter 9.

16   Over a good many years I have benefitted from talking with so many people
      about the issues raised in the discussion above that it would be unwise
      now to single any one out. But acknowledgment of my discussions cannot
      be passed by. First, I am much indebted to those who participated in the
      conference on "Religion and Liberalism" held at the University of Notre
      Dame in February 1996—and especially to Paul Weithman, organizer of
      the conference. Second, I have very much profited from the incisive, per-
      ceptive, and challenging comments of my dialogue partner in *Religion and
      the Public Square*, Robert Audi.

Chapter 8

1   I have taken this term from Gerald F. Gaus, who coined it (I think) in
     his *Justificatory Liberalism: An Essay on Epistemology and Political Theory*
     (New York: Oxford University Press, 1996), 3. I should warn the reader,
     however, that my use of that term is quite a bit broader than Gaus': Gaus
     distinguishes his position, "justificatory liberalism," from "political liberal-
     ism," the position Gaus associates most closely with Rawls. Consequently,
     I use "justificatory liberalism" to include Rawls' "political liberalism" as well
     as views that bear important similarities to Rawls' position, such as Gaus'.
     In spite of many significant differences between Rawls' and Gaus' positions,
     I regard the commonalities as far more important than those differences,
     particularly with respect to the implications of their positions for the proper
     role of religious convictions in politics.

2   Sometimes justificatory liberals and, perhaps even more commonly, critics
     of justificatory liberalism, conflate justificatory liberalism with a commit-
     ment to the various substantive political commitments mentioned in the
     prior paragraph. But that identification is neither historically accurate nor
     rationally compelling.

3   This defining commitment of justificatory liberalism raises a variety of
     questions. First, to *whom* does the obligation to provide a public justifica-
     tion apply? Second, what sort of obligation is the obligation to provide
     public justification? Is that obligation moral in nature, or legal as well? And
     if a moral obligation, what sort of moral obligation? Third, to which *kinds
     of political commitments* does the obligation to provide a public justification
     apply? Does it apply only to fundamental constitutional matters, to all
     coercive laws, or to all political commitments? Fourth, in which *contexts*
     does the obligation to provide a public justification apply? Must a citizen
     provide a public justification for her political commitments in any discus-
     sion of political matters (a "private" discussion around the dinner table, for
     example) or only those that most directly impinge on the political process?
     These questions admit of various reasonable but conflicting answers; con-
     sequently, as one might expect, there is no consensus among justificatory
     liberals as to how they ought to be answered. Nevertheless, in order to
     streamline my discussion, I will impute to the justificatory liberal a position
     on each question and, in so doing, construct an "ideal type" of justificatory
     liberalism. The core of that ideal type is as follows: each *citizen* has a moral

obligation to provide public justification for any *coercive* law she supports when *deciding* which coercive laws merit her support and when *advocating* for her favored coercive laws.

4   Amy Gutmann and Dennis Thompson, *Democracy and Disagreement* (Cambridge, Mass.: Belknap Press of Harvard University Press, 1996), 7.

5   This bald claim requires a number of significant qualifications, which I cannot pursue here.

6   Consider in this regard Bruce Ackerman's claim that

> If there is anything distinctive about liberalism, it must be in the kinds of reasons liberals rely on to legitimate their claims to scarce resources. Nazis are not liberals because there is something about the reasons they give in support of their claims that is inconsistent with the organizing principles of liberal power talk.

Bruce Ackerman, *Social Justice in the Liberal State* (New Haven: Yale University Press, 1980), 7. As I see it, the most crucial difference between mere liberalism and Nazism has *nothing* to do with the reasons on the basis of which Nazis and liberals support their characteristic policies, and everything to do with the sorts of policies they support. The defining characteristic of Nazism—*mere* Nazism—is its commitment to various racist policies, nationalism, authoritarianism, militarism, and the like. By contrast, the defining characteristic of liberalism—*mere* liberalism—is its commitment to the very freedoms Nazis are unwilling to support. Of course, liberals are free also to require that the substantive commitments that distinguish the liberal from the Nazi are amenable of a certain sort of rationale—a public justification. In that case, they are not mere but justificatory liberals. But the same basic move is open to the Nazi: as a conceptual matter, there is such a thing as *justificatory Nazism*, just as there is such a thing as justificatory communism, socialism, and the like.

7   Robert Audi, "Liberal Democracy and the Place of Religion in Politics," in *Religion in the Public Square: The Place of Religious Convictions in Political Debate*, ed. Robert Audi and Nicholas Wolterstorff (Lanham, Md.: Rowman & Littlefield, 1997), 1, 16. A 1999 essay by Charles Larmore also exemplifies the confusion between pursuing public justification and exercising restraint. At one point, Larmore claims that the "moral core of liberal thought" is the commitment "*to seek* principles that can be the object of reasonable agreement" among citizens of diverse points of view. Charles Larmore, "The Moral Basis of Liberalism," *Journal of Philosophy* 96 (1999): 602 (emphasis added). The moral core of liberal thought is here characterized as a commitment to pursuing public justification. But several pages later Larmore switches to the doctrine of restraint. He writes, "It is this coercive character of political principles which we have in mind, when we hold with the assurance that we do . . . that such principles must be the object of reasonable agreement. Our belief is that *only so* can the use of force to implement these principles be justified" (607 [emphasis added]). A bit later, Larmore claims that "thus, to respect another person as an end is *to require* that coercive or political principles be as justifiable to that person as they presumably are to us" (608 [emphasis added]). In these last two passages, Larmore claims that a given political principle is legitimate *only if* that principle is the object of reasonable agreement—and, thus, that citizens *should not* support political principles that are not the object of reasonable agreement. The first passage has to do with pursuing public justification, the second two with exercising restraint. Shortly after the third passage I have cited, Larmore reverts to the language

of pursuing public justification: "On the contrary, the idea of respect is what directs us to *seek* the principles of our political life in the area of reasonable agreement" (emphasis added).

8   Audi, "Liberal Democracy," 16 (emphasis added).

9   John Rawls is particularly explicit on this point. He writes:

> Suppose, then, that different combinations of values, or the same values weighted differently, tend to predominate in a particular fundamental case. Everyone appeals to political values but agreement is lacking and more than marginal differences persist. Should this happen, as it often does, some may say that public reason fails to resolve the question, in which case citizens may legitimately invoke principle appealing to nonpolitical values to resolve it in a way they find satisfactory. . . . The ideal of public reason urges us not to do this in cases of constitutional essentials and matters of basic justice. Close agreement is rarely achieved and abandoning public reason whenever disagreement occurs in balancing values is in effect to abandon it altogether.

John Rawls, *Political Liberalism* (New York: Columbia University Press, 1993), 240–41; see also Gaus, 182–84.

10   The distinction I have in mind is similar to that between the putative obligation to "prove that God exists" and the putative obligation not to believe in God if such proof is not in the offering. An agent can be fully committed to proving that God exists but reasonably refuse to cease believing in God because he doesn't enjoy that sort of evidence for her conviction that God exists. Now, perhaps it is the case that those who can't prove that God exists should cease believing in God, but that conclusion cannot be reached simply by showing that theists have an obligation to do what they can to prove that God exists.

11   I assume that abstaining from supporting coercive policies is not a realistic option.

12   Gaus, 162.

13   I fear that I argue in some detail for conclusions that might strike many as obviously true. But overcompensation is warranted, in my opinion, by the fact that many, if not most, of the extant attempts to articulate the argument from respect are insufficiently precise—they often amount to little more than an expression of the "intuition" that respect requires something or other by way of restraint or public justification.

14   Stephen L. Darwall, "Two Kinds of Respect," *Ethics* 88, no. 1 (1977): 36, 38–39. Darwall's distinction between appraisal and recognition respect is similar to Larmore's distinction between respect for beliefs and respect for persons as articulated in Charles Larmore, *Patterns of Moral Complexity* (New York: Cambridge University Press, 1987), 59–66.

15   Darwall, "Two Kinds of Respect," 45.

16   Not only am I willing to defend this claim, but so are most justificatory liberals. Thus, for example, Jeremy Waldron claims that liberals are committed to the "requirement that all aspects of the social should either be made acceptable or be capable of being made acceptable to every last individual." Jeremy Waldron, "Theoretical Foundations of Liberalism," *Philosophical Quarterly* 37 (1987): 127–28. Gerald Gaus is equally clear on this point: "To publicly justify a principle is to show that each and every member of the public has conclusive reason to embrace it." Gaus, 209. So is Bruce Ackerman:

> Like his contractarian comrade, the liberal is also dissatisfied with a utilitarian philosophy that makes an individual's rights depend upon the shifting preferences of his peers. Even if there were only a single person who questioned the legitimacy of his power position; even if the overwhelming majority passionately desired to suppress the questioner; the questioner's right to an answer remains fundamental in liberal theory. To silence this single dissenter would require the dominant coalition to declare that it has the right to treat the dissenter as merely a plaything for their own desires. Such a declaration breaks the dialogic bond that binds all citizens together to form a liberal state. (Ackerman, 340)

17   A complementary point. The quality of a person's beliefs can vary in just the same way that the quality of a person's character traits can vary: some people's beliefs deserve our appraisal respect, some do not. Since a citizen ought to respect each of her compatriots, the sort of respect a citizen owes to her compatriots does not consist in her positive evaluation of, much less agreement with, her compatriots' convictions. In the relevant sense of the notion of respect, a citizen can be thoroughly disgusted by her compatriots' convictions, or regard them as trivial or superficial, and nevertheless be committed to respecting her compatriots fully. In short, a citizen ought to respect each of her compatriots, not because she credits each compatriot's character or beliefs, but, if need be, *in spite of* their character or beliefs. See Larmore, *Patterns of Moral Complexity*, 64.

18   Darwall, "Two Kinds of Respect," 40.

19   I have no intention of articulating a conception of personhood or of identifying necessary and sufficient conditions for personhood. I am interested only in picking out a few relevant components about persons that serve my purposes. In the following account, I rely heavily on Charles Taylor's philosophical anthropology, although I have not incorporated the more controverted elements of his account—for example, his claim that there is an internal relation between personhood and "strong evaluation."

20   To be clear, it is not the fact of mattering itself that imposes moral constraints on us, but that fact in combination with certain moral platitudes that bear on that fact, e.g., that we ought not gratuitously frustrate another person's cares and concerns.

21   See Charles Taylor, *Human Agency and Language* (New York: Cambridge University Press, 1985), 60.

22   On the distinction between higher- and lower-level desires and commitments and the relation between that distinction and the concept of person, see Taylor, 15–44.

23   Appearances notwithstanding, I do *not* mean to endorse a thoroughgoingly proceduralist understanding of rationality. For example, in addition to forming their beliefs by adhering to the appropriate procedures, rationality presupposes that a citizen will enjoy cognitive faculties that function properly at least to a minimal degree. But that is too large a matter to discuss here. My thanks to Robert Audi for pressing this point.

24   Robert Merrihew Adams, *Finite and Infinite Goods: A Framework for Ethics* (New York: Oxford University Press, 1999), 326–27, 334–35.

25   Michael J. Perry, *Love and Power: The Role of Religion and Morality in American Politics* (New York: Oxford University Press, 1991), 135.

26   I take the argument in this section to answer a question forcefully put by Nicholas Wolterstorff, who writes:

> Once again, then, it is obvious that the role of citizen involves restraints on the legislation advocated. But what is the rationale for *epistemological* restraints on the decisions and debates of citizens? That is, why should epistemological restraints be laid on a person *when the legislation advocated by that person does not violate the restraints on content* [that is, is not illiberal]? What difference does it make what reasons citizens use in making their decisions and conducting their debates, if the positions they advocate do not violate the Idea of liberal democracy?

Nicholas Wolterstorff, "The Role of Religion in Decision and Discussion of Political Issues," in *Religion in the Public Square: The Place of Religious Convictions in Political Debate*, ed. Robert Audi and Nicholas Wolterstorff, 67, 77. I take it that Brutus fails adequately to respect his compatriots just in virtue of his willingness to flout the canons of rationality when deciding which coercive laws to support. (I do not think Wolterstorff would disagree, but statements such as the above might be read as a denial that Brutus violates the moral norms properly associated with the role of citizens.) Of course, it is quite another matter to infer from the claim that each citizen ought to withhold her support from coercive laws for which she lacks *rational justification*, the further claim that each citizen ought to withhold her support from coercive laws for which she enjoys only a *religious rationale*. It is the latter claim Wolterstorff is most interested in denying, an aim with which I am entirely sympathetic.

27   I take it that the relation between the obligation to pursue rational justification and the obligation not to support any law for which one cannot discern a rational justification is structurally the same as that between the obligation to pursue public justification and the obligation to exercise restraint. With respect to both sets of obligations, the first member of the set does not entail the second, whereas the second does entail the first.

28   Two brief notes about this point. First, I do not assume that Elijah's willingness to articulate a rationale for a favored coercive law by itself ameliorates his compatriots' distress: in fact, Elijah's articulation of a rationale could easily exacerbate his compatriots' distress if his rationale is particularly offensive. Rather, Elijah's articulation of a rationale ameliorates his compatriots' distress if he makes it clear why he addresses his compatriots, viz., because he accords significant value to the fact that his compatriots are agents. Second, mitigation is not compensation: the fact that Elijah articulates a rationale for a favored coercive law is highly unlikely to "outweigh" the distress generated by his support for that coercive law, particularly if his compatriots regard that law as quite objectionable.

29   William Galston, *Liberal Purposes* (New York: Cambridge University Press, 1991), 109.

30   This *disjunctive* conception of public justification is endorsed by Gerald Gaus: "We can think, then, of a public justification as a set of arguments for a proposal; sometimes the set may contain only one argument, at other times it may involve several." Gaus, 146.

31   The notion of remoteness is incurably vague, and I will not even attempt to render it more precise.

32   Michael J. Perry, *Religion in Politics* (New York: Oxford University Press, 1997), 64.

33   Nicholas Rescher, *Pluralism: Against the Demand for Consensus* (New York: Oxford University Press, 1993), 163.

34   Rescher, 164.

35   Robert Audi is clear about the intuitive pull of the doctrine of restraint, at least as relevant to religious convictions. He writes:

> For any of us who are religious, the prospect that we might be coerced by preferences based on some other religion is generally loathsome. Few have a similar reaction to coercion plausibly imposed for purposes of maintaining law and order or public health or a minimum level of education. Liberalism is in part a response to the intuitive difference nearly everyone feels in such cases.

Robert Audi, "Wolterstorff on Religion, Politics and the Liberal State," in Audi and Wolterstorff, *Religion in the Public Square*, 121.

36   "Colorado to Vote on Barring Gay-Rights Laws," *New York Times*, May 24, 1992, § 1, A31. McCartney is here alluding to Leviticus 18:22: "You shall not lie with a male as one lies with a female; it is an abomination" (RSV). According to one insider, the press conference at which McCartney expressed his support for Amendment 2 was crucial in jump-starting an otherwise moribund petition drive. See Stephen Bransford, *Gay Rights Vs. Colorado and America: The Inside Story of Amendment 2* (Cascade, Colo.: Sardis, 1994), 54.

37   Audi, "Liberal Democracy," 25.

38   Audi, "Wolterstorff on Religion," 141.

39   Robert Audi, *Religious Commitment and Secular Reason* (New York: Cambridge University Press, 2000), 201.

40   Audi, "*Liberal Democracy,*" 28. Audi formulates his role-reversal argument later on in the same essay as follows:

> What I may not do without adequate secular reason . . . is advocate or support *coercive* laws or public policies on this or other matters that concern me. That, too, is a kind of restraint I would wish to be observed by members of other religious groups who would want to coerce my behavior in the direction of their religiously preferred standards. (51)

41   See R. M. Hare, *Moral Thinking: Its Levels, Method and Point* (New York: Oxford University Press, 1981), 24–64 (discussing distinctions between two levels of moral thinking).

42   I hesitate to claim that I would feel resentment because there is a close relationship between resentment and blameworthiness: I resent others for performing some action only if I am willing to blame them for performing that action. And I feel no inclination at all to blame a citizen for supporting a coercive law if she is rationally justified to a sufficiently high degree in regarding that law as morally appropriate, pursues public justification for that law, is sufficiently accommodating, etc. Nevertheless, it seems to me that, if a law is sufficiently objectionable, I can resent being subject to that law even if I do not blame those who support that law. Thus, for example, it would be appropriate for a slave to feel resentment regarding his condition as a consequence of the sheer injustice of that condition even if he thought that his owner did not know any better.

43   Audi has suggested, in conversation, that his argument does not have this weakness; that it does not depend on the contingent reactions of just any

citizens. Rather, his role-reversal test is supposed to apply to fully rational and adequately informed citizens. Would fully rational and adequately informed citizens be willing to endorse a general policy permitting their compatriots to support coercive laws solely on religious grounds? But it seems likely to me that this move will ultimately turn out to beg the central question at issue: the manner in which we construe "full rationality" and "adequate information" will mirror our position on the merits of the doctrine of restraint. Thus, for example, those who believe that God exists and has authored an authoritative text (the Koran, for example) will naturally assume that adequately informed citizens will be aware that the Koran is divinely inspired and thus will assent to the claims revealed therein. After all, if one is firmly convinced that the Koran is authored by God, why would one believe that an adequately informed citizen could be ignorant of so important a fact?

44   Stephen Macedo, "Liberal Civic Education and Religious Fundamentalism: The Case of God v. John Rawls?" *Ethics* 105, no. 3 (1995): 468, 482.

45   Macedo, 480.

46   I know of no theorist who denies the claim that it is a good and desirable thing for citizens to cooperate with one another by trying to articulate a public justification for their favored coercive laws. However, I have seen that view attributed to critics of justificatory liberalism. For example, Paul Weithman makes the following claim: "Even the weak requirement seems plausible only if Rawls assumes the desirability and possibility of a society in which citizens cooperate on the basis of their common reasonability. But it is just these assumptions that Wolterstorff, like Quinn, calls into question." Paul J. Weithman, "Introduction: Religion and the Liberalism of Reasoned Respect," in *Religion and Contemporary Liberalism*, ed. Paul J. Weithman (Notre Dame: University of Notre Dame Press, 1997), 1, 21. As I read them, neither Nicholas Wolterstorff nor Philip Quinn denies the *desirability* of cooperation on the basis of common reasonability. They deny its *possibility* (in most cases) and therefore deny the desirability of *thinking* that we can cooperate on the basis of common reasonability when we cannot. This is, of course, consistent with the claim that such cooperation would be desirable if it were possible and that such cooperation is desirable in those instances when it is possible.

Chapter 9

1   John Rawls, *Political Liberalism* (New York: Columbia University Press, 1996), 13.

2   Rawls, 257–88.

3   Rawls, 254.

4   Rawls, 54–58.

5   Rawls, xxiv.

6   For just one example, see Stephen Carter, *The Culture of Disbelief* (New York: Basic Books, 1993), 53.

7   The best evidence that people will make such a slide is to be found in the scholarly literature on public reason itself. Despite Rawls' insistence that he defends an inclusive view, even well-informed readers commonly claim that his guidelines on public reason exclude religious reasons from political debate.

8   Christian Smith, *American Evangelicalism: Embattled but Thriving* (Chicago: University of Chicago Press, 1999).

9   A story titled "GOP retreating from hard stand against abortion," *New York Times*, Monday, June 21, 1999, A13, reported: "Even Pat Robertson, founder of the Christian Coalition, asserted last month that pressing for a constitutional amendment [banning abortion] was unrealistic, saying 'A strategic, incremental approach is much more effective.' He added, 'We must win an election.'"

10   For the American case, see generally Alan Wolfe, *One Nation, After All* (New York: Viking Penguin, 1998), 57–61.

11   [For these data, see chapter 2 of Paul Weithman, *Religion and the Obligations of Citizenship* (New York: Cambridge University Press, 2002)].

12   On idealization and abstraction, see Onora O'Neill, "Constructivisms in Ethics," in *Constructions of Reason* (New York: Cambridge University Press, 1989), 206–18, especially 210, where she remarks: "Idealization masquerading as abstraction produces theories that may appear to apply widely, but in fact covertly exclude from their scope those who do not match a certain ideal. They privilege certain sorts of human agents and life by presenting their specific characteristics as universal ideals."

13   Taylor Branch, "Uneasy Holiday," *New Republic*, February 3, 1986. The essay is reprinted in Dorothy Wickenden, ed., *The New Republic Reader* (New York: Basic Books, 1994), 419–48; the quoted passage is from 426. For a sophisticated attempt to find a basis of agreement in King's views, see Joshua Cohen, "The Arc of the Moral Universe," *Philosophy and Public Affairs* 26 (1997): 91–134, especially 133–34.

14   See Alan Wolfe's review of Taylor Branch's *Pillar of Fire: America in the King Years, 1963–65* (New York: Simon & Schuster, 1998), *New York Times Book Review*, January 18, 1998, 13.

Chapter 10

1   John Rawls, *Political Liberalism* (New York: Columbia University Press, 1993; paperback ed., 1996). Hereafter cited as PL. For a detailed account of the social contract as a set of principles "that could not reasonably be rejected, by people who were moved to find principles for the general regulation of behavior that others, similarly motivated, could not reasonably reject," see Thomas M. Scanlon, *What We Owe To Each Other* (Cambridge, Mass.: Harvard University Press, 1998), 4 and passim.

2   Nicholas Wolterstorff, "The Role of Religion in Decision and Discussion of Political Issues," in *Religion in the Public Square: The Place of Religious Convictions in Political Debate* (Lanham, Md.: Rowman & Littlefield, 1997), 94; emphasis in original.

3   John Rawls, *Collected Papers*, ed. Samuel Freeman (Cambridge, Mass.: Harvard University Press, 1999), 573–615. Hereafter cited as CP.

4   For useful criticism, see Kent Greenawalt, *Religious Convictions and Political Choice* (New York: Oxford University Press, 1988) and *Private Consciences and Public Reasons* (New York: Oxford University Press, 1995); and Wolterstorff, "The Role of Religion," 67–120. The most thorough and powerfully argued treatment of the general topic is now Christopher J. Eberle, *Religious Conviction in Liberal Politics* (New York: Cambridge University Press, 2002). See also Ronald F. Thiemano, *Religion in Public Life: A Dilemma for Democracy* (Washington, D.C.: Georgetown University Press, 1996).

5   Wolterstorff briefly discusses the relationship between entitlement and the Rawlsian sense of "reasonableness" in "The Role of Religion," 91.

6   Wolterstorff, "The Role of Religion," 105; emphasis in original.

7   Wolterstorff makes a related point about respect and particularity in "The Role of Religion," 110–18.

8   Notice that even on the amended version of Rawls' position, this would not be enough.

9   For illuminating remarks on the importance of attending to the "concrete" other, see Seyla Benhabib, *Situating the Self: Gender, Community, and Postmodernism in Contemporary Ethics* (New York: Routledge, 1992), esp. chap. 5.

10   Wolterstorff, "The Role of Religion," 109.

11   I am not addressing the distinctive issues surrounding the roles of judge, juror, attorney, or public official.

12   I . . . consider Hauerwas' arguments and give relevant references to his works in chapters 6 and 7 [of *Democracy and Tradition* (Princeton: Princeton University Press, 2004)].

13   One could also reasonably complain that the now rather baroque theory is simply too complicated to serve its intended public purpose as an action guide. If these scruples were to be followed by the masses, we would all need catechetical instruction from the Rawlsians.

14   The term *public* is to be understood here in its ordinary sense. Hauerwas was not speaking at a campaign rally or before a congressional committee. So Rawls might say that this case does not involve the "public forum" and that his scruples would therefore not apply. But why should this matter? Suppose another Christian pacifist did speak at a campaign rally for a political candidate representing the Green Party. Wouldn't it be good, all things considered, for her arguments to circulate publicly? How can we know in advance that they won't be persuasive? Suppose the speaker resists translating her arguments about the sanctity of human life into a Rawlsian vocabulary. Must we then condemn her for failing to satisfy the proviso?

15   The phrase appears as the title of chapter 4 in Stanley Hauerwas, *Dispatches from the Front: Theological Engagements with the Secular* (Durham: Duke University Press, 1994), where Hauerwas portrays Walter Rauschenbusch and Reinhold Niebuhr as complicit in "the exclusion from the politics of democracy of any religious convictions that are not 'humble'" (104). Hauerwas asks: "Does that mean I do not support 'democracy'? I have to confess I have not got the slightest idea, since I do not know what it means to call this society 'democratic.' Indeed, one of the troubling aspects about such a question is the assumption that how Christians answer it might matter" (105). In [*Democracy and Tradition*], I am trying to say what it might mean to call this society "democratic" and why it might matter how Christians answer that question.

16   John Rawls, *Lectures on the History of Moral Philosophy*, ed. Barbara Herman (Cambridge, Mass.: Harvard University Press, 2000), 329–71.

17   In the next several paragraphs, I will be relying on Robert Brandom, "Freedom and Constraint by Norms," in *Hermeneutics and Praxis*, ed. Robert Hollinger (Notre Dame: University of Notre Dame Press, 1985), 173–91. Brandom mentions arts and sports on 187.

18   Brandom, "Freedom," 185; emphasis in original.

19   Robert Brandom, "Some Pragmatist Themes in Hegel's Idealism: Negotiation and Administration in Hegel's Account of the Structure and Content

of Conceptual Norms," *European Journal of Philosophy* 7, no. 2 (1999): 164–89; emphasis in original.

20   Brandom, "Some Pragmatist Themes," 179.
21   Brandom, "Some Pragmatist Themes," 166; emphasis in original.
22   These expressivist considerations explain why Wolterstorff is right to say that we do not need a political basis of the kind that Rawls is seeking: "We aim at agreement in our discussions with each other. But we do not for the most part aim at achieving agreement concerning a political basis; rather, we aim at agreement concerning the particular policy, law, or constitutional provision under consideration. Our agreement on some policy need not be based on some set of principles *agreed on* by all present and future citizens and *rich enough* to settle all important political issues. Sufficient if each citizen, for his or her own reasons, agrees on the policy today and tomorrow— not for all time. It need not even be the case that each and every citizen agrees to the policy. Sufficient if the agreement be the fairly gained and fairly executed agreement of the majority" ("The Role of Religion," 114; emphasis in original).
23   Brandom, "Freedom and Constraint," 189.
24   Compare Wolterstorff, "The Role of Religion," 112–14.
25   Richard Rorty, "Religion as Conversation-Stopper," in *Philosophy and Social Hope* (London: Penguin Books, 1999), 168–74. Hereafter cited as PSH.
26   Robert B. Brandom, *Making It Explicit: Reasoning, Representing, and Discursive Commitment* (Cambridge, Mass.: Harvard University Press, 1994), 228; idem, *Articulating Reasons: An Introduction to Inferentialism* (Cambridge, Mass.: Harvard University Press, 2000), 105, hereafter cited as AR.
27   Greenawalt, *Religious Convictions*, chaps. 6–9.
28   Richard Rorty, *Contingency, Irony, and Solidarity* (New York: Cambridge University Press, 1989), 73.
29   Richard Rorty, *Philosophy and the Mirror of Nature* (Princeton: Princeton University Press, 1979).
30   Rorty, *Philosophy and the Mirror of Nature*, 389; emphasis in original.
31   Rorty, *Philosophy and the Mirror of Nature*, 389–90.
32   Johanna Goth made a similar point in her senior thesis for the Department of Philosophy at Princeton University (spring term, 2000).

Chapter 12

1   See Michael J. Perry, *The Idea of Human Rights: Four Inquiries* (New York: Oxford University Press, 1998), 11–41.
2   Samuel Brittan, "Making Common Cause: How Liberals Differ, and What They Ought to Agree On," *Times Literary Supplement*, September 20, 1996, 3–4. Cf. Charles Larmore, "The Moral Basis of Political Liberalism," *Journal of Philosophy* 96 (1999): 599, 624–25 (arguing that "our commitment to [liberal] democracy . . . cannot be understood except by appeal to a higher moral authority, which is the obligation to respect one another as persons").
3   Larmore, "The Moral Basis of Political Liberalism," 621.
4   The conference—a Calvin College Seminar in Christian Scholarship— took place May 27–29, 1999, at Calvin College, Grand Rapids, Michigan. Nicholas Wolterstorff, the Noah Porter Professor of Philosophical Theology at Yale University, organized and hosted the conference.

5   What about judges? Are they a special case? See Michael J. Perry, *Religion in Politics: Constitutional and Moral Perspectives* (New York: Oxford University Press, 1997), at 102–4; see also "Religion and the Judicial Process: Legal, Ethical, and Empirical Dimensions," *Marquette Law Review* 81 (1998): 177–567.

6   See Perry, *Religion in Politics*, 32–33. Cf. *McDaniel v. Paty*, 435 U.S. 618, 640–41 (1978) (J. Brennan concurring in judgment):

> That public debate of religious ideas, like any other, may arouse emotion, may incite, may foment religious divisiveness and strife does not rob it of constitutional protection. . . . The mere fact that a purpose of the Establishment Clause is to reduce or eliminate religious divisiveness or strife does not place religious discussion, association, or political participation in a status less preferred than rights of discussion, association, and political participation generally. . . . The State's goal of preventing sectarian bickering and strife may not be accomplished by regulating religious speech and political association. . . . Government may not as a goal promote "safe thinking" with respect to religion. . . . The Establishment Clause, properly understood, . . . may not be used as a sword to justify repression of religion or its adherents from any aspect of public life.

7   Mark Tushnet, "The Limits of the Involvement of Religion in the Body Politic," in *The Role of Religion in the Making of Public Policy*, ed. James E. Wood Jr., and Derek Davis (Waco, Tex.: J. M. Dawson Institute of Church-State Studies, Baylor University, 1991), 191, 213.

8   Richard Rorty, "Religion as Conversation-Stopper," in *Philosophy and Social Hope* (New York: Penguin, 1999), 168–69.

9   Jeffrey Siker, a Christian ethicist and ordained minister of the Presbyterian Church (USA), has persuasively criticized the effort to analogize homosexuality to alcoholism. See Jeffrey S. Siker, "Homosexual Christians, the Bible, and Gentile Inclusion: Confessions of a Repenting Heterosexist," in *Homosexuality in the Church: Both Sides of the Debate*, ed. Jeffrey S. Siker (Louisville, Ky.: Westminster John Knox, 1994), 178, 181–83.

10   Luke Timothy Johnson, "Religious Rights and Christian Texts," in *Religious Human Rights in Global Perspective: Religious Perspectives*, ed. John Witte Jr., and Johan David van der Vyver (The Hague: Martinus Nijhoff, 1996), 65, 72–73.

11   Indeed, American history does not suggest that debates about religious (theological) issues are invariably more divisive than debates about political issues. To the contrary: "Religious differences in this country have never generated the civil discord experienced in political conflicts over such issues as the Vietnam War, racial segregation, the Red Scare, unionization, or slavery." Michael W. McConnell, "Political and Religious Disestablishment," *Brigham Young University Law Review* (1986): 405, 413.

12   One might be tempted to claim that even if relying on religiously grounded moral argument, in public debate about whether to disfavor conduct, will usually *not* be more divisive than relying only on secularly grounded moral belief, the fact remains that the totality of the good consequences minus the totality of the bad consequences of relying only on secularly grounded moral belief is a number that is greater than the number reached by subtracting the totality of the bad consequences from the totality of the good consequences of relying on religiously grounded moral belief. But that

would be a difficult claim to sustain. As Chris Eberle has explained, in a July 21, 2000, e-mail message to me:

1. The argument to which you are objecting is a *consequentialist* argument: it mandates restraint regarding religion in virtue of the undesirable consequences of refusing to privatize religion. The undesirable consequences are, of course, the division, alienation, frustration, resentment, etc., religious believers cause when they bring their religious convictions into the public square.

2. I take your objection to the argument from divisiveness to be a point about consistency: religious discourse is no *more* divisive than secular discourse, so it is *arbitrary* to mandate restraint regarding the former but not the latter on grounds of divisiveness.

3. Regarding many formulations of the argument from divisiveness, I take your objection to be utterly compelling.

4. But I think that the version of the argument mentioned in 1 can't (or shouldn't) be the argument its proponents have in mind (in spite of the fact that they very often formulate it in the very terms you attack!). The reason why has to do with the nature of consequentialist arguments. As I understand them, a consequentialist argument requires a fair amount of "higher math": the proponent must identify *all* of the relevant alternatives, identify *all* of the relevant consequences of each alternative, "add" up all the positive consequences of each alternative, "subtract" the negative consequences from the sum just arrived at. The alternative that generates the higher net total of beneficial consequences, or at least the lower negative total, is the morally preferable alternative.

5. So as I see it, the two relevant alternatives are: to privatize religion or not to privatize religion. Otherwise put, the two relevant alternatives are: public discourse that is only secular or public discourse that is both secular and religious.

6. The next step is to identify the likely consequences of those alternatives, add, subtract, and compare.

7. One immediate consequence of this point about the nature of the argument from divisiveness: that argument can succeed even if you are correct that secular discourse is just as divisive as religious discourse. Indeed, it can succeed even if secular discourse is *more* divisive than religious discourse. The reason is, as I see it, as follows: even though secular discourse might generate a larger amount of division than religious discourse, it is counterbalanced by a large quantity of positive consequences that far "outweighs" the bad consequences of secular discourse (including divisiveness). And this seems right: the value of public deliberation regarding political policies is a very weighty good; public deliberation in at least secular terms is essential to healthy public deliberation; consequently, the deficits of secular discourse are far outweighed by the benefits of secular discourse.

8. Another implication of this point about the consequentialist nature of the argument from divisiveness. If it is going to work,

and if it is going to avoid the kind of consistency objection you level against it, its proponents will have to make good on the following claim: that the consequences of privatizing religion are more beneficial, all things considered, than are the consequences of refusing to privatize religion. That is, the relevant difference between religious and secular discourse is that the negative consequences of the former are *not* outweighed by the positive consequences of the former but the negative consequences of the latter *are* outweighed by the positive consequences of the latter (or something like that).

9. If this is correct, then it seems obvious that the argument from divisiveness is going to be a *lot* more complicated and difficult to pull off than its proponents often imagine. Regarding the formulations I am aware of, they almost always fail to recognize the implications of the fact that they are presenting a consequentialist argument and thus satisfy themselves with the observation that refusing to privatize religious commitments is very divisive. But that's nowhere nearly sufficient to make their case. They must also determine whether those divisive consequences are outweighed by the positive consequences. That's a *monumental* task, and no one I know of has come even close to doing it.

10. This might seem to be a small point, but, personally, I take it to be essential. If those who advocate restraint want to appeal to the consequences of refusing to privatize religion, then they have to do more than just selectively identify some of the negative consequences of refusing to privatize religion (which is what typically happens). And once they have to make that more complicated case, I think that it is plausible to suppose (and argue in my manuscript) that the argument from divisiveness fails.

The manuscript to which Eberle refers in his final sentence has now been published: Christopher J. Eberle, *Religious Conviction in Liberal Politics* (New York: Cambridge University Press, 2002).

13   John A. Coleman, SJ, *An American Strategic Theology* (New York: Paulist, 1982), 192–95. Coleman adds: "I am further strongly convinced that the Enlightenment desire for an unmediated universal fraternity and language (resting as it did on unreflected allegiance to *very* particular communities and language, conditioned by time and culture) was destructive of the lesser, real 'fraternities'—in [Wilson Carey] McWilliams' sense—in American life" (194).

14   See Daniel O. Conkle, "Different Religions, Different Politics: Evaluating the Role of Competing Religious Traditions in American Politics and Law," in *Journal of Law and Religion* 10, no. 1 (1993–1994).

15   David Tracy speaks for many of us religious believers when he writes:

For believers to be unable to learn from secular feminists on the patriarchal nature of most religions or to be unwilling to be challenged by Feuerbach, Darwin, Marx, Freud, or Nietzsche is to refuse to take seriously the religion's own suspicions on the existence of those fundamental distortions named sin, ignorance, or illusion. The interpretations of believers will, of course, be grounded in some fundamental trust in, and loyalty to, the Ultimate Reality both disclosed and concealed in one's own religious tradition. But fundamental trust, as any experience of friendship can teach, is not immune to either criticism or suspicion. A religious person will ordinarily fashion some hermeneutics of trust, even one of friendship and love, for the religious classics of her or his tradition. But, as any genuine understanding of friendship shows, friendship often demands both critique and suspicion. A belief in a pure and innocent love is one of the less happy inventions of the romantics. A friendship that never includes critique and even, when appropriate, suspicion is a friendship barely removed from the polite and wary communication of strangers. As Buber showed, in every I-Thou encounter, however transient, we encounter some new dimension of reality. But if that encounter is to prove more than transitory, the difficult ways of friendship need a trust powerful enough to risk itself in critique and suspicion. To claim that this may be true of all our other loves but not true of our love for, and trust in, our religious tradition makes very little sense either hermeneutically or religiously. (David Tracy, *Plurality and Ambiguity: Hermeneutics, Religion, Hope* [San Francisco: Harper & Row, 1987], 112).

To his credit, Richard Rorty insists that there is "hypocrisy . . . in saying that believers somehow have no right to base their political views on their religious faith, whereas we atheists have every right to base ours on Enlightenment philosophy. The claim that in doing so we are appealing to reason, whereas the religious are being irrational, is hokum." Rorty, "Religion as Conversation-Stopper," 172.

16   As David Tracy has written, religion is "the single subject about which many intellectuals can feel free to be ignorant. Often abetted by the churches, they need not study religion, for 'everybody' already knows what religion is: It is a private consumer product that some people seem to need. Its former social role was poisonous. Its present privatization is harmless enough to wish it well from a civilized distance. Religion seems to be the sort of thing one likes 'if that's the sort of thing one likes.'" David Tracy, *The Analogical Imagination* (New York: Crossroad, 1981), 13. See also Kent Greenawalt, *Religious Convictions and Political Choice* (New York: Oxford University Press, 1988), 6: "A good many professors and other intellectuals display a hostility or skeptical indifference to religion that amounts to a thinly disguised contempt for belief in any reality beyond that discoverable by scientific inquiry and ordinary human experience."

17   See Greenawalt, *Religious Convictions and Political Choice*, 159: "If the worry is open-mindedness and sensitivity to publicly accessible reasons, drawing a sharp distinction between religious convictions and [secular] personal bases [of judgment] would be an extremely crude tool."

David Tracy has lamented that "for however often the word is bandied about, dialogue remains a rare phenomenon in anyone's experience. Dialogue demands the intellectual, moral, and, at the limit, religious ability to struggle to hear another and to respond. To respond critically, and even suspiciously when necessary, but to respond only in dialogical relationship to a real, not a projected other." David Tracy, *Dialogue with the Other* (Grand Rapids: Eerdmans, 1990), 4. Steven Smith, commenting wryly that "'dialogue' seems to have become the all-purpose elixir of our time," has suggested that "[t]he hard question is not whether people should talk, but rather what they should say and what (among the various ideas communicated) they should believe." Steven D. Smith, "The Pursuit of Pragmatism," *Yale Law Journal* 100 (1990): 409, 434–35. As Tracy's observation suggests, however, there is yet another "hard" question, which Smith's suggestion tends to obscure. It is not *whether* but *how* people should talk—what qualities of character and mind they should bring, or try to bring, to the task.

18   David Hollenbach, SJ, "Civil Society: Beyond the Public-Private Dichotomy," *The Responsive Community* (1994/1995): 15, 22. One of the religious communities to which Hollenbach refers is the Catholic community. See David Hollenbach, SJ, "Contexts of the Political Role of Religion: Civil Society and Culture," *San Diego Law Review* 30 (1990): 877, 891:

> For example, the Catholic tradition provides some noteworthy evidence that discourse across the boundaries of diverse communities is both possible and potentially fruitful when it is pursued seriously. This tradition, in its better moments, has experienced considerable success in efforts to bridge the divisions that have separated it from other communities with other understandings of the good life. In the first and second centuries, the early Christian community moved from being a small Palestinian sect to active encounter with the Hellenistic and Roman worlds. In the fourth century, Augustine brought biblical faith into dialogue with Stoic and Neoplatonic thought. His efforts profoundly transformed both Christian and Greco-Roman thought and practice. In the thirteenth century Thomas Aquinas once again transformed Western Christianity by appropriating ideas from Aristotle that he had learned from Arab Muslims and from Jews. In the process he also transformed Aristotelian ways of thinking in fundamental ways. Not the least important of these transformations was his insistence that the political life of a people is not the highest realization of the good of which they are capable—an insight that lies at the root of constitutional theories of limited government. And though the Church resisted the liberal discovery of modern freedoms through much of the modern period, liberalism has been transforming Catholicism once again through the last half of [the twentieth] century. The memory of these events in social and intellectual history as well as the experience of the Catholic Church since the Second Vatican Council leads me to hope that communities holding different visions of the good life can get somewhere if they are willing to risk conversation and argument about these visions. Injecting such hope back into the public life of the United States would be a signal achievement. Today, it appears to be not only desirable but necessary.

See also Hollenbach, "Contexts of the Political Role of Religion," 892–96.

19   See Hollenbach, "Civil Society," 22:

> Conversation and argument about the common good [including religious conversation and argument] will not occur initially in the legislature or in the political sphere (narrowly conceived as the domain in which conflict of interest and power are adjudicated). Rather it will develop freely in those components of civil society that are the primary bearers of cultural meaning and

value—universities, religious communities, the world of the arts, and serious journalism. It can occur wherever thoughtful men and women bring their beliefs on the meaning of the good life into intelligent and critical encounter with understandings of this good held by other peoples with other traditions. In short, it occurs wherever education about and serious inquiry into the meaning of the good life takes place.

20   Hollenbach, "Contexts of the Political Role of Religion," 900. Cf. Kent Greenawalt, "Religious Convictions and Political Choice: Some Further Thoughts," *DePaul Law Review* 39 (1990): 1019, 1034 (expressing skepticism about "the promise of religious perspectives being transformed in what is primarily political debate").

21   Hollenbach, "Contexts of the Political Role of Religion," 900.

22   See chapter 2 [of Michael Perry, *Under God? Religious Faith and Liberal Democracy* (New York: Cambridge University Press, 2003)], note 25.

23   Paul G. Stern, "A Pluralistic Reading of the First Amendment and Its Relation to Public Discourse," *Yale Law Journal* 99 (1990): 925, 934.

24   No one suggests that presenting religiously grounded moral belief in *nonpublic* political argument—political argument around the kitchen table, for example, or at a meeting of the local parish's Peace and Justice Committee—is illegitimate. A practical problem with the position that presenting religiously grounded moral belief in public political argument is somehow illegitimate is that it might sometimes be difficult to say when "nonpublic" political argument has crossed the line and become "public." Moreover, it is no more possible to maintain "an airtight barrier" between the religiously grounded moral discourse that takes place in nonpublic political argument and that which takes place in public political argument than it is to maintain an airtight barrier between the religiously grounded moral discourse that takes place in "universities, religious communities, the world of the arts, and serious journalism" and that which takes place in "the domains of government and policy-formation." Why not, then, just welcome the presentation of religiously grounded moral belief in public as well as in relatively nonpublic political argument?

25   Michael J. Perry, *Morality, Politics, and Law* (New York: Oxford University Press, 1988), 183. The point is not that we must be open to the possibility of religious conversion, least of all conversion to a fundamentalist faith. What is the point, then? Jeremy Waldron articulates it well:

> Even if people are exposed in argument to ideas over which they are bound to disagree—and how could *any* doctrine of public deliberation preclude *that*?—it does not follow that such exposure is pointless or oppressive. For one thing, it is important for people to be acquainted with the views that others hold. Even more important, however, is the possibility that my own view may be improved, in its subtlety and depth, by exposure to a religion or a metaphysics that I am initially inclined to reject. . . . I mean . . . to draw attention to an experience we all have at one time or another, of having argued with someone whose worldview was quite at odds with our own, and of having come away thinking, "I'm sure he's wrong, and I can't follow much of it, but, still, it makes you think. . . ." The prospect of losing that sort of effect in public discourse is, frankly, frightening—terrifying,

even, if we are to imagine it's being replaced by a kind of "deliberation" that, in the name of "fairness" or "reasonableness" (or worse still, "balance") consists of bland appeals to harmless nostrums that are accepted without question on all sides. This is to imagine open-ended public debate reduced to the formal trivia of American televisions networks. . . . [This] might apply to *any* religious or other philosophically contentious intervention. We do not have (and we should not have) so secure a notion of public consensus, or such stringent requirements of fairness in debate, as to exclude any view from having its effect in the marketplace of ideas. (Jeremy Waldron, "Religious Contributions in Public Deliberation," *San Diego Law Review* 30 [1993]: 817, 841–42.)

See also Michael J. Sandel, "Political Liberalism," *Harvard Law Review* 107 (1994): 1765, 1794: "It is always possible that learning more about a moral or religious doctrine will lead us to like it less. But the respect of deliberation and engagement affords a more spacious public reason than liberalism allows. It is also a more suitable ideal for a pluralist society. To the extent that our moral and religious disagreements reflect the ultimate plurality of human goods, a deliberative mode of respect will better enable us to appreciate the distinctive goods our different lives express."

Kent Greenawalt and John Rawls have each defended a position (though not the same position) less congenial to the airing of religiously grounded moral belief in public political argument than the position I have defended here. I have explained elsewhere why I disagree both with Greenawalt's position and with Rawls'. See Perry, *Religion in Politics*, 49–61.

26   See note 8.
27   See Michael J. Perry, "Freedom of Religion in the United States: Fin de Siècle Sketches," *Indiana Law Journal* 75 (2000): 295, 327–29.
28   I therefore disagree with John Rawls (and others, such as Robert Audi) on this important point, as I have explained elsewhere. See Perry, *Religion in Politics*, 54–61.
29   Nicholas Wolterstorff, "Audi on Religion, Politics, and Liberal Democracy," in *Religion in the Public Square*, ed. Robert Audi and Nicholas Wolterstorff (Lanham, Md.: Rowman & Littlefield, 1997), 145, 147. See also Douglas Laycock, "Freedom of Speech That Is Both Religious and Political," *University of California, Davis Law Review* 29 (1996): 793; Michael W. McConnell, "Correspondence: Getting Along," *First Things*, June–July 1996, 2. Cf. Sanford Levinson, "Religious Language and the Public Square," *Harvard Law Review* 105 (1992): 2061, 2077 (suggesting that "liberal democracy give[s] everyone an equal chance, without engaging in any version of epistemic abstinence, to make his or her arguments, subject, obviously, to the prerogative of listeners to reject the arguments should they be unpersuasive").
30   See note 3.
31   See John Rawls, *Political Liberalism* (New York: Columbia University Press, 1993), 217.
32   Stephen Macedo, "Transformative Constitutionalism and the Case of Religion: Defending the Moderate Hegemony of Liberalism," *Political Theory* 26 (1998): 56, 71.
33   William A. Galston, *Liberal Purposes* (New York: Cambridge University Press, 1991), 108–9.

34   Michael J. Perry, "Religious Morality and Political Choice: Further Thoughts—and Second Thoughts—on *Love and Power*," *San Diego Law Review* 30 (1993): 703, 711 n. 23 (quoting Larmore).
35   Larmore, "The Moral Basis of Political Liberalism," 611 (emphasis added).
36   I have oversimplified. Eberle develops and defends this important position with great care in his excellent *Religious Conviction in Liberal Politics*.
37   See, e.g., Robert Audi, *Religious Commitment and Secular Reason* (New York: Cambridge University Press, 2000), 197.
38   Robert Audi, "The Place of Religious Argument in a Free and Democratic Society," *San Diego Law Review* 30 (1993): 677, 701. I wonder what it might mean for one to be "fully rational"—and also what "concepts we share as rational beings."
39   Gerald R. Dworkin, "Equal Respect and the Enforcement of Morality," *Social Philosophy & Policy* 7 (1990): 180, 193 (criticizing Ronald Dworkin). See also John M. Finnis, *Natural Law and Natural Rights* (Oxford: Clarendon, 1980), 221–22 (criticizing Ronald Dworkin). I concur in Nicholas Wolterstorff's critique of Audi's position on this point. See Wolterstorff, "Audi on Religion, Politics, and Liberal Democracy," 159–61. It seems to me that in his essay on "the moral basis of political liberalism," Larmore fails to close the gap to which Gerald Dworkin refers. See Larmore, "The Moral Basis of Political Liberalism," 608 and n. 13.
40   Put another way, it is altogether obscure why one does not show her compatriots the respect that is their due if she adheres to what Chris Eberle calls "the ideal of conscientious engagement." See Eberle, *Religious Conviction in Liberal Politics*, 104–8.
41   The argument from divisiveness, unlike the argument from respect, is a consequentialist argument. One might be tempted to mount a more complicated version of the argument, according to which even if basing a political choice on a controversial moral belief will *not* usually be more divisive if there is only a religious ground for the belief than if there is a secular ground, the fact remains that the totality of the good consequences minus the totality of the bad consequences of basing a political choice on a controversial moral belief that has a secular ground is a number that is greater than the number reached by subtracting the totality of the bad consequences from the totality of the good consequences of basing a political choice on a controversial moral belief that has only a religious ground. But so far as I know, no one has tried to make an argument in support of *that* claim—a claim that in any event would be difficult to sustain. See note 12.
42   Lawrence B. Solum, "Faith and Justice," *DePaul University Law Review* 39 (1990): 1083, 1096. Solum is stating the argument, not making it. Indeed, Solum is wary of the argument. See also 1096–97. Solum cites, as an instance of the argument, Stephen L. Carter, "The Religiously Devout Judge," *Notre Dame Law Review* 64 (1989): 932, 939. For another instance, see Maimon Schwarzschild, "Religion and Public Debate in a Liberal Society: Always Oil and Water or Sometimes More Like Rum and Coca-Cola?," *San Diego Law Review* 30 (1993): 903.
43   John Courtney Murray, *We Hold These Truths* (Kansas City, Mo.: Sheed & Ward, 1960), 23–24.
44   Kent Greenawalt, *Private Consciences and Public Reasons* (New York: Oxford University Press, 1991), 130.

45   A third argument—call it the argument from alienation—bears mention: Reliance on religiously grounded moral belief as a basis of political decision making makes many persons feel politically marginalized or alienated— namely, persons who do not subscribe to the supporting religious premise or premises. For Kent Greenawalt's version of the argument, see Greenawalt, *Private Consciences and Public Reasons*, 156–58. I have explained elsewhere why, in my judgment, the argument from alienation is implausible. See Perry, *Religion in Politics*, 50–52 (criticizing Greenawalt's argument). Cf. Mark V. Tushnet, "The Constitution of Religion," *Connecticut Law Review* 18 (1986): 701, 712 ("nonadherents who believe that they are excluded from the political community are merely expressing the disappointment felt by everyone who has lost a fair fight in the arena of politics"); Steven D. Smith, *Foreordained Failure: The Quest for a Constitutional Principle of Religious Freedom* (New York: Oxford University Press, 1995), 164–65 n. 66:

> [T]he very concept of "alienation," or symbolic exclusion, is difficult to grasp. How, if at all, does "alienation" differ from "anger," "annoyance," "frustration," or "disappointment" that every person who finds himself in a political minority is likely to feel? "Alienation" might refer to nothing more than an awareness by an individual that she belongs to a religious minority, accompanied by a realization that at least on some issues she is unlikely to be able to prevail in the political process. . . . That awareness may be discomforting. But is it the sort of phenomenon for which constitutional law can provide an efficacious remedy? Constitutional doctrine that stifles the message will not likely alter the reality—or a minority's awareness of that reality.

46   See Michael J. Perry, "What Is 'Morality' Anyway?" 45 *Villanova L. Rev.* 69 (2000) (the 1999 Donald M. Giannella Memorial Lecture).

47   See note 2 and accompanying text.

48   See Michael J. Perry, "The Putative Inviolability of 'The Other': A Nonreligious Ground?" (forthcoming). See also idem, "What Is 'Morality' Anyway?" 81–88; idem, *The Idea of Human Rights*, 11–41.

49   This is the relevant part of the *Oxford English Dictionary*'s definition of *inviolable*. See Oxford English Dictionary 51 (2nd ed., 1989).

50   In an otherwise laudatory review of a book by Frances Kamm, Jeff McMahan writes:

> The burden of the third and final part of the volume is to explain why it is generally not permissible for one to engage in killing even when, by doing so, one could prevent a greater number of killings from occurring. Here, Kamm's central contention is that people must be regarded as inviolable, as ends-in-themselves. . . . [Kamm's] arguments often raise difficult questions that the book fails to address. A conspicuous instance of this is Kamm's failure to identify the basis of our moral inviolability. Understanding the basis of our alleged inviolability is crucial both for determining whether it is plausible to regard ourselves as inviolable and for fixing the boundaries of the class of inviolable beings. (Jeff McMahan, "When Not to Kill or Be Killed," review of *Morality, Mortality*, vol. 2, *Rights, Duties, and Status* by Frances Kamm, *Times Literary Supplement*, August 7, 1998, 31.)

It is revealing that Kamm, one of the principal neo-Kantian moral philosophers among the younger generation of secular moral theorists, "conspicuously" fails in her otherwise rigorously argued book to tell her audience why—in virtue of what—persons are inviolable.

51   In the United States, liberal democracy's commitment to the true and full humanity of every person (without regard to race, etc.) is a constitutional commitment. See Michael Perry, *We the People: The Fourteenth Amendment and the Supreme Court* (New York: Oxford University Press, 1999), 48–87. For government to make any political choice even partly on the ground that some persons are not inviolable, that some are not subjects of justice, is to violate the Fourteenth Amendment.

Chapter 13

1   David Lewis, *King: A Critical Biography* (New York: Praeger, 1970), 228.
2   Quoted in Robert Bellah and Phillip Hammond, *Varieties of Civil Religion*, (New York: Harper & Row, 1980), 156.
3   Bellah and Hammond, *Varieties of Civil Religion*, 41.
4   John Courtney Murray, SJ, "The Church and Totalitarian Democracy," *Theological Studies*, December 1952, 531.
5   John Courtney Murray, SJ, "Return to Tribalism," *Catholic Mind*, January 1962.
6   The phrase is from Peter Berger, *Rumor of Angels* (Garden City, N.Y.: Doubleday, 1969).
7   Alasdair MacIntyre, *After Virtue: A Study in Moral Theory* (Notre Dame: University of Notre Dame Press, 1981), 245.
8   Reported in *Newsweek*, February 22, 1982.
9   *Forum Letter*, December 1982.
10   "Tass Denounces Group for Peace as West's Tool," *New York Times*, November 27, 1982.
11   "Christianity and Democracy," a statement of purpose drafted by Richard John Neuhaus and adopted by the Institute on Religion and Democracy, Washington, D.C.
12   For example, the symposium on the statement in the *Center Journal*.
13   Arthur Schlesinger Jr., *The Vital Center* (Boston: Houghton Mifflin, 1962), 188.
14   Schlesinger, 254.
15   Schlesinger, 240.
16   Schlesinger, 248.
17   Schlesinger, 176.
18   Sugarman and Coon; also David Sealey.
19   Martin E. Marty, *Righteous Empire* (New York: Dial, 1970).

Chapter 14

1   Only 20 percent of Americans believe they can trust the government in Washington to do what is right most of the time: *Gallup Poll Monthly*, February 1994, 12. Three-fourths say they are dissatisfied with the way the political process is working: *Gallup Poll Monthly*, September 1992. A similar percentage believe that government is run by a few big interests rather than for the benefit of all: Alan F. Kay et al., "Steps for Democracy," *Americans Talk Issues*, March 25, 1994, 9.

2   See John Rawls, *A Theory of Justice* (Cambridge, Mass.: Harvard University Press, 1971); Ronald Dworkin, "Liberalism," in *Public and Private Morality*, ed. Stuart Hampshire (New York: Cambridge University Press, 1978), 114–43; idem, *Taking Rights Seriously* (Cambridge, Mass.: Harvard University Press, 1977); Robert Nozick, *Anarchy, State, and Utopia* (New York: Basic Books, 1977); Bruce Ackerman, *Social Justice in the Liberal State* (New Haven: Yale University Press, 1980).

3   The term "procedural republic" was suggested to me by Judith N. Shklar.

4   On the meaning of "liberal" as used in contemporary American politics, see Ronald D. Rotunda, *The Politics of Language* (Iowa City: Iowa University Press, 1986).

5   Chapters 2–4 [of Michael Sandel, *Democracy's Discontent* (Cambridge, Mass.: Harvard University Press, 1996)] tell the first story; chapters 5–9 tell the second.

6   Aristotle, *The Politics*, trans. Ernest Barker, book 3, chap. 9 (London: Oxford University Press, 1946), 119.

7   Aristotle, 119–20.

8   In this section I draw on my introduction to Michael Sandel, ed., *Liberalism and Its Critics* (Oxford: Basil Blackwell, 1984), 1–11.

9   John Stuart Mill, *On Liberty* (1859), chap. 1.

10   For a sampling of arguments for and against utilitarianism, see Amartya Sen and Bernard Williams, eds., *Utilitarianism and Beyond* (New York: Cambridge University Press, 1982).

11   See Immanuel Kant, *Groundwork of the Metaphysics of Morals* (1785), trans. H. J. Paton (New York: Harper & Row, 1956); idem, *Critique of Practical Reason* (1788), trans. L. W. Beck (Indianapolis: Bobbs-Merrill, 1956); idem, "On the Common Saying: 'This May Be True in Theory, But It Does Not Apply in Practice,'" in *Kant's Political Writings*, ed. Hans Reiss (Cambridge, UK: Cambridge University Press, 1970), 61–92.

12   Rawls, *Theory of Justice*, 3–4.

13   Dworkin, "Liberalism," 136.

14   Rawls, *Theory of Justice*, 560.

15   George Kateb, "Democratic Individuality and the Claims of Politics," *Political Theory* 12 (August 1984): 343.

16   John Rawls, "Kantian Constructivism in Moral Theory," *Journal of Philosophy* 77 (1980): 543.

17   John Rawls, "Fairness to Goodness," *Philosophical Review* 84 (October 1985): 537.

18   Rawls, "Fairness to Goodness," 537.

19   Rawls, *Theory of Justice*, 312, and, generally, 310–15. See also Friedrich A. Hayek, *The Constitution of Liberty* (Chicago: University of Chicago Press, 1960), chap. 7; and Nozick, *Anarchy, State, and Utopia*, 155–60.

20   Rawls, *Theory of Justice*, 108–17.

21   Rawls, *Theory of Justice*, 114.

22   See Michael J. Sandel, *Liberalism and the Limits of Justice* (New York: Cambridge University Press, 1982), 179–83.

23   Alasdair MacIntyre, *After Virtue* (Notre Dame: University of Notre Dame Press, 1981), 204–6.

24   Lee quoted in Douglas Southall Freeman, *R. E. Lee* (New York: Charles Scribner's Sons, 1934), 443, 421. See also the discussions of Lee in Morton Grodzins, *The Loyal and the Disloyal* (Chicago: University of Chicago Press,

1965), 142–43; and Judith Shklar, *Ordinary Vices* (Cambridge, Mass.: Harvard University Press, 1984), 160.

25   Rawls, *Theory of Justice*, 101–2.

26   See Nozick, *Anarchy, State, and Utopia*, 228.

27   Ralph Waldo Emerson, "Self Reliance," in *Essays and Lectures* (New York: Library of America, 1983), 262.

28   The view I describe here as minimalist liberalism is represented by John Rawls' book, *Political Liberalism* (New York: Columbia University Press, 1993), and his article "Justice as Fairness: Political Not Metaphysical," *Philosophy & Public Affairs* 14 (1985): 223–51. It is also presented, in a somewhat different version, in Richard Rorty, "The Priority of Democracy to Philosophy," in *The Virginia Statute for Religious Freedom*, ed. Merrill D. Peterson and Robert C. Vaughan (New York: Cambridge University Press, 1988). The quotation is from Rawls, "Justice as Fairness," 230.

29   Rawls, *Political Liberalism*, 31; see generally 29–35.

30   Rawls, *Political Liberalism*, xvi–xxviii.

31   Rawls, "Justice as Fairness," 230; Rorty, "Priority of Democracy," 257.

32   I draw in this discussion from Michael J. Sandel's review of *Political Liberalism*, by John Rawls, *Harvard Law Review* 107 (1994): 1765–94.

33   Paul M. Angle, ed., *Created Equal? The Complete Lincoln-Douglas Debates of 1858* (Chicago: University of Chicago Press, 1958), 369, 374.

34   Angle, 390.

35   Angle, 392.

36   Angle, 389.

Chapter 15

1   September 2000 Harris Poll; September 2003 Time/CNN/Harris Interactive Poll; June 2003 Religion and Public Life Survey by Pew Research, Pew Forum on Religion and Public Life. All poll data provided by the Roper Center for Public Opinion Research, University of Connecticut, http://www.roperweb.ropercenter.uconn.edu/cgi-bin/hsrun.exe/Roperweb /iPoll.

2   November 2003 Gallup Survey, http://www.gallup.com/poll/9922/Bringing-Faith-Into-Voting-Booth-Part.aspx.

3   2005–2006 Gallup World Poll, http://www.gallup.com/video/28888/Bible-Sharia.aspx.

4   July 2006 Gallup Poll respectively, http://www.gallup.com/video/28888/Bible-Sharia.aspx.

5   See the essays in part I of this anthology.

6   See the essays in part II of this anthology.

7   The U.S. Supreme Court effectively upheld this decision when they refused to hear the case in October of 2005.

8   John Rawls, *Political Liberalism*, paperback ed. (New York: Columbia University Press, 1996), xlvi.

9   Jeremy Waldron, *Liberal Rights* (New York: Cambridge University Press, 1993), 37.

10   Bruce Ackerman, "Why Dialogue?" *Journal of Philosophy* 86 (1989): 16.

11   See, for instance, Stephen Holmes, "Gag Rules, or the Politics of Omission," in *Passions and Constraint* (Chicago: University of Chicago Press, 1995).

12   Rawls, *Political Liberalism*, li–lii; Cf. idem, "The Idea of Public Reason Revisited," *University of Chicago Law Review* 64, no. 3 (1997): 771.

13   Cf. Robert Audi's view in his "Liberal Democracy and the Place of Religion in Politics," in *Religion in the Public Square*, ed. Robert Audi and Nicholas Wolterstorff (Lanham, Md.: Rowman & Littlefield, 1997).

14   See for instance, Gerald Gaus, *Contemporary Theories of Liberalism* (Thousand Oaks, Calif.: Sage, 2003), 199–200. See also, Charles Larmore, "Public Reason," in *The Cambridge Companion to Rawls* (New York: Cambridge University Press, 2003), 387. Both Larmore and Gaus agree that the proviso fails to strengthen Rawls' view of public reason.

15   I take up this sort of argument in my *Religion and Democratic Citizenship* (Lanham, Md.: Lexington, 2008), especially 85–105.

16   See Sandel, *Democracy's Discontent*, 3–24.

17   Nicholas Wolterstorff, "The Role of Religion in Decision and Discussion of Political Issues," in Audi and Wolterstorff, *Religion in the Public Square*, 97.

18   Cass Sunstein, "The Law of Group Polarization," *Journal of Political Philosophy* 10, no. 2 (2002): 175–95. See also Sunstein, *Why Societies Need Dissent* (Cambridge, Mass.: Harvard University Press, 2003). For a helpful discussion of the implications of Sunstein's work, see Robert Talisse, "Dilemmas of Public Reason," in *The Legacy of John Rawls*, ed. Thom Brooks and Fabian Freyenhagen (New York: Continuum, 2005).

19   For example, imagine a group of fundamentalists who, for explicitly religious reasons, are opposed to abortion. Imagine that because they refuse to talk about abortion with liberal Christians, atheists, feminists, Jews, Muslims, or anyone not of their preferred worldview, they restrict themselves to discussing their pro-life views with only those of like mind. Conditions are now ripe for polarization. Not only will these citizens tend toward more extreme versions and of their predeliberative positions and strategies to execute their views, but they will probably also come to see themselves as marginalized and victimized. This will lead them to be dismissive of opposing views and to see those who disagree with them as simply evil, benighted, or unreasonable. And this is a recipe for shutting down the possibility of constructive public dialogue on the issue and filling the void with hatred and violence. (Witness something like the Eric Rudolph bombings of the late 1990s.)

20   See Jeffrey Stout, *Democracy and Tradition* (Princeton: Princeton University Press, 2004), 72–73.

21   Richard Rorty, "Religion as Conversation-Stopper," in *Philosophy and Social Hope* (New York: Penguin, 1999), 169.

22   Rorty, 170.

23   The religious citizen's R may be defeated because of the formulation and articulation of R. However, it may be the case that simply refining R in the light of certain objections allows R to be formulated again in a way that is no longer open to defeat by those objections. If such refinement takes place, then the religious citizen might bring that refined R out of privatization and into the public square. Here, I think it is important to understand that refining one's R is not the same as semantically reinterpreting one's R.

24   Michael Sandel, "A Response to Rawls's Political Liberalism," an appendix to the 2nd ed. of *Liberalism and the Limits of Justice* (New York: Cambridge University Press, 1998).

25   Socrates steadfastly admits his willingness to be refuted during a conversation in order to obtain truth. This willingness to be refuted is actually one of the ways that Socrates both identifies himself as a philosopher and distinguishes himself from the sophists. In the *Gorgias*, Socrates says that he is

more than willing to carry on more conversation with Gorgias if he is the "same kind of man as I am." Socrates goes on further to describe this "kind of man" in the following way: "And what kind of man am I? One of those who would gladly be refuted if anything I say is not true, and would gladly refute another who says what is not true, but would be no less happy to be refuted myself than to refute, for I consider that a greater benefit, inasmuch as it is a greater boon to be delivered from the worst of evils oneself than to deliver another" (458a). Hereafter, all citation to the Platonic dialogues will simply make reference to the specific dialogue and the appropriate Stephanus numbers. All citations to Plato are made to the translations in Edith Hamilton and Huntington Cairns, eds. *The Collected Dialogues* (Princeton: Princeton University Press, 1989).

26   Recall that Cleitophon tries to bolster Thrasymachus' argument against Socrates in Book I of the *Republic* by suggesting that justice is what *seems* to be the advantage of the stronger as opposed to the milder form of relativism advanced by Thrasymachus, which states that justice simply *is* the advantage of the stronger (340b). Thrasymachus, though, does not heed the suggestion of Cleitophon and ends up being refuted by Socrates. Interestingly, Socrates would not have been able to refute Cleitophon's reformulation of Thrasymachus' argument precisely because Cleitophon effectively rejects the truth/falsity distinction when he rejects the distinction between what *is* the advantage of the stronger and what *seems* to be the advantage of the stronger. Without such a truth/falsity distinction, no refuting arguments can be formulated by Socrates. At this point, Cleitophon simply steps out of the conversation (as he rejects the conditions for such a conversation), never to be heard from again in the *Republic*. See David Roochnik [*The Tragedy of Reason: Toward a Platonic Conception of Logos* (New York: Routledge, 1990)], 102–8 for an interesting discussion of this exchange.

27   The pronouncement of Parmenides here is essentially that one cannot say or think that what-is-not *is*. In order to challenge this pronouncement, then, one must effectively confront a contradiction.

28   Sandel, "Response to Rawls's Political Liberalism," 217–18.

29   Stout says, for instance: "And this consequence of theological plurality has an enormous impact on what our ethical discourse is like. It means, for example, that in most contexts it will simply be *imprudent*, rhetorically speaking, to introduce explicitly theological premises into an argument intended to persuade a religiously diverse public audience. If one cannot expect such premises to be accepted or interpreted in a uniform way, it will not necessarily advance one's rhetorical purposes to assert them" (Jeffrey Stout, *Democracy and Tradition* [Princeton: Princeton University Press, 2004], 98–99, emphasis added).

30   See Robert Talisse and J. Caleb Clanton, "Stout on Public Reason," *Soundings* 87, no. 3–4 (2004): 349–69.

31   Plato, *Meno* 80a.

32   Plato, *Apology* 30e.

33   C. S. Peirce, "The Scientific Essay and Fallibilism," in *The Philosophical Writings of Peirce*, ed. Justus Buchler (New York: Dover, 1955), 54.

34   Martin Luther King Jr., "Letter from a Birmingham Jail," no page, emphasis added.

35   Rawls, *Political Liberalism*, 4.

36   Sandel, "A Response to Rawls's Political Liberalism," 211.

37   There are obvious parallels between what I have identified as *act-now deliberative stalemate situations* and what William James calls "genuine options" in his essay, "Will to Believe" [in *Writings of William James*, ed. John McDermott (Chicago: University of Chicago Press, 1977), 718].

38   Rawls, *Political Liberalism*, 173ff.

39   Amy Gutmann and Dennis Thompson, "Why Deliberative Democracy Is Different," in *Democracy*, ed. Ellen Frankel Paul, Fred Miller, and Jeffrey Paul (New York: Cambridge University Press, 2000), 172. Cf. idem, "Deliberative Democracy Beyond Process," in *Debating Deliberative Democracy*, ed. James Fishkin and Peter Laslett (New York: Blackwell, 2003), 43.

40   Robert Talisse, *Democracy After Liberalism* (New York: Routledge, 2005), 105.

41   Cheryl Misak, "Making Disagreement Matter," *Journal of Speculative Philosophy* 18, no. 1 (2004): 9–22.

42   See, for instance, Misak, "Making Disagreement Matter"; idem, *Truth, Politics, Morality* (London: Routledge, 2000).

43   Misak, "Making Disagreement Matter," 12.

44   Misak, "Making Disagreement Matter," 12.

45   Christopher J. Eberle, *Religious Conviction in Liberal Politics* (New York: Cambridge University Press, 2002), 84–151.

46   Eberle, 10.

47   See David Estlund, *Democratic Authority: A Philosophical Framework* (Princeton: Princeton University Press, 2007), 19.

48   On this point, see Iris Marion Young, "Activist Challenges to Deliberative Democracy," *Political Theory* 29, no. 5 (2001): 676.

49   I am indebted to Wilfred McClay for posing this objection to me.

50   See, for instance, Michael Perry, *Under God: Religious Faith and Liberal Democracy* (New York: Cambridge University Press, 2003), 55, for a helpful discussion concerning how Christians might be able to interpret biblical passages relevant to homosexuality and same-sex marriage (e.g., Gen 19:1-29; Lev 18:22, 20:13; and 1 Cor 6:9) in at least two competing ways, while at the same time not denying the truth of the Bible itself.

51   This essay draws heavily from chapter 7 of my *Religion and Democratic Citizenship: Inquiry and Conviction in the American Public Square* (Lanham, Md.: Lexington, 2008), 123–47. Reprinted with permission of Lexington Books.

About the Contributors

THOMAS NAGEL is University Professor, Professor of Law, and Professor of Philosophy at New York University. He is the author of *The Possibility of Altruism* (Oxford, 1970, reprinted Princeton, 1978), *Mortal Questions* (Cambridge, 1979), *The View from Nowhere* (Oxford, 1986), *What Does It All Mean?* (Oxford, 1987), *Equality and Partiality* (Oxford, 1991), *Other Minds* (Oxford, 1995), *The Last Word* (Oxford, 1997), *The Myth of Ownership: Taxes and Justice* (with Liam Murphy) (Oxford, 2002), and *Concealment and Exposure* (Oxford, 2002).

JOHN RAWLS (1921–2002) was the James Bryant Conant University Professor, Emeritus, at Harvard University. He is the author of *A Theory of Justice* (Harvard, 1971), *Political Liberalism* (Columbia, 1993), *The Law of Peoples* (Harvard, 1999), *Collected Papers* (Harvard, 1999), *Lectures on the History of Moral Philosophy* (Harvard, 2000), *Justice as Fairness* (Harvard, 2001), and *Lectures on the History of Political Philosophy* (Harvard, 2007).

ROBERT AUDI is Professor of Philosophy and the David E. Gallo Professor of Business Ethics at the University of Notre Dame. He is the author of *Belief, Justification, and Knowledge* (Wadsworth, 1988), *Practical Reasoning* (Routledge, 1989), *The Structure of Justification* (Cambridge, 1993), *Action, Intention, and Reason* (Cornell, 1993), *Religion in the Public Square* (with Nicholas Wolterstorff) (Rowman & Littlefield, 1997), *Moral Knowledge and Ethical Character* (Oxford, 1997), *Epistemology: A Contemporary Introduction to the Theory of Knowledge* (Routledge, 1998), *Religious Commitment and Secular Reason* (Cambridge, 2000), *The Architecture of Reason: The Structure and Substance of Rationality* (Oxford, 2001), *The Good in the Right: A Theory of Intuition and Intrinsic Value* (Princeton, 2004), *Practical Reasoning and Ethical Decision* (Routledge, 2006), and *Moral Value and Human Diversity* (Oxford, 2007).

STEPHEN MACEDO is the Laurance S. Rockefeller Professor of Politics and the University Center for Human Values and the Director of the University Center for Human Values at Princeton University. His books include *The New Right v. The Constitution* (Cato Inst., 1987), *Liberal Virtues: Citizenship, Virtue, and Community in Liberal Constitutionalism* (Clarendon, 1990), and *Diversity and Distrust: Civic Education in a Multicultural Democracy* (Harvard, 2000).

BRUCE ACKERMAN is the Sterling Professor of Law and Political Science at Yale University. He is the author of *The Uncertain Search for Environmental Quality* (with Rose Ackerman, James Sawyer, and Dale Henderson) (Free Press, 1974), *Private Property and the Constitution* (Yale, 1977), *Social Justice in the Liberal State* (Yale, 1980), *Clean Coal/ Dirty Air* (with William Hassler) (Yale, 1981), *Reconstructing American Law* (Harvard, 1984), *We the People*, Vol 1: Foundations (Harvard, 1991), *The Future of Liberal Revolution* (Yale, 1992), *Is NAFTA Constitutional?* (with David Golove) (Harvard, 1995), *We the People*, Vol 2: Transformations (Harvard, 1998), *The Case Against Lameduck Impeachment* (Seven Stories, 1999), *The Stakeholder Society* (with Anne Alstott) (Yale, 1999), *Voting with Dollars* (with Ian Ayres) (Yale, 2002), *Deliberation Day* (with James Fishkin) (Yale, 2004), *The Failure of the Founding Fathers* (Harvard, 2005), and *Before the Next Attack* (Yale, 2006).

RICHARD RORTY (1931–2007) was Professor Emeritus of Comparative Literature at Stanford University. His many books include *Philosophy and the Mirror of Nature* (Princeton, 1979), *Consequences of Pragma-*

tism (University of Minnesota, 1982), *Contingency, Irony, and Solidarity* (Cambridge, 1989), *Objectivity, Relativism, and Truth* (Cambridge, 1991), *Essays on Heidegger and Others* (Cambridge, 1991), *Achieving Our Country* (Harvard, 1998), *Truth and Progress* (Cambridge, 1998), *Philosophy and Social Hope* (Penguin, 2000), *Against Bosses, Against Oligarchies* (Prickly Paradigm, 2002), and *Philosophy as Cultural Politics* (Cambridge, 2007).

NICHOLAS WOLTERSTORFF is the Noah Porter Professor of Philosophical Theology at Yale University. His books include *On Universals* (Chicago, 1970), *Reason with the Bounds of Religion* (Eerdmans, 1976), *Works and Worlds of Art* (Oxford, 1980), *Art in Action* (Eerdmans, 1980), *Until Justice and Peace Embrace* (Eerdmans, 1983), *Divine Discourse* (Cambridge, 1995), *John Locke and Ethics of Belief* (Cambridge, 1996), *Religion in the Public Square* (with Robert Audi) (Rowman & Littlefield, 1997), and *Thomas Reid and the Story of Epistemology* (Cambridge, 2001).

CHRISTOPHER J. EBERLE is Associate Professor of Philosophy at the United States Naval Academy. He is the author of *Religious Conviction in Liberal Politics* (Cambridge, 2002).

PAUL J. WEITHMAN is Professor of Philosophy at the University of Notre Dame. He is the author of *Religion and the Obligations of Citizenship* (Cambridge, 2002) and the editor or coeditor of *Religion and Contemporary Liberalism* (Notre Dame, 1997), *The Philosophy of Rawls*, vol. 1–5 (Garland, 1999), and *Liberal Faith: Essays in Honor of Philip Quinn* (Notre Dame, 2008).

JEFFREY STOUT is Professor of Religion at Princeton University. His books include *The Flight from Authority: Religion, Morality, and the Quest for Autonomy* (Notre Dame, 1981), *Ethics after Babel: The Languages of Moral and Their Discontents* (Beacon, 1988), and *Democracy and Tradition* (Princeton, 2004).

CORNEL WEST is the Class of 1943 Professor of Religion at Princeton University. His many books include *Prophesy Deliverance: An Afro-American Revolutionary Christianity* (Westminster John Knox, 1982), *Prophetic Fragments: Illuminations of the Crisis in American Religion and Culture* (Eerdmans, 1988), *The American Evasion of Philosophy: A Genealogy of Pragmatism* (University of Wisconsin, 1989), *The Ethical Dimensions of Marxist Thought* (Monthly Review, 1991), *Race Matters* (Beacon, 1993), *Keeping Faith* (Routledge, 1994), *The Future of the Race* (with Henry Louis

Gates Jr.) (Random House, 1997), *The Cornel West Reader* (Basic Civitas, 2000), and *Democracy Matters* (Penguin, 2004).

MICHAEL J. PERRY is the Robert W. Woodruff Professor of Law at Emory University. His many books include *Morality, Politics and Law* (Oxford, 1988), *Love and Power* (Oxford, 1991), *Religion in Politics: Constitutional and Moral Perspectives* (Oxford, 1997), *The Idea of Human Rights* (Oxford, 1998), *We the People: The Fourteenth Amendment and the Supreme Court* (Oxford, 1999), *Under God? Religious Faith and Liberal Democracy* (Cambridge, 2004), and *Toward a Theory of Human Rights: Religion, Law, Courts* (Cambridge, 2007).

RICHARD JOHN NEUHAUS (1936–2009) was the founder and editor of *First Things: A Journal of Religion, Culture, and Public Life*. His many books include *The Naked Public Square: Religion and Democracy in America* (Eerdmans, 1984), *America Against Itself: Moral Vision and the Public Order* (Notre Dame, 1992), and *Catholic Matters: Confusion, Controversy, and the Splendor of Truth* (Basic Books, 2006).

MICHAEL J. SANDEL is the Anne T. and Robert M. Bass Professor of Government at Harvard University. He is the author of *Liberalism and the Limits of Justice* (Cambridge, 1982), *Democracy Discontent: America in Search of a Public Philosophy* (Harvard, 1996), *Public Philosophy: Essays on Morality in Politics* (Harvard, 2005), and *The Case against Perfection: Ethics in the Age of Genetic Engineering* (Harvard, 2007).

J. CALEB CLANTON is Assistant Professor of Philosophy and Seaver Fellow in the Humanities at Pepperdine University. He is the author of *Religion and Democratic Citizenship: Inquiry and Conviction in the American Public Square* (Rowman & Littlefield's Lexington Books, 2008).

Credits

Thomas Nagel, "Moral Conflict and Political Legitimacy," from *Philosophy & Public Affairs* 16 (1987): 215–40. Reprinted with the permission of Blackwell Publishing.

John Rawls, "The Idea of Public Reason Revisited," from the *University of Chicago Law Review* 64, no. 3 (1997): 765–807. Reprinted with the permission of Copyright Clearance Center.

Robert Audi, "Religious Convictions and Secular Reasons," from *Religious Commitment and Secular Reason* (New York: Cambridge University Press, 2000), 81–115 and relevant notes on 230–36. Reprinted with the permission of Cambridge University Press.

Stephen Macedo, "Liberal Civic Education and Religious Fundamentalism: The Case of God v. John Rawls?," from *Ethics* 105, no. 3 (1995): 468–96. Reprinted with the permission of Copyright Clearance Center Rightslink.

Index

DATE DUE

MAY 24 2013

MAY 28 2013

JUN 10 2015

BRODART, CO.   Cat. No. 23-221